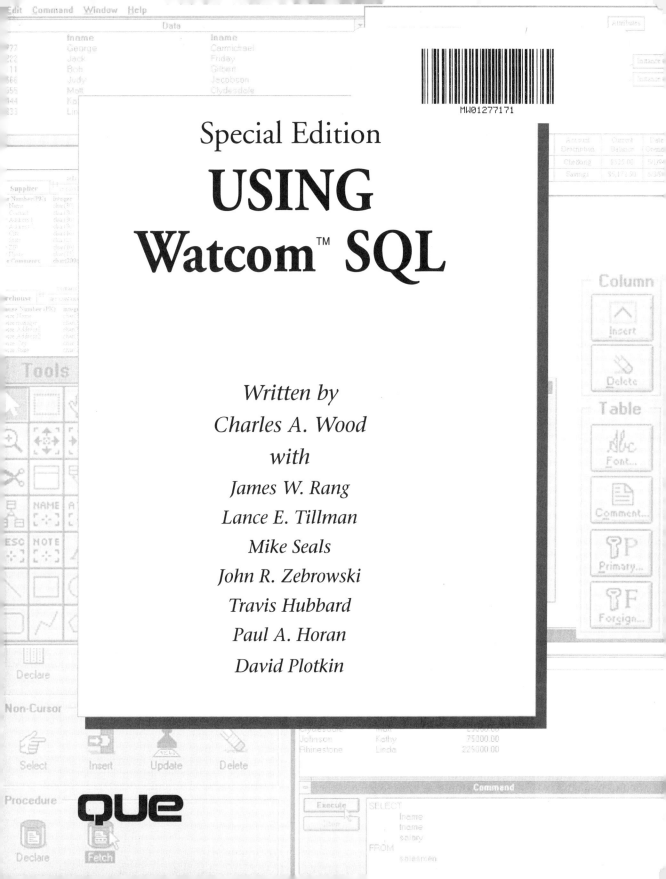

Special Edition
USING
Watcom™ SQL

Written by

Charles A. Wood

with

James W. Rang

Lance E. Tillman

Mike Seals

John R. Zebrowski

Travis Hubbard

Paul A. Horan

David Plotkin

Special Edition Using Watcom SQL

Copyright © 1995 by Que® Corporation

Library of Congress Catalog No.: 95-68914

ISBN: 0-7897-0103-0

97 96 95   4 3 2 1

Interpretation of the printing code: the rightmost double-digit number is the year of the book's printing; the rightmost single-digit number, the number of the book's printing. For example, a printing code of 95-1 shows that the first printing of the book occurred in 1995.

Publisher: Roland Elgey

Vice President and Publisher: Marie Butler-Knight

Associate Publisher: Don Roche, Jr.

Director of Product Series: Charles O. Stewart III

Editorial Services Director: Elizabeth Keaffaber

Director of Marketing: Lynn E. Zingraf

Dedication

This book is dedicated to my wife, Lyn, and my daughters, Kelly and Kailyn. I hope I can return all the love, patience, and understanding that you've given me.

Credits

Managing Editor

Michael Cunningham

Acquisitions Editor

Jenny L. Watson

Product Director

Kathie-Jo Arnoff

Product Development

Patrick Bogan, Anatec

Michael Watterud, Anatec

Technical Editor

Kevin Thompson, Anatec

Production Editor

Nancy E. Sixsmith

Editors

Theresa Mathias

Lynn Northrup

**Assistant Product
Marketing Manager**

Kim Margolius

Technical Specialist

Cari Skaggs

Acquisitions Assistant

Tracy M. Williams

Operations Coordinator

Patricia J. Brooks

Editorial Assistant

Jill Pursell

Book Designer

Ruth Harvey

Cover Designer

Dan Armstrong

Production Team

Claudia Bell

Chad Dressler

DiMonique Ford

George Hanlin

John Hulse

Barry Jorden

Bob LaRoche

Elizabeth Lewis

Kris Simmons

Michael Thomas

Indexer

Michael Hughes

Composed in *Stone Serif* and *MCPdigital* by Que Corporation

About the Authors

Charles A. Wood, author of Que Corporation's *Special Edition Using PowerBuilder™ 4*, is a senior programmer analyst at Indiana Farm Bureau Insurance. He graduated with bachelor's degrees in Computer Science and Finance from Ball State University in 1986. Along with developing software in PowerBuilder, C++, COBOL, and QuickBasic, Wood has instructed in C and C++ at Indiana Vocational Technical College. He is currently pursuing his MBA at Butler University.

James W. Rang is a consultant with NewMedia, Inc.—a PowerSoft Code Training Partner and Microsoft Solutions Provider. He earned a B.S. degree in Computer Information Systems from Ferris State University (Big Rapids, Michigan) in 1988. Rang has worked as an independent consultant and for various consulting firms. He was technical editor for Que's *Special Edition Using PowerBuilder™ 4*. He currently lives in Indianapolis, Indiana, with his wife, Jennifer, and their 16-month old daughter, Jessica (and one on the way). Rang can be contacted on the Internet at jrang@iquest.net, or on CompuServe at 73733,1747.

Lance E. Tillman is a programmer analyst at Indiana Farm Bureau Insurance. He graduated with a B.S. degree in Mathematics from Huntington College in 1987. He has worked as a computer programmer and systems analyst in the insurance industry for the past seven years. He resides in Fishers, Indiana, with his wife Julie and daughter, Jessica.

Mike Seals is a Senior Consultant at Source Consulting's Indianapolis, Indiana office. He has extensive experience in client/server and telecommunications technologies. He holds a degree in Entrepreneurship from Ball State University, is a Certified Netware Engineer and a Certified PowerBuilder Developer. He works with Visual Basic, Access, PowerBuilder, and other development tools. He can be reached on the Internet at mseals@iquest.net, and on CompuServe at 73753,274.

John R. Zebrowski is Manager of Technical Services with Visual Systems Development Group. He is a Certified PowerBuilder Instructor, a Certified PowerBuilder Developer, a Certified ERwin Instructor, and President of the Michigan PowerBuilder Users' Group. Zebrowski has taught PowerBuilder to hundreds of students and is consistently rated as one of the top PowerBuilder trainers in the Midwest. He has been developing client/server Windows applications for over two years, and has worked with various relational databases for eight years. Zebrowski graduated from Amherst College with a B.A. in Mathematics. He resides in Michigan with his wife, Lana, and their three boys: Adam, John-Paul, and Austin. Zebrowski can be reached on CompuServe at 74723,2155.

Travis Hubbard has been developing GUI applications since 1984 as a professional and hobbyist. He enjoys using PowerBuilder, Visual C++, and SmallTalk, and his current focus is on graphics applications for Windows NT. Hubbard is a Certified PowerBuilder Developer, and he has developed database applications for both corporate and government clients using PowerBuilder and SQL Server since 1992.

Paul A. Horan is a Manager with the Indianapolis, Indiana office of Ernst & Young's management-consulting practice. A Certified PowerBuilder Developer, he is the President of the Indianapolis PowerBuilder Users' Group. Horan has been a consultant for more than four years, working with client/server architectures and relational databases. He has worked exclusively with PowerBuilder since its initial release.

David Plotkin is a Business Area Analyst with Integral Systems in Walnut Creek, Calif. He has extensive experience in designing and implementing databases, both at the desktop and on Client Server systems. He writes extensively for various computer periodicals, and his favorite editor is his wife, Marisa.

Acknowledgments

Thanks to Don Roche, Jenny Watson, Nancy Sixsmith, and Kathie-Jo Arnoff for their tireless efforts to get this book done.

Thanks to Marv Taylor and the management of Farm Bureau Insurance of Indiana for giving me the time off to write this book.

Kudos to Tony Navarra from Anatec for putting me in touch with knowledgeable people.

Most of all, thanks to my wife, Lyn, for her infinite patience and understanding while this book was being written. I couldn't have done it without you.

Trademarks

Contents at a Glance

Techniques

Reference

Appendixes

Contents

II Fundamentals   105

5 Selecting Data   107

6 Understanding SQL   157

7 Using the ISQL Environment   201

IV Interfaces   311

12 Implementing Procedures and Triggers   313

13 Implementing Watcom SQL with PowerBuilder   349

14 Implementing Watcom SQL with SQLPP (C and C++)   383

15 Implementing Watcom SQL HLI   417

23 ISQL-Only SQL Commands   575

24 Using Watcom SQL Utilities 611

Index   **787**

Introduction

Watcom SQL is definitely on the rise as a power in the database community. As one of the most cost-effective client-server databases, Watcom SQL 4.0 also has great response time with SQL commands. With sales increasing, Watcom SQL is also being included in development products such as PowerBuilder 4.0 (available now) and CA-Realizer 3.0 (available sometime this year). Powersoft has even purchased Watcom SQL to ensure a close compatibility with the product.

> **Note**
>
> As many of you know, Sybase recently merged with Powersoft. Sybase is also an SQL database. Although you might expect this acquisition to hurt Watcom SQL, nothing could be further from the truth. Sybase is currently letting Watcom SQL run as an independent business unit. Watcom SQL is being marketed as a "shrink-wrapped" database that works right out of the box. Watcom SQL can also use the Sybase connections to become more prolific in corporate America.

As Watcom SQL increases its presence in the database world, *Special Edition Using Watcom SQL* becomes necessary for those trying to develop and administer Watcom SQL applications. This book contains valuable documentation and reference material not found in products that include Watcom SQL, such as PowerBuilder. Additionally, this book provides tips, techniques, and real-world examples not currently found anywhere else.

Understanding Client-Server Computing

One of the most important developments in today's business world is the evolution of *client-server applications*. Watcom SQL is a client-server database. Client-server computing allows several users (clients) to share one common database on a separate PC (called a server). This is as important in today's business environment as is the sharing of data with one another to increase efficiency.

In figure I.1, you see a client-server setup. Here, three client PCs are accessing a database on the server PC. Because they all can access and update the same data, there is more control over the database. Because the database is in one location, there needs to be only one backup procedure for the database, and all clients can access up-to-date information entered by other clients.

Fig. I.01
Client-server databases allow several PCs to process a central database.

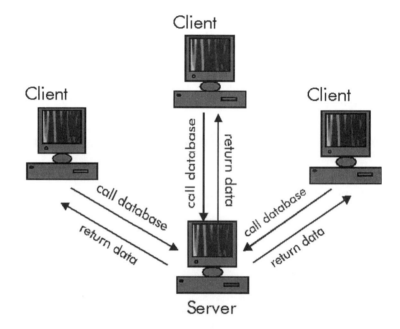

Using Watcom SQL, you can administer a client-server environment. Watcom SQL can run on the server and be accessed by several clients.

Understanding Trends in Database Development

Database technology has evolved significantly in the last few years. Databases have become easier to use, easier to move data in and out of, and easier to manipulate. Along with client-server development, there are several trends in database development:

■ Databases are now supporting SQL. (*SQL* stands for *Structured Query Language*.) SQL is an open language that allows developers to switch from database to database without having to retrain (too much) on the new platform.

■ Databases are now becoming ODBC-compliant. (*ODBC* stands for *Open DataBase Connectivity*.) ODBC is a standard developed by Microsoft to allow for easier database development. Now, developers can write Windows applications that can be ported to different databases without having to change their code! This is vital for applications like PowerBuilder that can be run on several database platforms.

■ Databases now include many features that aid in development and ensure database integrity. These features include:

  • *Referential integrity* (through the use of foreign keys) so that your foreign keys always contain a primary key.

  • *Stored procedures* (procedures defined in a database) that can be called from an application.

  • *Triggers*, which are stored procedures that are automatically called after a particular event occurs on a database, like adding a row or updating a specific column.

What To Expect from Watcom SQL

Watcom SQL contains all the features of a client-server database mentioned in the previous section:

■ Watcom SQL, as the name implies, was designed from the ground up as an SQL database. It has the highest level of compliance with the standard SQL language (set by the ANSI committee) and has added several functions and commands that aid the developer in administrating his or her database.

■ Watcom SQL was also designed as an ODBC database. If you're using ODBC, Watcom SQL performs better than most other databases.

■ Watcom SQL now includes procedures and triggers. In addition, Watcom SQL has greatly enhanced referential integrity to allow cascading deletes, cascading updates, and restrictive deletes and updates. Such enhancements ensure database integrity.

In addition, Watcom SQL also boasts one of the fastest response times on ad hoc database queries in the industry. (*Ad hoc queries* are queries done "on the fly," usually in a database window.)

Finally, Watcom SQL has one of the lowest cost-per-user and cost-per-transaction ratios in the industry. Therefore, Watcom SQL combines low cost with high efficiency to deliver an excellent database product.

Who Should Use This Book?

If you've used Watcom SQL, then this book is a must for your collection. With every edition of PowerBuilder and InfoMaker containing a copy of Watcom SQL (and containing very little documentation), this book can help the PowerBuilder/InfoMaker developers implement the Watcom SQL database included with their product. This product also includes special PowerBuilder coverage and applications for developers who use PowerBuilder.

> **Note**
>
> Even if you're using PowerBuilder with another client-server database like Oracle, Sybase, or DB2, you can use the Data Pipeline included with PowerBuilder 4 to create a similar database for work at home or away from the network.
>
> There is even a utility included on the CD that ports data as well as secutity information to and from Oracle with Watcom, and Sybase with Watcom.

Developers who own Watcom SQL as a stand-alone product will also find this book necessary. *Special Edition Using Watcom SQL* contains performance-tuning tips, database-design techniques, suggested backup procedures and methods, and references with understandable examples.

How this Book Is Organized

Special Edition Using Watcom SQL is (as far as we know) the first book on Watcom SQL in the industry. This book is not only a great reference book, but also discusses the finer points of database design, administration, and development. The following sections describe the book's contents in detail.

Part I: Database Design

This part talks about database fundamentals in Watcom SQL, relational database concepts, database normalization, and how to implement a database design using PowerBuilder. Included are the following chapters:

- Chapter 1, "Understanding Watcom SQL Fundamentals," discusses the new features in Watcom SQL: how to buy or upgrade Watcom SQL, the difference between ISQL and ESQL, accessing Watcom SQL through ODBC, and accessing Watcom SQL through PowerBuilder.

- Chapter 2, "Understanding Relational Database Concepts," discusses relational database theory and describes how to design a database.

- Chapter 3, "Understanding Normalization," discusses the six levels of normalization and how to determine the columns that belong to a table.

- Chapter 4, "Designing a Database Using PowerBuilder," discusses PowerBuilder's database painter and how to implement your design using PowerBuilder.

Part II: Fundamentals

This part discusses how to use SQL and the ISQL environment. Included are the following chapters:

- Chapter 5, "Selecting Data," describes the powerful SQL SELECT statement and the many ways to query a database.

- Chapter 6, "Understanding SQL," describes how to manipulate a Watcom SQL database using SQL. Also discussed are the COMMIT and ROLLBACK statements, ISQL, and ESQL.

- Chapter 7, "Using the ISQL Environment," describes how to use Watcom's ISQLW environment for Windows, as well as the ISQL environment for DOS, OS/2, and QNX environments.

Part III: Administration

This part discusses the ins and outs of database administration. Included are the following chapters:

- Chapter 8, "Understanding the Role of a Database Administrator," delves into the complicated task of administering a Watcom SQL database. In this chapter, security is discussed, as well as multiuser versions of Watcom SQWL, collating sequences, and importing and exporting data.

- Chapter 9, "Using SQL Table Commands," describes how to manipulate tables in your Watcom SQL database. CREATE, ALTER, and DROP commands are covered.

- Chapter 10, "Locking Tables," describes how to maintain database integrity in a multiuser environment using locks. Concepts like isolation levels, concurrency, and deadlock are described.

- Chapter 11, "Backing Up and Recovery," tells about the backup and recovery features of Watcom SQL. Included are discussions on logs, backup plans, and recovery from system failure.

Part IV: Interfaces

This part describes how to use Watcom SQL with PowerBuilder, C++, OS/2, and Windows development tools such as Visual BASIC. Included are the following chapters:

- Chapter 12, "Implementing Procedures and Triggers," describes the new procedure and trigger features of Watcom SQL 4.0. The procedural language is discussed, as well as error-handling, cursors, and creating and dropping procedures and triggers.

- Chapter 13, "Implementing Watcom SQL with PowerBuilder," describes how to develop a system using PowerBuilder with Watcom SQL.

- Chapter 14, "Implementing Watcom SQL with SQLPP (C and C++)," describes how to develop a C++ program with a Watcom SQL interface using SQLPP. Also covered is PowerBuilder's C++ interface.

- Chapter 15, "Implementing Watcom SQL HLI," describes how you can use Watcom SQL from any OS/2 or Windows program through DLL calls to Watcom SQL.

- Chapter 16, "Using Watcom SQL with Windows Tools," describes Watcom SQL as it is used with ODBC and DDE.

Part V: Techniques

This part contains interviews from industry leaders. Topics include: increasing Watcom SQL performance, using CASE tools to help with database design, distributing your Watcom SQL database application, mapping an object-oriented design onto a Watcom SQL relational database, and a preview of the upcoming CA-Realizer enhanced BASIC compiler, which will include the Watcom SQL development environment. Included are the following chapters:

- Chapter 17, "Performance Tuning," is an interview with David Yach of Watcom SQL. In this interview, David Yach describes ways to increase performance in your Watcom SQL environment.

- Chapter 18, "Distributing a Stand-Alone Version," is an interview with Marvin Taylor and Michelle Lehman of United Farm Bureau Insurance Companies. Discussed is the distribution of a stand-alone application using the Watcom SQL run-time version.

- Chapter 19, "Using CASE to Develop and Design Your Watcom SQL Database," is an interview with Dr. Ben Cohen, President and CEO of Logic Works, Inc., and Domenick Cilea, network manager of Set Marketing On, Inc. Discussed is the use of CASE tools (like LogicWorks' ERwin product) to develop a database.

- Chapter 20, "Using Watcom SQL with CA-Realizer," is an interview with Elvira Peretsman of Computer Associates International, Inc. Discussed are ways to develop a CA-Realizer application using Watcom SQL.

- Chapter 21, "Mapping an Object-Oriented Design onto a Relational Database," is an interview with design expert David O'Hearn from Computer Horizons Consulting. Discussed are ways to map an object-oriented design onto a relational database like Watcom SQL, and what features Watcom SQL 4.0 has to facilitate object-oriented design.

Part VI: Reference

This part lists and describes ESQL commands, ISQL commands, and the Watcom SQL utilities. Included are the following chapters:

- Chapter 22, "SQL Commands," is a reference chapter containing common SQL commands that can be used inside programs or inside the ISQL environment.

- Chapter 23, "ISQL-Only SQL Commands," is a reference chapter containing SQL commands available only within the ISQL environment.

- Chapter 24, "Using Watcom Utilities," is a reference chapter describing the utilities that come with Watcom SQL and how to use them.

Appendixes

The appendixes include listings of reserved words, Watcom SQL limitations, system messages, Watcom SQL system tables and system views, and PowerBuilder system tables. Included are the following:

- Appendix A, "Watcom SQL Reserved Words," lists the reserved words in Watcom SQL and where they are used in the SQL language.

- Appendix B, "Watcom SQL Limitations," lists the upper limits of data types inside Watcom SQL.

- Appendix C, "Database Error Messages," is a comprehensive list and description of all SQLDBCODEs and how each one should be interpreted.

- Appendix D, "SQL System Tables," describes all system tables and the columns on the system tables within Watcom SQL.

- Appendix E, "Watcom SQL System Views," describes all system views, how the views are formed, and the columns on the system views within Watcom SQL.

- Appendix F, "PowerBuilder System Tables," describes the PowerBuilder system tables.

- Appendix G, "What's on the CD?," describes the utilities, programs, and demos found on the CD-ROM included with this book.

The CD-ROM

Also included with the book is a CD-ROM filled with utilities, product demos, and programming examples with PowerBuilder. The CD-ROM also includes the run-time version of Watcom SQL, so you can test some of the features described in this book.

Conventions Used in This Book

Watcom enables you to use both the keyboard and mouse to select menu and dialog box items. You can press a letter, or you can select an item by clicking it with the mouse. Letters you press to activate menus, choose commands in menus, and select options in dialog boxes are printed in boldface type: **F**ile, **O**pen.

Names of dialog box options are written with initial capital letters. Messages that appear on-screen are printed in a special font: `Could not connect to database`. New terms are introduced in *italic* type. Text that you are to type appears in **boldface**.

Any programming code or SQL is printed in a special font:

```
SELECT * FROM mytable;
```

Chapters in this book contain some icons in the margins. You will notice the following icons:

This icon indicates features that are new in version 4.0 of Watcom SQL.

This icon indicates that the example being discussed is included on the CD-ROM that comes with this book.

You will also find a few other icons in the margin. These are icons you can click to perform various tasks in Watcom SQL.

You will find these visual aids that help you on your Watcom journey: **Notes, Tips, Cautions**, and **Troubleshooting**.

Note

Notes indicate additional information that may help you avoid problems or that should be considered in using the described features.

Tip
Tips suggest easier or alternative methods for executing a procedure.

Caution

Cautions warn you about hazardous procedures (for example, activities that delete files).

Troubleshooting

This question-and-answer format provides guidance on how to find solutions to common problems. Specific problems you may encounter are shown in italic. Possible solutions appear in the paragraph(s) following the problems.

Special Edition Using Watcom SQL uses cross-references to help you access related information in other parts of the book. Right-facing triangles point you to related information in later chapters. Left-facing triangles point you to information in previous chapters.

Part I

Database Design

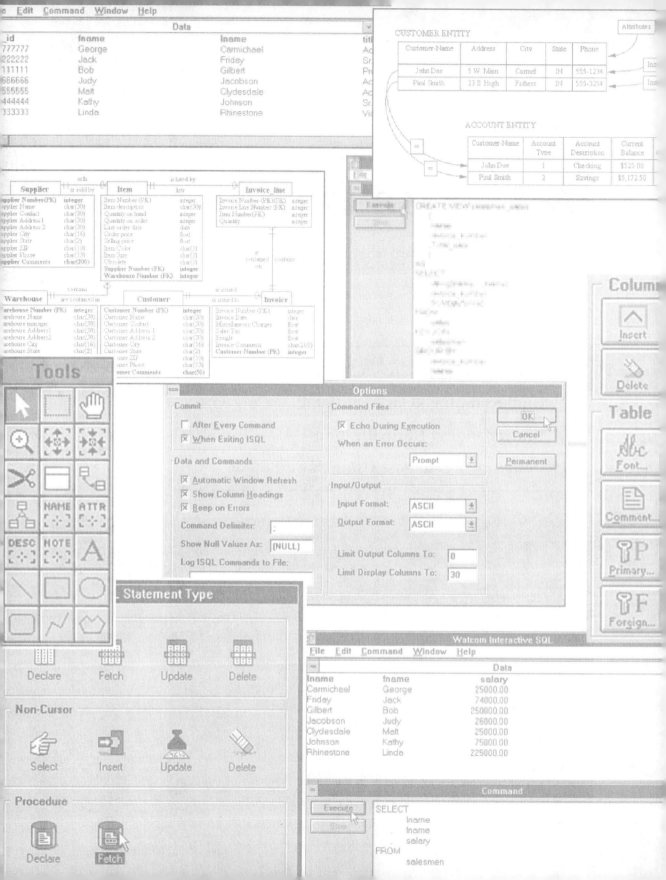

Chapter 1

Understanding Watcom SQL Fundamentals

by Charles A. Wood

In 1993, PowerSoft and Watcom merged companies. Now a development copy of Watcom SQL is included in every version of PowerBuilder, as well as other PowerSoft products such as InfoMaker.

Watcom SQL version 4.0 has some internal features that have a dramatic increase in performance. In addition, Watcom added several high-level features that are bound to make your database administration a simpler task.

According to a recent article on client-server databases in *PC Magazine*, Watcom SQL Version 3.2 had a faster response time on ad hoc queries (seen in many Windows programs such as PowerBuilder) than any other tested database! Watcom SQL 4.0 has made further speed improvements in on-line transaction processing.

▶ See "How Does Version 4.0 Performance Compare with Versions 3.0/ 3.2 Performance?," p. 466

Furthermore, the installation of Watcom SQL is the easiest in the industry. You can install the run-time version by running SETUP.EXE from the setup disk, and the Watcom development environment is automatically installed when you install PowerBuilder.

If money is a factor, you have a limited support staff coupled with a department-wide or peer-to-peer database, or you want to distribute a stand-alone copy of your work, Watcom is the database for you.

The Watcom SQL database is provided with PowerBuilder. There are many actions you can perform with Watcom SQL that are not included in the Watcom SQL documentation provided with PowerBuilder.

This chapter is designed to give you an overview of the features in Watcom SQL. By the end of this chapter, you should:

- Understand the new features of Watcom SQL

- Be able to install Watcom SQL

- Understand ISQL and ESQL

Reviewing New Features in Watcom SQL 4.0

Note

A *primary key* is the way you reference a row on a database. A primary key is a column or set of columns that uniquely identify the rows of a table.

A *foreign key* is a column or columns in a table that references a primary key in another table. Tables with foreign keys are often called *dependent tables*.

Referential integrity means that any foreign key has a corresponding primary key on a referenced table.

Restrictive referential integrity states that the user is not allowed to delete a row whose primary key is referenced by a foreign key on another table.

While the performance and features of Watcom SQL 3.2 satisfied the majority of users, version 4.0 adds a quantum leap in performance and features. Some of the significant improvements include those described in the following sections.

Cascading Deletes and Updates

When you established a foreign key in Watcom SQL 3.2, only restrictive referential integrity was allowed. In version 4.0, you can implement referential integrity using cascading deletes and updates.

A *cascading delete* means if you delete a row on a table, all rows on all other tables whose foreign key references the primary key on the row you deleted are also deleted.

A *cascading update* means that if you update the primary key on a table, all foreign keys that reference the primary key on the row you updated (depending on how the database is defined) do one of the following:

■ update with the same update value

■ update with a default value

■ set to NULL

This new functionality can save you, the developer, lots of work. It is also more robust than simple restrictive referential integrity. You can now use several types of referential integrity:

■ You would use restrictive referential integrity to force the developer and/or user to change all rows on a dependent table that reference the primary key you're about to change. Although this would not often be used, you could force the developer or user to review each row about to be changed before changing the master row.

  An example of this use can be seen in a company structure system. In this system, every employee in the employee table contains a foreign key to a department table. If that department were dissolved, you would want to reassign every employee and avoid automatically assigning employees to a new department or clearing their department key. Hence, the employee table would contain a foreign key with restrict referential integrity referencing department.

■ You would use cascading updates to update a key with NULL or a default value. This can be handy to indicate which rows on a table need attention, but not to cause the user to break from what he or she is doing to clean up rows on a dependent table.

  An example of this use can be seen in a salesperson/customer table. If a salesperson were to leave, all customers of that salesperson could receive a default value to indicate to another department that these customers need to be reassigned. Otherwise, you wouldn't be able to delete a salesperson from the salesperson table until all his customers were reassigned first.

■ You would use cascading updates to update a key with the changed primary key in the primary table.

  An example of this use can again be seen in a salesperson/customer table. If you wanted to reassign a salesperson's customers to another salesperson, you could update the primary key of that salesperson with a new salesperson's number. All dependent tables would then be updated with the new salesperson number.

▶ See "Under-
standing Keys,"
p. 48

Note

A *NULL* is a column that contains no data. Note that there is a difference between a NULL and a column with an empty string or zero in it. (NULLs are covered in more detail in Chapter 2, "Understanding Relational Database Concepts.")

An *empty string* is a string with no characters. It is different from a NULL in that an empty string is stored differently (internally), and is considered a value that can be entered into a string column; whereas a column containing NULL is considered to have no value.

Dependent tables are tables whose rows are dependent on another table. This is usually indicated with a foreign key on the dependent table that references the primary key of the primary table.

Auto-Increment Fields

Every developer knows the pain of setting up a unique key for each row on a table. Watcom lightens this burden with the addition of *auto-increment fields,* which automatically increment with each new row.

Dynamic Multi-Database Support

Watcom SQL now supports multiple databases on one server. In addition, Watcom SQL databases can be mounted and dismounted "on the fly." This is very handy for temporarily taking away multi-user access to a database for updates or fixes.

TCP/IP Support

TCP/IP is a network communication protocol used on the Internet and on Windows NT. Watcom SQL 4.0 now supports the TCP/IP access protocol.

Temporary Tables

Sometimes a table needs to be created that is temporary in nature. Without *temporary tables*, you not only need to make sure the table is empty when you start using it, you also don't want other users overwriting your temporary data with their own. This can cause a lockout of the database or, even worse, intermittent corruption of data in a multi-user environment.

Temporary tables simplify this a great deal. Temporary tables are set up to be unique for each user when she establishes a connection to the database. Any data left in this table is deleted when the user disconnects from the database. The automatic cleanup and individual tables greatly simplify many database procedures.

Buying Watcom SQL

According to an article on client-server databases in *PC Magazine*, Watcom SQL has the lowest price per user *for any number of users* than any other database tested! Now, version 4.0 increases performance even more for about the same cost. And the run-time version of Watcom SQL is available for an unlimited distribution at a relatively low price.

Watcom has run-time, single-user, and multi-user editions available. You can find out the price and availability for all versions of Watcom SQL by calling the Watcom/PowerSoft sales number at 1-800-265-4555.

> **Caution**
>
> The Watcom SQL run-time version *does not* support CREATE, COMMENT, ALTER, or DROP SQL commands. In addition, it does not support stored procedures or triggers. This can get a developer in trouble if he or she relies heavily on these new features of Watcom SQL.

> **Note**
>
> The Watcom SQL single-user version has all the features documented in this book except for networking utilities (DBWATCH, DBCLIENT, and DBSERVER). These utilities are available on the multi-user versions.

Using Watcom Utility Programs and ISQLW

You can implement Watcom SQL calls inside a PowerBuilder application by defining SQL for that application. However, you may find that you want to use the Watcom utility programs provided by Watcom.

> **Note**
>
> For the purposes of discussion, the program names listed are Windows programs. Watcom can also provide DOS, QNX, and OS/2 versions of these programs.

Table 1.1 lists all the Watcom Utility programs included with Watcom SQL Windows version, and gives a short description of each program. For a listing of programs with greater detail, see Chapter 24, "Using Watcom SQL Utilities."

▶ See "Implementing Watcom SQL as Multi-User Database," p. 222

Table 1.1   Watcom Utility Programs

Utility Program	Description
*BPATCH.EXE	Applies patches to Watcom programs. Available on the Watcom Forum on CompuServe when you download your patches.
DB32W.EXE, *RT32W.EXE, DBSTARTW.EXE, and *RTSTARTW.EXE	Database engines used to start your Watcom database.
DBBACKW.EXE	Backs up your Watcom database. For more information, see Chapter 11, "Backing Up and Recovery."
*DBCLIENT.EXE	Acts as a network requester. DBCOLLW.EXE applies a collating sequence. DBERASEW.EXE erases a database file, log file, or write file.
DBEXPANW.EXE	Expands a compressed database created by DBSHRINW.EXE.
DBINFOW.EXE	Displays information about a database or write file.
DBINITW.EXE	Creates a new database.
DBLOGW.EXE	Displays or changes the name of the transaction log.
DBSHRINW.EXE	Compresses a database.
*DBSTOPW.EXE	Stops a database engine or multi-user client (DBCLIENT).
DBTRANW.EXE	Translates a transaction log into SQL statements.
DBUNLOAW.EXE	Unloads a database into table files and SQL files.
*DBUPGRAD.EXE	Upgrades Watcom version 3.2 databases so they can use stored procedures.
DBVALIDW.EXE	Validates all indexes on a table.
*DBWATCH.EXE	Acts as a network server-monitoring facility.
DBWRITEW.EXE	Used to manage write files.
*ISQLW.EXE, RTSQLW.EXE	Processes interactive SQL commands.
*ODBCADM.EXE	Used to administer your ODBC environment. *ODBC* stands for *Open DataBase Connectivity* standards, set by Microsoft.

Utility Program	Description
*REBUILD.EXE	An automated procedure that calls DBUNLOAW and DERELOAW to rebuild one database from another.
*SQLPP.EXE	C/C++ precompiler and preprocessor for SQL commands to Watcom.
*TECHINFO.EXE	Displays technical information about your system.
*WSQLDDE.EXE	Invokes Watcom using the Dynamic Data Exchange.

These programs are not available with PowerBuilder but come with either the single-user version of Watcom or with the network version of Watcom (or both).

> **Note**
>
> An *index* is a column or set of columns that are specifically cataloged by the database to allow efficient searches on those columns.

Although we go into detail on each command in Chapter 24, "Using Watcom Utilities," right now you'll be able to see how some of these programs work.

Using DBINIT

You can create a Watcom SQL table outside of PowerBuilder by running the DBINIT (DBINITW.EXE) program. In figure 1.1, you can see the output of the DBINIT program when creating a table.

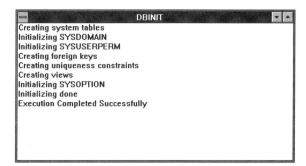

Fig. 1.1
By running DBINITW.EXE, you can create a table within the Windows environment.

Creating a Watcom SQL table outside of PowerBuilder by using DBINIT allows for a little more control of the table creation, including what to name log files, and controlling caching and performance issues.

▶ See "Using DBINITW.EXE," p. 628

Using ISQLW

The *ISQLW (Interactive SQL for Windows)* program allows the user to implement and/or test SQL statements. To get into the ISQLW environment, run ISQLW.EXE. If you are not already connected to a database and have not specified a database with an ISQLW.EXE command parameter, the Connect dialog box appears (see fig. 1.2).

Fig. 1.2

The Connect dialog box allows you to enter appropriate information needed to connect to your database.

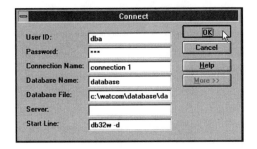

In the Connect dialog box, enter the following information:

■ Enter your user ID (usually **dba**).

■ Enter your password (usually **sql**).

■ You can enter your connection name, if you are using more than one connection to your database, to identify the connection you want to use. This is especially useful in a network environment.

■ The database name is the name of the database in the Microsoft ODBC (Open DataBase Connectivity) environment. The ODBC environment is used in Windows to let databases share a common interface.

■ The database file is the fully qualified path of the database file you want to access.

■ The server is the name of the server you are connecting to. (This is only needed in a network environment.)

■ The start line is the name of the database engine with the appropriate switches. Valid values are DB32W, RT32W, DBSTARTW, and RTSTARTW. You can review these engines and the switches they use in Chapter 24, "Using Watcom SQL Utilities."

When you're done entering your connection information, click OK. The ISQLW window opens, as shown in figure 1.3.

Menu bar   Data window

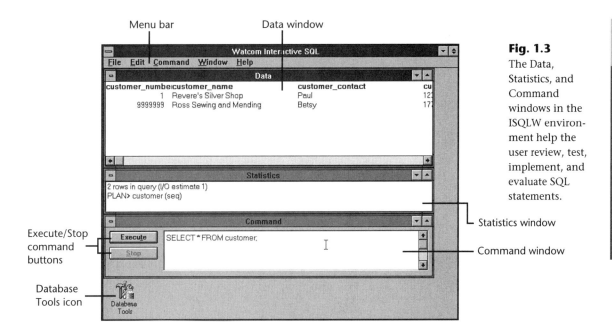

Fig. 1.3
The Data, Statistics, and Command windows in the ISQLW environment help the user review, test, implement, and evaluate SQL statements.

Execute/Stop command buttons

Database Tools icon

Statistics window

Command window

▶ See "Under-
standing and
Implementing
Security,"
p. 227

▶ See "GRANT,"
p. 555

The ISQLW window consists of five sections:

- **Command window.** The Command window is where you type the SQL command you want to implement.

- **Statistics window.** The Statistics window gives information that you can use to evaluate the efficiency of your SQL statement. Most SQL statements give the execution time.

- **Data window.** The Data window shows the results of an SQL statement. For instance, figure 1.3 shows that the SQL command Select * from customer was entered. The resulting columns and rows were displayed in the Data window.

> **Note**
>
> Don't confuse the Data window with a PowerBuilder DataWindow. The Data window in ISQLW shows the results of the SQL command, while a DataWindow is how PowerBuilder communicates with a database.

- **Database Tools icon.** The Database Tools icon with the Watcom SQL utilities (described in Chapter 24). You can do everything—from validating your database to backing up.

- **Execute and Stop command buttons.** These commands start your SQL and stop your SQL after you start processing.

- **Menu bar.** You use the menu bar to issue commands to the ISQLW environment. Like any good Windows 3.x program, you can access most of the popular menu commands with a shortcut key. For instance, to pull up a list of tables, you can open the **E**dit menu, and choose **L**ookup Table with the mouse (see fig. 1.4). Or you can press F7 from the keyboard.

Fig. 1.4
You can view the tables and columns of your database by clicking **E**dit, **I**nsert Table, or by pressing F7.

While you type your SQL command, you can look up database tables and columns. To do this, open the **E**dit menu and choose **I**nsert Table (or press F7). The Tables dialog box appears (see fig. 1.5). You can choose a table by selecting that table and clicking **I**nsert. The selected table pastes itself right in the command window where the cursor is placed.

Tip
The Columns dialog box is always renamed to be the name of the table whose columns are being displayed.

If you select a table in the Tables dialog box and then choose the **C**olumns button, the Columns dialog box appears (see fig. 1.6). The Columns dialog box lists all the columns for a table, and allows you to paste column names right in the Command window. Just select a column and then click OK.

Fig. 1.5
The Tables dialog box lets you examine and select a table from the tables already created on the database.

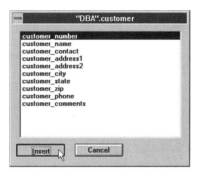

Fig. 1.6
The Columns dialog box lets you examine and select a column from a specific table.

Note

RTSQLW (Run Time SQL for Windows) is similar to ISQLW. Instead of being interactive, RTSQLW allows you to write a text file containing SQL statements and then implement them without input from the user.

▶ See "Using ISQLW.EXE," p. 641

▶ See "Using RTSQLW.EXE," p. 640

Understanding the Difference between ISQL and ESQL

SQL, as mentioned in the Introduction, stands for Structured Query Language. SQL has revolutionized the database industry because it enables developers to switch between databases without changing their database language. Many databases, including Watcom SQL, use SQL as their only database language.

In Watcom SQL, there are two distinctions of SQL commands: ESQL and ISQL.

- ESQL, or Embedded SQL, is the SQL found in programming languages. Certain SQL statements, like the cursor statements OPEN, FETCH, and CLOSE, are not needed in the external ISQLW utility, but come in handy when developing an application. These commands are considered "ESQL only."

- Some SQL commands (such as CONFIGURE) usually have no place inside a window's application; they are used in the ISQLW environment. This is because statements like CONFIGURE (used to set up your options inside your ISQLW environment), and DBTOOL DBBACKUP (used to back up your database) are used to administer your environment at the operating-system level rather than inside a program. These commands are considered "ISQL only."

- ISQL, or Interactive SQL, is the SQL used with the ISQLW and RTSQLW programs.

Most SQL commands can be used in the ISQLW environment and in a programming language.

PowerBuilder can use a subset of ESQL inside its Database Administration window (see "Accessing Watcom SQL with PowerBuilder," later in this chapter). PowerBuilder can also use a different subset of ESQL in PowerScript.

Note

PowerScript is the language used by PowerBuilder applications.

Using the Microsoft ODBC Administrator

 Watcom SQL comes with the Microsoft ODBC Administrator. To use the ODBC administrator, click the ODBCADM icon. The Microsoft ODBC Administrator dialog box appears (see fig. 1.7).

Note

ODBC is an acronym for the *Open DataBase Connectivity* standard established by Microsoft for Windows databases. Using ODBC, programs can connect to a Windows database without writing their own configuration programs for each database used.

Watcom SQL was written from the ground up as an ODBC database. While some databases have a "fast" version written in their native code and a "slow" version for ODBC, Watcom's native code *is* its ODBC code. By designing their database for ODBC, Watcom SQL has achieved some of the fastest times using ODBC in the industry!

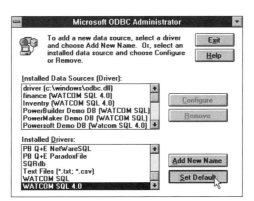

Fig. 1.7
You use the Microsoft ODBC Administrator to define tables for the ODBC interface.

In the Installed **D**rivers section, the ODBC Administrator may show many different database drivers. Select Watcom SQL 4.0 to see the databases supported by Watcom SQL.

By selecting Watcom SQL 4.0 and then choosing **S**et Default, the Watcom SQL ODBC Configuration dialog box appears (see fig. 1.8). Using the Watcom SQL ODBC Configuration dialog box, you define the connection parameters needed to connect to a Watcom SQL database.

In the Watcom SQL ODBC Configuration dialog box, you can enter the following database-connection information:

- **Data Source Name.** This is the name given to this configuration definition. The data source name allows a developer to identify the ODBC configuration from an application.

- **Description.** The description allows you to comment on your database from the ODBC administrator.

- **User ID.** The user ID is the connection name used to connect to the database. In this case, the user ID is dba.

- **Password.** The password allows you to define a default password to attach to a database file. Although all you see is ***, the password is actually sql.

■ **Database Alias.** The database alias, if used, allows you to use a different name for your database than the name entered as the data source
name.

■ **Database File.** The database file is the full path name of the database.

Fig. 1.8
The Watcom SQL
ODBC Configura-
tion dialog box
is used to set
configuration
defaults for your
Database.

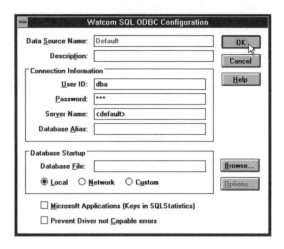

Note

As mentioned previously, dba and sql are the default user ID and password used
when Watcom SQL creates a database.

After you have entered all the fields needed in the Watcom SQL ODBC Configuration dialog box, choose whether you want the database to be a local
database (on your C: drive or personal hard disk drive) or a network database.
You can also define a custom database.

The Microsoft ODBC specification states that primary and foreign keys
should not be returned by SQLStatistics. Microsoft programs, like Microsoft
Visual Basic V3.0, assume that primary and foreign keys are returned by
SQLStatistics. If you check the Microsoft Applications (Keys in SQLStatistics)
checkbox, the Watcom SQL ODBC driver will mimic the required behavior so
that Visual Basic and other Microsoft applications work properly.

The Watcom SQL ODBC driver returns a Driver not Capable error code because it does not support qualifiers. Some ODBC applications do not handle
this error properly. If you are having problems with an ODBC application,
checking the Prevent Driver not Capable errors box disables this error code,
allowing these applications to work.

When you're done entering data on the Watcom SQL ODBC Configuration dialog box, click OK to save your configuration so that it's usable by ODBC languages (like PowerBuilder) and applications. This will return you to the Microsoft ODBC Administrator.

After you select a database in the Microsoft ODBC Administrator dialog box (refer to fig. 1.7), you can also choose **A**dd New Name. The Watcom SQL ODBC Configuration dialog box opens again (refer to fig. 1.8). This time, set the ODBC configuration for a new database. Choose **B**rowse to open the Select Database dialog box (see fig. 1.9).

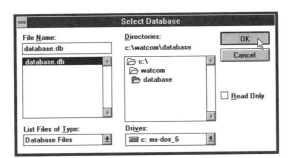

Fig. 1.9
The Select Database dialog box allows you to select a data source for your ODBC database definition.

Browse through the directories until you find the file you need as your data source. Select the database file you want, and click OK. This places the path and file name in the Watcom SQL ODBC Configuration dialog box (see fig. 1.10).

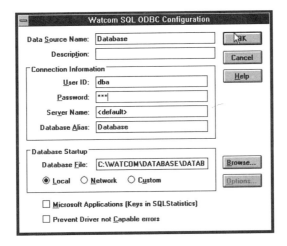

Fig. 1.10
Clicking **B**rowse allows you to add an existing database to the Watcom SQL ODBC Configuration dialog box.

Database Design

Accessing Watcom SQL with PowerBuilder

You can also access Watcom SQL from within PowerBuilder. You'll find that PowerBuilder's database painter can be a very intuitive database manager. In fact, even if you avoid developing in PowerBuilder, you might consider purchasing a copy just to help manage your database.

> **Note**
>
> A *painter* is a window in PowerBuilder that is associated with a given function. In this case, the *database painter* is a window that allows the developer to manipulate the database.

 When you're in the PowerBuilder environment, click the Database icon to open the database painter. Your current database tables, or the PowerBuilder Demo Database tables will appear in the Select Tables dialog box (see fig. 1.11). Click Cancel to clear your database painter and to begin creating your database.

Fig. 1.11
The Select Tables dialog box allows you to choose which database tables you want to view or modify.

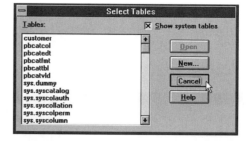

Creating a Watcom SQL Database from within PowerBuilder

To create a database, open the File menu and choose Create Database (see fig. 1.12).

> **Note**
>
> You can also open the ODBC Administrator dialog box, seen in figure 1.7, from inside PowerBuilder. Open the File menu and choose Configure ODBC inside the database painter.

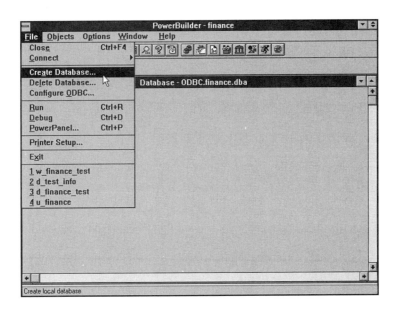

Fig. 1.12
In PowerBuilder's database painter, you can perform many database functions, including creating a database.

Now you should see the Create Local Database dialog box, as shown in figure 1.13. Type the Database Name, the User ID, the Password, and the name of the database engine used to start the database.

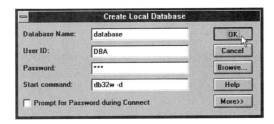

Fig. 1.13
The Create Local Database dialog box gives PowerBuilder all the necessary information needed to create a Watcom SQL database.

Although you created a database, you still need to connect to it through a PowerBuilder database profile. A PowerBuilder database profile contains information used by PowerBuilder to connect to a database.

To set up a PowerBuilder database profile and connect to your database through PowerBuilder, open the **F**ile menu and choose **C**onnect. A pop-up menu appears (see fig. 1.14). To choose an existing profile, choose that profile. If you have no existing profile yet, choose **S**etup.

If you chose **S**etup, you now see the Database Profiles dialog box (see fig. 1.15). Here, you can edit existing profiles by selecting the profile name and choosing **E**dit. You can also create new profiles by choosing **N**ew.

Fig. 1.14

You can connect to your database from PowerBuilder through a PowerBuilder database profile.

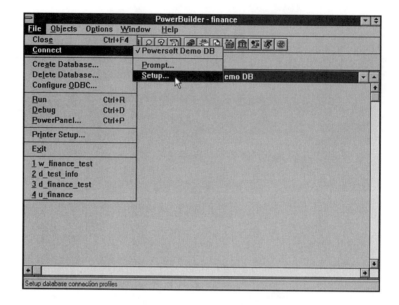

Fig. 1.15

You can add, change, or delete database profiles in PowerBuilder using the Database Profiles dialog box.

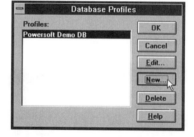

When you choose **N**ew in the Database Profiles dialog box, the Database Profile Setup dialog box opens, as in figure 1.16. Enter the Profile Name, the DBMS (ODBC for Watcom), the user ID (usually **dba**), the password (usually **sql**), and the database name. Click OK.

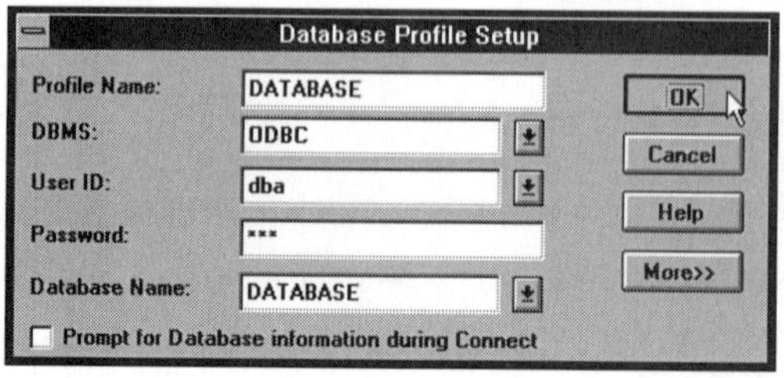

Fig. 1.16

Use the Database Profile Setup dialog box to give PowerBuilder the information necessary to connect to a database.

PowerBuilder then opens the SQL Data Sources dialog box (see fig. 1.17). In the SQL Data Sources dialog box, a list of ODBC databases that have already been defined appears. Click the database you want to use for this profile, and then click OK to close the SQL Data Sources dialog box and return to the Database Profiles dialog box.

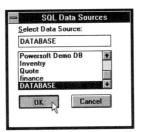

Fig. 1.17
Use the SQL Data Sources dialog box to associate a database with a PowerBuilder database profile.

Now the Database Profiles dialog box appears again (see fig. 1.18). This time, the database profile you just created is listed.

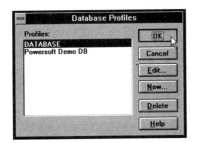

Fig. 1.18
The Database Profiles dialog box also lists newly-created database profiles.

Creating Database Tables from within PowerBuilder

You have created a database, but you don't have user-defined tables in the database. Click the Open icon in the database painter (or click on Options, **T**ables on the menu bar) to pull up the Select Tables dialog box. Notice that the Tables list is empty, as seen in figure 1.19.

Choose **N**ew, or click the Cancel command button and then click the New icon (or click on O**p**tions, **N**ew, **T**able on the menu bar).

Tip
A newly-defined database, while having no user-defined tables, does have system-defined tables.

You now see the Create Table dialog box, as shown in figure 1.20. Use this dialog box to define table names and fields, as well as to set up primary and foreign keys. After you enter the table name, enter each column name in the table—followed by the column's data type, width (if applicable), and decimals (if applicable). You can also define whether to allow a NULL to be placed in the column when storing a row.

Fig. 1.19
A newly created database has no user-defined tables.

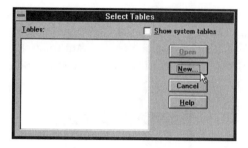

Fig. 1.20
Use the Create Table dialog box to create a table in your database.

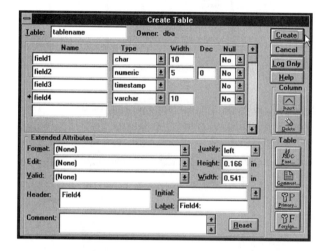

Note

You can also define extended attributes, such as format, labels, and comments, in the database painter. These are used internally for PowerBuilder use only—to display when accessing the database in PowerBuilder and to help set up your PowerBuilder DataWindows.

Tip
Primary keys cannot be NULL.

When you finish typing the fields, choose **P**rimary. The Primary Key Definition dialog box appears (see fig. 1.21). Simply click the table columns you want to be primary key columns, and then click OK.

Now you return to the Create Table dialog box (refer to fig. 1.20). Click OK. This opens the table you just defined in the database painter, as seen in figure 1.22.

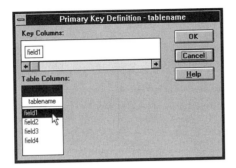

Fig. 1.21
In the Primary Key Definition dialog box, you can define a primary key for your database.

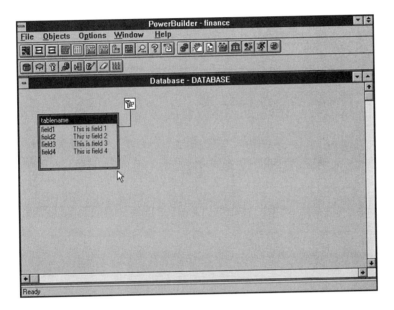

Fig. 1.22
Newly created tables open in the database painter.

Manipulating Your Watcom SQL Database Using PowerBuilder

You can manipulate your database when the tables are created from within the database painter. Using the database painter, you can do the following:

■ Issue ESQL commands using PowerBuilder's database administrator. From within the database painter, click the Admin icon. The Database Administration window opens (see fig. 1.23). From here, you can issue an ESQL command that can alter the database, create tables, or alter data in the tables.

34 Chapter 1—Understanding Watcom SQL Fundamentals

Fig. 1.23
The Database
Administration
window allows the
user to enter an
ESQL command.

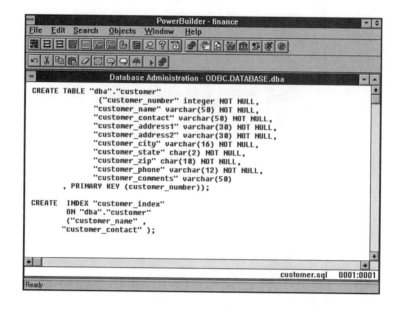

■ Enter data directly into the database tables without using SQL by using the Data Manipulation window seen in figure 1.24. You can enter the Data Manipulation window by clicking the Preview icon in the database painter.

Fig. 1.24
You can enter data
directly into the
tables in the Data
Manipulation
window.

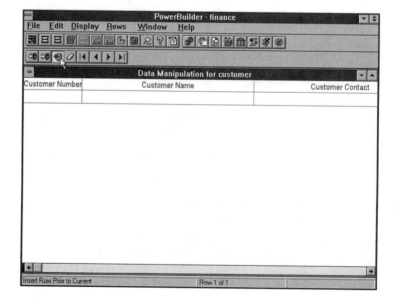

- To insert a row, click the Insert Row icon. This inserts a new row in which you can enter column data.

- Import data from an external source. Just open the **R**ows menu and choose **I**mport (see fig. 1.25).

Fig. 1.25
You can import data with the Select Import File dialog box by clicking on **R**ows, **I**mport.

- The Select Import File dialog box opens (see fig. 1.26). Select the import file type (either tab-delimited text (.txt) or dBase II or III only) and the name you want to add to your table.

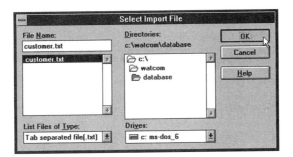

Fig. 1.26
Use the Select Import File dialog box to select an import file to import into a table.

- Export from within the Data Manipulation window. Open the **F**ile menu and choose Save **R**ows As (see fig. 1.27).

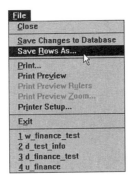

Fig. 1.27
To export your data, first click on **F**ile, Save **R**ows As.

Database Design

■ Now you can save your data in several different formats using the Save Rows As dialog box (see fig. 1.28). Select the proper **F**ile Format and then type the name of the output file. Click OK to begin the export.

Fig. 1.28

The Save Rows As dialog box allows you to save your data in several different formats.

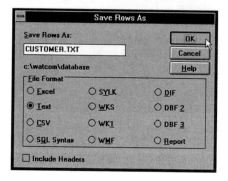

From Here...

This chapter showed you many ways to access your Watcom database, especially with PowerBuilder. Although every chapter touches on the information in this chapter, you might find the following chapters useful:

■ Chapter 4, "Designing a Database Using PowerBuilder," shows you how to implement a design using the PowerBuilder environment.

■ Chapter 6, "Understanding SQL," describes how to use SQL for database, table, and data manipulation.

■ Chapter 8, "Understanding the Role of a Database Administrator (DBA)," talks about implementing Watcom in a production environment.

■ Chapter 13, "Implementing Watcom SQL with PowerBuilder," tells you how to use Watcom SQL from within a PowerBuilder application.

Chapter 2

Understanding Relational Database Concepts

by Paul Horan with Charles A. Wood

Before you get into the details of working with Watcom SQL, it's important that you understand at least the basics of Relational Database Management System (RDBMS) theory. Believe me, this entire book could be devoted to the concepts of relational theory, but it'll stick to the basics.

In this chapter, you learn about the following:

- The history of relational database theory

- Understanding entities, attributes, and relationships

- How to diagram a logical database model

- The transition from a logical to a physical model

Relational Database Management System (RDBMS) Theory

In 1970, E. F. Codd published a paper that is widely recognized as the introduction of the relational database theory. Codd described a *relational algebra* that could be used to create models of data and information. The concepts outlined in Codd's paper were dramatically different from the established data management technologies in use in 1970.

The underlying concept of Codd's *relational* theory is that when you examine the business rules for a specific context or business area, certain patterns emerge that allow data and information to be arranged into like sets, or *entities*. These entities consist of one or more *attributes* that fully describe the entities. *Relationships* can be established between two entities that share common attributes. Codd also defined the concept of a universal retrieval "language" for relational database access, based on his relational algebra. However, it took about four years before an actual language, called SEQUEL, was introduced. By the late 1970s, IBM's San Jose Research Laboratory had implemented SQL (Structured Query Language) as the access language for its relational database system, System R.

Sequential file and hierarchical data storage systems both required the programmer to know intimate details about the physical characteristics of the data, such as file names, record and field lengths, the order of the fields on the record, the parent-child structures that had been specifically established, and so on. With relational databases, retrieving data is simply a matter of describing the desired answer set using a structured, English-like query language with real words such as SELECT, UPDATE, INSERT, and so on. The benefits of relational theory are evident: you are much less concerned with the physical storage aspects of the data than you would be with a record-based file structure, or a hierarchical DBMS. For those of you who have ever coded a Segment Search Argument in IMS-DB™, IBM's hierarchical DBMS, working with a relational database's structured query language is a breeze!

SQL has been adopted and adapted for many relational database management systems. It has been approved as the official relational query language standard by the American National Standards Institute (ANSI) and the International Standards Organization (ISO). Many RDBMS vendors, including Watcom, have developed specific extensions to ANSI-standard SQL, but all of them support at least the basic language. Although the "Q" in SQL stands for Query, the language also includes commands for adding new data, deleting and modifying existing data, creating new databases and database objects, and other functions. The specific syntax of SQL is examined in greater detail later. For now, we explore the basic building blocks of a Logical Relational Database Model: entities, attributes, and relationships.

Entities

An *entity* represents a set of real or abstract things (people, places, events, and so on) that have common attributes or characteristics. If you think of each database query as a sentence, entities would be the "nouns" of those sentences. The first step in developing a relational database model is to make a list of all the nouns that are important and need to be tracked.

> ### Note
>
> *Joint Application Development (JAD)*, the method used to systematically extract information from users, is a great technique for developing a Logical Database Model. These sessions usually involve key representatives from the business area, along with a session facilitator, sitting around a table and brainstorming together. JAD sessions help the users feel involved in the creation of the system that will eventually support them.

A good example of entities for a bank might be CUSTOMER, ACCOUNT, TRANSACTION, and so on. These are the important "things" that a bank might want to keep track of with a database.

You can view an entity as a two-dimensional table, consisting of rows and columns. The columns, which are also called *attributes*, represent the various characteristics of the entity. For the CUSTOMER entity, these characteristics might be Name, Address, and so on. The rows represent individual occurrences, or *instances*, of the entity.

Entities have the following properties:

- Each column contains values about the same attribute, and the attribute on a single row contains a single value. This means that the "Name" attribute only contains "Name" data, not "Address" or "Phone Number" data, and that only a single value for "Name" exists on any single instance of the CUSTOMER entity.

- Each attribute has a distinct name, and the order of the attributes across the entity is immaterial. This means that it makes no difference whether the "Name" attribute is defined before or after the "Address" attribute when writing an SQL statement.

- Each row is distinct; that is, one instance cannot duplicate another instance for selected key attribute columns.

- The sequence of the rows, or instances, is also immaterial.

It's important not to confuse the concept of an entity with the concept of occurrences, or instances, of that entity. In the bank example, CUSTOMER and ACCOUNT have been selected as entities. If Paul Smith and John Doe are customers of the bank, they would represent occurrences of the CUSTOMER entity. The same concept applies to ACCOUNT. Let's say that John and Paul both have checking accounts at the bank. There would be two instances of the ACCOUNT entity: one for John's checking account, and one for Paul's.

The entity is much like a "blueprint" for the creation of new occurrences, in the same way that many houses can be constructed from a single blueprint for a house.

A relational database must be able to distinguish between individual occurrences, or instances, of any entity. This is accomplished through the use of an entity's attributes. If entities are the nouns, attributes are the adjectives in a relational database. Instances of an entity are differentiated from each other by the values of their attributes at any one point in time.

> **Caution**
>
> Taking the noun-adjective analogy literally may result in a large number of single-attribute entities. Don't be concerned, nearly every logical model starts out this way. The techniques of normalization outlined in Chapter 3 will help weed out the attributes from the entities.

Attributes

An *attribute* represents a characteristic or property associated with a set of entities. It's easy to think of attributes as the fields of a record in a file-based structure. Back to the bank example, attributes of the CUSTOMER entity might be Name, Address, Phone Number, and so on. The ACCOUNT entity might be described with Customer Name, Checking Account Number, Current Balance, and so on.

An important part of the entity-attribute definition process is the identification of those attributes that can uniquely identify each occurrence. These specialized attributes are called *primary keys,* and should be chosen with care. Attributes that might initially seem to be unique may in fact be poor choices for primary keys. *Foreign keys* are attributes of an entity that are primary keys of a related entity. We'll spend more time on primary and foreign keys a little later in this chapter.

Relationships

The bank would also probably want to know which accounts belong to which customers. You certainly wouldn't want your bank to mix up its customers' accounts! By choosing a common attribute that can be shared on both the

CUSTOMER and ACCOUNT entities, a *relationship* can be established between specific instances of the two entities. Relationships are the heart and soul of a relational database. It is this capability that makes the relational algebra of E. F. Codd come to life. A relationship is a logical, meaningful connection between two separate entities, or from an entity to itself, and exists when the entities share common attributes or when dictated by business rules.

In the bank example, the CUSTOMER and ACCOUNT entities might share the common attribute of Customer Name. You can establish a relationship between the two entities by finding instances of CUSTOMER and ACCOUNT, where their Customer Name attributes are equal. Figure 2.1 illustrates the CUSTOMER and ACCOUNT entities, showing the various attributes that have been identified for each entity. There are two instances of each entity, and a relationship exists between the two entities on the Customer Name attribute.

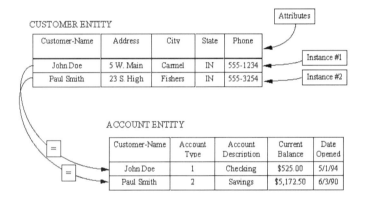

Fig. 2.1
This figure illustrates the concepts of entities, attributes, instances, and relationships.

Cardinality

Relationships also possess the concept of *cardinality*, which helps quantify the relationship. Suppose that there are two entities, A and B. A *zero-to-one* relationship from entity A to entity B means that a given instance of A has one and only one instance of B associated with it. However, each instance of B does not require a matching instance of A. In other words, the instance of B can exist without a matching instance of A, but each A requires a B. The example in figure 2.2 shows a common zero-to-one relationship, that of PERSON to SPOUSE.

A *one-to-one* relationship from entity A to entity B means that, at any point in time, a given instance of A has one and only one instance of B associated with it. Conversely, each instance of B has one and only one related instance

Tip
The diagramming notation used in figures 2.2 through 2.7 are defined more fully following figure 2.7.

of A. The two instances cannot exist without each other. One-to-one relation-ships are rarely used unless there's a good reason not to combine the two entities.

Fig. 2.2

This figure shows an example of zero-to-one relationship.

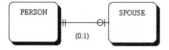

Figure 2.3 shows an example of a one-to-one relationship between the enti-ties STUDENT-ID and STUDENT-NAME. Obviously, a student can have one and only one name at a time. Therefore, a more concise representation of this relationship would be to combine the two entities as attributes of a single STUDENT entity.

Fig. 2.3

In this example of a one-to-one relationship, a STUDENT-ID can only have one STUDENT-NAME, and a STUDENT-NAME can only have one STUDENT-ID.

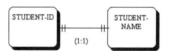

A *zero-to-many* relationship from A to B means that, at any period in time, a given instance of A may be related to zero, one, or more instances of B. How-ever, each instance of B must be related to one and only one instance of A. In other words, every B requires one and only one A, but an A can exist with zero, one, or more related B's. Figure 2.4 is an example of a common zero to many relationship, STUDENT to DEGREE.

Fig. 2.4

In this zero-to-many relationship, a student can have zero, one, or more DEGREEs, but a DEGREE does not exist unless it has been awarded to a STUDENT.

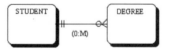

A *one-to-many* relationship from A to B means that, at any period in time, a given instance of A has one or more instances of B. However, each instance of B is associated with only one instance of A. This is the most prevalent type of relationship. Figure 2.5 shows a typical one-to-many relationship, from MAN-AGER to EMPLOYEE.

A *many-to-many* relationship from A to B means that, at any point in time, each instance of A has zero, one, or an arbitrary number of instances of B; the opposite is also true. These types of relationships are common in many initial relational models, but are impossible to maintain in a physical data model. Always avoid many-to-many relationships, if possible. The many-to-many relationship in figure 2.6 shows the association between STUDENT-ID and

COURSE-ID. Each STUDENT takes zero, one, or more COURSEs, and each COURSE can have zero, one, or more STUDENTs.

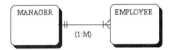

Fig. 2.5
In this example of a one-to-many relationship, each MANAGER has at least one or more EMPLOYEES, and each EMPLOYEE must have one and only one MANAGER.

Many-to-many relationships must be eliminated by creating a third entity, called an *associative entity,* that combines the primary keys of the two original entities. Each original entity then has a one-to-many relationship with the associative entity. For example, there would be one STUDENT-ID value in the original STUDENT-ID entity for possibly many values in the associative STUDENT-COURSE entity. Figure 2.7 shows the new associative entity STUDENT-COURSE, which contains both the STUDENT-ID attribute and the COURSE-ID attribute on the same row. This combination of attributes converts the many-to-many relationship from figure 2.6 into two one-to-many relationships.

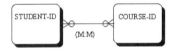

Fig. 2.6
In this example of a many-to-many relationship, a student can have many courses and courses can have many students.

Navigating through the new associative entity STUDENT-COURSE when constructing queries is rather simple. The relationship between STUDENT-ID and STUDENT-COURSE is on the STUDENT-ID attribute, and the relationship between COURSE-ID and STUDENT-COURSE is on the COURSE-ID attribute. By selecting a single STUDENT-ID row, you can then retrieve all the STUDENT-COURSE rows that match on STUDENT-ID. The COURSE-ID attribute on the rows that matched on STUDENT-ID can then be retrieved from the COURSE-ID entity. The navigation is exactly the same when starting with the COURSE-ID table, but in reverse.

Fig. 2.7
This illustrates the creation of the associative entity STUDENT-COURSE, to help resolve the many-to-many relationship between STUDENT-ID and COURSE-ID.

Designing a Database

Tip
Imagine that these
are the same
rounded rect-
angles used in
figures 2.2
through 2.7, but
now you can peek
inside the borders
and see the de-
scriptions of all
the attributes.

Designing a relational database is the process of defining entities and attributes, and determining the proper relationships between the entities. This
definition process is driven by a thorough analysis of the problems being
solved, and the business rules and processes that govern the subject area. The
product of all this analysis is called the *Logical Relational Database Model*, or
just the *Logical Model*.

Let's continue with our Bank example, and design a Logical Model for a basic
Customer Account tracking system.

Diagramming Entities, Attributes, and Relationships

The first step in creating the Logical Model is determining the entities and
taking a first-cut at their attributes. Let's start with an obvious choice, the
CUSTOMER entity.

Diagramming Notation for Entities and Attributes

Figure 2.8 shows a commonly used notation for diagramming a Logical
Model. A rounded rectangle represents each entity, with the list of attributes
inside the rectangle, and the entity name above the box.

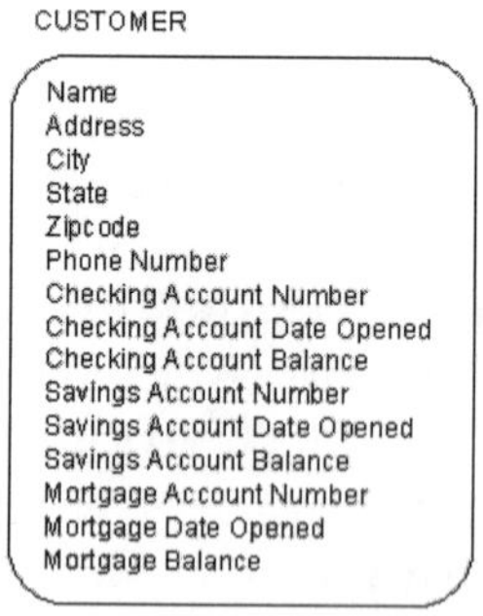

Fig. 2.8
This illustrates the
diagramming
techniques for
entity-attribute
definitions.

CUSTOMER

Name
Address
City
State
Zipcode
Phone Number
Checking Account Number
Checking Account Date Opened
Checking Account Balance
Savings Account Number
Savings Account Date Opened
Savings Account Balance
Mortgage Account Number
Mortgage Date Opened
Mortgage Balance

Note

Entity names should always be singular nouns, such as CUSTOMER and PERSON, not
CUSTOMERS and PEOPLE. The entity describes a singular concept, or class of entity,
that can have multiple occurrences or instances. The nature of the relationships
determines the cardinality of the entity.

The first cut of the CUSTOMER entity contains attributes that describe the customer (customer, name, address, and so on), and attributes that contain information about the various accounts a customer might have (Date Opened, Balance, and so on). This model is refined more in Chapter 3, when we cover a technique called *normalization*, but this is a good starting point.

The first thing that should be apparent from the initial cut of the CUSTOMER entity is the existence of a separate thing called "ACCOUNT." Pull the ACCOUNT-related attributes into a separate entity named ACCOUNT, and see what that looks like (see fig. 2.9). Remember that, in order for a relationship to be created between the entities, they must share a common attribute. To accomplish this, pull the Customer Name attribute into the ACCOUNT entity as well.

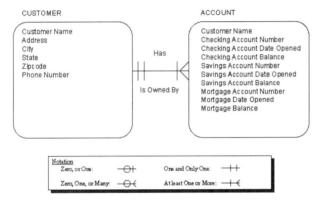

Fig. 2.9
This shows the creation of the ACCOUNT entity, and the relocation of the account-related attributes from the CUSTOMER entity.

Now the first relationship takes shape. The CUSTOMER and ACCOUNT entities share the common attribute Customer Name. We can now "join" the two entities when the Customer Name attributes are exactly equal.

Diagramming Notation for Relationships

A popular notation for diagramming entities and relationships is called *Chen notation*. It uses a verb phrase and several different symbols to denote the cardinality of the relationship. The way to read Chen notation is to start on one entity, and travel along the line connecting another entity, as follows:

```
"A(n)" <entity #1> <verb phrase> <symbol> <entity #2> "(s)".
```

Refer to the diagram in figure 2.9 to try it. Start on the CUSTOMER entity, and read to the right, using the verb Has. The result is: "A CUSTOMER has at least one or more ACCOUNT(s)." Going the other direction, start on the ACCOUNT entity and use the verb phrase is owned by. "An ACCOUNT is owned by one and only one CUSTOMER." (Ignore the possibility of a joint checking account for now.) Both of these statements are valid descriptions of the relationships between the two entities.

Further examination of the Logical Model reveals that the ACCOUNT entity really consists of three separate sets of attributes that depend on the type of account. The Account Balance and Date Opened attributes can be condensed into single attributes, and a new attribute can be created that identifies the type of account. Figure 2.10 shows the latest revision to the Logical Model. You can see that a new attribute, Account Description, was created to contain the values Checking, Savings, or Mortgage. For example, when the value of the Account Description attribute is Checking, the Account Number, Account Balance, and Date Opened attributes on that instance all pertain to the Customer's Checking account. This technique reduces the number of attributes from 10 to 5, and makes the Logical Model a great deal more flexible.

Fig. 2.10
This illustrates the changes to the Logical Model following the removal of attributes that are dependent on the Account Descrip-tion attribute.

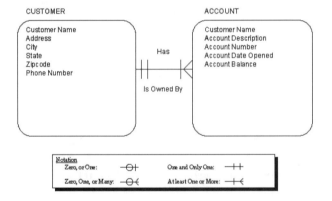

Understanding Tables

After the Logical Model is complete, it must be implemented into a Physical Model. The Logical Model consists of entities, attributes, instances, and rela-tionships; the Physical Model consists of tables, rows, and columns.

Entities are implemented in a relational DBMS as *tables*. Each table in a data-base must have a unique name; it can be the same name as in the Logical Model. Each row in a table represents a single occurrence, or instance, of the entity. Each column, also called an *attribute*, describes part of the entity.

Table 2.1 relates the Logical and Physical Model terms. Even though they're basically interchangeable, it's good practice to keep the terms straight.

Table 2.1 Logical Model and Physical Model Terms	
Logical Model	**Physical Model**
Entity	Table
Attribute	Column
Instance/Occurrence	Row
Relationship	Primary/Foreign Key

Figure 2.11 illustrates the transition from a Logical Entity-Attribute Definition to a Relational Table Definition.

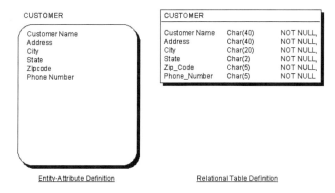

Fig. 2.11
This shows the difference in notation between a Logical Model and the Relational Table Definition used in a Physical Model.

Attributes of an entity are implemented as *columns* of the table. Each column has a name, which must be unique within the table; a data type, which describes the physical characteristics of the data stored in the column; and an indicator of whether the column can accept NULL values. Data types and the use of NULLs are explored in more detail shortly.

Exploring Rows and Columns

The easiest way to visualize a table's rows and columns is to think of a spreadsheet. Each spreadsheet consists of rows and columns that are uniquely identified. The columns are named A, B, C, and so on, and the rows are numbered. Each column can be set up to contain a specific data type, such as numeric or character data. As new rows are inserted, the columns on the new rows retain their definitions and data entered in the individual cells should conform to these definitions.

In a relational database table, the column names can be much more descriptive than A, B, and C, but still have to be unique in a single table. Each row represents a unique instance of the entity, and must be able to be uniquely identified. This is accomplished through the definition of a primary key, either a single column or a combination of several columns, that can uniquely identify a single row. A primary key that consists of several columns is called a *composite key*.

Understanding Keys

Keys are the columns, or combination of columns, that help identify specific instances of an entity. *Primary keys* uniquely identify each row in the table. Without a primary key, it's impossible for the DBMS to distinguish between specific rows in a table. *Foreign keys* are the columns in a table that are primary keys of a different table. (Refer to figure 2.10 for an example of foreign keys.)

Because Customer-Name is the primary key of the CUSTOMER entity, it functions as a foreign key in the ACCOUNT entity.

Let's revisit the Model for the Customer Account database, and see whether a primary key for the Customer and Account tables can be identified. Figure 2.12 shows the CUSTOMER and ACCOUNT tables, populated with rows of data.

Fig. 2.12

The physical tables CUSTOMER and ACCOUNT, with representative data.

CUSTOMER TABLE

Customer-Name	Address	City	State	Zip	Phone
John Doe	5 W. Main	Carmel	IN	46032	555-1234
Paul Smith	23 S. High	Fishers	IN	46038	555-3254

ACCOUNT TABLE

Customer-Name	Account Description	Account Number	Current Balance	Date Opened
John Doe	Checking	70020320211	$525.00	5/1/94
John Doe	Savings	90020320211	$1,315.29	5/1/94
Paul Smith	Savings	90020320439	$5,172.50	6/3/90

Using Primary Keys

What column or columns in the Customer table are potential candidates for a primary key? How about Name? This seems OK, but as soon as the bank has two Paul Smiths as customers, our model has a real problem. How about the combination of Address, City, and State? There certainly can't be two different houses at the same address! But the minute that Paul Smith's wife Paula opens her own Checking Account, we now have two distinct customers at the same address, and the uniqueness of our primary key is violated. Adding Name to the combination of Address, City, and State would probably do the trick, but a composite key consisting of these four columns becomes very unwieldy. What if Paul Smith and his family move to a new address? Now we've got to change the value stored in the primary key, which is a situation that should be avoided.

The answer here is to create a new column that will serve as a primary key, called Customer ID. This column can be a system-generated number, sequence of characters, or a well-established identifier such as the Social Security Number. In any case, the number assigned to Paul and Paula Smith can remain consistent, regardless of any change in another attribute. The columns that used to make up the primary key are now simply non-key columns.

Now look at the ACCOUNT table in figure 2.13. Because Customer Name has been replaced as the primary key of the CUSTOMER table with Customer ID, the relationship with the ACCOUNT table was affected. To restore the relationship, the Customer ID column has been propagated to the ACCOUNT table. The primary key of ACCOUNT now becomes the Customer ID column.

Tip
System-generated keys, used to replace a complex concatenated key, are often referred to as *obtuse keys*.

Database Design

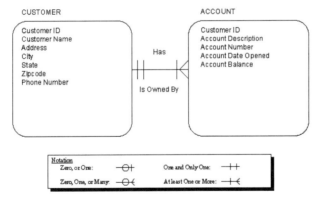

Fig. 2.13
This shows the changes in the Logical Model caused by the creation of an obtuse key called Customer ID.

Refer to figure 2.12 to see that the Customer ID attribute is no longer adequate as the primary key of the ACCOUNT table. Because there are now three different values for Account Description, each Customer can now have up to three related instances of the ACCOUNT table. The first reaction might be to combine the Customer ID and Account Description columns into a primary key. After all, the combination of these two columns uniquely identifies each row in ACCOUNT. This may not violate business rules, but there may be a better choice for a key—one that uses one column instead of two. A closer look at the business rules for the bank may reveal that the Account Number attribute must be unique for all Accounts. If this rule is true, then the Account Number column is a much better choice for the primary key of ACCOUNT. The Customer ID and Account Description columns would then become non-key attributes of the ACCOUNT table.

Because the Customer ID column is the primary key of the CUSTOMER entity, and also a non-key attribute of the ACCOUNT entity, it is designated as a foreign key in the ACCOUNT entity.

Using Foreign Keys

Foreign keys are of great benefit in ensuring the *referential integrity* (RI) of a relational database. For example, let's assume that Paul Smith decides to close his accounts. If the CUSTOMER row is deleted, without also deleting the related ACCOUNT rows, then the referential integrity of the model is violated. The business rule that states "Every ACCOUNT must be owned by one and only one CUSTOMER" would now be untrue. Another RI violation can occur if you insert a row in the ACCOUNT table, without first inserting a CUSTOMER row.

Many relational database systems, including Watcom SQL, have automatic support for referential integrity constraints through the definition of foreign keys. These automatic constraints help prevent the inadvertent corruption of the relationships between the tables in the database.

Indexing Your Table

Indexes allow the relational DBMS to quickly access individual rows in a table. Without indexes, the DBMS is forced to read each and every row to determine whether to include it in the desired result set. Indexes are created on a specific column or columns in a single table, and can be either "unique" or "duplicate" in nature. When a unique index exists, there cannot be two rows in the table that share the same value for the indexed columns. This is especially helpful for the columns that make up the primary key. Duplicate indexes are designed to allow one or more rows with the same value domain. These are generally used on the columns designated as foreign keys.

Indexes are used primarily to speed data retrieval. By storing binary pointers in either ascending or descending order of the indexed columns, the I/O required to get to any specific row in a table is greatly reduced. The downside of indexing comes during INSERT, UPDATE, and DELETE processing because every new row causes the indexes to be recalibrated. Too many indexes, or indexes on columns that really shouldn't be indexed, can significantly slow the transaction-processing part of the system. On the other hand, too few indexes can slow both transaction processing and query processing.

The following list is a set of general guidelines for designing an index on a table:

- Create a *unique* index that matches the primary key of the table.

- Create a *duplicate* index on each foreign key column in a table.

- Create *duplicate* indexes on each additional column that you may use in a WHERE clause of a SELECT statement.

- DON'T create indexes on columns with low *selectivity*. For example, a column that can have only three or four possible values will have a low selectivity ratio. SEX can have only two possible values, so the selectivity ratio is about 50 percent. Don't index a column with a selectivity ratio over 10 to 15 percent. The database has to do more work to handle these indexes than the system will gain by having them!

Understanding Nulls

Null values are the relational DBMS's way of saying, "I don't know!" A NULL value in a numeric column does not mean zero, nor does it mean "the empty string" in a character column. NULL is a distinct value that means that the database was not supplied with a proper value for a column.

The DBMS automatically uses the NULL value whenever a real value is required, but not specified. For example, if I tried to insert a new row into the CUSTOMER table, and left out the value for Zip Code, the DBMS would try and place the NULL value into that column. If the Zip Code column is not capable of accepting a NULL, then the INSERT command fails.

When you create a table, you must state whether each column will be capable of accepting a NULL value. If you choose the NOT NULL option, then that column *must* have a definite value supplied before an INSERT command will process successfully. Attempting to INSERT a row with a NULL value in a NOT NULL column always results in an SQL error.

Nulls have some peculiar properties. First, any equality comparison using a NULL value returns FALSE. Even NULL = NULL evaluates to FALSE. For this reason, exercise caution when using nullable columns in WHERE clauses.

Database Design

Second, several arithmetic aggregate database functions exclude NULL. For example, the average of (0, 3, 4, 5) is (12/4), or 3. The average of (NULL, 3, 4, 5) is (12/3) or 4. The row with the NULL value is excluded from the aggregate computation, but the row containing the zero is not.

Using Views

A *view* is a logical table composed of columns from two or more physical tables. Views are special database objects that behave just like tables, but don't really contain any data. Think of a view as a "template" through which you can see the data you're really interested in.

Views are derived from one or more real tables, the *base tables,* whose data is physically stored in the database. Views can also be derived from other views. The only part of a view that is actually stored in the database is its definition; it is simply a SELECT statement, that can include one or more joined tables, or other views. The data is not copied and stored with the associated view definition; the data you see is really still stored in the base tables. Other than that, views behave exactly like database tables when you query them. You can even modify data in the base tables through a view, but there are a few restrictions on creating updateable views.

Views offer several advantages:

■ *Combining information from multiple tables to facilitate access.*

Some entity relationships will be used more commonly than others. In the bank example, the relationship between the CUSTOMER and ACCOUNT entities will probably always be on the Customer ID column. We can define a view that pre-joins the two tables based on the Customer ID column. Call the new view CUST_BALANCES. The view definition would look something like:

```
CREATE VIEW Cust_Balances AS
SELECT
      Customer Name,
      Account Balance,
      Date Account Opened
FROM CUSTOMER, ACCOUNT
WHERE CUSTOMER.Customer ID = ACCOUNT.Customer ID
```

The data is still really stored in the CUSTOMER and ACCOUNT tables, called the *base tables.* To the user, though, CUST_BALANCES looks and behaves like a brand new table, containing only the three columns listed above.

- *Limiting access to data in a table.*

  Assume there are certain users who need to be prevented from seeing savings or mortgage balances, but can see checking account balances. A view can be defined that excludes certain conditions or columns from the SELECT statement, effectively eliminating access to the sensitive data.

  Call the new view CHECKING_BALANCE. The view definition would look something like:

  ```
  CREATE VIEW Checking_Balance AS
  SELECT
        Customer Name,
        Account Balance,
        Date Account Opened
  FROM CUSTOMER, ACCOUNT
  WHERE CUSTOMER.Customer ID = ACCOUNT.Customer ID AND
        ACCOUNT.Account Description = 'CHECKING'
  ```

  By granting access to the view, and revoking access to the base tables, I restricted the users from seeing anything but checking accounts.

- *Encapsulation of business rules or logic.*

  A view definition can include calculated columns that implement business-specific calculations. This encapsulates the logic in the database definition instead of program code, and ensures that all users get the same definition of the calculation. The following view definition, Savings_Interest, retrieves the Customer Name, current Savings Account balance, and calculates the five percent monthly interest deposit that will be credited to the account.

  ```
  CREATE VIEW Savings_Interest AS
  SELECT
        Customer Name,
        Account Balance,
        (Account_Balance * .05) / 12
  FROM CUSTOMER, ACCOUNT
  WHERE CUSTOMER.Customer ID = ACCOUNT.Customer ID AND
        ACCOUNT.Account_Description = 'SAVINGS'
  ```

  With the interest calculation located in the view definition, it is no longer necessary to replicate the calculation in application code.

Stored Procedures

Stored procedures are collections of SQL statements and flow-of-control language elements. Stored procedures differ from ordinary SQL statements and from "batches" of SQL statements because they are precompiled and stored in the database (hence the name "stored procedures"). Stored procedures can offer significant performance improvements over ordinary SQL statements.

When you execute an ordinary SQL statement, the DBMS spends some of its time just figuring out how to execute the query. For example, the SQL statement is parsed to check for syntax errors; the list of objects in the query is examined to make sure they all exist, and that the user executing the query has the authority to access them; the index structure of the tables is examined to determine the optimal path to the desired data; and finally, the DBMS starts to access the tables and return the result set. The optimal path to the data for any single query is called the *execution plan*, and it is recalculated each time you execute an SQL statement, even when you execute them in a batch.

The execution plan for a stored procedure calculates once when the procedure is initially created, and is stored along with the procedure in a system table. Subsequently, whenever the procedure is invoked, it executes according to the precompiled plan. Because most of the work is already completed, stored procedures execute almost immediately.

Stored procedures offer incredible flexibility by creating small "programs" that encapsulate database interaction. Stored procedures are capable of the following:

- Taking parameters or arguments

- Calling other stored procedures

- Returning a status value to a calling procedure or batch to indicate success or failure

- Returning values of parameters to a calling procedure

Here are a few guidelines for working with stored procedures:

- You can create tables in a procedure, but the CREATE TABLE statements must come before any SQL statements that reference the tables.

- Procedures cannot create other database objects, including views, triggers, and stored procedures.

- In a single stored procedure, you cannot create an object, drop it, and then re-create it with the same name.

- Tables that are created in a stored procedure are created when the procedure executes, not when it is compiled.

The following is an example of a simple stored procedure that takes no parameters and doesn't generate a return status code:

```
CREATE PROCEDURE all_customers
          AS SELECT name, city
                 FROM customer
                 ORDER BY name ;
```

To invoke this procedure, use the keyword `execute` or `exec`, and the name of the procedure. (Of course, you must have been granted the authority to execute the procedure by the person that created it.)

```
exec all_customers ;
```

The result set returned from this stored procedure call is no different than that returned from the underlying SELECT statement, but because the DBMS didn't have to recalculate the execution plan, it probably executed much faster.

Stored procedures can also serve as security mechanisms, because a user can be granted permission to execute a stored procedure without having explicit permissions on the tables or views referenced in the procedure. The person that creates the procedure must either own the tables or views that are referenced in the procedure, or must have been granted explicit permissions on the objects.

```
GRANT EXECUTE
        on all_customers
        TO Smith;
```

To delete a procedure, use the keyword `drop` and the name of the procedure.

Triggers

A *trigger* is a special kind of stored procedure that is associated with a single table, and executes whenever you insert, delete, or update data in that table. The major difference between stored procedures and triggers is that you must explicitly execute a stored procedure, and a trigger executes automatically. Triggers can assist in maintaining the referential integrity of the database by ensuring that the logical relationships between tables are kept intact.

The real power of triggers is that they get kicked off, no matter what caused the data modification. It could be a data-entry operation, a batch-update program, or even another trigger. Each table in the database can have up to three triggers defined, corresponding to the three modification operations: UPDATE, INSERT, and DELETE. The associated trigger executes, or "fires," immediately after you complete the original data-modification statements (or before, if you use the appropriate option).

A trigger executes once per SQL statement, and is considered to be part of the overall *transaction,* or logical unit of work. This means that even if the original SQL statement executes successfully, if the trigger itself causes an error, then every update to the table can be backed out by the DBMS.

A trigger can help enforce the referential integrity of the database by:

- "Cascading" changes throughout related tables when a related key is modified or deleted. For example, a delete trigger on the STUDENT table would cause a corresponding deletion of matching rows in the STUDENT_GRADE table, using the student_id column as the related column.

- Restricting, or "rolling back" changes that would otherwise violate referential integrity, which cancels the attempted modification. An example of this might be an insert trigger on the STUDENT_GRADE table, that rolls back attempts to insert rows without a corresponding row in the STUDENT table.

- Rolling back updates that violate established business rules. An insert trigger on the STUDENT_COURSE table that prevents a student from scheduling a course that overlaps another, already scheduled, course.

There are currently two popular implementations of referential integrity support in many of today's database management systems: *explicit triggers* and *foreign key constraints.* Some database systems support both methods, while others only offer one type of RI support.

Explicit Triggers

With explicit triggers, the trigger is manipulated as a separate database object, much like a view or stored procedure. You create them with a CREATE TRIGGER statement, and drop them with a DROP TRIGGER statement. The following code illustrates the creation of a simple trigger:

```
CREATE TRIGGER cascade_cust_delete
ON CUSTOMER
FOR DELETE
AS
    If (SELECT count(*)
       FROM ACCOUNT, deleted
       WHERE ACCOUNT.customer_id = deleted.customer_id)> 0
       BEGIN
```

```
            DELETE FROM ACCOUNT
            WHERE ACCOUNT.customer_id = deleted.customer_id
            PRINT "Customer and related Accounts have been deleted"
      END
   else
            Print "Customer has been deleted."
```

With this simple trigger, whenever you delete a row from the CUSTOMER table, all of that Customer's related ACCOUNT rows are also deleted, and an appropriate message is displayed. This trigger will fire automatically whenever a row is deleted from the CUSTOMER table. Some important things to note about the explicit trigger method:

- The trigger is created with the CREATE TRIGGER statement, and is given a specific name that must be unique to the table.

- Each table can have up to three triggers, one each for INSERT, UPDATE, and DELETE processing.

- The trigger body can contain any number of SQL statements with flow-of-control language. If any SQL statement in the trigger fails, the original SQL statement that caused the trigger to fire will also fail.

- Triggers make use of two important temporary system tables: *inserted* and *deleted*. These tables will exist only during the actual processing of a data modification SQL statement, and can only be referenced from a trigger. During an INSERT statement, the *inserted* table contains an exact copy of each entire row being inserted, no matter what table is being modified. During a DELETE statement, the *deleted* table contains an exact copy of each row being deleted. During an UPDATE statement, the *deleted* table contains the "before" image of each updated row, and the *inserted* table contains the "after" image. In the previous example, the *deleted* table contains each CUSTOMER row or rows being deleted, and is joined to the ACCOUNT table on Customer_ID to determine whether the Customer had any corresponding Accounts.

Foreign Key Constraints

Explicit triggers are extremely flexible, but have two major disadvantages:

- Even though triggers are associated with a single table, they are separate database objects, and are manipulated with their own CREATE and DROP statements. This introduces another level of database maintenance for the database administrator.

■ Explicit triggers are associated with the entire table; not on the individual columns in the table. Consequently, if a table contains two or more foreign keys to two or more separate tables, the UPDATE trigger can get unnecessarily complex. All the code to maintain each foreign key relationship must be placed in a single UPDATE trigger.

To solve this problem, several DBMS vendors introduced the concept of *foreign key constraints,* sometimes known as *declarative referential integrity.* With this method, the referential integrity rules are encapsulated in the table definition, and are bound to the individual columns that serve as foreign keys. The syntax for the CREATE TABLE statement was enhanced to provide for the declaration of RI rules (hence the name "declarative referential integrity"). The DELETE trigger from above can be restated with a foreign key constraint as:

```
CREATE TABLE ACCOUNT
      (Account_Number      integer        NOT NULL,
       Account_Description char(10)       NOT NULL,
       Customer_ID         char(10)       NOT NULL,
       Account_Balance     numeric(9,2)   NOT NULL,
       Date_Opened         date           NOT NULL,
      PRIMARY KEY (Account_Number),
      FOREIGN KEY cust_id
          (Customer_ID)
      REFERENCES CUSTOMER
          ON DELETE   CASCADE
      );
```

With this new CREATE TABLE statement, the following business rules were encapsulated into the definition of the ACCOUNT table:

■ The primary key of the ACCOUNT table is the Account_Number column.

■ The foreign key named `cust_id` links the ACCOUNT table to the CUSTOMER table on the Customer_ID column.

■ Prevent the insertion of any new ACCOUNT rows, until there's a corresponding CUSTOMER row that matches on Customer ID.

■ Prevent the modification of the Customer_ID column to a value that doesn't already exist in the CUSTOMER table.

■ Whenever a row in the CUSTOMER table is deleted, check to see if there are matching rows in the ACCOUNT table and delete those as well.

The advantages of declarative referential integrity are two-fold. The business rules are bound to the definition of the table, not stored as separate objects. The logic that was once spread across INSERT, UPDATE, and DELETE triggers is now found in one place.

The major disadvantage associated with declarative referential integrity rules that the capability to use flow-of-control language and BEGIN/END statement blocks is lost. You can't use declarative referential integrity to write complex logic. For example, the complex logic in the statement, "Cascade the delete to only those Accounts whose Account_Balance column is zero, and restrict the deletion of all others," will still require an explicit trigger.

> **Note**
>
> When a table has both a constraint and an explicit trigger, the constraint is always checked first. If the constraint is violated, the statement fails and the trigger is never fired.

From Here...

This chapter has presented an introduction to basic relational database theory. We looked at the process of developing a Logical Database Model by examining business rules and the relationships that exist between entities, and transitioning that Logical Model into a Physical Database Model.

For more information, refer to these chapters:

- Chapter 3, "Understanding Normalization," explores the technique of normalization, to help refine and optimize the Logical and Physical Database Models even further.

- Chapter 6, "Understanding SQL," presents the basic structure of the SQL statement and covers specific Watcom SQL syntax.

- Chapter 8, "Understanding the Role of a Database Administrator," covers items such as referential integrity, stored procedures, and triggers, as well as database security.

- Chapter 9, "Using SQL Table Commands," describes the syntax for the CREATE, DROP, and ALTER statements.

Database Design

Chapter 3

Understanding Normalization

by Charles A. Wood

Before starting to develop your database, you must first obtain the application requirements from the client in order to analyze what data the database should contain and how it should be contained. Determining what data should be contained consists of defining your entities needed for a system. Determining how the data should be contained in your database is called normalization.

Normalization is the act of defining your database tables in their most logical and broken-down form. Normalization is a key part of database analysis. Using normalization, you add primary keys to your table and remove any repeating data.

In 1972, a professor named E. F. Codd defined three normal forms that lead to database normalization. (*Normal forms* are stages or steps an analyst would take to normalize a database.) Codd's "steps," or normal forms, were (appropriately) described as first normal form (1NF), second normal form (2NF), and third normal form (3NF).

Later, Codd was joined by Robert Boyce to define the Boyce-Codd normal form (BCNF), which defined a further step that is sometimes needed in normalization. Finally, in 1977 and 1979, another professor named Robert Fagin furthered the study of normalization by adding two more normal forms: fourth normal form (4NF) and fifth normal form (5NF).

This chapter deals with normal forms: defining them and showing you how to use them with an example. In this chapter, you learn:

■ Determine a table's columns that are needed in a database, based on a given set of requirements

■ Normalize the database using the six normal forms

> **Note**
>
> Although the requirements start out differently, the data model described here will eventually mirror the Inventory Tracking system defined in the *Special Edition Using PowerBuilder 4* book, published by Que Corporation. Although you do not need to buy it to understand this chapter, it is a nice companion volume if you are developing in PowerBuilder with Watcom SQL.

Determining a Database's Tables and Columns

The first step in database analysis is to determine the tables you need and the columns contained in those tables. Let's assume that your users want an inventory-tracking system that is invoice-driven.

> **Note**
>
> Experienced developers know that there are many different analysis methodologies. In addition, each methodology is implemented slightly differently from developer to developer. The methodology I use is a hybrid of several different methodologies, and is well suited for system analysis by hand into PowerBuilder if no CASE (Computer Aided Software Engineering) tool is available.
>
> The analysis methodology mentioned in this chapter is designed to give developers without an analysis tool a methodology that they can evolve (or mutate) to meet their specific needs.
>
> Keep in mind that your analysis methodology should be flexible enough to support iterative design, and you should organize your system so that you can deliver a quality system with a minimum amount of time.
>
> If possible, use CASE tools, which help with analysis and system documentation.

In the analysis phase of a project, the language you're using (PowerBuilder or CA-Realizer), the operating system (DOS, OS/2, or Windows), and the computer you're using (a PC) are not considered. *Analysis* deals only with description of the current business activities and the software that needs to be developed. In the next chapter, you'll see how to implement design using PowerBuilder's database painter.

Finding the Entities (Tables)

The first step in analysis is finding all the entities in a system (an *entity* is someone or something associated with a system). In the Inventory Tracking system, we need to show the basic item listing, as well as a link to an invoice. These entities are shown in figure 3.1.

Fig. 3.1
Here, you see every entity in a box.

Eventually, each entity you find turns into a database table. Using analysis, you need to define which tables you'll need.

> **Note**
>
> Remember that entities are always nouns (a person, place, or thing). It can, however, be an entity relationship. (See the next section for details.)

> **Caution**
>
> You could name about 80 percent of the entities in any system in a few minutes. The last 20 percent, however, require some in-depth research. Be prepared for a long and laborious process of interviews, research, and analysis to name all of the entities.

> **Note**
>
> Some of you probably already see some additions to the number of entities needed for this system. This entity-relationship model has left out some entities on purpose to show the way normalization will show entities that need to be created.

Database Design

Determining Relationships

After determining the entities, you must find out how the entities relate to each other. This is done with *functions*. In other words, entities relate to each other by doing some action. Draw lines with words on them between the entities to show the relationship, as seen in figure 3.2. *Relationship* describes the number of values in one entity that may match a value in a related entity.

Fig. 3.2
Now you see the relationships between the entities. When displaying relationships, connect the two entities with a line and describe the relationship.

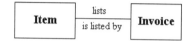

Tip
Remember that functions are always verbs! If you write down a relationship between two entities that is not an action, rethink your entities.

When developing in traditional languages such as C, COBOL, or BASIC, each relationship translates into a function, subroutine, or paragraph. Using PowerBuilder, you can also code relationships as functions, as command buttons on a window, or as menu-bar items.

Notice that the relationship, or function, of the left (or top) entity is listed above (or on the left side of) the line connecting the entities, as shown in figure 3.2. The relationship of the right (or bottom) entity is listed below (or on the right side of) the line connecting the entities. Therefore, you can read the relationship between item and invoice in figure 3.2 as "The Item is listed by the Invoice" and "The Invoice lists the Item."

Showing Ordinality

After you define the entities and relationships, you need to define *ordinality*, which describes the number of entities that can exist with another entity. For example, how many Warehouses can exist for each Item? (The answer is: one—and only one—Warehouse can exist for each Item.) How many Items can exist for each Warehouse? (The answer is: zero to many items can exist for each warehouse.)

Thus, Items and Warehouses have a one-to-many relationship, or a one-to-many ordinality.

In figure 3.3, Item has a many-to-many relationship with Invoice.

Fig. 3.3
Now we add all of the ordinalities.

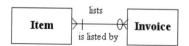

Note

I have heard many people use *cardinaltiy* as opposed to *ordinality* when referring to relationships in design, but I think ordinality fits the definition better. If you look up *ordinal number* versus *cardinal number* in the Random House College Dictionary like I did, you'll see that:

- A *cardinal number* is defined as any of the numbers that express amount: one, two, three, etc.

- An *ordinal number* is defined as any of the numbers that express degree, quality, or position in a series: first, second, third, etc.

You could argue that relationships like "one-to-one" are cardinal in nature, while relationships like "many-to-many" are ordinal in nature. However, I think "ordinality" fits a little better than "cardinality" because ordinal numbers seem more relational, degree, and series oriented than cardinal numbers, which are isolated and stand alone.

Tip

Two entities can have more than one relationship between them. Don't be afraid to draw more than one relationship, and don't feel forced to choose between two valid relationships.

Note

Notice how the Inventory Tracking system seems to revolve around the Item. You should try to find out which entities your system revolves around, and (in the Inventory Tracking system) ask "How do my entities revolve around the Item?" (instead of trying to find all entities that relate to any other entity). This is a good way to limit the size of your system and to avoid programming for entities that really have no place in your system.

Did you notice the new type of lines drawn in figure 3.3? This is one way of identifying your ordinality. Figures 3.4 through 3.7 identify the symbols used to denote notation.

Figure 3.4 indicates that each instance of Entity 1 can have no (zero) corresponding instance of Entity 2, or it can have one corresponding instance of Entity 2. (This is referred to as a *none-or-one relationship*. None of these exist in the Inventory Tracking system.)

Fig. 3.4
Entity 1 has a none-or-one relationship with Entity 2.

The symbol shown in figure 3.5 indicates that each instance of Entity 1 can have one and only one corresponding instance of Entity 2. This is referred to as a *one-and-only-one relationship*. In this Inventory Tracking system, an Item entry must be stored in only one Warehouse.

Fig. 3.5

Entity 1 has a one-and-only-one relationship with Entity 2.

Figure 3.6 indicates that each instance of Entity 1 can have no (zero) corresponding instance of Entity 2, but it can have many corresponding instances of Entity 2. This is referred to as a *zero-through-many relationship*.

Fig. 3.6

Entity 1 has a zero-through-many relationship with Entity 2.

In this Inventory Tracking system, a warehouse can be empty (not have any item entries), but a warehouse also can store many items (and therefore have several item entries).

Figure 3.7 indicates that each instance of Entity 1 must have at least one corresponding instance of Entity 2, but it can have many corresponding instances of Entity 2. This is referred to as a *one-through-many relationship*.

Fig. 3.7

Entity 1 has a one-through-many relationship with Entity 2.

In this Inventory Tracking system (as denoted in fig. 3.3), each invoice must list at least one item. However, an invoice might list several items.

Defining First Normal Form (1NF)

◄ See "Understanding Keys," p. 48

First Normal Form (or 1NF) occurs when you have defined a column that can identify any row in your database table. This column is the primary key. It can be denoted with a (PK) added after the primary key column name, as seen in figure 3.8.

1NF also is the phase where you determine what tables are *dependent* on other tables. Dependency occurs when you can't have a row on one table without having a related row on another table, making one table dependent on the other table. The column that is related to the other table is the foreign key. In this instance, Invoice has six dependencies on Item! These dependencies can be shown with an (FK) after the foreign key column name, as seen in figure 3.10.

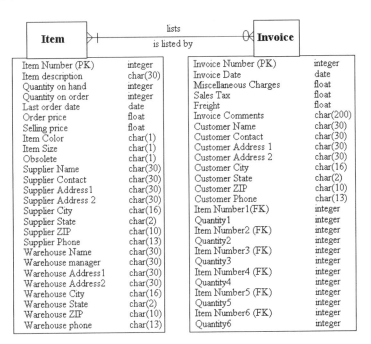

Database Design

Fig. 3.8
1NF entails identifying the column that uniquely defines rows on your table.

Caution

Often, you won't find any unique column that defines your table. This occurs when an entity can have duplicates. If that's the case, for design purposes, you must generate a number, timestamp, etc., to become the primary key. Otherwise, both your database and your analysis will run into difficulties in areas that require tables to relate to each other.

1NF forces the analyst to determine an *atomic* identifier for each table. This means that each table must have one identifier that identifies the row. You are not allowed to have "groups" of information contained in several rows and related to each other in a single table. You are also not allowed to have a table without a primary key.

If dependencies between the tables are not defined by now, they should also be defined in 1NF via the use of foreign keys.

> **Note**
>
> Some analysts define dependencies via foreign keys when determining the ordinality of a table, as opposed to adding a step to 1NF. Either way is OK; it's a matter of preference. I like to define the columns before I start listing the foreign keys, which is why I define foreign keys during 1NF.

Defining Second Normal Form (2NF)

By now, some of you may have recognized some inefficiencies with the entity model (or *data model,* as we'll start to call it). Primarily, you are always forced to have six items on your invoice. There is no storage for more than six items on your invoice, and if you have fewer than six, your invoice table must contain blank fields. This is not only cumbersome to the developer, but probably unacceptable to the user.

This inadequacy can be dealt with by using second normal form (2NF). 2NF deals with removing any repeating dependencies within a table and separating them out into their own dependent table. Figure 3.9 shows the removal of dependent information by creating a new table called Invoice_line.

Fig. 3.9

2NF separates dependent information within a table into its own dependent table.

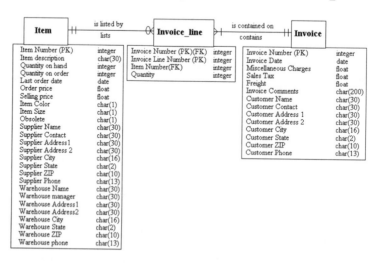

Notice how 2NF also tends to eliminate many-to-many relationships. Now there is a many-to-one relationship between Item and Invoice_line (every Invoice_line can list only one item; every item can be listed by several Invoice_lines) and a one-to-many relationship between Invoice_line and

Invoice (every Invoice_line can be contained on only one invoice; every Invoice can contain many Invoice_lines).

> **Note**
>
> Eliminating many-to-many relationships is easier while you are modeling your entity. Although many-to-many relationships exist in the "real world," they cannot exist (for long) on a data model. Since a many-to-many relationship should alert the analyst to a potential design flaw, it is often easier to take steps to prevent them immediately. (This was not done here so we could illustrate 2NF.)

> **Note**
>
> It's very important to normalize all tables created during the normalization process. Even though we are finished with 1NF, we still must return to 1NF momentarily to assign keys to the new Invoice_line table we just created.

2NF eliminates recurring information that is a subset of a table by creating a new dependent table based on the recurring columns. By splitting Invoice_line out of Invoice, we can have as many (or as few) Invoice_lines per Invoice as we need.

> **Note**
>
> Since the city, state, and ZIP code parts of an address would repeat often, should we should split them out to a new table? Obviously, this would cause more problems than it would solve since the address of the customer would be split into two different tables and would make maintenance more difficult. I have chosen not to do this.
>
> Some analysts believe that a database should be *fully normalized*, no matter what concerns the analyst may have, and that the analyst should not be concerned with such details until design. This seems a little odd (and time-consuming) to me. Analysis should help the design process as much as possible and not purposefully normalize data just to add a denormalize step later.

Defining Third Normal Form (3NF)

Although 2NF has removed the most glaring deficiency of the data model, there are still problems to resolve. Throughout the table, there is a tendency to repeat data, making maintenance more difficult. For instance, if the same customer orders from us twice, his entire customer information (name, address, phone) is repeated. If a warehouse holds more than one item, the warehouse information is repeated. If a supplier supplies us with more than one item, the supplier information is repeated. Also, there's no way to leave comments about supplier or customer—there isn't a table available to do this.

If viewed from an entity standpoint, you can see that customer should not be part of the invoice entity. Similarly, warehouse and supplier should not be part of the item entity. Third normal form (3NF) takes care of this. In 3NF, we remove any *nondependent* information from tables. You could say that a customer is not dependent on a single invoice. Rather, an invoice is dependent upon a customer. A customer could exist without being on any invoice. This is similar to warehouse and supplier information not needing to be contained on the item table.

Figure 3.10 shows how we split out customer from invoice, leaving a customer number on the invoice table to show which customer the invoice is dependent on. This allows us to store customer comments. Similarly, we removed warehouse and supplier information from Item, set up dependencies from Item to Supplier and Warehouse, and placed foreign keys inside Item that indicate which warehouse and which supplier the item comes from.

Fig. 3.10

3NF separates nondependent information from a table into its own table. Then dependencies are added from the original table to the new table. New fields are added in bold.

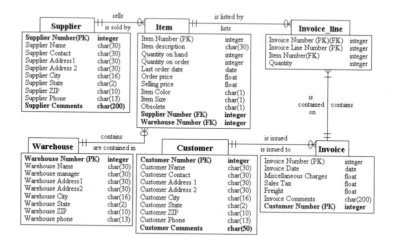

Defining Boyce-Codd Normal Form (BCNF)

Codd noticed a deficiency in 3NF. Codd and Robert Boyce enhanced 3NF to eliminate some of these deficiencies. This new 3NF is called Boyce-Codd Normal Form, or BCNF.

Suppose you were developing a system with the following system requirements:

- All salespeople work for one or more counties.

- All salespeople-county relationships are serviced by a branch office.

You could develop the model shown in figure 3.11. Indeed, the model is in 3NF since all repeating dependencies have been resolved.

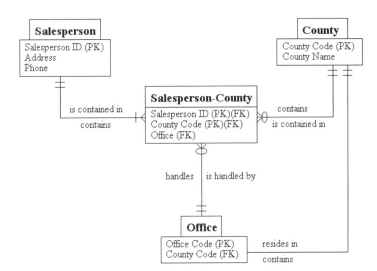

Fig. 3.11
This model is in 3NF because all dependencies have been resolved. However, there are still problems with the design.

This model has some problems. An office resides in a county. Each salesperson/county relationship is handled by an office. However, that data model does not ensure that the branch office that handles the salesperson/county relationship resides in the same county.

With a BCNF violation, there is usually a circular relationship once all foreign keys have been mapped out on the entity relationship model. Usually, this can be resolved by reorganizing the foreign keys in the tables.

In figure 3.12, we change the Salesperson-County table to the Salesperson-Office table. We then force any inquiries about County to first go through the Office table. Now all branches servicing a salesperson are guaranteed to be a valid branch for that county.

Fig. 3.12
BCNF resolves all
conflicting
determinants.

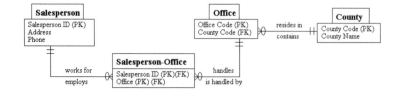

Defining Fourth Normal Form (4NF)

All previous normal forms dealt with the way entities looked on a entity-relationship model. Fourth normal form (4NF) and fifth normal form (5NF) deal with the way data is stored on a table, rather than the relationship between two tables. Consider the many-to-many-to-many relationship with Office, Salesperson, and Item in figure 3.13.

Fig. 3.13
The many-to-
many relationship
violates 2NF and
must be resolved.

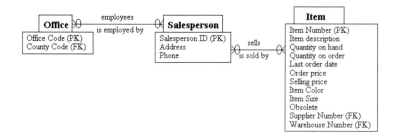

Tip
An *associate table*
is a table specifi-
cally designed to
resolve a many-to-
many relationship.

You can resolve the relationship with a three-way associative table that relates to all three tables, as seen in figure 3.14.

Fig. 3.14
The Sales/Office
Information table
resolves the many-
to-many relation-
ships, but creates
other problems.

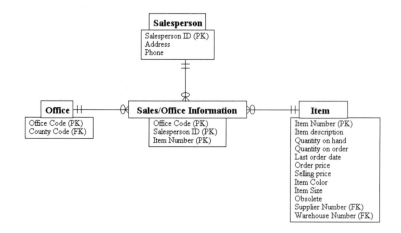

The design in figure 3.14 meets BCNF. However, the design has some flaws:

■ There is no way to assign a salesperson to an office before he or she sells anything.

■ The salesperson has to list every item-office combination, which would could create a very large and cumbersome table.

4NF states that you should not resolve more than one many-to-many relationships in one table. This is shown in figure 3.15, in which two associative tables were added to the design in figure 3.13 to achieve 2NF.

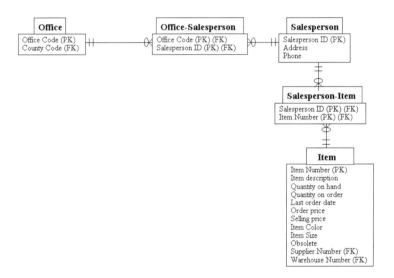

Fig. 3.15
Adding two associative tables resolves the many-to-many relationships.

You should analyze a table for 4NF violations if both the following conditions apply:

■ The table has three or more columns in the primary key

■ The table has relationships to three or more other tables

Defining Fifth Normal Form (5NF)

The fifth normal form (5NF) is more rule-based than entity-based. 5NF deals with when you should stop normalizing. If you had the requirement that investment brokers have to be certified to trade a type of securities on an exchange, table 3.1 could describe a table to meet this requirement.

Table 3.1   Investment Table

Investment Broker	Exchange	Security Type
Jones	Nikkei	Bonds
Jones	Nikkei	Stocks
Jones	NYSE	Stocks
Jones	NYSE	T-Bills
Smith	Nikkei	Bonds
Smith	NYSE	Stocks

You may see some duplicate data on the Investment Broker, Exchange, and Security Type columns. You can normalize the data by splitting this table into three tables (see tables 3.2, 3.3, and 3.4).

Table 3.2   Investment Broker—Exchange Table

Investment Broker	Exchange
Jones	NYSE
Jones	Nikkei
Smith	NYSE
Smith	Nikkei

Table 3.3   Investment Broker—Security Type Table

Investment Broker	Security Type
Jones	Bonds
Jones	Stocks
Jones	T-Bills
Smith	Bonds
Smith	Stocks

Table 3.4 Exchange—Security Type Table	
Exchange	**Security Type**
NYSE	Stocks
NYSE	T-Bills
Nikkei	Stocks
Nikkei	Bonds

By separating these tables, however, you may conclude the following (through the entity relationships):

- Smith can sell on the Nikkei exchange (table 3.2).

- Smith can sell stocks (table 3.3).

- Stocks are sold on the Nikkei exchange (table 3.4).

- Thus, Smith can sell stocks on the Nikkei exchange.

The conclusion that Smith can sell stocks on the Nikkei exchange based on the information in tables 3.2, 3.3, and 3.4 contradicts the information found in table 3.1, in which Smith cannot sell stocks on the Nikkei exchange.

Fifth normal form (5NF) specifies that you should not normalize *join dependencies* out of tables. A join dependency occurs when every column of a key in a table is dependent on every other key column. In this case, Investment Broker, Exchange, and Security Type all are dependent on each other and should not be normalized into separate tables without losing some information.

There is no easy method for determining whether there are 5NF violations. The analyst must make sure that the requirements given to him or her are reflected in the table design.

Note

Sometimes, especially with small tables, the designer of a system must undo the normalization that was done earlier for increased efficiency. This is not a bad thing to do, but must be done carefully so as to not significantly hurt the integrity of the entity-relationship model.

From Here...

By now, you should have a good feel for how to design your database. Normalization is an important part of database analysis, and it should not be ignored if your application is to be designed and developed quickly and efficiently.

Some related chapters that you may want to review are as follows:

- Chapter 2, "Understanding Relational Database Concepts," discusses relational database theory. You must understand the concepts presented in this chapter before attempting to understand normalization.

- Chapter 4, "Designing a Database Using PowerBuilder," shows how to implement your analysis using PowerBuilder 4. If you use PowerBuilder, this chapter will show you how to easily design your database with your entity-relationship model. (If you don't use PowerBuilder, you must use the SQL statement CREATE TABLE to develop your database.)

- Chapter 7, "Using the ISQL Environment," shows you how to issue SQL commands (such as CREATE TABLE) to implement your design (if you don't have access to PowerBuilder).

Chapter 4

Designing a Database Using PowerBuilder

by Charles A. Wood with Paul Horan

Although Watcom SQL's ISQLW can be used to turn your design into a database, many developers use PowerBuilder to actually implement their design into a Watcom SQL database.

Using PowerBuilder gives many advantages to the database administrator:

- PowerBuilder makes data definition easier with drop-down list boxes for data types, comments, and easy-to-use tools for foreign and primary key definition (just to name a few).

- PowerBuilder is graphical. You can actually see a line between related databases.

- PowerBuilder comes with an SQL painter that writes your SQL statements for the developer.

- You can view the contents of any table with the click of a mouse button. Futhermore, you can enter data in the PowerBuilder environment without resorting to SQL statements.

> **Note**
>
> If you need to learn PowerBuilder, a good source is *Special Edition Using PowerBuilder 4*, available from Que Corporation. The Inventory Tracking system mentioned in this chapter is the same Inventory Tracking system developed for *Special Edition Using PowerBuilder*.

In this chapter, you learn how to:

- Create a Watcom SQL database in PowerBuilder

- Connect to your Watcom SQL database in PowerBuilder

- Customize your Watcom SQL database in PowerBuilder

- Create, modify, and drop a table in PowerBuilder

- Manipulate data in the PowerBuilder environment

Creating a Database

To get into the database painter, double-click the PowerBuilder icon and then click the Database icon. As soon as you click the Database icon for the first time, you see the tables from the PowerSoft Demo DB appear (as shown in fig. 4.1). This is the database that PowerBuilder uses for its sample application. (Of course, it's not the database you need—you must create a new database.)

Fig. 4.1
The first database that opens when you click the database icon is not the database you need—you need to create a new database.

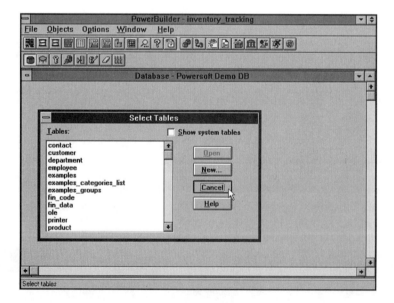

To create a new database, click the Cancel button (see fig. 4.1). Then choose File, Create Database, as shown in figure 4.2.

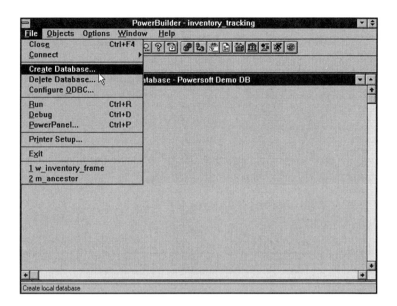

Fig. 4.2
In the database
painter, open **F**ile
to find Cre**a**te
Database.

The Create Local Database dialog box appears (see fig. 4.3). You must type the
full path of your database name. It is a good idea to end it with a .db extension; remember that the first part of the name must not contain more than
eight characters. (Hence, the name Inventry for Inventory Tracking.) The user
ID defaults to DBA, and the password to SQL. You should change these if
security is an issue. Finally, the Start command defaults to db32w -d when
using a Watcom database. The Start command tells PowerBuilder which program to run to start the database engine.

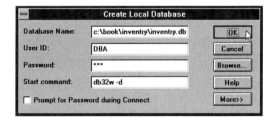

Fig. 4.3
Use this dialog box
to create your
database.

By selecting the Prompt for Password during Connect checkbox, you are telling PowerBuilder to ignore the Password setting, and to always prompt the
user for his password when establishing the connection to the Watcom database. This is an additional security mechanism, but it can be very annoying
during system development.

Clicking the **M**ore button expands the Create Local Database dialog box and presents some additional options, as shown in figure 4.4.

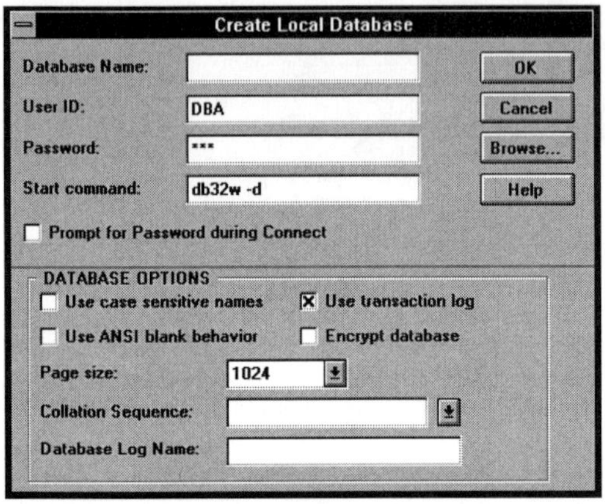

Fig. 4.4
The Create Local Database dialog box has additional options that control advanced features of the Watcom database.

Note

Once a database is created, these settings cannot be altered. In order to change settings, you must create a new database with the desired settings changed, create the database objects in the new database, and copy over the data from the old database.

Generally, the defaults provided will be adequate, but it is important to understand the implications of each of the following settings:

- **Use case-sensitive names.** Select this checkbox if you want all the names in the database (tables, columns, views, and so on) to be case-sensitive. For example, the Empname column is not the same as the EMPNAME column. The default is that all names and comparisons are not case-sensitive.

- **Use ANSI blank behavior.** Select this checkbox to use ANSI conventions when dealing with blanks, that is, ignore trailing blanks for comparison purposes. For example, "Smith" and "Smith   " would be treated equally. The default is that blanks are significant for comparisons.

▶ See "Using Log Files to Back Up and Restore," p. 290

- **Use transaction log.** Select this checkbox to use a transaction log to record all database activities. The transaction log maintains a record of all changes to database records, and is critical for robust database recovery in the event of a failure. The default is to use a log.

> **Caution**
>
> The run-time version of Watcom SQL used for distribution of your database *does not* support the use of log files. If you plan to distribute your database, disable the transaction logs.

- **Encrypt database.** Select this checkbox to encrypt your database, making it much more difficult for someone to decipher the data in it using a disk utility to look at the file.

- **Page size.** This refers to the page size of your database. A *page* is the physical unit of data that is read from the database. Page size can be 512, 1024, 2048, or 4096 bytes (1024 is the default). If your database contains very large tables, or tables whose rows exceed 1024 bytes, then you may realize a performance boost by increasing the page size. For the majority of databases, the 1024 default is sufficient.

Tip

File-compression utilities do not work well on encrypted database files.

- **Collation Sequence.** A collating or sorting sequence is used for all string comparisons in the database. By default, normal ASCII (binary) ordering will be used for the lower 128 characters. For the upper 128 characters (the extended characters), the characters that are accented forms of a letter in the lower 128 are sorted to the same position as the unaccented form. The determination of whether or not an extended character is a letter is based on code page 850 (multilingual code page).

▶ See "Making Different Collating Sequences," p. 238

- **Database Log Name.** The fully qualified path and file name of the transaction log that will be used to record all database activities. If you do not specify a path, the transaction log is placed in the same directory as the database file. If this option is left blank and the Use Transaction Log option is checked, a transaction log will be created that has the same first eight characters as the database file with the file extension .LOG.

▶ See "Using DB32W.EXE, DBSTARTW.EXE, RT32W.EXE, and RTSTARTW.EXE," p. 612

Your database is created.

Connecting and Customizing Your Database

Even though you can't create databases with names longer than eight characters, your database can be renamed with a longer and more descriptive name by using the profile setup. By choosing **F**ile, **C**onnect, **S**etup in the database painter, as seen in figure 4.5, you allow PowerBuilder to edit your database profiles.

Fig. 4.5

You can help configure your database by choosing **F**ile, **C**onnect, **S**etup.

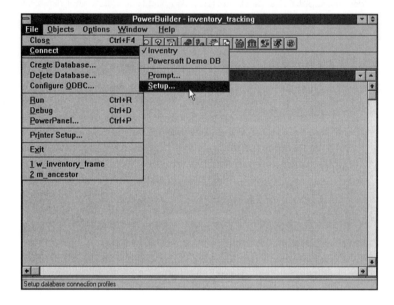

PowerBuilder now displays all valid database profiles for you to choose from in the Database Profiles dialog box, as shown in figure 4.6. To edit your Inventry profile, pick Inventry, and choose **E**dit.

Fig. 4.6

The Database Profiles dialog box allows you to choose which profile you want to edit, or to create or delete database profiles.

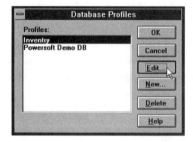

The Database Profile Setup dialog box appears (see fig. 4.7). In the Profile Name field, you can change the name to Inventory Tracking. Type the name, the user ID, the password, and click OK.

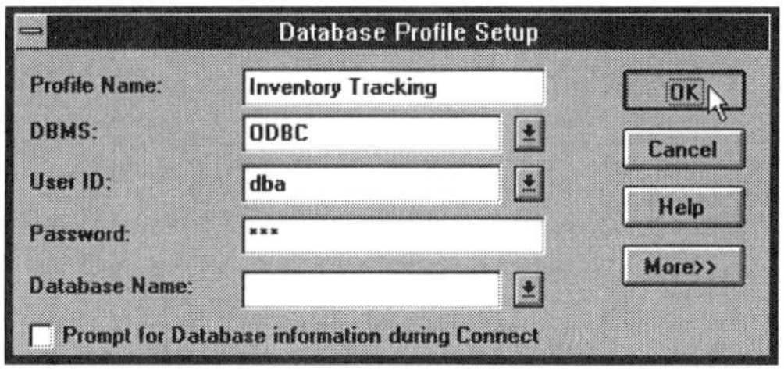

Fig. 4.7
Changing the name in the Database Profile Setup dialog box.

Database Design

> **Note**
>
> PowerBuilder allows you to type in a user ID and a password into the Database Profile Setup dialog box. This defaults in PowerBuilder to a user ID of dba and a password of sql. If you assign the user ID and password when you connect to your database, your users will not be forced to enter a user ID and password every time they use your system.

The Database Profiles dialog box appears after you click OK (see fig. 4.8). Notice that Inventory Tracking appears. By clicking OK here, Inventory Tracking will be brought up in the database painter.

Fig. 4.8
Inventory Tracking now shows in the Profile Name field.

Creating Tables

Right now, you have an empty database. That is, you have a database that contains no *tables,* which are groups of data inside a database. Think of a database as a file cabinet; each table represents a file within that file cabinet. In any system, the entities developed in analysis track directly to each table. Therefore, you will have a supplier table, an item table, a customer table, and so on.

To create a table, either click the Open icon (the one that looks like a canister) and click the **New** button, or click the New icon.

The Create Table dialog box displays, as seen in figure 4.9. Enter the name of your table (in this case, **Item**) in the **T**able text box. The table and field (column) names can be entered in lowercase letters only.

Fig. 4.9
The Create Table dialog box is where you create tables for the database.

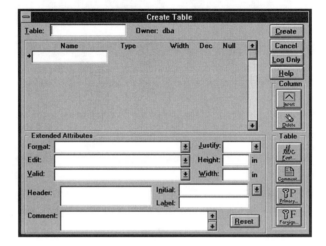

Determining a Table's Columns

Using database terminology, a *column* is a field on a table. Although determining a table's columns is done in the analysis of a project, this process can be automated to go right into the design of your system. When dealing with PowerBuilder applications, do all database-column analysis in the database painter.

In database terminology, a *row* is a record on a table. Two different types of items have two corresponding rows on the Item table.

Use the following guidelines to help you determine which columns to put in your database:

- Any variable that changes from row to row that you want to report. For instance, the cost a supplier charges for an item is important to record and report. Include order_price in each row to report this.

◀ See "Understanding Keys," p. 48

- A column (or set of columns) that makes this row unique from other rows (this is called a *primary key*). For instance, item_number is unique to each item row.

■ A column (or set of columns) indicating that rows have either a zero or one, or a one-and-only-one correspondence to a row in another table (this is called a *foreign key*). For instance, because each Item is stored in one and only one Warehouse, you can include warehouse_number in every Item row.

Your columns for items are shown in the Create Table dialog box (see fig. 4.10).

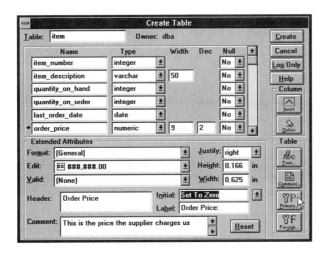

Fig. 4.10
Now enter all the columns needed for the item table.

Here, you enter all your fields, their data type (such as character, integer, and date), width (if applicable), number of decimals (if applicable), and whether or not you allow NULLs in your database for this field.

◄ See "Understanding Nulls," p. 51

> **Caution**
>
> In the database painter, the database data types are the same as the ones used in the database. They are not the same data types as in PowerBuilder (often, the different data types have different valid ranges).
>
> Furthermore, little checking is done to make sure numbers are still within the range for a data type. For instance, in Watcom SQL, an *integer* is defined as any value from –2,147,483,648 through 2,147,483,647. In PowerBuilder, an integer is defined as any value from –32,768 through 32,767. If you were to read an integer from Watcom SQL into an integer in PowerBuilder, a wraparound might occur, and you would end up with a random number some of the time. This is a hard bug to catch. (By the way, if you define an integer in Watcom SQL, make sure that any values do not exceed the PowerBuilder limit, or use a long data type in PowerBuilder. A long data type in PowerBuilder has the same range as an integer data type in Watcom SQL.)

> **Note**
>
> *NULLs* are not zeros; they are empty columns in a row on your database. (An empty column contains nothing—no zeros, no spaces, no anything!) Most columns require some entry, so most databases allow you to define a column as Not NULL when you create it. By declaring a column Not NULL, you force the database to not allow an update when the column in question is NULL.

If you're following along on your computer as you're reading this, do not click the Create button yet! You still have a little work to do on this database.

Picking Primary Keys

After entering all of your fields into your table, you need to tell your database what sets every row in a table apart from each other. For this you need a *primary key*, which is a unique indicator that allows you to address individual table entries. Every table needs to have a primary key defined.

Click the **P**rimary button on the lower right corner of the window. This opens the Primary Key Definition dialog box for your table. Choose the field (or fields) that you want for your primary key for this table by clicking the appropriate field name. By choosing item_number as your primary key, you are saying that item_number can't ever be duplicated on the item table (as seen in fig. 4.11). Now you can use item_number to identify an item.

Fig. 4.11
Choose
item_number as
your primary key.

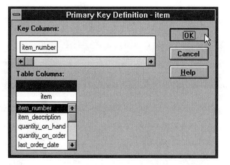

When you're finished, click OK to return to the Create Table dialog box. Click OK again in the Create Table dialog box to return to the database painter. Notice that you now have a table window containing the column name and comments of the item table (see fig. 4.12). This window can be resized, especially if you want to display several table windows at a time.

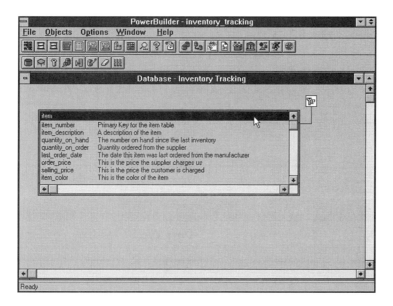

Database Design

Fig. 4.12
You now have a
resizable table
window describing
your item table.

> **Note**
>
> A lot can be added to this inventory system to make it more fully featured (for ex-
> ample, backorders, order points, economic order quantities, and items supplied by
> several suppliers and stored in several warehouses). Keep in mind that your goal is to
> learn how to design Watcom SQL databases using PowerBuilder, and that we are
> merely using a scaled-down inventory system to illustrate all our points.

A table sometimes will have more than one column in the primary key
(known as a *composite key*). In the invoice_line table, the primary key consists
of invoice_number and invoice_line. Invoice_number tells you which invoice
this invoice_line is a part of, as seen in figure 4.13. Invoice_line tells you
which line of the invoice this table entry represents.

Notice that you can also name a field with the same name as the table.
(Although you should usually avoid such ambiguity, in this case it is the
best way to identify the field.)

Now repeat the process of creating tables for the rest of the Inventory Tracking system. I have done this for you, as seen in table 4.1 and figure 4.14.

If you're following along, you may want to see what data types all of these
have. Table 4.1 shows all of the data types used. Note that all columns don't
allow NULLs.

Tip
See Table 14.1 for a
complete listing of
all columns on the
Inventory Tracking
tables.

Tip
Use the scroll bars
on the table win-
dows to see any
columns that may
have scrolled off.

Fig. 4.13
The invoice_line
table has two
columns for a
primary key!

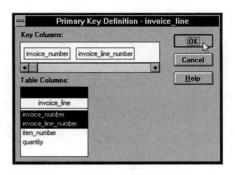

Table 4.1	Inventory Tracking Database Definition			
Table	**Column Name**	**Data Type**	**Width**	**Decimals**
*customer	customer_number	integer		
	customer_name	varchar	50	
	customer_contact	varchar	50	
	customer_address1	varchar	30	
	customer_address2	varchar	30	
	customer_city	varchar	16	
	customer_state	char	2	
	customer_zip	char	10	
	customer_phone	varchar	12	
invoice	invoice_number	integer		
	invoice_date	date		
	miscellaneous_charges	numeric	9	2
	sales_tax	numeric	9	2
	freight	numeric	9	2
	invoice_comments	varchar	200	
	customer_number	integer		
invoice_line	invoice_number	integer		
	invoice_line_number	integer		
	item_number	integer		

Table	Column Name	Data Type	Width	Decimals
	quantity	integer		
item	item_number	integer		
	item_description	varchar	50	
	quantity_on_hand	integer		
	quantity_on_order	integer		
	last_order_date	date		
	order_price	numeric	9	2
	selling_price	numeric	9	2
	item_color	char	10	
	item_size	char	1	
	obsolete	char	1	
	supplier_number	integer		
	warehouse_number	integer		
supplier	supplier_number	integer		
	supplier_name	varchar	50	
	supplier_contact	varchar	50	
	supplier_address1	varchar	30	
	supplier_address2	varchar	30	
	supplier_city	varchar	16	
	supplier_state	char	2	
	supplier_zip	char	10	
	supplier_phone	varchar	12	
	supplier_comments	varchar	200	
warehouse	warehouse_number	integer		
	warehouse_name	varchar	50	
	warehouse_manager	varchar	30	

(continues)

Database Design

Table 4.1	Continued			
Table	**Column Name**	**Data Type**	**Width**	**Decimals**
	warehouse_address1	varchar	30	
	warehouse_address2	varchar	30	
	warehouse_city	varchar	16	
	warehouse_state	char	2	
	warehouse_zip	char	10	
	warehouse_phone	varchar	12	

*Customer comments are to be added in the "Modifying Tables" section, later in this chapter.

Fig. 4.14
All of the fields
have been entered
on all of the
tables, and all of
the primary keys
have been chosen.

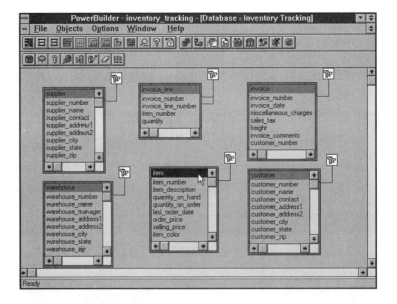

Adding Foreign Keys

Now that you have defined all of the primary keys, you can start working on
your foreign keys. As mentioned previously, a foreign key is a field (or set of
fields), indicating that table entries have either a zero or one, or a one-and-
only-one correspondence to a table entry in another table. Foreign keys are
defined by taking the corresponding table's primary key and duplicating it in
the related table.

For example, because every entry in the item table has one-and-only-one corresponding warehouse entry, and because every entry in the item table has one-and-only-one corresponding supplier entry, item will have foreign keys to warehouse and supplier.

To add a foreign key, you must first double-click one of the open tables in your database painter, which opens the Alter Table dialog box. Now click For**ei**gn to open the Foreign Key Selection dialog box for your table. To add a foreign key, click **N**ew, as shown in figure 4.15. Often, foreign keys stop you from making a grievous error and help you track down bugs caused by database irregularities.

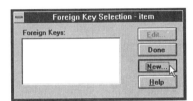

Fig. 4.15
It's important to relate the tables together with a foreign key.

The Foreign Key Definition dialog box opens for your table. To define a foreign key, perform the following steps:

1. Enter a foreign key name. (This will probably be a name ending in _key.)

2. Choose the columns you want to relate by clicking a column in the Select Columns list box.

3. Choose the table you want to relate in the Primary Key Table drop-down list box. (The primary key of the Primary Key Table is shown automatically. See fig. 4.16.)

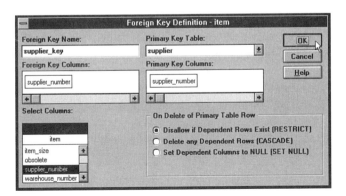

Fig. 4.16
`Supplier_number` is chosen as one of the foreign keys for the item table.

4. Choose the type of referential integrity you want to enforce in the On Delete of Primary Table Row group box. Your choices are as follows:

- You can't allow a primary key table row to be deleted if a foreign key table row (dependent row) exists. This is called *Restrict* referential integrity.

- You can delete dependent rows if a primary key table row is deleted. This is called *Cascade referential integrity*.

- You can set the foreign keys to NULL if the foreign keys reference a deleted row. This is called *Set NULL referential integrity*.

> **Caution**
>
> If you use Set NULL referential integrity, make sure you did not define your column as NOT NULL when you created it. Otherwise, you'll receive an error.

5. Click OK to return to the Foreign Key Selection dialog box.

6. Click Done to return to the Alter Table dialog box.

7. Click Alter to save your changes to this table. Now you have established a foreign key.

Establishing a foreign key in PowerBuilder enforces a somewhat complicated universal database concept called referential integrity. *Referential integrity* implies that if you have a foreign key in table 1 referencing a primary key in table 2, that primary key will definitely be in table 2, or you will not be allowed to add your table entry in table 1. Furthermore, you will not be able to delete your entry in table 2 until all corresponding foreign keys in table 1 have been either deleted or changed to another entry in table 2.

For example, suppose that you have several entries in your supplier table (table 2). If you try to add an item entry in the item table, Watcom SQL automatically makes sure that the supplier_number you entered in the item table corresponds to an existing entry in the supplier table. Otherwise, Watcom SQL will not allow the item to be added, and will return an error to PowerBuilder giving some cryptic message that referential integrity has been violated.

If you try to delete an entry in your supplier table and that entry has a corresponding `supplier_number` in the item table, Watcom SQL will not allow you to delete the supplier. With restrictive referential integrity defined, Watcom SQL will return a referential-integrity error to PowerBuilder or, with update or set NULL referential integrity defined, Watcom SQL will automatically alter all `supplier_number` columns in the item table that relate to the deleted supplier row.

In any case, using foreign keys is a good way to catch your errors during development, and ensures that future developers do not make mistakes that can mess up your database. Foreign keys also maintain the integrity of your database for your users and any third-party database packages that can alter the contents of your database.

Using the same methods, define all the foreign keys listed in table 4.2.

Table 4.2   Foreign Key Definitions in the Inventory Tracking System

Dependent Table	Foreign Key Column Name	Parent Table
item	supplier_number warehouse_number	supplier warehouse
invoice	customer_number	customer
invoice_line	invoice_number item_number	invoice item

When you return to the database painter, foreign keys will be noted, as seen in figure 4.17.

Note

Although the screen in figure 4.17 looks complicated, it is even more so when you first open it. After opening all of the tables, the foreign key lines looked like spaghetti! I took a lot of time to resize the table windows and move the table windows and key boxes around so that the window was more readable. You should not pull up more than three tables at a time if you want to check out foreign key relationships.

Fig. 4.17
Barring any future changes, you have defined your database and all foreign keys have been noted.

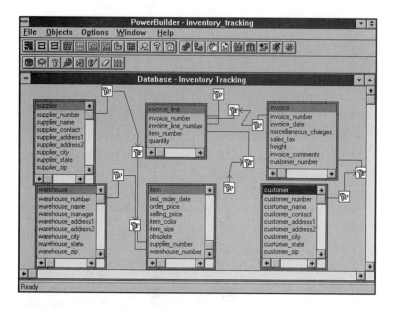

Modifying Tables

Now you can create tables. As development goes on, however, you need to modify your tables. You can increase the size of a column, and add or delete columns, but you can't decrease the size of a column.

Opening and Modifying a Table

To open an existing table, use the Select Tables dialog box, as shown in figure 4.18. It automatically displays when you enter the database or when you select the Open Table icon. Although several tables can be opened at once, for the following example, you only need to open the customer table.

Fig. 4.18
By using the Select Tables dialog box, you can modify your database,

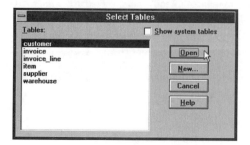

The customer table now shows in the database painter. To alter the table, choose **O**bjects, **E**xtended Definition. The Alter Table dialog box appears

(see fig. 4.19). From here, you can add other columns, like customer comments, to your Watcom SQL database.

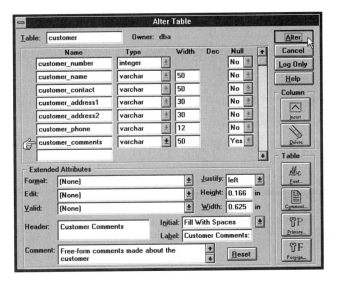

Fig. 4.19
You can add
customer com-
ments to the
customer table in
the Alter Table
dialog box.

> **Note**
>
> Like most PowerBuilder menu bar functions, there are several ways to open the Alter
> Table dialog box. You can double-click the customer table shown in the database
> painter on the table name (this is the one I use most). You can also right-click the
> table name and choose Definition. This may be preferable to some, though it is
> probably less intuitive. Finally, you can select **O**bjects, **E**xtended Definition from
> your menu to open the Alter Table dialog box.

The database painter now reflects the changes made in the Alter Table dialog
box.

Using Table Indexes

Sometimes, you'll want to look up data using criteria other than the primary
or foreign key. For instance, even though you have declared `customer_number`
for your primary key, you are more likely to look up people by name. Hence,
you should probably have names indexed.

Indexing speeds up data retrieval immensely! If you often use a field to look
up data, an index on that field speeds things up. To index a field, open a
table (as described in the last section), and click the Index icon on your

PainterBar. This opens the Create Index dialog box (as shown in fig. 4.20), in which you choose the field or fields you want indexed, the index name, whether you want the index to be ascending or descending, and whether or not the index should be unique.

Fig. 4.20
Clicking the Index (Key) icon opens the Create Index dialog box. Here you can define another key for your table.

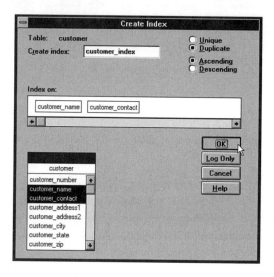

> **Note**
>
> Indexes decrease querying time in a database, so you can retrieve records faster by using an index. However, indexes increase the time needed to update or add to your tables, so use them only when you need them.
>
> Also, the longer the key, the longer both queries and updates are, so try to keep your keys reasonable in length. For instance, if you only need customer_name and customer_contact as keys, don't also include customer_phone.
>
> Because graphical applications tend to run slower than old-style, text-based applications, you should do what you can to speed things up!

Manipulating Data in a Table

Now that you've created the table, you need to know how to get data inside it. Normally, this is done through the application in either a DataWindow or through PowerScript. However, PowerBuilder gives you two ways to access and alter data in your PowerBuilder environment: through the Data Manipulation dialog box, and through the database administrator painter and SQL.

Using the Data Manipulation Dialog Box

You get to the Data Manipulation window (as shown in fig. 4.21) through the database painter. Click the Preview icon, which opens the Data Manipulation window for the table you selected.

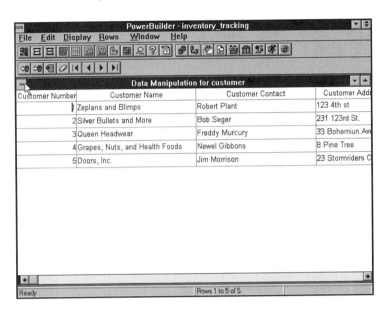

Fig. 4.21
In the Data Manipulation window for your table, you can add, change, or delete table entries.

Database Design

This window contains the following utilities for quick updates to your table:

Retrieve. Retrieve lets you re-retrieve your data in your table. It's handy if you want to start over on your manipulations.

Update Database. Update Database lets you write any changes you've made to your table.

Insert Row. Insert Row lets you add a new row to your table.

Delete Row. Delete Row lets you delete the current row from your table.

Scroll to First Page. Scroll to First Page allows you to go to the beginning of your table.

Scroll to Last Page. Scroll to Last Page brings you to the end of your table.

Scroll to Previous Page. Scroll to Previous Page pages up for you.

Scroll to Next Page. Scroll to Next Page pages down for you.

In addition to the PainterBar commands, you will find the menu bar commands very helpful. Within **F**ile, you will find many commands that help you print your table. Within **R**ows, you have two commands that are particularly helpful: **F**ilter and **S**ort.

Clicking on **R**ows, **F**ilter opens up the Specify Filter dialog box, as shown in figure 4.22. The Specify Filter dialog box screens out certain rows so that you're only working with the rows you want.

Fig. 4.22
Use the **F**ilter command in the **R**ows menu to specify which rows on your table you want to work with.

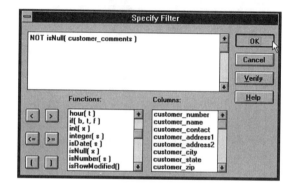

Clicking on **R**ows, **S**ort opens the Specify Sort Columns dialog box, as shown in figure 4.23. Using your mouse, drag each field from the Source Data area to the Columns area. The Specify Sort Columns dialog box allows you to display the rows in any order you want.

Fig. 4.23
In the Specify Sort Columns dialog box, you can specify the row order in which you want to display your table.

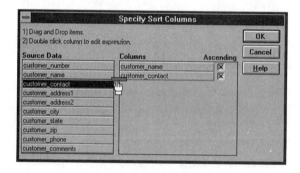

Troubleshooting

I'm trying to change or delete a row on a table, but my database and PowerBuilder won't let me. I keep getting this cryptic message:

```
"SQLSTATE = 23000
[WATCOM][ODBC Driver]Integrity contraint violation: primary key
for row in table <<tablename>> is referenced in another table

No changes made to database.".
```

How do I drop a row I don't want?

Sometimes, you will try to delete or alter a primary key on a table that has foreign keys attached to it. This can be maddening because you can have several tables with corresponding foreign keys to your table's primary key. All foreign keys must be tracked down before you make any alterations to a primary key.

To do this quickly in the database painter, maximize the table you are working on (so that the fields and keys are all displayed). Then right-click the primary key. This displays a pop-up menu with an Open Dependent Tables selection, as shown in figure 4.24. If you click this choice, all tables that have foreign keys that relate to this primary key are displayed, as shown in figure 4.25.

You need to reassign or delete all rows containing foreign keys that reference the primary key of the row you are trying to delete before you can delete that row.

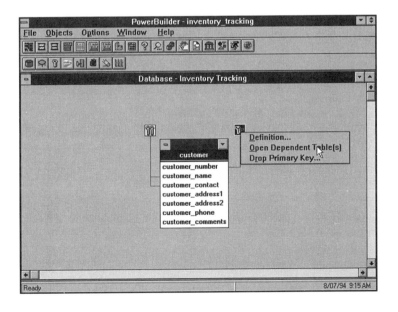

Fig. 4.24
Open Dependent Tables opens any table with a foreign key that relates to a table.

Fig. 4.25
After clicking on
Open Dependent
Tables, all tables
that relate to the
primary key you
right-clicked on
will open.

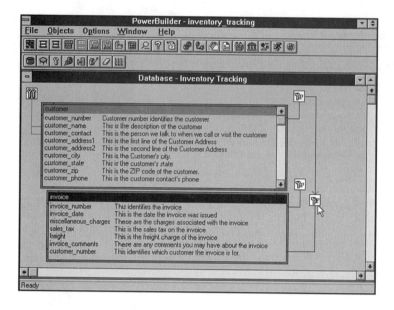

Using the Database Administration Painter and SQL

If you know SQL pretty well, you will spend a lot of your development time
in the Database Administration painter, which allows you to issue SQL
commands to your database. To enter the Database Administration painter
pictured in figure 4.26, click the Admin icon.

Fig. 4.26
From the Database
Administration
window, you can
alter any table in
the database you
are connected to.
For example, you
can delete all
records from the
customer table.

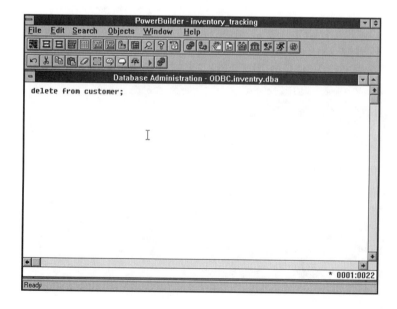

Note

DELETE is an SQL statement that deletes all the records in your table denoted by table_name. Here is the syntax:

```
DELETE FROM table_name [WHERE condition];
```

If you specify a WHERE condition (for example, **WHERE customer_name = "Smith"**), only those records that fit the criteria are be deleted. Note that SQL statements such as DELETE require a semicolon (;) at the end.

Implementing Database Changes with a Spreadsheet

It may be easier to implement changes into a database by going outside of PowerBuilder, especially in a spreadsheet. This is done by doing the following:

1. Back up your database! This is probably the most important step. That way, if all your manipulation destroys needed data, you'll have a backup to return to.

2. Drop all foreign keys. This can be done in several ways, but the easiest is to pull up your table, open dependent tables, and then drop the foreign keys.

3. Go into the Data Manipulation window, and choose File, Save Rows As.

   The Save Rows As dialog box displays, which allows you to save your database rows in several popular formats (see fig. 4.27). If you check Include Headers, the headers are displayed for easier manipulation.

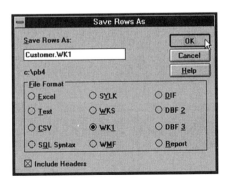

4. Go to the Database Administration painter, and type a delete command to delete all rows off the table, as shown earlier in figure 4.26.

Tip

The Database Administration painter is good for massive operations on huge tables that would be impractical using the Data Manipulation window.

Tip

Use the Data Manipulation painter to do minor data manipulation; use SQL to do major data manipulation.

Fig. 4.27

In the Save Rows As dialog box (or what I like to call the Export dialog box), you can save your table in several formats, such as the Lotus .WK1 format.

5. Work on your data in the spreadsheet. After you complete your changes, save the data in tab-delimited format. (You can also use dBASE II or dBASE III format. These are the only formats that PowerBuilder imports.)

6. Go to the Data Manipulation window. Choose **R**ows, **I**mport.

   The Select Import File dialog box appears, in which you can enter the name of your new file, as shown in figure 4.28. Save data from the spreadsheet into tab-separated format.

Fig. 4.28
You import the data in this dialog box.

Tip
If you mess up during this process, restore immediately! This seven-step process will help out if you are proficient with a spreadsheet.

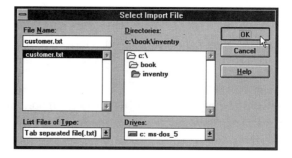

7. Go back to your Alter Table window, as shown in figure 4.19, and reassign all your foreign keys.

Dropping a Table

Of course, there will be times when a table is no longer needed, so it must be dropped.

To drop a table from within PowerBuilder, click the Drop icon to drop a table from your database. This will remove the table, as well as any references to the table or table columns from within the PowerBuilder system tables.

Troubleshooting

What happened to my foreign key references when I try to delete a table?

PowerBuilder and Watcom SQL will allow you to delete a table whose primary key is referenced by another table. When a table has a foreign key relationship to a table that is deleted, that foreign key relationship is also deleted.

From Here...

PowerBuilder can be of great use when administrating your Watcom SQL database. To find out more about PowerBuilder and database administration, check out the following chapters:

■ Chapter 6, "Understanding SQL," gives you a clear understanding of how to use SQL commands to administer your database.

■ Chapter 8, "Understanding the Role of a Database Administrator," tells you about a DBA's role when using a database and how to accomplish the DBA's tasks.

■ Chapter 13, "Implementing Watcom SQL with PowerBuilder," shows a PowerBuilder application being developed using the Watcom SQL database.

■ Appendix F, "PowerBuilder System Tables," describes the PowerBuilder system tables that you may want to access.

I

Database Design

Part II

Fundamentals

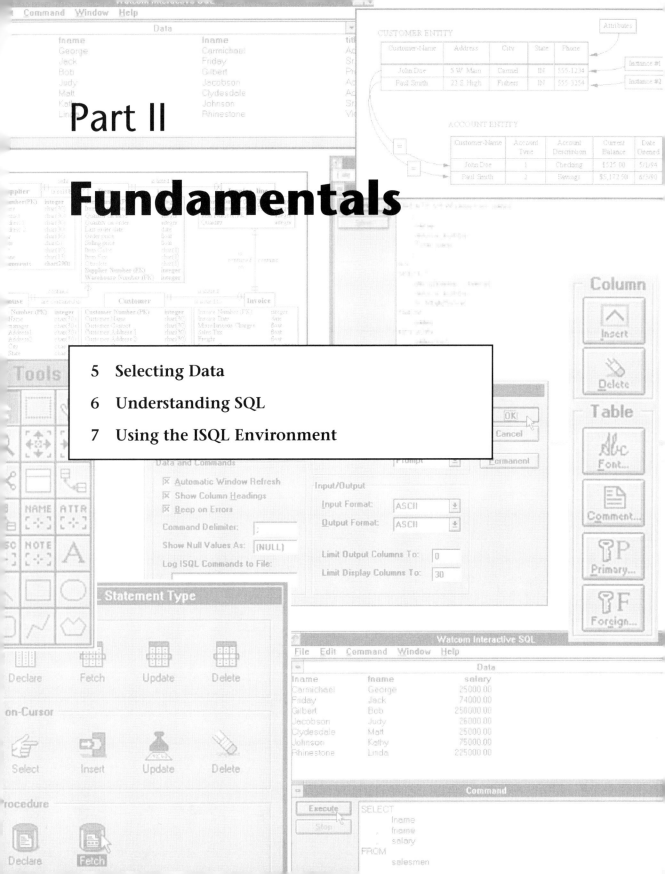

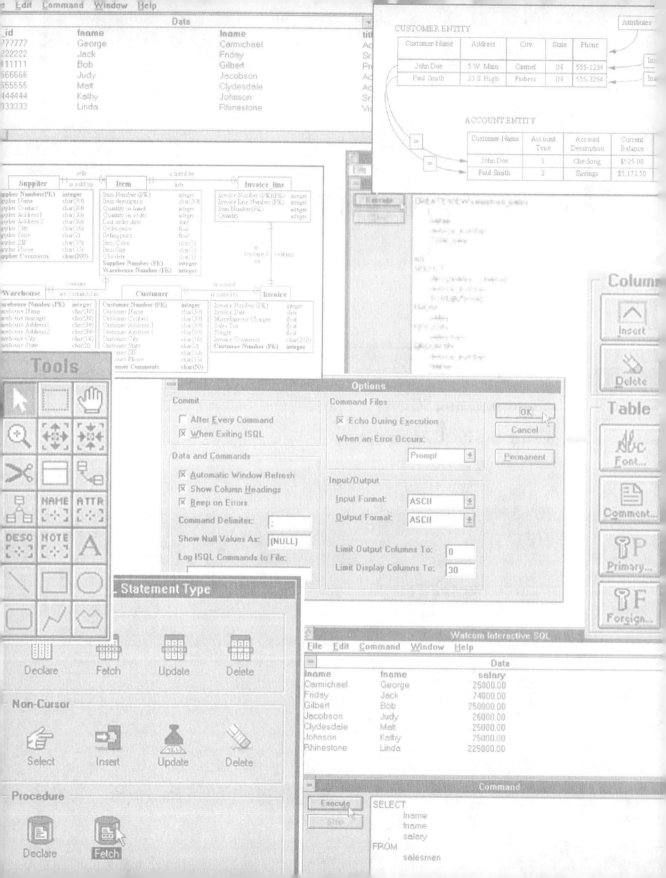

Chapter 5

Selecting Data

By James W. Rang

A very important topic of discussion for a book about any database is, of course, the data: In what formats can you store it, how can you retrieve it, and what operations can you perform against it to best meet the needs of the user. Towards that end, this chapter discusses the following:

- ■ Retrieving information with the SQL SELECT statement

- ■ Understanding Watcom SQL data types

- ■ Defining Watcom SQL functions

Understanding the SQL SELECT Statement

As a foundation for the rest of the chapter, the SQL SELECT statement and how you use it to retrieve data from the database is discussed first. You will probably use the SQL SELECT statement the most often. It retrieves information from the database.

> **Note**
>
> To illustrate how to use and to show the result sets of the SQL statements, the SQL statements will be submitted in the ISQL environment.

▶ See "Using ISQL with DOS and QNX," p. 202

▶ See "Using ISQL with Windows and Windows NT," p. 205

▶ See "Using ISQL with OS/2," p. 208

Syntax-at-a-Glance

The SQL SELECT syntax is as follows:

```
SELECT [ALL¦DISTINCT] select-list
[
¦INTO      host-variable-list            ¦      ]
¦INTO      variable-list                 ¦
FROM       table-list
[WHERE          search condition         ]
[GROUP BY  column-name,...               ]
[HAVING    search-condition              ]
¦[ORDER BY expression  [ASC¦DESC], ...]  ¦
¦[ORDER BY integer          [ASC¦DESC],..] ¦
```

The following are options for select list:

```
¦table-name.*                            ¦,...
¦expression [expression [AS alias-name]¦
¦*                                       ¦
```

For a basic SELECT statement, you only need to tell the database what you want to see (what columns) and where to find the data (what table). See figure 5.1 to see how you can obtain a listing of all the people in the Salesmen table. In the Command window, I wrote a SELECT statement to display the information in all of the rows in the Salesman table. To see more information, use the scrollbar to scroll to the right.

Fig. 5.1
In the Data window, you can see the results of the execution of the SELECT statement.

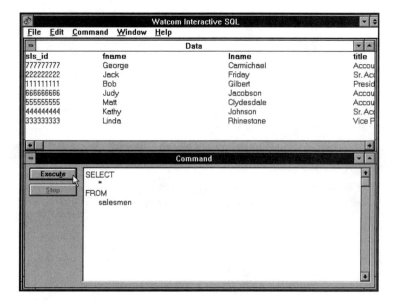

Figure 5.2 shows the tables referenced in this chapter. Even though you can
see a listing of all the people in the Salesmen table, you may not want to
see all of the columns in the table. If you just want to see the name of each
person and their salary, you can specify in the SELECT statement only the
columns you want to see. The SELECT statement in the Command window
of figure 5.3 specifies that only the last name, first name, and salary for each
salesmen should be displayed. The Data window in the figure shows the
results.

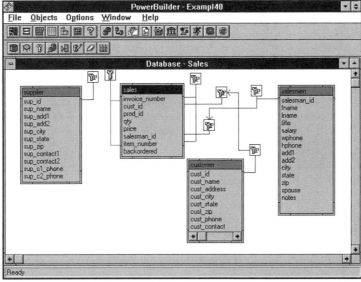

Fig. 5.2
These are the table
layouts for the
Supplier, Sales,
Customer, and
Salesmen tables
mentioned
throughout this
section.

II

Fundamentals

Fig. 5.3
You can specify
that you only want
to see three
columns (first
name, last name,
and salary) from
the table by using
the SELECT
statement.

Clauses

If you want to make the display of information more meaningful, you can sort the list by specifying the column to be sorted in an ORDER BY clause. To see the list of Salesmen in alphabetical order, you can add the ORDER BY clause to the SELECT statement, and specify that the rows be sorted by lname (see fig. 5.4). The execution of the statement displays the information as seen in the Data window.

Fig. 5.4

You can add an ORDER BY clause to display the salesmen in alphabetical order.

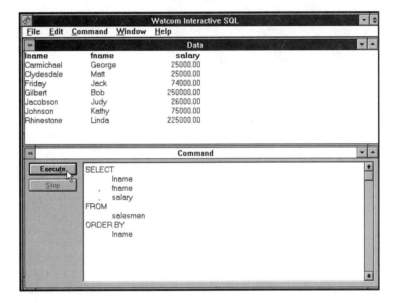

If you want to get more specific and see the information of just a particular salesman, you can add the WHERE clause. Or, if you want to see the salary information for all the Gilbert's in the Salesmen table, you can add a WHERE clause to the SELECT statement that specifies the rows that have Gilbert in the lname field (see fig. 5.5).

Joins

So far, you've only seen information from one table, the Salesmen table. But, what if you want to look at Sales information? The Sales table contains the salesman's ID, but wouldn't it be more meaningful to show the salesman's name instead? You can easily obtain that result by joining the tables together.

Creating a join is a way of combining information from two (or more) tables to make the result set more meaningful. There are different ways to do a join, discussed in the following sections.

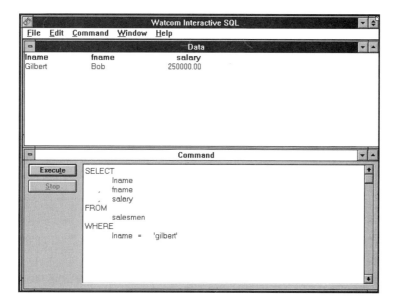

Fig. 5.5
I added a WHERE clause to SELECT all the salesmen with the last name of Gilbert. In the Data window, you can see the results of the SELECT statement.

II

Fundamentals

Cross Product

A Cross Product join occurs when you specify more than one table in the FROM clause and you did not add clauses to the SELECT statement (such as WHERE) to restrict the number of rows returned from either table. Figure 5.6 shows an example of a Cross Product join using the Sales and Salesmen tables. To get a cross product join, you do not need foreign keys, nor do they affect the result if they are present.

Fig. 5.6
The Command window shows an example of a Cross Product join. In the Data window, you can see the results of this type of join.

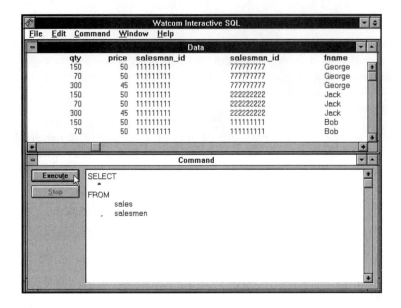

Because the join wasn't restricted, the SQL statement returned every sale once for every salesperson. If there were three sales (invoices) in the Sales database and seven salesmen in the Salesmen database, then twenty-one rows would be returned. If you want to see the salesperson's name for each sale, restrict the join by specifying criteria using the WHERE clause.

Restricting a Join

To find the information you need, restrict the join by using information from a column that resides in both tables: In the examples with the sales and salesmen's tables, they both have `salesman_id` in common. By specifying a WHERE clause using the `salesman_id` to match rows in both tables, you can obtain related information. Figure 5.7 shows a join that displays every `invoice_number` (from the Sales table) and the salesman's name (from the Salesmen table) WHERE the `salesman_id` in the Sales table matches the `salesman_id` in the Salesmen table.

The information retrieved is also limited to three columns so you can see the invoice number as well as the name of the salesman for each sale. In the example, Bob Gilbert was the salesman who made each sale.

You may have noticed some other differences in the SQL syntax. Because the salesman_id column is in both tables, it needs to be qualified with both table names. Otherwise, Watcom SQL will report an error. Instead of typing out the full table names, I made use of correlation names. By specifying the characters that I was going to use to correlate to each table in the FROM clause, I was able to use those correlation names in the WHERE clause. Because invoice_number, lname, and fname are not found in both tables, correlation names were not needed.

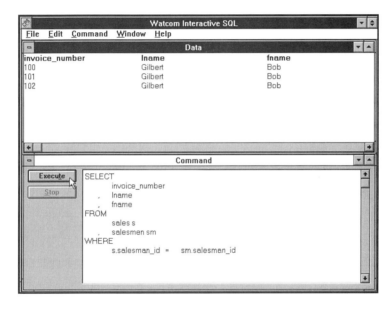

Fig. 5.7
You can restrict a join by using a WHERE clause to match rows in one table to rows in another table. Specify a column used in both tables, such as the salesman_id column in this figure.

Joining a Table to Itself

If you need to compare values in a column with values in the same column in a table , you can do so by specifying the table name twice in the FROM clause and by specifying a different correlation name for each reference of the table name. Logically, this creates two instances of the same table. As seen in figure 5.8, the Salesmen table is being joined to itself by specifying the Salesmen table twice and joining the first instance of the Salesmen table with the second instance of the Salesmen table wherever the salesman_id is the same in both tables.

Fig. 5.8
You can join a table to itself by specifying the table name twice in the FROM clause and assigning two different correlation names to it.

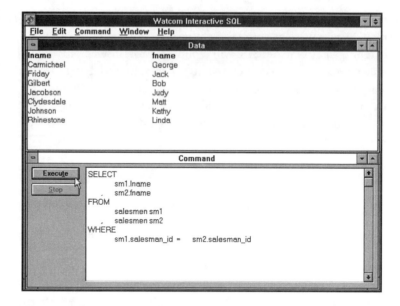

Using Primary Keys, Foreign Keys, and Indexes

In the joins previously discussed, salesman_id was used in the WHERE clause to restrict the join. It was used to display the salesman's name next to his sales (invoice) records. Salesman_id is actually the primary key in the Salesmen table and a foreign key in the Sales table. (Invoice_number is the primary key in the Sales table.) Instead of specifying the salesman_id column name in the WHERE clause, you could have used the KEY JOIN operator to achieve the same results (see fig. 5.9). The advantage of creating a join in this way is that you don't have to specify a WHERE clause or the key fields. Watcom SQL does this work for you. You can only use the KEY JOIN when there is one foreign key between two tables. If there is more than one, Watcom SQL does not know which columns to join and displays an error message.

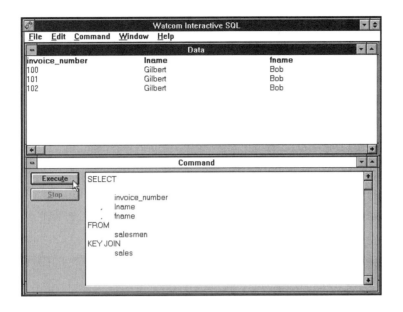

Fig. 5.9
Use the KEY JOIN
operator to restrict
a join instead of
specifying the key
or foreign key
explicitly.

Subqueries

A *subquery* (also called a SubSELECT) is essentially one or more SELECT statements inside a SELECT statement. It is used to SELECT data and then perform
another SELECT on the returned result set.

For example, I want to find all the customers located in the same state as any
of our suppliers. I do this with a subquery (see fig. 5.10). The SELECT statement executes first against the Supplier table to determine in what state each
supplier is located. The results are GA and FL. Now, the statement that issues
the SELECT against the Customer table executes. This statement uses the
keyword IN. In the example, the statement selects all the customers located
in a state that was IN the list generated earlier (GA and FL). Two customers
were found in Georgia, and none were in Florida.

Fig. 5.10
Subqueries are
embedded SELECT
statements, where
one SELECT
statement relies on
the results from
another SELECT
statement as part
of its selection
criteria.

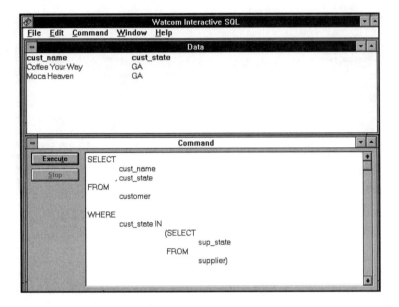

Understanding Watcom SQL Data Types

When you define a field in a table, you must choose a data type for the field. You first need to understand how you will use each field so you can make the right decision about its data type. The business needs for the data may also dictate the data type required. If you choose an incorrect data type, it can waste space in the database. Incorrect data types can also make the application using the data take extra steps to convert the data into a format that it needs.

To make it easier to decide what data type you need, Table 5.1 compiles the relevant aspects of each data type. Identical data types are listed together, separated by commas. Although the size of the data often dictates the choice of data type (you can tell by using the following table), you may need to take something else into account when storing character data. Use a variation of the CHAR data type for fields that contain character data unless you intend to make case-sensitive comparisons. Then you should use the BINARY data type.

Table 5.1   Data Type Specifications

Data Type	Minimum/Maximum Value	Maximum Size Length
Character		
CHAR, CHARACTER, CHARACTER VARYING, VARCHAR	n/a	32,767 bytes
LONG VARCHAR	n/a	2G
BINARY	n/a	32,767 bytes
LONG BINARY	n/a	2G
Numeric		
INT, INTEGER	-2,147,483,648 to 2,147,483,647	4 bytes
SMALLINT	-32,767 to 32,767	2 bytes
DECIMAL, NUMERIC		*
FLOAT, DOUBLE	2.22507385850720160e-308 to 1.79769313486231560e+308	8 bytes
REAL	1.175494351e-38 to	4 bytes
	3.402823466e+38	
Date/Time		
DATE	0001 to 9999 (year)	4 bytes
TIMESTAMP	N/A	8 bytes
TIME	N/A	8 bytes

For the formula used to figure out the number of bytes used for the DECIMAL and NU-MERIC data types, see the explanation in the DECIMAL data type section.

II

Fundamentals

▶ See "ALTER TABLE," p. 259

▶ See "Using ISQL with DOS and QNX," p. 202

▶ See "Using ISQL with Windows and Windows NT," p. 205

▶ See "Using ISQL with OS/ 2," p. 208

Note

After you create a column's length, it cannot be reduced, nor can it's data type be changed using PowerBuilder's database painter. One way to make these modifications is to use the ALTER TABLE command in PowerBuilder's Database Administrator or in the ISQL environment. Be aware, however, that truncation of data or conversion problems may occur. Another way to change a column is to delete and add the columns again using the correct attributes. If you do this, you lose all data in the column, so back up your data first. It is always a good idea to back up information before altering a table.

Troubleshooting

I found that if I hadn't set up a column to hold enough information and after I altered the column width to be much wider, the field doesn't allow me to enter more characters than I could before. Why?

When a column width is first determined, the Limit attribute of the PowerBuilder object is set to the width of the field. When the column width is later changed, the Limit attribute of the object is not automatically adjusted. To update the Limit attribute, right-click the object you want to change, and then choose **E**dit Styles from the popup menu (if the object is a datawindow, choose **M**odify DataWindow, then right-click the object and follow these steps from there). Choose the edit style checked, type in the new Limit, and that should take care of the problem. For more information on how to change the Limit attribute of a PowerBuilder object, look at the reference manuals that came with PowerBuilder.

Note

To specify the size value after the data type, enclose the value in parenthesis.

Example: VARCHAR (20)

BINARY [(size)]

The BINARY data type can contain any type of character. The maximum length of data in this field is 32,767 characters. If you do not specify a size, it will default to 1. This data type is much like the CHAR data type (see the following section). The only difference is that a compare using BINARY data types is case-sensitive where using CHAR data types is not.

CHAR [(size)]

The CHAR data type can contain any type of character. As far as Watcom SQL is concerned, this data type is identical to VARCHAR and LONG VARCHAR (except for the maximum length of LONG VARCHAR, which is currently 2G). The maximum length of data in this field is 32,767 characters. If you do not specify a size, it defaults to 1. Values up to 254 characters (considered short strings) are stored with a preceding length byte—so the number of bytes that a value uses for storage is the number of characters + 1. Values of 255 characters or more (considered long strings) have characters from the 256th on, stored separately from the first 255.

It is important to note that SOUNDEX, SIMILAR, and all of the date functions will ignore all characters after the 255th. This data type is much like the BINARY data type (see BINARY earlier in this section). The only difference is that a compare using CHAR data types is not case-sensitive, where using BINARY data types is.

CHARACTER [(size)]

Same as CHAR [(size)].

CHARACTER VARYING [(size)]

This is the same as CHAR [(size)].

> **Note**
>
> As you can see, Watcom SQL lets you use more than one data type name to reference the same data type. This was most likely done to ease the transition from other SQL environments. I suggest that you devise a standard data type name to use for data types with multiple names. This will help avoid confusion now and in the future, as new developers join your team.

DATE

The DATE data type stores a calendar date (year, month, and day). Valid years are from 0001 to 9999. You need four bytes to store a value of this type. This data type also includes the hour and minute as part of its value. If you do not specify the hour and minute, the default is 0:00 (12:00 am—midnight).

> **Note**
>
> If a column is set up as a DATE data type and is used as a timestamp, or if some of the values in the database have time stored as part of the date, you do not receive a match if you compare it to a date that does not include the time as part of it's value. In these instances, use a date function such as DATEFORMAT to make sure the time is not used in the comparison.
>
> Example:
>
> ```
> dateformat(sales_date,'yyyy/mm/dd') = '1995/01/01'
> ```

> **Note**
>
> A DATE data type represents a constant as a string (the date enclosed in quotes), such as '1995/02/05'. It is retrieved from the database as a string and is sent to the database as a string, but is stored internally as a number. When comparing a string to a date within the database, the string is automatically converted to a date for the comparison.

DECIMAL [(precision [,scale])]

The DECIMAL data type is used for numbers with decimals. Precision refers to the total digits in the field, including the digits to the right of the decimal point. Scale refers to the number of digits to the right of the decimal point. The defaults are precision=30 and scale=6.

The amount of storage a decimal value uses is based on the actual value—not the default precision and scale values. The formula is as follows:

```
2+int((before+1)/2)+int((after+1)/2)
```

> **Note**
>
> before refers to the number of significant digits before the decimal point, after refers to the number of significant digits after the decimal point, and int refers to the integer part of the result.

For example, a value of 10,000.50 would be stored in six bytes and is computed as follows:

```
2 + int( (5+1) / 2) + int( (2+1)/2 )
.
.
.
2 + int(3) + int(1.5) = 6
```

DOUBLE

The DOUBLE data type is a double precision, floating-point number that is stored in eight bytes. The range of values is 2.22507385850720160e-308 to 1.79769313486231560e+308.

FLOAT

Same as DOUBLE.

INT

The INT data type uses four bytes of storage and has a maximum value of 2,147,483,647 and a minimum value of -2,147,483,648. If you attempt to move a value larger than the allowed maximum from a data type such as DOUBLE, Watcom displays a conversion error and does not change the value in the column with the INT data type.

INTEGER

Same as INT.

LONG BINARY

The LONG BINARY data type can contain any type of character. The maximum length depends on the restrictions of the database which is currently 2G. See the BINARY data type for more information.

LONG VARCHAR

The LONG VARCHAR data type can contain any type of character. As far as Watcom SQL is concerned, this data type is identical to CHAR and VARCHAR (except for the maximum length of CHAR and VARCHAR, which is 32,767 characters). The maximum length of data in this field is 2G. If you do not specify a size, it defaults to 1. Values up to 254 characters (considered short strings) are stored with a preceding length byte—so the number of bytes that a value uses for storage is the number of characters + 1. Values of 255 characters or more (considered long strings) have characters from the 256th on, stored separately from the first 255. SOUNDEX, SIMILAR, and all date functions ignore all characters from the 256th on.

NUMERIC [(precision [,scale])]

Same as DECIMAL [(precision [,scale])].

REAL

The REAL data type is a single precision, floating-point number that is stored in four bytes. The range of values is 1.175494351e-38 to 3.402823466e+38.

SMALLINT

The SMALLINT data type requires two bytes of storage and is a signed integer (stores whether the value is positive or negative) with a maximum value of 32,767 and a minimum value of -32,767.

TIME

The TIME data type requires eight bytes of storage. It is composed of hours, minutes, seconds, and fractions of a second. It is carried out to six decimal places. The following example shows how 2:00 a.m. would be stored:

```
02:00:00.000000
```

TIMESTAMP

The TIMESTAMP data type is similar to the TIME data type except that it also includes date information. It takes up eight bytes and is composed of years, months, days, hours, minutes, seconds, and fractions of a second. It is carried out to six decimal places. The following example is one second after midnight:

```
01/01/1995 00:00:01.000000
```

VARCHAR [(size)]

This is the same as CHAR [(size)].

Understanding Watcom SQL Functions

After you define the columns of your database, you might need to compare columns that have different data types. Or you might need to find a part of a date field such as the day of the month. That is where Watcom SQL functions come into play.

There are two different types of functions: normal and aggregate. *Normal* functions use parameters that you supply, and they return a result based on those parameters. *Aggregate* functions perform their operations over a group of rows from the database that meets the grouping criteria specified in the GROUP BY clause in the SELECT statement. It is important to note that aggregate functions are only allowed in the HAVING and ORDER BY clauses of the SELECT statement and in the select list. The select list is the list of what will be retrieved from the database—usually columns or aggregate functions—and is listed immediately after the SELECT command. In the following example, `lname` and `fname` make up the select list. The values from these columns will be retrieved from the database.

```
SELECT
                lname
        ,       fname
FROM
                salesmen
        ;
```

Because Watcom SQL functions expect parameters of a certain type (that you can determine by looking at the type of expression listed next to each function), Watcom SQL automatically converts a parameter of a different type to the expected type. The following sections list the functions in alphabetical order. The type of function (normal or aggregate) is identified under each function name.

Note

Watcom functions need data to act upon. That data is noted next to the function names and is called an *expression*. An expression can be a column name, a variable supplied in PowerBuilder, or a hard-coded value. Most of the functions will be supplied column names as the input expression because they need to access information in multiple rows in a table, such as MAX, MIN, COUNT, SUM, and so on.

Other functions (such as NOW and TODAY) can't use any of the information in a table, and can be executed against the SYS.DUMMY table by referencing a SELECT statement. This is a table with only one row; therefore, the NOW function can only retrieve the current time once, instead of a thousand times—as would happen if the table had a thousand rows. Some functions can have the evaluated expression be a column in a table or any other data provided (such as HOUR, MINUTE, DAY, LTRIM functions, and so on).

The following example shows that the command SELECT HOUR(*column-name*) FROM *table-name* returns the HOUR from the datetime value in *column-name* for every row. The example returns a value of 5.

```
SELECT HOUR('05:10:00') FROM SYS.DUMMY
```

Caution

Make sure the parameters sent to a function are not NULL, because in most cases a NULL result will be returned from the function.

II

Fundamentals

ABS (numeric-expr)
(Normal)

The ABS function returns the absolute value of the input expression.

Example:

```
SELECT
        ABS(columnx)
FROM
        table-name
        ;
```

Columnx has the values: 15, -5, 0, -9.7

The results would be: 15, 5, 0, 9.7

ACOS (numeric-expr)
(Normal)

The ACOS function returns the arc-cosine of the input expression in radians.

Example:

```
SELECT
        ACOS(columnx)
FROM
        table-name
        ;
```

Columnx has the values: .57, .785, .729843, .1

The results would be: .96429047, .6681002, .75270407, 1.4706289

ARGN (integer-expr, expression [, ...])
(Normal)

Using the first input expression as n, the ARGN function returns the nth input parameter from the remaining list of parameters.

```
SELECT
        ARGN(value1, value2, value3, value4, value5)
FROM
        sys.dummy
        ;
```

value1 = 2

value2 = first

value3 = second

value4 = third

value5 = fourth

The result would be *second*.

ASCII (string-expr)
(Normal)

The ASCII function returns the ASCII integer representation of the first character of the input expression. It returns 0 if the input expression is an empty string.

Example:

```
SELECT
        ASCII(columnx)
FROM
        table-name
        ;
```

Columnx has the values: Rang, Wood, Ohearn, Seals

The results would be: 82, 87, 79, 83

ASIN (numeric-expr)
(Normal)

The ASIN function returns the arc-sine of the input expression in radians.

ATAN (numeric-expr)
(Normal)

The ATAN function returns the arc-tangent of the input expression in radians.

AVG (numeric-expr)
(Aggregate)

The AVG function is an aggregate function that returns the average of the input expression for each group of rows selected from the database. If a value in a row is NULL, it is not included in computing the average. The result returned is the NULL value if no rows were selected.

Example 1: (The average of all columnx values in the table)

```
SELECT
        AVG(columnx)
FROM
        table-name
        ;
```

II

Fundamentals

`Columnx` has the values: 20, 40, 60, 80.

The result would be: 50.

Example 2: (Average of `columnx` values in each group)

```
SELECT
        AVG(columnx)
FROM
        table-name
[GROUP BY
        columny]
        ;
```

`Columnx` has the values: 20, 40, 60, 80.

`Columny` has the values: 10, 10, 20, 20.

The results would be: 30, 70.

AVG (DISTINCT column-name)
(Aggregate)

This version of the AVG function is an aggregate function that returns the average of the unique values of the input expression for each group of rows selected from the database. A NULL value in `columny` would be treated like any other value being grouped together, so an average would also be computed for a group of NULL values. A NULL value in `columnx` would be ignored.

Example: (Average of unique columnx values in each group)

```
SELECT
        AVG(DISTINCT columnx)
FROM
        table-name
[GROUP BY
        columny]
        ;
```

`Columnx` has the values: 20, 20, 40, 60, 60, 80, 40.

`Columny` has the values: 10, 10, 10, 20, 20, 20, NULL.

The results would be: 40, 30, 70.

CEILING (numeric-expr)
(Normal)

The CEILING function returns the smallest integer that is greater than or equal to the input expression.

Example:

```
SELECT
        CEILING(columnx)
FROM
        table-name
        ;
```

Columnx has the values: 14.9, -5, 0, -9.7.

The results would be: 15, -5, 0, -9.

CHAR (numeric-expr)

(Normal)

The CHAR function returns the character represented by the ASCII representation of the value in the input expression.

Example:

```
SELECT
        CHAR(columnx)
FROM
        table-name
        ;
```

Columnx has the values: 83, 82, 115, 121.

The results would be: S, R, s, y.

COALESCE (expression, expression [, ...])

(Normal)

The COALESCE function returns the value of the first expression that is not NULL.

Example:

```
SELECT
        COALESCE(columnx, columny, columnz)
FROM
        table-name
        ;
```

Columnx has the values: NULL, NULL, 10, 10, NULL.

Columny has the values: 20, NULL, 20, 20, NULL.

Columnz has the values: 30, 30, NULL, 30, NULL.

The results would be: 20, 30, 10, 10, NULL.

II

Fundamentals

COS (numeric-expr)
(Normal)

The COS function returns the cosine of the input expression in radians.

COT (numeric-expr)
(Normal)

The COT function returns the cotangent of the input expression in radians.

COUNT (*)
(Aggregate)

The COUNT function is an aggregate function that returns the number of rows selected in each group.

Example:

```
SELECT
        COUNT(*)
FROM
        table-name
[WHERE
        columnx < 75]
[GROUP BY
        columny]
        ;
```

Columnx has the values: 20, 40, 60, NULL, 100.

Columny has the values: 10, 10, 20, 20, 20.

The results would be: 2, 1.

COUNT (expression)
(Aggregate)

This version of the COUNT function is an aggregate function that returns the number of rows in each group where the expression is not NULL.

Example:

```
SELECT
        COUNT(columnx)
FROM
        table-name
[GROUP BY
        columny]
        ;
```

Columnx has the values: 20, 40, 60, NULL, 100.

Columny has the values: 10, 10, 20, 20, 20.

The results would be: 2, 2.

COUNT (DISTINCT column-name)
(Aggregate)

This version of the COUNT function is an aggregate function that returns the number of rows in each group where the expression is unique and not NULL.

Example:

```
SELECT
        COUNT(DISTINCT columnx)
FROM
        table-name
[GROUP BY
        columny]
        ;
```

Columnx has the values: 20, 20, 40, 60, NULL, 60.

Columny has the values: 10, 10, 10, 20, 20, 20.

The results would be: 2, 1.

DATE (expression)
(Normal)

The DATE function returns a date converted from the input expression. All time information (hours, minutes, and seconds) is stripped off. If a conversion error occurs, it will be reported.

Example:

```
SELECT
        DATE(columnx)
FROM
        table-name
        ;
```

Columnx has the values (in a form of the CHAR data type):

1995-01-01, 02-05-1995, 01/20/1995 10:00:00

The results would be (in a DATE data type):

01-01-1995, 02-05-1995, 01-20-1995

II

Fundamentals

► See "SET OP-
TION," p. 176

> **Note**
>
> The resultant date is in the format that has been set for the database (using Set
> Option Date-Format) or the default (YYYY-MM-DD).

DATEFORMAT (date-expr, string-expr)

(Normal)

The DATEFORMAT function returns the string representation of the input
date in the format specified by the string expression.

Example:

```
SELECT
        DATEFORMAT(columnx, 'mm/dd/yy')
FROM
        table-name
        ;
```

Columnx has the values (in a form of the CHAR data type):

1995-01-01, 02-05-1995, 01/20/1995, NULL

The results would be (in a DATE data type):

01/01/95, 02/05/95, 01/20/95, NULL

DATETIME (expression)

(Normal)

The DATETIME function returns a timestamp converted from the input expression. If a conversion error occurs, it will be reported.

Example:

```
SELECT
        DATETIME(columnx)
FROM
        table-name
        ;
```

Columnx has the values (in a form of the CHAR data type):

1995-01-01, 02-05-1995 04:10, 01/20/1995 16:30:15, NULL

The results would be (in a DATE data type):

1995-01-01 00:00:00.000, 1995-02-05 04:10:00.000,

1995-01-20 16:30:15.000, NULL

DAY (date-expr)

(Normal)

The DAY function returns the day of the month extracted from the input date expression. Values are from 1 to 31.

Example:

```
SELECT
        DAY(columnx)
FROM
        table-name
        ;
```

Columnx has the values (in a form of the CHAR data type):

1995-01-01, 02-05-1995, 01/20/1995, NULL

The results would be: 1, 5, 20, NULL.

DAYS (date-expr)

(Normal)

This version of the DAYS function returns the number of days between 00/00/0000 and the input date-expression.

Example:

```
SELECT
        DAYS(columnx)
FROM
        table-name
        ;
```

Columnx has the values (in a DATE data type):

1995-01-01, 02-05-1995, 01/20/1995, NULL

The results would be: 728600, 728635, 728619, NULL.

DAYS (date-expr, date-expr)

(Normal)

This version of the DAYS function returns the number of days between the two input date expressions. Because the first parameter is subtracted from the second, if the first parameter is a later date, a negative number will result. Time information (hours, minutes, and seconds) is ignored.

Example:

```
SELECT
        DAYS(columnx, columny)
FROM
        table-name
        ;
```

`Columnx` has the values:

01/01/1995, 02/05/1995, 01/20/1995, NULL

`Columny` has the values:

01/20/1995, 01/20/1995, 01/20/1995, 01/20/1995

The results would be: 19, -16, 0, NULL.

DAYS (date-expr, integer-expr)

(Normal)

The DAYS function returns the date in the input date expression plus or minus the number of days in the input integer expression. Time information (hours, minutes, and seconds) is ignored.

Example:

```
SELECT
        DAYS(columnx,10)
FROM
        table-name
        ;
```

`Columnx` has the values:

01/01/1995, 02/05/1995, 01/20/1995, NULL

The results would be:

01/11/1995 00:00:00.000, 02/15/1995 00:00:00.000,

01/30/1995 00:00:00.000, NULL

DOW (date-expr)

(Normal)

The DOW function returns the day of the week of the input date expression in the format of 1=Sunday, 2=Monday, and so on.

Example:

```
SELECT
        DOW(columnx)
FROM
        table-name
        ;
```

`Columnx` has the values:

01/01/1995, 02/05/1995, 01/20/1995, NULL

The results would be: 1, 1, 6, NULL.

EXP (numeric-expr)

(Normal)

The EXP function returns the exponential function of the input numeric expression.

FLOOR (numeric-expr)

(Normal)

The FLOOR function returns the largest integer that is less than or equal to the input expression.

Example:

```
SELECT
        FLOOR(columnx)
FROM
        table-name
        ;
```

`Columnx` has the values: 14.5, -14.5, 0, 20, NULL

The results would be: 14, -15, 0, 20, NULL.

HOUR (datetime-expr)

(Normal)

The HOUR function returns the number of the hour extracted from the input datetime expression. Values are from 0 to 23.

Example:

```
SELECT
        HOUR(columnx)
FROM
        table-name
        ;
```

`Columnx` has the values:

01/01/1995 10:05:00, 02/05/1995 17:00:00,

01/20/1995 06:00:01, NULL

The results would be: 10, 17, 6, NULL.

HOURS (datetime-expr)

(Normal)

This version of the HOURS function returns the number of hours between 00/00/0000 00:00:00.000 and the input datetime-expression.

Example:

```
SELECT
        HOURS(columnx)
FROM
        table-name
        ;
```

`Columnx` has the values:

01/01/1995 10:05:00, 02/05/1995 17:00:00,

01/20/1995 06:00:01, NULL

The results would be: 17486410, 17487257, 17486862, NULL.

HOURS (datetime-expr, datetime-expr)

(Normal)

The HOURS function returns the number of full hours between the two datetime parameters. Because the first parameter is subtracted from the second, if the first parameter is a later datetime of more than one full hour, a negative number will result.

Example:

```
SELECT
        HOURS(columnx,columny)
FROM
        table-name
        ;
```

`Columnx` has the values:

01/01/1995 10:05:00, 02/05/1995 17:00:00,

01/20/1995 06:01:00, NULL

`Columny` has the values:

> 01/02/1995 10:05:00, 02/04/1995 15:00:00,
>
> 01/20/1995 07:00:00, 01/01/1995 01:00:00

The results would be: 24, -26, 0, NULL.

HOURS (datetime-expr, integer-expr)
(Normal)

The HOURS function returns the datetime resulting from the addition or subtraction of the input integer expression (number of hours) to/from the input datetime expression.

Example:

```
SELECT
        HOURS(columnx,25)
FROM
        table-name
        ;
```

`Columnx` has the values:

> 01/01/1995, 02/05/1995, 01/20/1995, NULL

The results would be:

> 01/02/1995 01:00:00.000, 02/06/1995 01:00:00.000,
>
> 01/21/1995 01:00:00.000, NULL

IFNULL (expression, expression [, expression])
(Normal)

The IFNULL function returns the second expression if the first expression is NULL, or it returns the third expression if it is not. If the third expression is not specified and the first expression is not NULL, then the NULL value is returned.

ISNULL (expression, expression [, ...])
(Normal)

Same as the COALESCE function. The ISNULL function returns the value of the first expression that is not NULL.

LCASE (string-expr)
(Normal)

The LCASE function returns the input string expression in lowercase characters.

Example:

```
SELECT
        LCASE(columnx)
FROM
        table-name
        ;
```

Columnx has the values: Rang, Wood, O'Hearn, Seals.

The results would be: rang, wood, o'hearn, seals.

LEFT (string-expr, numeric-expr)
(Normal)

The LEFT function returns the specified number of characters starting at the left side of the input string expression.

Example:

```
SELECT
        LEFT(columnx, 4)
FROM
        table-name
        ;
```

Columnx has the values: Rang, Wood, O'Hearn, Seals.

The results would be: Rang, Wood, O'He, Seal.

LENGTH (string-expr)
(Normal)

The LENGTH function returns the number of characters in the input string expression.

Example:

```
SELECT
        LENGTH(columnx)
FROM
        table-name
        ;
```

Columnx has the values: Rang, Wood, O'Hearn, Seals.

The results would be: 4, 4, 7, 5.

LIST (column-name)

(Aggregate)

The LIST function is an aggregate function that returns a list separated by commas of all the values in the specified column for each group of rows meeting the criteria of the GROUP BY clause.

Example:

```
SELECT
        LIST(columnx)
FROM
        table-name
[GROUP BY
        columny]
        ;
```

`Columnx` has the values: Rang, Wood, O'Hearn, Seals.

`Columny` has the values: 10, 10, 10, 20.

The results would be: Rang, Wood, O'Hearn and Seals.

LIST (DISTINCT column-name)

(Aggregate)

The LIST function is an aggregate function that returns a comma-separated list of all the unique values in the specified column for each group of rows meeting the criteria of the GROUP BY clause.

Example:

```
SELECT
        LIST(DISTINCT columnx)
FROM
        table-name
[GROUP BY
        columny]
        ;
```

`Columnx` has the values: Rang, Wood, WOOD, O'Hearn, Seals.

`Columny` has the values: 10, 10, 10, 10, 20.

The results would be: Rang, Wood, O'Hearn, and Seals.

> **Note**
>
> When using DISTINCT with the LIST function, the case of the characters in the value is not taken into account. Therefore, if there are values of ADAMS and Adams, only ADAMS will show in the list.

II

Fundamentals

LOCATE (string-expr, string-expr [,numeric-expr])

(Normal)

The LOCATE function returns the position (the first character being 1) where the string specified in the second string expression is found in the first string expression. If the numeric expression is used, the search starts at that specified position.

Example:

```
SELECT
        LOCATE(columnx,'O')
FROM
        table-name
        ;
```

Columnx has the values: Rang, Wood, O'Hearn, Seals.

The results would be: 0, 2, 1, 0.

Example:

```
SELECT
        LOCATE(columnx,'O',3)
FROM
        table-name
        ;
```

Columnx has the values: Rang, Wood, O'Hearn, Seals.

The results would be: 0, 3, 0, 0.

LOG (numeric-expr)

(Normal)

The LOG function returns the logarithm of the numeric input parameter.

LOG10 (numeric-expr)

(Normal)

The LOG10 function returns the logarithm base 10 of the numeric input parameter.

LTRIM (string-expr)

(Normal)

The LTRIM function returns the input string parameter after stripping off leading spaces.

MAX (expression)

(Aggregate)

The MAX function an aggregate function that returns the largest value found in the group of rows. A NULL value is returned if there are no rows in the selected group of rows.

Example:

```
SELECT
        MAX(columnx)
FROM
        table-name
[GROUP BY
        columny]
        ;
```

Columnx has the values: 14.5, -14.5, 0, 20.

Columny has the values: 10, 10, 10, 20.

The results would be: 14.5, 20.

MAX (DISTINCT column-name)

(Aggregate)

The MAX function is the same as the MAX (expression) function. It is an aggregate function that returns the largest value found in the selected group of rows. A NULL value is returned if there are no rows in the group.

MIN (expression)

(Aggregate)

The MIN function is an aggregate function that returns the smallest value found in the group of rows. A NULL value is returned if there are no rows in the group.

Example:

```
SELECT
        MIN(columnx)
FROM
        table-name
[GROUP BY
        columny]
        ;
```

Columnx has the values: 14.5, -14.5, 0, 20.

Columny has the values: 10, 10, 10, 20.

The results would be: -14.5, 20.

MIN (DISTINCT column-name)

(Aggregate)

The MIN function is the same as the MIN (expression) function. It is an aggregate function that returns the smallest value found in the group of rows. A NULL value is returned if there are no rows in the group.

MINUTE (datetime-expr)

(Normal)

The MINUTE function returns the minute extracted from the input datetime expression. The valid values are from 0 to 59.

Example:

```
SELECT
        MINUTE(columnx)
FROM
        table-name
        ;
```

Columnx has the values:

01/01/1995 10:05:00, 02/05/1995 17:00:00,

01/20/1995 06:10:01, NULL

The results would be: 5, 0, 10, NULL.

MINUTES (datetime-expr)

(Normal)

This version of the MINUTES function returns the number of minutes between 00/00/0000 00:00:00.000 and the input datetime-expression.

Example:

```
SELECT
        MINUTES(columnx)
FROM
        table-name
        ;
```

Columnx has the values: 01/01/1995 00:00:00, 01/01/1995 00:01:00.

The results would be: 1049184000, 1049184001.

MINUTES (datetime-expr, datetime-expr)
(Normal)

The MINUTES function returns the number of whole minutes between the two input parameters. Because the first parameter is subtracted from the second, if the first parameter is a later datetime of more than one full minute, a negative number will result.

MINUTES (datetime-expr, integer-expr)
(Normal)

The MINUTES function returns the result of adding or subtracting the integer parameter to or from the datetime parameter.

Example:

```
SELECT
        MINUTES(columnx,10)
FROM
        table-name
        ;
```

Columnx has the values:

01/01/1995 00:00:00.000, 01/01/1995 00:55:00.000

The results would be:

01/01/1995 00:10:00.000, 01/01/1995 01:05:00.000

MOD (dividend, divisor)
(Normal)

The MOD function returns the remainder after dividing the dividend by the divisor. If the dividend is negative, the result will be either a negative number or zero, whichever applies. The sign of the divisor is not taken into account.

Example:

```
SELECT
        MOD(columnx, expressionx)
FROM
        table-name
        ;
```

Columnx has the values: 3, -3, 3.

Expressionx has the values: 2, 2, -2.

The results would be: 1, -1, 1.

MONTH (date-expr)

(Normal)

The MONTH function returns the number of the month extracted from the input date expression. The valid values are from 1 to 12.

MONTHS (date-expr)

(Normal)

This version of the MONTHS function returns the number of months between 00/00/0000 and the input date expression.

Example:

```
SELECT
        MONTHS(columnx)
FROM
        table-name
        ;
```

Columnx has the values: 01/01/1995, 02/01/1995.

The results would be: 23940, 23941.

MONTHS (date-expr, date-expr)

(Normal)

The MONTHS function returns the number of full months between the two date parameters. Because the first parameter is subtracted from the second, if the first parameter is a later date of more than one full month, a negative number will result. Time values (hours, minutes, and seconds) are ignored.

Example:

```
SELECT
        MONTHS(columnx,columny)
FROM
        table-name
        ;
```

Columnx has the values:

01/01/1994, 02/05/1996, 01/21/1995 06:01:00, NULL

Columny has the values:

01/02/1995, 02/04/1995, 01/20/1995, 01/01/1995

The results would be: 11, -12, 0, NULL.

MONTHS (date-expr, integer-expr)

(Normal)

The MONTHS function returns the input date after adding or subtracting the input integer (number of months) to and from the input date. If the result happens to be past the end of the month, the day of the month is automatically adjusted to be the last day of the month. Time values (hours, minutes, and seconds) are ignored.

Example:

```
SELECT
        MONTHS(columnx,13)
FROM
        table-name
        ;
```

Columnx has the values:

01/01/1995, 02/05/1995, 01/31/1995, NULL

The results would be:

02/01/1996, 03/05/1996, 02/29/1996, NULL

NOW (*)

(Normal)

The NOW function returns the current datetime. Because this function returns the current date and time for every row in the table, use the SYS.DUMMY table that has only one row and was created for purposes like this.

Example:

```
SELECT
        NOW(*)
FROM
        SYS.DUMMY
        ;
```

The result would be the something like: 02/15/95 15:32:14.325.

NUMBER (*)

(Normal)

The NUMBER function returns a number starting at one and is incremented by one for each row in the resulting set.

Example:

```
SELECT
         NUMBER (*)
FROM
         table-name
         ;
```

If there are 10 rows in the table, then the result would be:

1, 2, 3, 4, 5, 6, 7, 8, 9, 10

PI (*)
(Normal)

The PI function returns the numeric value of PI. Use the SYS.DUMMY table when using this function because it only has one row.

Example:

```
SELECT
         PI(*)
FROM
         SYS.DUMMY
         ;
```

The result would be 3.1415927.

PLAN (string-expr)
(Normal)

The PLAN function returns the optimization strategy of the SELECT statement input string expression. The optimization strategy is Watcom's estimate about how many times the disk will be accessed to get the required data using the SELECT statement in the input expression.

Example:

```
SELECT
         PLAN('Select * from salesmen')
FROM
         Salesmen
         ;
```

Let's say there are seven rows in the table. The results listed once for each row in the table would be:

Estimate 1 I/O operations|Scan Salesmen sequentially|Estimate getting here 7 times|

REMAINDER (dividend, divisor)

(Normal)

The REMAINDER function is the same as the MOD function. It returns the remainder after dividing the dividend by the divisor. If the dividend is negative, the result will be either a negative number or zero, whichever applies. The sign of the divisor is not taken into account.

Example:

```
SELECT
        REMAINDER(columnx, expressionx)
FROM
        table-name
        ;
```

Columnx has the values: 3, -3, 3.

Expressionx has the values: 2, 2, -2.

The results would be: 1, -1, 1.

REPEAT (string-expr, numeric-expr)

(Normal)

The REPEAT function returns a string with the value in the input string parameter repeated the number of times listed in the input number parameter.

Example:

```
SELECT
        REPEAT(columnx, 2)
FROM
        table-name
        ;
```

Columnx has the values: IN, MI, GA.

Results would be: ININ, MIMI, GAGA.

RIGHT (string-expr, numeric-expr)

(Normal)

The RIGHT function returns the specified number of characters starting at the right side of the input string expression.

Example:

```
SELECT
        RIGHT(columnx, 2)
FROM
        table-name
        ;
```

Fundamentals

`Columnx` has the values: Rang, Wood, O'hearn, Seals.

Results would be: ng, od, rn, ls.

RTRIM (string-expr)
(Normal)

The RTRIM function returns the input string parameter after stripping off trailing spaces.

SECOND (datetime-expr)
(Normal)

The SECOND function returns the number of seconds extracted from the input datetime parameter. The valid values are from 0 to 59.

Example:

```
SELECT
        SECOND(columnx)
FROM
        table-name
        ;
```

`Columnx` has the values:

01/01/1995 10:05:10, 02/05/1995 17:00:59,

01/20/1995 06:10:01, NULL

The results would be: 10, 59, 1, NULL.

SECONDS (datetime-expr)
(Normal)

The SECONDS function returns the number of seconds from an arbitrary starting date and time.

Example:

```
SELECT
        SECONDS(columnx)
FROM
        table-name
        ;
```

`Columnx` has the values: 01/01/1995 00:00:00, 01/01/1995 00:00:10.

The results would be: 62951040000, 62951040010.

SECONDS (datetime-expr, datetime-expr)

(Normal)

The SECONDS function returns the number of full seconds between the two datetime parameters. Because the first parameter is subtracted from the second, if the first parameter is a later datetime of more than one full second, a negative number will result.

Example:

```
SELECT
        SECONDS(columnx,'1995/01/01 00:00:00')
FROM
        table-name
        ;
```

Columnx has the values:

01/01/1995 00:01:00, 01/01/1995 00:00:00,

12/31/1994 23:59:00, NULL

The results would be: -60, 0, 60, NULL.

SECONDS (datetime-expr, integer-expr)

(Normal)

The SECONDS function returns the input date after adding or subtracting the input integer (number of seconds) to or from the input date.

Example:

```
SELECT
        SECONDS(columnx,10)
FROM
        table-name
        ;
```

Columnx has the values:

01/01/1995 00:00:00.000, 01/01/1995 00:00:55.000

The results would be:

01/01/1995 00:00:10.000, 01/01/1995 00:01:05.000

SIGN (numeric-expr)

(Normal)

The SIGN function returns -1 if the sign of the numeric expression is negative, 1 if the sign is positive, and 0 if the numeric expression is 0.

Example:

```
SELECT
        SIGN(columnx)
FROM
        table_name
        ;
```

The values in columnx are: 20, -4, NULL, 60, 0

The results would be: 1, -1, NULL, 1, 0

SIMILAR (string-expr, string-expr)
(Normal)

The SIMILAR function returns a number from 0 to 100 representing the percentage of the two strings that are similar. The function returns 0 if the two strings have nothing in common and 100 if they are identical. The comparison is case-insensitive.

Example:

```
SELECT
        SIMILAR(columnx,'Bob')
FROM
        table-name
        ;
```

Columnx has the values: Don, BOB, bob, Jack, Robin.

The results would be: 0, 100, 100, 0, 43.

SIN (numeric-expr)
(Normal)

The SIN function returns the sine of the numeric input parameter in radians.

SOUNDEX (string-expr)
(Normal)

The SOUNDEX function returns a number that represents the sound of the string expression. The number is determined by values given for the first letter and the next three consonants that are not H, Y, or W.

Example:

```
SELECT
        SOUNDEX(columnx)
FROM
        table-name
        ;
```

`Columnx` has the values: Smith, Smythe, James, Jones.

The results would be: 3827, 3827, 2794, 2794.

SQRT (numeric-expr)

(Normal)

The SQRT function returns the square root of the input parameter.

Example:

```
SELECT
        SQRT(columnx)
FROM
        table_name
        ;
```

`Columnx` has the values: 16, 0, 7, NULL

The results would be: 4, 0, 7, NULL

STRING (string-expr1, [string-expr2,..., string-expr99])

(Normal)

The STRING function returns a concatenated string of all values passed in. Numbers and dates are automatically converted to strings and NULL values are converted to empty strings ('').

Example:

```
SELECT
        STRING(columnx,', ', columny)
FROM
        table-name
        ;
```

`Columnx` has the values: Smith, Smythe, James, Jones, Harris.

`Columny` has the values: Don, BOB, bob, Jack, Robin.

The results would be: Smith, Don

                                     Smythe, BOB

                                     James, bob

                                     Jones, Jack

                                     Harris, Robin

SUBSTR (string-expr, start [, length])

(Normal)

The SUBSTR function returns a substring of the entered string expression using the start position and the length (if supplied). If the start position is a negative number, the substring is obtained starting at the right. If the length is a negative number, the substring is obtained starting at the start position and moving left.

`Columnx` has the values: Smith, Smythe, James, Jones, Harris.

Example:

```
SELECT
        SUBSTR(columnx, 1,4)
FROM
        table-name
        ;
```

The results would be: Smit, Smyt, Jame, Jone, Harr.

Example:

```
SELECT
        SUBSTR(columnx,-5,5)
FROM
        table-name
        ;
```

The results would be: Smith, mythe, James, Jones, arris.

Example:

```
SELECT
        SUBSTR(columnx,3,-2)
FROM
        table-name
        ;
```

The results would be: mi, my, am, on, ar.

SUM (numeric-expr)

(Aggregate)

The SUM function is an aggregate function that returns the total of all values in the selected group of rows. It returns NULL if there are no rows in the group.

Example:

```
SELECT
        SUM(columnx)
FROM
        table-name
[GROUP BY
        columny]
        ;
```

`Columnx` has the values: 20, 40, 60, 80.

`Columnx` has the values: 10, 10, 20, 20.

The results would be: 60, 140.

SUM (DISTINCT column-name)
(Aggregate)

The SUM function is an aggregate function that returns the total of all the unique values in the selected group of rows.

Example:

```
SELECT
        SUM(columnx)
FROM
        table-name
[GROUP BY
        columny]
        ;
```

`Columnx` has the values: 20, 20, 60, 80.

`Columnx` has the values: 10, 10, 20, 20.

The results would be: 20, 140.

TAN (numeric-expr)
(Normal)

The TAN function returns the tangent of the input parameter in radians.

TODAY (*)
(Normal)

The TODAY function returns today's date once for every row in the table. Perform SELECT against the SYS.DUMMY table which only has one row.

II

Fundamentals

Example:

```
SELECT
           TODAY(*)
FROM
           SYS.DUMMY
           ;
```

The result would be similar to: 02/05/1995.

TRACEBACK (*)

(Normal)

▶ See "Using
Procedures,"
p. 313

▶ See "Using
Triggers,"
p. 344

The TRACEBACK function returns a traceback (a list) of the procedures and triggers that were being executed when the most recent error occurred. This function is basically used for debugging purposes. In the following example, I created a procedure by the name of get_date. When I pass in an actual date, instead of a string containing a date format, an error occurs.

Example:

```
CREATE PROCEDURE   get_date(IN a CHAR, OUT b DATE)
         BEGIN
                             // Return date converted from string
                     SET b = DATE(a)
         END
```

Statement to call procedure: CALL get_date(10-01-95)

After the error, I issued the following command:

```
SELECT TRACEBACK(*) FROM sys.dummy
```

I received the following result (the line where the error occurred):

```
set b="date"(a)
```

TRIM (string-expr)

(Normal)

The TRIM function returns the input string parameter after stripping leading and trailing spaces.

Example:

```
SELECT
           TRIM(columnx)
FROM
           table_name
           ;
```

The following values are in quotes only to show that there are spaces in the value.

Values for columnx are: ' Fred', 'Wilma ', NULL, ' Betty '

The results are: 'Fred', 'Wilma', NULL, 'Betty'

UCASE (string-expr)

(Normal)

The UCASE function returns the input string expression in uppercase characters.

Example:

```
SELECT
        UCASE(columnx)
FROM
        table-name
        ;
```

Columnx has the values: Rang, Wood, O'Hearn, Seals.

The results would be: RANG, WOOD, O'HEARN, SEALS.

WEEKS (date-expr)

(Normal)

This version of the WEEKS function returns the number of weeks between 00/00/0000 and the input date. Weeks are considered to start on a Sunday and end on a Saturday.

Example:

```
SELECT
        WEEKS(columnx)
FROM
        table-name
        ;
```

Columnx has the values: 01/01/1995, 01/08/1995.

The results would be: 104086, 104087.

WEEKS (date-expr, date-expr)

(Normal)

The WEEKS function returns the number of full weeks between the two date expressions. Because the first expression is subtracted from the second, if the first expression is a later date of more than one full week, a negative number will result. Time values (hours, minutes, and seconds) are ignored.

Example:

```
SELECT
        WEEKS(columnx, '01/01/1995')
FROM
        table-name
        ;
```

`Columnx` has the values: 02/01/1995, 12/01/1994.

The results would be: -4, 4.

WEEKS (date-expr, integer-expr)

(Normal)

The WEEKS function return the date after adding or subtracting the number of weeks passed in. Time values (hours, minutes, and seconds) are ignored.

Example:

```
SELECT
        WEEKS(columnx,4)
FROM
        table-name
        ;
```

`Columnx` has the values: 01/01/1995, 12/01/1994.

The results would be: 01/29/1995, 12/29/1994.

YEAR (date-expr)

(Normal)

The YEAR function returns a four-digit year that is extracted from the input date.

Example:

```
SELECT
        YEAR(columnx)
FROM
        table-name
        ;
```

`Columnx` has the values: 01/01/1995, 12/01/1994.

The results would be: 1995, 1994.

YEARS (date-expr)
(Normal)

This version of the YEARS function returns the number of years between 00/00/0000 and the input date expression.

YEARS (date-expr, date-expr)
(Normal)

The YEARS function returns the number of full years between the two date parameters. Because the first parameter is subtracted from the second, if the first parameter is a later date of more than one full year, a negative number will result. Time values (hours, minutes, and seconds) are ignored.

Example:

```
SELECT
        YEARS(columnx,'01/01/1995')
FROM
        table-name
        ;
```

`Columnx` has the values: 02/01/1996, 02/01/1994.

The results would be: -1, 0.

YEARS (date-expr, integer-expr)
(Normal)

The YEARS function returns the date after adding or subtracting the number of years passed in. Time values (hours, minutes, and seconds) are ignored.

Example:

```
SELECT
        YEARS(columnx,1)
FROM
        table-name
        ;
```

`Columnx` has the values: 01/01/1995, 12/01/1994.

The results would be: 01/01/1996 00:00:00.000

                         12/01/1995 00:00:00.000

YMD (year-num, month-num, day-num)
(Normal)

The YMD function returns a date value computed from the year, month, and day expressions passed in. Values do not have to be in their usual ranges, such as months 1-12 and days 1-31; they can be any number with extra days and months rolling over.

Example:

```
SELECT
         YMD(columnx,columny, columnz)
FROM
         table-name
         ;
```

`Columnx` has the values: 1995, 1994.

`Columny` has the values: 13, 05.

`Columnz` has the values: 01, 12.

The results would be: 01/01/1996, 05/12/1995.

From Here...

This chapter covered some of the Watcom SQL basics with the discussion of Watcom SQL data types, functions, and SELECT statements. Many other chapters build on this chapter.

For more information about designing and creating a Watcom SQL database, other Watcom SQL statements, and manipulating data through the ISQL environment, refer to the following chapters:

- Chapter 2, "Understanding Relational Database Concepts," guides you on your way to creating an efficient database.

- Chapter 6, "Understanding SQL," covers views; Watcom SQL data manipulation commands; transactions and why it is important to understand them; and ISQL and ESQL commands.

- Chapter 7, "Using the ISQL Environment," shows you how to use the ISQL environment where you can do most, if not all, of your data manipulation.

- Chapter 17, "Performance Tuning," is a good place to learn about getting the most efficiency out of your database with information from the Watcom company itself.

Chapter 6

Understanding SQL

by James W. Rang

What is SQL? SQL stands for Structured Query Language. It is the language used by many databases to create, modify, and delete tables and their data. SQL is a popular language that is used on machines from PCs to mainframes. So, after you have a good knowledge of SQL, your experience can be transferred to a variety of platforms and database management systems. If you don't already know how to code in SQL, I strongly recommend that you become proficient; it will make you more marketable, and that is something we all need to be.

If you have little to no experience with SQL, read this chapter to get a good understanding of the most common SQL commands, as well as some of the concepts about SQL and transactions.

If you are proficient with SQL, browse the chapter to see structured coding techniques that you may want to use for easier code maintenance. You should also review the following sections in particular: "Understanding Transactions," "Using ISQL Commands," and "Using ESQL Commands."

In this chapter, I will discuss the following:

- Understanding SQL data manipulation commands
- Using views
- Understanding transactions
- Using ISQL commands (Interactive SQL)
- Using ESQL commands (Embedded SQL)

Understanding SQL Data Manipulation Commands

The best way to begin is by listing characteristics common to most SQL statements:

- Most statements need to end with a semicolon (;).

- All columns and values are separated by a comma (,). The only exception is that the last column or value in the list does not have a comma.

- All variables referenced need to be preceded with a colon (:).

> **Note**
>
> Some data manipulation utilities, such as ISQL, included with PowerBuilder 4, do not require that you use the semicolon.

Tip

You need to place quotes (") around column names that happen to be Watcom SQL (or PowerBuilder) reserved words.

In addition, here is a list of optional characteristics of SQL statements:

- Quotes (") around table names and *most* column names.

- All columns and values can be on one line.

- Each column or value can be on its own line—you *do not* use a continuation character, such as the ampersand (&), to do this.

- A *correlation (or alias) name* can be used in place of a table name (after it is defined). Figure 6.1 shows an example of specifying a correlation name for a table name.

- Table names do not have to precede column names *unless* there are two or more columns with the same name or ownership referenced in the query.

◀ See "Understanding the SQL SELECT Statement," p. 107

The most common SQL commands that you will use are SELECT, INSERT, UPDATE, and DELETE. The SELECT command was discussed in Chapter 5. I will be talking about the other three commands in this chapter.

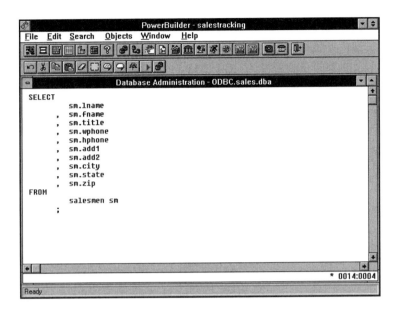

Fig. 6.1
To qualify a column name, you can use the correlation name sm instead of the table name salesmen. After you define a correlation name in an SQL statement, the full table name can no longer be used as a qualifier.

INSERT Statement

You use the INSERT statement to add data (rows) to a table. You don't have to specify every column when INSERTing a row to a table. When you specify the columns in the statement, the values need to be in the same order as the columns. If you do not specify a column in the statement, the default value or null of the column is inserted. You can specify default values for a column when you issue the CREATE TABLE and ALTER TABLE commands in the PowerBuilder Database Administration painter or ISQL environments. You can also specify default values for a column in the Initial field of a column in an open table in the PowerBuilder Database painter. If you do not specify a default value, then the null value is inserted. An error occurs if you attempt to insert a null value in a column that does not allow null values (such as any column that is part of the primary key).

Because of referential integrity, when you insert a value in a field defined as a foreign key, the value must match a corresponding primary key value in the other table. If the value does not match, an error occurs.

▶ See "Understanding Referential Integrity," p. 236

▶ See "CREATE TABLE," p. 243

▶ See "ALTER TABLE," p. 259

II

Fundamentals

The INSERT statement has the following format:

```
INSERT INTO
    <table name>
    (
        columnname1
    ,   columnname2
    ,   columnname3
    ,
    .
    .
    .
    ,   columnnamex
    )
VALUES
    (
        value1
    ,   value2
    ,   value3
    ,   .
    ,   .
    ,   .
    ,   valuex
    );
```

Note

You do not have to specify the column names. If you don't, the values are inserted in the columns in the order they were created. You can determine the order of column creation by doing a SELECT * (select everything) on the table. This displays the columns in the order they were created. I recommend that you specify the column names. That way, if you add a column to or delete a column from a table, the SQL statement continues to write values to the correct columns.

You can see an example of an INSERT statement in figure 6.2. In the example, I added a new salesman by the name of Joseph French to the salesmen table. His id number is 234532334, his title is NAM Representative and his salary is $75,000 a year. Because id is the first column, Joseph's id of 234532334 must be the first value inserted and because lname is the second column listed, Joseph's last name must be the second value inserted.

Note

The syntax and examples are formatted in such a way as to make *maintainability*—addition of columns/values and debugging—as easy as possible. But, of course, you can place the commas at the end of the previous line of code instead (which seems to be the most common way to do it), if you want to.

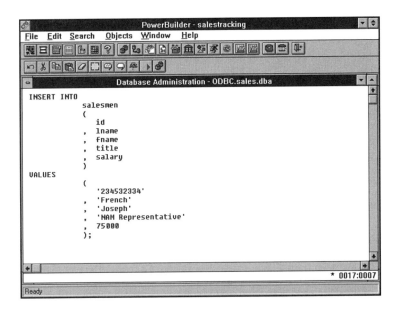

Fig. 6.2
A new salesman
row was inserted
to the salesmen
table.

> **Note**
>
> You can also have PowerBuilder code your SQL for you by selecting the Paste SQL button in the Database Administrator. You can write the following SQL commands this way: SELECT, INSERT, UPDATE, and DELETE. However, I highly recommend that you learn to do it yourself. After you learn how to write SQL statements, you can use the Paste SQL button. This button is good for when you can't remember how the table or column names are spelled—and you don't want to waste valuable time looking them up.

As a general note, if you precede applicable fields with a comma, you can comment out—by using two forward slashes (//) at the beginning of the line of code—lines of SQL, or add or delete column/value references at the first or last line. If you do this, you don't have to worry about too many or too few commas and other syntactical problems.

If you write SQL syntax as it is shown in the examples in this chapter, it will be very easy to read, maintain, and debug during development and when production problems occur. You can also add parenthesis when using AND/OR and other operators to make the syntax easier to read and to determine processing order.

Tip
By using the Tab key instead of spaces, you spend less time lining up SQL syntax in most areas where SQL is coded.

Because Windows treats the Tab character and spaces differently when printing (as opposed to viewing on-screen), five spaces on-screen might *look* as though they are lined up with a line of code where the Tab key was used. When you print it, however, it may not line up at all. By using the Tab key consistently—instead of using the Tab key to indent some lines of code and the space bar to line up others—you will have a cleaner look to your code when you or someone else needs to print it because your different levels of indentation should line up. This is especially helpful when you are trying to debug a pressing production problem where a long intricate SQL statement is the culprit.

Another reason to use the Tab key to line up code in general, is that functions can only contain so many bytes. If you have a long function, you may not be able to add any more code to it. The Tab key uses one byte, whereas five spaces use five bytes.

Note

Whether you create a case-sensitive or case-insensitive table, the case of the data in the table looks the same as when you inserted or updated it. When you code a WHERE clause on a SELECT or UPDATE statement, however, the case must match exactly on case-sensitive tables. For example, if you type John in the WHERE clause, and there are two Johns in the table—spelled JOHN and John—a case-sensitive table retrieves one row, and a case-insensitive table returns two rows. Watcom SQL creates case-insensitive tables by default.

Troubleshooting

When I attempt to compile my script, PowerBuilder says that it found a syntax error in my SQL, but it flags the last line as the line with the error. Everything looks right. How can I determine which line is in error?

It helps if your SQL is written the same way shown in this chapter's figures: one row/value on a line, a comma preceding the line of code, and so on.

Try the following:

- Refer to the syntax needed for each type of statement. Is your syntax correct?

- Do you have parenthesis, if they are needed?

- Do you have a semicolon after the last line of your SQL statement?

- Do you have commas between all of your column names and all of your values, and not at the end of a list?

- Comment out (by typing two slashes at the beginning of the line so it does not get executed) one line of code at a time, along with the column's associated data/field. Compile the script after each new line is commented out until you can determine which line of code is in error. Of course, you can't do this with only one of the columns of a multi-column key or any statements where order is important.

- Do you have a colon preceding each variable in your statement?

- Put quotation marks around all the column names to see whether one happens to be a reserved word.

- Have someone else look at your code.

UPDATE Statement

You may code UPDATEs about as much as you code INSERTs. You use the UPDATE statement to change information in one or more rows in the database. Generally, you code a WHERE clause in the UPDATE that limits the rows being updated to those that meet the criteria in the WHERE clause. (If you're not careful, you can make the specified change to all the rows in the database by forgetting to add the WHERE clause.)

The UPDATE statement has the following format:

```
UPDATE
        <table name>
SET     columnname1 =  value1
      , columnname2 =  value2
      , columnname3 =  value3
[WHERE   columnnamex =  valuex]
[ORDER BY expression [ASC¦DESC],...];
```

For example, I changed the first name of salesman 234532334 to James, his title to Account Rep, and his salary to $80,000. I did this by specifying that I want to make the changes in the salesmen table WHERE the salesman id = 234532334 (see fig. 6.3).

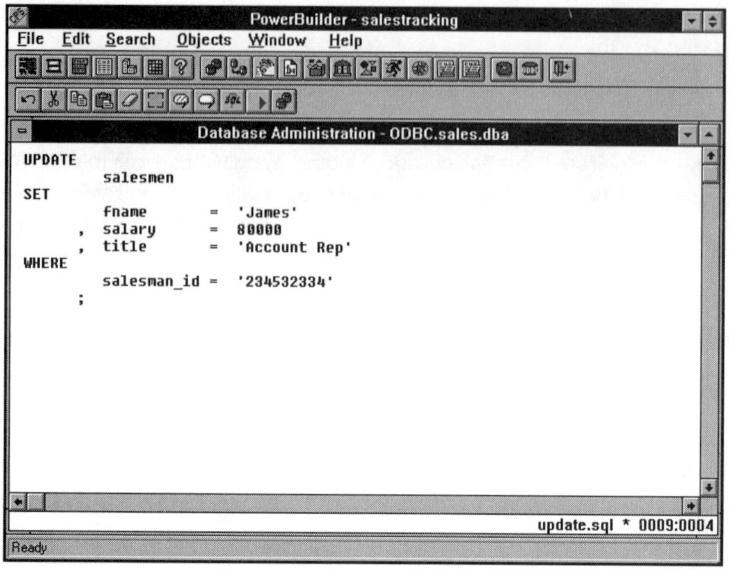

Fig. 6.3

You can use the UPDATE statement to change information in a table.

You may not see much use in the ORDER BY clause when using the UPDATE statement. You update rows in a particular order, for example, when you need to add a number to the primary key of all the rows in the table. You do this if you started your primary key at the number 1, but you now want the primary key to start at 1001 and the other rows to update incrementally. To do this, you have to update the largest primary key first, then the next largest, and so on until the smallest primary key is updated. This way you can avoid having problems with a duplicate key. In this case, you need to do the updates in descending order.

For example, say you have a table called Addresses that stores addresses and phone numbers of friends and family. Because there really isn't a good column to have as a primary key (people are moving all the time, so you shouldn't use phone number), you created a column called address_key as the primary key with the default value of AUTOINCREMENT. The primary key started out at one, and added one to the highest key value each time, but now you decide to add 100 to each record's primary key. You can do this with the following code:

Example:

```
UPDATE
        addresses
SET
        address_key = address_key + 100
ORDER BY
        address_key DESC;
```

DELETE Statement

Now that you know how to use the INSERT and UPDATE SQL statements, it is time to learn about the DELETE statement. If you need to get rid of rows in a table, you can use the DELETE statement. You may need to think about referential integrity when coding DELETE statements, because the tables may be set up in such a way that if a row is deleted in one table, it may automatically delete rows in other tables.

▶ See "Under-standing Referential Integrity," p. 236

The DELETE statement has the following format:

```
DELETE    FROM
        <table name>
    [WHERE
    (       columnname1 =  value1
    AND
        columnname2 =  value2
    AND
            .
            .
            .
        )];
```

Notice the parenthesis in the DELETE statement format previously shown. Parenthesis are often used in WHERE clauses when logical operators such as AND and OR are used to visually group conditions together. They may also be necessary when various AND/OR conditions are used to clarify which conditions go together and to ensure processing order.

For example, I want to delete the rows where the first name is either James or Joseph and the salesman has a title of Account Rep (see the following code). If I don't use the parenthesis, it isn't clear what condition I am looking for in the DELETE statement. Without the parenthesis, it might seem as though I wanted to delete all the salesmen that had a first name of James OR all the salesmen where the first name was Joseph AND the title was Account Rep.

```
DELETE FROM
        SALESMEN
    WHERE
        (fname  =       'James'
    OR
        fname  =       'Joseph')
    AND
        title  =       'Account Rep'
        ;
```

Figure 6.4 shows an example of a DELETE statement where I deleted all the rows in the salesmen table that have a first name of James and a title of Account Rep. In the test table, there is only one row that matches this information.

Fig. 6.4
You can use the DELETE statement to delete an entry from a table that meets particular criteria.

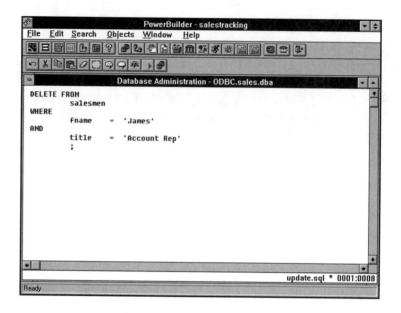

To actually save the changes you make, or to back out (not apply) the changes, you need to know about and use a couple of other SQL Commands. These commands are discussed in the section "Understanding Transactions," later in this chapter.

▶ See "CREATE VIEW," p. 255

▶ See "DROP VIEW," p. 272

Using Views

What is a view? It is a SELECT statement that is predefined to a name and, when referenced, creates a table populated with the information defined by the SQL. The word *view* may lead you to believe that views are only used to browse tables, but they can also be used to update tables as long as the view was not defined using a GROUP BY clause, aggregate function, or UNION command. Figure 6.5 shows a view being created. A view only needs to be created once. In the figure, if Hclub is accessed, it populates a table with the first and last names of all the salesmen that have a salary of $100,000 or more.

Tip
The table created by the view is not a physical table stored in the database. It is a logical table that gets populated with data by executing its associated SQL each time you access the view.

You can use a view to combine information from multiple tables to facilitate access, or you can use a view to limit a certain category of users to only view and/or update columns in a table without giving them access to confidential (or even non-confidential) information. Say that department A of a company needs access to information that is owned by department B. Because some of the columns contain confidential information and information is needed from several different but related tables, department B decides to create a view that contains all the relevant information. Part of the beauty of this arrangement is that now department A only has to do a SELECT against one source, and department B doesn't have to worry about releasing confidential information.

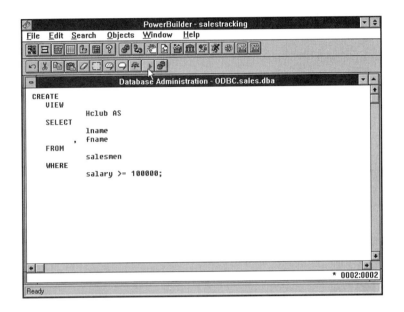

Fig. 6.5
This view displays all the salesmen who have a salary of $100,000 or more.

After you create a view, you can use its name in place of a table name in SE-LECT, DELETE, UPDATE, INSERT, and DROP statements. Figure 6.6 shows a view that limits columns from being accessed. In this example, I created a view to only allow access to a salesman's name, title, phone numbers, and home address. This would allow an administrative assistant to see or change this information without seeing any salary information. I could have created this view to allow everyone in the company limited access to salesmen information.

When you *define* a view, you can use any SELECT SQL syntax except ORDER BY. If you want to sort the selected data, use the ORDER BY command when you *access* the view (see fig. 6.7). In this example, I wanted access to sorted salesman information but a view does not allow you to include an ORDER BY clause. Therefore, when I actually access the view SalesMaint using a SELECT command, I also specify the desired ORDER BY clause.

Fig. 6.6
This view lets you access basic information about the salesmen in the salesmen table, but does not include confidential information such as salary.

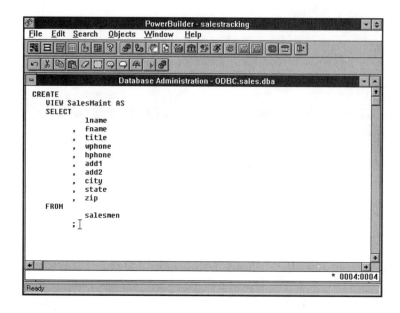

Fig. 6.7
I have to add the ORDER BY clause to the SELECT statement that uses this view whenever I access it and want to have the information sorted.

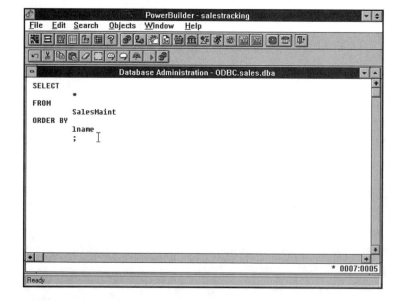

Understanding Transactions

Multiple SQL statements can make up a *transaction* or unit of work. A unit of work is one or more SQL statements that are related. In a unit of work, all the SQL statements need to be executed successfully (unless a non-zero return code might be a valid code). If one is not successful, then all of the database changes that were made in that unit of work are backed out.

In the following example, when a product is ordered on an invoice, the quantity of the item ordered must also be subtracted from the quantity of the product on hand. In the example, I hard-coded the values to be inserted in the table for clarity (variables would probably be used in an application). I first attempted to insert a row in the sales table for a product listed on the sales invoice. It was successfully written to the sales table, so I then attempted to reduce the quantity of the product in the product table.

If the INSERT to the sales table is not successful, a ROLLBACK issues, a message box displays, and the script exits without attempting to reduce the product quantity in the product table. If the INSERT to the sales table is successful, and the attempt to update the product quantity in the product table is not successful, then a ROLLBACK issues so that data inserted in the sales table is backed out. This is done so that one table will not have information in it that is not properly reflected in another table. If the INSERT to the sales table and the UPDATE to the product table are both successful, then the database is updated using the COMMIT command. This command applies the information to the database. (A database is not actually updated when the SQL commands are executed, but when the COMMIT command is successfully issued.)

So, how do you know whether an SQL statement is successful? You check the SQLCode for the transaction you used for the statement. As in the next example, you should check the SQLCode after every statement with code similar to the following:

```
If SQLCA.SQLCode <> 0 then
    MessageBox("SQL error",SQLCA.SQLErrText,StopSign!)      ROLL-
BACK;
    RETURN
End If
```

If the SQLCode is not zero (and it wasn't an SQLCode that you may have expected), then ROLLBACK the changes, display a message to the user, and prevent more SQL statements from being executed (if applicable). If you reference SQLErrText (as in the previous example), you will have more details about the error.

```
INSERT INTO
    sales
    (
            invoice_number
    ,       cust_id
    ,       prod_id
    ,       qty
    ,       price
    ,       salesman_id
    ,       item_number
    )
```

```
       VALUES
         (
                 104
         ,       '002'
         ,       104
         ,       150
         ,       70
         ,       '222222222'
         ,       001
         );

If SQLCA.SQLCode <> 0 then
   MessageBox("SQL error",SQLCA.SQLErrText,StopSign!)
   ROLLBACK;
   RETURN
End If

UPDATE
   products
SET
   prod_qty        = prod_qty - 150
WHERE
   prod_id = 104;

If SQLCA.SQLCode <> 0 then
   MessageBox("SQL error",SQLCA.SQLErrText,StopSign!)
   ROLLBACK;
Else
   COMMIT;
   If SQLCA.SQLCode <> 0 then
           MessageBox("SQL error",SQLCA.SQLErrText,StopSign!)
   End If
End If
```

A transaction begins when you connect to the database. It ends after a COM-MIT or ROLLBACK and the next one begins with the next SQL statement. In PowerBuilder, this is only true if the AutoCommit is set to false, which is the default.

COMMIT Statement

A COMMIT is used to apply the changes done in your transaction to the database. It is also important to test the SQLCode to see if the COMMIT was successful. Otherwise, you might think that your changes were made, when they actually weren't.

So, what do you do if one of your SQL statements is not successful—whether the user entered bad values for some of the columns, or the row was already locked by someone else (and you weren't expecting a non-zero SQLCode)? You issue a ROLLBACK.

ROLLBACK Statement

A ROLLBACK is used to back out (not apply) your changes. Most of the time, if you have an unsuccessful SQL statement, you need to issue a ROLLBACK and let the user know. At other times, you may get a bad SQL return code, but it may be one you expected. For example, if you allow a user to enter new data or update existing data on the same window, you may want to try doing an UPDATE first. If that fails with a SQLCode of +100 (row not found), then you issue an INSERT because you now know that it is a new record.

> **Caution**
>
> Be sure you complete a transaction (issue a COMMIT or ROLLBACK) before you return control to the user. If not, the user's session might "time out"—or something else might happen to prevent a COMMIT from taking place. Another unwanted result can occur if you exit a script (that executes some SQL statements) early because one of the statements received a bad return code and you didn't issue a ROLLBACK. If you issue a COMMIT later (and do not issue ROLLBACKs in between), then the changes that you weren't intending to COMMIT are now saved.

Using ISQL Commands

ISQL stands for Interactive SQL (or more precisely, Interactive Structured Query Language). It is used in the ISQL program supplied with Watcom SQL. It is its own environment where you can create, alter, and delete tables as well as manipulate data in many ways.

▶ See "Starting the ISQL Environment," p. 202

▶ See "Exiting the ISQL Environment," p. 205

There are three different groups of ISQL commands:

- Standard SQL commands, including data manipulation and data definition commands

- ISQL commands that manipulate the ISQL environment

- Commands that impact the ISQL data window—the window that holds the result set from commands executed in the command window

Standard SQL commands are SQL commands that you can type into the ISQL environment to manipulate databases and their data. They work the same way as they do embedded in PowerScript, except they can be executed immediately. There are two subgroups here: data manipulation and data definition.

Data Manipulation SQL Commands

The following are the data manipulation SQL commands to which you have access, along with a short explanation of each. These commands impact data directly. Some of the commands send changes (INSERT, UPDATE, and DELETE) to the database, and some apply or undo changes (COMMIT and ROLLBACK).

CALL

You use this command to call a procedure that has been created using the CREATE PROCEDURE command. When calling a procedure, you can send and receive arguments according to how the procedure defined them. Input arguments are mandatory, but output arguments are optional.

For example, if a procedure was defined (created) with the name of `find_average` with two integer input parameters and one integer output parameter, a call to it would look like this:

```
CALL find_average(15,7, average_found)
```

The 15 and 7 are the values of the integers sent, and `average_found` is where the result is received.

CHECKPOINT

To speed up database access, transactions are not immediately written to the database. They are stored in memory until they are sent to update the database when the memory is full or when the database engine is idle long enough. The CHECKPOINT command writes all the database changes that are currently being cached in memory to the disk. It is not usually explicitly called in an SQL statement because the database itself usually handles it.

But in case you do want to issue the CHECKPOINT command, simply type:

```
CHECKPOINT;
```

COMMIT

COMMIT ends a transaction by writing the changes made throughout the transaction to the database. The following is an example:

```
COMMIT;
```

DELETE

This command deletes rows from the database. In the following example, I deleted the salesman whose id is 222222222 from the salesmen table.

```
DELETE FROM
        salesmen
WHERE
        salesmen_id = '222222222';
```

INSERT

This command inserts a row or rows into the database. The following example adds the new coffee bean grinder product to the products table.

```
        INSERT INTO
                products
                (
                        prod_id
                ,       prod_desc
                ,       sup_id
                ,       prod_qty
                ,       unit_cost
                )
VALUES
                (       106
                ,       'Coffee bean grinder'
                ,       500
                ,       20
                ,       50
                );
```

PREPARE TO COMMIT

The PREPARE TO COMMIT command checks to see whether doing a COM-
MIT at that moment would be successful. The following example deletes the
product with an id of 106 from the products table and then goes through the
motions of COMMITing the changes to the database to see whether a COM-
MIT would be successful. This command is useful when you have the foreign
key option for a table set to CHECK ON COMMIT, and you decide to see
whether a particular SQL statement violates referential integrity. CHECK ON
COMMIT specifies that the database should not check the integrity of a foreign key until a COMMIT statement is issued.

```
        DELETE FROM
                products
        WHERE
                prod_id = '106'
        ;
        PREPARE TO COMMIT;
```

RELEASE SAVEPOINT

This command removes a SAVEPOINT. The following is an example:

```
        RELEASE SAVEPOINT       (Releases the most recent SAVEPOINT)
```

ROLLBACK

The ROLLBACK command removes from a database all updates that have
occurred since the last COMMIT or ROLLBACK. See the following example:

```
        ROLLBACK;
```

ROLLBACK TO SAVEPOINT

This command undoes any changes made to the database since you initiated the specified SAVEPOINT. Changes made before the SAVEPOINT (and since the last COMMIT or ROLLBACK) are not undone. Any SAVEPOINT commands issued after the named SAVEPOINT are released. If you do not identify a SAVEPOINT name, the last SAVEPOINT is used.

Example:

```
ROLLBACK TO SAVEPOINT savepoint1;
```

SAVEPOINT

This is a point to which a transaction can be rolled back. It is also referred to as a subtransaction. This is an example:

```
SAVEPOINT savepoint1;
```

SELECT

You can use this command to select data from a database or to export data to an external file. In the following example, lv_number_of_salesmen refers to a local variable that holds the number of salesmen in the company or the number of rows in the salesmen table.

```
SELECT
        count(*)
INTO
        :lv_number_of_salesmen
FROM
        salesmen;
```

UPDATE

This command updates values in rows that meet the specified criteria. In the following example, it looks like a shipment of product number 105 came in, because I added 350 to the quantity I currently had.

```
UPDATE
        products
SET
        prod_qty = prod_qty + 350
WHERE
        prod_id = 105;
```

▶ See "SQL Commands," p. 521

Data Definition SQL Commands

Data definition SQL commands apply more to the entities that hold data and allow access to data than to data in the database itself.

ALTER TABLE

This command adds, deletes, or modifies columns in a table. In the following example, I modify the `cust_name` field in the customer table so that it cannot be null (I have to specify a value when I insert a new row). Because of the nature of the ALTER TABLE command, the table must be empty for this specific example to be executed. For information about other constraints and more specific information about this command, see the "ALTER TABLE" section later in this chapter.

```
ALTER TABLE
        customer
MODIFY
        cust_name NOT NULL;
```

COMMENT

You use this command to add a comment to a table. After executing the code in the example, when you look at the comments on the salesmen table, you can see `Information about all the salesmen in the company`. This is true until it is changed.

```
COMMENT ON TABLE
        salesmen
IS
        "Information about all the salesmen in the company.";
```

CREATE

This command creates databases, indexes, views, procedures, tables, and triggers. In the following example, I created a view that contains a list of all the states in which there are customers.

```
CREATE VIEW cust_state AS
SELECT DISTINCT
        cust_state
FROM
        customer;
```

DROP

The DROP command deletes databases, indexes, views, procedures, tables, and triggers. In the following example, I deleted the `cust_state` view.

```
DROP VIEW
        cust_state;
```

GRANT

This command gives different levels of database access to users. You can use it to give different privileges to users such as: CONNECT, DBA, RESOURCE, GROUP, and MEMBERSHIP IN GROUP, or to give permissions to specific

► See "Understanding Triggers," p. 237

► See "CREATE INDEX," p. 256

► See "CREATE VIEW," p. 255

► See "CREATE TABLE," p. 243

► See "Implementing Procedures and Triggers," p. 313

II

Fundamentals

► See "Using the
GRANT and
REVOKE SQL
Commands,"
p. 229
tables, such as: ALTER, DELETE, INSERT, REFERENCES, SELECT, UPDATE, and
ALL. The following example creates a new user id `jrang` and assigns `PB4` as the
password.

```
GRANT
        CONNECT TO
                jrang
        IDENTIFIED BY
                PB4;
```

REVOKE

The REVOKE command removes levels of database access from users that
were given access by the GRANT statement. The following example removes
the access given to the id `jrang`.

```
REVOKE CONNECT
FROM
        jrang;
```

SET OPTION

This command changes database and ISQL options. The following example
sets the format for the date data type to the format `'MM-DD-YYYY'`. (The default
is 'YYYY-MM-DD.')

```
SET OPTION
        DATE_FORMAT = 'MM-DD-YYYY';
```

VALIDATE TABLE

You can use the VALIDATE TABLE command to have the system access all
rows in a table through every index to see whether there is any database corruption. In the following example, the validity of the data in the salesmen
table is being checked.

```
VALIDATE TABLE
        salesmen;
```

Commands that Manipulate the ISQL Environment

You use the commands in this section to set up everything so that data manipulation can be done from within the ISQL environment. These commands
perform functions such as creating, populating, and connecting to desired
tables.

CONFIGURE

When you execute the CONFIGURE command, the ISQL Environment Configuration dialog box appears (see fig. 6.8). Here, you can select options such
as whether changes made by a successful SQL statement will automatically be

committed, or if the COMMIT will only be done automatically upon exit from the environment. You can change such things as the command delimiter, that is used to separate SQL statements. To make any changes permanent, click the **P**ermanent button. To bring up the configuration window, you only have to execute the following code:

```
CONFIGURE;
```

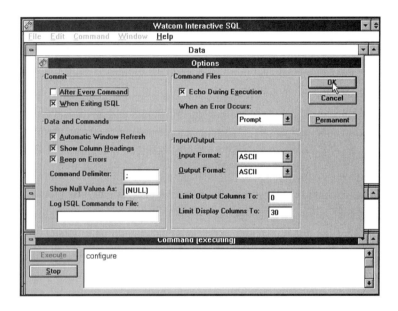

Fig. 6.8
The Options dialog box shows currently defined options.

There are four sections in the Options dialog box. The first section concerns committing changes made while in the ISQL environment.

COMMIT

- *After Every Command.* Denotes that you want database changes committed after every successful SQL statement execution.

- *When Exiting ISQL.* Denotes that you want database changes committed when exiting the ISQL environment.

Data and Commands

- *Automatic Window Refresh.* When you select this option, the result set displayed in the data window is refreshed from the database after any INSERT, UPDATE, or DELETE. In this way, if you INSERT a row into the table that has a result set displayed in the data window, it will immediately be updated with the new row if it qualifies the conditions that returned the result set.

- *Show Column Headings.* Denotes whether headings will show for a result set.

- *Beep on Errors.* Denotes whether the computer will beep when an error is made.

- *Command Delimiter.* Specifies the character that is the SQL statement delimiter. The default is the semicolon (;).

- *Show NULL Values AS.* Specifies how null values will be displayed in the data window.

- *Log ISQL Commands to File.* Denotes whether the SQL commands issued are being logged to a file.

Command Files

- *Echo During Execution.* Denotes whether commands are displayed (echoed) before they are executed.

- *When an Error Occurs.* Denotes action to be taken if an error occurs while reading commands from a command file.

  STOP. Stops reading from the command file and returns to the command window.

  PROMPT. Asks if the user wants to continue.

  CONTINUE. Continue to read SQL statements from the command file.

  EXIT. Exit the ISQL environment.

Input/Output

- *Input Format.* Specifies the default format for input files from the following list:

  ASCII, DBASEII, DBASEIII, DIF, FIXED, FOXPRO, LOTUS, WATFILE.

- *Output Format.* Specifies the default format for output files from the following list:

  ASCII, DBASEII, DBASEIII, DIF, FIXED, FOXPRO, LOTUS, WATFILE.

- *Limit Output Columns To.* Denotes the maximum width of the output columns.

- *Limit Display Columns To.* Denotes the maximum width of the display columns.

CONNECT

Connects to the specified database, or the local one, if none is specified. This is a very important command, because no other database commands will run until it has executed successfully.

Syntax-At-A-Glance

CONNECT TO <database name> USER <user id> IDENTIFIED BY <password>

If you specify all the parameters in this way, you don't have to be prompted for the ID and password.

It is possible to have more than one connection to the same database, or simultaneous connections to different databases, by using the CONNECT AS clause. In the following example, I connected to the SALES database engine and assigned the connection name sales1. I also supplied the user id and password.

```
CONNECT TO SALES
AS
        sales1
USER jrang
IDENTIFIED BY PB4;
```

DBTOOL

This command invokes any of the following ISQL utilities:

ALTER DATABASE

You use this command to remove or point the database to a new log file. The syntax is as follows:

Syntax-At-A-Glance

ALTER DATABASE name

... | NO [TRANSACTION] LOG
                   |
                            | SET [TRANSACTION] LOG TO filename |

The following example alters the sales database so that it writes to a new log file called `sales2.log`:

```
DBTOOL ALTER DATABASE
        d:\pb4\sales\sales.db
SET LOG TO
        d:\pb4\sales\sales2.log;
```

ALTER WRITEFILE

This command is used to associate a write file to a different copy of the database.

Note

A write file is a file that is attached to a database. It allows SQL commands to be executed against it instead of the database, and is generally used for testing purposes.

The syntax is as follows:

Syntax-At-A-Glance

ALTER WRITEFILE name [REFER TO dbname]

In the following example, I attached the write file `sales.wrt` to a copy of the sales database called `sales2.db`.

```
DBTOOL ALTER WRITEFILE
        d:\pb4\sales\sales.wrt
REFER TO
        d:\pb4\sales\sales2.db;
```

BACKUP TO

This command is used to back up all or part of a database.

The syntax is as follows:

Syntax-At-A-Glance

BACKUP TO directory

      | [DBFILE] [WRITE FILE] TRANSACTION LOG |

      | [ALL FILES]

                                     |

```
...              | [ RENAME [ TRANSACTION ] LOG ]
|

                          | [ TRUNCATE [ TRANSACTION ] LOG ]
|

...              [ NOCONFIRM ] USING connection-string
```

Note

When you reference using connection-string in the syntax of any of the commands, it refers to a string that is needed to connect to the database engine. The following are the elements that you can specify:

- Userid (UID)

- Password (PWD)

- ConnectionName (CON)

- EngineName (ENG)

- DatabaseName (DBN)

- DatabaseFile (DBF)

- DatabaseSwitches (DBS)

- AutoStop (AutoStop)

- Start (Start)

- Unconditional (UNC)

The format for using these parameters is:

KEYWORD = value delimited by semicolons-colons (;)

Example: DBF=c:\wsql\sample.db;UID=admin;PWD=school

COMPRESS DATABASE

You use this command to compress the named database.

The syntax is as follows:

Syntax-At-A-Glance

COMPRESS DATABASE filename [TO filename]

In the following example, the sales database is compressed and saved as salesc.db:

```
DBTOOL COMPRESS DATABASE
        d:\pb4\sales\sales.db
TO d:\pb4\sales\salesc.db;
```

CREATE DATABASE

You use this command to create a database.

The syntax is as follows:

Syntax-At-A-Glance

CREATE DATABASE filename

```
...            | [ NO [ TRANSACTION ] LOG ]
|

               | [ [ TRANSACTION ] LOG TO filename ] |

...            | [ IGNORE CASE ]
                             |

               | [ RESPECT CASE ]
                        |

...            [ PAGE SIZE n ] [ COLLATION name ]

...            [ ENCRYPT ] [ TRAILING SPACES ]
```

The following example creates a database called temp.db in the d:\pb4 directory, and also creates a log file for it called temp.log:

```
DBTOOL CREATE DATABASE
        d:\pb4\temp.db
LOG TO
        d:\pb4\temp.log;
```

CREATE WRITEFILE

You can use this command to create a write file for the named database.

The syntax is as follows:

Syntax-At-A-Glance

CREATE WRITEFILE name FOR DATABASE name

...[[TRANSACTION] LOG TO logname] [NOCONFIRM]

In the following example, I created a write file in the d:\pb4\sales directory. It is called sales.wrt and is attached to the sales.db database.

```
DBTOOL CREATE WRITEFILE
        d:\pb4\sales\sales.wrt
FOR DATABASE
        d:\pb4\sales\sales.db;
```

DBINFO DATABASE

You use this command to display information about the database.

The syntax is as follows:

Syntax-At-A-Glance

DBINFO DATABASE filename TO filename [[WITH] PAGE USAGE]

DROP DATABASE

You can use this command to delete a database.

The syntax is as follows:

Syntax-At-A-Glance

DROP DATABASE name [NOCONFIRM]

In the following example, I deleted the temp.db database.

```
DBTOOL DROP DATABASE
        d:\pb4\temp.db;
```

TRANSLATE

This command converts a database log file into an SQL command file.

II

Fundamentals

The syntax is as follows:

Syntax-At-A-Glance

```
TRANSLATE [ TRANSACTION ] LOG FROM logname
...             [ TO sqlfile ] [ WITH ROLLBACKS ]
...             | [ USERS u1, u2, ... , un ]      |
                | [ EXCLUDE USERS u1, u2, ... , un ]      |
...             [ LAST CHECKPOINT ] [ ANSI ] [ NOCONFIRM ]
```

The following example converts the log file for the sales database to an SQL command file called `sales.sql`:

```
DBTOOL TRANSLATE LOG
FROM
        d:\pb4\sales\sales.log
    TO
        d:\pb4\sales\sales.sql;
```

UNCOMPRESS DATABASE

This command uncompresses a database that was compressed using the COMPRESS DATABASE command.

The syntax is as follows:

Syntax-At-A-Glance

```
UNCOMPRESS DATABASE filename [TO filename][NOCONFIRM]
```

The following statement uncompresses the compressed `salesc.db` database with the resultant uncompressed database named `salesu.db`:

```
DBTOOL UNCOMPRESS DATABASE
    d:\pb4\sales\salesc.db
TO d:\pb4\sales\salesu.db;
```

UNLOAD COLLATION

You use this command to extract the sorting sequence of a table and place it in a file.

The syntax is as follows:

Syntax-At-A-Glance

UNLOAD COLLATION [name] TO filename

...   [EMPTY MAPPINGS] [HEXIHEXADECIMAL] [NOCONFIRM]

UNLOAD TABLES

This command unloads data from tables into files that are comma-delimited, ASCII-formatted files, and creates a file called `reload.sql` that contains the SQL to completely rebuild the database and table structures and reload the data from the ASCII files.

The syntax is as follows:

Syntax-At-A-Glance

UNLOAD TABLES TO directory [RELOAD FILE TO filename]

... | [DATA] |

           | [SCHEMA] |

...   [UNORDERED] [VERBOSE] USING connection-string

VALIDATE TABLES

This command validates the indexes of tables in a database.

The syntax is as follows:

Syntax-At-A-Glance

VALIDATE TABLES [t1, t2, ..., tn] USING connection-string

DISCONNECT

You use DISCONNECT to break a connection to a database and release all resources used by it. The following is an example:

    DISCONNECT   (Defaults to current connection)

    DISCONNECT ALL   (Drops all connections)

EXIT

This command exits ISQL and automatically does a COMMIT unless COMMIT_ON_EXIT is false. (This option is found in the Configuration menu.)

In the ISQL environment, simply type the following in the command window and execute it:

    EXIT;

HELP

You use this command to access on-line help. If you want, you can specify a keyword to jump directly to that topic in the help system.

Syntax-At-A-Glance

HELP

or

HELP <topic>

For example, typing **HELP INPUT** shows the Help window in figure 6.9. The Help window shows that there are two ways to input data interactively: using the INSERT or INPUT command.

▶ See "Starting the ISQL Environment," p. 208

While you are in the Help window, you can click the Search button to type another command with which to get help. You can also click the Contents button to see a table of contents of help topics. For more information on using the help feature of Watcom SQL, choose **U**sing Help from the Help window while in the ISQL environment.

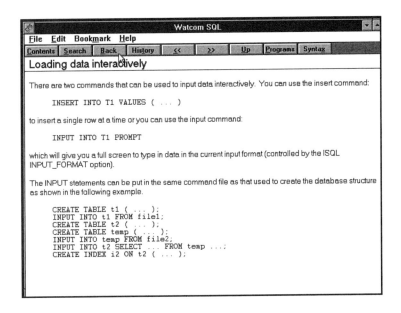

Fig. 6.9
Typing HELP
INPUT obtains the
help information
on the INPUT
command.

INPUT

This command adds many rows to a table. The syntax is as follows:

Syntax-At-A-Glance

INPUT INTO table-name

       [FROM filename|PROMPT

       [FORMAT input-format]

       [BY ORDER|BY NAME]

       [DELIMITED BY string]

       [COLUMN WIDTHS (integer,...)]

       [NOSTRIP]

       [(column-name, ...)]

The input-format can be one of the following file formats:

- *ASCII.* ASCII characters with one row per line and values separated by commas.

- *DBASEII.* DBASEII format.

- *DBASEIII.* DBASEIII format.

- *DIF.* Data Interchange Format.

- *FIXED.* The input lines are in fixed format. With this format, column widths can either be set by using the COLUMN WIDTHS clause, or the column widths are assumed to be the length of the maximum number of characters required by the corresponding database column's type.

- *FOXPRO.* FoxPro format.

- *LOTUS.* Lotus 1-2-3 worksheet format. It is assumed that the first row of the file has the column header names.

- *WATFILE.* WATFILE format. WATFILE is a tabular file management tool available from WATCOM.

Example:

```
INPUT INTO
    salesmen
FROM
    d:\pb4\sales\salesmen.dbf
FORMAT
    DBASEIII;
```

OUTPUT
This command writes the current result-set into a file. The following is an example:

```
OUTPUT TO
    d:\pb4\sales\salesmen.dbf
FORMAT
    DBASEIII;
```

PARAMETERS

▶ See "Using Command Files with RTSQL and READ," p. 216

This command specifies what parameters are used in a command file. If all of the parameters are not passed in, you'll be prompted for the rest.

Command files are files that contain SQL statements that can manipulate databases and their data and are run using the following syntax:

```
READ filename [parameters]
```

An example of a command file is as follows:

```
PARAMETERS  salary;

SELECT
    lname, fname
FROM
    salesmen
WHERE
    salary >= {salary}

>#d:\pb4\sales\salsales.dat;
```

QUIT

This command makes you leave the ISQL environment. Type the following in the command window and execute it by one of the various methods available, such as clicking the Execute button:

```
QUIT;
```

READ

This reads (and executes) ISQL code in a command file. You can code nested reads. This means that from within a command file, you can execute other command files using the READ command. The syntax for this command is as follows:

```
READ filename [parameters];
```

Say you created a command file that contained ISQL to retrieve all the salesmen who had a salary that fell between two numbers that were passed in. In the following example, I executed the command file named `salary.sql`, using the salary range of $100,000 to $150,000.

In `salary.sql`, I specified that the two input parameters are named `min_salary` and `max_salary`. The last name, first name, and salary display for all the salesmen who meet the salary criteria.

```
parameters min_salary, max_salary;
SELECT
        lname
      , fname
      , salary
```

Tip

If you want the result set to display in the data window, don't specify a file name. (You can comment out the file name using two slashes.)

Fundamentals

```
FROM
        salesmen
WHERE
        salary >= {min_salary}
AND
        salary <= {max_salary}
        ;
```

To execute the `salary.sql`, I used the following code and passed in the minimum salary of `100000` and the maximum salary of `150000`:

```
read salary [100000] [150000]
```

SET CONNECTION

You use this command to switch between database connections. For example, if you defined two transactions to the same database (using the CONNECT AS command), and one connection is called `sales1` and the other is called `sales2`, you can connect to `sales2` by issuing the following command:

```
SET CONNECTION sales2;
```

SET OPTION

Used to set database and ISQL options. The syntax is as follows:

Syntax-At-A-Glance

SET OPTION option-name = option-value

To set the DATE_ORDER to month/day/year format, issue this command:

```
SET OPTION date_order='MDY';
```

The database options that you can change include the following:

- *Blocking.* If a user locks data and another user tries to get it, this command determines whether the second user will be locked out or receive an error message right away. The default is ON (block second user).

- *Checkpoint_time.* The number of minutes specified here is the maximum length of time that the database engine waits to do a checkpoint. The default is 60 minutes.

- *Conversion_Error.* Determines whether data conversion errors will report an error or ignore them (setting the field to NULL). The default is ON (report an error).

- *Date_Format.* This option specifies the date format for dates retrieved from the database. The default is YYYY-MM-DD. This default is new for version 4.

- *Date_Order.* This option specifies in what order the database will recognize a date that has a month, day, and year in it. For example, a date of 95/01/02 would be interpreted as January 2, 1995 if you use the default format. The default is YMD. This default is new for version 4.

- *Isolation_Level.* This is used to control the locking isolation level.

- *Precision.* Used to specify the largest number of digits (includes both sides of the decimal point) resulting from an arithmetic equation. The default is 30 digits.

- *Recovery Time.* Sets the maximum amount of time in minutes to recover from a system failure. The default is two minutes

- *Row Counts.* Specifies whether a query will always count the number of rows or make an estimate. The default is OFF.

- *Scale.* Specifies the minimum number of digits after a decimal point when an arithmetic equation is truncated to the maximum precision. The default is six digits.

- *Thread_Count.* This is the number of concurrent requests that the database engine will process. The default is 0. (Meaning that it takes an operating system specific value: 16-bit DOS = 3, 16-bit QNX = 8, 16-bit Windows = 8, all 32-bit = 20.)

- *Time_format.* This setting determines the format for time values retrieved from the database. The default is HH:NN:SS.SSS.

- *Timestamp Format.* Sets the format for timestamps retrieved from the database. The default is YYYY-MM-DD HH:NN:SS.SSS.

- *Wait For COMMIT.* If this is set to ON, it does not check the integrity of foreign keys until the next COMMIT statement. If it is set to OFF (and foreign keys were not created with the CHECK ON COMMIT option), integrity will be checked as they are inserted, updated, or deleted. The default is OFF.

II

Fundamentals

SYSTEM

This command is only usable in the DOS and QNX versions of the ISQL environment. It allows you to shell out to DOS or QNX to execute some commands, or execute DOS or QNX commands from within the ISQL environment. If you shell out to the DOS environment by just typing **SYSTEM**, you return to ISQL by typing **exit**. Press Ctrl+D to return from the QNX environment.

Commands that Impact the ISQL Data Window

You can use the following commands to manipulate the data window. You can clear it, or move its result set (the data retrieved by executing a data retrieval SQL statement like SELECT) up and down a specified number of lines.

CLEAR

This command clears the result set in the data window returned from previous SQL execution.

DOWN [n]

This allows you to move the result set down [n] number of lines at a time.

UP [n]

This allows you to move the result set up [n] number of lines at a time.

Using ESQL Commands

There are a few other embedded SQL commands that you are bound to use sooner or later. Embedded SQL commands are executed from within a programming environment such as SQL in PowerBuilder PowerScript.

- CREATE TABLE

- ALTER TABLE

- DROP TABLE

CREATE TABLE

You can create tables using embedded SQL. The following is the syntax for creating a table, after which the clauses that can be used when creating a table are covered:

Syntax-At-A-Glance

CREATE [GLOBAL TEMPORARY] TABLE[creator.]table-name

... (

    |column-def[column-constraint...]|,...)

    |table-constraint

                    |

    ...   [IN [creator.]dbspace-name]

    ...   [|ON COMMIT DELETE ROWS
                   |]

                            |ON COMMIT PRESERVE ROWS

                   |

Column-definition

Column-definition breaks down into separate parts. Each part is discussed in more detail in the following sections. Those parts are:

Column-name data-type [NOT NULL] [DEFAULT default-value]

Column-name
This is the name of the column. Column names in a table must be unique.

Data-type
Any of the allowable data types, which include the following:

- BINARY

- CHAR

- DATE

- DECIMAL

- DOUBLE

- FLOAT

- INT

- INTEGER

◄ See "Under-standing Watcom SQL Data Types," p. 116

II

Fundamentals

- LONG BINARY

- LONG VARCHAR

- NUMERIC

- REAL

- SMALLINT

- TIME

- TIMESTAMP

- VARCHAR

NOT NULL

This option is used to specify whether the column can be NULL. If it is defined as UNIQUE or is part of the primary key, then it cannot be NULL. A benefit of allowing a column to be NULL, is that if you do not supply a value for it, then the row still writes on an SQL statement such as INSERT.

Why would you want to have a NULL value in a column? There are a couple of business reasons. Say you insert a row in an audit table every time a row in one of your application tables changes, and you only want to write the columns that change. If you had a number column specified as NOT NULL, then you have to put some value in there unless you specify the default value for the column as 0. If you do this, however, you do not know whether the user changed the value to 0, or if the column defaulted to this value. If you define the field to accept NULL values, though, and the user does not change the column, then it is very obvious that the user didn't change the field because it would be NULL instead of having a 0 in it.

Another business reason for allowing NULL values is if you are going to use a column in an aggregate function (summarize data over a group of rows). For example, say you want to find the average value for a column in a table. If you have values of 200, 100, and 0 in the column, and the 0 is just a default value and not an actual value that a user entered, the average comes out to 100 ((200 + 100 + 0)/3), when actually it should be 150 ((200 + 100)/2). You would receive the correct answer of 150 if the NULL value is allowed and is the default because NULL values are ignored in aggregate functions.

◀ See "Understanding NULLS," p. 51

A drawback of allowing a column to be NULL is that, generally speaking, when you pass a NULL value into a function, the result will also be NULL.

DEFAULT default-value
This specifies what value will be placed in the column if you do not assign a value to the column. If the DEFAULT option is not specified, the default-value will become NULL.

For example:

```
...(
mailing_list CHAR(1) DEFAULT 'Y'
...);
```

Table-Constraint
There are four types of constraints that can be set up for tables so that the integrity of the database is not compromised: Unique, Primary Key, Foreign Key, and Check.

Unique Constraints
You can identify one or more columns in a table that will uniquely identify each row of data. A constraint is used so that you don't accidentally have two rows with the same value, if by nature the value should be unique. For example, because a social security number is often used as a source of identification, it is important to ensure that it is unique. If a duplicate social security number ever appeared, it would be necessary to research the information to see if there was a typographical error or attempted fraud.

For example:

```
...(
ssn     CHAR(9) UNIQUE
...);
```

Primary Key Constraint
The primary key should always uniquely identify each row of a table.

For example:

```
...(
drivers_lic_num CHAR Primary Key
...);
```

Foreign Key Constraint
With this constraint, the value in a column that is defined as a foreign key must already exist in another table.

Check Constraint
A constraint that allows only certain values in a particular column.

◀ See "Using Primary Keys, Foreign Keys, and Indexes," p. 114

▶ See "Understanding Referential Integrity," p. 236

ALTER TABLE

This command is an important one. You will find that over the course of developing an application, you will need to ALTER a table in order to change some of its attributes. I highly recommend that you backup your data before you alter a table. The syntax is as follows:

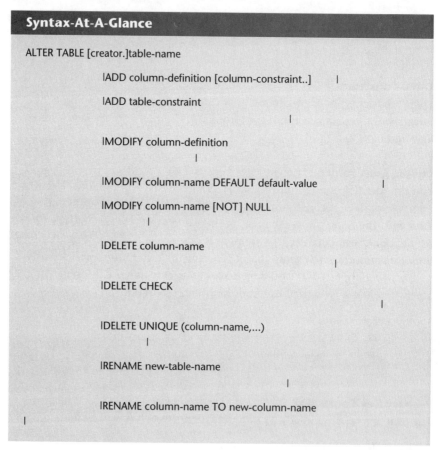

Syntax-At-A-Glance

```
ALTER TABLE [creator.]table-name

            |ADD column-definition [column-constraint..]      |

            |ADD table-constraint
                                                     |

            |MODIFY column-definition
                        |

            |MODIFY column-name DEFAULT default-value          |

            |MODIFY column-name [NOT] NULL
                        |

            |DELETE column-name
                                                 |

            |DELETE CHECK
                                                        |

            |DELETE UNIQUE (column-name,...)
                        |

            |RENAME new-table-name
                                            |

            |RENAME column-name TO new-column-name
|
```

The following are more detailed descriptions of the ways that you can ALTER a table.

Note

It is important to note the following restrictions and potential problems when altering tables:

- ADD(ing) a column defined as NOT NULL. The table must be empty.

- ADD(ing) a primary key. An existing primary key must first be deleted.

- MODIFY(ing) a column's length or data type. Existing values will be converted to the new type. If a conversion error occurs, the column data type changes, all data changes are undone, and the conversion process ends.

- MODIFY(ing) a column. If the column is currently defined as UNIQUE, as a foreign key, or as a primary key, these constraints must be deleted first. If a primary key is deleted, all of the foreign keys referencing the table will also be deleted.

- MODIFY(ing) table and column constraints. This cannot be done; they need to be deleted and then added.

- DELETE(ing) a column. If the column is currently defined as UNIQUE, as a foreign key, as a primary key, or as part of any index, these constraints must be deleted first.

- DELETE(ing) a table's UNIQUEness constraint. If there are any foreign keys referencing the uniqueness constraint, they also must be deleted.

- DELETE(ing) a table's primary key. If there are any foreign keys referencing the primary key, they will also be deleted.

- RENAME(ing) a table name. Any code references to the old table name need to be changed.

- RENAME(ing) a column name. Any code references to the old column name need to be changed.

▶ See "Understanding Referential Integrity," p. 236

Fundamentals

ADD column-definition

This command adds a new column to a table. In the following example, a new column named `backordered` is being added to the sales table.

```
ALTER TABLE sales
        ADD backordered CHAR(1);
```

ADD table-constraint

These consist of the table constraints mentioned in the earlier section, "CREATE TABLE." In the following example, the `prod_id` column is being specified as a UNIQUE column.

```
ALTER TABLE products
        ADD UNIQUE (prod_id);
```

MODIFY column-definition

This specification changes to the length or data type of a column. In the following example, I change the length of the prod_desc column in the products table to VARCHAR(200).

```
ALTER TABLE products
        MODIFY prod_desc VARCHAR(200);
```

MODIFY column-name DEFAULT default-value

This command allows you to change the default value for a column. The following is an example:

```
ALTER TABLE products
        MODIFY backordered DEFAULT 'N';
```

MODIFY column-name [NOT] NULL

This command allows you to change whether a column can be null. In the following example, the sup_id column in the products table is being modified to allow the NULL character.

```
ALTER TABLE products
        MODIFY  sup_id NULL;
```

DELETE column-name

This command deletes a column from a table. In the following example, I had a lic_plate column in the salesmen table because that information was needed at one time. No one uses the information now, so it can be deleted. I deleted it with the following statement.

```
ALTER TABLE salesmen
        DELETE lic_plate;
```

DELETE CHECK

If you want to delete all table and column check constraints, this command does it. The following statement deletes all checks from the salesmen table:

```
ALTER TABLE salesmen
        DELETE CHECK;
```

DELETE UNIQUE (column-name,...)

This command deletes a constraint that makes sure the value in a column(s) is unique. I wanted to remove the UNIQUE constraint (that was added in an earlier example) from the `prod_id` column in the products table—even though it's the primary key, and is unique by nature. I executed the following statement:

```
ALTER TABLE products
        DELETE UNIQUE (prod_id);
```

DELETE PRIMARY KEY

If you guessed that this would delete the primary key constraint on a column, then you are correct. If you want to remove the primary key, `prod_id`, from the products table, you could do it with the following statement:

```
ALTER TABLE products
        DELETE PRIMARY KEY;
```

DELETE FOREIGN KEY role-name

For the given role name, delete the foreign key constraint. The role name is the name of the foreign key field if you specified it when you created the foreign key. If you did not specify it, it defaults to the name of the primary table (the table that the foreign key references). If you want to remove the `salesman_id` foreign key constraint from the Sales table, code the following:

```
ALTER TABLE sales
        DELETE FOREIGN KEY salesman_id;
```

RENAME new-table-name

By using this command, you can change the name of a table. In the following example, the table name `salesmen` is renamed to `employees`:

```
ALTER TABLE salesmen
        RENAME employees;
```

RENAME column-name TO new-column-name

This command allows you to rename a column name. If you want to rename the `prod_desc` column to the longer description of `prod_description`, you could do this by coding the following:

```
ALTER TABLE products
        RENAME prod_desc TO prod_description;
```

DROP TABLE

This command deletes the table and all of its data. If you want to delete a table called `temp`, you could do so by issuing the following command:

```
DROP TABLE temp;
```

▶ See "Under-standing Referential Integrity," p. 236

From Here...

Now that you've seen how to use the most commonly used SQL commands, and have some examples to refer to, there are other places in this book that you can go to learn more about the other SQL commands and refer back to previous chapters for reference on some of the basic concepts:

■ Chapter 1, "Understanding Watcom SQL Fundamentals," gives you a general introduction to using Watcom SQL.

■ Chapter 5, "Selecting Data," describes the different Watcom SQL data types and functions, as well as explains SQL SELECT statements and performing subqueries. Joins are also discussed in this chapter.

■ Chapter 7, "Using the ISQL Environment," shows how to begin and end a session in the ISQL environment, as well as using the ISQL environment on different platforms.

■ Chapter 22, "Embedded SQL Commands," goes into more detail about SQL by discussing all of the embedded SQL commands.

Chapter 7

Using the ISQL Environment

Previous chapters discussed various Watcom SQL commands and showed them being executed in the ISQL environment. Now it's time to discuss the ISQL environment in greater detail. ISQL stands for Interactive Structured Query Language. It's an environment that allows the developer to execute SQL statements to create, delete, and manipulate database structures and their data.

This chapter covers Watcom SQL's ISQL environment and its use in the following operating systems: DOS, QNX, Windows, Windows NT, and OS/2. Aspects of ISQL in operating systems that have similar interfaces are discussed together.

In this chapter, you learn:

- How to use ISQL in the DOS and QNX environments

- How to use ISQL in the Windows and Windows NT environments

- How to use ISQL in the OS/2 environment

- How to create and connect to a database

- How to create a table and manipulate its data

- How to configure the ISQL environment

- How to save SQL commands to a file...and easily re-execute them later

Using ISQL with DOS and QNX

ISQL is an excellent tool to manipulate the various components of a database, and it's a welcome addition to the DOS and QNX environments. To run ISQL for DOS, you need a 386, 486, or Pentium IBM PC, IBM AT, IBM PS/2, or compatible machine; and at least 4M of memory is suggested. Now let's discuss some of the basics of using ISQL in the DOS and QNX environments.

Starting the ISQL Environment

To start the ISQL environment in DOS, you need to change to the directory where ISQL resides. If you used the default directory, it's: c:\wsql40\dos.

To start the ISQL environment in QNX, you need to change to the directory where ISQL resides.

Now you can start the ISQL environment in either environment by typing **ISQL**.

The Command Window

The Command window in the ISQL environment is at the bottom of the screen. This is the place where you type ISQL commands to manipulate the environment, as well as database structures and data. Initially, you can type only four lines of ISQL commands before the window automatically begins scrolling to accept more lines. You can resize the window by using the key combinations described in Table 7.1.

> **Note**
>
> The ISQL environment does not force you to end an SQL command with a semi-colon, as many other environments do. But if you want to enter multiple ISQL commands in the Command window, you need to separate the commands with a semicolon so that ISQL will recognize them as separate statements.

Table 7.1   Resizing the Command Window

Action	Command	Description
Expand window	Ctrl+G	(Grow) Expands the window one line at a time. The maximum size is half of the screen.
Decrease window	Ctrl+S	(Shrink) Decreases the window size one line at a time to a minimum of three lines.
Maximize window	Ctrl+Z	(Zoom) Toggles between the current size and a maximum sized window.

After you connect to a database, you can see a list of all available tables and columns in those tables by pressing the F7 key. A list of all tables appears. Highlight the table you want to see, and then click the **C**olumns button to see a list of columns in that table. If you ever need to paste a table or column name into an ISQL statement, you can do the above, then choose the table or column, and click the **I**nsert button. The name appears back in the Command window where the insertion point was located when you pressed the F7 key. For more information, see the sections, "Creating a Database," and "Connecting to a Database," later in this chapter.

Because you execute your ISQL statements through the Command window, you need to know about another window that's accessible from the Command window (and is a very helpful feature). If you need to execute a particular ISQL statement often, you'll be happy to know that the DOS ISQL environment keeps track of the last 15 ISQL commands you use. You can access them by opening the **C**ommand menu and choosing **R**ecall. Use the cursor keys to select the command line you want to paste back to the Command window, and then press Enter. The command is pasted in the Command window. If you need to modify the command line, go ahead and do so; then Execute the command you just recalled.

You can use the keyboard shortcuts shown in Table 7.2 to access previously executed commands.

Table 7.2 Working in the Command Recall Window	
Action	**Command**
Open command recall window	Ctrl+R
Cycle backward through commands	Ctrl+P
Cycle forward through commands	Ctrl+N
Cancel a command in process	Ctrl+Break

Note

You use Ctrl+P and Ctrl+N to cycle through previously executed commands without pulling up the Command Recall window. They let you cycle through the commands, displaying one command in the Command window at a time.

II

Fundamentals

The Data Window

The Data window is at the top of the screen. It holds the result set of ISQL commands executed from the Command window or command file.

Unless you specify that only a few columns be displayed in your result set, the returned data probably will not fit in the Data window. You can scroll left and right in the window to display values in other columns by opening the **D**ata menu and choosing **L**eft or **R**ight. You can also use the scroll bar (if the mouse is available).

Other Keyboard Shortcuts

You can use the keyboard shortcuts in Table 7.3 to perform particular tasks in the ISQL environment.

Table 7.3 Keyboard Shortcuts	
Key(s)	**Description**
F1	Brings up the Help file.
F5	Moves the data left by one column in the Data window.
Shift+F5	Moves the data left by one character in the Data window.
F6	Moves the data right by one column in the Data window.
Shift+F6	Moves the data right by one character in the Data window.
F7	Displays a list of all the tables in the database. After you highlight the desired table, press Enter to copy the table name to the cursor location in the Command window. If you want to display column names, press the F7 key again. Choose one of the column names and press Enter to copy the name to the cursor position in the Command window.
F9	Executes the commands in the Command window.
F10	Activates the menus.
PgUp	Moves the information up one page.
PgDn	Moves the information down one page.
Ctrl+PgUp	Moves to the top of the data.
Ctrl+PgDn	Moves to the bottom of the data.

Exiting the ISQL Environment

To exit the ISQL environment, open the **F**ile menu and choose E**x**it, or execute the EXIT command in the Command window.

Using ISQL with Windows and Windows NT

The hardware needed to run ISQL in these environments includes an IBM PC, IBM AT, IBM PS/2, or compatible machine running Windows 3.0 or later, and any version of Windows NT. It is recommended that you have at least 8M of memory. The ISQL environment is one that's fairly easy to learn by accessing the menu options and experimenting, but to get a quick jump on the basics of using ISQL in Windows or Windows NT, read this section.

Starting the ISQL Environment

To start the ISQL environment, double-click the ISQL icon that was set up when you installed the ISQL environment. After the ISQL environment starts, you need to connect to a database. For more information on how to do this, see "Connecting to a Database," later in this chapter.

The Command Window

The Command window in the ISQL environment is at the bottom of the screen, as shown in figure 7.1. (Your screen may look different than the one in the figure—I closed the Statistics window.) Initially, you can see only a certain number of lines at a time for coding ISQL commands. When you go beyond the last line, the window automatically begins scrolling to accept more lines. You can easily resize the Command window by using the mouse to drag the edges of the window where you want them to be.

When entering multiple ISQL commands in this window, you need to separate the commands with a semicolon.

After you connect to a database, press the F7 key to see a list of all available tables and the columns in those tables. Highlight the table you want to see, and then click the **C**olumns button to see a list of columns in that table. If you want to paste a table or column name into an ISQL statement, choose the table or column, and click the **I**nsert button.

Because you execute your ISQL statements through the Command window, you need to know about another window that's accessible from the Command window (and is a very helpful feature). If you need to execute a particular ISQL statement often, you'll be happy to know that the DOS ISQL environment keeps track of the last 20 ISQL commands you use. You can access them by opening the **C**ommand menu and choosing **R**ecall. Use the cursor keys to select the command line you want to paste back to the Command window, and then press Enter. The command is pasted in the Command window. If you need to modify the command line, go ahead and do so; then Execute the command you just recalled. If you need to paste a table or column name into an ISQL statement, you can do the above, and then choose the table or column, and click the **I**nsert button. The name appears back in the Command window where the insertion point was located when you pressed the F7 key.

Fig. 7.1
As part of the ISQL environment, the Command window is where ISQL commands are executed against database structures and their data.

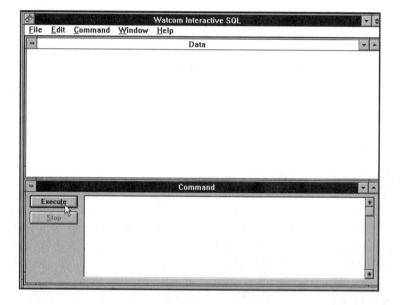

Tip
You can also double-click the highlighted row or click the **R**ecall button to copy the selected ISQL statement back to the Command window.

You can use the keyboard shortcuts shown in Table 7.4 to recall commands. If the ISQL environment is in the middle of performing a command you want to cancel, click the Stop button.

Table 7.4 Working in the Command Recall Window

Action	Command
Open Command Recall window	Ctrl+R
Cycle backward through commands	Ctrl+P
Cycle forward through commands	Ctrl+N

> **Note**
>
> You use Ctrl+P and Ctrl+N to cycle through previously executed commands without pulling up the Command Recall window. They let you cycle through the commands, displaying one command in the Command window at a time.

The Data Window

The Data window is the window at the top of the screen (refer to fig. 7.1). It displays the result set of ISQL commands executed from the Command window or Command file.

Unless you specify that only a few columns be displayed in your result set, the returned data will not fit in the window. You can scroll left or right in the window to display values in other columns. You do this by scrolling the Data window left and right. To scroll up and down, use the mouse on the scroll bar.

Other Keyboard Shortcuts

You can use the keyboard shortcuts in Table 7.5 to perform particular tasks in the ISQL environment.

Table 7.5 Keyboard Shortcuts	
Key(s)	**Description**
F1	Brings up the Help file.
F7	Displays a list of all the tables in the database. After you highlight the desired table, press Enter to copy the table name to the insertion point in the Command window. If you want to display column names, click the **C**olumns button or double-click the table name. Choose one of the column names and press Enter to copy the name back to the insertion point in the Command window.
F9	Executes the commands in the Command window.
PgUp	Moves the information up one page.
PgDn	Moves the information down one page.
Ctrl+PgUp	Moves to the top of the data.
Ctrl+PgDn	Moves to the bottom of the data.

II

Fundamentals

Using ISQL with OS/2

The OS/2 version of ISQL works with OS/2 versions 2.0, 2.1, and 3.0 (Warp). The hardware requirements include an IBM PC, IBM AT, IBM PS/2, or a compatible machine running OS/2. It is recommended that you have at least 8M of memory. Now, assuming that you have the required hardware and have installed the software, let's move on to the discussion on entering and becoming familiar with using ISQL in the OS/2 environment.

Starting the ISQL Environment

To start the environment, double-click the ISQL icon that was set up when you installed the ISQL environment. After the ISQL environment starts, you need to connect to a database.

The Command Window

The Command window in the ISQL environment is at the bottom of the screen. Initially, you can see only a certain number of lines at a time for coding ISQL commands. When you go beyond the last line, the window automatically begins scrolling to accept more lines. You can easily resize the Command window by using the mouse to drag the edges of the window where you want them to be.

When entering multiple ISQL commands in this window, you need to separate the commands with a semicolon.

After you connect to a database, if you want to see a list of all available tables, and columns in those tables, press the F7 key. This brings up a list of all the tables. Highlight the table you want to see, and then click the **C**olumns button to see a list of columns in that table.

If you want to paste a table or column name into an ISQL statement, choose the table or column, and click the **I**nsert button. The ISQL environment keeps track of the last 20 ISQL commands you use. You can access them by opening the **C**ommand menu and choosing **R**ecall. Use the cursor keys to select the command line you want to paste back to the Command window, and then press Enter. The command is pasted in the Command window. If you need to modify the command line, go ahead and do so; otherwise **Ex**ecute the command you just recalled.

You can use the keyboard shortcuts shown in Table 7.6 to recall commands from the Command window. If the ISQL environment is in the middle of performing a command you want to cancel, click **S**top.

Table 7.6 Recalling Commands

Action	Command
Open Command Recall window	Ctrl+R
Cycle backward through commands	Ctrl+P
Cycle forward through commands	Ctrl+N

Note

You use Ctrl+P and Ctrl+N to cycle through previously executed commands without pulling up the Command Recall window. They allow you to cycle through the commands, displaying one command in the Command window at a time.

The Data Window

The Data window is at the top of the screen. It holds the result set of ISQL commands executed from the Command window or Command file.

Unless you specify that only a few columns display in your result set, the returned data probably will not fit in the window. You can scroll left or right in the window to display values in other columns. You do this by scrolling the Data window left and right. To scroll up and down, use the mouse on the scroll bar.

Other Keyboard Shortcuts

You can use the keyboard shortcuts in Table 7.7 to perform particular tasks in the ISQL environment.

Table 7.7 Keyboard Shortcuts

Key(s)	Description
F1	Brings up the Help file.
F7	Displays a list of all the tables in the database. After you highlight the desired table, press Enter to copy the table name to the cursor location in the Command window. If you want to display column names, click the **C**olumns button. Choose one of the column names and press Enter to copy the name back to the cursor position in the Command window.
F9	Executes the commands in the Command window.

(continues)

Tip
You can also
display column
names by double-
clicking the table
name.

Table 7.7 Continued	
Key(s)	**Description**
PgUp	Moves the information up one page.
PgDn	Moves the information down one page.
Ctrl+PgUp	Moves to the top of the data.
Ctrl+PgDn	Moves to the bottom of the data.

Using the ISQL Environment to Manipulate Database Structures and Data

> **Note**
>
> In case you are not running ISQL in the Windows environment, be aware that the figures in the rest of this chapter may look slightly different than your screens because they've been shot in the Windows environment

Now that you've become familiar with starting the ISQL environment and have seen a little of the Command and Data windows, you need to learn about working with databases.

Creating a Database

Before you create any tables, you need to create the database (or databases) where the tables will be stored. You can do this from the Command window in the ISQL environment by using the DBTOOL command (see fig. 7.2).

Fig. 7.2
Using the
DBTOOL com-
mand is one
way to create a
database in the
ISQL environ-
ment.

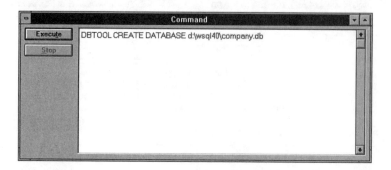

In figure 7.2, I created a database in d:\wsql40 called company.db. After you type the command line, execute it by opening the **C**ommand menu and choosing **E**xecute. You can also click the Execute button or press Alt+T. It takes a few seconds to create the database.

Another way to create a database is to open the **W**indow menu and choose Database **T**ools. The Database Tools dialog box appears. In the Tools section, choose the Create Database option. Enter the database path and name in the Database File text box, and then click the **C**reate button, as seen in figure 7.3.

▶ See "Database Tools," p. 590

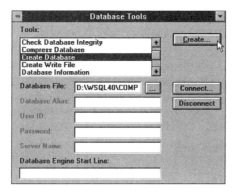

Fig. 7.3
The Database Tools window, where you have easy access to ISQL database tools.

The Create Database dialog box appears (see fig. 7.4). In this dialog box, you can specify database characteristics. After selecting the desired options, click the OK button.

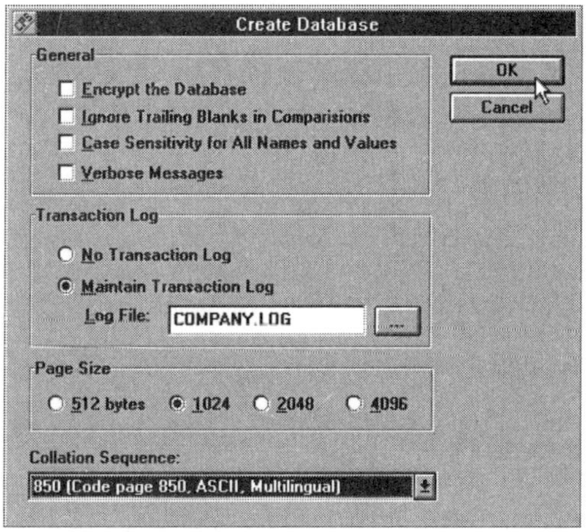

Fig. 7.4
In this dialog box, you can specify the options you want the Company database to have.

II

Fundamentals

After you use the DBTOOL command or the Create Database selection from the Database Tools dialog box to create a database, Watcom populates the database with system tables, as seen in figure 7.5.

Fig. 7.5
This figures shows a partial list of system tables that were automatically created after you created the new database Company.

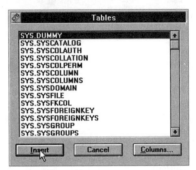

The following is a list of all the actions you can perform using the Database Tools window:

- Backup database files

- Change a transaction log name

- Change a write file's database

- Check database integrity

- Compress a database

- Create a database

- Create a write file

- Erase a database or write file

- Extract collation from a database

- Get database information

- Rebuild a database

- Translate a transaction log to SQL

- Uncompress a database

- Unload a database

- CONNECT to a database (using a button)

- DISCONNECT from a database (using a button)

▶ See "Database Tools," p. 590

Connecting to a Database

You can connect to a database by typing **CONNECT** in the Command window and clicking the Execute button, or by opening the Command menu and choosing Connect. You can also press the F11 key, or use the Database Tools window. The Connect dialog box appears (see fig. 7.6).

▶ See "Using the GRANT and REVOKE SQL Commands," p. 229

Fig. 7.6
When the Connect window appears, you enter the user ID and password to gain access.

Note

If you do not specify the user ID and password using a GRANT statement, the user ID defaults to DBA and the password defaults to SQL. You need to know this when you attempt to CONNECT to the database in the ISQL environment.

Caution

If you don't specify the full database path and name when you issue the CONNECT statement, you connect to the last database to which you were previously connected. When you successfully connect to a database, the database engine starts and is represented by an icon with the same name as the database. Say you connect to a database successfully. Sometime later you connect to a different database. The database engine still remains running, but its name doesn't change, so it looks as if the old database is still running. This is very misleading.

There are a couple of things you can do to avoid typing a path name every time you need to connect to a database in the graphical environments (Windows, Windows NT, and OS/2). First, after you create a database, you can

II

Fundamentals

assign an icon to it. Use your favorite Windows method to do this. On the command line for the icon, type the following information (depending on the environment you use).

In the Windows, Windows NT, and OS/2 environments, type:

DBSTARTW drive:\path\databasename.db

For example, to have the icon execute the command line to start a database named COMPANY.DB located in the D:\WSQL40 subdirectory, type:

DBSTARTW d:\wsql40\company.db

You should also specify the working directory. To find out what the working directory should be, look at the properties of the database icons that were set up when Watcom SQL was installed. To do this, click the icon once and then press Alt+Enter, or open the **F**ile menu and choose **P**roperties. This tells you where Watcom SQL will be searching for the needed components. If you installed the software on drive D in the Windows environment, the default is d:\wsql40\win\.

When you double-click the icon, the database engine runs the database—which is then minimized to an icon at the bottom of your screen. Even though the database engine is now running, there is no connection to the database. The database engine is a separate program that manages and provides access to the database. (The following section describes how to connect to a database.)

▶ See "Database Tools," p. 590

The second thing you can do to avoid typing in a path name to your database every time you need to connect to it, is to connect to it from the Database Tools dialog box. After you find your database in the Database File field, click the **C**onnect button.

▶ See "Understanding Connection Parameters," p. 579

To specify more details about the database connection, such as the location and name of the database, click the **M**ore button. The Connect dialog box expands with more options (see fig. 7.7).

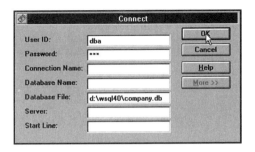

Fig. 7.7
Sometimes the database needs more information to connect—the Connect dialog box expands to allow this.

Troubleshooting

I get an error message when I attempt to connect to my database in ISQL. Why?

There are various reasons why connections to a database may not be successful. Answer the following questions to find other solutions to try.

- Did you use the correct logon ID and password? Try dba for the logon_id and sql for the password.

- Try connecting to another database that you've been able to connect to before. If the connection is successful, compare the database file structures. File name, log or lack thereof, and so on. What's different about the two tables?

- Did you reboot after installing Watcom SQL so that the path changes are in effect?

- Even if you did reboot, verify that the path contains the subdirectory where ISQL is located (if your environment uses a path) because your path may be too long.

- Did you move or rename the database, log file, or directory they were in? If so, find the option in the Database Tools dialog box to change a log file and make sure the log and database file is located where ISQL thinks it is.

- Are you trying to reference a database that was created in another version of Watcom SQL? If so, follow the procedures necessary to upgrade to version 4.0.

- Try shutting down all your applications and rebooting your machine. Try connecting again before opening any unecessary applications.

▶ See "Upgrading Existing Watcom 3.2 Databases to Version 4.0," p. 382

Creating Tables

▶ See "Using SQL Table Commands," p. 241

Now that you know how to create a database in the ISQL environment, you can create tables.

Configuring the ISQL Environment

▶ See "CONFIGURE," p. 575

You can change certain aspects of the ISQL environment in the Options dialog box (see fig. 7.8). Type **CONFIGURE** in the Data window to open the Options dialog box. Click Execute to execute the command. You can also open the Command menu and choose Options to open the Options dialog box.

> **Note**
>
> Any changes you make only apply to the current session unless you choose the Permanent button.

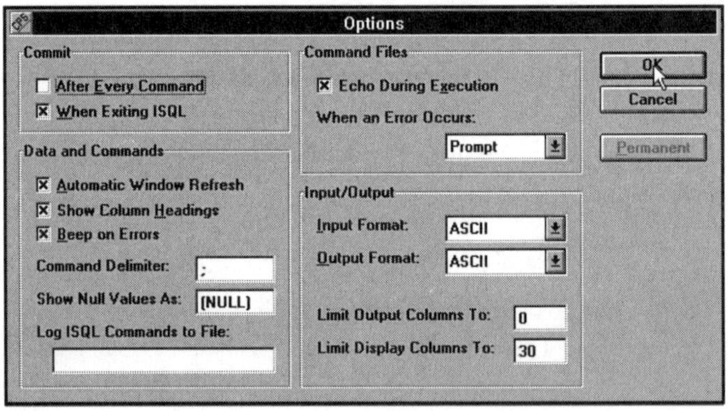

Fig. 7.8
You can specify some of the attributes of the ISQL environment.

Using Command Files with RTSQL and READ

Command files are nothing more than database and data manipulation ISQL commands that are stored in and executed from a file by using the READ command. You can use Command files for such things as creating tables, exporting table data to files, or importing table data from files.

Using the READ Command

You can execute the READ command in the ISQL environment by explicitly coding it, or by embedding it in a Command file. The syntax for the READ command is as follows:

```
READ filename [parameters]
```

The following example is a theoretical file that contains the commands to recreate the Employee table:

```
READ cremp
```

Command files are flexible enough to allow nested code, embedded READ commands, and parameters.

Note

You can use comments in a Command file by prefacing the comments with a percent sign (%) or a double slash (//). Example:

```
// The following command deletes the employee table

DROP TABLE

    employee;
```

The ISQL environment doesn't require the use of a semicolon after a single ISQL statement, but if you are executing multiple statements with one execute command, then you must use a semicolon between each ISQL statement.

Using RTSQL and RTSQLW (Windows)

RTSQL and RTSQLW (Windows) are runtime SQL processor programs that execute Command files containing ISQL statements. You can use this feature to set up an icon in Windows that performs a particular set of Watcom SQL commands. You can use something like this to import data in one format, say dBASE III, to a Watcom SQL table. The valid data formats are ASCII, dBASE II, dBASE III, DIF, Fixed, Foxpro, Lotus, SQL, Text, and Watfile.

◄ See "INPUT," p. 187

From Here...

This chapter covered the basics of using the ISQL utility in a variety of environments. The following chapters discuss SQL commands and how to execute them in the ISQL environment.

- ■ Chapter 5, "Selecting Data," describes how to select data to meet your testing and application needs.

- Chapter 6, "Understanding SQL," goes into detail about other SQL commands you can use, such as INSERT, UPDATE, and DELETE. This is a good chapter if you want to go beyond just selecting data.

- Chapter 9, "Using SQL Table Commands," discusses the ISQL environment commands to CREATE, ALTER, and DROP various database structures, such as dbspaces and tables.

Part III

Administration

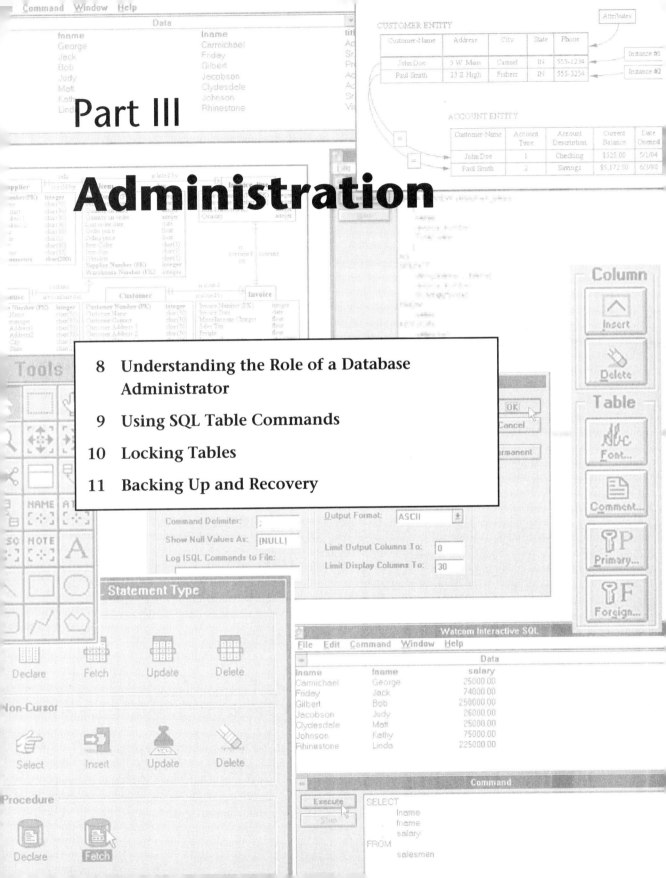

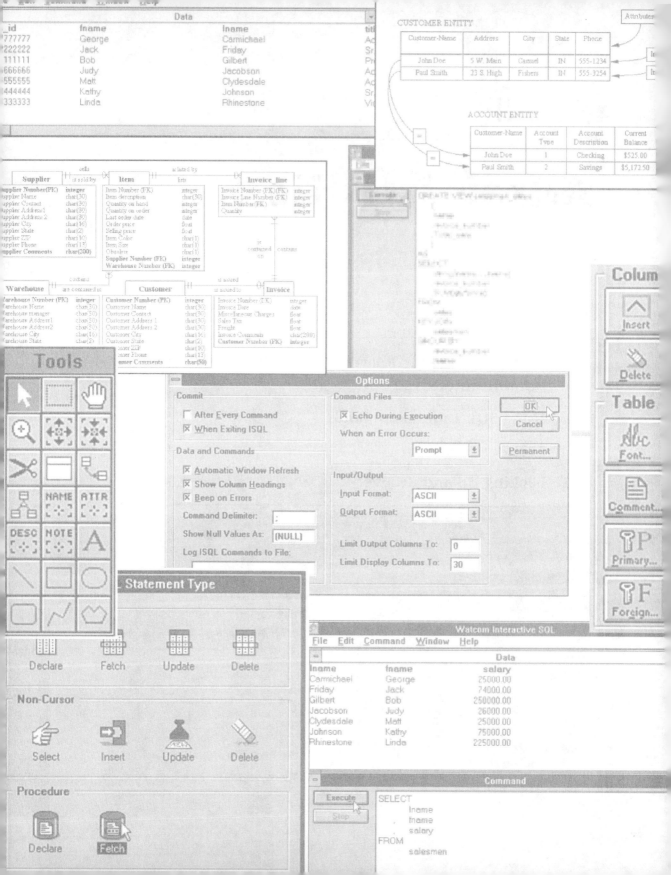

Chapter 8

Understanding the Role of a Database Administrator

by Travis Hubbard

Database administration is one of the most critical jobs in the world. Think about the time it takes to acquire all the raw data used to forecast inventory requirements at a supermarket or the amount of transactions created daily by bond traders on Wall Street. Our world depends on these databases.

Economies are based on data: banks, commodities markets, hospitals—the list is endless. Almost every business you can think of depends on its data to remain operational. Who manages this information; who keeps it secure? As the Database Administrator (DBA) for your organization, it's your responsibility to maintain the security and integrity of the corporate database.

But the fun doesn't stop there. You might also be involved in database design as part of a development team. In this role, you help the developers effectively utilize the database. You help optimize queries, create stored procedures, and create triggers. You specify transaction logs and table spaces, and establish policies for backing up and restoring databases.

In this chapter, you learn about the following:

- Implementing Watcom SQL as a single or multi-user system

- Implementing support for multiple database connections

- Basic networking concepts

- Ways to implement security in your database

- Managing the space used by your database

- Defining how the data in your database is sorted by using standard or custom collating sequences

Implementing Watcom SQL as a Single-User Database

Tip
Installing a single-user version of Watcom SQL on your PC is a safe way to practice your DBA skills.

Watcom SQL, if used as a single-user database, is one of the most robust desktop Database Management Systems (DBMS) available. Most database-administration activities in this type of setup can be less formal than in a multi-user configuration. However, you should still follow some basic practices such as regular backups and database security.

> **Note**
>
> If you're developing an application against a single-user database, and you plan to deploy it in a multi-user environment, take a rigorous approach to database administration.

Implementing Watcom SQL as a Multi-User Database

This section discusses some of the issues of implementing Watcom SQL as a multi-user database. In the current release, Watcom SQL supports all features typically found in the more expensive competing DBMSs. These include:

- Declarative referential integrity

- Stored procedures and triggers

- An optimizing compiler

Watcom SQL is available for DOS, OS/2, NetWare, Windows, Windows NT, and QNX.

> **Note**
>
> All of the features available in the multi-user configuration are also available in single-user systems.

In a multi-user database environment, you must ensure that the users will be accessing valid data. Watcom SQL provides *automatic row-level locking*. This prevents a user from writing over the transaction of another user or reading data that is inconsistent. There are four different isolation levels available in Watcom SQL: RU, RC, RR, and TS. You can set these levels using the lock element of SQLCA. For example, if you want to set the isolation level to TS (the highest level), you set the lock element of SQLCA to:

► See "Under-standing Concurrency," p. 281

```
SQLCA.LOCK="TS";
```

If two users are competing for the same resources, a condition called a *deadlock* may occur. When this happens, Watcom SQL terminates the transaction that caused the condition and returns an error code to the application. Two types of deadlocks can occur:

- Transaction A is waiting for Transaction B to release a lock on a table, and Transaction B is waiting on Transaction A to release its lock on the same table.

◄ See "Under-standing the SQL Select Statement," p. 107

- All active database threads are in use and Transaction A is waiting on a thread.

Another topic that affects performance on multi-user systems is the way you issue SQL queries. WATCOM SQL has a built-in optimizing compiler that "learns" about the way you work. It can only learn so much, though, and could still get bogged down with an improperly designed query. For example, if tables A and B each contained 50 rows, how many rows would be returned by the following query?

Tip

If your users are creating complex SQL queries, you should check them for efficiency.

```
SELECT * FROM A,B;
```

Your user might be suprised to see 2,500 rows returned, when he was only expecting about 15. The problem is that he forgot to include a WHERE clause on this statement. Imagine the result set that would be returned from a join of two huge tables: it could possibly bring your system to its knees.

Watcom SQL as a Client-Server Database

Because Watcom SQL supports multi-user access, it lends itself well to performing in a client-server architecture. Remember that multi-user access alone does not qualify a database to be used in a client-server system. Watcom SQL offers plenty of reasons to select it as your client-server database; it has several features to use in a client-server environment.

Companies are realizing financial benefits by offloading processing and database systems from mainframes onto Local Area Network (LAN) environments.

III

Administration

They're saving a lot based on a number of factors, the most important of which is that companies are no longer bound to a few select vendors for support. They can acquire quality workstations and peripheral devices from a number of sources. Powerful, high-quality development tools and multi-user relational databases are becoming incredibly inexpensive. The days of multi-million dollar service and license agreements, and paying for CPU nano-seconds, are over.

The whole principle of client-server architecture is based on the distribution of processing across workstations and servers. Using this model, you can install high-speed servers that perform a great deal of the processing, and you can install lower-end workstations that are primarily used for the execution of applications. There are also several other benefits associated with the client-server architecture, although not necessarily unique to the environment, which include the following:

- The capability to enforce corporate-wide security mechanisms by controlling who can access your resources

- The capability to decentralize data and applications

- The establishment of a core set of business logic in modules or objects that can be shared by many applications

- The realization of significant time and cost savings in application development and maintenance through the sharing of data and application objects

The corporate data is the most valuable component in the processing system. The front-end (application) is the vehicle used to present data to the user in a meaningful format. A database should be flexible enough to switch front-ends at any time to take advantage of further cost savings and technological advances.

The capability to quickly change front-ends or effectively develop new applications is a primary goal. To meet this goal, the methods to turn the data into information must be stored in the database. This prevents the unnecessary duplication of code and wasting of an application developer's time and effort. To satisfy this requirement, Watcom SQL allows you to do such things as:

- Create triggers to enforce special cases of referential integrity, or automatically update control or accumulator tables

- Create stored procedures to return result sets used for reporting

- Place column-validation rules in the tables

Implementing Multiple Database Support

Watcom SQL offers support for simultaneous connections to multiple database files. Using the DBSTART command, you can specify what database files to load.

When using multiple databases, consider the implications of a committed transaction on all of the connected databases. You use a *two-phase commit* to handle this situation. The two-phase commit allows you to post a `prepare to commit` message to all of your connections. Based on the return value from this message, you can either COMMIT or ROLLBACK the transaction.

Using Shared Data

With the migration towards development on the PC platform, many organizations are developing applications to meet their specific needs. For example, the following departments created applications and databases to perform the following activities:

- Accounting departments record sales figures and the activities of sales personnel

- Personnel departments kept track of current staff and recruiting activities

In this environment, many of the data elements stored by these separate departments were duplicated across separate databases. This made it impossible to generate reports that require the extraction of data from these independent sources.

For example, suppose I want to determine the effectiveness of the training classes my sales personnel attended. I compare sales figures for each employee, both before and after the class. If the data is stored in three separate unconnected systems, I need to do the following:

- Send a request for a Training Report to Personnel to see what employees attended a training class

- Send a request for a Sales Report to Accounting

- Cross-reference the reports and look for trends

All of this activity seems like a waste of time and effort. Why isn't there a facility in place to access all the data at the same time?

It takes time to perform an analysis to determine what data elements are similar across the groups. The time spent on creating a common database

III

Administration

would be recovered in reduced application-development time. I'll also be able to quickly and accurately report on the state of the organization by collecting data from all departments.

So, using the above example, I can create my own report in less time, and the individual departments can still run their specialized applications. Another benefit of shared databases is that the ability to change front ends is in place. Data validation is done at the server level, I have procedures in place to return result sets for reports, and all database activity is recorded in a common audit table.

Understanding Networking Issues

Just as insects and flowering plants developed as a result of each others' existence, so have networks and database servers. Understanding the concepts of networking is a great benefit if you're involved in the design and implementation of multi-user databases. There are volumes of published text that discuss network technology, but a discussion of basic networking issues will get you started.

> **Note**
>
> If you're in a relatively small shop, administering the network might be another one of your responsibilities. Take the time to read the manuals that came with your network operating system: your reward will be an exponential return on the investment of your time.

When discussing networks, refer to the Open Systems Interconnect (OSI) model. The International Standards Organization (ISO) developed OSI in the 1970's. The goal of the OSI model is to define the activities performed by similar equipment built by different vendors. The OSI model is made up of seven layers, and each layer depends on the one directly below it.

Application Layer	Layer 7
Presentation Layer	Layer 6
Session Layer	Layer 5
Transport Layer	Layer 4
Network Layer	Layer 3
Datalink Layer	Layer 2
Physical Layer	Layer 1

This discussion focuses on *Local Area Networks (LANs)*. A LAN is a collection of devices that connect to provide data communication in a small geographical area. The devices typically include workstations, printers, modems, fax machines, and other peripherals.

The primary parts of a network are the servers and the workstations. You can set up many different types of servers on your LAN. These can include print servers, file servers, communication servers, and database servers.

Typically, an installation will have one or more Network Administrators. It is the responsibility of this individual (or team) to set up the network hardware and software, and monitor its performance. They also assign network user IDs and passwords for all of the users' of the network and maintain these accounts.

As a DBA for an organization, you should be aware of the *topography,* or physical layout of the LAN. This will help you to better understand the environment in which your users will be operating. Based on the layout of the network, you can determine the best place to store your data. The physical location of data can be an important factor when trying to evaluate the performance of your users' applications. For example, if the network has a very slow data-transfer rate, it's best to avoid placing data in remote locations.

Implementing the TCP/IP Protocol

Transmission Control Protocol/Internet Protocol (TCP/IP) is the transport layer (layer 4) of the OSI model, and consists of a suite of protocols developed by the Department of Defense. TCP/IP is not something you implement by itself. You implement one of the associated protocols such as Internet Protocol (IP), Domain Name System (DNS), Simple Mail Transfer Protocol (SMTP), or one of the numerous others in the suite.

You may be responsible for setting up the workstation that will be the database server. If you are not familiar with the network in your site, seek assistance from knowledgeable personnel.

Understanding and Implementing Security

Placing all of your data on a network database server gives you the power to analyze data and make decisions in a timely manner. This access is great for legitimate users, but it also places the company's most valuable asset at risk.

Realizing this risk, Watcom SQL has built-in security features you can apply to your database. You have the ability to restrict access to your data through the use of user ID's and passwords, and to only allow certain types of processing to be performed against your tables.

If your application runs on a network, your first line of defense is the security mechanisms built into the network operating system. However, after a user logs onto the network and accesses the database files, it's up to you to make sure they can't compromise your data.

User IDs and Passwords

Your first step to a secure database is the assignment of user ID's and passwords to all of your users. All of these users will not have the same access rights and will not be able to perform the same actions on the data.

To create a user ID and password combination, use the GRANT statement. For example, to create a user ID and password for a user, run the following command in ISQL:

```
GRANT CONNECT TO <userid> IDENTIFIED BY <password>;
```

Note

You may want to set up a method of expiring passwords after a certain amount of time (Watcom doesn't include this feature). This ensures that if a person illicitly uses someone's logon parameters, she'll be locked out sooner or later.

When you create a database, the default user ID is DBA and the default password is SQL. This is the user ID and password combination for the Database Administrator. This combination has full access rights and resource authority for the database. Upon creation of a database, create a new user ID and password combination for you to use as the DBA (see fig. 8.1). This prevents your savvy users (who will probably read this book) from logging on as the DBA by using the defaults.

Note

If you specified case sensitivity during database initialization (by using the -c switch) you must enter the default user ID and password in uppercase.

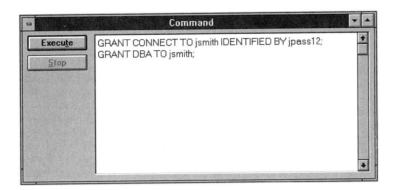

Fig. 8.1
When you create
a new database,
create a new user
ID and password
combination—this
is your DBA login.

> **Caution**
>
> When you create a new database in Watcom SQL, be sure to change the user ID
> and password from DBA and SQL to the user ID and password you'll use as the
> administrator.

Using the GRANT and REVOKE SQL Commands

After you establish a user ID and password for every user of your database,
then what? By creating a user ID and password, you've only taken a small
step in the right direction. Now you have to determine what each new user
can do while connected to your database (after you allow them to connect!).

> **Note**
>
> New users created in your database do not have the permission to perform any
> action against the database until you give it to them.

You use the GRANT command to perform the following (see fig. 8.2):

- Create user groups

- Create user ID's and passwords

- Authorize actions that can be performed on a database, table, or
  column by individuals or groups.

Tip
Create an ISQL
batch file that will
perform GRANT's
on your tables. If
you have to re-
create your tables,
you can run this
file and save lots
of time.

III

Administration

Fig. 8.2
Using the GRANT
command to allow
a user to UPDATE
a table.

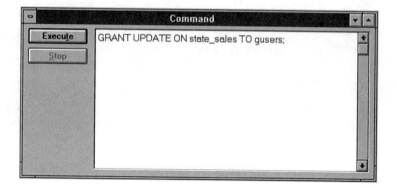

The REVOKE command reverses any actions you performed using GRANT
(see fig. 8.3).

Fig. 8.3
Using the REVOKE
command to
reverse the action
of a GRANT.

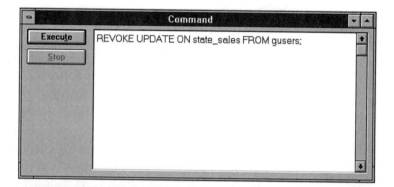

> **Note**
>
> The GRANT and REVOKE keywords are SQL commands used to allow or deny
> individuals or groups the right to access and/or manipulate your data.

DBA and Resource Authority

When you create a database, you have the authority to perform any activity
against that database. This is called *resource authority*. You need resource authority to create:

- Tables and views
- Stored procedures and triggers

Only DBAs should have resource authority, and those users designated as "superusers" of your database. If regular users have resource authority, they may perform actions that would adversely affect the performance or integrity of your database. For example, you do not want users to be able to create triggers on a table without determining the impact on the rest of the database.

> **Caution**
>
> You typically do not want anyone except the DBA to have resource authority.

Encryption

You may store sensitive information in your database, such as personal information about employees, proprietary sales information, or the company's financial status. This is the kind of information your competitors (or unscrupulous users) would love to get their hands on. To prevent unauthorized viewing of your data, you can *encrypt* your database.

You might wonder why you should encrypt your database since you need the proper tools to retrieve the data. The only tool you need is a disk editor. Even though the information is stored in binary format, a disk editor can convert the values to text.

You encrypt your database by using the -e switch in DBINITW.

> **Caution**
>
> One drawback of using the encryption option is that file-compression techniques are not as effective.

Tip
Encryption is a good way to prevent someone from viewing your data by using a disk-editing utility.

User Groups

In your application, there are three types of users that can connect at any one time (see fig. 8.4 and fig. 8.5).

First, there are the administrators, who have the authority to perform almost any action they desire. This is the only group that can delete from the database. Name this group GADMIN.

The regular users are second—they use the database every day. Regular users typically query tables, add records, and update information to the database. Only allow them to delete records from specific tables in the database. Name this group GUSERS.

Tip
Create groups based on the types of users accessing your database.

III

Administration

The third group of users connects to the system daily to view reports. This group of users only issues selects and will not be able to update, insert, or delete any records from the database. Name this group GVIEW.

Fig. 8.4
One use of the GRANT command is to create user groups.

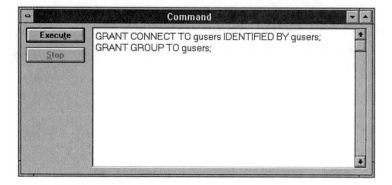

Fig. 8.5
You also use the GRANT command to assign users to a group that you have defined.

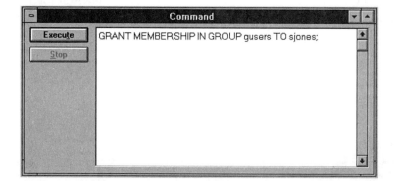

Group Tables

You can find the groups defined in your database in the tables SYSGROUPS and SYSGROUP. There is an entry in these tables for every member of a group. The data in SYSGROUPS will make more sense to you because the data in SYSGROUP is the integer value assigned to the group. SYSGROUPS actually contains the text name of the group that you assigned on creation of the group.

Group Permission

You can grant or revoke permission for entire groups of users. This is where the GRANT and REVOKE commands become valuable time-savers. Instead of performing these actions for every user, assign all of the individuals to one or more groups. The GRANT or REVOKE command applies to the group, and any individual assigned to the group has the permissions defined.

GRANT permissions to the following groups (see fig. 8.6):

- The GADMIN group has the authority to perform almost any action they desire. This is the only group that can delete records from all of the tables in the database.

- The GUSERS group can SELECT, INSERT, and UPDATE the customer table but not DELETE any records.

- The GVIEW group can only issue SELECT statements.

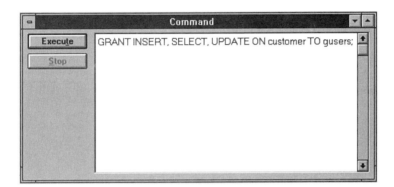

Fig. 8.6
You use the GRANT command to specify permission on a database or table.

Understanding Space Management

Space management is a required part of database design. As you design your database, you need to consider resource allocation. Fortunately, if you do not take space management into consideration at design time, you can add table space as needed.

Tip
Place your transaction log on a separate physical device than your database files. In the event of a media failure, you can roll-forward transactions committed before the failure.

> **Note**
>
> For a personal or workgroup database, this isn't a critical issue. For databases of this type, it's relatively safe to use the default table space created on database initialization.

For multi-user installations, many factors affect how you lay out your table spaces. Common considerations include:

- How many records will be in a table

- How often those tables will be accessed

- The amount of data to be returned from the queries

III

Administration

■ The physical location of your users in relation to the database server

■ Transaction log placement

If your table will contain huge amounts of information, create a separate table space. This will allow your database to span physical devices.

Using Table Spaces

When you initialize a database, it creates one database file. All tables and indexes you define are placed in that initial file. If you established an enterprise data model, multiple applications share data. You should create separate space for these shared tables.

The reason for separate table space is that you may have data that is secure or only applicable to your application. The shared tables can be accessed by anyone who has rights to the device on which it is stored. Secure your stored data so only authorized users can access the tables.

The syntax for creating a table space is:

```
CREATE DBSPACE [creator.]dbspace-name AS filename
```

In this example, there is a shared data directory on the network server. Every application has access to this directory and sees it as N:\ENTDATA. The table contains data on regional sales figures. Create a space named regsales in this directory as:

```
CREATE DBSPACE regsales AS 'N:\ENTDATA\regsales.db';
```

> **Caution**
>
> The more remote your database files are, the more susceptible they are to security violations. Make sure you have appropriate security mechanisms in place before placing database files on shared network directories.

Tables are contained entirely in one database file. This means that a database table and its indexes can't use more space than one file. The IN clause of the CREATE TABLE command specifies into which file a table will go (see fig. 8.7). If you don't specify table space, the table will be created in the base database file by default.

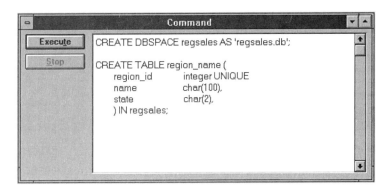

Fig. 8.7
You create a table in a specific database file when you are tracking how your resources are distributed.

Understanding Temporary Tables

As the DBA, you can create temporary tables for use in applications by specifying GLOBAL TEMPORARY in the CREATE TABLE command. Temporary tables are not really temporary; they exist in the database until deleted by the DROP TABLE command. What is temporary is the data in the tables.

The rows in a temporary table are only visible to the connection that created the rows. Multiple connections from the same or different applications can use the same temporary table simultaneously and each connection will only see its own rows.

The rows of a temporary table are deleted when the connection ends or you issue a COMMIT. The exception to this is if you specify to keep the rows on COMMIT by using the PRESERVE ROWS ON COMMIT option during temporary table creation (see fig. 8.8).

Tip
The rows in a temporary table are only visible to the connection that created the rows. This makes temporary tables ideal as work spaces for report data.

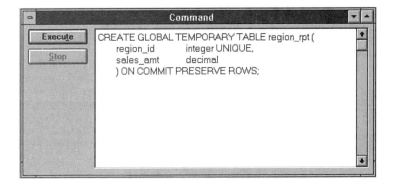

Fig. 8.8
The syntax to create a temporary table and keep the records on COMMIT.

III

Administration

> **Note**
>
> The *temporary* part of a temporary table is the data contained in that table.

Understanding Referential Integrity

Data stored in the tables of a relational database do not contain explicit pointers to related data. These relationships are designated through the use of foreign keys. The foreign key columns in one table must match the primary key columns of another table. A foreign key may be wholly null.

When you create a table in WATCOM, and declare a foreign key on the new table, there are two options you are typically concerned with: to RESTRICT or CASCADE from the foreign key table when the referenced primary key record is deleted. RESTRICT was the only option prior to version 4.0 of WATCOM SQL and is the current default for foreign keys.

For example, an employee table may reference a department table. If an employee record references a particular department, that department must exist. An employee may be assigned to one or more departments, or none. The departments that employees are assigned to may not be deleted until those relationships are eliminated. In this case, you would place a foreign key on the employee table that references the primary key of the department table.

If the department ID changes, then all the records that use that ID can be updated to reflect the new department ID or left alone. In the first case, restrict on update; second case, cascade on update and change all the foreign key values to the updated primary key value.

One way that referential integrity can be enforced in your database is through the use of triggers.

Understanding Stored Procedures

Stored procedures are basically "little programs" that you create and are stored with the database. WATCOM SQL has a built-in procedural language that you use to define stored procedures and triggers. Stored procedures offer many advantages to you as the DBA. Some of these advantages are:

- They exist independently of applications, so you can change front-ends and migrate a significant amount of functionality.

- They are executed on the server, and only a condition code or result set is returned, thereby reducing network traffic.

- When a procedure is called, it is compiled and stored in virtual memory, so subsequent calls will be much faster.

Understanding Triggers

Triggers are a special kind of stored procedure that you do not explicitly call. Because they're stored procedures, you have access to the same functionality that you have in procedures. In Watcom SQL, triggers can be declared to execute on an INSERT, DELETE, or UPDATE to a table. You have the option of specifying whether the trigger fires before or after the action.

You can use triggers to:

- Enforce referential-integrity constraints that cannot be met with primary or foreign key relationships

- Write modified data to a history log for archival or auditing purposes

- Write records to a control table that records database activity such as date and time of modification and the user that performed the action

Loading and Moving Data Using INPUT and OUTPUT

You'll eventually need to move a large amount of data into, or out of, your database. The data may be an export from another database or application.

One possible solution to this requirement is to create an ISQL batch that contains hundreds of INSERT statements. Editing the file would most likely make you go insane. An easier solution is to use the INPUT command from ISQL (see fig. 8.9).

To move data out of your database to be used by another application, you can use the OUTPUT command (see fig. 8.10). It writes the data from a query to the file that you designate. The OUTPUT command allows you to export data in a variety of formats, using the FORMAT option.

III

Administration

Fig. 8.9
The INPUT
command allows
you to import
large amounts of
data into your
tables.

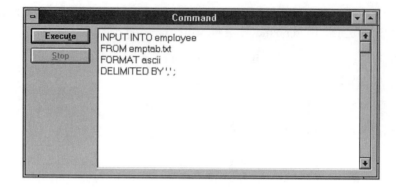

Fig. 8.10
The OUTPUT
command allows
you to export data
that is returned
from a query.

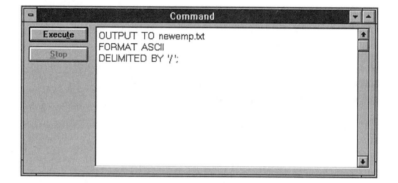

Making Different Collating Sequences

Tip
You can find the
available collating
sequences in the
system table
SYSCOLLATION.

Watcom SQL uses *collating sequences* to determine the sort order of your data. There are many collating sequences included with the database that support many languages. You have the capability to create custom collating sequences if the ones provided do not meet your needs.

> **Note**
>
> To specify a collating sequence when creating the database with DBINIT, use the -z switch.

If the collating sequence specified after the -z switch is not found, it's assumed to be a custom collating sequence file. The file will be parsed and, if no errors are found, will be applied to your database.

Using Standard Collations

When you create a database, you have the option of specifying which collating sequence you want to use as the default. If you do not specify a collation sequence, the standard ASCII is used by default.

Using Customized Collations

If none of the supplied collating sequences is suitable for your requirements, you can create your own. It helps to have a template to work from; you can create one using the DBCOLLW statement.

An easier way to extract the collating sequence from the database is to use the ISQL utility. In ISQL, there is a collection of database tools available that automate frequently performed actions. To get to these tools, follow these steps:

1. Start ISQL.

2. Double-click the database tools icon in the ISQL workspace.

3. Scroll through the Tools list box in the Database Tools dialog box, and select Extract Collation from Database (see fig. 8.11).

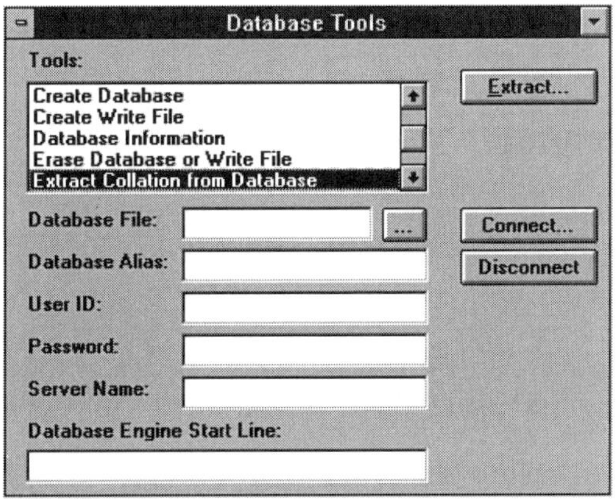

Fig. 8.11
The Database Tools dialog box allows you to perform some DBA activities that have been automated for you.

4. Provide the database connection parameters for the database you want to extract from.

III

Administration

5. Choose **E**xtract. The Extract Collation from Database dialog box appears.

6. Choose the correct Extract Collating Sequence, and enter the name for the Output File (see fig. 8.12). Choose OK when you're finished.

Fig. 8.12

You define your output parameters in the Extract Collation from Database dialog box.

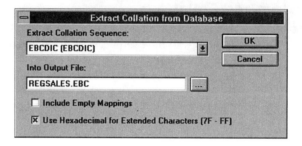

The file created by the export process contains the format for the collating sequence you selected. You can now edit this file and create your own collating sequence. The format for a line is:

```
[sort-position] : character [lowercase uppercase]
```

To apply the custom collating sequence to your database, use the -z switch with DBINIT.

From Here...

Database administration is one of the key roles in a modern organization. Through careful implementation and use of your tools, you can provide up-to-date and accurate information to your user community.

The following chapters provide additional information that will assist you in your database administration tasks:

- Chapter 10, "Locking Tables," provides a detailed discussion of multi-user issues you need to consider.

- Chapter 11, "Backing Up and Recovery," describes how to use log files, schedule backups, and what to do if everything goes wrong.

- Chapter 12, "Implementing Procedures and Triggers," has a complete discussion on the creation and implementation of stored procedures.

- Chapter 17, "Performance Tuning," teaches you many actions to take as an Administrator to get optimum use of your database.

Chapter 9

Using SQL Table Commands

by James W. Rang

Earlier chapters discuss how to retrieve, update, insert, and delete rows from and into tables. But how do you create, alter, or delete the tables? Although you can do all of this from PowerBuilder's graphical database environment, the database painter, that environment is somewhat limited. For example, you can't modify the data type, shorten the length, or change the NULL/NOT NULL attribute for a column after it's created. By knowing SQL table commands and using the ISQL environment that comes with PowerBuilder, you have the ability to store SQL table commands in a *command file* (a text file created in the ISQL environment), and execute them from within the ISQL environment at a later date.

◀ See "Understanding Watcom SQL Data Types," p. 116

With this ability, you can store all the table commands used to create a table in its own command file. Then, if you need to create the table again, all you have to do is execute the command file. If you do this in PowerBuilder's database painter, you have to enter the various specifications for each column, which can be very time-consuming.

Also, before you create a table, you're sure to have the desired names, data types, and lengths of each column already written down somewhere—possibly in a text file. If the information is in a text file, all you need to do is format it into the proper SQL syntax, read it into the ISQL environment, and execute the statements. With this in mind, you can design all future tables in your favorite text editor, using the proper SQL syntax. When the time comes to create the tables, all the work is already done! After knowing all this, you see how important it is to learn and understand SQL table commands.

The following areas are discussed in this chapter:

- How to use the CREATE statement to create dbspaces, tables, views, and indexes

- How to use the ALTER statement to change dbspaces and tables

- How to use the DROP statement to delete tables, views, and more

CREATE Statements

You can use the CREATE statements to specify such things as the name of a table or view being created, as well as the names and attributes of columns. CREATE statements are very important to understand because they specify the details about what you are creating—whether it's a dbspace, table, view, or index. For example, when you create a dbspace, you need to specify its name and also the name of the file that is used to store the dbspace. The file is created when the CREATE DBSPACE command is executed.

CREATE DBSPACE

Unlike dBase, where one or more files make up each table (such as salesmen.dbf, salesmen.ndx, or salesmen.mdx), Watcom SQL *usually* stores all of its tables in a database that is a single file. Because a file cannot span two disk drives (a file partially on drive C and partially on drive D), you would think that your database can't be larger than the available free space on the physical storage device where it's located. But, that's where the CREATE DBSPACE command comes into play. It creates another file—that can be on another storage device—which expands the amount of space you have in which to store the tables in your database. Although a database can span multiple files, a table and all of its indexes cannot. They must all reside in the same file.

> **Note**
>
> Another time to use the CREATE DBSPACE command is when you want to keep tables containing read-only information separate from tables that hold information that the user updates, inserts, or deletes. Say you have tables that contain annually updated information (such as makes and models of vehicles), and your users are at remote locations using your system on laptops. When you update those tables, you have to find a way to update the necessary tables without overwriting what the users updated (such as client information). You can't just overwrite the user's database file with the one that has the updated tables. By using the CREATE DBSPACE command, you create a separate database file that holds the tables that only you, the developer, can update. You can overwrite that file on the user's machine without affecting user-updated data.

◀ See "Creating a Database," p. 78

Syntax-at-a-Glance

The following is the syntax for CREATE DBSPACE:

```
CREATE DBSPACE [creator.]dbspace-name
    AS filename
```

To use the CREATE TABLE statement, you need to create a database file. Following the CREATE TABLE syntax, the various parts of the CREATE TABLE statement are discussed in greater detail.

By default, when you create a table, it is stored in the original database file. To place a table in the new file you created with the CREATE DBSPACE command, you need to specify the new dbspace file name when you create the table. In the example below, I created a dbspace by the name of Sales2 and also used that name for the file. Then, I created a table by the name of employees and stored it in the newly created Sales2 database file.

```
CREATE DBSPACE sales2
    AS 'sales2.db';
CREATE TABLE
        employees
        (empl_id char(9) NOT NULL,
        fname varchar(20) ,
        lname varchar(20) ,
        title varchar(20) ,
        salary numeric(9,2) ,
        wphone char(10) ,
        hphone char(10) ,
        add1 varchar(25) ,
        add2 varchar(25) ,
        city varchar(25) ,
        state char(2) ,
        zip varchar(9) ,
        spouse varchar(20) ,
        notes long varchar
        )
        IN sales2
        ;
```

CREATE TABLE

The data used by your application is stored in tables, but how are the tables created? Use the CREATE TABLE statement to create a table and to define the attributes about the data stored in it. For example, you use this statement to define the following information about the table:

- The name of the table
- Whether the table is permanent or temporary

Administration

III

- Where it's stored and to what database file

- What action to perform when a COMMIT statement is executed (temporary tables only)

- If there are any unique constraints

- If there are any check constraints

- If there is a primary key

- If there are any foreign keys and the action to perform if the column(s) being referenced is updated or deleted

The CREATE TABLE statement is used to define the following information about individual columns in a table:

- The column name

- The type of data stored in the column

- The maximum size of the data

- If the column value can be NULL

- If the column value must be unique

- If the column has a check constraint

- If the column is a primary key

- If the column references a primary key or a column defined as having unique data in another table (in other words, if it's a foreign key), and the action to perform if the column being referenced is updated or deleted

- The column's default value

Syntax-at-a-Glance

The general syntax for using the CREATE TABLE statement is as follows:

```
CREATE [GLOBAL TEMPORARY] TABLE[creator.]table-name
... (
        ¦column-def[column-constraint...]    ¦,...
        ¦,table-constraint                   ¦)
...    [IN [creator.]dbspace-name]
...    [ ¦ON COMMIT DELETE ROWS              ¦    ]
         ¦ON COMMIT PRESERVE ROWS            ¦
```

Now, the above syntax is broken into greater detail, explaining the available options for column definition, column constraints, and so on.

column-def:

```
column-name data-type[NOT NULL][DEFAULT        default-value]
```

column-constraint:

```
¦UNIQUE ¦
¦PRIMARY KEY    ¦
¦REFERENCES table-name[(column-name)]
   [actions]                               ¦
¦CHECK (condition)                         ¦
```

default-value:

```
¦string                                   ¦
¦number                                   ¦
¦AUTOINCREMENT      ¦
¦CURRENT DATE                             ¦
¦CURRENT TIME                             ¦
¦CURRENT TIMESTAMP                        ¦
¦NULL                                     ¦
¦USER                                     ¦
```

table-constraint:

```
¦UNIQUE (column-name,...) ¦
¦PRIMARY KEY (column-name,...)     ¦
¦CHECK (condition)                       ¦
¦foreign-key-constraint   ¦
```

foreign-key-constraint:

```
[NOT NULL] FOREIGN KEY [role-name] [(column-name,...)]
...REFERENCES table-name[(column-name,...)]
...[actions][CHECK ON COMMIT]
```

actions:

```
[ON UPDATE action][ON DELETE action]
```

action:

```
¦CASCADE                                  ¦
¦SET NULL                                 ¦
¦SET DEFAULT                              ¦
¦RESTRICT                                 ¦
```

III

Administration

GLOBAL TEMPORARY

You use this option when you want a table (or more specifically, the data in a table) to be temporary. Contrary to what you would think about the word *temporary*, when you create a temporary table, it remains in the database until you use a DROP statement to delete it. If you use a temporary table, the data in it is automatically deleted when the connection that inserted the data ends. There can be multiple connections to a temporary table from one or multiple applications just as with a base table. Each connection only sees the rows that it inserts into the table. If you omit the GLOBAL TEMPORARY option, the table defaults to a *base* table. A base table is the most often used of the two types of tables and resides in a database—along with its data—until it is explicitly deleted.

◄ See "Understanding Temporary Tables," p. 235

◄ See "Understanding Transactions," p. 168

In the following example, I created a temporary table with a single field called *text*. I can insert rows into this table whenever I'm connected to the database that contains it. When you end the connection or issue a COMMIT for the current connection (unless the ON COMMIT PRESERVE ROWS option is defined for the table), the data in the table is automatically deleted:

```
CREATE GLOBAL TEMPORARY TABLE temp
    (
    text   long varchar
    );
```

ON COMMIT

You can only use the ON COMMIT DELETE ROWS and ON COMMIT PRE-SERVE ROWS options with temporary tables. By default, when you issue a COMMIT, it deletes all of the rows inserted into a temporary table by that transaction. To keep the rows from being deleted on a COMMIT, you must use the ON COMMIT PRESERVE ROWS option.

In the following example, I created a temporary file called Temp. Because I used ON COMMIT PRESERVE ROWS, the data in the table is not deleted when I execute the COMMIT command:

```
CREATE GLOBAL TEMPORARY TABLE temp
    (
    text   long varchar
    )
    ON COMMIT PRESERVE ROWS
    ;
```

IN [creator.]dbspace_name

You use this option to specify the name of the database file in which you want to store a new table. The root database file holds tables by default.

The following example creates a table named Comments and stores it in the dbspace named Sales2:

```
CREATE TABLE Comments
      (
       text    long varchar
      )
       IN sales2
      ;
```

COLUMN-DEFINITION

You use the COLUMN-DEFINITION option of the CREATE TABLE statement to specify the column name, data type, column length, default value (if any), and whether the column can be NULL.

In the following example, I created a table called Temp. It has a column called `salesman_id` that is defined as containing character data and can be a maximum of nine bytes:

```
CREATE TABLE temp
      (
       salesman_id CHAR(9)
      );
```

COLUMN-CONSTRAINT

There are four types of column constraints possible for a column. They are: UNIQUE, PRIMARY KEY, CHECK, and REFERENCES. These constraints are discussed in the following sections.

UNIQUE. You specify the UNIQUE option when you want to make sure the value entered in a column is unique (no other rows have that value in the named column). When this is specified for a column, the column cannot contain a null value.

In the following example, I defined the `salesman_id` as being unique. An error would occur if I attempted to add a second row with the same `salesman_id`:

```
CREATE TABLE temp
      (
       salesman_id CHAR(9) UNIQUE
      );
```

PRIMARY KEY. The primary key is similar to the unique constraint. It is different in that Watcom has built-in facilities to make a search using a primary key go quickly. The developer doesn't need to do a sort on the primary key (it isn't even recommended).

III

Administration

A primary key generally signifies a column (or group of columns) that uniquely identifies each row in a table and is usually the field(s) used to select a particular row. For example, a Social Security number is often used as the primary key for tables that hold information about people (such as students and employees). Because of the vast amount of information available for one person, the Social Security number is the only information that is guaranteed to differentiate them. By default, a primary key must be unique and cannot contain null values. Because a primary key automatically sorts a table, only one primary key per table is allowed.

In the following example, I defined `salesman_id` as the primary key:

```
CREATE TABLE temp
       (
        salesman_id CHAR(9) PRIMARY KEY
       );
```

◀ See "Understanding Referential Integrity," p. 236

REFERENCES primary-table-name [(primary-column-name)]. You use this option to denote that a particular column is a foreign key that directly relates to the primary key or unique constraint in another table. If the primary-column-name is specified, that column must be the primary key or specified as being unique in the other table. If the primary-column-name is not specified, the column reference defaults to the primary key in the other table.

In the following example, the foreign key is `cust_id` and it must contain a value that matches a value in the `cust_id` column of the Customer table:

```
CREATE TABLE SALES
(
.
    ,cust_id CHAR(10) REFERENCES customer (cust_id)
.
.
);
```

> **Note**
>
> A temporary table cannot have a foreign key that references a base table. Likewise, a base table cannot have a foreign key that references a temporary table.

CHECK (condition). You can use the CHECK option to examine the results of a condition. If the condition returns a value of true or unknown, the operation (INSERT, UPDATE, and so on) is allowed to continue. If it is false, the operation is canceled and changes already made are rolled back.

TABLE-CONSTRAINT

Specify this option when you want to make sure the value entered in the specified columns is constrained in a particular way. There are four types of table constraints: Unique, Primary Key, Foreign Key, and Check.

Unique. You use this to specify that one or more columns uniquely identify each row. If you are constraining only one column, the UNIQUE constraint could be specified as part of the column definition. See UNIQUE in the COL-UMN-CONSTRAINT section, earlier in this chapter.

In the following example, I placed a UNIQUE table constraint on the `salesman_id` column:

```
CREATE TABLE temp
      (
       salesman_id CHAR(9)
      ,UNIQUE (salesman_id)
      );
```

Primary Key. The primary key option is the same as the UNIQUE table constraint, except that there can only be one primary key per table (though the primary key can be made up of more than one column).

In this example, I defined the `invoice_number` and `item_number` as a primary key:

```
CREATE TABLE invoices
      (
       invoice_number INTEGER
      ,item_number             INTEGER
      ,PRIMARY KEY (invoice_number, item_number)
      );
```

Foreign Key. You use the foreign key to make sure the values entered in the columns match the values of the primary key in another table, or that the value entered in the column matches a column in another table that has a UNIQUE constraint. Multiple foreign keys are allowed.

In the following example, I defined the `salesman_id` as a foreign key. The value in this column must match the value in the `salesman_id` column of the Salesmen table:

III

Administration

```
CREATE TABLE invoices
    (
     salesman_id CHAR(9)
    ,FOREIGN KEY (salesman_id)
            REFERENCES salesmen(salesman_id)
    );
```

Check. Use the check to make sure that values in a column (or columns) meet specific criteria, such as M or F in a gender column.

DEFAULT-VALUE

If you specify the DEFAULT option, the column sets to the value specified for the default value when you execute an Insert statement and have not specified a value for the column. There are eight possible default value types: string, number, AUTOINCREMENT, CURRENT DATE, CURRENT TIME, CURRENT TIMESTAMP, NULL, and USER. If you do not specify a default value, the NULL value is placed in the column—unless the column is defined as not being able to contain the NULL value, in which case an error would be reported to the user and the insert will not be performed.

String. You use this option to specify a default value that is a string.

In this example, the default value for the mail_list column is the string value Y:

```
CREATE TABLE temp
    (
     mail_list CHAR(1) DEFAULT 'Y'
    )
    ;
```

Number. Use this option to specify a numeric value.

In this example, the family_members column defaults to 1 if you do not specify another value when a row is inserted into the table:

```
CREATE TABLE temp
    (
     family_members INTEGER DEFAULT 1
    )
    ;
```

AUTOINCREMENT. You can use this option to obtain a unique number that can be used as a key, instead of using datetime to generate a unique key. The data type of this column must be one of the following: INTEGER, SMALLINT, FLOAT, or DOUBLE.

You can still specify a particular value for this column without adversely affecting the operation of the defaulted AUTOINCREMENT value. Say that the last default value was 78, and you specified 100 for the value of a row on an INSERT statement. If the next INSERT statement didn't specify a value for this column, the value 101 would be used. If a row is deleted, it will leave a gap in the numbers.

For performance reasons, the best scenarios to use this type of default with are columns defined as a PRIMARY KEY, a column with a UNIQUE constraint, or the first column of an index.

In this example, the column `members` is given a value of one more than the largest value in the table if no other value is specified when an INSERT is performed:

```
CREATE TABLE temp
        (
          members INTEGER DEFAULT AUTOINCREMENT
        )
        ;
```

CURRENT DATE. If you specify CURRENT DATE for the default value, the column defaults to the current year, month, and day in the DATE data type if a value is not also specified.

For this example, when I inserted a row in the table Temp and the `date_created` column value was not specified, the current date was used:

```
CREATE TABLE temp
        (
          date_created DATE DEFAULT CURRENT DATE
        )
        ;
```

CURRENT TIME. If you do not specify a value, and the column default is CURRENT TIME, the column defaults to the current hour, minute, second, and fraction of a second in the TIME data type.

III

Administration

In this example, `time_created` defaults to the current time if a value is not supplied:

```
CREATE TABLE temp
       (
        time_created TIME DEFAULT CURRENT TIME
       )
       ;
```

CURRENT TIMESTAMP. If you specify a column default value of CURRENT TIMESTAMP, the column defaults to a combination of CURRENT DATE and CURRENT TIME. This results in the current year, month, day, hour, minute, second, and fraction of a second.

In this example, the column `date_time_created` is given the current date and time value if no other value is specified when a row is inserted:

```
CREATE TABLE temp
       (
        date_time_created TIMESTAMP DEFAULT CURRENT TIMESTAMP
       )
       ;
```

NULL. If the column default is NULL, the column defaults to the NULL value. This option is automatically selected if the column can be null and the default is not specified for a column.

◀ See "Understanding Nulls," p. 51

For this example, the salesman's middle initial defaults to NULL if you do not specify a value when a row is inserted into the Temp table:

```
CREATE TABLE temp
       (
        salesman_mi CHAR(1) DEFAULT NULL
       )
       ;
```

◀ See "UserIDs and Passwords," p. 228

USER. This option defaults the column to the user's ID. You use this option when you want to keep track of who made changes to a particular record. For example, if a user makes a change, you can insert a row in an audit table that contains the changes just made. One of the columns in the audit table could be `userid_modified`. USER could be specified as the type of default for this field. In this case, you don't have to insert the user's ID into this field because it is done automatically by Watcom.

In the following example, the user's ID is inserted into the `create_id` column if no other value is specified:

```
CREATE TABLE temp
        (
        create_id CHAR(10) DEFAULT USER
        )
        ;
```

Note

If a column's default value is not specified, it sets to the null value.

FOREIGN-KEY-CONSTRAINT

You use this option to make sure the values entered in the columns match the values of the primary key in another table, or the value entered in the column matches a column in another table that has a UNIQUE constraint. There is also a referential integrity action that can be specified whenever an UPDATE or DELETE is being done, by specifying ON UPDATE, ON DELETE, or both. The four possible actions for this type of constraint include: CASCADE, SET NULL, SET DEFAULT, and RESTRICT.

CASCADE. CASCADE updates the foreign key to match the updated primary key when ON UPDATE is specified. When ON DELETE is specified, it deletes the rows where the foreign key matches the primary key that is being deleted.

In the following example, whenever a `salesman_id` in the Salesmen table is changed, any value in the `salesman_id` column of the Temp table that matches the old value is changed to the new value. For example, if a salesman's ID is changed from 123456789 to 123456788 in the Salesmen table, then any row in the Temp table that has a value of 123456789 in the `salesman_id` column is changed to 123456788:

```
CREATE TABLE temp
        (
        salesman_id CHAR(9)
        ,FOREIGN KEY (salesman_id)
        REFERENCES salesmen (salesman_id)
                ON UPDATE CASCADE
        );
```

III

Administration

SET NULL. This option sets the foreign key to NULL whenever a primary key is updated and ON UPDATE is specified, or whenever a primary key is deleted and ON DELETE is specified.

In the following example, whenever a salesman's ID changes in the Salesmen table, any row in the Temp table that has a value that matches the old salesman's ID is set to NULL:

```
CREATE TABLE temp
       (
        salesman_id CHAR(9)
       ,FOREIGN KEY (salesman_id)
        REFERENCES salesmen (salesman_id)
ON UPDATE SET NULL
       );
```

SET DEFAULT. SET DEFAULT sets the foreign key to its DEFAULT value when a primary key is updated and ON UPDATE is specified, or when a primary key is deleted and ON DELETE is specified.

In the following example, a salesman's ID was changed in the Salesmen table from 123456789 to 123456788. Any values in the salesman_id column of the Temp table that are equal to 123456789 are changed to the default value of 000000000:

```
CREATE TABLE temp
       (
        salesman_id CHAR(9) DEFAULT '000000000'
       ,FOREIGN KEY (salesman_id)
        REFERENCES salesmen (salesman_id)
ON UPDATE SET DEFAULT
       );
```

RESTRICT. An error occurs if a foreign key matches the value of a primary key that is being updated or deleted. If you do not specify another option, RESTRICT is the default.

In the following example, a salesman's ID was changed in the Salesmen table from 123456789 to 123456788. An error would result if any values in the salesman_id column of the Temp table were equal to 123456789 and the change would not be allowed:

```
CREATE TABLE temp
        (
         salesman_id CHAR(9)
        ,FOREIGN KEY (salesman_id)
        REFERENCES salesmen (salesman_id)
ON UPDATE RESTRICT
        );
```

CREATE VIEW

You use a *view* to select data that may reside in different tables. A view makes the data available as if the data was from the same table. A view is not actually stored in the database, as base and temporary tables are. It is actually just a SELECT statement that executes each time the view is accessed.

Syntax-at-a-Glance

The following is the syntax for creating a view:

```
CREATE VIEW [creator.]view-name [(column-name, ...)]
   AS select-without-order-by
```

If you often want to find out how much selling your salesmen are doing, and you also want to make the information accessible to all the salesmen without allowing access to confidential information, then you create a view (see fig. 9.1). This view gathers information from two tables, one containing sales information, and the other containing salesmen information. First, I specified the name of the view, `salesmen_sales` and then I specified names for the column headings: `name`, `invoice_number`, and `Total_sale`. Next, I coded the select statement that I needed to get the desired information. I concatenated the first and last names together to make the data more presentable. I also selected `invoice_numbers` and added up all the sales on each invoice to arrive at an invoice total. By specifying a KEY JOIN, I linked all the invoices with the salesman that created the invoice.

In figure 9.2, I accessed the view by using the view name and specifying the columns to be retrieved—just as I would if I were accessing a table. In this example, I also wanted the results to be sorted, and all the items of an invoice summarized to give the total for each invoice.

◄ See "Using Views," p. 166

III

Administration

Fig. 9.1

In this figure, I created a view that obtains information from two tables to display sales information.

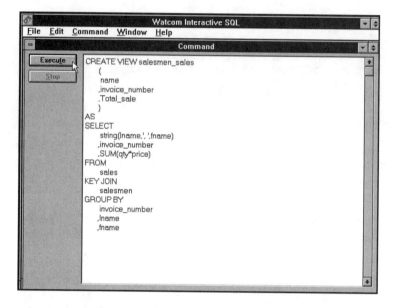

Fig. 9.2

You can access the data in a view just as you would a table—by using a SELECT statement.

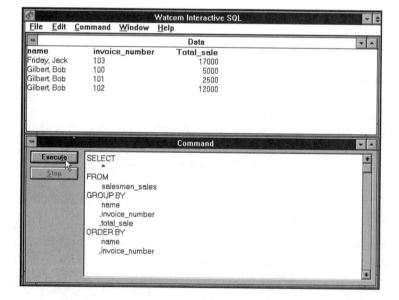

CREATE INDEX

◀ See "Indexing Your Table," p. 50

To improve database performance, create an index on your tables. When you create an index, Watcom creates a sorted index using the column(s) you specify. After you create an index, Watcom automatically uses it to increase performance when you retrieve information from a table or use an ORDER BY clause to sort information retrieved for a table. The index is used even if you define the index in ascending order and later decide to sort some information in descending order. It does matter whether you specified ascending or descending on your index when you have multiple columns in your index, some ascending and some descending. In that instance, a future ORDER BY clause only uses the index if it specified the same ascending/descending sequence. If you specify UNIQUE when creating the index, the column(s) that make up the index must be unique.

Syntax-at-a-Glance

Here is the syntax of the CREATE INDEX statement:

```
CREATE   [UNIQUE] INDEX [creator.]index-name
   ON    [creator.]table-name
   (column-name [ASC¦DESC],...)
```

When you create an index, you must specify the name of the index, the table that will use the index, and the column(s) that make up the index. Specifying the index sort order and whether the index should be unique are optional. If they are not specified, the index defaults to be sorted in ascending order and the index does not have to be unique. Figure 9.3 shows an example of creating an index.

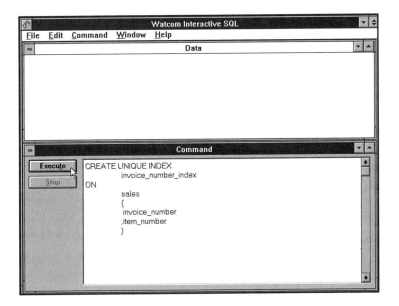

Fig. 9.3
In this example, I created an index on the Sales table. I specified that the invoice number and item number are the index, and that together they must be unique. By default, this index is sorted in ascending order.

III

Administration

ALTER Statements

◀ See "Loading and Moving Data Using INPUT and OUTPUT SQL Commands," p. 237

You can use the ALTER statement to change an existing DBSPACE or TABLE without having to DROP and CREATE it again. If you didn't know SQL, you may have needed to DROP and then re-create a table if you wanted to change columns of a table because PowerBuilder only allows limited alteration of tables from the database painter. If you drop a table, you lose all the data that it contains—unless you save the data to a file first. The ALTER TABLE statement is very useful if you already have data in a table and you need to make modifications to some of its columns. Know that if some modifications are made to a table, such as changing the data type, reducing the size of a column, and so on, some data loss may occur.

ALTER DBSPACE

◀ See "Using Table Spaces," p. 234

A DBSPACE is hard drive space allocated for a database. You can use the ALTER DBSPACE command to change the name or location of the main database file or an extra DBSPACE file that was created. You can also use this command to increase the space allocated to the database file by adding the number of pages specified. A *page* is a unit of measurement for databases—the default is 1024 bytes.

Syntax-at-a-Glance

Here is the syntax for the ALTER DBSPACE statement:

```
ALTER DBSPACE
    [creator.]dbspace-name
    |ADD number                          |
    |RENAME filename                     |
```

You can use the ADD number option to increase the number of pages of the DBSPACE by adding the number of pages specified. If the DBSPACE file name needs to be changed or it has moved physical locations, use the RENAME command to make the change.

In the following example, I told Watcom SQL that the sales2 DBSPACE is now located in C:\sales and that the file name is sales2.db.

Example:

```
ALTER DBSPACE sales2
        RENAME 'C:\sales\sales2.db'
        ;
```

ALTER TABLE

Use the ALTER TABLE command to add, modify, and delete column attributes. It is important to know how to alter column attributes because you have to modify attributes of columns in a table from time to time. The following sections describe each part of the ALTER statement in more detail.

Note

It is important to note the following restrictions and potential problems when altering tables:

- ADDing a column defined as NOT NULL. The table must be empty.

- ADDing a primary key. You must first delete an existing primary key.

- MODIFYing a column's length or data type. Existing values convert to the new type. If a conversion error occurs, the column data type changes, all data changes are undone, and the conversion process ends.

- MODIFYing a column. If UNIQUE currently defines the column as a foreign key, or as a primary key you must first delete these constraints. If you delete a primary key, all of the foreign keys referencing the table also get deleted.

- MODIFYing table and column constraints. This cannot be done; they need to be deleted and then added.

- DELETEing a column. If UNIQUE currently defines the column as a foreign key, as a primary key, or as part of any index, you must first delete these constraints.

- DELETEing a table's UNIQUEness constraint. If there are any foreign keys referencing the uniqueness constraint, you must also delete them.

- DELETEing a table's primary key. If there are any foreign keys referencing the primary key, you must also delete them.

- RENAMEing a table name. You need to change any code references to the old table name.

- RENAMEing a column name. You need to change any code references to the old column name.

Syntax-at-a-Glance

The following is the required syntax for ALTER TABLE:

```
ALTER TABLE [creator.]table-name
   |ADD column-definition [column-constraint..]
 |
 |
   |ADD table-constraint   |
   |MODIFY column-definition                   |
   |MODIFY column-name DEFAULT default-value
 |
   |MODIFY column-name [NOT] NULL          |
   |DELETE column-name   |
   |DELETE CHECK   |
   |DELETE UNIQUE (column-name,...)                |
   |DELETE PRIMARY KEY   |
   |DELETE FOREIGN KEY role-name   |
   |RENAME new-table-name   |
   |RENAME column-name TO new-column-name              |
```

The above syntax is explained even further to give more information about attributes such as: column definition, column constraints, table constraints, and so on.

column-definition:

```
      column-name data-type[NOT NULL][DEFAULT default-value]
```

column-constraint:

```
      |UNIQUE                                 |
      |PRIMARY KEY                            |
      |REFERENCES table-name[(column-name)]
         [actions]                            |
      |CHECK (condition)                      |
```

default-value:

```
      |string                                 |
      |number                                 |
      |AUTOINCREMENT                          |
      |CURRENT DATE                           |
      |CURRENT TIME                           |
      |CURRENT TIMESTAMP                      |
      |NULL                                   |
      |USER                                   |
```

table-constraint:

```
      |UNIQUE (column-name,...)   |
      |PRIMARY KEY (column-name,...)      |
      |CHECK (condition)                          |
      |foreign-key-constraint   |
```

```
foreign-key-constraint:

   [NOT NULL] FOREIGN KEY [role-name] [(column-name,...)]
   ...REFERENCES table-name[(column-name,...)]
   ...[actions][CHECK ON COMMIT]

actions:

   [ON UPDATE action][ON DELETE action]

action:

   |CASCADE                                              |
   |SET NULL                                             |
   |SET DEFAULT                                          |
   |RESTRICT                                             |
```

The following descriptions of column definition, column constraint, table constraint, foreign key constraint, and default value are almost identical to those listed in the CREATE TABLE section, but are listed again for your convenience.

ADD column-definition

You use this part of the ALTER statement to specify a new column name, data type, length, and default value. The column can only be designated as NOT NULL if the table is empty.

In the following example, I added the column salesman_mi to the Temp table and defined it as a one-character column:

```
ALTER TABLE temp
       ADD salesman_mi CHAR(1)
       ;
```

ADD table-constraint

Specify this option when you want to add a constraint so that the value entered in the specified column(s) is constrained in a particular way. The four types of table constraints are: UNIQUE, PRIMARY KEY, FOREIGN KEY, and CHECK.

UNIQUE. If you want to specify that one or more columns uniquely identify each row, use the UNIQUE option. If you are constraining only one column, and that column doesn't already exist, you can specify the UNIQUE constraint as part of the column definition. See UNIQUE in the COLUMN-CONSTRAINT section, later in this chapter. You must constrain the column to NOT NULL before using this command.

III

Administration

In this example, I specified that values in the salesman_id column must be unique:

```
ALTER TABLE temp
        ADD UNIQUE (salesman_id)
        ;
```

PRIMARY KEY. The PRIMARY KEY option specifies that a unique column cannot contain a null value. Though a primary key can be made up of more than one column, you can only have one primary key per table. You generally use a primary key to signify a column (or group of columns) that uniquely identifies each row in the table and is usually the field(s) used to select a particular row. For example, a Social Security number is often used as the primary key for tables that hold information about people (such as students and employees). Because of all the information available for people, the Social Security number is the only information that is guaranteed to differentiate between them.

In the following example, the Temp table did not have a primary key. I added one and specified that the salesman_id column is the primary key:

```
ALTER TABLE temp
        ADD PRIMARY KEY (salesman_id)
        ;
```

Foreign Key Constraint. The foreign key constraint option is used to make sure the values entered in the columns match the values of the primary key in another table, or that the value entered in the column matches a column in another table that has a UNIQUE constraint.

In this example, I specified that salesman_id is a foreign key. This signifies that it's value must match a value in the salesman_id column of the Salesmen table:

```
ALTER TABLE invoice
        ADD FOREIGN KEY (salesman_id)
                REFERENCES salesmen (salesman_id)
        ;
```

CHECK. Use the check option to make sure the values in a column (or columns) meet specific criteria, such as M or F in a gender column.

MODIFY column-definition

You use this statement to change the data type and/or length of the specified column. You can use NOT NULL as part of the statement. If a data type change is specified, and any of the data cannot be successfully changed to the new type, an error occurs and the change does not take affect. If you are attempting to modify a column that is part of a primary or foreign key or is defined as being unique, the keys need to be deleted before the column can be modified. If a primary key is deleted, all foreign keys that reference the table are also deleted.

In this example, I changed the size of the salesman_id column from 9 to 10:

```
ALTER TABLE temp
      MODIFY salesman_id CHAR(10)
      ;
```

MODIFY column-name DEFAULT default-value

Use the MODIFY DEFAULT statement to change the default value of a column. If you want to remove a default value altogether, specify that the column should default to NULL.

In this example, I set the default value for the salesman_mi column to one space:

```
ALTER TABLE temp
      MODIFY salesman_mi DEFAULT ' '
      ;
```

MODIFY column-name [NOT] NULL

Use this statement to switch between allowing and not allowing the NULL value in a column.

In this example, I specified that the salesman_mi column can be NULL:

```
ALTER TABLE temp
      MODIFY salesman_mi      NULL
      ;
```

DELETE column-name

This delete option deletes the named column from the table. If the column is part of a primary key, foreign key, index, or unique constraint, it must be deleted before the column. Be aware that you will not be warned if the column is referenced in a CHECK statement.

III

Administration

In this example, we are deleting the salesman_mi column:

```
ALTER TABLE temp
        DELETE salesman_mi
        ;
```

DELETE CHECK

This part of the ALTER statement deletes all table and column constraints on the table.

This example shows all the CHECK constraints for the Temp table:

```
ALTER TABLE temp
        DELETE CHECK
        ;
```

DELETE UNIQUE (column-name, ...)

This option deletes a UNIQUE constraint that is on a table. If referenced by a foreign key, the foreign key is deleted.

In this example, I removed the unique constraint from the salesman_id column of the Temp table:

```
ALTER TABLE temp
        DELETE UNIQUE (salesman_id)
        ;
```

DELETE PRIMARY KEY

This option deletes the primary key from a table. Any foreign keys referencing this column will also be deleted.

In this example, I removed the primary key from the Temp table:

```
ALTER TABLE temp
        DELETE PRIMARY KEY
        ;
```

DELETE FOREIGN KEY role-name

Use this option to delete the foreign key for a table using the given *role name*, which is the name of the foreign key. This name is used in case there is more than one foreign key to the same table. If the role name is not specified, it defaults to the name of the table to which the foreign key refers.

In the following example, I removed the foreign key designation from the
`salesman_id` column of the Temp table:

```
ALTER TABLE temp
        DELETE FOREIGN KEY salesman_id
        ;
```

RENAME new-table-name
Use this statement to rename a table. If the old table name is referenced anywhere, you need to change that code so it uses the new name in order to
access the table.

In the following example, I renamed the `Temp` table to `employees`:

```
ALTER TABLE temp
        RENAME employees
        ;
```

RENAME column-name TO new-column-name
You use this statement to rename a column. If the old column name is referenced anywhere, you need to change that code so it uses the newly named
column.

Here I renamed the `salesman_mi` column to `mi`:

```
ALTER TABLE employees
        RENAME salesman_mi TO mi
        ;
```

COLUMN-CONSTRAINT
The following optional information is used to specify column-constraint
information about the column from among the following: UNIQUE, PRI-
MARY KEY, REFERENCES, and CHECK.

UNIQUE. You can specify the UNIQUE option when you add a new column
and you want to make sure the value entered in the column is unique. The
table must be empty if you want to use this command. When you specify this
for a column, the column cannot contain a null value.

> **Note**
>
> If you want to add the UNIQUE constraint to a column that currently exists, or if the
> table already has data, you must use the table-constraint version of this command
> discussed earlier in this chapter.

III

Administration

In this example, I created a student_id column and specified that its value must be unique.:

```
ALTER TABLE temp
        ADD student_id CHAR(9) UNIQUE
    ;
```

PRIMARY KEY. The PRIMARY KEY option specifies that a column is a unique column that cannot contain a null value. The column(s) that are to be part of the primary key cannot already exist. If they do exist, use the table-constraint version of this command, discussed earlier in the chapter. The table must be empty if you want to use this command. Though a primary key can be made up of more than one column, you can only have one primary key per table.

In this example, I created the primary key on the student_id column:

```
ALTER TABLE temp
        ADD student_id CHAR(9) PRIMARY KEY
    ;
```

REFERENCES primary-table-name [(primary-column-name)]. This option denotes that a particular column is a foreign key that directly relates to the primary key or unique constraint in another table. If you specify the primary-column-name, that column must be the primary key or be specified as unique in the other table. If you do not specify the primary-column-name, this column reference defaults to the primary key in the other table. You can only use this command if the foreign key column doesn't already exist. If it does, use the foreign-key-constraint in the table-constraint section discussed earlier.

Here, I defined salesman_id as a foreign key. Any value placed in this column must have a matching value in the Salesmen table:

```
ALTER TABLE invoices
        ADD salesman_id CHAR(9)
                REFERENCES salesmen (salesman_id)
        ;
```

Note

A temporary table cannot have a foreign key that references a base (permanent) table, and a base table cannot have a foreign key that references a temporary table.

CHECK (condition). The CHECK option verifies the results of a condition. If the condition returns a value of true or unknown, the operation (INSERT, UPDATE, and so on) is allowed to continue. If it is false, the operation is undone.

DEFAULT-VALUE

If this option is specified, it sets the column to the default value on an IN-SERT if you do not give information for the column. There are eight possible default value types: string, number, AUTOINCREMENT, CURRENT DATE, CURRENT TIME, CURRENT TIMESTAMP, NULL, and USER.

String. You use the string option to specify a string value. In this example, the default value for the mail_list column is the string value Y:

```
ALTER TABLE temp
      ADD mail_list CHAR(1) DEFAULT 'Y'
      ;
```

Number. Use this option to specify a numeric value for the default value. In this example, the family_members column defaults to 1 if no other value is specified when a row is inserted into the table:

```
ALTER TABLE temp
      ADD family_members INTEGER DEFAULT 1
      ;
```

AUTOINCREMENT. Use AUTOINCREMENT to obtain a unique number to use as a key, instead of using datetime to generate a unique key. The data type of this column must be one of the following: INTEGER, SMALLINT, FLOAT, or DOUBLE.

You can still specify a particular value for this column and not adversely affect the operation of the defaulted AUTOINCREMENT value. Say the last default value was 78, and you specified 100 for the value of a row on an IN-SERT statement. If the next INSERT statement didn't specify a value for this column, the value 101 would be used.

For performance reasons, the best scenarios in which to use this default are with columns defined as a PRIMARY KEY, a column with a UNIQUE constraint, or the first column of an index. If a row is deleted, it leaves a gap in the numbers.

In this example, the column members is given a value of one more than the largest value in the table if no other value is specified when an INSERT is performed:

```
ALTER TABLE temp
        ADD members INTEGER DEFAULT AUTOINCREMENT
        ;
```

CURRENT DATE. When you use this option, the column defaults to the current year, month, and day in the DATE data type.

For this example, whenever a row is inserted into the table Temp and the date_created column value is not specified, the current date is used:

```
ALTER TABLE temp
        ADD date_created DATE DEFAULT CURRENT DATE
        ;
```

CURRENT TIME. Use this option to default the column to the current hour, minute, second, and fraction of a second in the TIME data type.

In this example, time_created defaults to the current time if a value is not supplied:

```
ALTER TABLE temp
        ADD time_created TIME DEFAULT CURRENT TIME
        ;
```

CURRENT TIMESTAMP. This option defaults the column to a combination of CURRENT DATE and CURRENT TIME to return the current year, month, day, hour, minute, second, and fraction of a second.

In this example, the column datetime_created is given the current date and time value if no other value is specified when a row is inserted:

```
ALTER TABLE temp
        ADD datetime_created TIMESTAMP DEFAULT CURRENT TIMESTAMP
        ;
```

NULL. If you select this option, the column defaults to NULL. If you do not select another default type, this one is used.

For this example, the salesman's middle initial defaults to NULL if a value is not specified when a row is inserted in the Temp table:

```
ALTER TABLE temp
        ADD mi CHAR(1) DEFAULT NULL
        ;
```

USER. This option defaults the column to the user's ID. Use this option when you want to keep track of who made changes to a particular record. For example, if a user makes a change, you may want to insert a row into an audit table which contains the changes just made. One of the columns in the audit table could be userid_modified. USER could be specified as the type of default for this field. In that case, you don't have to insert the user's id in this field because it is done automatically by Watcom SQL.

Note

If you do not specify a column default value, the column sets to NULL.

In the following example, the user's ID is inserted in the `create_id` column if no other value is specified:

```
ALTER TABLE temp
      ADD create_id CHAR(10) DEFAULT USER
      ;
```

FOREIGN-KEY-CONSTRAINT

Use this constraint to make sure the values entered in the columns match the values of the primary key in another table, or the value entered in the column matches a column in another table that has a UNIQUE constraint. There is also a referential-integrity action that can be specified whenever an UPDATE or DELETE is being done by specifying: ON UPDATE, ON DELETE, or both. The four possible actions include the following: CASCADE, SET NULL, SET DEFAULT, and RESTRICT.

CASCADE. CASCADE updates the foreign key to match the updated primary key when you specify ON UPDATE. When you specify ON DELETE, it deletes the rows where the foreign key matches the primary key that is being deleted.

In the following example, whenever a `salesman_id` in the Salesmen table is changed, any value in the `salesman_id` column of the Temp table that matches the old value changes to the new value. For example, if a salesman's ID was changed from 123456789 to 123456788 in the Salesmen table, then any row in the Temp table that has a value of 123456789 in the `salesman_id` column changes to 123456788:

◄ See "Understanding Referential Integrity," p. 236

III

Administration

```
ALTER TABLE temp    ADD FOREIGN KEY salesman_id
       REFERENCES salesmen (salesman_id)
          ON UPDATE CASCADE
    ;
```

SET NULL. This option sets the foreign key to NULL whenever a primary key is updated and ON UPDATE is specified, or whenever a primary key is deleted and ON DELETE is specified.

In the following example, whenever a salesman's ID changes in the Salesmen table, any row in the Temp table that has a value that matches the old salesman's ID sets to NULL:

```
ALTER TABLE temp
   ADD FOREIGN KEY salesman_id
      REFERENCES salesmen (salesman_id)
         ON UPDATE SET NULL
    ;
```

SET DEFAULT. SET DEFAULT sets the foreign key to its DEFAULT value when a primary key is updated and ON UPDATE is specified, or when a primary key is deleted and ON DELETE is specified.

In the following example, I changed a salesman's ID in the Salesmen table from 123456789 to 123456788. Any values in the salesman_id column of the Temp table that are equal to 123456789 change to the default value specified for the salesman_id column. If a default value is not specified, the NULL value inserts into the column:

```
ALTER TABLE temp
   ADD FOREIGN KEY salesman_id
      REFERENCES salesmen (salesman_id)
         ON UPDATE SET DEFAULT
    ;
```

RESTRICT. With this option, an error occurs if a foreign key matches the value of a primary key that is being updated or deleted. If you do not specify another option, RESTRICT is the default.

In the following example, I changed a salesman's ID in the Salesmen table from 123456789 to 123456788. An error results if any values in the salesman_id column of the Temp table were equal to 123456789 and the change was not allowed:

```
ALTER TABLE temp
   ADD FOREIGN KEY salesman_id
      REFERENCES salesmen (salesman_id)
         ON UPDATE RESTRICT
;
```

DROP Statements

You use the DROP statement to delete database entities such as dbspaces, tables, views, and so on. If data loss occurs from dropping an entity, it is noted in the following section.

DROP DBSPACE

Use the DROP DBSPACE command to delete a physical file that contains tables, indexes, and so on. You may want to do this if you created a new dbspace to hold some of your tables and then later decided to put all the tables in the original dbspace.

Syntax-at-a-Glance

The following is the syntax for the DROP DBSPACE statement:

```
DROP DBSPACE
   [creator.]dbspace-name
```

In the following example, I deleted the dbspace `Sales`:

```
DROP DBSPACE
   sales;
```

Before you issue the DROP statement for a dbspace, all of the tables with the dbspace must be dropped. See the following section for more information about dropping tables.

DROP TABLE

You use this command to delete a table. When you use the DROP TABLE statement, it deletes all data and it automatically drops all indexes and keys associated with the table.

III

Administration

> **Syntax-at-a-Glance**
>
> Here is the syntax for the DROP TABLE statement:
>
> ```
> DROP TABLE
>     [creator.]table-name
> ```

In the following example, I removed the Customers table along with any data or indexes that were part of the table:

```
DROP TABLE
    customers;
```

DROP VIEW

You cannot change a view with the ALTER statement. If you need to change a view, you must first use the DROP VIEW statement to delete it. Then use the CREATE VIEW statement to create the view the way you need it to be.

> **Syntax-at-a-Glance**
>
> ```
> DROP VIEW
>     [creator.]view-name
> ```

In the following example, I deleted the Salesmen_sales view.

```
DROP VIEW
    salesmen_sales;
```

DROP INDEX

Tip

If an index is associated with a table that you are going to delete, you can just DROP the table. This automatically deletes the index.

You use the DROP INDEX command to remove an index from a table. You cannot change an index with the ALTER command. If the index needs to be changed, first use the DROP INDEX command to remove the index. Then use the CREATE INDEX command to create the new index.

> **Syntax-at-a-Glance**
>
> The following is the syntax for dropping an index:
>
> ```
> DROP INDEX
>     [creator.]index-name
> ```

In the following example, I deleted the Invoice_number_index:

```
DROP INDEX
    invoice_number_index;
```

From Here...

This chapter described how to use SQL table commands to CREATE, ALTER, and DROP various database structures. To obtain more information concerning database creation and manipulation, refer to the following chapters:

■ Chapter 3, "Understanding Normalization," describes why and how you should normalize your data so you can design a more efficient database—before you actually create tables for your application.

■ Chapter 4, "Designing a Database Using PowerBuilder," shows you how to use the PowerBuilder environment to develop a database.

■ Chapter 7, "Using the ISQL Environment," tells you how to use the excellent ISQL environment that comes with Watcom SQL to do immediate database structure and data manipulation.

■ Chapter 13, "Implementing Watcom SQL with PowerBuilder," discusses integrating Watcom SQL with the PowerBuilder environment.

III

Administration

Chapter 10

Locking Tables

by Lance E. Tillman

The purpose of this chapter is to inform you about ways to keep your data correct and consistent in a multi-user environment. Keeping your data correct and consistent is known as *data integrity*. Data integrity is the accuracy, completeness, and internal consistency of the information stored in a database.

In a multi-user environment, it might seem difficult to keep data integrity when more than one transaction attempts to use the same data at the same time. This process of executing more than one transaction at a time on a computer system is referred to as *multitasking* or *concurrent processing*. Concurrency is the capability that allows more than one transaction to run and access data at the same time without corrupting the data files.

This chapter will teach you what locks are and how to use them. You will also learn how to plan around the inconsistencies of multi-user processing and how to avoid their pitfalls.

In this chapter, you learn:

- What locks are and when to use them
- How to apply the locks in a multi-user environment
- How to avoid blocking in a multi-user environment
- How to apply the locks to processing on a laptop

One of the main purposes of your database is to be able to use the data in an efficient manner. This includes being able to retrieve, update, insert, and delete the data. When you use this data, you want it to be valid according to the rules that have been set. This would be using a central database. This way, you don't have multiple copies of the data that are being changed. The only reason there would be a need to have copies of the database would be if you are not connected to the central database.

With multi-user database systems, transactions can overlap. When transactions overlap, and common data is involved in the database, the outcome is uncertain. If you do not take care of this properly, your data can become corrupted. When these transactions overlap, they are said to be after the same data *concurrently*, or at the same time.

Maintaining Consistency and Integrity through Isolation Levels

With the multi-user database or database system, the relational model needs to be concerned with data integrity. If a relational database has data integrity, then all of the data in the database is valid, according to a set of rules.

This set of rules can be built into the relational database model. They can be broad rules, dealing with everyday processing, or they can be more narrow rules, such as dealing with every individual detail within everyday processing. Every company's database has its own set of business guidelines that are just as important as the standard set of data-integrity rules. For example, a security administrator might want to disallow changes to a table except during normal business hours.

◀ See "Understanding Keys," p. 48

When dealing with tables in a database, keeping the data valid is a major concern. Carefully consider how to set up your tables. One of the standard data-integrity rules of the relational model deals with this concern. The rule is called *entity integrity*. This implies that you can uniquely identify each row in a table from all others.

Trying to keep the integrity of the data when there are many users after the same data can be a problem. When there is overlap in the transactions, the system needs to decide who gets the data first, and what to do with others who try to retrieve the data later. And this has to be done in an efficient and valid manner.

Without some sort of locking system, inconsistencies can occur, which can result in loss of data integrity. The following are three examples of inconsistencies that can occur during the execution of concurrent transactions without some sort of lock:

■ **Dirty read.** This can occur when the transaction A modifies a row. Transaction B then reads that row before transaction A performs a COMMIT. If transaction A then performs a ROLLBACK, transaction B will have read a row that was never committed.

◄ See "COMMIT Statement," p. 170

◄ See "ROLL-BACK Statement," p. 171

■ **Non-repeatable read.** This can occur when the transaction A reads a row. Transaction B then modifies or deletes the row and performs a COMMIT. If transaction A then attempts to read the same row again, the row will have changed or been deleted.

■ **Phantom row.** This can occur when the transaction A reads a set of rows that satisfy some condition. Transaction B then executes an INSERT or an UPDATE (that generates one or more rows that satisfy the condition used by transaction A), and then performs a COMMIT. Transaction A then repeats the initial read and obtains a different set of rows.

Just as a lock on an airport locker will prevent two people from using the same locker at the same time, locks on a table allow only one user at a time to access the table. Alternately, locks can also allow more than one user at a time to access the table. This is where the isolation levels can be used.

The *isolation level* defines the degree to which the operations in one transaction are visible to the operations in a concurrent transaction. Watcom SQL has four isolation levels that prevent all or some inconsistent behavior.

All of the isolation levels guarantee that each transaction will execute completely or not at all. They also guarantee that no updates will be lost. The isolation levels are different with respect to each of the inconsistencies that previously listed.

In table 10.1, the different isolation levels are shown across the top of the table—they correspond to the inconsistencies that can occur. The isolation levels are from 0 to 3; the higher the number, the more inconsistencies are prevented from occurring. In the table, an - means that the behavior is prevented, and a x means the behavior can occur.

Table 10.1 Isolation Levels

Inconsistencies	0	1	2	3
Dirty reads	X	-	-	-
Non-repeatable reads	X	X	-	-
Phantom rows	X	X	X	-

III

Administration

The default isolation level is set to 0. You can change the SET command in the database options. Because the isolation level is a database option, it can be different for each user. For example:

```
SET
ISOLATION_LEVEL 3
```

▶ See "OPEN Command," p. 423

Also, by using Embedded SQL, you can control the isolation level on a per-cursor basis. Because cursors deal with retrieving more than one row from a table at a time, it needs more attentiveness to data integrity. Any row that a cursor is currently positioned in will not be modified until the cursor leaves the row. This is called *cursor stability*. Watcom SQL automatically provides cursor stability at isolation levels 1, 2, and 3. The cursor level for the cursor is set in the OPEN statement. For example:

```
OPEN cursor-name
    ...
ISOLATION_LEVEL 3;
```

When choosing what isolation level to use, take into account the volume of the processing and the time it takes each transaction to complete its task. Transactions that involve browsing or performing data entry should use isolation level 0 or 1. This type of transaction frequently reads a large number of rows and lasts several minutes.

Applications that involve a high volume of small transactions can use isolation level 3 without sacrificing concurrency. Concurrency that is the execution of more than one program at a time will be discussed later in this chapter in the "Understanding Concurrency" section. It is still a good idea to get a grasp of concurrency while discussing isolation levels and locks.

The isolation level can be changed by a transaction within a transaction. This can be accomplished with the ISOLATION_LEVEL option. When the ISOLATION_LEVEL option is changed in the middle of a transaction, the new setting affects cursors opened after the change and statements executed after the changes.

Troubleshooting

I am having difficulty deciding which ISOLATION_LEVEL to use in different situations.

The choice of an ISOLATION_LEVEL depends on the nature of the transaction. There will be a trade-off in all of your decisions. The higher the ISOLATION_LEVEL number, the more secure your database will be. On the other hand, the transaction will run slower than an ISOLATION_LEVEL that is lower. If you have a single-user environment, an ISOLATION_LEVEL of zero would suit your purposes.

The ISOLATION_LEVEL clause allows the cursor to be opened at an isolation level that is different from the current setting of the ISOLATION_LEVEL option. All operations on the cursor will be performed at the specified isolation level, regardless of the option setting. If the clause is not specified during the OPEN statement, the cursor's isolation level for the entire time the cursor is open is the value of the ISOLATION_LEVEL option when the cursor is first opened.

Understanding Locks

Consider what can happen if you and your spouse want to withdraw the remaining balance from your joint checking account at the same time from different ATMs. If the database server permits you both to update the checking balance at exactly the same time, two things can happen: either the bank loses one of the updates or the account has a negative final checking balance. The latter means that you receive more money than you have each time you pull off this trick. This might be fine for you and your spouse, but the bank would not be very happy about the situation.

This scenario is referred to as *destructive interference*. This occurs when two operations contending for the same data interfere with each other to produce inaccurate results or sacrifice data integrity. The use of locks prevent destructive interferences in a multi-user database system.

Locking tables is a method that Watcom SQL uses to prevent concurrent transactions from interfering with each other. One of the most important and possibly the most apparent job of a database server is to solve the problem of managing concurrent access to the same set of data.

The responsibility of the Database Administrators is to determine what kind of locks need to be applied to the transactions. They need to determine, among other things, what the transaction will be performing and what tables will be accessed. The inconsistencies that were described in the previous section will need to be taken into consideration.

Watcom SQL uses automatic row level locking to prevent concurrent transactions from interfering with each other. What the *automatic row level lock* means is that Watcom SQL acquires a lock on the data to prevent the possibility of destructive interference. All locks for a transaction are held until the transaction is completed. The transaction is completed when a COMMIT or a ROLLBACK is performed.

III

Administration

Watcom SQL also will acquire a *read lock* on the data, if doing so leaves no possibility of destructive interference. At isolation levels 2 and 3, read locks are used whenever a transaction reads a row. A read lock allows other transactions to acquire read locks on the same data, thereby maximizing the level of concurrency in the database. Maximizing concurrency will be discussed later in this chapter in "Understanding Concurrency."

If a read lock leaves open the possibility of destructive interference, Watcom SQL needs to acquire a more exclusive lock. The read locks are non-exclusive. The possibility for destructive interference could be a transaction performing an insert, update, or delete to a row. A *write lock* is needed.

A write lock is used at all isolation levels. It prevents other locks of any type on the same data to preserve data integrity—at the expense of eliminating concurrent access to the same data. The write lock is exclusive.

To preserve data integrity, a transaction cannot acquire a read lock on a row that already has a write lock by a different transaction. Conversely, write locks are not allowed on any row that is already read-locked.

One more lock deals strictly with the phantom rows: the *phantom lock*. The phantom lock is made up of read locks that have been acquired by a transaction with an isolation level of 3. These locks are used to prevent phantom rows.

To illustrate how these locks work, assume that you want to update the balance in the ACCOUNT table. You need to balance account 69. When you perform an UPDATE, INSERT, or DELETE to account 69, a write lock is put on the row. If another transaction wants to perform an update to another account, say account 70, a write lock is placed on account 70. Watcom SQL will allow both transactions to be performed because the transactions are not interfering with each other.

Another example would be if another transaction wants to read or update account 69 at the same time you are updating it. Because you were attempting to update account 69 first, the write lock gives your transaction exclusive rights to the data. You have this exclusive right to the data until you decide to COMMIT or ROLLBACK your transaction.

On the other hand, if you were trying to read account 69, a read lock would be placed on the row. If a second transaction attempts to read account 69, there is no chance for destructive interference. Thus, the second transaction would be able to read the data for account 69. No transaction would be able to update the data for account 69 until all of the locks were removed. This would include both write and read locks.

Watcom SQL has a "first come, first serve" approach to locking data. The first transaction that calls for the data receives priority. The transaction holds the data until you decide to release it.

This example also illustrates how Watcom SQL creates *serializability* in a multi-transaction environment. When you can serialize transactions, they act as though they were run one after another, even if they were run at the same time. Transactions of this type read few or no rows and last only a few seconds.

Understanding Concurrency

It would be convenient from a Database Administrator's view if only one user would update a table at one time. This would be a much simpler process and it would be easier to control data integrity. If a statement violates an integrity constraint or an integrity rule in a trigger, the statement would be rolled back to preserve database integrity.

Of course, from a business standpoint, this would not be acceptable. The single-user database just doesn't cut it for today's workplace. There are too many users out there who need the same information at the same time. This can cause some major problems if you are not prepared.

Consider the problem of interfacing with a filing cabinet. If a file is in use, what do you do? Should you wait for the file to be returned or should you make a copy of the file and hope that there aren't any changes made by anyone else? Either decision could cost you time and accuracy. If you wait to see what changes might have been made, you have lost valuable time. If you do not wait and the other user makes changes to the file, your data could be invalid. This example illustrates the *concurrency* problems involved when there are multiple users attempting to use the same database.

Tip
When you can use a low ISOLATION_LEVEL without giving up data integrity, do so. It allows more users to use read access to the information at one time.

Concurrency is the degree to which many transactions can be active at the same time. A database server must manage data so that contending users wait the least amount of time for each other to complete work without sacrificing data integrity. If a database server fails at either objective, users will notice the repercussions as many transactions contend for the same data. Users can observe poor application performance or get inaccurate results from their work. The capability to improve response time when several users are accessing the same database will improve concurrency.

III

Administration

Blocking Transactions

A conflict can arise when dealing with locks. You have seen an illustration of the conflict in the example with the ACCOUNT table. The conflict is referred to as a *blocked* transaction.

A blocked transaction can take place when a transaction locks a row of data. When another transaction tries to access the same data and has to wait for your transaction to complete, the second transaction is said to be blocked.

Blocking will occur more frequently with higher isolation levels because there is more locking and more checking being done. This leads to less concurrency. Fewer transactions can run at the same time when transactions are waiting on other transactions.

Lower isolation levels provide a higher degree of concurrency. For example, transactions running at an isolation level of 0 perform mostly reads on a particular row. When a transaction only has a read lock on a row, many different transactions can access the data on the row as long as the other transactions acquire a read lock. The only time a locking conflict will arise is when one of the other transactions attempts to update or delete a row. The transaction will then need to wait for it to acquire a write lock.

There is a database option that will change the behavior of the transactions. This can be set with the SET OPTION command. When the database option BLOCKING is set to ON, a transaction will wait until the lock can be acquired for itself. When BLOCKING is set to OFF, the request that caused the locking conflict will get an error.

Tip

For a single-user environment, you might want to set BLOCKING to OFF. This will save disk space and enable the transaction to run faster.

Unlike a transaction waiting until a resource is available, the transaction is terminated and an error is produced if the BLOCKING is set to OFF. Therefore, if a transaction acquires a write lock on a row and a second transaction tries to access the data, the second transaction will be terminated with an error.

Handling Deadlock

In a multi-tasking environment, the possibility of blocking is very common. A larger problem can occur when transactions are being locked out of data that is needed. This problem is a *deadlock*. A deadlock occurs when it is impossible to complete a transaction because there is a lock on the data.

A deadlock can occur for two reasons:

- **A cyclical blocking conflict.** This is when transaction A is blocked by transaction B, and transaction B is blocked by transaction A. Without intervention, neither transaction will complete. More time will not solve the problem. The cycle of conflict can expand to many transactions that are being blocked. One or more of the transactions need to be canceled to allow other transactions to complete.

- **All active database threads are blocked.** When a transaction becomes blocked, its database thread is not relinquished. If the database is configured with three treads and transactions A, B, and C are blocked on transaction D, which is not currently executing a request, then a deadlock situation has arisen because there are no available threads.

Watcom SQL automatically cancels the last transaction that becomes blocked. This eliminates the deadlock situation. When the transaction is canceled, an error message is sent to the canceled transaction. From the error message, you can determine what kind of deadlock situation you have encountered.

Other Considerations

When trying to deal with locks and concurrency, there are circumstances that need to be considered. The multi-user environment has made keeping accurate data more challenging. Of course, the benefits of the multi-user environment help offset this minor inconvenience.

It is not as hard to handle if you know what to expect. The following are a few considerations to watch for when dealing with locks and concurrency.

Generating Primary Keys

The need for primary keys is obvious. How do you generate a primary key in a multi-user environment? Many applications generate the primary key automatically. For example, if you use a policy number as the primary key, the new primary key is the next policy number. This can easily be accomplished by adding one to the last policy number.

This is sufficient for a single-user environment. The problem in a multi-user environment is that there is a chance of two people updating the table at the same time. If occurs, the primary key is no longer unique.

There are ways around this scenario. Here are a few solutions:

III

Administration

■ A different range of policy numbers can be used for each person who adds new policy numbers. This can be accomplished by having a table with two columns: the user's name and policy number. The table would have one row for each user who adds policy numbers. Each time a user adds a policy number, the number of the policy in the table is incremented and used for the new policy number.

■ Create a new table that has two columns: the table name and the last key value. There should be one row in this table for the last policy number used. Each time a user adds a policy number, establish a new connection, increment the number in the table, and COMMIT. The incremented number can be used for the new policy number. Other users can grab policy numbers because you updated the row with a separate transaction that only lasted an instant.

■ Probably the best solution is to have the system default the value for you. This can be done when you create the table. By placing the AUTOINCREMENT on the CREATE command, the system automatically increments the primary key for you. For example:

```
CREATE table POLNO (
policy_number    integer not null default
➥autoincrement,
issue_date       date,
...
primary key (policy_number)
);
```

The AUTOINCREMENT option is only the default. When you want to INSERT into the table, the AUTOINCREMENT option only increments if there is not a value for the policy_number. If there is not a value specified, the autoincrement column is given a unique value.

If a value is specified, the value supplied by the user is used. If the value supplied is larger than the current maximum value for the column, that value will be used as a starting point for subsequent INSERTs.

Creating and Altering Tables

When you are dealing with major alterations in your tables and indexes, you must consider concurrency. Creating an index, altering a table, or dropping a table are time consuming and bad for concurrency. CREATE INDEX, ALTER TABLE, and DROP will be prevented whenever the command affects a table that is currently being used by another transaction. The server will not process requests referencing the same table while the command is being processed.

The CREATE TABLE command will not cause any concurrency conflicts. When you create a table, there should not be any transactions trying to access the table. After the table is created, then there can be some conflicts. Of course, they should be only normal conflicts due to the multi-user environment.

The GRANT, REVOKE, and SET commands will not cause concurrency conflicts. These commands will affect any SQL statements sent to the database engine. They will not affect existing outstanding statements.

Applying Changes from Multiple Databases

So far, I have only discussed the use of a central database. The central database allows you to keep more control of the data to prevent corruption. This control is only held if the users are connected to the central database. This is not always possible in today's workplace.

The use of personal computers and laptops are ever-increasing. Especially with laptops, the user is not expected to be connected to the database at all times. But at the same time, there may be several database applications that the user would like to use while not connected to the network.

It is obvious that the user cannot update the database server if he is not connected to the network. The user would need to make the changes to a temporary copy of the database that was put onto the user's laptop or PC. The changes could then be uploaded to the server's database. If we were running a single-user database at all times, this would not be a problem. The trouble is that the server's database is in a multi-user environment.

The way around this problem is to take a copy of the database files; you can make changes to the copy using the single user run-time Watcom SQL database engine (running on a laptop or personal computer). When you are able to connect back to the server, the transaction log can be translated into an ISQL command file and applied to the database server.

Note

To use the single user run-time database engine on an unlimited number of machines, you need to have the Watcom SQL Runtime System for DOS, Windows, OS/2, or Windows NT. For more information on this topic, refer to the CD-ROM that accompanies this book.

CD-ROM

III

Administration

Applying Updates to the Server

There could be a problem when you try to apply the transactions from a laptop or personal computer to the server. Because you made changes to the copy of the database on the laptop, other users might have made changes to the data that you have been working with.

When the users are connected to the server, locks can be placed on data that is being worked on. Without being connected to the server, these locks cannot prevent conflicting updates to records within the database. Without some sort of strategy to update the database with the changes from the laptop, data integrity cannot be assured. Consider what would happen if two users updated the same record, or one user deleted a record that another user updated.

To assure data integrity, you must have a plan to handle these situations. Frequently, you can design applications to avoid this situation. It is still a good idea to be aware of the possibility.

One way to avoid this problem is to use the –v option when starting the database engine on the portable computer. This causes the engine to record the previous values of every column whenever a row of the database is updated. These values are kept in the transaction log. When the transaction log is translated, every UPDATE will have a WHERE clause that specifies the value of every column in the row.

> **Note**
>
> The transaction log is translated by using the DBTRAN command. This puts the log into an SQL command file.

▶ See "Using DBTRANW.EXE," p. 635

These rows will not be updated if any value has been changed by another user. ISQL will issue a warning if an UPDATE does not find any rows. This will indicate that the particular database row has already been updated or deleted by someone else. When this happens, your update procedures will need manual intervention to resolve the potential conflict. This might be tedious, but it is the only way to assure data integrity. It is a small price to pay for the freedom to be disconnected from the database.

Handling Large Databases

When you copy over the database from the server to your personal computer, you might have a space problem. When you are dealing with large databases, it might be beneficial to be able to shrink the database. To accomplish this, you can use the DBSHRINK command.

The DBSHRINK command compresses the database before making a copy of the database. The compressed database is usually 40 to 60 percent of the original size. The database engine cannot update the compressed database file. The only way to write to this compressed database is by using the DBWRITE command.

▶ See "Using DBSHRINW.EXE," p. 634

▶ See "Using DBWRITEW.EXE," p. 639

Another way to deal with large databases is to create a subset of the large database. This can be accomplished by creating an extraction procedure that builds a database containing only the data needed by one person. As long as the table names and column names are identical, the translation log from the smaller database can be applied to the main database.

From Here...

This chapter taught you the basics of locking: when you should use a lock and what type of locks to use. This chapter also explained concurrency. In a multi-user environment, locks and concurrency go hand-in-hand. Without locks on a system that is running more than one user at a time, data integrity will be compromised. This will help you keep your databases correct and running smoothly and it will help you fine-tune your transactions. Many of the processes discussed in this chapter are handled automatically by Watcom SQL, but it is wise to always keep in mind what could happen.

If you want to learn more about locking and concurrency, refer to the following chapters:

- Chapter 1, "Understanding Watcom SQL Fundamentals," shows you how Watcom SQL operates.

- Chapter 8, "Understanding the Role of a Database Administrator," tells about the other functions of a DBA and how to administer a database.

- Chapter 22, "SQL Commands," lists the SQL commands discussed in this chapter.

III

Administration

Chapter 11

Backing Up and Recovery

by Lance E. Tillman

The need to back up your data is usually rather obvious. If the data you're putting on your database ever needs to be used again, you need to set a backup plan. A database can be corrupted at any time and in many different ways. With a backup and recovery plan established, you can avoid many problems.

When I think about backup and recovery, I think of my main-frame experience with *disaster recovery*. This was a process of backing up all files in the event of an emergency or disaster. When this disaster occurred and the data was lost, I could recover the data from the backups. An emergency or disaster that corrupts or destroys your database is unpredictable. It's like a natural disaster. You don't always know when one will happen. You just know they happen, and you need to be prepared.

A disaster doesn't have to be a natural disaster, although that is a good reason to have a backup. It could be as simple as hitting the Reset button during processing, encountering a power outage, or the system locking up. Any of these can corrupt your database, and a backup might be the only way to recover your data. The only other alternative is to manually enter the data back into the database. But, unless you've stored all the paper that has the information on it, that may be impossible.

Because there is no guarantee that a system is fail-proof, Watcom SQL has features that protect your data from two categories of failures: system failures and media failures.

System failures occur when the machine goes down before the completion of a transaction, such as accidentally turning off the power during a transaction. This can corrupt the data or even wipe it out.

Media failures happen when the database file, the file system, or the device storing the database file become unusable. This could be as simple as a corrupted file or as serious as a disk crash. Either way, you can't use the data on the file in its present state.

In this chapter, you learn how to:

- Complete a full backup of your database

- Perform daily backups of your logs

- Set up a back-up and recovery strategy

- Recover your database

Using Log Files to Back Up and Restore

◀ See "COMMIT Statement," p. 170

When a failure occurs, the recovery mechanism must treat the transactions as *atomic units of work:* any transaction that wasn't successfully completed and committed must be rolled back, and any transaction that was committed must not be lost. This is why you perform commits; they save the data to the database, so it should not be lost.

Watcom SQL uses three different logs to protect your data from being lost due to system or media failure: the checkpoint log, the rollback log, and the transaction log. These log files exist for each database running on a database engine or network server.

The Checkpoint Log

Checkpoints are milestones that regularly occur to write all modified data in memory back to a database's data files. Watcom SQL database files are composed of *pages*. When a page updates, it is made *dirty*. Dirty means that a change was made to the page. But before the page is made dirty, Watcom copies the original page. These copied pages make up the *checkpoint log*.

Because these dirty pages are not written to the disk immediately, you could have some efficiency problems down the road if you don't address them.

For improved performance, the dirty pages are written to disk when the cache is full or the server has no pending requests. Checkpoints also indicate how much of the transaction log to apply to the data files if crash recovery is necessary.

A checkpoint is a point at which all of the dirty pages are written to disk. After all of the dirty pages are written to disk, the checkpoint log deletes.

There are many reasons for a checkpoint to occur:

- A transaction issues a CHECKPOINT command

- The database engine is idle long enough to write all of the dirty pages to disk

- The database engine is running without a transaction log, and a transaction commits

- The database engine stops

- The amount of time since the last checkpoint exceeds the database option CHECKPOINT_TIME

- The estimated time to do a recovery operation exceeds the database option RECOVERY_TIME

When you're first developing your database-backup strategy, the need to write dirty pages might not seem too high on the priority list. The checkpoints take care of themselves early on. When the cache is full or the database engine is idle, the dirty pages write to disk. But as the time and the amount of processing grows since the last checkpoint, the priority to establish consistent checkpoints also grows.

To establish consistent time intervals between checkpoints, you can use the database option CHECKPOINT_TIME. This option controls the maximum desired time between checkpoints. Another database option you can use is RECOVERY_TIME. This option controls the maximum desired time for recovery in the event of system failure. These options are not required—the checkpoints issue automatically—but they can help fine-tune your processing.

▶ See "Using DB32W.EXE, DBSTARTW.EXE, RT32W.EXE, and RTSTARTW.EXE," p. 612

When the database engine is running with multiple databases, the CHECKPOINT_TIME and RECOVERY_TIME options specified by the first database started are used. This is, of course, if the options are not overridden by command-line switches.

III

Administration

The Rollback Log

◀ See "ROLL-
BACK State-
ment," p. 171

A *rollback log* cancels any changes made to the contents of tables. It has a two-fold purpose: it's used to process ROLLBACK requests and for recovering from a system failure. There's a separate rollback log for each transaction. When a transaction completes, the rollback log is deleted.

The Transaction Log

The database's *transaction log* is a vital component of an efficient database recovery plan. The transaction log immediately records the changes made by ongoing application transactions in a database in the order in which they occur. The transaction log is also referred to as a *forward log* file.

You don't have to use a transaction log. When running Watcom SQL without a transaction log, a checkpoint occurs whenever a transaction commits. You need to have the checkpoint to ensure that all committed transactions write to the disk. This process is time-consuming and inefficient. Use the transaction log to improve performance, as well as protect against media failure and corrupted databases.

When you use the transaction log, remember to use good documentation. The order of the transaction logs is important when it comes time to recover a database. Figure 11.1 shows the transaction logs from Monday through Wednesday.

Fig. 11.1
The order in which the transaction logs are created.

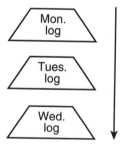

The need to perform at the peak of performance and still protect the database should be a major concern to you and your application. The Database Administrator needs to take careful consideration when designing the transaction log. The transaction log structure needs to adequately and efficiently safeguard the ongoing transaction processing.

A key point when configuring a transaction log is protection. By default, the transaction log is on the same device and in the same directory as the database. This has some major drawbacks when it comes to the protection of your transaction log. If there is a media failure, the transaction logs could be lost or corrupted. Without usable transaction logs, it's tough to re-create the database.

You should keep the transaction log on a device separate from the main database file. This minimizes the risk of losing your transaction log during a media failure. You can set the file name of the transaction log in one of two places. The first is where you initialize the database with the DBINIT command. The second is where the database engine is not running; use the DBLOG command.

Caution

Never place the transaction log and the database file on the same devices if at all possible. The transaction log could be vulnerable to a single point of failure or a media failure; both are unrecoverable situations.

While protection is a major concern, there are also performance considerations. If the database server has more than one disk drive, you need to carefully consider the file-structure needs. With an efficient file structure, you can minimize the disk I/O contention and maximize the performance for the database server. With transaction logs and database files on separate disks, reads and writes do not contend with each other for disk-access time.

Note

Placing the transaction log and the database file on separate devices can result in improved performance by eliminating the need for disk head movement between the transaction log and the main database file.

Before using the transaction logs for recovery, they must be converted into an SQL command file. The transaction log cannot be read otherwise. The most common way to convert is to use the DBTRAN command. Because the transaction log contains all of the records of everything processed, it can also serve as an audit trail. Files that have not been committed by the user can also be recovered when you convert the transaction log to SQL. Do this by including the -a switch to the DBTRAN command.

▶ See "Using DBTRANW.EXE," p. 635

Note

If you omit the -a switch from the DBTRAN command, all transactions that were rolled back are omitted from the SQL.

III

Administration

Establishing Database Backups

Because failures can happen at any time or on any device, periodic backups are a priority. You can perform backups either while the database is running or when it is shut down. Another part of backing up files to consider is how much and how often to backup. A full backup involves making a copy of the database file. Another back up might be a daily or partial backup. This can include only making a copy of the transaction log, and saves time and resources compared to always making a full back up. You can accomplish both updates using an on-line or off-line backup.

On-line Backup

Many database systems cannot afford to frequently shut down to make backups. The *on-line backup* makes a copy of the database file while the database engine is still running. You can run the DBBACKW command against a single-user or multi-user database server. The DBBACKW command is equivalent to copying the database file when the database is not running.

The DBBACKW command copies all files to make a single database. The copied database can be of a simple nature. These consist of the main database and the transaction log. The more complicated databases can store tables in multiple files. These files are commonly called *dbspaces*. The naming convention used by DBBACKW is rather convenient: all file names are the same as the file names on the server.

▶ See "Using DBBACKW.EXE," p. 621

Each file of the database copies to the identical file of the same name in the specified output directory. This lets you back up a database while other applications or users are using the database.

Troubleshooting
When I do an on-line backup, my database is too large, and I cannot get a good backup. The DBBACKW is the only command that can be used during an online backup. When your database becomes too large to copy to your storage device, you need to shut down the database engine and perform an offline backup.

Off-line Backup

▶ See "DBSERVEW," p. 631

Off-line backup is when you shut down the database engine before copying the database files. It's important that you take down the database engine cleanly. If the database does not come down cleanly, unforeseen problems could occur. It's also a good idea to do off-line backups at a consistent time. To set a time to shut down the database engine, use Watcom SQL's DBSERVEW command.

After you complete the backup, you'll have a complete set of files that make up the database with respect to an instant in time. Unlike the on-line backup, no updating of the database is done during the off-line backup. This process is commonly referred to as a *consistent database backup*.

Determining Backup Frequency

Now that you know how to backup, you need to answer some questions. These questions need to be discussed by the Database Administrator, the client, and the developer:

- When should you make database backups?

- How often should you make database backups?

- How long should you keep older database backups?

Like many other administrative operations, database backup strategies vary with each database and installation, depending on such things as transactions and database size. However, the following key points remain constant when dealing with backup strategy:

- *Back up a database frequently*. The longer the time between backups, the longer it takes to complete the database-recovery process. If you need multiple transaction logs for recovery, you need to apply the transaction logs to the older version of the database file. Even if there is only one transaction log, but it's extremely large, it can still take quite a bit of time to recover.

- *Back up a database regularly*. The time between backups does not have to be too complicated. You can back up nightly, every other night, or every weekend. The important part is to be consistent.

- *Back up a database after making structural modifications*. For example, if you add a new tablespace or data file to the database, alter your database script to address the new tablespace, and then back up the database that day. The most recent database backup includes the new data files added to the database. Back up a database after it's created, after creating or dropping a tablespace, after adding or renaming data files, and after modifying the configuration of the database's transaction log.

■ *Keep the two most recent database backups, at least.* If something happens to the current database and the previous database is corrupt, then you can still re-create the database. If the data is very sensitive and vital to your company, it might be wise to make a second copy. This copy could be kept off-site. In the event that something happens to the site where the original copy is kept, you still have a valid copy to recover the database with.

Performing Daily (Transaction Log File) Backups

With constraints on your time and resources, it isn't always possible to make a copy of the database and the transaction log. This is where a daily backup comes in handy. The *daily backup* means that you're only backing up the transaction log. You can do this either on-line or off-line.

▶ See "Using DBBACKW.EXE," p. 621

The off-line daily backup makes a copy of the transaction log with all of the transactions completed by the application since the last full backup. The on-line backup gets the same results as the off-line, but you don't have to shut down the database engine. The command for the on-line daily backup is:

```
DBBACKW   -t
```

> **Note**
>
> If the transaction log becomes exceptionally large, the on-line backup might not work. After the storage area you're using for the backup is full, the process fails. When this happens, you need to shut down the database engine and perform an off-line backup. This way you have the ability to either shrink the transaction log or have the transaction log span disks.

Use daily backups for added protection against failures. The need for daily backups is greater if the transaction log and the database reside on the same device. If there's a media failure, both files could possibly be lost. By doing daily backups, the worst that can happen is that you lose one day's transactions.

Now, I know the theory of backups and the everyday workplace do not always see eye-to-eye. The need for a daily backup is determined by the needs of the business: your business may not need daily backups. It might be every other day or every third day. You need to take this into consideration when you set up your backup strategy.

Another reason for daily backups is the size of the transaction log. The transaction log can grow to unmanageable sizes, depending on how many transactions are processed by your application. By doing daily backups, you save on larger storage devices or on more frequent full backups. After you archive the transaction log, delete the current transaction log, and you're ready to start again.

The down side of deleting the current transaction log after archiving is the chance that the backup of the transaction log is corrupt. You need to apply the archived versions of the transaction log to the database in the sequence they were archived in the event of a recovery. If you think the transaction log may be corrupt, either make another backup of the transaction file or do a full backup.

Performing Full Backups

A *full backup* makes a copy of the current database and the transaction log. After you complete a full backup, the transaction log deletes, and another transaction log is produced. Because full backups make a copy of the current database, verify that the data in the database is not corrupt.

File-system errors or software errors in any software you're running can corrupt a small portion of the database file without you ever knowing. Before the backup, run a validation check against the database. Imagine how you would feel if you attempt a database recovery, and you find out that for weeks your database was corrupted. Your most recent database backups would be useless.

To take care of validating your data, Watcom SQL has the following on-line validation command that checks the database:

```
dbvalid -c dba,sql
```

The validation command scans every record in every table and looks up each record in each index on the table. If the database is corrupt, you need to recover from the previous database file.

▶ See "Using DBVALIDW.EXE," p. 638

III

Administration

► See "VALIDATE TABLE," p. 572 Another way to validate the data of a table in the database is with the VALI-DATE TABLE command. This command also scans every row of a table and looks up each row in each index on the table. If the database file is corrupt, it reports an error. If this happens, you can drop all of the indexes and keys on a table and re-create them. Any foreign keys to the table also need to be re-created. If this doesn't work, or you're uncomfortable with the procedure, recover the database from the previous database file, and then do a full backup.

Now that you've validated the database file, you can do a full backup. It does not matter what backup method you want to use. If you want to do the backup while the database engine is running, use the DBBACKW command:

DBBACKW

Depending on what your specific needs are, you may want to see which connection parameters are available to you.

Whenever you back up the database file, you no longer need the current transaction log. It's only used to recover from the previous database to the current database. Archive the transaction log as a history or audit trail; you won't need it as long as the database was backed up successfully.

> **Note**
>
> Archiving the transaction log might also give added protection in the event that you cannot restore the most recent full backup.

The DBBACKW command can accommodate any path you take. If you want to delete the transaction log and restart, use the -x option. If you want to rename (archive) the transaction log and restart, use the -r option. You can accomplish all of this on-line.

It's a good idea to keep some of the backups off-site—depending on how important your data is to you. If something happens to your server and you can't recover the backup files, you can restore your database to the previous database state.

Another good idea when backing up your database is to use some type of documentation—it's a great help when it comes time to recover. Even simple messages help, such as the date of the backup, the database name, and any information that might make it easier when the pressure is on to recover the database.

Testing Database Backups

Before you assume that the backup process is correct, test to make sure that both the daily and full backups are performing correctly. Imagine the horror when you lose a disk and attempt a database recovery, only to find that your drive has been working incorrectly. Your most recent backups are useless! You can easily avoid this scenario, or at least minimize the risk, if you perform regular test database recoveries. You guarantee that your backup methods and all of the involved hardware components perform as expected.

The key to checking the backup system is to take the previous backup and apply the transaction log or logs. After you do this, the database you just recovered should equal the current production database. If they are not equal, either the backup procedures are not working or one or more of the backup files is corrupt.

Follow these steps to test your backup strategy:

1. Pick a time when you can shut down the database for a period of time (to allow a recovery to take place).

2. Make a copy of the production database files, and place it on a temporary backup location using the operating system commands established to backup the database. This copy needs to be at another location to ensure that the data does not get corrupted during the test.

3. Verify the temporary database file to ensure that it is intact and valid. This shows you whether the current database is corrupt.

4. Restore the database from the most recent backup. This is accomplished by a copy from the backup to the database name that you are using.

5. Perform a database recovery to see if everything works correctly. To do this, apply the daily transaction logs back to the database. Apply the oldest transaction log first, followed by the next oldest, and so on, until you apply all of the transaction logs to the database. Figure 11.2 shows the order in which you must apply the transaction logs.

> **Note**
>
> You can find an example of these commands in the section "Recovering from Media Failure on the Database File," later in this chapter.

III

Administration

Fig. 11.2
The order in
which the
transaction logs
need to be applied
to the database.

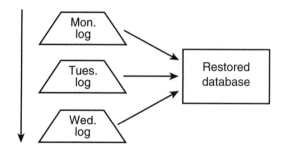

6. Compare the recovered database to the current database you copied to temporary storage. The best way to compare the two databases is to check their sizes and to validate the databases. If the validation is verified and the sizes are equal, the test was a success.

If everything goes well, you know that the backups are performing correctly. Also, you know that you have the experience to recover the databases. This will come in handy when you have to recover a database during a real failure.

If the database does not recover successfully, you must determine the cause. It can take awhile to determine the problem, or it might take just seconds, so have a large window to perform the recovery. When you determine the problem, you need to test the database recovery again to make sure that the problem is fixed. Continue this process until the database recovery is successful. If you don't have enough time to complete your testing, recover the database with the production database in temporary storage.

> **Caution**
>
> It's dangerous to recover the database with the production database in temporary storage: it means you don't have a working database recovery system. Fix this problem as soon as possible.

Using Alternative Backups

There's no one way to back up your database. Just as there are many different ways to copy a file, there are many ways to copy your current files to backup files. The following sections briefly describe other ways to back up your files.

DBSHRINW

The DBSHRINW command is handy if you're trying to save space. It compresses the database file, usually to 40—60 percent of the original size.

DBSHRINW reads the given database file and creates a compressed database file.

Another advantage to DBSHRINW is that the compressed database file is read-only. The database engine cannot update the compressed database file. This could be an advantage since it prevents the unauthorized update of backups.

When it comes time to recover your database file, you need to uncompress the database to be able to apply the transaction log(s) to the backup database file. You can accomplish this using the DBEXPANW command. DBEXPANW reads the compressed database file and creates an uncompressed database file.

▶ See "DBEXPANW.EXE," p. 627

Using the DOS Copy Command

The DOS COPY command copies the current database file to the backup file. It doesn't compress the file. Depending on the size of your current database file, this can cause some problems. You will need to evaluate your resources along with your methods when you determine your strategy.

For more information, see the DOS programmer's reference material.

Using File Manager to Copy

Copying the database file using the File Manager works similarly to the COPY command from DOS: the database file copies to another file without being compressed.

Your clients (or whoever does the backup) might be more familiar with copying in Windows than in DOS. If you make the backup process into an executable, the client doesn't need to know what process you use to back up the database files.

This is a viable option to backing up your database file. You need to evaluate your resources along with your methods when you determine your strategy.

For more information, see your Windows reference material.

INPUT and OUTPUT Commands Using ISQL

The INPUT and OUTPUT commands allow you to put the data in a database table and retrieve from the database table. ISQL inserts lines of input into a named table. ISQL uses the OUTPUT command to retrieve from the named table and put the results into a file.

▶ See "INPUT," p. 602

▶ See "OUTPUT," p. 605

III

Administration

Recovering the Database

When it comes to backup and recovery, the role of the Database Administrator is one of preparation. The backups of the files, the testing of the files after they're backed up, and mock recoveries of the database are all in preparation for something the DBA hopes will never occur: a failure or corruption of the database.

As experience will show, sometimes the system will fail you. It's best to be prepared for the worst. If you follow set rules to back up and recover the database, you'll be ready.

As discussed earlier in the chapter, there is an order to recovering databases. Figure 11.3 shows the process that generally occurs when recovering a database. The following sections will help explain the order in which to back up the databases during certain failures.

Fig. 11.3
The process for recovering the database.

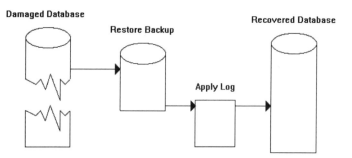

Recovering from System Failure

The aftermath of a system failure can be damaging to both your database files and your system. It can either be a minor problem or very damaging. If the system failure occurs during a transaction, your transaction is left in limbo.

After you bring the system back up, run a disk-verification program. This will correct minor errors caused by the system failure. Perform the process before running any software. Some examples of the verifications are as follows:

Operating System	Verification Method
DOS, Windows, OS/2	Type **chkdsk /f**
NetWare	Load the Novell VREPAIR.EXE to repair any volume that will not mount due to errors.
Windows NT	Automatically done by Windows NT

After the system failure, Watcom SQL automatically recovers when you re-start the database. The results of all transactions not committed prior to the system failure are intact, and all changes by transactions not committed prior to the system failure are canceled. You can recover the transactions not committed prior to the failure manually (see "Recovering Uncommitted Changes," later in this chapter).

During the automatic recovery done by Watcom SQL, the database engine takes the following three steps to recover from the system failure:

1. Restores all pages to the most recent checkpoint by using the checkpoint log.

2. Applies any changes made between the checkpoint and the system failure. These changes are in the transaction log.

3. Rolls back all uncommitted transactions by using the rollback logs. There's a separate rollback log for every transaction.

The use of more frequent checkpoints will make the recovery from a system failure take less time. There is a down side, though. Frequent checkpoints will create extra work for the database engine: the database engine will be writing out more dirty pages. You need to evaluate this during your database setup.

There are two database options that allow you to control the frequency of checkpoints: CHECKPOINT_TIME controls the maximum desired time between checkpoints, and RECOVERY_TIME controls the maximum desired time for recovery in the event of a system failure.

RECOVERY_TIME specifies an estimate for steps 1 and 2 only (see previous numbered list). Step 3 may take a long time if there are long uncommitted

▶ See "SET OPTION," p. 565

transactions that have already done a great deal of work before the last checkpoint.

When you're running Watcom SQL without a transaction log, it does a checkpoint whenever a transaction is committed. In the event of a system failure, the database engine uses steps 1 and 3 to recover a database file (see previous numbered list). Step 2 is not necessary because there will be no committed transactions since the last checkpoint. The disadvantage of running without a transaction log is that the system will usually run slower; the database engine will need to perform more frequent checkpoints.

Recovering from Media Failure

A media failure can be as simple as a corrupt database or as complex as a crashed hard drive; regardless, your database files are unusable. This is a good reason to have your transaction logs on a different device than the database file. If the transaction log and the database file are on the same device, you could lose them both in the event of a media failure.

When a media failure occurs, your first step is to clean up, reformat, or replace the device that failed. This is another reason to keep your database file and your backups on different devices. If the device is unusable, you can switch temporarily to a different device.

Regular backups of the database file and the transaction log will reduce the time required to recover from a media failure. Frequent backups will mean fewer transaction logs to apply to the recovered database. The frequent backups should also give you a sense of security that, even if you cannot recover to the current database, you should not lose too much data.

A media failure can occur in two areas: on the database file or the transaction log.

Recovering from Media Failure on the Database File

This occurs when your current database file is lost or unusable. Depending on when the failure has happened, there could be one or more transaction log(s). They're handled in relatively the same manner.

One Transaction Log

When there's only one transaction log to apply to the database, this means that you have not deleted or restarted the transaction log since the last full backup. If you have been doing frequent and regular full backups, this should contain every transaction that has been attempted since the last full backup.

To recover the database, perform the following steps:

1. Make a copy of the transaction log.

2. Restore the database file with the most recent full backup. When the transaction log has been applied to this database, the current database file will be restored:

   ```
   copy -r previous.db example.db
   ```

3. Use the database engine to apply the transaction log to the recovered database file. Use the following commands:

   ```
   dbstart   example.db -a example.log
   dbservew  example.db -a sample.log
   ```

   After the database engine applies the transaction log to the recovered database, the database file will be up-to-date.

4. From here, you can start the database in the normal manner. The database engine will come up normally and any new activity will be appended to the current transaction log.

▶ See "Using DB32W.EXE, DBSTARTW.EXE, RT32W.EXE, and RTSTARTW.EXE," p. 612

Back up the current database after the recovery is complete. From that point, you can either delete or archive the transaction log.

▶ See "DBSERVEW.EXE," p. 631

Caution

If you performed the last full backup after a system failure, and you have archived the transaction log, you will get an error message because the archived transaction log is required in recovery.

Troubleshooting

When I attempt to restore a corrupted database using the DOS copy command without first resetting the read-only attribute, I am not able to.

Watcom SQL sets a read-only attribute to the corrupted database. You need to reset the attribute with the DOS ATTRIB command using the following commands before copying over the database:

```
Attrib -r database.db
Attrib -r database.log
```

You could also use the File Manager to copy the database. File Manager asks if you want to continue your processing and resets the attribute for you.

III

Administration

Multiple Transaction Logs

You need to apply multiple transaction logs to the database if you have archived transaction logs, which probably happened if you've been performing daily backups. The daily backups back up the transaction log and delete the current one. This allows you to do less frequent full backups, but still recover the database.

The key to recovering the database file with multiple transaction logs is to apply the transaction logs in the order they were archived. First, apply the oldest transaction log to the database, followed by the next oldest, and so on until you have applied all of them.

To recover the database, perform these steps:

1. Make a copy of each transaction log.

2. Restore the database file with the most recent full backup. When you have applied all of the transaction logs to the database, the current database file will be restored:

   ```
   copy previous.db example.db
   ```

3. Use the database engine to apply the transaction logs to the recovered database file. Start with the oldest transaction log. (This would be the first transaction log after the most recent full backup.) Each archived transaction log follows in the same manner. Use the transaction log switch (-a); for example, if your last full backup was on Sunday and the database file is lost during the day on Thursday. This takes into consideration that you did daily backups.

   ```
   dbstart    example.db -a mon.log
   dbstart    example.db -a tue.log
   dbstart    example.db -a wed.log
   dbstart    example.db -a example.log (current transaction log)
   dbservew   example.db -a mon.log
   dbservew   example.db -a tue.log
   dbservew   example.db -a wed.log
   dbservew   example.db -a example.log (current transaction log)
   ```

▶ See "Using DB32W.EXE, DBSTARTW.EXE, RT32W.EXE, and RTSTARTW.EXE," p. 612

▶ See "DBSERVEW.EXE," p. 631

Watcom SQL does not allow you to apply the transaction logs in the wrong order or to skip a transaction log in the sequence. This is a good example of why it helps to use good documentation—order is very important when it comes to recovering with multiple transaction logs.

After the database engine applies the transaction logs to the recovered database, the database file will be up-to-date.

4. From here, you can start the database in the normal manner. The database engine comes up normally and any new activity appends to the current transaction log.

Back up the current database after the recovery is complete. From that point, you can either delete or archive the transaction log.

Recovering from Media Failure on the Transaction Log

If a media failure only affects the transaction log, your database file should still be intact and usable. The only problem could be that you no longer have a record of what took place when the transaction log was working correctly.

When there are one or more transaction logs since the last full backup, you cannot recover from the last database file if a transaction log is corrupt. Transaction logs need to be applied to the database in the order they were created. If a transaction log is corrupt, it cannot be applied to the previous database file to recover to the current database file.

Media failure on a transaction log could be more damaging than media failure on the database file. When media failure occurs on a transaction log, all uncommitted transactions that were on the transaction log are lost. This means that all changes to the database since the last checkpoint are unrecoverable. This is a problem if you have a system failure and a media failure at the same time. This can happen if a power failure causes a head crash that damages the disk. Hopefully this will never happen, but you must keep it in mind when designing your backup strategy.

Perform the following procedures in the event of a media failure on the transaction log:

1. Make a copy of the database file. The current database file is usable and correct. If you don't back up the database file immediately and your database file becomes corrupted later, you won't be able to recover it from a previous backup.

2. Restart the database using the -f switch. Do this with the following commands:

```
dbstart   example.db -f
dbservew  example.db -f
```

The database engine restores the database to the most recent checkpoint and rolls back any transactions that were not committed at the time of the checkpoint. If you start the database engine without the -f switch, it will complain about the lack of the transaction log.

4. From here, you can start the database in the normal manner. The database engine will come up normally and any new activity will be appended to the current transaction log.

▶ See "Using
DB32W.EXE,
DBSTARTW.EXE,
RT32W.EXE, and
RTSTARTW.EXE,"
p. 612

▶ See
"DBSERVEW.EXE,"
p. 631

Back up the current database after the recovery is complete. From that point, you can either delete or archive the transaction log.

Recovering Uncommitted Changes

The transaction log keeps a record of all changes made to the database. Included in these changes are changes that were not yet committed. Because these changes are on the transaction log, they can be recovered. This can be handy if you accidentally uncommit a change.

To recover uncommitted changes, use the DBTRAN command. If you add the -a switch, it recovers the uncommitted changes. The DBTRAN command with the -a switch translates the transactions that were not committed. You can then recover changes that were not committed by editing the SQL command file and picking out the changes you want to recover.

> **Note**
>
> Editing the SQL command line would allow you to only recover the uncommitted transactions that you want. Otherwise, all of the uncommitted transactions will be recovered.

From Here...

In this section, you have learned the importance of having a backup and recovery plan. You have seen how to make full and daily backups. You have also learned how to recover from a failure.

Backup and recovery strategies are important to your peace of mind. If you would like more information that will help you with backup and recovery, refer to the following chapters:

■ Chapter 1, "Understanding Watcom SQL Fundamentals," shows you how Watcom SQL operates.

■ Chapter 4, "Designing a Database Using PowerBuilder," describes the structure of the database so you can recover when a failure occurs.

■ Chapter 22, "Embedded SQL Commands," teaches you SQL commands and how to use them. For backup and recovery, take a good look at the COMMIT and ROLLBACK commands. These commands are very important to determine what data will be rolled back during a recovery.

■ Chapter 23, "ISQL-Only SQL Commands," encompasses the INPUT and OUTPUT commands you can use to back up and retrieve data in a database table.

■ Chapter 24, "Using Watcom SQL Utilities," shows the many executables that you can use when backing up and recovering your database. This chapter is a *must* to read.

III

Administration

Part IV

Interfaces

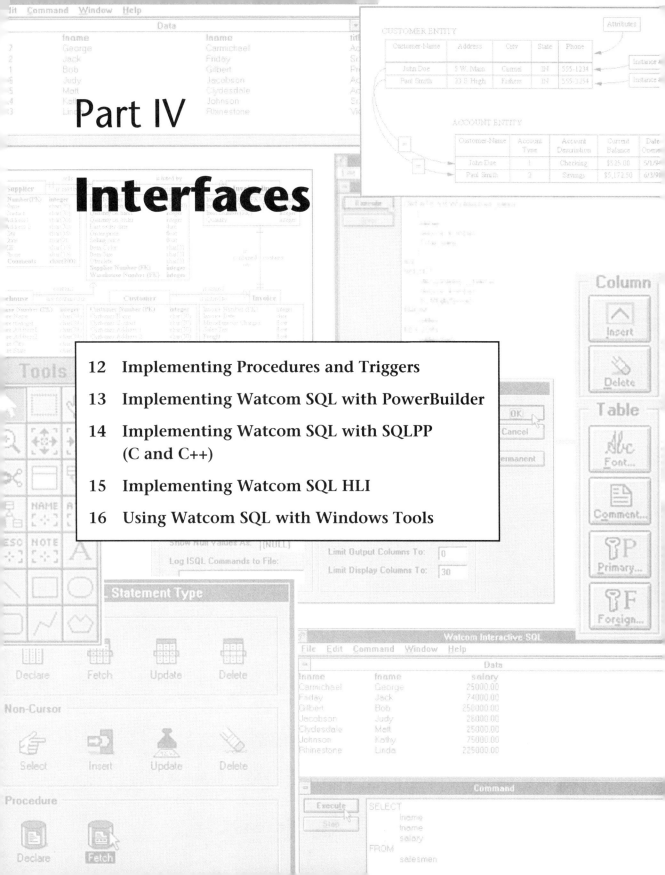

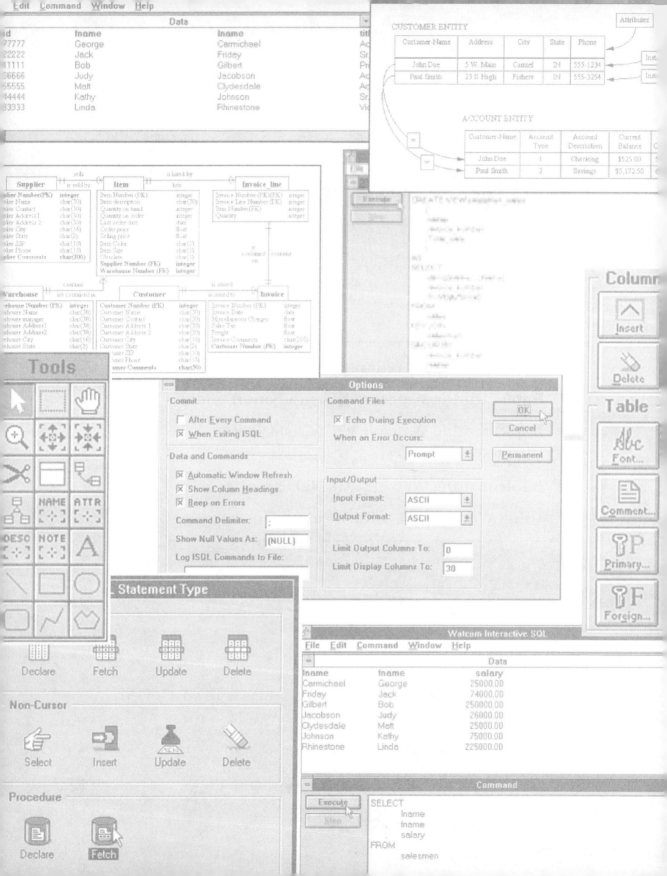

Chapter 12

Implementing Procedures and Triggers

by Charles Wood

You use procedures and triggers to store SQL and database-related tasks for use with all applications. Along with all embedded SQL, procedures and triggers allow the use of the Watcom SQL Procedural Language. The Watcom SQL Procedural Language allows the use of loops and conditional expressions.

In this chapter, you learn:

- The importance of procedures and how to use them

- How to use the Watcom SQL Procedural Language

- Uses for embedded SQL

- What to do with a cursor

- How to define and use a trigger

- Different types of triggers

Using Procedures

Procedures (also called *Watcom SQL procedures* or *stored procedures*) are written to be separate from any program or language accessing a Watcom SQL database. Procedures incorporate embedded SQL commands with the Watcom SQL Procedural Language. This separation from the accessing language has several benefits:

■ Procedures allow database functionality to be modularized so that any program can call a procedure without extensive design and coding for each SQL statement.

■ Standard procedures allow for a much tighter control of the database without losing any of the functionality. A database analyst or programmer can define bullet-proof procedures that can be accessed by others with little risk of bugs or data corruption.

■ Windows programs tend to have slower access to any database due to the extensive use of DLLs. Operations such as cursor processing, bulk updates, and serial queries often make several requests of the Watcom SQL engine through DLLs.

Watcom SQL compiles any procedure into the database engine's virtual memory after it executes once. It can then be executed several times, by many different applications, with little overhead. This has the potential to dramatically speed up database access.

■ Procedures are executed at the server level rather than the host level. This causes a lot less line traffic over any network. Not only is your access faster, but every other person on the network is not impacted as greatly.

■ You can administer security at the procedure level. That way, anyone can access a procedure they've been given authority to *even if* they have not been given access to the tables that the procedure accesses. You control security by *function* rather than table or column. Procedures can make a DBA's job a lot easier.

Creating, Dropping, and Granting Access to Procedures

Like other database constructs, you can create and drop procedures. You can also grant security to a procedure.

Creating Procedures

To create a stored procedure, use the CREATE PROCEDURE command. The CREATE PROCEDURE statement contains two parts: the CREATE statement declares the procedure and the result set (if desired); the COMPOUND statement defines the procedure. The syntax for the CREATE PROCEDURE command is as follows:

```
CREATE PROCEDURE procedure_name ([parm1, parm2, ...])
        [RESULT (result_column1, result_column2, ...)]
        compound_statement
```

- **CREATE PROCEDURE...** The CREATE PROCEDURE clause allows you to define the procedure_name, the parameters, and the result set. The CREATE PROCEDURE clause is divided as follows:

  procedure_name (parm1, parm2, ...). Procedure_name is the name of the procedure. Included in the procedure_name are any parameters needed by the procedure. If the procedure doesn't need any parameters, an empty parenthesis follows the procedure_name. Valid parameter formats are:

  parm_mode parm_name data_type. A parameter clause uses this syntax to define each of the parameters. Each parameter is defined as follows:

  parm_mode. Parm_mode is the mode of the parameter. The mode of the parameter describes how the parameter is used in the stored procedure. Valid values for parm_mode are IN (for parameters passed to the stored procedure), OUT (for parameters returned to the calling procedure or program), or INOUT (for parameters that are both passed to the procedure, modified, and then returned to the calling procedure).

  parm_name. Parm_name is the name of the variable used as a parameter.

  data_type. Data_type describes the data type of the parameter (such as INTEGER, DECIMAL, and so on).

  SQLCODE | SQLSTATE. Specifying SQLCODE or SQLSTATE as the parameter returns the SQLCODE or SQLSTATE to the calling procedure upon completion of the procedure.

  > **Tip**
  > The SQLCODE and SQLSTATE parameters use OUT as the parameter mode.

  RESULT (result_column1, result_column2, ...). The RESULT command, if used, passes a set of result columns (as a cursor does) back to the calling procedure or program.

- **compound_statement.** A compound statement is the body of the procedure. Compound statements can be nested. Compound statements always start with a BEGIN statement and finish with an END statement.

The following is an example of the CREATE PROCEDURE statement. In the procedure, customer_number is sent to the procedure while a formatted customer_name and an error return code return to the program. Components of the COMPOUND statement that follows the BEGIN statement are explained as the discussion continues in the section called "Defining a Procedure with a Compound Statement."

```
CREATE PROCEDURE GetCustName (IN custnum INT, OUT  custname CHAR
(30), OUT error INT)
BEGIN
   DECLARE no_db_error EXCEPTION FOR SQLSTATE '00000';
   SET error = 0;
   SELECT customer_name
          INTO custname
          FROM customer
          WHERE customer_number = custnum;
   IF SQLSTATE <> no_db_error THEN
          SET error = 1
   END IF;
END
```

Troubleshooting

I'm trying to write a procedure using ISQLW, but keep getting this error message:

```
"syntax error near ('end of line')"
```

I know I have the correct syntax! Why can't I create a procedure?

Because Watcom SQL procedures allow compound statements, separated by semicolons, there is a problem when using ISQLW. In the ISQLW environment, semicolon is also the default SQL command delimiter. When ISQLW encounters a semicolon, it assumes that your CREATE PROCEDURE command is finished, and a new command is beginning. This not only causes errors, but it can also make unwanted SQL commands issued to your database.

To solve this problem, you must change the default command delimiter when using your ISQLW environment before creating your procedure. Either execute the CONFIGURE command or click on **C**ommand, **O**ptions, which displays the Options dialog box seen in figure 12.1.

You will see a semicolon in the Command Delimiter text box. Change this to another character, like a tilde (~). Now your ISQLW commands will need to be separated with the character you have chosen (i.e. "~"); your stored procedure commands will still be separated with a semicolon.

Dropping Procedures

As you can probably guess, based on other CREATE commands, there is also a DROP PROCEDURE command that deletes a stored procedure. That command is as follows:

```
DROP PROCEDURE procedure_name
```

The `procedure_name` is the name given the procedure in the CREATE PROCEDURE statement.

▶ See "CONFIGURE," p. 575

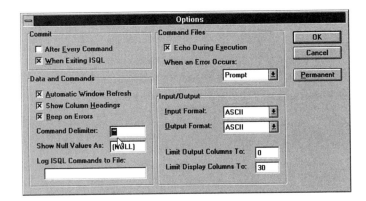

Fig. 12.1
You can change many of your command options using the Options dialog box.

Granting Access to Procedures

Finally, the creator of a procedure can grant access to a procedure, as well as revoke access to that procedure, with the GRANT and REVOKE commands using the following syntax:

```
GRANT EXECUTE ON procedure_name TO user_id
REVOKE EXECUTE ON procedure_name FROM user_id
```

The `procedure_name` is the name given the procedure in the CREATE PROCEDURE statement. The `user_id` is the login identification of the user.

Note

Procedures are granted authority at the function level. If you GRANT a user access to a procedure, he can use that procedure even if he doesn't have authority to use tables accessed in that procedure! This gives the DBA authority at the *function level* as opposed to the *data level*. Often, this eases the burden on DBAs who want to GRANT users some (but not all) rights to certain elements on a table.

Defining a Procedure with a Compound Statement

As mentioned previously, a procedure consists of two main components: a CREATE statement used to declare a procedure, and a compound statement that defines the procedure. The compound statement is actually a series of *atomic* (stand-alone) SQL statements grouped together by a BEGIN and an END. These statements use a combination of embedded SQL and Watcom SQL Procedural Language statements.

Using Embedded SQL

You can use embedded SQL statements (such as SELECT, INSERT, UPDATE, DELETE, DECLARE, and so on) inside a Watcom SQL stored procedure. The following is an example of how to use embedded SQL inside a stored procedure compound statement:

```
CREATE PROCEDURE ChangeInvoiceDate (IN invnum INT, IN newdate DATE,
➥OUT invoice_count INT)
BEGIN
   UPDATE invoice
          SET invoice_date = newdate
          WHERE invoice_number = invnum;
   SELECT count(*)
          FROM invoice
          WHERE invoice_number = invnum;
END
```

This is a stored procedure to set a column on an invoice table to a new date (that was provided by the calling program or procedure), and then to count all invoices with a given invoice number. As you can see, two SQL statements that are closely related were combined into one procedure.

As shown in the previous code segment, you can use procedures to group SQL statements together that should not be executed apart. In this manner, the Database Administrator can control the integrity of the database while at the same time making SQL coding easier for the developer.

Using the Watcom SQL Procedural Language

Watcom allows the use of the Watcom SQL Procedural Language inside a stored procedure. Table 12.1 describes the types of Watcom SQL Procedural Language constructs.

Table 12.1 Watcom SQL Procedural Language Statements	
Type of Statement	**Description**
Declarative Statements	Use declarative statements to declare a stored procedure or variables in the stored procedure. You can also use them to declare blocks of statements in a procedure.
Conditional Expressions	Conditional statements allow Watcom SQL to follow an execution path based on the result of previous statements.
Iterative (Looping) Expressions	Use iterative expressions to execute the same instructions several times.
Branching Instructions	Use branching instructions to go to a specific area in the procedure or to leave the procedure.
Error Handling Instructions	Error handling instructions deal with any unwanted situations that may occur in the procedure.

Declarative Statements: DECLARE, SET, BEGIN, and END

DECLARE, SET, BEGIN, and END are the declarative Watcom SQL statements. Use DECLARE to declare a variable inside a stored procedure:

```
DECLARE total_sales DECIMAL;
```

Use SET, in conjunction with a DECLARE variable statement, to assign a value to a variable inside a stored procedure:

```
DECLARE total_sales DECIMAL;
SET total_sales = 0;
```

BEGIN starts a procedure or compound statement and END terminates the procedure or compound statement. The syntax for BEGIN and END are as follows:

```
[label:]
BEGIN [ATOMIC]
...
END
```

In the above statement, BEGIN and END signify the beginning and end of a procedure. `label:` is the name of the procedure (used with the LEAVE command described later in this chapter in the "Branching Instructions" section).

If you specify ATOMIC, Watcom SQL treats the compound statement as a single, atomic statement. Therefore, in an ATOMIC compound statement, if one statement fails, all of the statements in the compound statement fail and roll back.

Conditional Expressions

Conditional expressions allow Watcom SQL to change the execution path of the SQL if certain conditions occur. The Watcom SQL Procedural Language allows two types of conditional expressions: the IF statement and the CASE statement.

IF ... ELSE IF ... ELSE ... END IF. The IF statement is similar to IF statements found in other languages. A developer can test for a condition with a simple IF statement using the following syntax:

```
CREATE PROCEDURE CheckItemStatus (IN itemnum INT, OUT status CHAR
➡(10))
BEGIN
   DECLARE ObsoleteCode CHAR(1);
   SET status = '';
   SELECT obsolete
          INTO ObsoleteCode
          FROM item
          WHERE item_number = itemnum;
   If ObsoleteCode = 'Y' THEN
          SET status = 'Obsolete';
   END IF;
END
```

In this example, we declare an ObsoleteCode variable and select the obsolete status from the item table for an item matching a given item number. We then return an empty string if the item is obsolete, or obsolete if the item's obsolete status has been checked.

In an either-or scenario, the developer can add an ELSE clause to the IF statement to allow for all other situations. For instance, if you wanted status to be "Active" unless it was determined to be inactive, you could add an ELSE to the syntax as follows:

```
CREATE PROCEDURE CheckItemStatus (IN itemnum INT, OUT status CHAR
➡(10))
BEGIN
   DECLARE ObsoleteCode CHAR(1);
   SELECT obsolete
          INTO ObsoleteCode
          FROM item
          WHERE item_number = itemnum;
```

```
      IF ObsoleteCode = 'Y' THEN
              SET status = 'Obsolete';
      ELSE
              SET status = 'Active';
      END IF;
   END
```

You often need to test a third (or fourth, or fifth) scenario. For this, add an
ELSE IF clause to your existing IF statement, as the following example
illustrates:

```
CREATE PROCEDURE CheckItemStatus (IN itemnum INT, OUT status CHAR
➥(10))
BEGIN
   DECLARE ObsoleteCode CHAR(1);
   SELECT obsolete
           INTO ObsoleteCode
           FROM item
           WHERE item_number = itemnum;
   IF ObsoleteCode = 'Y' THEN
           SET status = 'Obsolete';
   ELSEIF ObsoleteCode = 'N' THEN
           SET status = 'Active';
   ELSE
           SET status = 'Unknown';
   END IF;
END
```

The previous code now tests for active as well as obsolete item status. If an
unknown code is placed in the obsolete column on the item table, the above
procedure will set status to 'Unknown'.

Note

You never need to code an ELSE or an ELSEIF with an IF statement unless the situation warrants it. You can code an ELSEIF clause without coding an ELSE clause.

CASE ... WHEN ... ELSE ... END CASE. When tests are similar, as in the previ-
ous IF statement tests, you can use a CASE structure to test for conditions.
Developers often find that CASE structures are easier to develop and easier to
read than lengthy IF...ELSE IF...ELSE...END IF clauses.
To perform the IF test on the obsolete status of an item, code the following
CASE statement:

```
CREATE PROCEDURE CheckItemStatus (IN itemnum INT, OUT status CHAR
➥(10))
BEGIN
```

```
DECLARE ObsoleteCode CHAR(1);
SELECT obsolete
        INTO ObsoleteCode
        FROM item
        WHERE item_number = itemnum;
CASE  ObsoleteCode
        WHEN  'Y'  THEN
                    SET status = 'Obsolete';
        WHEN  'N'  THEN
                    SET status = 'Active';
        ELSE
                    SET status = 'Unknown';
    END  CASE;
END
```

Branching Instructions

Branching instructions cause the Watcom SQL procedure language to skip over certain areas of code usually based on a condition, or to execute a set of commands in the middle of another set of commands. The two branching instructions in the Watcom SQL Procedural Language are LEAVE and CALL.

LEAVE. LEAVE allows you to end a procedure, or to end a loop with a label. The format for the LEAVE command is as follows:

```
LEAVE label
```

Tip

Examples of the LEAVE command as it relates to loops can be viewed during the discussion of iterative commands described in the "WHILE ... LOOP ... END LOOP" section.

Label is the name of the compound statement or loop that you want to exit. An example of the LEAVE command is as follows:

```
mylabel:
BEGIN
. . .
        IF SQLSTATE <> no_error THEN
                LEAVE mylabel
        END IF
. . .
END
```

CALL. CALL is the command to execute a procedure. Use CALL in ISQLW, inside embedded SQL, or inside one procedure to call another procedure. The format for the CALL statement is as follows:

```
CALL  procedure-name  ( [parameter-name =] expression [ ,... ] )
```

The procedure name is the name of the procedure. The expressions are either constants or variables that correspond to the parameter list of the procedure. The expressions must be in the same order as the corresponding parameter name unless the parameter name is supplied with each parameter.

Using Cursors

Before the discussion of the Watcom SQL Procedural Language can continue, you need a clear understanding of cursors. Queries using the SELECT statement must only return one row when executed inside embedded SQL. To browse through (or process) several rows in a table (or tables) that all meet a specified criteria, you have to use a cursor. A cursor is a temporary table set up by SQL databases to handle SELECTs that return more than one row.

You must first DECLARE the cursors and then OPEN them. Cursor rows are FETCHed one at a time, and then the cursor is CLOSEd. Cursors are available with stored procedures or inside stored procedures.

Declaring Cursors. To declare a cursor, you must use the DECLARE CURSOR command as follows:

```
DECLARE   cursor-name
[ SCROLL ¦ NO SCROLL ¦ DYNAMIC SCROLL ]
CURSOR FOR   select_statement
[ FOR UPDATE ¦ FOR READ ONLY ]
```

- **DECLARE cursor_name.** DECLARE cursor_name allows you to design and name a cursor for later use in your stored procedure (or embedded SQL).

- **SCROLL | NO SCROLL | DYNAMIC SCROLL**. Watcom SQL version 4.0 has added backward scrolling and absolute positioning of a cursor. To only allow traditional scrolling forward, specify NO SCROLL. A cursor declared NO SCROLL is restricted to a FETCH NEXT and FETCH RELATIVE 0 seek. To allow all types of cursor positioning, specify SCROLL or DYNAMIC SCROLL. DYNAMIC SCROLL is the default.

> **Note**
>
> DYNAMIC SCROLL cursors and NO SCROLL cursors have about the same overhead. However, SCROLL is not as efficient as DYNAMIC SCROLL, so only use SCROLL when you need to.
>
> SCROLL is different from DYNAMIC SCROLL in the way SCROLL handles positional UPDATEs and DELETEs. If you don't use positional UPDATEs and DELETEs, then use DYNAMIC SCROLL or NO SCROLL as the scrolling preference in your cursor.
>
> If you do use positional UPDATEs and DELETEs, you still may want to use DYNAMIC SCROLL. Read about positional UPDATEs and DELETEs in the "Positional UPDATEs and DELETEs" section.

▶ See "PREPARE,"
p. 423

- **CURSOR FOR select_statement**. Use CURSOR FOR select_statement to define the SELECT statement used with the procedure. The select_statement can actually be a SELECT command, a string using the PREPARE command, or a call to a procedure that returns a multi-row column listing.

- **FOR UPDATE | FOR READ ONLY**. FOR UPDATE | FOR READ ONLY tells how this cursor is supposed to be used. FOR UPDATE allows the use of positional UPDATEs and DELETEs.

OPENing Cursors. After declaring a cursor, you must OPEN it. OPENing a cursor executes the select_statement found in the cursor declaration and stores the results in a temporary buffer. The format for the OPEN command is as follows:

```
OPEN  cursor-name
[USING DESCRIPTOR  sqlda-name | USING host-variable,]
[WITH HOLD ]
[ ISOLATION LEVEL n ]
[ BLOCK n ]
```

- **OPEN cursor–name**. OPEN cursor-name allows you to identify the cursor (DECLAREd earlier) you want to open. The OPEN clause is the only required clause in the OPEN statement. By OPENing a cursor, the select_statement defined in the DECLARE statement for this cursor executes.

- **USING DESCRIPTOR sqlda–name | USING host–variable**. The USING clause allows the developer to declare a SQLDA (SQL Descriptor Area) to store the information about the cursor. The USING clause is only available in embedded SQL and not usable inside stored procedures.

- **WITH HOLD**. WITH HOLD keeps the cursor active for subsequent transactions until disconnected from the database.

◀ See "Maintaining Consistency and Integrity through Isolation Levels," p. 276

- **ISOLATION LEVEL n**. ISOLATION LEVEL n allows you to set the isolation level for this cursor.

- **BLOCK n**. In multiuser environments (networks), cursors retrieve multiple rows at a time. The number of rows retrieved depends on the size of the row and the size of the transmission size set by your network administrator.

BLOCK n overrides the default block to retrieve a given number of rows at a time. If you know the number of rows and intend to process them at once, specifying BLOCK can increase your efficiency.

FETCHing a Cursor Row. The FETCH command retrieves a single row from a cursor. The syntax for the FETCH command is as follows:

```
FETCH [position] cursor-name
[USING DESCRIPTOR sqlda-name]
INTO variable-list
[PURGE]
[BLOCK n]
[FOR UPDATE]
```

- **FETCH [position] cursor-name.** FETCH [position] cursor-name retrieves a row from the cursor after the cursor is OPEN. position defaults to NEXT, which allows sequential processing of the cursor. position can also be PRIOR to retrieve the prior row in the cursor, FIRST to retrieve the first row in the cursor, or LAST to retrieve the last row in the cursor.

  You can use RELATIVE row-count for the position to indicate what position is relative to the current row of the cursor. RELATIVE can be positive to move further down the cursor, or negative to move up the cursor. A row_count of 0 re-retrieves the current row.

  ABSOLUTE row-count can be used as the position to retrieve the row at the absolute row_count relative to the start of the cursor. If row_count is negative, ABSOLUTE retrieves the row that is at the absolute row count relative to the last row in the cursor.

- **USING DESCRIPTOR sqlda-name.** USING DESCRIPTOR sqlda-name allows you to use a predefined SQLDA area. This clause is used only with embedded SQL and not with stored procedures.

- **INTO variable-list.** INTO variable-list lets you declare the target variables where the results of the select_statement are defined in the DECLARE PROCEDURE command.

> **Caution**
>
> Each variable in the variable_list must match each column in the SELECT statement in both size and data type. If the variables don't match, you receive an error.

- **PURGE**. PURGE flushes all Watcom SQL buffers before executing the FETCH command. Use it for embedded SQL only and not with stored procedures.

- **BLOCK n**. BLOCK n instructs Watcom SQL to block the transactions using n as the number of rows to block. This clause is for embedded SQL only and not used with stored procedures.

- **FOR UPDATE**. FOR UPDATE indicates you should use this cursor to allow updates to a row using the UPDATE WHERE CURRENT OF CURSOR statement.

CLOSEing a Cursor. Every cursor that is OPENed should also be CLOSEd when cursor processing is finished. CLOSE deallocates memory used to process the cursor. To CLOSE a cursor, use the following syntax:

```
CLOSE cursor_name
```

Cursor_name can be the name of the cursor or a variable containing the name of the cursor.

Caution

Don't forget to close your cursor. Not only is the memory allocated by a cursor not released unless a CLOSE is issued, but an OPEN ... FOR UPDATE can lock other users from database tables.

Cursor Processing through PowerBuilder. Generating cursors can be time-consuming and tedious. PowerBuilder has a cursor generator, known as the *cursor painter*, that allows you to develop bug-free complex cursors graphically, while providing you with instant access to all your database tables and columns.

Note

Although not part of stored procedures, developing cursors through PowerBuilder is an easy and bug-free way to write declare statements through cursors. However, a certain knowledge of PowerBuilder is assumed for this section. For a clear, comprehensive coverage of PowerBuilder, check out Que's *Special Edition Using PowerBuilder*, by Charles Wood. It's the definitive work on PowerBuilder 4.

 The following example uses a sales database to select all customers who ordered more than $100 from my company. Ordinarily, coding this cursor would be difficult and time-consuming. However, using the PowerBuilder cursor painter, our job eases up considerably.

To open the cursor painter, you first open an event or function in an object. After you do this, choose **D**eclare, **I**nstance Variables (see fig. 12.2).

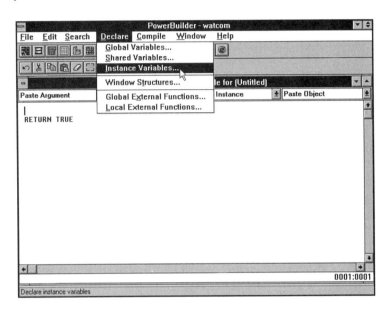

Fig. 12.2
You enter your PowerBuilder cursor painter through your instance, shared, or global variable declarations.

When the Declare Instance Variables dialog box opens, double-click the cursor icon, as shown in figure 12.3. This opens the PowerBuilder cursor painter.

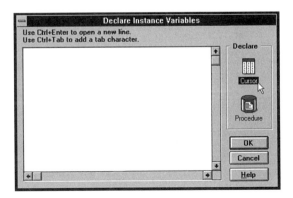

Fig. 12.3
You can paint both cursor and procedure declarations inside your instance, shared, and global variable painters.

Now, PowerBuilder displays the SQL painter that it used to paint SQL commands used in PowerBuilder queries and DataWindows, as seen in figure 12.4. In the SQL painter, choose the tables you want to use in a query.

Fig. 12.4

You use the SQL painter to define any SQL construct (including cursors) inside PowerBuilder.

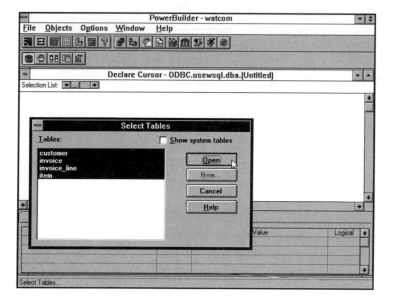

Now choose what tables you want to use. I definitely need the customer table because I'm selecting customer names. I need to know what items each customer bought so I can compute the price; therefore, I also need the item table. Finally, because I need to join the selling prices to the customers, I need to include all tables used to relate a customer with an item. In this case, I need to include the invoice and invoice_line tables.

After you choose your tables, choose **O**pen. Figure 12.5 shows how each table's columns display. I can choose what columns I want to add to my cursor.

Using the SQL toolbox at the bottom of the window, you can also define GROUP BY clauses (GROUP BY customer_name), HAVING clauses (HAVING SUM(selling_price) > 100), and computed columns (SUM(selling_price)). Of course, you can use the usual WHERE and ORDER BY clauses as well, but this exercise doesn't call for them.

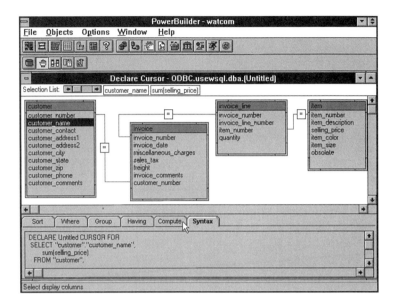

Fig. 12.5
Using your cursor painter, you can define the SELECT statement needed for your cursor.

When you're finished graphically "painting" your SQL definition, click the Design button. PowerBuilder returns your cursor to the instance painter. The Save Declare Cursor dialog box appears, and you can save your cursor (see fig. 12.6).

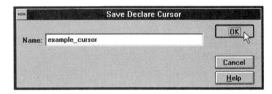

Fig. 12.6
Type the cursor name in the Save Declare Cursor dialog box.

You return to the Declare Instance Variables dialog box with the DECLARE CURSOR statement already coded for you, as shown in figure 12.7. Because the DECLARE CURSOR is coded and bug-free by the time you get it, you save a lot of time using the cursor painter.

An Example of Cursor Processing. You may wonder why the cursor painter is discussed in the middle of a stored procedures section. The answer is that you can use the cursor you declared inside a stored procedure with a simple cut and paste using the Windows Clipboard.

Tip
Cut and paste a cursor declaration from an instance (or shared or global) variable painter to a local function or event; it is then processed as a local cursor.

Fig. 12.7

The cursor painter can paint a complex cursor statement in a fraction of the time it takes you to code and test it.

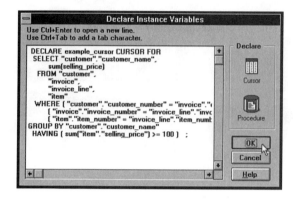

The following code segment shows a cursor written using the PowerBuilder cursor painter:

```
DECLARE example_cursor CURSOR FOR
    SELECT "customer"."customer_name",
           sum(selling_price)
    FROM   "customer",
           "invoice",
           "invoice_line",
           "item"
    WHERE ( "customer"."customer_number" =
"invoice"."customer_number" ) and
           ( "invoice"."invoice_number" =
"invoice_line"."invoice_number" ) and
           ( "item"."item_number" = "invoice_line"."item_number" )
    GROUP BY "customer"."customer_name"
    HAVING ( sum("item"."selling_price") >= 100 );
```

It takes about five minutes to paint this statement. To write it from scratch could take as many as several hours, when you consider testing. You can now add the simpler processing code around the statement for use in a stored procedure. The following stored procedure returns the sum of sales of all customers who have bought more than $100 of merchandise:

```
CREATE PROCEDURE GetBigCustomers (OUT total_sales DECIMAL )
BEGIN
    DECLARE no_error EXCEPTION FOR SQLSTATE '00000';
    DECLARE current_sales DECIMAL;
    DECLARE name_holder CHAR(30);
    DECLARE example_cursor CURSOR FOR
        SELECT "customer"."customer_name",
               sum(selling_price)
        FROM   "customer",
               "invoice",
               "invoice_line",
               "item"
        WHERE ( "customer"."customer_number" =
"invoice"."customer_number" ) and
```

```
                            ( "invoice"."invoice_number" =
"invoice_line"."invoice_number" ) and
                            ( "item"."item_number" =
"invoice_line"."item_number" )
              GROUP BY "customer"."customer_name"
              HAVING ( sum("item"."selling_price") >= 100 );
        OPEN example_cursor;
        SET total_sales = 0;
        FETCH example_cursor INTO name_holder, current_sales;
        WHILE SQLSTATE = no_error LOOP
              SET total_sales = total_sales + current_sales;
              FETCH example_cursor INTO name_holder, current_sales;
        END LOOP;
    END
```

As you can see from the previous code, the cursor painter generated the majority of the code inside PowerBuilder. You can often manage your Watcom SQL database better by using PowerBuilder in conjunction with Watcom SQL.

Positional UPDATEs and DELETEs. Often when scrolling through a cursor, you may want to either alter or erase the related row from a table. SQL allows you to easily do this through a positional DELETE or a positional UPDATE. A positional UPDATE or positional DELETE alters the contents of the table row associated with a cursor row.

A *positional statement* contains the clause WHERE CURRENT OF cursor_name. The syntax for a positional DELETE and a positional UPDATE is as follows:

```
DELETE FROM invoice_line WHERE CURRENT OF example_cursor;
UPDATE table-list
      SET column1 = value1, column2 = value2, . . .,
      WHERE CURRENT OF cursor;
```

> **Note**
>
> You can also use a user-defined SQLDA area to perform a positional UPDATE, but not in a stored procedure. Using a user-defined SQLDA is complicated, hard to maintain, usually not necessary, and beyond the scope of this book.

For instance, if you want to DELETE a row currently being accessed by the example cursor, use this command:

```
DELETE FROM invoice_line WHERE CURRENT OF example_cursor;
```

If you want to mark the item currently being accessed by a cursor as `obsolete` (using the example cursor), use the following command:

```
UPDATE item
      SET obsolete = 'Y'
      WHERE CURRENT OF example_cursor;
```

After a positional UPDATE, an application must FETCH the row again before you can do another UPDATE or DELETE. An update to any column causes a warning/error, even if the cursor doesn't reference the column.

SCROLL and DYNAMIC SCROLL are identical unless you use a positioned UPDATE or a positioned DELETE on a row. When you specify SCROLL, positioned DELETEs leave a "hole" in the cursor. If, using dynamic scrolling techniques, the row in question is FETCHed again, it returns a SQLSTATE_NO_CURRENT_ROW error. DYNAMIC SCROLL does not keep deleted records on the cursor, but then cursor positions of certain rows change with every positioned DELETE.

Note

Cursors defined and compiled using Watcom SQL version 3.0 are equivalent to DYNAMIC SCROLL cursors in version 4.0.

In addition, a fetch on a SCROLL cursor returns a SQLSTATE_ROW_UPDATED_WARNING warning if you updated that row with a positional UPDATE since the last FETCH on the cursor.

If some other user updated a row since the FETCH but before the positioned UPDATE or DELETE, a SQLSTATE_ROW_UPDATED_SINCE_READ error occurs, and the row does not update.

Iterative (Looping) Expressions

A developer often wants to execute the same set of code until it meets a certain condition. This is done through iterative expressions, also known as *loops*. There are two types of loops used in the Watcom SQL Procedural Language—WHILE loops and FOR loops.

WHILE … LOOP … END LOOP. The major looping construct of the Watcom SQL Procedural Language is the LOOP…END LOOP construct. The format for the LOOP command is as follows:

```
[LBL:]
[WHILE condition] LOOP
      statement-list
END LOOP [LBL]
```

LOOP and END LOOP surround a statement-list that's one or more SQL statements. LBL is an optional label that identifies the loop. If LBL is defined, the developer can use the LEAVE command to exit the loop. To use the LEAVE command, however, LBL has to be defined before the LOOP clause, as well as added to the end of the END LOOP clause. The WHILE condition clause terminates the loop if the condition declared is not true.

> **Note**
>
> If the WHILE clause is not included in a LOOP statement, an infinite loop will result. An *infinite loop* is a loop that continues executing but never terminates. You can get around the infinite loop by coding a LEAVE statement inside the LOOP.

Two examples of stored procedures that execute a cursor follow. The following example (which you saw during the cursor discussion) uses the WHILE clause to test for an SQL error. When the loop hits an SQL error, it terminates.

```
. . .
DECLARE no_error EXCEPTION FOR SQLSTATE '00000';
. . .
FETCH example_cursor INTO name_holder, current_sales;
WHILE SQLSTATE = no_error LOOP
      SET total_sales = total_sales + current_sales;
      FETCH example_cursor INTO name_holder, current_sales;
END LOOP;
. . .
```

You could accomplish the same task by avoiding the WHILE clause and using a LEAVE command to exit the loop:

```
. . .
myloop:
LOOP
      FETCH example_cursor INTO name_holder, current_sales;
      IF SQLSTATE = no_error THEN
            LEAVE myloop
      END IF
      SET total_sales = total_sales + current_sales;
END LOOP myloop;
. . .
```

> **Note**
>
> Most developers end up preferring a loop with the WHILE clause over an infinite loop with a LEAVE clause. WHILE clauses are always at the beginning of a loop and tend to make the loop easier to understand. Also, infinite loops that lock the system are less likely when using a WHILE clause.

FOR loops

FOR loops are different in stored procedures than in other languages. Using stored procedures, a FOR loop combines iteration with cursor processing. The format for a FOR statement is as follows:

```
[LBL:]
FOR  for-loop-name  AS  cursor-name CURSOR FOR  statement
        [ FOR UPDATE ¦ FOR READ ONLY ]
        DO
                statement-list
END  FOR  [LBL]
```

The following is a WHILE statement:

```
. . .
DECLARE example2_cursor CURSOR FOR
        SELECT "customer"."customer_name"
                FROM  "customer";
FETCH example2_cursor INTO name_holder;
WHILE SQLSTATE = no_error LOOP
        SET total_customers = total_customers + 1;
        FETCH example2_cursor INTO name_holder;
END LOOP;
. . .
```

It can be written more concisely with the following FOR statement:

```
FOR  for-loop-name  AS  example_cursor2 CURSOR FOR  SELECT
➥"customer"."customer_name" FROM "customer";
        DO
                SET total_customers = total_customers + 1;
END  FOR
```

The FOR loop automatically terminates when the cursor is finished processing. After you get used to the FOR statement, FOR becomes a clear and easy way to combine a cursor with a loop.

Error Handling

Every language has some means to handle unexpected situations, and the Watcom SQL procedure language is no exception. There are many ways to track errors in Watcom SQL, and many levels of error correction.

TRACEBACK(*). If you don't code any error exception handling, you can still see what made your procedure stop by using the TRACEBACK (*) function. The command

```
SELECT TRACEBACK(*) FROM dummy;
```

returns a list of procedures and triggers that were executed before the error occurred.

EXCEPTION ... WHEN   WHEN OTHERS ... RESIGNAL. We have already
used the DECLARE statement to declare an error situation with the following
command:

```
DECLARE not_found EXCEPTION FOR SQLSTATE '02000';
```

In the previous statement, you declare the not_found variable to be the
SQLSTATE of '02000'. After you declare the exception, you can use the exception with an IF test:

```
. . .
IF SQLSTATE = not_found THEN
      LEAVE loop
END IF
. . .
```

The previous method works with warnings. However, if serious errors occur,
your procedure immediately terminates unless you declared an EXCEPTION
section in your procedure. An EXCEPTION section allows you to trap serious
errors or warnings and handle them appropriately.

The EXCEPTION section in a procedure begins with the EXCEPTION declaration:

```
. . .
BEGIN
      DECLARE row_not_found EXCEPTION FOR SQLSTATE '02000';
      DECLARE column_not_found EXCEPTION FOR SQLSTATE '52003';
. . .
      procedure logic goes here
. . .
      EXCEPTION
            WHEN row_not_found THEN
                  row not found logic goes here
            WHEN column_not_found THEN
                  column not found logic goes here
            WHEN OTHERS THEN
                  RESIGNAL.
END
```

When your procedure logic encounters an error exception, your procedure
branches to the EXCEPTION declaration. The EXCEPTION declaration consists of several WHEN statements that handle the logic for specific errors.

The WHEN OTHERS THEN clause is executed for all other exceptions. The
RESIGNAL command returns the error to Watcom SQL so that the default
error procedures in the database can take place.

If an EXCEPTION clause is not coded, you must test immediately after each
SQL statement. Declaring an EXCEPTION can save some time, especially with
large procedures.

SIGNAL. The SIGNAL command lets you force an error exception. You can use SIGNAL to generate your own specific errors. SIGNAL lets your procedure pretend that an error occurred. The format for the SIGNAL command is as follows:

```
SIGNAL exception-condition
```

The exception-condition is a user-defined exception. For instance, the lines

```
DECLARE column_not_found EXCEPTION FOR SQLSTATE '52003';
. . .
SIGNAL column_not_found
```

force a `column_not_found` error on your procedure.

Returning Result Sets

Procedures can also return *result sets*. A result set is a series of rows returned by a procedure. In this manner, a procedure acts as a type of cursor to the calling procedure or program.

You then need to execute the following CREATE PROCEDURE statement so that `items_purchased()` can be called:

```
CREATE PROCEDURE items_purchased()        RESULT (item_description
CHAR (30), customer_name CHAR(30))
      BEGIN
            SELECT  "item". "item_description",
"customer"."customer_name"
            FROM    "item" , "invoice_line",   "invoice",
"customer"
            WHERE ( "item"."item_number" =
"invoice_line"."item_number" ) and
                ( "invoice"."invoice_number" =
"invoice_line"."invoice_number" ) and
                    ( "customer"."customer_number" =
"invoice"."customer_number" );
      END
```

The previous routine returns a *single result set*. A single result set returns related values of a singular nature. In this case, `items_purchased()` returns all item descriptions and the name of the customer who purchased them.

It is also possible to return a multiple result set, in which the two sets of columns returned are unrelated. Consider the following rewrite of `items_purchased()` (now called `items_purchased2()`):

```
CREATE PROCEDURE items_purchased2()
    RESULT (item_description CHAR (30), customer_name CHAR(30))
    BEGIN
        SELECT "item","item_description" FROM  "item";
        SELECT "customer"."customer_name" FROM "customer";
    END
```

The previous procedure returns a list of items and a list of customers. The SELECT statements are performed simultanenously, but the items and customers that are returned from the procedure are not related.

> **Caution**
>
> Multiple result sets are hardly ever used. The problem with using a multiple result set is that the FETCH used to retrieve the columns starts retrieving NULLs when it runs out of one column's values.

Using Procedures Inside PowerBuilder

Watcom SQL procedures can be accessed from PowerBuilder via several different methods. This section discusses how PowerBuilder can guide you through calling a stored procedure from PowerScript, how PowerBuilder can let you "paint" a cursor that uses a procedure, and how you can use a procedure as your DataWindow data source.

Calling a Procedure from PowerScript

PowerBuilder will let you declare a stored procedure inside your PowerScript to retrieve information using a procedure call. To declare a procedure, you can use the SQL painter. Click on the SQL Paste icon to open the SQL Statement Type dialog box, as seen in figure 12.8.

Double-click on Declare in the Procedure group box. This opens the Select Procedure dialog box shown in figure 12.9.

In the Select Procedure dialog box, choose the procedure that you want to call, and click OK. This will open the Parameters dialog box shown in figure 12.10.

After entering values for each of the parameters used in the procedure, click on OK. This opens the Save Declare Procedure dialog box shown in figure 12.11.

Fig. 12.8
The SQL Statement Type dialog box lets you choose what type of SQL statement you want to paint using the PowerBuilder SQL painter.

Fig. 12.9
The Select Procedure dialog box displays all the procedures for a database and their source code.

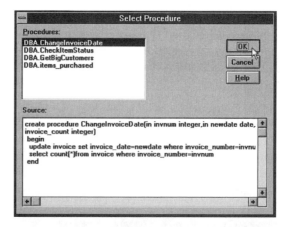

Fig. 12.10
Enter the program variables used to call the procedure using the Parameters dialog box.

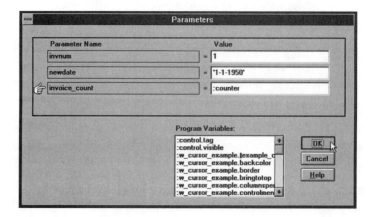

Fig. 12.11
Name your
procedure using
the Save Declare
Procedure dialog
box.

After entering the name of your procedure and clicking Yes, return to the painter with your procedure defined. Now, you have your procedure defined. Add any variables used in the declaration and an EXECUTE statement to actually call the procedure you declared, and you'll have a working stored procedure from within Watcom SQL. The following code is the result of a painted procedure declaration and two added lines (in bold):

```
long counter;

DECLARE ChgInvDate PROCEDURE FOR ChangeInvoiceDate
        invnum = 1,
        newdate = '1-1-1950',
        invoice_count = :counter  ;

EXECUTE ChgInvDate;
```

▶ See "GRANT,"
p. 555

Troubleshooting

When I try to save the PowerScript containing my procedure call, I keep getting a message similar to this error message:

```
Database Warning C0038: SQLSTATE = 37000
[WATCOM][ODBC Driver]Syntax error: near 'dba' in
[dba].ChangeInvoiceDate...
```

I did exactly what you said! What went wrong?

Many times, you'll use Watcom SQL as a stand-alone environment for development. If this is the case, you probably didn't define security for your database and use the default user ID of dba, which is also a keyword that can be used in the GRANT command. As a result, Watcom returns an error to PowerBuilder, saying that you can't use the keyword dba in this command.

To get around this, either type **"dba"** in quotes, or delete the user ID from the procedure name.

Of course, you could just type in the cursor declaration without using the SQL painter, but the SQL painter delivers a syntactically correct procedure with development speed that is hard to match.

Using a Procedure as a Cursor in PowerScript

In addition to explicitly EXECUTEing a procedure in PowerScript, you can also declare a procedure as a cursor. A procedure with a RESULT set defined can return many rows of information, and therefore is treated identically to a cursor using Watcom SQL.

To declare a procedure as a cursor, click on **D**eclare on the menu bar, and then choose **G**lobal Variables, **S**hared Variables, or **I**nstance Variables. This opens a Declare Instance Variables dialog box (or the Declare Shared Variables dialog box, or the Declare Global Variables dialog box), as seen in figure 12.12.

Fig. 12.12

The Declare Instance Variables dialog box is used to declare instance variables, or to enter the cursor or procedure painters.

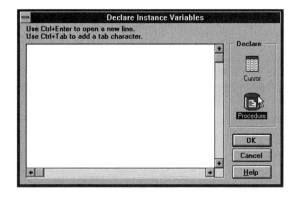

Double-click on Procedure to enter the procedure painter. You should once more see the Select Procedure dialog box, as seen in figure 12.13. Click on the procedure you want to use for a cursor, and then click on OK.

Caution

Be sure the procedure you want to use for a cursor has a RESULT set defined. Otherwise, you can only use the procedure as a callable function, as defined in the "Calling a Procedure from PowerScript" section.

The Save Declare Procedure dialog box appears, as seen in figure 12.11. Here, enter the name you want to call your cursor, and click on Yes. PowerBuilder will then return your cursor declaration to your Instance Variable Declaration dialog box, similar to the following declaration:

```
DECLARE ItemsPurchased PROCEDURE FOR items_purchased  ;
```

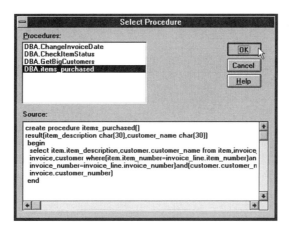

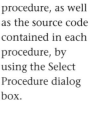

Fig. 12.13
You can view each procedure, as well as the source code contained in each procedure, by using the Select Procedure dialog box.

> **Caution**
>
> Once more, if you are using **"dba",** you will receive the following message when you try to save your instance variable:
>
> ```
> Database Warning C0038: SQLSTATE = 37000
> [WATCOM][ODBC Driver]Syntax error: near 'dba' in [dba].items_purchased
> ```
>
> To get around this, do what I did in the example above and delete the user ID (dba) from the procedure declaration or place **"dba"** in quotes.

Now, return to the function or event that you want to use as a procedure. You can now use the SQL painter. Click on the SQL Paste icon to open the SQL Statement Type dialog box. Double-click on Fetch in the Procedure group box, as shown in figure 12.14.

This will open the Select Declared Procedure dialog box, shown in figure 12.15. Your declared procedure should be listed here.

Click on the declared procedure you want to use as a cursor and click on OK. PowerBuilder will then open the Into Variables dialog box, shown in figure 12.16.

The SQL painter then returns to your function or event with a working FETCH statement, although you still have to add the appropriate DECLARE, OPEN, and CLOSE commands for the cursor (in bold):

```
string item_description
string customer_name
DECLARE ItemsPurchased CURSOR FOR CALL items_purchased() ;

OPEN ItemsPurchased;
```

Fig. 12.14
The SQL Statement Type dialog box allows you to paint SQL procedure commands using the PowerBuilder SQL painter.

Fig. 12.15
The Select Declared Procedure dialog box shows all procedures that have been declared in the Declare Instance (or Shared, or Global) Variable dialog box.

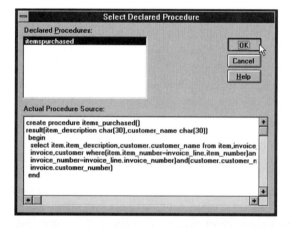

Fig. 12.16
The Into Variables dialog box allows you to declare your variables used in the FETCH.

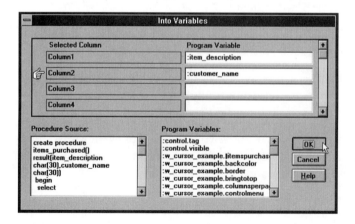

```
// ...
   FETCH itemspurchased
    INTO :item_description,
         :customer_name  ;
// ...
CLOSE itemspurchased;
```

> **Note**
>
> Notice that we still have to DECLARE our procedure with a DECLARE CURSOR state-
> ment. PowerBuilder's DECLARE statement returned from the SQL painter is only used
> so we can paint our FETCH:
>
>   DECLARE ItemsPurchased PROCEDURE FOR items_purchased ;
>
> To use an OPEN statement, you must have a DECLARE CURSOR statement. If you use
> the SQL painter to paint your declaration, you must name your cursor with the same
> name as your declaration.

Using a Procedure as a Data Source for a DataWindow

You can also use a procedure as a read-only data source for a DataWindow in
PowerBuilder. To declare your DataWindow, click on the DataWindow icon.
This will open the Select DataWindow dialog box seen in figure 12.17.

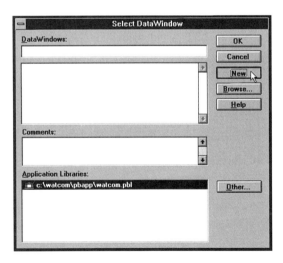

Fig. 12.17
You choose to
create a new
DataWindow or
edit an existing
DataWindow
in the Select
DataWindow
dialog box.

Click on New. This will open the New DataWindow dialog box seen in
figure 12.18.

Fig. 12.18

The New
DataWindow
dialog box lets you
determine the
type and data
source of your
data window.

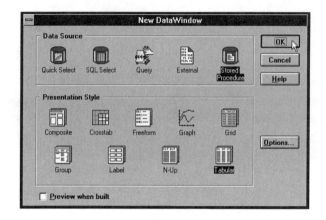

Click on Stored Procedure as your data source, and then pick one of the presentation styles. Then click on OK. The Select Stored Procedure dialog box,
seen in figure 12.19, opens. Choose your procedure, and click on OK.

Fig. 12.19

The Select Stored
Procedure dialog
box lists all stored
procedures
available for your
DataWindow
source.

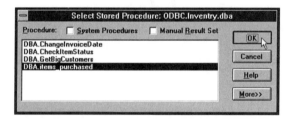

Finally, your DataWindow painter is opened with the appropriate columns
from your procedure RESULT set placed on your data window, as shown in
figure 12.20. From here, you use this DataWindow like any other except that
no updates are allowed.

Using Triggers

Triggers are a lot like stored procedures because they are developed using the
same Watcom SQL procedure language. However, triggers are *event driven* as
opposed to *function driven*. Function driven modules (such as stored procedures) require an explicit call to execute. Event driven modules (such as triggers) occur when an event takes place. Often, the developer has no idea that
a trigger is being executed.

Examples of events that could execute a trigger are when a row in a particular
table gets deleted or when a specific column gets modified. If a trigger was

defined for this event, then the trigger gets executed automatically. This can aid the Database Administrator in maintaining data integrity and audit tracking.

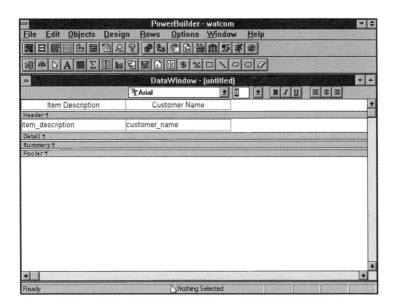

Fig. 12.20
You can manipulate the format of the newly created DataWindow from the DataWindow painter.

Another key difference between triggers and procedures is that procedures are GRANTed authority based on functionality. Triggers take their authority from the table to which they are assigned.

> **Caution**
>
> Your procedure or trigger can fail if a trigger that you have access to calls a procedure that you don't have access to.

Types of Triggers

There are four types of trigger events:

Trigger Event	Description
INSERT	INSERT triggers are executed if a row is inserted into a table associated with the trigger.
DELETE	DELETE triggers are executed if a row is deleted from the table associated with the trigger.

(continues)

Trigger Event	Description
UPDATE	UPDATE triggers are executed if a row is updated in the table associated with the trigger.
Column UPDATE	Column UPDATE triggers are executed if a column or columns in the table associated with the trigger is UPDATEd.

Each trigger can be executed before or after the trigger event.

Creating and Deleting Triggers

Use the CREATE TRIGGER command to create a trigger and associate a table with it. The syntax for the CREATE TRIGGER command is as follows:

```
CREATE TRIGGER trigger_name
      trigger_time
      trigger_event
      [ORDER num]
      ON table_name
      [REFERENCING OLD AS old_name]
      [REFERENCING NEW AS new_name]
      FOR EACH ROW [WHEN search_condition]
      compound_statement
```

■ **trigger_name**. `Trigger_name` is the name of the trigger; it's used for referencing.

■ **trigger_time**. `Trigger_time` can be BEFORE or AFTER. `Trigger_time` indicates whether your trigger occurs before or after the desired `trigger_event`.

■ **trigger_event**. `Trigger_event` is the event of the trigger. Valid values are INSERT, DELETE, UPDATE, or UPDATE OF column_list. The column_list is a list of columns on the associated table that, when modified, start the trigger.

■ **ORDER num**. `ORDER num` is an optional clause. Use it to order the execution of the triggers if more than one trigger will execute at one time.

■ **ON table_name**. `ON table_name` is a required clause that associates the trigger with a table.

■ **REFERENCING OLD AS old_name**. `REFERENCING OLD AS old_name` lets you use old values (before `trigger_event`) in your `compound_statement`. This has no effect on nor is affected by `trigger_time`.

- **REFERENCING NEW AS new_name**. REFERENCING NEW AS new_name lets you use new values (after trigger_event) in your compound_statement. This has no effect on nor is affected by trigger_time.

- **WHEN search_condition**. WHEN search_condition lets you run a trigger only if a certain condition evaluates to TRUE.

- **compound_statement**. compound_statement allows you to define a procedure that occurs when this trigger is executed.

An example of the CREATE TRIGGER command is as follows:

```
CREATE TRIGGER audit_trail BEFORE UPDATE OF salary
      ON payroll_table
      REFERENCING OLD AS old_payroll
FOR EACH ROW
BEGIN
      CALL INSERT_INTO_AUDIT_TRAIL (old_payroll.name,
old_payroll.salary, old_payroll_date)
END
```

This example calls an audit trail procedure to record old salaries if the salary on the payroll table is modified.

Triggers remain on the database until they are deleted or dropped. To drop a trigger, use the DROP TRIGGER command as follows:

```
DROP TRIGGER triggername
```

From Here...

This chapter took a comprehensive look at stored procedures. For more information, check out the following sources:

- Chapter 17, "Performance Tuning," provides performance tuning tips and techniques from David Yach, the Watcom Vice President and co-developer of Watcom 1.0. No one knows more about the inside of Watcom SQL.

- Chapter 22, "SQL Commands," contains of listing of all SQL, most of which you can use in a stored procedure.

- Appendix C, "Database Error Messages," gives a description of SQLSTATE and error codes. This is useful when developing your procedures.

IV

Interfaces

Chapter 13

Implementing Watcom SQL with PowerBuilder

by Mike Seals

Imagine this scenario: you open your new PowerBuilder or InfoMaker package and discover that Watcom SQL 4.0 is bundled with it for *free*. You distinctly remember that old adage, "You get what you pay for," and because you didn't pay anything extra for Watcom, you're suddenly suspicious. "How powerful could it be, anyway?"

Well, as you have learned in this book, Watcom SQL is a powerful relational database management package with features that rival the top-of-the-line Relational Database Management Systems (RDBMS). Applications developed in PowerBuilder or InfoMaker can be distributed with a run-time version on Watcom, making the pair a powerful platform for developing any number of useful applications.

You can scale up the applications you develop with this pair of power tools to a multi-user server version without changing any code because the single-user and server versions share the exact same SQL syntax, stored procedures, and table layouts. Your clients, in-house or out, can scale your application up to DOS, Windows, Windows NT, OS/2, QNX, or Netware NLM server implementations of Watcom SQL.

> **Note**
>
> Your clients must purchase their own copies of these Watcom multi-user servers. The single-user version that comes bundled with PowerBuilder is the only one that can be distributed royalty-free.

Watcom SQL allows you to develop a single PowerBuilder application that can access any of these Watcom Server implementations simply by making changes to a database profile (in an INI file).

Developing in an RDBMS that offers this range of scalability allows you to offer solutions to your clients that are likely to fit within their existing systems.

You're beginning to think that Watcom may be *the* development platform of choice for scalable applications, and you want to create an application in PowerBuilder that uses Watcom as the underlying database. "Just tell me what I need to know to get these things to work together!"

Well, it *is* fairly easy to get a Watcom database application up and running quickly. In fact, you can do this in PowerBuilder while writing only a few lines of code. In this chapter, you'll create the database equivalent of the "hello world" application common in many programming tutorials. This is the minimum amount of code and objects needed to create a database maintenance application in PowerBuilder using Watcom as the database.

In this chapter, you learn how to:

- Install the single-user version of Watcom SQL from the PowerBuilder installation disk(s).

- Set up a PowerBuilder application framework on which to build the examples.

- Set up a connection "profile" to an existing Watcom SQL database (the demo database) from within PowerBuilder.

- Use the PowerBuilder Database Administration Painter to create a new table in the currently selected database.

- Create a datawindow and tie it to several Watcom tables using the DataWindow Painter.

- Create a minimum application including the datawindow just created.

- Upgrade existing Watcom databases from version 3.2 to version 4.0.

Installing the Single-User Version of Watcom SQL from the PowerBuilder Installation Disks

A single-user version of Watcom SQL 4.0 comes bundled with PowerBuilder Desktop and Enterprise Editions, as well as with InfoMaker. All of these products also include a sample database and a sample application.

The examples in this chapter assume that you have Watcom 4.0 and the sample database installed. While I will not refer to the sample application itself, it includes many examples of well-written PowerBuilder code, and is probably worth the hard disk real estate investment of 10M. PowerBuilder *requires* a current application before you can open any painter. If you install the code examples, PowerBuilder opens to the sample application by default.

The easiest way to install the version of Watcom SQL that comes with these tools is to accept the default installation settings. By default, when these tools are installed, the single-user version of Watcom SQL will also be installed, along with a sample Watcom database.

You can choose to prevent it from being installed by removing it from the options screen. If you have already installed PowerBuilder without Watcom, follow these steps to install Watcom by itself:

1. Insert the PowerBuilder installation CD-ROM or the first installation disk.

2. From the Program Manager window, choose **F**ile, **R**un. The Program Managers Run dialog box displays.

3. Click the **B**rowse button. This displays a standard Windows dialog box that you probably recognize.

4. Select the path to the disk you inserted in step 1. The SETUP.EXE file appears in the file list.

5. Select the file named SETUP.EXE, and click **O**K.

6. In the Program Manager's Run dialog box, click OK. You will be running the Setup program for PowerBuilder. It looks similar to figure 13.1.

Fig. 13.1
This dialog box displays a list of products that can be installed.

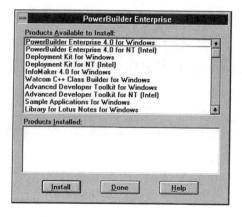

7. Select either PowerBuilder Enterprise 4.0 for Windows or PowerBuilder Desktop 4.0, and then choose **I**nstall. After asking for and confirming your name and company, the installation options window appears (see fig. 13.2).

Fig. 13.2
This window shows the PowerBuilder installation options. The options available might be slightly different if you are installing the desktop version.

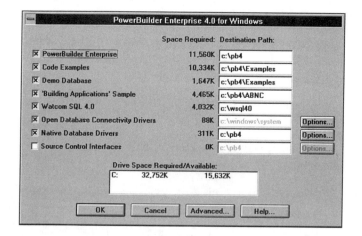

8. The next step is to *deselect* the installation of PowerBuilder, and leave only the installation of Watcom 4.0 and the ODBC deployment kit (because Watcom uses the ODBC interface). Deselect the following checkboxes:

PowerBuilder Enterprise

'Building Applications' Sample

This leaves the following checkboxes selected:

Code Examples

Demo Database

Watcom SQL 4.0

Open Database Connectivity Drivers

Native Database Drivers

9. Click the Options button beside the Destination Path for Native Database Drivers edit box, and make sure that ODBC is the only one selected. Click on OK to return.

10. Click the Options button beside Open Database Connectivity Drivers, and make sure that Watcom SQL is the only one selected.

11. Click the OK button and follow any additional prompts for disks as needed.

You have now installed Watcom SQL 4.0 from the PowerBuilder Setup utility. If you want to go directly to PowerBuilder at this point, you can work in the Powersoft Demo DB database and the sample code application; however, you first need to create an empty library and application object for the following examples.

Setting Up a PowerBuilder Application Object

Start PowerBuilder by double-clicking the PowerBuilder icon.

PowerBuilder

You must specify an application to work in before doing anything in PowerBuilder. If you specified during installation that you wanted to install the sample application, that is what appears when you first open PowerBuilder.

Click the Application painter Powerbar button (see fig. 13.3).

After you are in the Application painter, choose **F**ile, **O**pen.

You are presented with the Select Application Library dialog box.

Fig. 13.3
The PowerBuilder
Powerbar, showing
the Application
painter button on
the far left.

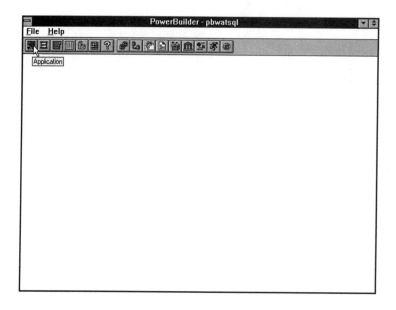

> **Note**
>
> If you chose not to install the sample code, this is the first window to appear. You can
> start following the tutorial here.

Now you can create a new library with an application object to use throughout the rest of this chapter. PowerBuilder 4.0 gives you an easy way to accomplish this by offering to create an application framework when you try to
create a new application.

Type **pbwatsql.pbl** in the File **N**ame edit box, and click OK. Because the
PowerBuilder Library you typed in does not exist, the warning dialog box
shown in figure 13.4 displays.

Fig. 13.4
Because the library
name you typed
does not exist, this
dialog box appears
to offer to create
an application
shell in the new
library file.

You *are* trying to create a new library, so click **Y**es. The dialog box that appears looks similar to the Select Application Library dialog box, but it is for new libraries. Again, type **pbwatsql.pbl** in the File **N**ame edit box, and click OK. The Save Application dialog box appears. Fill in the application name **pbwatsql** and a comment, as illustrated in figure 13.5.

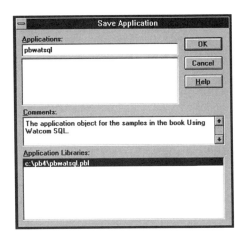

Fig. 13.5
This dialog box allows you to name the application object that will be saved when you press OK, along with a comment containing a description of its purpose.

After you fill in these two fields, click OK. Now PowerBuilder understands that you are creating a new application and offers to create a complete MDI application framework for you (see fig. 13.6). This framework includes several objects that are useful for creating MDI applications, such as an MDI frame window and menu, an MDI sheet window and menu, and an application object with startup code in the application open event.

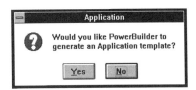

Fig. 13.6
PowerBuilder is offering to save you the time and effort of creating many of the basic objects and code needed to create an MDI application. Choose Yes!

This is one of the nicest new features in PowerBuilder 4.0! It is a great time-saver. Choose **Y**es. You will use this application framework later in this chapter.

PowerBuilder generates a complete MDI application framework in the specified directory. This saves you a lot of time; you can concentrate on using Watcom SQL within PowerBuilder, and not spend your time creating a PowerBuilder application to work in.

Setting Up a PowerBuilder Profile for an Existing Watcom SQL Database

Now that you have installed Watcom SQL 4.0, and created a library and application to work in, you need to get into PowerBuilder and define a database connection to the sample Watcom SQL database you installed. This logical description of a database is called a *database profile*. It is stored as a section in the PowerBuilder PB.INI file. It contains information that tells PowerBuilder how to connect to a database: either through a native database connection or through ODBC.

Native database connections serve as a direct interface between PowerBuilder and a vendor's database. For example, Sybase SQLServer is one of the most popular RDBMSs, so Powersoft includes a direct connection between PowerBuilder and the DBLib interface to SQLServer.

An *ODBC database connection* is used to connect to a database driver that conforms to the Microsoft ODBC specification. ODBC handles the details of routing database calls to the appropriate database server (local or remote) and returning the result.

Database vendors must create an ODBC driver that converts industry standard ODBC calls into the specific commands necessary for their particular database. Its ODBC driver converts the incoming command syntax to the native syntax of the database, and the call is finally processed and returns a result set or generates an error code.

Now that you know a little about how ODBC works, it should be easier for you to configure a Watcom SQL database profile. One was created for you automatically when you installed the sample database. Open it and see what it contains (see fig. 13.7).

Click the Database painter button to display the database selection dialog box if no database has been selected. However, because you installed the sample database in the installation of Watcom SQL, the default database, Powersoft Demo DB database, will already be selected.

> **Note**
>
> This is the first time in this demonstration that the Watcom database engine has been started. Up to now, you have been in PowerBuilder but have not attempted to perform any database operations. So if you receive an error message at this point, you may want to verify that you installed the Sample Database as described in "Installing the Single-user version of Watcom SQL from the PowerBuilder Installation Disks," earlier in this chapter, and that Watcom SQL is installed properly.

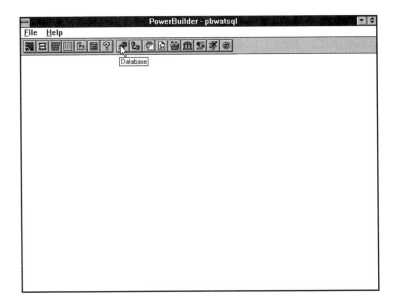

Fig. 13.7
The PowerBuilder
Powerbar,
showing the
pointer on the
database painter
icon.

If all goes well, you will be presented with a list of the tables in the sample database. Verify that these include tables such as contact, customer, and so on. I will get back to this list of tables when I discuss the creation of a new table, later in this chapter. For now, click Cancel. You are left with an empty database painter screen.

Right now, you want to look at the current database profile settings for the PowerBuilder sample database. This will tell you much about how to set up a database profile of your own for a different Watcom SQL database.

Perform the following steps to view the database profile for the sample database:

1. Choose **F**ile, **C**onnect, **S**etup.

2. Choose Powersoft Demo DB from the list in the Database Profiles dialog box that appears (see fig. 13.8).

3. Because you want to view the contents of this profile, click the **E**dit button.

4. Pressing the **E**dit button displays the PowerBuilder Database Profile Setup dialog box. The **M**ore button expands this dialog box to reveal profile-configuration fields used only by ODBC drivers. Because Watcom SQL is accessed through ODBC, you want to see these fields, so click the **M**ore button now. The Watcom SQL sample Database Profile Setup dialog box looks similar to figure 13.9.

Fig. 13.8
Use the PowerBuilder Database Profiles dialog box to select a database profile to view, modify, or connect to.

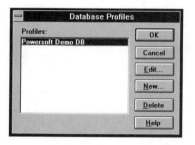

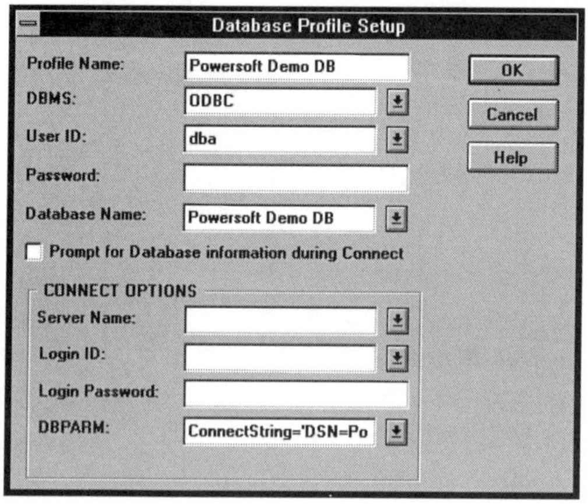

Fig. 13.9
The database profile created in this dialog box allows you to configure a connection to a database, including a user ID and password, and to store it for future use.

Keep in mind that the database profile is for an entire database, in which there will usually be multiple tables. If you create new tables in a database, there is no need to modify the database-connection profile. If you create an entirely new database in PowerBuilder or InfoMaker, a database profile will be created for you. It will simply appear in the list with the other profiles. However, if you create a database from outside PowerBuilder, such as from Watcom's ISQL or ERWin, you must create a profile yourself in order to connect to the database from within PowerBuilder.

Profile Name

This is an arbitrary name given to the *profile.* You have already chosen a database profile from the PowerBuilder Database Profiles dialog box. This profile name is the name that displays in this listbox. If all users have the same privileges in a database, then only one database profile would be required. This is usually the case when you are developing for a local database.

If you had several database scenarios, you would want multiple profiles pointing to the same database. This would be useful when developing for the multi-user server version of Watcom SQL.

While they are creating multi-user database applications, most developers have full access rights to the database they are developing for. The end users, however, may have several restrictions on their database login ID. In this case, the developer can create two profiles for the same database: one that has his own login in the user ID field, and another with a sample user's user ID with restrictions. The profile name for the developer might be called Marketing DB for Developer, while the sample user's profile might be called Marketing DB for User. This would allow the developer to quickly switch back and forth between development and user-testing modes.

If you use several ODBC sources for different projects, you may want to consider adding a prefix as the first few characters of a profile name to indicate what type of database it is, such as DBF for dBASE files and WAT for Watcom files. When you use one ODBC registry for many different projects, this helps you distinguish between them.

DBMS

This field specifies the database interface PowerBuilder must use to access the database for which you are setting up a profile. For Watcom SQL, this field is always ODBC.

User ID

This field specifies the *database* user ID of the user account on the database. For a local Watcom SQL 4.0 database that you created yourself, this user ID is dba. By default, the password is defined as sql. If you intend to use database security in your application, don't forget to change this password before rolling out your new application.

You can leave this field blank, and the ODBC driver will prompt you for a user name.

Password

This is the password associated with the previous user ID. You can leave this field blank, even if a user ID is defined, and the ODBC driver will prompt you for it.

When you type your password into this field, it is displayed as asterisks so that someone in the same room cannot see it.

Database Name

This is the name of the Watcom database as defined in the database's ODBC configuration. It is the Data Source Name in the ODBC configuration screen. You can select from a drop-down list of all ODBC databases currently defined (including non-Watcom ODBC databases) by clicking the arrow beside this field.

Prompt for Database Information During Connect

Checking this box allows you to omit the specific user ID, password, and database information; and force the ODBC driver to prompt for it when a database connection is attempted. If you select this box, it will prompt for a new data source on each attempt to connect to ODBC using this profile, including when you are saving this profile by pressing OK. At that time, you must select a data source to be saved as part of the profile, even if it is just a "dummy" data source that will not be available in the distributed application.

> **Note**
>
> Use the SetTransObject function in your scripts instead of SetTrans if you check this option. The SetTrans function disconnects the PowerBuilder transaction object after each SQL statement, which forces you to specify a database and to log in repeatedly during the execution of your program.

Connect Options

These fields are used by ODBC drivers. The server version of Watcom SQL 4.0 requires that you specify the name of the machine that is acting as the database server, and the user name and password to log onto that machine. You record other configuration parameters for the Watcom SQL ODBC driver that are not specified in the above configuration fields in the DBPARM field. It usually is not necessary to modify this parameter.

Click OK when you are done making changes to a database profile, and PowerBuilder attempts to connect using these parameters. If successful, you return to the Database Profiles dialog box to select a database profile. You were simply looking at an existing profile, but if you were creating a new one, it would now appear in the list of ODBC data sources.

You have already edited an existing database profile. You can also delete an existing profile by highlighting it and pressing the **D**elete button. You can also create an entirely new database profile by clicking on the **N**ew button.

Profile information is stored in the PB.INI file in your PowerBuilder directory. Because an INI file is a standard ASCII text file, you can view its contents via Windows' Notepad application.

The [DBMS_PROFILES] section records the names of all installed profiles. In the example, it looks like this:

```
[DBMS_PROFILES]
CURRENT=
PROFILES='Powersoft Demo DB'
History='Powersoft Demo DB'
```

There is a separate section in the PB.INI file for each profile. The section name is the keyword Profile plus the Profile Name. For our example, it looks like this:

```
[Profile Powersoft Demo DB]
DBMS=ODBC
Database=Powersoft Demo DB
UserId=dba
DatabasePassword=
LogPassword=
ServerName=
LogId=
Lock=
DbParm=ConnectString='DSN=Powersoft Demo DB'
Prompt=0
```

Note the one-to-one relationship between the profile editor fields and the PB.INI file. You can pull this profile information into your PowerBuilder applications in the application open script. Then, if the database moves from a local file to a server, or even to a different database platform, you can simply distribute a new PB.INI file, and they can connect without distributing a new version of the application.

Troubleshooting

How do I establish a database connection from within a PowerBuilder application?

This is usually done in the application open script by retrieving a specific database profile section using PowerBuilder's INI functions. The application framework gives a good example of this. The following code is in the application open script of the application framework created by PowerBuilder 4.0:

(continues)

(continued)

```
/* Populate sqlca from current PB.INI settings */
sqlca.DBMS       = ProfileString ("pb.ini", "database", "dbms",        "")
sqlca.database   = ProfileString ("pb.ini", "database", "database",    "")
sqlca.userid     = ProfileString ("pb.ini", "database", "userid",      "")
sqlca.dbpass     = ProfileString ("pb.ini", "database", "dbpass",      "")
sqlca.logid      = ProfileString ("pb.ini", "database", "logid",       "")
sqlca.logpass    = ProfileString ("pb.ini", "database", "LogPassWord", "")
sqlca.servername = ProfileString ("pb.ini", "database", "servername",  "")
sqlca.dbparm     = ProfileString ("pb.ini", "database", "dbparm",      "")

connect;
```

This code simply pulls the entries out of the current database connection section of the PB.INI file, and assigns them to the appropriate property of the SQLCA default transaction object. You could also point to a specific database connection by changing the string database to the actual name of a database profile section in PB.INI. You could even point to a section in your own application INI file by changing PB.INI to the name of your own INI file, such as MYAPP.INI.

In the PowerBuilder development environment, the currently selected profile is saved in a section called [Database]. This section changes if you select a new database profile. It is used by PowerBuilder to allow it to restore the database environment when you exit and then return. You never need to modify the parameters in the [Database] section of the PB.INI file, and the PB.INI file that you distribute to your users does not need it.

Using the PowerBuilder Database Administration Painter

Now that you know how to configure a database profile for Watcom, let's see how to use the Database Administration painter to create new tables, add columns to tables, and add PowerBuilder extended attributes to tables.

You looked at the database profile from the Database Administration painter, so it should already be open in PowerBuilder.

The Database Administration painter allows you to graphically create tables, set attributes of tables (such as primary and foreign keys), add new columns, and set attributes of columns. All of these are functions of the database itself and have the effect of modifying its internal system tables.

Creating a New Database

If you are authorized, you can create a new database from within the Database Administration painter. Try adding a new database now.

First, choose **F**ile, Cre**a**te Database from the Database Administration painter window's menu. The Create Local Database dialog box appears, as shown in figure 13.10.

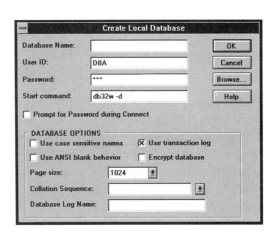

Fig. 13.10

Using the Create Local Database dialog box is a quicker method of creating a new database than trying to remember the exact syntax of the CREATE DATA-BASE command.

Browse Button

The Browse button in this dialog box is handy as a way to specify the exact subdirectory and file name of the database to be created. Clicking the Browse button opens a standard Windows new file dialog box, allowing you to browse for a location for the database and enter a name for it. The path and file name are entered in the Database Name field when the dialog box is closed.

Database Name

You can keep the name returned by the Browse button or replace the entire database name with a more descriptive one that can be longer than the eight-character DOS limitation. This may be desirable because if you let the database name default to the path and file name, PowerBuilder will create a database profile to match the database name, and you will end up with database profile names with an embedded path! This makes it confusing when you later decide to move the database to a different directory or to a database server. Do not use spaces in the database name. Watcom will truncate the name to eight characters plus the default extension of DB when creating the database file itself. The ODBC configuration file and the database profile will have the longer descriptive name.

Tip

Use only DB as the extension for a Watcom database, even though it lets you use anything! If you use something other than DB, the file will not show up in the file browse list in the ODBC configuration dialog box.

User ID

The single-user version of Watcom supports only a single database account. You must specify this one "user database account" at the time the database is created. The default is dba.

Password

The password that is associated with the previous user ID. The default is sql.

Start Command

▶ See "Using DB32W.EXE, DBSTARTW.EXE, RT32W.EXE, and RTSTARTW.EXE," p.612

This is the command line to be used by PowerBuilder to start the database engine.

Prompt for Password during Connect

When you enter a password in the password field, it is saved in the ODBC.INI file, where anyone can view it using a simple text editor (such as Windows Notepad). This is convenient, but not very secure! To prevent this from happening with sensitive files, you can leave the Password field blank and check this box. Then the ODBC driver will prompt you for the password, as needed. This is less convenient, but more secure.

Use Case-Sensitive Names

Checking this box makes the database case-sensitive when searching for tables. You do not want to use this configuration option unless you have no other choice. For example, if you are upgrading to Watcom from an existing database that is already case-sensitive, *and* it contains two tables with the same name in different case (such as Sales and SALES), you can still use the tables in Watcom.

▶ See "Using DBINITW.EXE" p.628

This checkbox is equivalent to using the -c switch with the DBINIT.EXE utility.

> **Note**
>
> Enabling the Use Case Sensitive Names option also affects comparison operations in a SELECT statement.

Use ANSI Blank Behavior

This option ignores trailing spaces in comparisons. The default is deselected, which does *not* ignore trailing spaces.

This checkbox is the equivalent to using the [TRAILING SPACES] parameter with the CREATE DBSPACE command.

Use Transaction Log

This is the same as using the [[TRANSACTION] LOG TO filename] parameters with the CREATE DBSPACE command.

Encrypt Database

This checkbox is the equivalent to the [ENCRYPT] parameter of the ISQL CREATE DBSPACE command, or the DBINIT utility.

Page Size

A large database can benefit from larger page sizes because it reduces the number of disk accesses by retrieving larger chunks of data. The default is usually sufficient for most databases.

This option is equivalent to the [PAGE SIZE n] parameter of the CREATE DBSPACE command.

Collation Sequence

Specifies the name of the desired collation sequence (determines the rules used for sorting result sets).

Database Log Name

This is the log name to be used when the Use Transaction Log option is checked. If blank, a file with the same name as the database with an extension LOG will be used for the transaction log. Use this field only if you want to record the transaction log on a physically separate disk device so that the database can be recovered in the event of a primary disk failure. For example, if you have a C: drive and a D: drive on your machine, you may want to keep the database file on the C: drive and the transaction log on the D: drive.

OK Button

The new database is not created until you press the OK button. If there is a problem with the database name or with database creation authority, you get an error message at this point.

When a new database is created for the first time from within PowerBuilder, the database itself is created, and then special PowerBuilder system tables are added to it to hold the PowerBuilder extended attributes. There is no place in most databases, including Watcom, for recording the default header of a column or its default formatting, such as font and color. PowerBuilder stores these extra attributes in its own system tables so they are available to everyone developing in PowerBuilder against that database.

PowerBuilder also maintains special tables in the database to allow format, validation, and edit styles to be defined once, and then made available to any developer working in that database.

Table 13.1 shows the tables that PowerBuilder adds to all databases created from within PowerBuilder.

> **Note**
>
> If you attempt to attach to a database that does not contain these tables, PowerBuilder tries to create them. Be sure you are signed on as a user that has table creation authority when attaching to a database for the first time. This would only apply if the database were created in a tool other than PowerBuilder, such as ISQL, ERWin, or the DBINIT utility. The Synchronize Extended Attributes menu option will re-synchronize these extended attribute tables with any new tables or columns added outside of PowerBuilder.

Table 13.1 PowerBuilder Extended Attribute Tables

Table	Key	Comments
pbcattbl	Owner, Table Name	One row for each table in the database, with the default font, color, size, and any table comments.
pbcatcol	Owner, Table Name, Col Name	Contains the default column heading text, alignment, formatting, font and color, and other column information.
pbcatvld	Validation Style Name	Contains all validation styles stored in PowerBuilder while using this database.
pbcatfmt	Format Style Name	Contains all saved format styles stored in PowerBuilder while using this database.

You can view these system tables in PowerBuilder by checking the Show System Tables checkbox in the Select Tables dialog box (choose **O**bjects, **T**ables... from the Database Administration painter).

Creating New Tables

Now return to the Powersoft Sample Database, and create a new table. From within the Database Administration painter, choose **F**ile, **C**onnect, Powersoft

Demo DB. The list of tables appears in the Select Tables dialog box shown in figure 13.11.

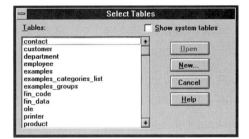

Fig. 13.11
The PowerBuilder Select Tables dialog box shows all of the tables in a database. Click **N**ew to add a new table.

PowerBuilder displays the Create Table dialog box (see fig. 13.12).

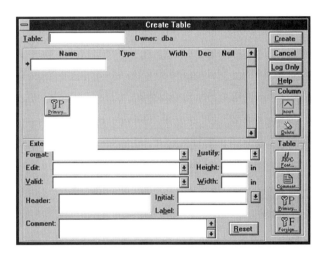

Fig. 13.12
The PowerBuilder Create Table window allows you to define the columns, keys, indexes, and extended attributes of a new table.

This dialog box contains some fields that you will be familiar with from other chapters of this book, and other fields that you will not find elsewhere because they are PowerBuilder-specific extended attribute fields. The following parts of the dialog box are standard Create Table fields.

◀ See "CREATE TABLE" p.243

Table

This is the name to be given to the new table. In the example, you will create an inventory table with one row for each item in inventory, along with its cost and location information. You will also add a related table of inventory locations. Enter **inventory** as the table name on this screen.

Name

In this field, type the name of each column to be created when the table is created. PowerBuilder creates a table in Watcom the same way you would do it from ISQL or any other tool. It constructs a CREATE statement from your selections in this dialog box and sends it to the database engine, whether the engine is running locally or remotely. You can alter the table layout and some properties later, but you cannot alter column types if the table already contains data, and you cannot change the nullable property of a column after a table has been created for the first time.

Enter **inv_id** as the name of the first column in the table. This column will be incremented each time a row is inserted into the table. It uniquely identifies a specific item in inventory.

Type

This is the Watcom-defined data type. Keep in mind that a Watcom smallint is equivalent to PowerBuilder's integer type, and Watcom's Integer type is the same size as PowerBuilder's Long data type. You must be careful to use a Powerbuilder datatype that is compatible with the Watcom data type of a column when writing scripts that will operate on the contents of a datawindow column. Columns in a datawindow are stored in the database's data type. You can get the current contents of a column using the Powerbuilder GetItem( ) functions. There are six of these functions, one for each general type of data: decimal, numeric, string, date, time, and datetime. The following table illustrates the Watcom data types in the left column, the compatible Powerbuilder data types in the middle column, and the correct GetItem( ) function to use with that data type:

Table 13.2	Watcom Data Types	
Watcom Data Type	**Recommended Powerbuilder Data Types**	**Datawindow support[2]**
BINARY	String, Char[1]	(Not supported in DW's)
CHAR	String, Char	GetItemString( )
DATE	Date	GetItemDate( )
NUMERIC	Decimal	GetItemDecimal( )
DOUBLE	Double	GetItemNumber( )
FLOAT	Double	GetItemNumber( )

Watcom Data Type	Recommended Powerbuilder Data Types	Datawindow support[2]
INTEGER	Long	GetItemNumber( )
LONG BINARY	Blob, OLE columns	(Supported as OLE column only)
LONG VARCHAR	String	GetItemString( )
NUMERIC	Decimal	GetItemDecimal( )
REAL	Double	GetItemNumber( )
SMALLINT	Int	GetItemNumber( )
TIME	Time	GetItemTime( )
TIMESTAMP	DateTime	GetItemDateTime( )
VARCHAR	String, Char[1]	GetItemString( )

(1)   The PowerBuilder Char datatype can store only a single character. If you use the Char datatype in conjunction with a database column, ensure that the length of the database column is 1; otherwise, the GetItemString( ) function will return only the first character from the column.

(2)   The PowerBuilder SetItem( ) function is used to set the value of a datawindow column using any PowerBuilder datatype supported by that column.

Integer is sufficient for the data type of the inv_id column. To set the type of the column to integer, drop down the list on the type column and select integer from the list. You could also type the word **integer** into the edit box.

Width

If a column you are entering is CHAR or VARCHAR, this Width field would be used to define the length of CHAR columns and the maximum length of VARCHAR character columns. Since we are entering an integer (**inv_id**), which does not require us to specify a width, the width field is disabled for this particular column.

Dec

Think of the Watcom NUMERIC data type as a sequence of characters containing only numbers, a decimal point, and a specified number of numeric digits after the decimal point. Use the Dec field to specify the number of numeric places that appear after the decimal point when using the NUMERIC data type. The NUMERIC data type is equivalent to the Decimal datatype in PowerBuilder. In this example, we are entering an Integer type column.

Null

You can change this field only when a column is initially inserted in either a new or existing table. Generally, the columns that make up the primary key, plus any required columns are set to No, while all others are set to Yes. The inv_id field will be the primary key for this table, so set it to No to indicate that it cannot be saved as a null value.

Troubleshooting

What do I do if I need to change the Null property after the table has been created?

Export the table's contents as a comma-delimited file using the Database Administration painter's data-manipulation feature. Drop the table and re-create it with the new setting for the Null field, then import the data back in.

Entering PowerBuilder Extended Attributes

Clicking any column displays its PowerBuilder Extended Attributes in the lower portion of the dialog box. You can modify these; PowerBuilder will include the appropriate INSERT or UPDATE statements to keep the PowerBuilder extended attribute tables up-to-date. You can see this INSERT and UPDATE syntax if you use the **L**og Only button instead of the Create button.

Enter the following columns in the inventory table:

Column Name	Type	Width	Dec	Null
inv_id	Integer			No
prod_id	Integer			No
cost	Numeric	10	2	Yes
location	Char	20		Yes
create_date	Date			Yes

Creating a Primary Key for a Table

You have not created a primary key field for this new table, so that will be your next step. Click on the Primary Key button, which is in the lower right hand corner of the dialog box.

◀ See "Using Primary Keys" p.48

Because the inv_id column will increment automatically when a new row is inserted into the inventory table, it is the only column needed to uniquely identify a row in this table. Select inv_id from the Table Columns list, and press OK.

Although it is not necessary in this table, you could select several columns as the primary key. In this case, it would be the combination of all of the selected key columns that uniquely identified a row in the table.

Creating a Foreign Key for a Table

Click the Foreign Key button to add a foreign key for the current table (see fig. 13.13).

◀ See "Using Foreign Keys" p.50

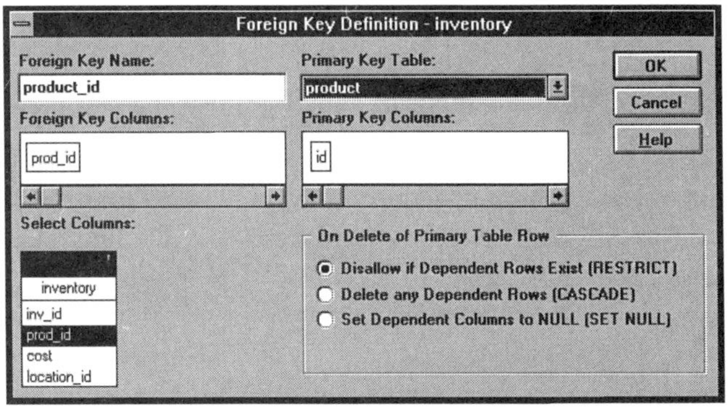

Fig. 13.13
The PowerBuilder Foreign Key Definition dialog box allows you to identify those columns in your table that contain key fields in a foreign table.

You must name the foreign key yourself, in the Foreign Key Name field. Below that, select the field(s) in the currently selected table that point to fields in other (foreign) tables. Select the name of the other table in the Primary Key Table field: product. Select from the list below that the column(s) to be linked to the foreign key field: id. Now determine what action the database is to take if the primary key pointed to by this foreign key definition is ever deleted and exists as a foreign key in this table. The default radio button selection of RESTRICT is sufficient for this example.

Using the Create Button

PowerBuilder does not interactively support all of the table-creation options available in Watcom SQL 4.0. For example, you can specify DEFAULT *value* after a column in the CREATE statement, or DEFAULT AUTOINCREMENT. If you do not need to take advantage of additional table-creation options such as these, you can simply click the Create button, and the table will be immediately created. If you need to modify the CREATE statement before it is actually executed, you can click the **L**og Only button, instead.

Using the Log Only Button

Tip

Because the log is appended with all database activity, clear the log before going into the Create Table dialog box. Now, only the syntax of the most recent command is captured in the log.

When you click this button, the CREATE statement is constructed but not executed. Instead, it is appended to a log in the Database Administration Painter. You can open this edit box to see exactly what syntax would have been executed had you pressed the Create button. This also gives you an opportunity to add phrases to the statement that PowerBuilder's painter does not support, such as the DEFAULT AUTOINCREMENT feature available for key columns. To demonstrate this technique, press the Log Only button now.

Save the text to a standard ASCII file by selecting O**p**tions, **S**ave Log As.

You can edit the resulting log file with any text editor, such as Windows Notepad.

In the example, you want the inventory ID to increment automatically and the Create Date column to reflect the current date, so modify it like this (the changes are in bold):

```
CREATE TABLE "dba"."inventory"
                        ("inv_id" integer NOT NULL DEFAULT
AUTOINCREMENT,
                        "prod_id" integer NOT NULL,
                        "cost" numeric(10,2) ,
                        "location" char(20) ,
                        "create_date" date DEFAULT CURRENT DATE
        , PRIMARY KEY (inv_id)
        , FOREIGN KEY product_id (prod_id)
            REFERENCES "dba"."product");

insert into "dba".pbcattbl
        (pbt_tnam,
         pbt_ownr,
         pbd_fhgt,
    .
    .
    .
```

Save the changes. Now choose **O**bjects, Data**b**ase Administration. This editor accepts any SELECT, CREATE, UPDATE, or any other SQL statement. It will accept the text of the statement from a text file like the one you just saved. Choose **F**ile, **O**pen. Find the text file you just saved, select it, and click OK. The text file appears in the Database Administration window ready to execute. Select the Execute button on the sheet toolbar to execute the SQL in the painter.

This technique allows you to use Watcom features that are not directly supported in PowerBuilder. You have used the example of setting a default date value for a column and of using the AUTOINCREMENT feature on a key column. The Data window you will create will use this table, joined with the products table, as an illustration of how the Update characteristics of a Data window must be set in order to take advantage of the DEFAULT parameter.

Modifying Existing Tables

You can add columns to any existing table by opening the table in the Database Administration painter and double-clicking the table's heading. You can also highlight an open table definition and choose **O**bjects, **E**xtended Definition from the Database Administration painter window's menu. This opens a dialog box identical to the Create Table dialog box, except that the Create button has been replaced with the Alter button. You can append or delete columns, or change any extended column attributes. You cannot delete columns that are defined as part of the primary key, or that have indexes on them. You can change the nullable property of any new columns, but not of existing columns.

Creating a Simple DataWindow

Now that you have created a new table in the Database Administration painter, you can build a datawindow object that uses the table as its data source. First, go to the DataWindow painter.

Opening the DataWindow Painter

From the frame or any painter, select the Powerbar DataWindow button (see fig. 13.14).

This opens the Select DataWindow dialog box (see fig. 13.15).

Fig. 13.14
The DataWindow
toolbar button.

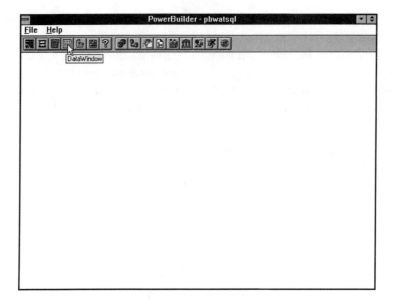

Fig. 13.15
Use the Select
DataWindow
dialog box to
browse for and
open a data-
window, or to
create or inherit a
new datawindow.

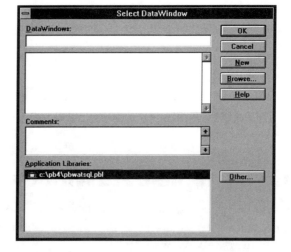

There are no datawindow objects in the PBWATSQL.PBL library. Click **New** to
create a new datawindow.

Choosing the DataWindow Data Source and Style

The New DataWindow dialog box asks for the source of data for the
datawindow, and the general type of datawindow to be created, such as
grouped, freeform, tabular, and so on. For the example, choose SQL Select as
the data source and Freeform as the style. Then click the OK button.

> **Note**
>
> You can also choose Stored Procedure as the data source for a datawindow. You must first create the stored procedure in the Database Administration painter. It then appears in the list of stored procedures available when Stored Procedure is the data source for a new datawindow.

Choosing Tables and Drawing the Select Statement

After you have selected the data source and the presentation style, the Select Tables dialog box appears. Select and open the tables that will be used in the SELECT statement that will be the source of data to the datawindow you are creating. For the example, select the inventory table you just created and the product table that already existed in the sample database, then choose the Open button.

Because you defined a foreign key when you created the inventory table, PowerBuilder links the foreign key in the inventory table with the primary key in the products table. These table joins are included in any WHERE clause that PowerBuilder initiates. You simply select the columns you want to include in your result set. Keep in mind that you may want a particular column returned to the datawindow, even if it does not normally appear on the datawindow itself. For example, the primary key value of the inventory table might not convey any meaning to a user, and so you might not want to display it as a field on the datawindow. To update it, however, you must include it in the result set. Select the following columns:

Table	Column
inventory	inv_id
inventory	prod_id
product	name
product	description
inventory	cost
inventory	location
inventory	create_date

You are selecting product name and description only, so they can be included on the datawindow for information to the user. Select them in the order specified in the previous table.

Now that you have defined the data source, you can further define the visual appearance of the detail area of the datawindow. Choose **F**ile, **D**esign to move to design mode.

You would normally hide a key value like the inv_id field by deleting its edit box from the datawindow (it would still be in the result set). Leave it in place so you can see Watcom assigning these key values as rows are inserted. Set the tab order for the fields (by choosing **D**esign, Tab **O**rder) so that only the prod_id, cost, and location fields are editable. Set all others to tab order zero. I like to give the user the visual indication that a field is non-editable by removing the border. If a field is required, I give it a shadow box—if it is optional, I give it a box style border. Assign the border style to the fields (by right-clicking the field and choosing **B**order), as follows:

Column	Tab Order	Border
inventory_inv_id	0	None
inventory_prod_id	10	Shadow box
product_name	0	None
product_description	0	None
inventory_cost	20	Shadow box
inventory_location	30	Box
inventory_create_date	0	None

Setting the Update Characteristics of a New Datawindow

Now you must set the update characteristics of the datawindow. In the example, you join two tables together to bring along the product name and description. These are for convenience only; you do not intend to maintain these fields using this datawindow. The update characteristics screen allows you to specify which columns on a specific table can be updated. Choose **R**ows, **U**pdate from the datawindow painter menu. This brings up the Specify Update Characteristics dialog box (see fig. 13.16).

By default, if the select contains more than one table, then no columns can be updated. Check the **A**llow Updates checkbox to enable updating on a table. First, select the table to be updated. Select the inventory table from the **T**able to Update drop-down list box. In the **U**pdateable Columns list, select all columns from the result set that are in the inventory table, except the key value, `inventory_inv_id`, and `inventory_create_date` fields. You do not want to select these for update because if they were included, PowerBuilder would include null values for them in an INSERT statement. Watcom will only include the default value for them if they are not included in the column list of the INSERT statement. Select the following columns:

Columns
inventory_prod_id
inventory_cost
inventory_location

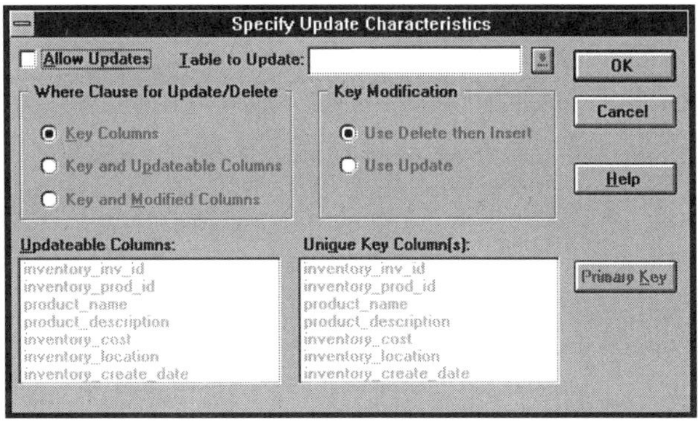

Fig. 13.16
The Specify Update Characteristics dialog box.

In the Unique Key Columns list, select the `inventory_inv_id` field. Click OK and then save the datawindow as `d_inv`.

A significant improvement over this primitive datawindow would be a drop-down datawindow on the `inventory_prod_id` field. For now, viewing the products table shows inventory items in the 300 range that you can type in directly.

Creating a Minimum Application

Now that you have created a table and a datawindow to perform editing, you need to build a few objects for a small application in which to display it. You will use the PBWATSQL.PBL library that you created at the beginning of this chapter as the basic framework. This will allow you to add only two new objects, in addition to the datawindow you just created. Follow these steps to create the necessary objects:

1. In the application open script, uncomment the connect and return code checking.

> **Note**
>
> While you are in this code, notice that the script sets attributes of the SQLCA transaction object from the current database connection information stored in the PB.INI file. These attributes are set in the profile editor. The Database section is for the current connection, but these connection attributes could be pulled from a specific database profile section, such as Powersoft Sample DB. You can also copy the entire profile section into a different application INI file, such as PBWATSQL.INI.

2. Add the following menu items to the m_genapp_frame menu. Be sure to name the new edit menu item **m_edit1**, because the inherited sheet menu already contains an m_edit menu item for cut, copy, and paste functions. Adding the menu items to the frame menu allows them to be available to any inherited sheet menus.

    Add the following menu items to the m_edit1 menu:

```
MenuItem: m_insert
Text = "&Insert"
ToolBarItemName = "Insert!"
ToolBarItemText = "Insert"

Script for: clicked event of m_insert
// If a sheet is open, trigger the appropriate event on the window.
// If a datawindow is open on the window, the event will be for-
warded
// to it.
If IsValid(w_genapp_frame.GetActiveSheet()) = true then
    w_genapp_frame.GetActiveSheet().TriggerEvent("ue_rowinsert")

end if

MenuItem: m_delete
Text = "&Delete"
ToolBarItemName = "Custom009!"
ToolBarItemText = "Delete"

Script for clicked event of m_delete:
// If a sheet is open, trigger the appropriate event on the window.
// If a datawindow is open on the window, the event will be for-
warded
```

```
// to it.
If IsValid(w_genapp_frame.GetActiveSheet()) = true then
   w_genapp_frame.GetActiveSheet().TriggerEvent("ue_rowdelete")
end if
```

MenuItem: m_save
```
Text = "&Save"
ToolBarItemName = "Custom008!"
ToolBarItemText = "Save"
```

Script for: clicked event of m_save
```
// If a sheet is open, trigger the appropriate event on the window.
// If a datawindow is open on the window, the event will be for-
warded
// to it.
If IsValid(w_genapp_frame.GetActiveSheet()) = true then
   w_genapp_frame.GetActiveSheet().TriggerEvent("ue_rowsave")
end if
End of Script
```

MenuItem = m_-5   " - "
```
Visible = true      Enabled = true
```

```
MenuItem = m_next
```
Text = "&Next Row"
```
ToolBarItemName = "VCRNext!"
ToolBarItemText = "Next Row"
ToolBarItemSpace = 1
```

Script for: clicked event of m_next
```
// If a sheet is open, trigger the appropriate event on the window.
// If a datawindow is open on the window, the event will be for-
warded
// to it.
If IsValid(w_genapp_frame.GetActiveSheet()) = true then
   w_genapp_frame.GetActiveSheet().TriggerEvent("ue_rownext")
end if
```

MenuItem: m_previousrow
Text = "&Previous Row"
```
ToolBarItemName = "VCRPrior!"
ToolBarItemText = "Prev. Row"
```

Script for: clicked event of m_previousrow
```
// If a sheet is open, trigger the appropriate event on the window.
// If a datawindow is open on the window, the event will be for-
warded
// to it.
If IsValid(w_genapp_frame.GetActiveSheet()) = true then
   w_genapp_frame.GetActiveSheet().TriggerEvent("ue_rowprev")
end if
```

MenuItem: m_nextpage
```
Text = "Next P&age"
```

(continues)

```
ToolBarItemName = "VCRLast!"
ToolBarItemText = "Next Page"

Script for: clicked event of m_nextpage
// If a sheet is open, trigger the appropriate event on the window.
// If a datawindow is open on the window, the event will be for-
warded
// to it.
If IsValid(w_genapp_frame.GetActiveSheet()) = true then
    w_genapp_frame.GetActiveSheet().TriggerEvent("ue_rownextpage")
end if


MenuItem: m_priorpage
Text = "Prior Pag&e"
ToolBarItemName = "VCRFirst!"
ToolBarItemText = "Prior Page"

Script for: clicked event of m_priorpage
// If a sheet is open, trigger the appropriate event on the window.
// If a datawindow is open on the window, the event will be for-
warded
// to it.
If IsValid(w_genapp_frame.GetActiveSheet()) = true then
    w_genapp_frame.GetActiveSheet().TriggerEvent("ue_rowpriorpage")
end if
```

3. Create a datawindow user object that can respond to the insert, delete, save, and row scrolling user events triggered from the menu:

```
User Object: u_base_dw

Properties for User Object:

DataObject = "d_inv"
VScrollBar = true
Border = true
LiveScroll = true
BorderStyle = stylebox!

!!!Kathie-Jo: I have removed the entire section in an attempt to
simplify this 'minimum' application.  I suffered a slight case of
'mission creep' - Mike

Script for: ue_rowinsert  event
// Insert a row into the datawindow.
This.InsertRow(This.getRow())

Script for: ue_rowdelete  event
// delete current row from the datawindow.
This.DeleteRow(This.getRow())

Script for: ue_rowsave  event
// delete current row from the datawindow.
This.Update()
```

```
Script for: ue_rownext  event
// Move to next row in the datawindow.
This.ScrollNextRow()

Script for: ue_rowprev  event
// Move to previous row in the datawindow.
This.ScrollPriorRow()

Script for: ue_rownextpage  event
// Move to next page in the datawindow.
This.ScrollNextPage()

Script for: ue_rowpriorpage  event
// Move to prior page in the datawindow.
This.ScrollPriorPage()
```

4. Now inherit a new sheet from the w_genapp_sheet window, place a
   u_base_dw on the window, and set the datawindow to the datawindow
   object you created, d_inv:

```
Window: w_autoinc inherited from w_genapp_sheet
Window Properties:
Title = "Sheet"
MenuName = "m_genapp_sheet"

Script for: open event of w_autoinc
// Retrieve the dw on this window.
dw_1.SetTransObject(SQLCA)
dw_1.Retrieve()

User Object Control: dw_1 (The datawindow control on the window)

User Object Control Properties:
TabOrder = 1
DataObject = "d_inv"
VScrollBar = true
```

5. Last, we need to modify a line in the wf_newsheet function on the
   w_genapp_frame window. Change line 2 of the function to:

```
/* w_genapp_sheet lw_Sheet */
w_autoinc lw_Sheet
```

Pulling It All Together

Now run the application. It opens a new sheet, which retrieves the
datawindow in the open event. Click the Insert button. A new row is inserted
in the datawindow. Enter **300** as the product ID, **10.00** as the cost, and
Warehouse in the Location field. Now click the Save toolbar button. Close
the sheet and then reopen the sheet by choosing **F**ile, **N**ew. When it retrieves
the data, you can see that the inv_id = 1, and the create_date field contains
the current date!

Upgrading Existing Watcom 3.2 Databases to Version 4.0

When Watcom is installed, it searches your existing database profiles for existing 3.2 databases on your machine. If it finds any, it will ask whether you want them migrated to version 4.0. If you choose to migrate the databases, they can no longer be read by version 3.2 runtimes or servers.

You can run this utility from the DOS command line or from within Windows. To run from the DOS command line, first exit Windows. At the DOS command prompt, enter the following command:

```
DBUPGRAD [switches] databasename
```

From within Windows, choose **F**ile, **R**un from the Program Manager. Type the following in the Command Line field.

```
DBUPGRDW [switches] databasename
```

You can use the following switches with either the DOS or Windows version:

```
[-c "keyword1=value1;keyword2=value2...keywordn=valuen] [-q]
```

The -c switch is the connection parameters supplied in the database's profile, and -q switch instructs Watcom to perform the operation in quiet mode, with a minimum of messages displayed. In the -q mode, only error messages are displayed.

From Here...

We have covered a lot of ground in this chapter, including how to install Watcom, a discussion of configuring database profiles, and some techniques for using Watcom with PowerBuilder. You might also find the following chapters of interest:

- Chapter 6, "Understanding SQL," gives you a good basis for the clear understanding of how to construct concise SQL statements.

- Chapter 12, "Implementing Procedures and Triggers," discusses how to write stored procedures, which can be used as the direct data source for a datawindow.

Chapter 14

Implementing Watcom SQL with SQLPP (C and C++)

by Charles A. Wood

Embedded SQL combines the C and C++ programming languages with Watcom SQL statements. The SQL statements are translated into C code via the SQLPP utility. The SQLPP calls interface with a dynamic link library to access the database. This preprocessor must be run before actual C or C++ compilation can occur.

This chapter covers the following:

- Implementing SQLPP in a C++ environment

- Accessing the C++ Interface in PowerBuilder 4

- Understanding the SQLCA structure

- Implementing static and dynamic SQL calls

Note

Using SQLPP implies that you have some understanding of the C or C++ languages. This chapter does not intend to teach you C or C++. The purpose of this chapter is to show you how to link SQLPP to your C or C++ program.

Using SQLPP with C and C++ Compilers

You can use SQLPP in conjunction with the following C and C++ compilers:

DOS and Windows	Borland C++ 2.0
	Borland C++ 3.0
	Borland C++ 4.0
	Borland Turbo C 2.0
	Microsoft C 4.0
	Microsoft C 5.0
	Microsoft C 5.1
	Microsoft C 6.0
	Microsoft C ++ 7.0
	Microsoft Visual C++ 1.0
	Microsoft Visual C++ 1.5
	Watcom C/C++ 9.0
	Watcom C/C++ 9.5
	Watcom C/C++ 10.0
OS/2	Borland C++ for OS/2 1.0
	IBM C Set ++ 2.0
	Watcom C/C++ 9.0
	Watcom C/C++ 9.5
	Watcom C/C++ 10.0
Windows NT	Microsoft Visual C++ 1.0
	Microsoft Visual C++ 1.5
	Watcom C/C++ 9.5
	Watcom C/C++ 10.0
QNX	Watcom C/C++ 9.5
	Watcom C/C++ 10.0

Caution

Some C++ compilers allow you to pass C++ data structures or classes by address only. Others allow you to pass the entire structure pack. This allows the programmer to pass a copy of the entire structure to a function. Watcom SQL requires that you be allowed to pass an entire structrure pack. All embedded SQL programs must be compiled with the structure-packing option of the compiler turned on. This is usually the default, but you should check to make sure. If the structure-packing option is not turned on, a *general protection fault (GPF)* will probably occur.

Understanding the SQLPP Development Process in C++

PowerBuilder has always been used for fast Windows development with minimal training. PowerBuilder is difficult to beat for development time and maintainability. However, PowerBuilder applications tend to run slower than equivalent C++ Windows applications. C++, while delivering extremely fast execution time, is hard to learn and somewhat difficult to maintain.

In PowerBuilder 4.0, C++ was merged with the PowerBuilder Enterprise edition for fast development, as well as close integration with C++ to speed up those slow functions. Using the Watcom C++ interface built into Power-Builder 4.0, C++ development has become easier, as well as more maintainable.

For the purposes of the example in this chapter, you will be using the Watcom C++ compiler that comes with the PowerBuilder Enterprise edition. This will show you how to incorporate C++ with your PowerBuilder application, while at the same time showing you how to incorporate SQL calls inside your C++ DLL or application.

With normal C++ development, you simply compile source code into an object file, and link the object file with other object files and libraries to get an executable file. This executable file is the actual application that runs and calls dynamic link libraries (DLLs) during execution.

With PowerBuilder development, your PowerBuilder application compiles into your executable file. Any C++ modules are compiled into DLLs that the PowerBuilder application calls during run time.

Finally, adding the SQL Preprocessor (SQLPP) adds a step before the actual compilation to change SQL statements into function calls. After running a program through SQLPP, the SQL statements can be accepted by the C++ compiler (see fig. 14.1).

The SQLPP step is important because it allows SQL calls to be present inside your C++ compiler. The following sections will show you how to compile a DLL in Watcom C++ to be used with your PowerBuilder application.

Tip
Using C++ inside a PowerBuilder application can really speed up that application without adding *too* much maintenance—if you use the PowerBuilder C++ interface.

Fig. 14.1
This is the flow of
C++ application
development
when using
SQLPP.

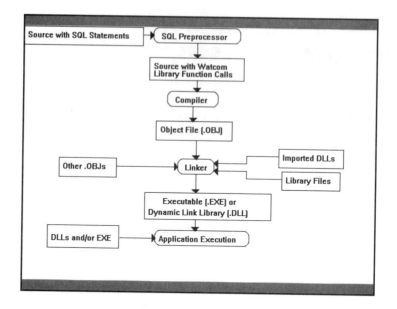

Running the SQL Preprocessor (SQLPP)

SQLPP.EXE is the SQL preprocessor program that comes with Watcom SQL. You need to run your C++ program containing SQL statements through SQLPP before compiling it. The SQLPP program has the following syntax:

```
SQLPP [switches] SQL_program_name [output_program_name]
```

The SQL_program_name is the name of your input program. If your input program doesn't have an extension, an SQC extension is assumed. If you don't specify an output_program_name, your output_program_name will be the same name as the SQL_program_name with a C extension. If you already have a file with that name, then your default output file will change to a CC extension.

The switches used in the SQLPP are shown in Table 14.1.

Table 14.1 Switches Used with the SQLPP Program	
Switch	**Description**
-c	Generates code that favors code size and execution speed over data space size. This is the default.

Switch	Description
-d	Generates code that reduces the data space size. With this option, data structures are reused and reinitialized at execution time before use. This option increases the EXE size and can slow down an application. However, this option tends to take up more lower memory resources during execution.
-f	This places the far keyword before any character declarations in the preprocessor generated program area. This is necessary for Borland and Turbo C++ products when using the large memory models. This option forces data into another data segment when using Microsoft or Watcom C++ products. With the Borland C/C++ family of compilers, this forces a larger character address so that data can be addressed from a different data segment in memory.
-l user_id, password	Use the user_id and password for static SQL statements.
-n	This switch enables the #line metacommand in C and C++ to be active for the generated code. This way, if you have an error in your SQL, the compiler will tell you the line number of that error.
-o operating_system	This switch allows you to choose your operating systems. Valid values for operating_system are: **DOS.** MS-DOS or DR-DOS **DOS32.** 32-bit DOS extended program **DOS286.** 286 DOS extended program **WINDOWS.** Microsoft Windows **WIN32.** 32-bit Microsoft Windows **OS232.** 32-bit OS/2 **WINNT.** Microsoft Windows NT **NETWARE.** Novell NetWare **QNX.** 16-bit QNX **QNX32.** 32-bit QNX
−r	This switch forces the preprocessor to generate re-entrant code. This means that your program can be used by more than one individual at a time. −r is very important for Windows programs because, usually, Windows programs can be run several times from the same machine.
−q	Operate quietly. Don't print the banner.
−s string_len	Sets the maximum string length. Many compilers have a string length limit. This lets you choose your limit for any strings that may be created during compilation. The default is 500.

A typical example of an SQLPP to compile a Windows application is:

```
SQLPP -o WINDOWS -r -n EXAMPLE.SQC EXAMPLE.CPP
```

> **Note**
>
> You must specify -o WINDOWS when running SQLPP in a Windows environment. Because SQLPP is a DOS program, it assumes you will be compiling a DOS program.

The previous SQLPP DOS command takes EXAMPLE.SQC, which is a C++ program with embedded SQL, converts all SQL calls into re-entrant Microsoft Windows calls while keeping the #line directive for debugging purposes, and stores the result in EXAMPLE.CPP.

Tip

For more complete coverage of user objects and the C++ interface in PowerBuilder, check out the Que book *Special Edition Using PowerBuilder 4.*

Accessing the C++ Interface in PowerBuilder 4

This section shows how to access the C++ interface and code a C++ DLL from within your PowerBuilder environment. If you want to code a C++ executable or don't use PowerBuilder, this section will provide some background information and source modules for your C++ program.

The first step in accessing the C++ library is to click the User Object icon. This pulls up the Select User Object dialog box, as seen in figure 14.2. From here, click New to create a new user object.

Fig. 14.2
Use the Select User Object dialog box to edit or create user objects in PowerBuilder.

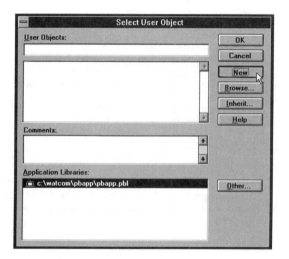

You should see the New User Object dialog box (see fig. 14.3). Choose the C++ icon to create a C++ class user object.

Fig. 14.3
The New User Object dialog box allows you to define the characteristics of your new user object in PowerBuilder.

Troubleshooting

I did what you said, but I can't see any C++ icon on my New User Object dialog box. What gives?

To use the C++ interface in PowerBuilder, you need to install Watcom C++. Watcom C++ is included with PowerBuilder Enterprise edition version 4.0, or you can get a copy by calling the Watcom sales line at 1-800-395-3525.

Now you should see the Select C++ DLL Name dialog box (see fig. 14.4). Select a DLL name and a directory for your DLL.

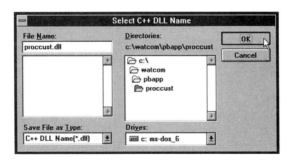

Fig. 14.4
The Select C++ DLL Name dialog box lets you choose the name of the DLL that will be accessed by PowerBuilder 4.

Caution

The C++ interface will build a project containing *all* C++ programs in your specified directory. Consequently, make sure that each DLL gets its own directory, or else you'll have bloated DLLs and could possibly have ambiguous references during compilation.

Now you have to declare your C++ functions. You do this by choosing Declare, **U**ser Object Functions (see fig. 14.5).

Fig. 14.5
Declaring a C++
function inside
PowerBuilder sets
up that C++
function to be
later called from
the PowerBuilder
environment.

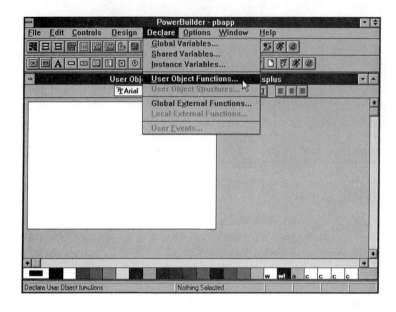

The Select Function in User Object dialog box appears. Choose New to declare a new function for your soon-to-be-developed C++ DLL (see fig. 14.6).

Fig. 14.6
This dialog box
lets you set up or
edit the prototype
of your C++ DLL
function.

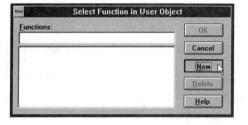

Now you can set up your C++ function prototype by naming your C++ function, its parameters, and its return variable in the New Function dialog box (see fig. 14.7). When you're finished, click OK.

Now you should be back in PowerBuilder's user object painter. Click the C++ interface icon. PowerBuilder asks you to name your C++ user object (see fig. 14.8). Choose **Yes**.

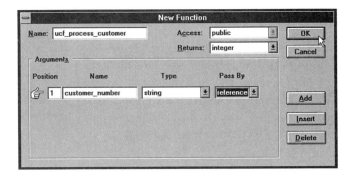

Fig. 14.7
This dialog box allows you to set up your C++ function prototype within PowerBuilder 4.

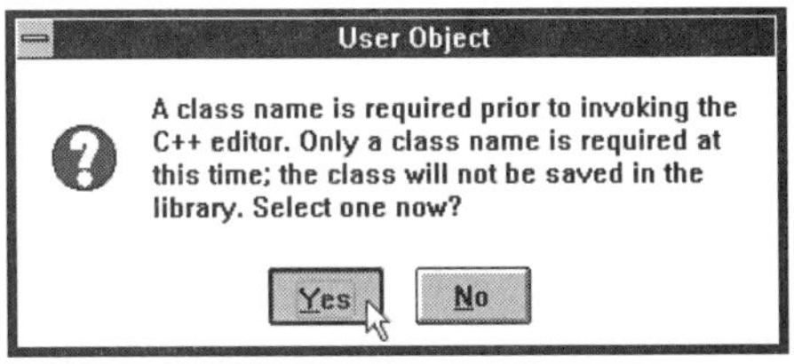

Fig. 14.8
PowerBuilder will not let you enter the C++ environment until you've named your C++ user object.

The Save User Object dialog box appears, as seen in figure 14.9. This dialog box lets you name your C++ user object. The name you give your C++ user object is then also used for your C++ class name, which will contain all of your C++ functions you have declared.

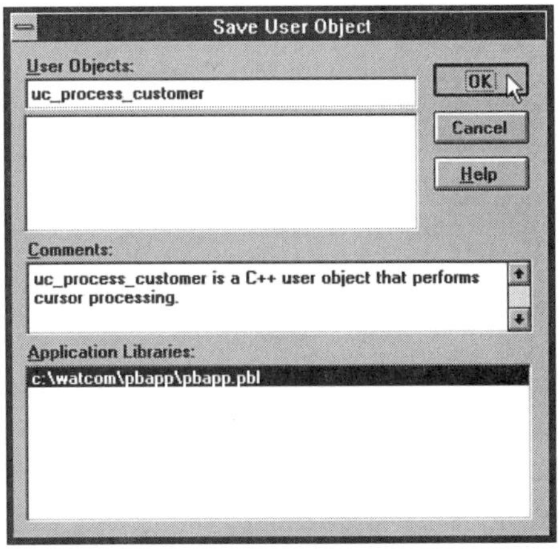

Fig. 14.9
You can save your user object and name your C++ class. A prefix of uc_ lets other developers know that this is a PowerBuilder C++ user object.

Setting Up Your C++ Code

Now you get to see why you would generate the C++ object this way instead of typing it in yourself. PowerBuilder generated all of the header files, the LIBMAIN functions, and the function shell of all PowerBuilder functions declared in the user object painter. This saves you a *ton* of overhead and typing. Also, because the code generated is bug free, you only have to worry about the body of the functions you are declaring.

For those of you who are not using PowerBuilder, I will now list the generated code. (Have fun typing. If you want to avoid this headache, this C++ code is available on the CD that comes with this book.) The C++ header file (UC_CUSR3.HPP) that contains all function declarations and class variables declared in the user object painter, was generated as follows:

```
UC_CUSR3.HPP

/* WATCOM Interface Generator    Version 1.0 */
/* Created:  Mon Mar  6 05:24:41 1995
 */
/* This file contains code generated by PowerBuilder.
 * Do not modify code delimited by comments of the form:
 * // $PB$ — begin generated code for object <>.  Do not modify
this code
 * // $PB$ — end generated code for object <>.
 * This file contains the C++ class definition for your user
object.
 */

#include <string.hpp>
#include <windows.h>


// $PB$ — begin generated code for object <uc_customer_number>.
Do not modify this code
class uc_customer_number {
public:
    virtual int ucf_process_customer( char *customer_number );
// $PB$ — end generated code for object <uc_customer_number>.

    /*
     * PUT YOUR DECLARATIONS HERE
     */

};
```

Notice the bold comment. Place any additional declarations you might need here. The LMAIN.CPP file contains the overhead functions you need to allow your DLL to be called by other Windows programs. It was generated as follows:

LMAIN.CPP

```
/* This file is generated by PowerBuilder.
 * You may modify it in any way you wish but do not remove
 * Libmain and WEP.  Without them you will be unable to link your
DLL.
 */

#include <windows.h>
#include "pbdll.h"


int PB_EXPORT LibMain( HANDLE hmod, WORD dataseg, WORD heap,
LPSTR cmdline )
{
    hmod = hmod; // these assignments generate no code
    dataseg = dataseg;  // but prevent compiler warnings about
    heap = heap;               // unreferenced variables
    cmdline = cmdline;
    return( 1 );
}

int PB_EXPORT WEP( int res )
{
    res = res;
    return( 1 );
}
```

You probably don't want to change LMAIN at all. PowerBuilder has set it up so that all you need to worry about are your own functions. The CUC_CUR3.CPP file contains the constructor and destructor for the C++ class. Again, all of this is generated by PowerBuilder 4. PowerBuilder constructs your class for you during a C++ call, so you don't have to worry about it. You probably don't want to modify anything unless you are very familiar with C++ and need to perform specific actions during the construction and destruction of your C++ class. The code for CUC_CUR3.CPP is as follows:

```
CUC_CUR3.CPP

/* WATCOM Interface Generator   Version 1.0 */
/* Created:  Mon Mar  6 05:24:42 1995
 */
/* This file is generated by PowerBuilder.
 * Do not modify this file.
 * This file contains interface code called by PowerBuilder.
 */

#include <pbdll.h>

#include "uc_cusR3.hpp"

extern "C" {
int PB_EXPORT uc_customer_numberucf_process_customADF0(
uc_customer_number *this_hdl, char *customer_number );
uc_customer_number *PB_EXPORT
uc_customer_number_CPP_CONSTRUCTOR();
void PB_EXPORT uc_customer_number_CPP_DESTRUCTOR(
uc_customer_number *this_hdl );
}

int PB_EXPORT uc_customer_numberucf_process_customADF0(
uc_customer_number *this_hdl, char *customer_number ) {
    return( this_hdl->ucf_process_customer( customer_number ) );
}

uc_customer_number *PB_EXPORT
uc_customer_number_CPP_CONSTRUCTOR() {
    return( new uc_customer_number );
}

void PB_EXPORT uc_customer_number_CPP_DESTRUCTOR(
uc_customer_number *this_hdl ) {
    delete this_hdl;
}
```

PowerBuilder comes with a pbdll.h header file that it includes in several of its
modules. pbdll.h simply defines PB_EXPORT as a pascal export data type.
pbdll.h is listed as follows:

```
#define PB_EXPORT       __pascal __export
```

Now we get to the module, UC_CUSR3.CPP, where you add your C++ code.
However, as you can see, the UC_CUSR3.CPP code is already set up so that all
you need to add is the body of your ucf_process_customer function that you
declared in the PowerBuilder painter.

UC_CUSR3.CPP

```
/* WATCOM Interface Generator    Version 1.0 */
/* Created:  Mon Mar  6 05:24:42 1995
 */
/* This file contains code generated by PowerBuilder.
 * Do not modify code delimited by comments of the form:
 * // $PB$ — begin generated code for object <>.  Do not modify
this code
 * // $PB$ — end generated code for object <>.
 * This file contains the bodies the functions for your user
object.
 */



#include <pbdll.h>

#include "uc_cusR3.hpp"


// $PB$ — begin generated code for object <uc_customer_number>.
Do not modify this code
#if 1
int uc_customer_number::ucf_process_customer( char
*customer_number ) {
// $PB$ — end generated code for object <uc_customer_number>.
//===================================

    /*
     * PUT YOUR CODE HERE
     */

    return( 0 );
}
#endif // PowerBuilder code, do not remove
```

Notice the bold area. Replace these comments with your customized code.

Understanding the SQLCA Structure

The *SQL Common Area (SQLCA)* is an area inside a program that contains all of the SQL information. The format for the SQLCA structure is as follows:

```
typedef long int  an_sql_code;

typedef char      an_sql_state[6];
```

```
struct sqlwarn{
    unsigned char   sqlwarn0;
    unsigned char   sqlwarn1;
    unsigned char   sqlwarn2;
    unsigned char   sqlwarn3;
    unsigned char   sqlwarn4;
    unsigned char   sqlwarn5;
    unsigned char   sqlwarn6;
    unsigned char   sqlwarn7;
    unsigned char   sqlwarn8;
    unsigned char   sqlwarn9;
};

typedef struct sqlca{
    unsigned char   sqlcaid[8];
    long            sqlcabc;
    an_sql_code     sqlcode;
    short           sqlerrml;
    unsigned char   sqlerrmc[70];
    unsigned char   sqlerrp[8];
    long            sqlerrd[6];
    struct sqlwarn  sqlwarn;
    an_sql_state    sqlstate;
} SQLCA;

extern SQLCA        *sqlcaptr;

#define SQLCODE     sqlcaptr->sqlcode
#define SQLSTATE    sqlcaptr->sqlstate
#define SQLIOCOUNT_F    sqlerrd[1]
#define SQLCOUNT_F      sqlerrd[2]
#define SQLIOESTIMATE_F sqlerrd[3]
#define SQLIOCOUNT      sqlcaptr->SQLIOCOUNT_F
#define SQLCOUNT    sqlcaptr->SQLCOUNT_F
#define SQLIOESTIMATE   sqlcaptr->SQLIOESTIMATE_F
```

Table 14.2 contains a description of the SQLCA structure variables.

Table 14.2   SQLCA Structure Variables

SQLCA Structure Variable	Description
SQLCA.sqlcaid	The sqlcaid field is the SQLCA ID. It is an eight-byte string containing SQLCA as a debugging tool to show where the SQLCA structure begins in memory.
SQLCA.sqlcabc	The sqlcabc field is the SQLCA byte count. It contains 136 as its value: the number of bytes in the SQLCA structure.
SQLCA.sqlcode	The sqlcode field is the return code of any SQL statements used in your program. The sqlcode field is reset with each SQL command.

IV

Interfaces

SQLCA Structure Variable	Description
SQLCA.sqlerrml	The sqlerrml field contains the length of the sqlerrmc field.
SQLCA.sqlerrmc	Many SQL error messages have a place for a column name or other string. The sqlerrmc field contains one or more strings to be inserted in the SQL error message.
SQLCA.sqlerrd[0]	The sqlerrd[0] field is reserved by Watcom SQL.
SQLCA.sqlerrd[1]	The sqlerrd[1] field is the SQL input-output count. These are the total input and output calls for any command. The constant defined for sqlerrd[1] is SQLIOCOUNT.
SQLCA.sqlerrd[2]	The sqlerrd[2] field is the count of the rows affected by any INSERT, DELETE, or UPDATE SQL command. It also contains the number of rows in a cursor after an OPEN command. In the case of a syntax error, SQLE_SYNTAX_ERROR, this field will contain the approximate character position in the command string where the error was detected. The constant defined for sqlerrd[2] is SQLCOUNT.
SQLCA.sqlerrd[3]	The sqlerrd[3] field is the SQL row estimate. This field is the estimated number of input/output operations required to complete the command, and is filled in on an OPEN or EXPLAIN command. The constant defined for sqlerrd[3] is SQLIOESTIMATE.
SQLCA.sqlerrd[4]	The sqlerrd[4] field is reserved by Watcom SQL.
SQLCA.sqlerrd[5]	The sqlerrd[5] field is reserved by Watcom SQL.
SQLCA.sqlerrp	The sqlerrp field is reserved by Watcom SQL.
SQLCA.sqlwarn	The sqlwarn field is reserved by Watcom SQL.
SQLCA.sqlstate	The sqlstate field is a character string containing the SQLSTATE variable returned by Watcom SQL.

SQLCA is a global structure available to all programs using Watcom SQL. The sqlca.h header file (where the SQLCA structure resides) needs no #include metacommand because the #include metacommand is generated by the SQLPP preprocessor by using the command:

```
EXEC SQL INCLUDE SQLCA;
```

The EXEC SQL INCLUDE SQLCA command and Watcom SQL header (.h) files are described later in this chapter in the section titled "Formatting Your SQL Statements." You can find the listing for values for SQLCA.sqlcode and SQLCA.sqlstate in Appendix C, "Database Error Messages." Also see "Understanding Embedded SQL Header Files," later in this chapter.

Understanding the Difference between Static and Dynamic Statements

Dynamic SQL calls are formed at run time, rather than at link time like traditional static SQL calls. Although dynamic SQL calls take more time to execute than static SQL calls, dynamic SQL calls allow you some flexibility in your C++ program to form the SQL calls after the program has begun to execute.

A good use of dynamic SQL calls is an application that contains a report writer or a program that allows the user to query the database using any criteria.

Using dynamic SQL calls requires an understanding of the SQLDA structure, the PREPARE SQL command, and the DESCRIBE SQL command.

Understanding the SQLDA Structure

The SQLDA structure is used to make dynamic SQL calls.

```
#define        SQL_MAX_NAME_LEN      30

#define        _sqldafar             _sqlfar

typedef        short int             a_sql_type;

struct sqlname {
   short int   length;                  /* length of char data */
   char        data[ SQL_MAX_NAME_LEN ];         /* data
*/
};

struct sqlvar {                         /* array of variable descrip-
tors */
   short int   sqltype;                 /* type of host variable
*/
   short int   sqllen;                  /* length of host variable
*/
   void _sqldafar                       *sqldata;   /* address of
variable       */
   short int _sqldafar                  *sqlind;    /* indicator
variable pointer */
   struct sqlname                       sqlname;
};

struct sqlda{
   unsigned char                        sqldaid[8]; /* eye catcher
"SQLDA" */
```

```
    long  int   sqldabc;              /* length of sqlda structure */
    short int   sqln;                 /* descriptor size in number of
entries */
    short int   sqld;                 /* number of variables found by
DESCRIBE */
    struct sqlvar               sqlvar[1];  /* array of vari-
able descriptors */
};

#define     SCALE(sqllen)        ((sqllen)/256)
#define     PRECISION(sqllen)    ((sqllen)&0xff)
#define     SET_PRECISION_SCALE(sqllen,precision,scale)  sqllen
= (scale)*256 + (precision)
#define     DECIMALSTORAGE(sqllen)          (PRECISION(sqllen)/
2 + 1)

typedef struct sqlda            SQLDA;
typedef struct sqlvar           SQLVAR, SQLDA_VARIABLE;
typedef struct sqlname          SQLNAME, SQLDA_NAME;

#define     SQLDASIZE(n)    ( sizeof( struct sqlda ) + (n-1) *
sizeof( struct sqlvar) )
```

Table 14.3 contains a description of the SQLDA structure variables.

Table 14.3 SQLDA Structure Variables

SQLDA Structure Variable	Description
sqldaid	The sqldaid field is the SQLDA ID field. It contains the string SQLDA.
sqldabc	A long integer, containing the length of the SQLDA structure in bytes. The formula for sqldabc is $16 + 44 \times n$ (where n is the number of host variables).
sqln	The number of variable descriptors in the sqlvar array. This value is set in advance, and has no actual bearing on how many host variables were used in the dynamic SQL statement.
sqld	The sqld field contains the number of variable descriptors that are used, and contain information describing a host variable. This field can be set by a programmer, but usually is set by the DESCRIBE statement.
sqlvar[ ]	An array of descriptors of type struct sqlvar, each describing a host variable. Although initially set to one, this variable can be reset using the SQLDA functions, described later in this chapter.

(continues)

Table 14.3 Continued

SQLDA Structure Variable	Description
sqlvar[n].sqltype	The sqltype field is filled by the DESCRIBE statement. It contains an integer that denotes what data type the host variable is. These host variable data type indicators can be found in sqldef.h. Valid sqltypes are described in the "Using Host Variables and Embedded SQL Data Types" section, later in this chapter.
sqlvar[n].sqllen	The sqllen field contains the number of bytes contained in the field. For decimal types, sqllen is divided into two one-byte fields: the high byte is the precision and the low byte is the scale. The precision is the total number of digits, and the scale is the number of digits that appear after the decimal point.
sqlvar[n].*sqldata	The sqldata field is a four-byte pointer to the variable defined by sqlvar. The variable that sqldata points to must be the same data type and length as is defined in the sqltype and sqllen fields. For UPDATE and INSERT commands, the sqldata pointer will not be involved in the operation if the sqldata pointer is NULL (in C++). For a FETCH, no data is returned if the sqldata pointer is NULL (in C++).
sqlvar[n].*sqlind	The sqlind field is a four-byte pointer to an indicator variable. Indicator variables can be found later in the section, "Using Indicator Values to Handle NULLs in C++." If the sqlind pointer is NULL (in C++), then no indicator variable is used. When using a DESCRIBE SELECT LIST SQL command, the sqlind contains one of three pre-defined constants (in sqldef.h): DT_UPDATABLE indicates that the field is updatable, DT_DESCRIBE_INPUT indicates that the variable is for input on using a DESCRIBE statement, DT_PROCEDURE_IN indicates the variable is an input variable in a stored procedure, and DT_PROCEDURE_OUT indicates that the variable is an output variable in a stored procedure. These values can be logically ORed together (DT_PROCEDURE_IN | DT_PROCEDURE_OUT would indicate an INOUT variable in a stored procedure) to test for several conditions.
sqlvar[n].sqlname	The sqlname field is a VARCHAR structure, containing a length and character buffer. It is filled in by a DESCRIBE statement and is not otherwise used. This field has a different meaning for the two formats of the DESCRIBE statement. Using the DESCRIBE SELECT LIST SQL command, the name buffer is filled with the column heading of the corresponding item in the select list. Using the DESCRIBE BIND VARIABLES SQL command, the name buffer is filled with the name of the host variable that was used as a bind variable, or "?" if an unnamed parameter marker is used.

Tip

Bind variables are host variables used to pass information to the database.

Using PREPARE and EXECUTE

The PREPARE SQL statement is used to form a dynamic SQL statement, while the EXECUTE SQL statement is used to implement a previously PREPAREd SQL statement.

The format for the PREPARE statement is as follows:

```
EXEC SQL PREPARE sql_statement FROM :comm;
```

The sql_statement is the statement name given to the PREPAREd statement. :comm is a host variable string containing the dynamic SQL statement. PRE-PARE can be used to dynamically form statements using the following SQL commands: ALTER, CALL, COMMENT ON, CREATE, DELETE, DROP, GRANT, INSERT, REVOKE, SELECT, SET OPTION, UPDATE, and VALIDATE TABLE.

> **Caution**
>
> The COMMIT and ROLLBACK SQL commands are also supported by PREPARE: how-ever, Watcom recommends that you do all transaction-management operations (COMMIT and ROLLBACK) with static Embedded SQL because certain application environments may require it. Also, other Embedded SQL systems do not support dynamic transaction-management operations.

The format for the EXECUTE statement is as follows:

```
EXEC SQL EXECUTE sql_statement USING DESCRIPTOR sqlda;
```

The sql_statement is the previously PREPAREd sql_statement. The sqlda de-scriptor is the SQLDA variable used to implement dynamic statements.

You can use the following code to dynamically update the customer table on a database:

▶ See "PREPARE Command," p. 423

▶ See "EXECUTE Command," p. 422

```
EXEC SQL BEGIN DECLARE SECTION;
      char  comm[200];
      int   empnum;
      char  address[30];
      char  city[17];
EXEC SQL END DECLARE SECTION;
SQLDA *sqlda;            // Declare the sqlda pointer

   sprintf( comm, "UPDATE customer SET address1 = :address, city
= :city WHERE employee_number = :empnum");
   EXEC SQL PREPARE sql_statement FROM :comm;
   sqlda = alloc_sqlda( 10 );   // Allocate the SQLDA memory.
Assume that there are NEVER more than 10 host variables.
   EXEC SQL DESCRIBE INPUT FOR sql_statement INTO sqlda; // Set
up the SQLDA area
```

```
                    // Fill in SQLDA_VARIABLE fields with values based on name
            fields in sqlda
                    EXEC SQL EXECUTE sql_statement USING DESCRIPTOR sqlda;
                    free_sqlda( sqlda );            // Free the SQLDA memory
```

You can implement dynamic statements using the PREPARE and EXECUTE SQL commands and the SQLDA area in conjunction with the sprintf C++ command and the SQLDA functions described later in this chapter.

The alloc_sqlda(10) statement allows for 10 host variables to be used with your dynamic SQL statement. When viewing the DESCRIBE statement below, you can dynamically allocate your sqlda area. See "SQLDA Management Functions," later in this chapter.

Using DESCRIBE with C++

The DESCRIBE SQL statement will fill the SQLDA area with the appropriate values. You can DESCRIBE INPUT for INSERT, UPDATE, and DELETE SQL commands, or DESCRIBE OUTPUT for SELECT and CALL commands. Also, if you just want the host variable count, you can use DESCRIBE BIND VARI-ABLES instead of DESCRIBE INPUT, or DESCRIBE SELECT LIST in place of DESCRIBE OUTPUT.

The following code shows you how to use DESCRIBE to dynamically allocate the proper amount of storage for an SQL command, and then use DESCRIBE to fill in the appropriate SQLDA area with a dynamic UPDATE command.

```
        EXEC SQL BEGIN DECLARE SECTION;
            char   comm[200];
            int    empnum;
            char   address[30];
            char   city[17];
        EXEC SQL END DECLARE SECTION;
        SQLDA *sqlda;                // Declare the sqlda pointer

        sprintf( comm, "UPDATE customer SET address1 = :address, city =
        :city WHERE employee_number = :empnum");
        EXEC SQL PREPARE sql_statement FROM :comm;
        sqlda = alloc_sqlda(1 );     // Allocate the SQLDA memory.  Assume
        that there are NEVER more than 1 host variable.
        EXEC SQL DESCRIBE BIND VARIABLES FOR sql_statement USING DESCRIPTOR
        sqlda;
        // sqlda->sqld will tell you how many host variables there were.
        if( sqlda->sqld != sqlda->sqln ) {        // There's more than 1
        host variable.
            int actual_size = sqlda->sqld;        // Get the actual size
            free_sqlda( sqlda );
            sqlda = alloc_sqlda( actual_size );
            EXEC SQL DESCRIBE INPUT FOR employee_statement INTO sqlda;
            }
        ...
```

As you can see, DESCRIBE is necessary and useful for memory management while using dynamic SQL statements. DESCRIBE takes the SQLDA management burden away from the developer.

Understanding Embedded SQL Libraries

Libraries must be linked to your C++ program when you make your executable or DLL. These libraries contain functions used internally by Watcom SQL, as well as functions the programmer can call.

You must link different Watcom SQL libraries when you are making your executable, depending on what compiler you are using for Watcom SQL. Table 14.1 lists the Embedded SQL libraries.

Table 14.4 Embedded SQL Libraries			
Library	**Path**	**OS**	**Description**
dblibwcc.lib	\wsql40\dos\lib	DOS	Watcom C compact memory model library.
dblibwch.lib	\wsql40\dos\lib	DOS	Watcom C huge memory model library.
dblibwcl.lib	\wsql40\dos\lib	DOS	Watcom C large memory model library.
dblibwcm.lib	\wsql40\dos\lib	DOS	Watcom C medium memory model library.
dblibwcs.lib	\wsql40\dos\lib	DOS	Watcom C small memory model library.
dblibmcc.lib	\wsql40\dos\lib	DOS	Microsoft C compact memory model library.
dblibmch.lib	\wsql40\dos\lib	DOS	Microsoft C huge memory model library.
dblibmcl.lib	\wsql40\dos\lib	DOS	Microsoft C large memory model library.
dblibmcm.lib	\wsql40\dos\lib	DOS	Microsoft C medium memory model library.

(continues)

Table 14.4	Continued		
Library	**Path**	**OS**	**Description**
dblibmcs.lib	\wsql40\dos\lib	DOS	Microsoft C small memory model library.
dblibbcc.lib	\wsql40\dos\lib	DOS	Borland C compact memory model library.
dblibbch.lib	\wsql40\dos\lib	DOS	Borland C huge memory model library.
dblibbcl.lib	\wsql40\dos\lib	DOS	Borland C large memory model library.
dblibbcm.lib	\wsql40\dos\lib	DOS	Borland C medium memory model library.
dblibbcs.lib	\wsql40\dos\lib	DOS	Borland C small memory model library.
dblibwfg.lib	\wsql40\dos\lib	DOS	32-bit Rational DOS4G DOS Extender Watcom C library.
dblibwfp.lib	\wsql40\dos\lib	DOS	32-bit Pharlap DOS Extender Watcom C library.
dblibwfa.lib	\wsql40\dos\lib	DOS	32-bit ADS (AutoCAD) Watcom C library.
dblibw.lib	\wsql40\win\lib	Windows	Import library for DBLIBW.DLL.
dblibwfw.lib	\wsql40\win\lib	Windows	32-bit Watcom C library.
dblibfws.lib	\wsql40\win\lib	Windows	32-bit Watcom C stack calling convention library.
dblib2.lib	\wsql40\os2\lib	OS/2	Import library for DBLIB2.DLL.
dblibtw.lib	\wsql40\nt\lib	Windows NT	Watcom C/C++ import library for DBLIBT.DLL.
dblibtm.lib	\wsql40\nt\lib	Windows NT	Microsoft Visual C++ import library for DBLIBT.DLL.
dblibs.lib	\wsql40\qnx\lib	QNX	Watcom C small memory model library.

Library	Path	OS	Description
dblibm.lib	\wsql40\qnx\lib	QNX	Watcom C medium memory model library.
dblibl.lib	\wsql40\qnx\lib	QNX	Watcom C large memory model library.
dblibc.lib	\wsql40\qnx\lib	QNX	Watcom C compact memory model library.
dblib3r.lib	\wsql40\qnx\lib	QNX	32-bit Watcom C library.

In the case with PowerBuilder, you should probably link in dblibwfw.lib.

Note

With Watcom SQL for Windows, you can statically link your Watcom SQL library with your executable. All other Windows compilers require DLL calls. Because static calls are faster than dynamic calls, your Watcom SQL will run faster with your Watcom C++ than with any other Windows compiler.

Using SQL Inside Your C++ Program

In this section, you finally get to start coding Watcom SQL C++ commands inside your program. First, you must rename your C++ program from UC_CUSR3.CPP to UC_CUSR3.SQC. Adding Watcom SQL calls to your C++ program requires some preprocessing, using UC_CUSR3.SQC as the input file and UC_CUSR3.CPP as the output file.

This section will show you how to modify and then process UC_CUSR3 to contain SQL statements.

Understanding Embedded SQL Header Files

Watcom provides several header files that help you with your SQL access. These are listed in Table 14.5.

Table 14.5 Header Files Included with Watcom SQL	
SQL Header File	**Description**
sqlca.h	sqlca.h contains the most widely used embedded SQL structures and functions. Included is the sqlca structure definition for the SQL Communications Area used by all embedded SQL commands. Also included are function prototypes for interfacing with the SQL libraries, such as db_init and db_fini, which are required by all programs containing embedded SQL. However, you don't have to include sqlca.h because the EXEC SQL INCLUDE SQLCA command includes it for you.
sqlda.h	sqlda.h contains functions and structures used by programs that use dynamic SQL. Dynamic SQL is discussed in "Understanding the Difference between Static and Dynamic Statements," earlier in this chapter. You don't have to include sqlda.h because the EXEC SQL INCLUDE SQLCA command includes it for you.
sqldef.h	sqldef.h is a header file that contains data type information that defines SQL interface data types. sqldef.h is useful when connecting to a database or network while in C++ or when using the DESCRIBE SQL command.
sqlerr.h	sqlerr.h contains the definition for the error codes returned in the sqlcode field of the SQLCA. This is handy for displaying text about an error.
sqlstate.h	sqlstate.h contains constants that make coding for SQLSTATE codes easier. SQLSTATE codes are returned in the sqlstate field of the sqlca structure.

Your applications will have sqlca.h and sqlda.h already included. You'll probably find that no more header files are needed for your application.

Formatting Your SQL Statements

Every SQL command used in C++ must begin with EXEC SQL and end with a semicolon (;). The first SQL statement in every SQL C++ should include SQLCA, as follows:

```
EXEC SQL INCLUDE SQLCA;
```

This statement goes *outside* of any function declarations. Before any SQL calls are made in your function, you must first initialize your SQLCA area. This is done with the db_init function and the following call:

```
db_init(&sqlca);
```

SQLCA is a variable that's defined after the preprocessor is finished executing the INCLUDE SQLCA command previously mentioned. You must also connect to your ODBC database. This is done through the CONNECT command, as follows:

```
EXEC SQL CONNECT DATABASE c:\watcom\database\database.db USER dba
IDENTIFIED BY sql;
```

Note

You would replace c:\watcom\database\database.db with the database you want to access. dba and sql are my user ID and password.

Using Host Variables and Embedded SQL Data Types

To include host variables in your C++ code, you must use a declare section. The syntax for a declare section is as follows:

```
EXEC SQL BEGIN DECLARE SECTION;
      . . .
EXEC SQL END DECLARE SECTION;
```

To declare variables in C++ to be used as host variables, you can use the following syntax:

```
EXEC SQL BEGIN DECLARE SECTION;
      long customer_number;
EXEC SQL END DECLARE SECTION;
```

In the previous example, customer_number can now be used both in the C++ body and as a host variable in SQL statements. Certain host variable types don't have a corresponding data type in C++. For these, Watcom provided macros in sqlca.h that try to pick up the slack. These variable macros are DECL_VARCHAR(size), DECL_BINARY(size), DECL_DECIMAL(prec, scale), DECL_FIXCHAR(size), and DECL_DATETIME. These macros are used as follows:

```
EXEC SQL BEGIN DECLARE SECTION;
      DECL_VARCHAR(30)  customer_name;
      DECL_BINARY(30)    customer_address;
      DECL_DECIMAL(10, 2)     salary;
      DECL_FIXCHAR(2)    customer_state;
      DECL_DATETIME     order_date;
EXEC SQL END DECLARE SECTION;
```

The macro in sqlca.h automatically changes these variables to the appropriate type for use with a Watcom SQL database.

> **Note**
>
> If you look at sqlca.h, you can see how each macro is defined. Right away, you notice that DECL_VARCHAR(size) and DECL_BINARY(size) have the same conversion format:
>
> ```
> #define DECL_VARCHAR(size) \
>         struct { unsigned short int len; \
>                 char array[size]; \
>         }
>
> #define DECL_BINARY( size )  \
>         struct { unsigned short int len; \
>                 char array[size];  \
>         }
> ```
>
> Hence, the variable type you choose (between these two) is irrelevant—in terms of efficiency. However, you might want to define your C++ variable the same as your Watcom SQL variable for documentation purposes.
>
> You also notice that the scale in DECL_DECIMAL is not used:
>
> ```
> #define DECL_DECIMAL( prec, scale )  \
>         struct { char   array[ (prec/2) + 1 ]; \
>         }
> ```
>
> Although you still need to enter *anything* (even a letter) for scale, the SQLPP preprocessor ignores it. So the following DECL_DECIMAL declarations all are identical:
>
> ```
> DECL_DECIMAL(10, 2)     salary;
> DECL_DECIMAL(10, 20)    salary;
> DECL_DECIMAL(10, abc)   salary;
> ```
>
> All of the above DECL_DECIMAL statements give you a decimal precision of 10 but ignore the second value.

Table 14.6 lists the data types in C++ and their corresponding Watcom SQL data types.

Table 14.6   C++ Data Types Used with Watcom SQL

C Data Type	SQLDA Data Type Constant	Watcom SQL Data Type	Description
short short int unsigned short int	DT_SMALLINT	SMALLINT	16 bit, signed integer

C Data Type	SQLDA Data Type Constant	Watcom SQL Data Type	Description
long long int unsigned long int	DT_INT	INT	32 bit, signed integer
float	DT_FLOAT	FLOAT	4-byte floating point number
double	DT_DOUBLE	DOUBLE	8-byte floating point number
DECL_DECIMAL(p,s)	DT_DECIMAL	DECIMAL(p,s)	packed decimal
char (n = 1) DECL_FIXCHAR(n) a; DECL_FIXCHAR a[n]; char a[n]; char *a;	DT_STRING DT_FIXCHAR	CHAR(n)	blank padded fixed length character string
DECL_VARCHAR(n);	DT_VARCHAR DT_DATE* DT_TIME* DT_TIMESTAMP*	VARCHAR(n)	varying length character string with 2- byte length field
DECL_BINARY(n)	DT_BINARY	BINARY(n)	varying length binary data with 2-byte length field
DECL_DATETIME	DT_TIMESTAMP _STRUCT	TIMESTAMP	Timestamp

Using Indicator Values To Handle NULLs in C++

One of the thorniest problems with embedded SQL is how to handle a column containing NULL. This is done through indicator variables.

◀ See "Understanding NULLS," p. 51

> **Note**
>
> In C++, a NULL is often an ASCII zero placed at the end of a string. The phrase NULL terminated string refers to a string of variable length with a NULL at the end.
>
> In SQL, a NULL is *not* an ASCII zero. NULL represents an unknown or "empty" value in a column. This section deals with the SQL NULL.

Indicator variables are used in SELECT, INSERT, and UPDATE statements to either report that a NULL has been detected in a column or to place a NULL in a column. A NULL is a short integer that is used in addition to the column host variable to indicate whether a NULL was detected. Review the following code:

```
EXEC SQL BEGIN DECLARE SECTION;
      DECL_VARCHAR(300) customer_comments;
      short int         comment_indicator;
      long              customer_number;
EXEC SQL END DECLARE SECTION;
. . .
EXEC SQL
      SELECT customer_comments comment_indicator
      INTO :customer_comments :comment_indicator
      FROM customer
      WHERE customer_number = :customer_number;
if (comment_indicator < 0) {
      // comments are NULL
}
. . .
comment_indicator = -1                      // Set column to NULL
EXEC SQL
      UPDATE customer
      SET customer_comments = :customer_comments :comment_indicator
      WHERE customer_number = :customer_number;
. . .
```

In the previous code segment, the first SQL statement declares the variables you'll be using as host variables. The second SQL statement uses `comment_indicator` to test whether the retrieved value is NULL. The third SQL statement updates `customer_comments` and sets it to NULL by using a –1 in the customer indicator.

NULL indicators are host variables that immediately follow the column host variable (without a comma) in a SELECT, INSERT, or UPDATE statement. When the `comment_indicator` is –1, it either indicates that the last query retrieved a NULL in that column, or that you want the column you are updating or inserting set to NULL.

Error Processing with SQL

Catching the errors inside SQL can be done in one of two ways. The first (and probably the best) is to test SQLCA.sqlcode after every SQL command. A listing of error codes is available in Appendix C.

The following example illustrates the use of SQLCA.sqlcode:

```
EXEC SQL CONNECT DATABASE c:\watcom\database\database.db USER dba
IDENTIFIED BY sql;
if (SQLCA.sqlcode != 0) {
        char message[50];
        sprintf(message, "Could not connect to database.  SQL error
code is %d", SQLCA.sqlcode);
        MessageBox(0, message, "CONNECTION ERROR", MB_ICONHAND);
        return SQLCA.sqlcode;
}
```

As you can see by the previous code, if the sqlcode is not zero, then an error
has occurred and you are not connected.

Another way to catch errors is to have an error interrupt handler. Interrupt
handlers are more generic in nature than individual error messages. The following code shows the use of the WHENEVER clause to handle errors in C
and C++:

► See "Error
Message
Descriptions,"
p. 673

```
#include "stdio.h"
EXEC SQL INCLUDE SQLCA;

main() {
   db_init( SQLCA );
   EXEC SQL WHENEVER SQLERROR GOTO error;
   EXEC SQL CONNECT DATABASE c:\watcom\database\database.db USER
dba IDENTIFIED BY sql;
   EXEC SQL UPDATE customer SET customer_name = 'Chuck Wood'
        WHERE customer_number = 1;
   EXEC SQL COMMIT WORK;
   EXEC SQL DISCONNECT;
   db_fini( SQLCA );
   return( 0 );

   error:
        printf( "Update DID NOT WORK!!! sqlcode = %ld\n",
sqlca.sqlcode );
        return( -1 );
}
```

In the above code, the WHENEVER clause causes the program to branch to
the error: label when an SQL error occurs anywhere in the program.

Using SQLPP Library Functions

In addition to internal function calls used to support your Watcom SQL application, Watcom SQL libraries also include several developer-accessible
functions. The interface functions (db_init and db_fini) are required for every
Watcom SQL interface. Other functions might make your SQL programming
a little easier, but most can be accomplished using embedded SQL.

Interface Functions

Interface functions are the only functions required when using embedded SQL. The two interface functions are db_init (used before any SQL statements) and db_fini (to clean up after all SQL statements). These functions are described in Table 14.7.

Table 14.7 Interface Functions	
Library Function	**Description**
db_init(SQLCA *sqlca)	db_init must be called before you access an SQLCA variable. db_init sets up the Watcom SQL interface in the SQLCA area.
db_fini(SQLCA *sqlca)	db_fini must be called at the end of your program or function for every SQLCA variable you set up. db_fini frees up allocated memory used in your SQLCA variable.

Connection Functions

▶ See "Under-standing Con-nection Param-eters," p. 579

Connection functions can be used to control the connection to the database without using the embedded SQL CONNECT statement. The connection functions each require a connection string filled with connection parameters (denoted by char *parms in the function prototypes). Valid connection parameters are listed in Table 14.8.

Table 14.8 Connection Parameters		
Verbose Form	**Short Form**	**Description**
Userid	UID	Defines the user ID of the person accessing the database.
Password	PWD	Password defines the password of the user accessing the database.
ConnectionName	CON	You are allowed to name your connection. This is needed if you access multiple SQLCA sessions at once.
EngineName	ENG	EngineName is the name of the database engine that will be called after starting. If not specified, the EngineName will default to the DatabaseName.

Verbose Form	Short Form	Description
DatabaseName	DBN	The DatabaseName is the name you have given your database when defining it by using the ODBC administrator or in the ODBC.INI file.
DatabaseFile	DBF	The DatabaseFile is the exact path and file location of the database you want to access. This is not needed if you use DatabaseName.
DatabaseSwitches	DBS	DatabaseSwitches are switches used to start your database.
AutoStop	AutoStop	AutoStop determines whether the database engine will automatically terminate when the database is disconnected.
Start	Start	Start lists the program used to start the database. Valid values are DB32W.EXE, DBSTARTW.EXE, RT32W.EXE, and RTSTARTW.EXE.
Unconditional	UNC	Unconditional tells the database to start, regardless of the existence of a log file. This is useful if the log file has been corrupted but the database is intact.

▶ See "Using DB32W.EXE, DBSTARTW.EXE, RT32W.EXE, and RTSTARTW.EXE," p. 612

IV

Interfaces

> **Note**
>
> When you use connection parameters, you can use the long form or the short form. For example, the following two connection strings are equivalent:
>
>   :
>
>   UID=dba;PWD=sql;DBF=c:\wsql40\sample.db
>
> and
>
>   UserID=dba;Password=sql;DatabaseFile=c:\wsql40\sample.db

Table 14.9 lists the connection functions, their parameters, and a brief description of each function.

Table 14.9   Connection Functions

Function Name	Description
db_string_connect (SQLCA *sqlca, char *parms)	Connects to the database like the SQL CONNECT command, except it also uses the SQLCA variable to define the database, the engine, the AutoStop choice, the User ID, and the Password.
db_string_disconnect (SQLCA *sqlca, char *parms)	Disconnects the SQLCA specified by the ConnectionName parameter. All other parameters are ignored.
db_start_engine (SQLCA *sqlca, char *parms)	Starts a database engine, but can also be used to connect to a database or set database switches based on the SQLCA area.
db_start_database (SQLCA *sqlca, char *parms)	Connects to a database. If an engine is not already running, db_start_database will start the engine defined in the SQLCA area.
db_stop_engine (SQLCA *sqlca, char *parms)	Stops the engine specified by the EngineName parameter. If Unconditional is specified, db_stop_engine will shut down the database engine, even if there are existing connections.
db_stop_database (SQLCA *sqlca, char *parms)	Stops the database specified by the DatabaseName parameter. If Unconditional is specified, db_stop_engine will shut down the database, even if there are existing connections.

SQLDA Management Functions

In addition to the DESCRIBE SQL command, Watcom SQL includes several functions to manage your SQLDA area. These functions are described in Table 14.10.

Table 14.10   SQLDA Management Functions

Function Name	Description
struct sqlda *alloc_sqlda (unsigned numvar)	Allocates an SQLDA with descriptors for numvar variables. The sqln field of the SQLDA will be initialized to numvar. Space is allocated for the indicator variables, the indicator pointers are set to point to this space, and the indicator value is initialized to zero. A null pointer will be returned if memory cannot be allocated.

Function Name	Description
struct sqlda *alloc_sqlda_noind (unsigned numvar)	Allocates an SQLDA with descriptors for numvar variables. The sqln field of the SQLDA will be initialized to numvar. Space is not allocated for indicator variables; the indicator pointers are set to the null pointer. A null pointer will be returned if memory cannot be allocated.
struct sqlda *fill_sqlda (struct sqlda *sqlda)	Allocates space for each variable described in each descriptor of sqlda, and assigns the address of this memory to the sqldata field of the corresponding descriptor. Enough space is allocated for the database type and length indicated in the descriptor. Returns sqlda if successful, and returns the null pointer if there is not enough memory available.
unsigned long sqlda_string_length (struct sqlda *sqlda, int varno)	Returns the length of a C string required to hold the variable sqlda -> sqlvar[varno] (no matter what its type).
unsigned long sqlda_storage (struct sqlda *sqlda, int varno)	Returns the amount of storage required to store any value for the variable described in sqlda -> sqlvar[varno].
struct sqlda *fill_s_sqlda (struct sqlda *sqlda, unsigned int maxlen)	Much the same as fill_sqlda, except that it changes all of the data types in sqlda to type DT_STRING (see SQLDEF.H header file). Enough space is allocated for the strings to hold the string representation of the type originally specified by the SQLDA, up to a maximum of maxlen bytes. The length fields in the SQLDA (sqllen) are modified appropriately. Returns sqlda if successful, and returns the null pointer if there is not enough memory available.
void free_filled_sqlda (struct sqlda *sqlda)	Frees all space allocated to this sqlda, including the memory allocated to each sqldata pointer. Any null pointer will not be freed. The indicator variable space is also freed as allocated in fill_sqlda.
void free_sqlda_noind (struct sqlda *sqlda)	Frees the space allocated to this sqlda, but does not free the memory referenced by each sqldata pointer. The indicator variable pointers are ignored.
void free_sqlda (struct sqlda *sqlda)	Frees the space allocated to this sqlda, but does not free the memory referenced by each sqldata pointer. The indicator variable space is also freed as allocated in fill_sqlda.

Pulling It All Together

The following code is a simple example of how to use embedded SQL inside your C++ program.

```
/* WATCOM Interface Generator    Version 1.0 */
/* Created:  Mon Mar  6 05:24:42 1995
 */
/* This file contains code generated by PowerBuilder.
 * Do not modify code delimited by comments of the form:
 * // $PB$ — begin generated code for object <>.  Do not modify
this code
 * // $PB$ — end generated code for object <>.
 * This file contains the bodies the functions for your user
object.
 */

#include <pbdll.h>

#include "uc_cusR3.hpp"

EXEC SQL INCLUDE SQLCA;

// $PB$ — begin generated code for object <uc_customer_number>.
Do not modify this code
#if 1
int uc_customer_number::ucf_process_customer( char *customer_number
) {
// $PB$ — end generated code for object <uc_customer_number>.
//==================================

    EXEC SQL BEGIN DECLARE SECTION;
         DECL_VARCHAR(300)          customer_comments;
         float              customer_sales;
    EXEC SQL END DECLARE SECTION;
    EXEC SQL CONNECT DATABASE c:\watcom\database\database.db USER
dba IDENTIFIED BY sql;
    return( 0 );
}
#endif // PowerBuilder code, do not remove
```

From Here...

This chapter taught you how to use embedded SQL inside your C++ program. To further increase your knowledge on this topic, check out the following sources:

■ Chapter 16, "Using Watcom SQL with Windows Tools," teaches you how to implement Watcom SQL using DLLs and ODBC interfaces with computer languages other than C++.

■ Chapter 22, "Embedded SQL Commands," lists and describes all SQL commands available to you inside your program.

■ In Appendix C, "Database Error Messages," you get a listing of all error messages and warnings inside your C++ program.

Implementing Watcom SQL HLI

SQLPP is used for C and C++ compilers to take advantage of the Watcom SQL database, as described in Chapter 14. However, Watcom SQL does not include preprocessors for any other language. To access Watcom SQL from Windows, Windows NT, or OS/2 programs, you can use the *host language interface (HLI)*.

The HLI is a set of functions contained within a Dynamic Link Library (DLL) that can be called from outside programs. In this chapter, the following topics are discussed:

- The difference between static and dynamic linking

- What is required to run Watcom SQL's HLI

- The functions contained inside the HLI

- Using the HLI with Visual BASIC

- Using the HLI with REXX and OS/2

Understanding Dynamic and Static Linking

Conventional DOS and QNX applications require programs to be linked together to form one executable. *Static linking* is when you develop an executable program by linking all object modules together (see fig. 15.1). Notice the way all source modules are compiled into object modules and then all linked together (statically) to make a single executable.

Note

Static linking refers to linking all your modules together to form one stand-alone executable program.

Dynamic linking refers to allowing your executable program to link to other libraries at run time.

Fig. 15.1
The traditional way to develop an application was to compile all modules and statically link them together.

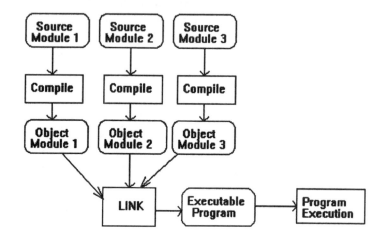

The HLI makes use of Dynamic Link Libraries (DLLs). Dynamic Link Libraries are available through Windows and OS/2. They allow you to defer linking until run time, as shown in figure 15.2.

Fig. 15.2
By using Dynamic Link Libraries, you reduce executable size and let your executable program call functions at run time, rather than statically linking all modules together.

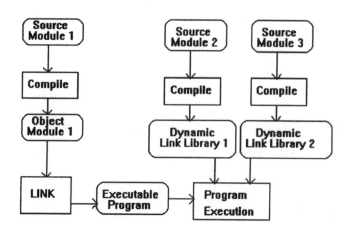

Dynamic Link Libraries let you make generic libraries that can be used with several different programs—even programs written in different languages. Therefore DLLs have several advantages over traditional linking:

- DLLs can be shared between several programs.

- Because DLLs are stand-alone modules, they are completely encapsulated: upgrading is easily accomplished, and changes to your code do not effect the functionality of the DLL.

- DLLs are easy to use. Often, you merely need to declare them in a program and then treat them as a regular function. Plus, the DLL's high level of abstraction means that the DLL does all the work after being called. The developer can simply call the DLL to start its function.

The tradeoff to using DLLs is speed. Because of their dynamic nature, DLLs require additional run-time setup that statically linked modules don't require, possibly slowing down an application.

Watcom makes use of DLLs in its HLI. By providing DLLs that can be accessed by any Windows or OS/2 program, Watcom has made its database accessible to programs in which a specific interface has not been developed.

> **Note**
>
> Although you *could* use the Watcom SQL HLI to interface with a Windows or OS/2 C or C++ program, you can accomplish the same task a lot quicker *and* have more efficient code by using the C/C++ preprocessor, SQLPP, that comes with Watcom SQL. Not only will SQLPP run faster, but your SQL syntax is checked at compile time rather than run time, making it easier to catch errors. If you are developing in C or C++, see Chapter 14, "Implementing Watcom SQL with SQLPP (C and C++)," for more details.

Understanding Watcom SQL HLI Requirements

Setting up a program to access the Watcom SQL HLI is different for different operating systems:

- *In Windows,* the Watcom SQL HLI functions are found in WSQLCALL.DLL and you use the FAR PASCAL function prototype to declare all functions.

■ *In Windows NT,* the Watcom SQL HLI functions are found in WSQLCALT.DLL for Windows NT programs, and you use the _stdcall declaration to declare all functions.

■ *In OS/2,* the Watcom SQL HLI functions are found in WSQLLCAL2.DLL, and you use the _System declaration to declare all functions.

The following line of code is an example of a call to a Watcom SQL HLI function in both C/C++ and Visual Basic:

```
ret = wsqlexec ("START USING DATABASE sample AS first_connection
USER dba IDENTIFIED BY sql");
```

> **Note**
>
> C/C++ requires a semicolon at the end of statements; Visual BASIC does not.

In all the Watcom SQL HLI functions, the value returned is the SQLCode of the last SQL function.

Using Watcom SQL HLI Functions

Watcom SQL HLI consists of seven functions. These functions are robust enough to perform all of your database access.

> **Note**
>
> Examples of the Watcom SQL HLI can be found in the "Using Watcom SQL with Visual Basic" and "Using Watcom SQL with REXX and OS/2" sections.

wsqlexec and wsqlexec Functions

You use wsqlexec to execute one of 13 commands that allow the user to execute any SQL statement except the SELECT statement. The C declaration for the wsqlexec function is as follows:

```
extern long _entry wsqlexec (char *command);
```

The command can be CLIP, CLOSE, COMMIT, DECLARE, DROP, EXECUTE, FETCH, OPEN, PREPARE, ROLLBACK, SET CONNECTION, START USING DATABASE, or STOP USING DATABASE. (The following sections describe these commands.)

An example of the wsqlexec function (one you've seen before) is as follows:

```
ret = wsqlexec ("START USING DATABASE sample AS first_connection
USER dba IDENTIFIED BY sql")
```

The previous command connects to the sample database with a dba user
ID and an sql password. The return code is the SQLCode returned by the
CONNECT command called by the START USING DATABASE command.

CLIP Command

The CLIP command copies the contents of a cursor to the Clipboard in Windows or Windows NT. The syntax for CLIP is as follows:

```
CLIP clip_type cursor_name
```

The cursor_name is the name of the cursor. The cursor must be OPENed first.
See the "OPEN Command" section, later in this chapter.

The clip_type can be NAMES, DATA, or BOTH. If you specify NAMES, the
Clipboard will contain a single row of column names SELECTed by a cursor.
If you specify DATA, the Clipboard will contain all the cursor rows in column
format. If you specify BOTH, the Clipboard will contain both the column
names and the data.

Specifying DATA (or BOTH) causes the cursor pointer to be positioned after
the last row in the cursor.

CLOSE Command

CLOSE closes a cursor. The syntax for HLI CLOSE is:

```
CLOSE cursor_name
```

where cursor_name is the name of the OPENed cursor.

▶ See "CLOSE,"
p. 533

COMMIT Command

Similar to normal SQL, the HLI COMMIT makes changes to the database
permanent. Unlike the SQL commit, you are not allowed to specify the
USING sqlca_area clause. The format for the HLI COMMIT is:

```
COMMIT
```

Notice that no additional parameters are allowed.

▶ See "COMMIT,"
p. 534

DECLARE Command

As with the SQL DECLARE, the HLI DECLARE declares a cursor. The syntax
for the HLI DECLARE is:

```
DECLARE cursor_name CURSOR FOR statement_name
```

▶ See "DECLARE
CURSOR,"
p. 543

The main difference between the HLI DECLARE and the SQL DECLARE is that the statement_name in the HLI DECLARE must have been used in a previous HLI PREPARE statement. See the "PREPARE Command" section, later in this chapter.

DROP Command

▶ See "DROP," p. 548

The HLI DROP command frees resources previously declared with a PREPARE statement. The syntax for the HLI DROP statement is as follows:

```
DROP statement_name
```

You must have used the statement_name in a previous HLI PREPARE statement. (See the "PREPARE Command" section, later in this chapter.) If a cursor is associated with the statement_name, the cursor closes.

EXECUTE Command

EXECUTE allows the developer to execute any SQL statement. The HLI EXECUTE statement has two formats:

Format 1:

```
EXECUTE statement_name [USING host_variable_list]
```

Format 2:

```
EXECUTE IMMEDIATE statement
```

In format 1, you must have used the statement_name in a previous HLI PRE-PARE statement. (See the "PREPARE Command" section, later in this chapter.) You can omit the host_variable_list, but if you include it, it must contain host variable parameters.

In format 2, the statement following the EXECUTE IMMEDIATE command is PREPAREd, EXECUTEd, and DROPped. The statement in format 2 is a string or a host variable containing any SQL command except the SELECT statement.

▶ See "FETCH," p. 551

FETCH Command

As with the SQL FETCH, the HLI FETCH retrieves a row from a cursor. The syntax for the HLI FETCH is as follows:

```
FETCH [offset_type offset_amount]
      cursor_name
      [INTO host_variable_list]
```

The cursor_name is the name of the OPENed cursor. The host_variable_list is a list of host variables used to store the contents of the FETCH. If you don't provide a host_variable_list, the data from the FETCH can be retrieved using the wsqlgetfield HLI function discussed in the "wsqlgetfield Function" section.

The `offset_type` can be ABSOLUTE or RELATIVE, depending on whether you want to get the absolute row number or the row number in relation to your current cursor position:

- ABSOLUTE fetches the row at that absolute row number. The following statement fetches the row at position 5 of the `customer_cursor` and places the results in `customer_number` and `customer_name`:

```
FETCH ABSOLUTE 5 customer_cursor INTO :customer_number,
:customer_name
```

- RELATIVE fetches the row in relation to the current cursor position. The following statement fetches the row at a position that is five rows after the current cursor position of the `customer_cursor` and places the results in `customer_number` and `customer_name`:

```
FETCH RELATIVE 5 customer_cursor INTO :customer_number,
:customer_name
```

The following statement fetches the row prior to the current position of the `customer_cursor` (negative numbers scroll up the cursor; positive numbers scroll down the cursor):

```
FETCH RELATIVE -1 customer_cursor INTO :customer_number,
:customer_name
```

The default for the FETCH statement (if both ABSOLUTE and RELATIVE are not specified) is to FETCH RELATIVE 1, which retrieves the row after the current cursor position.

OPEN Command
The HLI OPEN command is similar to the SQL OPEN statement: they both open a cursor for use with a FETCH at a later time. The syntax for the OPEN command is as follows:

```
OPEN cursor_name
```

The `cursor_name` is the name of the cursor DECLAREd using a PREPARE statement. See the "DECLARE Command" and "PREPARE Command" sections for further reference.

PREPARE Command
The HLI PREPARE command is functionally identical to the PREPARE SQL statement. The syntax for the HLI PREPARE command is as follows:

Tip
Although you can't issue a SELECT in Watcom SQL HLI, you *can* OPEN a single-row cursor and FETCH the results. This is functionally equivalent to using a SELECT.

IV

Interfaces

▶ See "OPEN," p. 558

▶ See "PREPARE TO COMMIT," p. 559

```
PREPARE statement_name FROM statement_string
```

Tip
Although you
can't use SELECT
with the HLI, you
can use SELECT
inside a prepared
statement with the
HLI.

The PREPARE statement allows a statement to be dynamically built and executed at run time. The `statement_name` is the identifier of the PREPAREd statement to be used with other commands (such as DROP and DECLARE). The `statement_string` is a string containing an SQL statement. SQL commands supported are ALTER, CALL, COMMENT ON, CREATE, DELETE, DROP, GRANT, INSERT, REVOKE, SELECT, SET OPTION, UPDATE, and VALIDATE TABLE.

ROLLBACK Command

▶ See "ROLL-
BACK," p. 562

Like the ROLLBACK SQL statement, the HLI ROLLBACK undoes changes made since the last COMMIT. The syntax for the HLI ROLLBACK is:

```
ROLLBACK
```

Notice that no parameters are allowed when using the HLI ROLLBACK.

SET CONNECTION Command

▶ See "SET CON-
NECTION,"
p. 570

SET CONNECTION allows you to change the current connection. A new connection is formed every time you run the START USING DATABASE command. Using the SET CONNECTION command, you can flip between open connections.

The syntax for the SET CONNECTION command is:

```
SET CONNECTION connection_name
```

The `connection_name` is the name supplied for the connection during the START USING DATABASE command.

START USING DATABASE Command

▶ See "CON-
NECT," p. 535

This command begins a new connection to a database engine or server. The format for the START USING DATABASE command is as follows:

```
START USING DATABASE [database_name]
    [AS connection_name]
    [USER] user_id IDENTIFIED BY password
```

The `database_name` is the name of the database to which you want to connect. If you omit `database_name`, Watcom SQL uses the default database environment. You can optionally name the connection with the `AS connection_name` clause. This is a good idea if you are connecting to many databases at one time. The `user_id IDENTIFIED BY password` identifies the user who is logging on to the database.

STOP USING DATABASE Command

The STOP USING DATABASE command disconnects the database. The syntax for the STOP USING DATABASE command is as follows:

▶ See "DISCON-
NECT," p. 548

```
STOP USING DATABASE [connection_name]
```

If you specify connection_name, that specific connection disconnects. If you omit connection_name, the current database connection disconnects.

wsqlgetcolumnname Function

You use the wsqlgetcolumnname function to retrieve a column name from a cursor. The C function prototype for the wsqlgetcolumnname function is as follows:

```
extern long _entry wsqlgetcolumnname(char *cursor_name, int
column_num, short *ind, char *result, int len );
```

In the wsqlgetcolumnname function, cursor_name is the name of a cursor that has been opened. Column_num is the number of the column you want. Columns are numbered from left to right, starting at 0. Ind is the length indicator variable. If the result buffer is too small, then the required length is put in the ind. Otherwise, it is set to zero. The result is a pre-allocated string of length len that is to hold the name of the column. The result should be allocated and deallocated by the calling program.

wsqlgetfield Function

You use the wsqlgetfield function to retrieve the value from one column of the most recently FETCHed row. The C function prototype is:

```
extern long _entry wsqlgetfield(char *cursor_name, int column_num,
short *ind, char *result, int len);
```

The cursor_name is the name of a cursor that is opened and positioned at the row of the query result set that you want to examine. The column_num is the column number you want to examine. Columns are numbered from left to right, starting at 0. The ind is the length indicator variable. If the result buffer is too small, then the required length is put in the ind. If the requested item is NULL, then the indicator is set to –1. If there is a conversion error, then the indicator is set to –2. Otherwise, it is set to zero. The result is a string buffer of length len that will be filled in with the requested column data value. The result buffer should be allocated and freed by the calling application.

wsqllasterror Function

The wsqllasterror function returns a text message describing the last SQL error that occurred. The C function prototype is:

```
extern long _entry wsqllasterror(char *buffer, int len);
```

The `buffer` is a pre-allocated string of length `len` that will hold the returning error message.

wsqlquerytomemdelim and wsqlquerytomem Functions

The wsqlquerytomemdelim and wsqlquerytomem functions are similar. (In fact, the wsqlquerytomem function consists of a single call to the wsqlquerytomemdelim function.) The wsqlquerytomemdelim function returns the rows of an OPEN cursor delimited to the developer's specification.

The syntax for wsqlquerytomemdelim is as follows:

```
extern long _entry wsqlquerytomemdelim(char *cursor_name, char
*result, int len, bool data, bool names, char *column_delim, char
*row_delim);
```

The variables used in wsqlquerytomemdelim are as follows:

- **cursor_name.** The name of the OPENed cursor. You must point the cursor pointer of `cursor_name` at the first row of the cursor unless you don't want data or don't want the entire cursor.

- **result.** The character buffer where the rows of the cursor will be stored. It is of length `len` and will be filled in with as many rows as possible, starting with the current cursor position until the size of the rows returned exceeds the len.

- **len.** The length of the result character buffer.

- **data.** A flag (0 for no or 1 for yes), indicating whether you want data returned in the result buffer.

- **names.** A flag (0 for no or 1 for yes), indicating whether you want column names returned as the first row in the result buffer.

- **column_delim.** A character string of the delimiter to place between columns in the result character buffer.

- **row_delim.** A character string of the delimiter to place between rows in the character buffer.

Wsqlquerytomem is identical to wsqlquerytomemdelim, except that instead of being able to choose your column and row delimiters, wsqlquerytomem fills them in for you. Column delimiters in wsqlquerytomem are tabs; row delimiters in wsqlquerytomem are carriage return/line feeds.

The syntax for wsqlquerytomem is as follows:

```
extern long _entry wsqlquerytomemdelim(char *cursor_name, char
*result, int len, bool data, bool names);
```

The definition for these variables is identical to the wsqlquerytomemdelim function.

wsqlregisterfuncs Function

You use the wsqlregisterfuncs function to register host variables for SQL commands. The C prototype for wsqlregisterfuncs is as follows:

```
extern long _entry wsqlregisterfuncs(p_callback PutHostVar,
p_callback GetHostVar);
```

The p_callback data type is a structure defined (in C/C++) as the following:

```
struct p_callback {
       char *name,
       short ind,
       char *value,
       int len
};
```

The following describes each variable in the structure for PutHostVar and GetHostVar:

Variable	Description
PutHostVar.name	The name of the host variable that the Watcom SQL HLI will affect.
PutHostVar.ind	The indicator variable for the host variable.
PutHostVar.value	The new value for the host variable. It is always a null-terminated string.
PutHostVar.len	The length of the new value.
GetHostVar.name	The name of the host variable whose value is needed by the Watcom SQL HLI.
GetHostVar.ind	The indicator variable for the host variable (if one exists).
GetHostVar.value	A string containing the value of the host variable.
GetHostVar.len	The length of the host variable.

> **Note**
>
> *Indicator variables* are short integers used to indicate what type of value (if any) is retrieved or placed in the database. The actual value of an indicator variable is as follows:

Indicator Value	Value Supplied to Database	Meaning of Indicator Value
> 0	host variable	The received value was truncated to fit in the length. The actual length is in the indicator value.
0	host variable	The FETCH was successful.
–1	NULL	NULL resulted from the FETCH.
–2	NULL	A conversion error occurred. (The wsqllasterror function displays a conversion error message.)
< –2	NULL	NULL resulted from the FETCH.

Using Watcom SQL with Visual Basic

Tip

If you are using Visual Basic for DOS, be sure to use the SETMEM function.

In Visual Basic, place the following lines in the global area in your Visual Basic project:

```
Declare Function wsqlexec Lib "wsqlcall.dll" (ByVal cmd$) As Long
Declare Function wsqlgetfield Lib "wsqlcall.dll" (ByVal cur$, ByVal
i As Integer, ind As Integer, ByVal buf$, ByVal l As Integer) As
Long
Declare Function wsqlgetcolumnname Lib "wsqlcall.dll" (ByVal cur$,
ByVal i As Integer, ind As Integer, ByVal buf$, ByVal l As Integer)
As Long
Declare Function wsqllasterror Lib "wsqlcall.dll" (ByVal buf$,
ByVal i As Integer) As Long
Declare Function wsqlquerytomem Lib "wsqlcall.dll" (ByVal cur$,
ByVal buf$, ByVal length As Integer, ByVal names As Integer, ByVal
dta As Integer) As Long
Global fields(1 To 6)  As String * 110
```

> **Note**
>
> You can find these declarations in the WSQLDLLT.GLB file. This file is probably in the \WSQL40\ACCXMP\VB directory (if you're using the Windows environment).

The following implements the HLI inside a Visual Basic program:

```
' Start using the customer database

DIM CustomerName[100] AS STRING
DIM CustomerPhone[100] AS STRING

' Start using the customer database

ReturnCode% = wsqlexec( "START USING DATABASE customer AS
connection1 USER dba IDENTIFIED BY sql" )
IF ReturnCode% <> 0 THEN
     GOSUB sqlerror
END IF
ReturnCode% = wsqlexec( "SET CONNECTION connection1" )
IF ReturnCode% <> 0 THEN
     GOSUB sqlerror
END IF

' Now declare your customer_cursor

ReturnCode% = wsqlexec( "PREPARE statement1 FROM SELECT CustomerName,
CustomerPhone FROM customer_table" )
IF ReturnCode% <> 0 THEN
     GOSUB sqlerror
END IF
ReturnCode% = wsqlexec( "DECLARE customer_cursor CURSOR FOR statement1" )
IF ReturnCode% <> 0 THEN
     GOSUB sqlerror
END IF

' Now fetch customer_cursor into custname$(30 byte string) and
custphone$(15 byte string)

ReturnCode% = wsqlexec( "OPEN customer_cursor" )
IF ReturnCode% <> 0 THEN
     GOSUB sqlerror
END IF
FOR counter% = 1 TO 100
     ReturnCode% = wsqlexec( "FETCH customer_cursor")
     IF ReturnCode% > 0 THEN
         EXIT FOR
     ELSEIF ReturnCode% < 0 THEN
         GOSUB sqlerror
     END IF
     wsqlgetfield( "customer_cursor", 0, ind%, custname[counter%], 30)
     wsqlgetfield( "customer_cursor", 1, ind%, custphone[counter%], 15)
NEXT counter%

' close cursor
```

IV

Interfaces

```
ReturnCode% = wsqlexec( "CLOSE customer_cursor" )
IF ReturnCode% <> 0 THEN
      GOSUB sqlerror
END IF
ReturnCode% = wsqlexec( "DROP statement1" )
IF ReturnCode% <> 0 THEN
      GOSUB sqlerror
END IF

' EXECUTE an INSERT command immediately

ReturnCode% = wsqlexec( "EXECUTE IMMEDIATE INSERT INTO
customer_table VALUES ('Chuck Wood', '(317) 555-1212')" )
IF ReturnCode% <> 0 THEN
      GOSUB sqlerror
END IF

' Terminate Database Connection

ReturnCode% = wsqlexec( "STOP USING DATABASE connection1" )
EXIT SUB


' Error handler

:sqlerror

' Get error message and display it.

      wsqllasterror( buffer$, 100 )
      MessageBox("Error number " + str$(ReturnCode%) " — " +
      buffer$)
      return
```

In the program segment, we use a loop containing a FETCH to fill the
CustomerName and CustomerPhone arrays with values from a customer database.
When we run out of rows, we exit the loop and immediately close the cursor.
We then execute an INSERT command. Throughout the program, we check
for errors and GOSUB to an error handler if an error occurs.

> **Note**
>
> Although we use a GOSUB here to make a single cohesive subroutine, you should
> make a separate subroutine to be called after any SQL errors that occur in any func-
> tions or subroutines in your Visual Basic project.

> **Troubleshooting**
>
> *I get syntax errors whenever I try to use host variables in my VB project. What can I do?*
>
> The HLI supports host variables only in languages that support callback functions. *Callback functions* are hidden, internal, automatically generated functions that allow Watcom SQL (or other programs) to determine the host variables in a program that's executing.
>
> Visual Basic does not support callback functions, and therefore cannot use host variables with the Watcom SQL HLI.
>
> To retrieve information from your Watcom SQL database to your program, write your FETCH statement without an INTO clause. Then use the wsqlgetfield function, as shown in the previous example, to retrieve previously FETCHed information.

Using Watcom SQL with REXX and OS/2

Watcom offers a graphical REXX development tool called VX-REXX, which makes REXX development easier for most OS/2 programmers.

OS/2's REXX environment can also be used to access a Watcom SQL database using the HLI. Unlike Visual Basic, OS/2's REXX *does* support host variables. Host variable support makes coding using the HLI a little easier.

The following REXX code shows how to integrate the Watcom SQL HLI with REXX:

```
/* Using Watcom SQL HLI programming example */

/* Declare your Watcom SQL HLI function */

call RXFUNCADD 'SQLEXEC', 'WSQLCAL2', 'WSQLEXECREXX'

/* Start your database */

call sqldbs 'START DATABASE MANAGER'
call sqldbs 'START USING DATABASE customer USER dba IDENTIFIED BY sql'

/* Make your SELECT statement for your cursor */

stmt = "SELECT CustomerName, CustomerPhone FROM customer_table"
call sqlexec "PREPARE statement1 FROM :stmt"
call CheckSQLError
```

```
/* DECLARE and OPEN your cursor */

call sqlexec "DECLARE customer_cursor CURSOR FOR statement1"
call CheckSQLError
call sqlexec "OPEN customer_cursor"
call CheckSQLError

/* FETCH 20 customers and display them */

do 20
     /* fetch a row */
     call sqlexec "FETCH customer_cursor INTO :CustName, :CustPhone"
     call CheckSQLError
     say :CustName :CustPhone
end

/* DROP your statement, CLOSE your cursor, and disconnect from your database */

call sqlexec "DROP statement1"
call CheckSQLError
call sqlexec "CLOSE customer_cursor"
call CheckSQLError
call sqldbs "STOP USING DATABASE ALL"
exit

/* SQL Error Handler */

CheckSQLError:
     if SQLCA.SQLCODE \= 0 then do
          say SQLCA.SQLCODE SQLMSG
     end
     return
```

This statement declares a customer_cursor to contain the customer name and customer phone. Then a loop is executed that displays 20 customer name-phone combinations. Finally, the statement is dropped, the cursor is closed, and the program disconnects from the database. There is also an error handler that displays an error message when one occurs.

OS/2 REXX development with Watcom SQL is somewhat easier than Watcom SQL development with Visual Basic. REXX provides the callback functionality needed for Watcom SQL to evaluate and set host variables. As shown in the example, host variables allow you to FETCH directly into your variables without the need for the wsqlgetfield function.

From Here...

In this chapter, you learned about Watcom SQL's host language interface (HLI). Host languages can access Watcom SQL through other means as well:

- Chapter 12, "Implementing Procedures and Triggers," teaches you how to write stored procedures that you can access from any Watcom SQL program.

- Chapter 14, "Implementing Watcom SQL with SQLPP (C and C++)," describes how to incorporate Watcom SQL before compilation by using the Watcom SQL SQLPP preprocessor for C and C++.

- Chapter 16, "Using Watcom SQL with Windows Tools," teaches you how to access the Microsoft Windows DDE (Dynamic Data Exchange) function to access Watcom SQL through other Windows programs.

Chapter 16

Using Watcom SQL with Windows Tools

by Mike Seals

Now that you have learned how to install, set up, and manage Watcom databases and tables, take a look at using Watcom with Windows tools.

In the early days of the PC, database sharing was not an issue because there were so few applications available. Only a few databases, such as dBASE and Paradox, were popular enough to be considered de facto standards. A software vendor could support multiple database formats, and their applications could work with data in most databases. DOS programs ran one at a time, so intra-application integration was not an issue, either.

The industry quickly became more competitive, with each new database product introducing a new, proprietary file format for application vendors to support. LAN gateways introduced the PC to the wide variety of databases running on mainframes and minicomputers, and users immediately began looking for ways to tap into these storehouses of data.

At about the same time, Windows was introduced and provided a way of running multiple applications at the same time. Two problems emerged: how to simplify the task of integrating an application with dozens of data-base formats without writing code to support each one individually, and how to manage the transfer of information between two running applica-tions without writing special code to support each and every application.

ODBC was developed to solve the first problem, and DDE was designed to solve the second one. OLE is an even higher level of application interactivity built on top of the message-passing capabilities of DDE.

Many personal-productivity applications today support either ODBC for database access, or DDE (or both) for cross-application data sharing. In addition to the direct HLI API discussed in Chapter 15, Watcom supports both ODBC and DDE connections to the database engine, allowing it to be integrated with a wide variety of database clients and applications.

Watcom has a utility to configure ODBC for an installation, and supports DDE calls to the database engine through a special server program.

In this chapter, you learn how to:

- Install, set up, and maintain ODBC database configurations.

- Run the DDE server, and send and receive commands and data using the DDE protocol.

Using ODBC

ODBC operates as a database request *broker.* When an application wants to connect to a database through ODBC, it places a standard call to a function in the ODBC.DLL library that is a part of Windows 3.1, requesting a connection to a named data source. The ODBC connect function looks into the ODBC.INI file to see which database engine should be used for this particular data source, starts the engine (if necessary) using startup information in an INI file called ODBCINST.INI, and forwards the connection request to the engine. Requests for data are handled similarly, with requests sent to the ODBC.DLL library first, and then forwarded to the database engine.

There is a separate entry in the ODBCINST.INI file for each database engine. This entry defines how to start the database engine *driver,* with the name of the program or DLL to load for this purpose. It also includes an entry that defines the DLL or EXE to be used for configuration setup. In this way, an ODBC-enabled application can include a button that allows the user to configure data sources for any ODBC database. This Configure button is included somewhere in most ODBC applications, and each one is different. I will use the ODBC configuration utility that comes with PowerBuilder.

Installing ODBC for Watcom SQL 4.0

The ODBC drivers are installed when you install any Windows or Windows NT version of Watcom SQL 4.0. An entry is made in the ODBCINST.INI file that defines the library name to be used to start and configure Watcom. If you chose to install the Powersoft sample database, an entry is made in the ODBC.INI file defining a data source entry for it.

IV

Declaring Data Sources

Normally, a data source points to a database. The database must exist before a data source can be defined for it, and you can define multiple data source definitions for a single database. For example, you may want to define separate ODBC data sources to a single database, one with read and write access, the other with read-only access.

The exact process used to declare data sources differs from one application to another. If you installed Watcom SQL 4.0 as a native product, then the installation process will install an ODBC configuration icon in the Watcom SQL Program Manager group. It will also install the ODBC configuration icon to the control panel. If Watcom was installed as part of another program, such as PowerBuilder or InfoMaker, then these icons will not be visible. PowerBuilder itself provides an ODBC administrator. You can add it to the PowerBar by following these steps:

1. Start PowerBuilder 4.0.

2. Choose **W**indow, Tool**b**ars... from the frame menu. The dialog box shown in figure 16.1 displays.

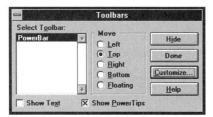

Fig. 16.1
The PowerBuilder Toolbars dialog box allows you to specify the visibility and position of the PowerBar and the various painter toolbars.

3. Click the **C**ustomize... button. The Customize dialog box appears, as shown in figure 16.2.

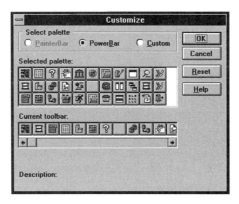

Fig. 16.2
The PowerBuilder Customize dialog box.

4. Drag the ODBC icon down to the toolbar. It makes sense to drop it next to the existing database icon.

5. Click OK to save the change.

6. Click Done after you return to the Toolbars dialog box. The ODBC configuration icon will now appear on the PowerBar.

Click the new ODBC Power**B**ar button. The PowerBuilder Configure ODBC dialog box appears, shown in figure 16.3.

Fig. 16.3
PowerBuilder's Configure ODBC dialog box. The exact layout of the ODBC configuration dialog box for your application may be different, but will include many of these same configuration fields.

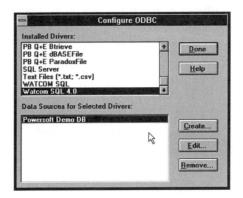

This dialog box may be different from one application to another. The ODBC configuration editor that comes with the native implementation of Watcom SQL 4.0 includes all data sources in a single list box.

To add, configure, or remove a Watcom SQL ODBC configuration using the Configure ODBC dialog box, you must first select the driver. Choosing the Watcom SQL 4.0 driver from the Installed Drivers list displays the available data sources for this type of database. If you just installed Watcom (and also chose to install the sample database), then the Powersoft Demo DB configuration is available. If you did not install the sample database, then the Data Sources for Selected Drivers list area may be blank (and the only option available to you is to create a new data source). Otherwise, you can add, edit, or delete any existing data source.

Adding a Data Source

Note

The database must already exist before you can create a new data source definition. Many Windows tools that allow the creation of databases, such as PowerBuilder, automatically create a default ODBC data source configuration of the same name.

In the Configure ODBC dialog box, be sure that Watcom SQL 4.0 is selected in the upper list box. Click **C**reate. The Watcom SQL ODBC Configuration dialog box appears (see fig. 16.4).

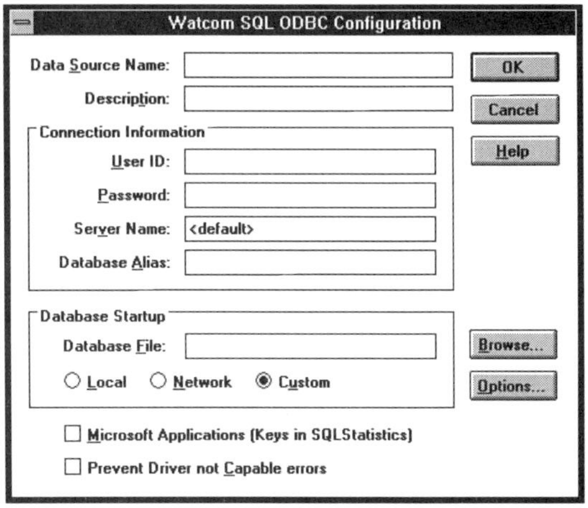

Fig. 16.4
An ODBC connection must have a configuration defined for it. This dialog box allows you to specify the ODBC configuration for a Watcom database.

The dialog box in figure 16.4 includes several ODBC configuration fields:

Data Source Name
This is a required field. Enter a short, 10- to 15-character description for the data source name. This can be any meaningful description you want, but keep it brief by using abbreviations where possible.

Description
This field is also required. Enter a more descriptive name than the short name entered in the Data Source Name field above. For example, if you entered **Corp AP** as the Data Source Name, you might enter **Corporate Accounts Payables** as the Description.

User ID
This field is optional, but if you omit it, the driver will prompt for it each time you connect. This is the user ID of the database user, not the network user (if you are logged into the network). For the single-user version of Watcom, this name defaults to dba.

Password
This field is also optional, and if omitted, the driver will prompt for it on each connect to the database. If you are running the single-user version of Watcom, the default password is sql.

Server Name

This field is initially set to `<default>`, which uses the default database server. You can also specify the name of a specific single-user engine or the name of a Watcom SQL network server. You can start multiple instances of the Windows single-user engine with commands like:

```
dbclienw engine1

dbclienw engine2
```

Then, you can specify `engine1` or `engine2` in the Server Name field to specify which engine received the connection and data request commands when using this ODBC data source.

Database Alias

This optional field allows you to specify an alias name for the database. If you had two database files in different directories, but with the same name, opening two connections to them would result in two engines with the same database name. Because this could be very confusing, this field allows you to distinguish between them, if necessary.

Database File

This field contains the path and file name of the data source. You can click **B**rowse to search for the database file. A standard file open dialog box appears. The field will contain a path similar to:

```
C:\wsql\sample.db
```

Local

If you are running the single-user version of Watcom, select this radio button. When you select Local, the command line used to start the data source is

```
db32w -ga
```

This starts the database engine using the automatic shutdown command-line switch. If you have other command-line switches to set when the database engine starts, select the C**u**stom Database Startup option.

Network

Select the **N**etwork radio button if you are using the network server version of Watcom SQL.

```
dbclienw -ga
```

This command line starts the database client engine using the autostop command-line switch. If you have other command-line switches to set, use the C**u**stom Database Startup option.

Custom

Select this option when you want to specify a particular path for the executable in the command line, if you do not want the autostop command-line switch, or if you want to specify other command-line startup options. You must click the **O**ptions button to display the custom Startup Options dialog box (see fig. 16.5).

Fig. 16.5
The Start Command field and the Database Switches field are combined to construct the database engine startup command. Checking Autostop Database adds the -ga switch to the command line.

Because you are specifying the database name in a separate field, you do not include it in the Start Command field as you would if you were actually constructing a command line. In the Start Command field, specify only the name of the executable. If the path to the database engine is not included in the DOS path, include the drive and path, also.

A separate edit field is available to specify the command-line switches, if any, minus the –ga switch, which is appended to the switch list automatically if you select the A**u**tostop Database checkbox.

At execution time, the Watcom ODBC driver constructs a startup command line using the Start Command field, the Autostop Database switch, the Database Switches field, and the Database File field.

Microsoft Applications

Microsoft Visual Basic version 3.0 and Microsoft Access require the SQLStatistics ODBC command to return primary and foreign keys, while most other ODBC-compatible applications do not. Check the **M**icrosoft Applications (Keys in SQLStatistics) box only when you need to communicate with those Microsoft products that require it.

This may require you to create two data sources if you intend to access a database from multiple tools, such as accessing a data source from within Lotus 1-2-3 and from Microsoft Access. The data-source configuration would be identical, except the Access configuration would have this field checked.

Prevent Driver Not Capable Errors

When ODBC services are initiated for a client application, the client calls a series of ODBC functions to determine the features that are supported by a particular database. These may include an inquiry as to whether or not the database supports the use of qualifiers. *Correlation name qualifiers* are the "nicknames" given to owner/table names in the FROM clause of an SQL statement. For example, the following statements are equivalent in Watcom:

```
SELECT authors.author, books.bookname
FROM authors, books
WHERE authors.author_id = books.author_id
```

```
SELECT a.author, b.bookname
FROM authors as a, books as b
WHERE a.author_id = b.author_id
```

As you can see, the second format can save a lot of typing, and is fully supported in Watcom SQL.

◀ See "Understanding the SQL SELECT Statement" p. 107

However, the ODBC implementation for Watcom SQL does not support the use of correlation name qualifiers. When the client application queries the Watcom SQL driver about this capability, ODBC will return a Driver not Capable Error to the client. Some client applications do not handle this response well.

If you configure an ODBC data source for a client application, and you receive the error message `Driver not Capable Error`, check this box to prevent the Watcom ODBC driver from returning the error message.

The client will still operate normally, but you must be careful not to send SQL statements to the Watcom ODBC connection with qualifiers in the statement.

Troubleshooting

I used a correlation name in the FROM clause of the following SQL statement:

```
SELECT a.author, b.bookname
FROM authors as a, books as b
WHERE authors.author_id = books.author_id
```

But, I am getting an error message when I try to execute this SQL. What am I doing wrong?

When you use a qualifier on a table name in the FROM clause, you must use the qualifier throughout the entire SQL statement, including the column list and the WHERE clause. You cannot refer to the exact table name anymore, like you did in the WHERE clause of the statement above. The WHERE clause should have read:

```
WHERE a.author_id = b.author_id
```

Note that you cannot use qualifiers when accessing Watcom through the ODBC interface.

Configuring a Data Source

In the Configure ODBC dialog box, click the **E**dit... button to display the Watcom SQL ODBC Configuration dialog box for the highlighted data source. This is the same as a Setup button in many other applications' ODBC configuration editors.

Removing a Data Source

The last button on the Configure ODBC dialog is the **R**emove... button. Click **R**emove... to delete an ODBC data source. Deleting the ODBC data source configuration entry in the ODBC.INI file does not delete the database, and in most cases, deleting a database does not remove its corresponding data source entry. Creating a Watcom database from within PowerBuilder automatically creates an ODBC data source for it, but does not automatically remove an ODBC data source when a database is deleted.

You will be prompted to confirm the delete operation.

Using DDE

DDE is an intra-application communication protocol. It is available only in Windows applications. You can use it to create solutions using the features of various applications. For example, most spreadsheet applications have sophisticated graphing capabilities. If you have a database with large sets of data you want to graph, you can create a DDE link to the database server, run a query and retrieve the result into rows of the spreadsheet, then graph the results.

If an application has an ODBC interface available, that will be the fastest way to access data in a Watcom database. However, many more applications support DDE than support ODBC. For many solutions, DDE is the only automated option available for sharing data between applications.

DDE Concepts

DDE works by setting up named conversation channels through which data can flow between applications. There are always two sides to a DDE conversation: a DDE client and a DDE server. DDE clients request conversations of DDE servers. DDE servers respond when DDE clients request a particular *service* that it understands. Some examples of service names are EXCELDOCUMENT, WORDDOCUMENT, and so on. Watcom SQL's DDE server responds to the service name WSQLDDE.

A particular DDE server can service requests from multiple client applications to different files or databases. A *topic* more narrowly defines the data being requested. In Excel and Word, the topic is usually the file name of the spreadsheet or document that contains the information being requested. In Watcom's DDE server, the topic is the database from which you want information. The topic always includes at least the user ID and password, and usually the database, separated by commas.

An *item* narrows down the exact information (or command) desired from the server. In a spreadsheet, this could be a range of rows and columns. In Watcom, this is the command to be executed, such as CONNECT or CLEAR.

In addition to the three identifiers above, a *text* parameter specifies the data itself. This is always in the form of a string.

There are three *flavors* of DDE that determine how data gets updated when it changes on the server; Hot, Warm, and Cold.

Hot
In a *hot* link, when data is requested of a server, the server supplies the data to the client, then monitors the data it sent to see if it changes. If it does, it sends the data again.

Warm
A *warm* link is similar to a hot link except that the server only informs the client that data has changed, it does not send the data automatically; the client can decide for itself if it wants to request the data again.

Cold
In a *cold* DDE link, data is never updated; it is returned to the client when the client requests it. If it then changes on the server, the client is not informed that it has changed. This is the only type of DDE that Watcom supports.

DDE is implemented in Watcom through a special executable that runs in addition to the database engine in the single-user version of Watcom, or in addition to the client executable in the network server versions of Watcom. This executable acts as a DDE request broker by responding when client applications request a channel with a service name of WSQLDDE.

Sending and Receiving Commands Using DDE
Most applications and languages that support DDE include three kinds of DDE commands. All three require that a DDE channel already be established

by specifying a service name and a topic. Usually, an INITIATE command specifying the service name and topic returns a number that uniquely identifies a *channel* to be used in subsequent communications. The channel is then supplied along with an item and text parameter. DDE communications can be broken down into five general types of *transactions*; INITIATE, POKE, REQUEST, EXECUTE, and TERMINATE.

The INITIATE Command

Watcom WSQLDDE can act only as a DDE server, not as a client. As a result, it can respond to initiate commands sent from DDE clients, but does not support initiating conversations itself. The application macro language or programming language used to develop DDE clients have the INITIATE command instead. The INITIATE function requires a service name and topic, and usually returns a channel number *handle* to be used in future DDE calls on the same channel. The service name is always WSQLDDE when INITIATing a channel to the Watcom DDE Server. The topic is a string with the user ID, password, and data source in a single string separated by commas or periods. For example, in Excel, the command is as follows:

```
=INITIATE("WSQLDDE","dba,sql,sample")
```

The previous macro function returns the channel number of the initiated DDE conversation. Multiple channels can be initiated in a single client, if desired.

The INITIATE command merely sets up the DDE channel of communication between the client and server; it does not perform a connect to the database.

The POKE Command

As its name implies, the POKE command is used to send data from the client to the server. This data can be a part of a query, or a connect or disconnect or other command.

CONNECT. As previously stated, simply initiating a DDE conversation does not cause a connect to be issued to the database. This must be done before any other POKE command. This form of the POKE command has the following syntax:

```
POKE CONNECT
```

> **Note**
>
> The actual function name and syntax used will vary from one application and language to another. In Excel, the previous POKE command would include the channel number returned by the INITIATE command:
>
> ```
> =POKE(chnl,"CONNECT","")
> ```
>
> In Visual Basic, the connect command is POKEd by setting the LinkItem property to "CONNECT," and then triggering the POKE event of the edit control.
>
> These represent two very different implementations of the DDE pseudo-code POKE CONNECT. Your particular application or language syntax will also differ. The important thing to know about this command is the transaction type (POKE), the channel, (which is maintained internally by Visual Basic), and the text or data-buffer (a string).

CLEAR. WSQLDDE works by allowing a client application to construct a command string to be executed by "building up" a command string by one or more POKE commands. In some client DDE implementations, a POKE command cannot carry text longer than 255 characters. Many complex SELECT statements can be longer than this, so WSQLDDE allows the command string to be POKEd to the server a few lines at a time. The POKE CLEAR command clears the contents of the current query buffer (if any) and inserts the string contained in the text parameter to the query buffer.

This form of the POKE command has the following syntax:

```
POKE CLEAR text
```

Where *text* is the first part of the SELECT, INSERT, UPDATE, CREATE TABLE, or other commands.

ADD. The POKE ADD command is similar to the POKE CLEAR command, except that it does not clear the current contents of the query buffer; instead, it appends the contents of *text* onto the end of whatever already happens to be in the query buffer.

This form of the POKE command should only be used after clearing the contents of the command buffer by using one POKE CLEAR text followed by as many POKE ADD text commands as it takes to complete the long command. For example, you might use the following statements to send a very long command to the DDE server:

```
POKE CLEAR SELECT
POKE ADD * FROM
```

```
POKE ADD AUTHORS

POKE REQUEST DATA
```

The POKE REQUEST DATA DDE command would return the entire AUTHORS table in a single string, containing tabs between each column and a newline character at the end of each row of data.

> **Caution**
>
> The query buffer is not reset when you issue commands such as POKE CLIP or REQUEST. Use POKE ADD only when your application or language does not support *text* arguments longer than 255 characters, and you believe your statement could exceed this limitation.

The POKE CLEAR and POKE ADD commands are used only to construct the query statement to be executed. The statement is not executed until a POKE CLIP or REQUEST DDE command is issued.

CLIP. After a query statement has been POKEd into the query buffer, it can be executed and the results placed on the Clipboard with these POKE CLIP commands:

- CLIP_COLUMN_NAMES

  This places a string on the Clipboard representing the column names of the result set (separated by tabs) without any data.

- CLIP_DATA

  This places a single string on the Clipboard that contains the result set of the SELECT statement, with the columns of each row of data separated by commas and each row terminated by a newline character.

- CLIP_COLUMN_NAMES_AND_DATA

  This also returns a single string value, with the column names returned in the first row, and the result set returned in subsequent rows.

All three POKE CLIP commands destroy the current contents of the Clipboard and replace it with a single string in a table format. This "comma delimited" Clipboard format is widely recognized by most Windows word processors and spreadsheets.

DISCONNECT. POKE DISCONNECT drops any pending query buffer and immediately performs a disconnect from the database. Disconnecting from the database does not terminate the DDE conversation. You can issue other commands before terminating the DDE channel, such as an EXECUTE command to perform some action with the transaction log or another CONNECT command.

The REQUEST Command

REQUEST is another method of retrieving data after a SELECT or other statement has been constructed using POKE CLEAR and POKE ADD commands. It uses the same three commands as the POKE CLIP commands, except that the data is returned directly to the calling application in the form of a string. The current contents of the Clipboard are not disturbed. Because it leaves the Clipboard intact, unless you are placing data onto the Clipboard for the user to paste, it is a good idea to use the REQUEST command instead of the equivalent POKE CLIP command.

Your REQUEST command can include the following ITEM verbs:

```
DATA

COLUMN_NAMES

COLUMN_NAMES_AND_DATA
```

These items return the same result as the corresponding POKE CLIP items.

The EXECUTE Command

The EXECUTE command can be used to execute any command that does not return a result set (a table). Generally, any command that can be used with PowerBuilder's EXECUTE IMMEDIATE command can be used by the EXECUTE command. The Excel macro function has the form:

```
=EXECUTE(chnl,"Any EXECUTE statement")
```

The cell that contains this function will contain the SQLCA return code of the command.

The TERMINATE Command

Just as it is the DDE client's responsibility to initiate a conversation, it is also the DDE client's responsibility to terminate the conversation. The macro language will contain a function to terminate the DDE channel. For example, in Excel, this macro command performs the terminate action:

```
=TERMINATE(chnl)
```

A disconnect command should be issued using the POKE command before terminating the channel.

Using the Sample Application

The CD-ROM contains a sample application, written in Visual Basic, which demonstrates connecting to the Watcom DDE server, running a SELECT statement, and displaying the result in a grid. You can experiment with the CONNECT parameters, and the SELECT statement.

Installing VBCLIP, the sample application

To install the sample application, VBCLIP, follow these steps:

1. From File Manager, select **F**ile Run...

2. In the command line field, type **E:\ch16\vbclip\setup.exe.**

3. Press **O**K. The following installation window displays:

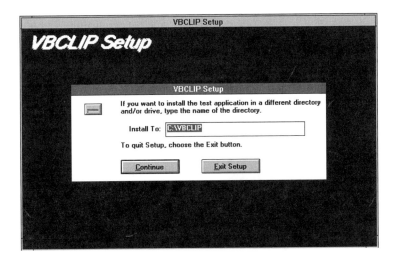

Fig. 16.6
You can install the sample application to any drive or directory. It will offer to create a Program Manager Group when all of the files have been copied.

4. You can choose to install to the default directory, or choose a different drive or directory for installation. Press OK when you are ready to continue.

5. When all files have been copied, the setup utility offers to create a Program Manager Group called VBCLIP.

Running VBCLIP

The sample application is written in Visual Basic. It contains several buttons marked Go, one for each step that is performed in the process of establishing a DDE link with Watcom. This allows you to perform the operation, one step at a time, while looking at the commands echoed in the WSQLDDE application, and the database commands forwarded from WSQLDDE to the database server engine. Before starting VBCLIP, the sample database must be started. Start VBCLIP by double-clicking on its icon. The following main window will appear:

Fig. 16.7

The sample app allows you to establish a DDE connection to Watcom's DDE server one step at a time so you can see the results of each step.

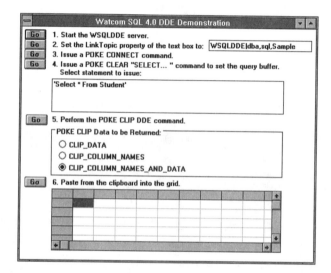

Now perform the following steps by pressing Go beside each one:

1. This step assures that the WSQLDDE server application is started.

2. This step sets the LinkTopic property of the edit box with the SELECT statement to WSQLDDE|dba,sql,Sample.

3. This step performs the CONNECT DDE command on the textbox control by setting the LinkItem property to CONNECT, then performing the LinkPoke method on the textbox.

4. This step sets the LinkItem property of the textbox control to CLEAR, and then performs the LinkPoke method on the textbox.

5. While the last step merely poked a statement to be executed into the DDE servers command buffer, this step is the one that actually requests

IV

the data by setting the LinkItem property to `CLIP_COLUMN_NAMES_AND_DATA`, and again performing the LinkPoke method on the textbox. When the DDE server receives this command, it performs the SELECT, and places a copy of it on the Clipboard. It opens the Clipboard viewer so you can verify that the SELECT, data is actually there.

6. This step merely pastes the Clipboard contents into a spreadsheet-like grid for viewing. The columns can be resized so you can see all of a column, if you like.

This should give you a good idea of how to interface with the Watcom DDE server. Keep in mind that you could also pass the results data directly back to VB without using the Clipboard by using the REQUEST method instead of the POKE, as described earlier in this chapter.

From Here...

In this chapter, you learned how to configure the Watcom ODBC interface and how to use the DDE server WSQLDDE.EXE. A sample application, written in Visual Basic, was demonstrated to illustrate the technique in action. (The code used to create the sample application is also included on the CD-ROM.)

If you have read this chapter with the intention of interfacing Watcom SQL with other applications, you may also find the following areas of this book useful:

■ Chapter 1, "Understanding Watcom SQL Fundamentals," includes a section on using Microsofts ODBC Administrator.

■ Chapter 5, "Selecting Data," includes discussions of the elements of a SQL statement, which you must understand in order to pass the statements through DDE to the database engine.

■ Chapter 6, "Understanding SQL," discusses how to construct INSERT and UPDATE statements, which can also be passed to Watcom through ODBC or DDE.

■ Chapter 8, "Understanding the Role of a Database Administrator," includes a section on implementing the Watcom Server editions and a general discussion of networking technology.

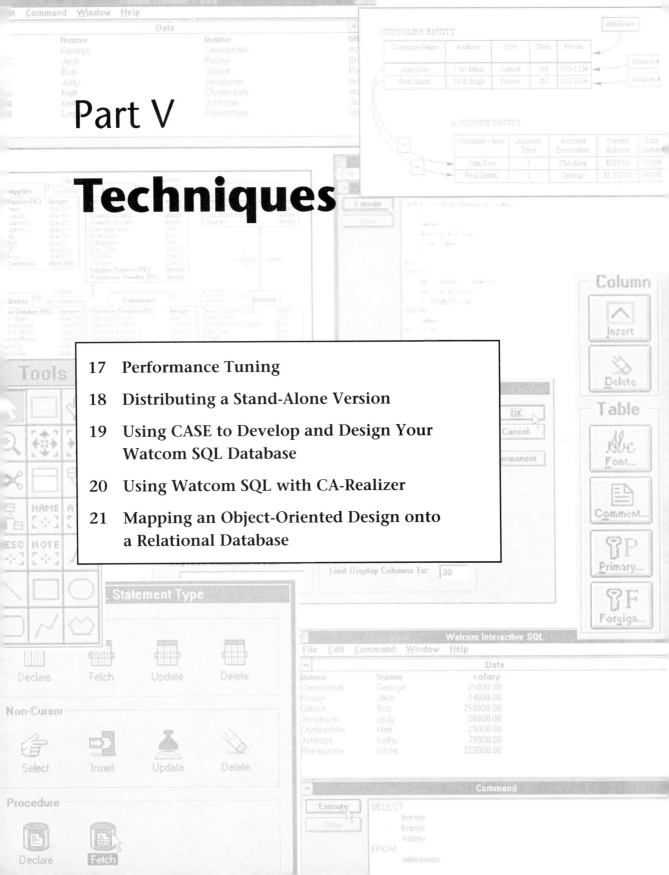

Part V

Techniques

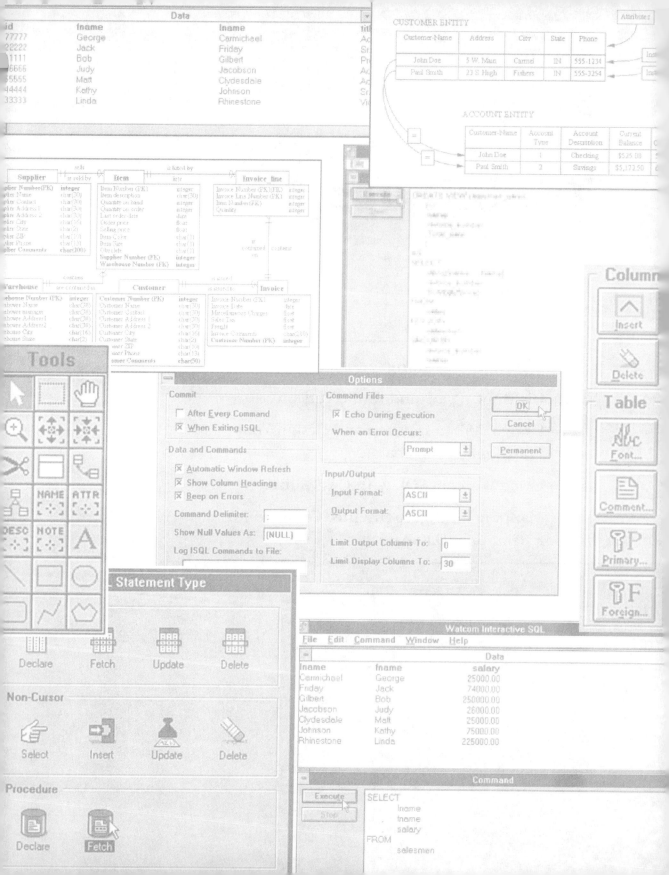

Chapter 17

David Yach is the Vice President of engineering at Watcom and the original architect of the Watcom SQL database.

Performance Tuning

With any database, there are performance tips and techniques that can be applied to significantly increase response time. In this interview, David Yach, Vice President of Engineering at Watcom and co-developer of the original Watcom SQL product, shares his vast knowledge of Watcom SQL performance tuning.

Q In what ways can you examine the performance of your database?

With the Watcom SQL database, you can get some simple statistics by running our Interactive SQL (ISQLW.EXE). It will tell you some timing and the number of actual I/O operations that happen. It will give you a detailed access plan for queries and other operations that you do. What we don't have is a lot of the detailed statistics used for setting everything from cache performance to network I/O performance. That's partly by design because we're trying to fit the model of a "shrink-wrapped," "don't-have-to-tune" database, but we are hearing more requests for that all the time.

Techniques from the Pros

Interview with David Yach by Charles A. Wood

Q Why (or how) would you use the optimizer statistics and the DROP OPTIMIZER STATISTICS SQL command?

The Watcom SQL optimizer uses a self-tuning algorithm where it keeps track of information used in previous optimizations. To optimize performance, "efficient tests" will then be run before other tests to reduce the number of qualifying rows as much as possible. After the "efficient tests" are run, the "inefficient tests" follow on the remaining rows.

For example, if you were to test for SEX = FEMALE, Watcom SQL will figure out (by running the test once) that this test is inefficient because it only removes half the rows. However, if you were to test for Birthdate='1995-01-30', Watcom SQL will figure out (again, by running the test once) that this test is efficient because it removes a significant percentage of the rows.

Watcom SQL's recorded optimization can become inefficient if a significant amount of data is changed, loaded, or deleted. You should consider using the DROP OPTIMIZER STATISTICS if the following situations apply:

- If you feel the current optimization plan is not efficient, perhaps dropping the optimizer statistics will force the statistics to be recomputed and may increase database efficiency.

- If you're planning to deploy an application, you may want to drop statistics so everyone starts from the same efficiency starting point.

- If you load a significant amount of data or delete a significant amount of data from your database, you might want to drop statistics because your efficiency rules may have changed.

Q What role do primary and foreign keys have in database organization?

It is common knowledge that indexes are important in terms of being able to optimize queries, as well as sorting. Because the referential integrity was important in terms of having a consistent database, we decided to implement foreign keys and primary keys as slightly modified indexes.

We observed that many applications do a lot of joins and lookups on primary and foreign keys, so designed a modified index structure that allows us to do the referential integrity checking with minimal extra work. At the time, people were leery about using referential integrity for performance reasons, so we wanted INSERTs, UPDATEs, and DELETEs to modify foreign key information, and check for validity with virtually no performance penalty.

Q How can the incorrect key definition degrade performance?

The mechanism we used is to actually store primary keys and the associated foreign keys for that primary key in the same index structure. This allows for the efficient modifications while checking for integrity constraints. It also allows the index to be used for lookups while ignoring other key information. For example, if you're looking for the primary key, you can just ignore all the foreign key entries in the index.

The down side is that if you have a primary key table that doesn't have many rows and a foreign key table with lots of rows, a sorted query can take additional time because there are many foreign key index entries to ignore. For instance, if you have a Parts table with 100 rows and an Invoice_line table with 100,000 rows, you have 100,100 entries in the primary key/foreign key index, but only 100 unique primary keys. To produce a list of parts sorted by primary key, Watcom SQL must ignore 100,000 foreign key entries while finding the 100 primary key entries.

To resolve this problem, you need to create a *separate unique index* on the primary key columns in situations where there are a lot of foreign keys that point to a primary key. By establishing a separate index on the primary key, the optimizer performs queries on these records much more quickly.

Q Should you index a primary key if there are few entries in the primary key table, but many foreign key tables referencing this primary key?

Not exactly. The important question is how many other rows in the database reference each primary key row, not how many tables have foreign keys. This is something we came across in the last few months as more people started using Watcom SQL. We discovered positive results when indexing primary keys in this situation.

Q We've already talked about the ways in which indexes optimize your database. Can indexes degrade performance if there are too many of them or if they're too long?

Basically, the rule of thumb is that an index improves your speed on SELECTs as long as it's a useful index (it's on the column that you often put in the WHERE clause or a column you often use in an ORDER BY clause). Indexes add costs to INSERTs, UPDATEs, and DELETEs because every extra index requires extra work whenever you modify the table.

The performance benefit or cost of indexes depends on how you are using the table. There's no performance cost associated with an index on a table that's just loaded and never modified, and there's very little cost if you don't do many modifications. However, if you're doing a lot of modifications to a table, you should pay attention to the cost of maintaining the indexes. Normally, you would not create an index on columns that are involved in primary or foreign keys because the index structure is already there (except for the case I mentioned previously).

Another important point is that order is important to multi-column indexes and primary keys. Often, developers don't understand the importance of column placement when defining primary keys.

For example, suppose you have an invoice table with two columns for customer number and date. A query that produces a list of invoices for one customer ordered by date could use a combined index on customer number and date (in that order) to both select the customer's invoices and order by date. Note that reversing the order of the columns to be date followed by customer number makes the index almost useless for this query.

Most developers aren't aware that the primary keys in Watcom SQL are in the order that the columns are declared in the table, not in the order that they are declared in the primary keys.

 You were talking about a primary key. Is this true with a foreign key also?

Foreign key columns are in the same order as primary key columns. If you need to reorder the columns in your primary key (especially if you're starting with a fairly fresh database), you need to actually create the columns in a different order on the table and then rearrange the columns in the primary key clause.

 Does the ASCENDING or DESCENDING clause that's used when defining an index affect performance?

It most cases, there's no impact on performance. The only case in which you might want to decide the direction you want your index ordered is when using an ORDER BY clause with column A ASCENDING and column B DESCENDING. If the index is defined the same as the ORDER BY clause, you can do a query without re-sorting the results. Otherwise, there's not a lot of use for having a descending index since Watcom SQL can go backward through an index as efficiently as going forward. This capability makes it possible for Watcom SQL to support bi-directional scrollable cursors.

Q You can use JOINs or subqueries to combine information during a database SELECT. Which one's better? And how do you optimize SELECT statements in terms of joining two tables together?

The Watcom SQL optimizer does a very good job on JOINs. In fact, subqueries in the WHERE clause are converted into JOINS where possible because it gives the optimizer more freedom. Watcom SQL uses some algorithms that can determine whether or not a subquery can be transformed to a JOIN to get an equivalent query .

If a subquery can't be converted to a JOIN, the subquery is optimized separately from the main query and then implemented in a straightforward way. If it's a *correlated subquery*, in which something in the subquery relates to the main query, the subquery potentially gets evaluated once for every row in the main query. The optimizer will try to filter the rows in the main query by using other conditions in the WHERE clause before trying to evaluate the subquery because subqueries are a relatively expensive operation.

In Watcom SQL, search conditions involving IN, = ANY, and = ALL subqueries are treated as correlated subqueries. The clause on the left side of the IN/ANY/ALL subqueries is part of the correlated subquery.

One thing Watcom SQL does not do is materialize the set for a correlated subquery. *Materialize the set* means that the valid values of the subquery are stored so that other rows in the main query don't have to process the subquery again. Instead, Watcom SQL converts all those queries to an equivalent EXISTS clause, and then optimizes the EXISTS subquery. If it happens to be correlated, Watcom SQL will first try to see whether the queries can be converted to JOINS. If not, the subquery is evaluated for each separate row of the main query, which is sometimes inefficient.

> **Note**
>
> Relational database purists might point out that IN, ALL and ANY subqueries use three-valued logic (TRUE, FALSE, and UNKNOWN)'. EXISTS subqueries use two-valued logic (TRUE and FALSE only). Internally, Watcom SQL supports a three-valued EXISTS to properly handle IN, ALL, and ANY subqueries.

One of the things on our to-do list is to implement, in certain cases, materialization of the list for efficiency. The problem is determining cases where our current optimization method is more efficient, and cases where materializing the subquery is better, since neither solution is best all of the time. Right now, subqueries are converted into an EXISTS clause and then, if possible, converted into JOINS.

Q Does the order of columns in your WHERE clause affect performance?

The development team at Watcom has made a great deal of effort to make equivalent queries optimize identically, in most cases. So the ordering of the WHERE clause, the ordering of the FROM clause, etc., shouldn't matter. The fact that we optimize the EXISTS clause the same as the IN clause is because they're equivalent queries, and we like them to be optimized the same way. Developers don't like getting different optimizations from basically the same SQL statement just because of the order of the clauses. Watcom's optimization techniques in this area come from our compiler backgrounds.

There are cases right now where identical clauses are optimized differently. Those cases use what I would call "nonsense" clauses (for example, WHERE sex = sex or WHERE SALARY = SALARY + 0), in which meaningless operations (such as + 0) are used. In fact, you can use these "nonsense" clauses to control the optimization of your SQL statement.

If the optimizer's not doing what you're expecting it to do, there are two ways to give it some direction:

- The preferred method is using something we call *estimates*. Using estimates, you can put a condition in the WHERE clause in parentheses. Before the last parenthesis, you put a comma and then a number representing a percentage, indicating how often the condition in the parentheses will be true. Valid values range from zero percent up to 100 percent.

  Usually, the estimates don't affect performance because Watcom SQL has an estimate stored for the WHERE clause in question. Therefore, the optimizer is not affected if you put "average" numbers in the parenthesis (such as 25 or 35). As long as you get the same optimization plan, you'll get the same performance. In most cases, you end up putting in a number like 0, 1, 99, or 100 where a value is pervasive. If you put in a 0, it really means the assumption that the condition uniquely identifies a row. Sometimes, you'll use columns that are not unique, but are almost always unique, like a full name or address. Here, you would put a 0 after the WHERE condition to let the optimizer know that, for the most part, this column should be treated as unique.

The statistics information discussed earlier is only used when you compare a column to a constant or host variable. Complicated expressions (like conditions comparing two columns in the same table), SOUNDEX functions, or string and numeric functions can all benefit by the use of estimates.

■ If estimates fail, you can use those "nonsense clauses," like adding zero to a numeric expression or concatenating (with the ‖ symbol) an empty string ("") to a string variable. This will force Watcom SQL to ignore the optimizer statistics. For example, if you use `WHERE INVOICE.CUSTOMER_NUMBER + 0 = 12345`, Watcom SQL will never look up the customer number in the index table by index because Watcom SQL no longer recognizes `customer_number` as a column; it looks at `customer_number + 0` as an expression.

Caution Typically, the indexes in a table increase performance. Be sure you have a really good reason to bypass indexing with a "nonsense clause." Otherwise, your SQL statement may take a relatively long time to complete.

Do not use expressions too freely. They can cause a performance penalty.

Q But usually, you wouldn't want to override the optimizer, right?

No. Typically you wouldn't. The optimizer will usually get things right, but because the optimizer's an heuristic, there are occasions where it will get it wrong. The cases where the optimizer is inefficient are rare, but they do exist. Sometimes, we'll find customers who write a query that throws the optimizer off for whatever reason. We do try to keep track of those queries that cause problems for the optimizer and make changes to the optimizer to improve performance.

There's a time cycle involved where the optimizer is constantly improving, but because the optimizer is heuristic, I don't know if you could ever get all situations to be absolutely optimal. "Optimizer" is a misnomer because an heuristic will probably never be optimal in all circumstances.

Q **Returning to subqueries: if you have one or two in a SELECT statement that aren't converted to JOINS, that could really take a huge hit on your performance or SELECT statement, right?**

Right. Depending on the subquery, the worst kind of subquery from a performance perspective is a subquery in which you end up scanning the table in the main query sequentially while checking the subquery for every row.

Q **How does array processing in PowerBuilder and other host languages like C++ optimize your performance?**

We don't support any array FETCHing or INSERTs or UPDATEs right now, so I guess the answer is that it doesn't affect us at all. If you're using Watcom SQL network servers, they will automatically FETCH a buffer full of rows and send them back to your client machine; returning them, one-by-one, to your application as it requests rows.

Q **So, cursors can be executed on the server, and then the result can be returned to the client?**

It's actually not all executed, but rather executed ahead. There's all the appropriate code in Watcom SQL FETCH to keep track of the rows it has retrieved. If you decide to back up in a cursor, Watcom SQL knows how far ahead it is and will restore the database to its pre-FETCH condition. So it doesn't affect response time (you don't have to wait any longer for retrieval), but after you get the first row, maybe the next 10 will come really quickly because you don't have any network communication after the initial bundle is passed to the client PC. If your program then wants the eleventh row, Watcom SQL will instruct the server to get rows 11 through 20.

Q **If you're SELECTing one row at a time, the result is negligible, but if you're FETCHing tons of rows at once, it really helps on network traffic. Right?**

Yes, and even if your application program is FETCHing one row at a time, this happens for you automatically without any additional programming. You can still write your program the same way, FETCHing rows one at a time, but you're only going to have network traffic every 10 rows, 20 rows, or five rows, depending on the size of the rows.

Q Is there any way to increase the bundle that's sent over the network?

You can adjust the packet size. Each platform has a different way to do this, depending on your operating system and whether you're using TCP/IP, IPX, or NetBIOS. Check your network administration guide. There's a command-line switch on the server and the client, and you set both to increase the packet size. Depending on what network you're using, there may be some network setup that you need to do to get a larger packet size, thereby increasing the speed of the client application.

You can turn blocking off entirely if you determine that it's not adequate, and you can limit the number of rows that come back in a block from Embedded SQL through the OPEN CURSOR statement. By using the blocking flag with the OPEN statement, you set a maximum block. In addition to the size of the packet, which limits the number of rows you get, there are also some timing parameters. If the rows are really taking a long time (between each one) to FETCH, and your client's waiting for a response, Watcom SQL will not return as many rows at one time.

Q How should you use stored procedures and triggers to optimize performance in host languages like C++, and especially in PowerBuilder?

There are a number of advantages to stored procedures and triggers:

■ Procedures reduce network traffic. Since triggers and procedures are run on the server computer, more work is done on the network server computer than on the client computer.

■ Even in the stand-alone environment, stored procedures and triggers can reduce communication between the host language and Watcom SQL. If you are doing a lot of communication between the two, the effect should be noticeable, especially in a language like PowerBuilder, where several dynamic link libraries (DLLs) are often called to process database information.

■ Procedures and triggers give you consistency with the way operations are done. If you have a set of operations involving UPDATEs to tables, deletions, etc., stored procedures give you a consistency for all your applications. Triggers are even better because all operations are done automatically so the application doesn't need to be aware that the operation is done.

For example, whenever the salary table gets UPDATEd, a trigger can insert a row into a history table to keep track of all salary modifications. (If somebody wants to sneak in using Interactive SQL to UPDATE the salary information, the changes are recorded.)

- People also use procedures for integrity constraints and security. For example, suppose there's a procedure that UPDATEs two tables and INSERTs a row into a third table. You can set it up so a user does not have permission to do this directly, but the procedure does. The user has permission to execute the procedure so modifications are implemented in a consistent way. In fact, you can set it up so that the user cannot look at the tables.

In another scenario, the security is there to prevent you from accidentally making an inconsistent change.

Normal security is granted by table. Procedures allow you to grant authority by function.

- Finally, using procedures can increase performance. If you're running a network server, it is probably a more powerful machine than your client machines. So, in addition to saving network traffic, you're running the procedure on powerful computers that will run more quickly.

How do auto increment columns affect your database performance?

Auto increment columns save execution time when you consider alternative ways of providing the same functionality; that is, to perform a query that computes the next available number. There are also a number of concurrency issues that you have to deal with to achieve the same result.

A simple (yet flawed) solution is to SELECT MAX plus one on the primary key. The problem, however, is that if two people INSERT at the same time, they get the same MAX and end up INSERTing the same number. One of these users will receive an error because the column value is not unique.

Often, you end up doing all sorts of tricks like opening a second connection and having a table containing the next available number. Auto increment columns automatically find the next available value and handle all the concurrency features.

Q How do log files affect database performance, and how can you optimize the use of log files?

The basic impact of log files is that COMMITs run a lot faster by reducing the I/O done for COMMIT. This is especially true in the single-user environment. One of the attributes of a COMMIT is that if the machine crashes or you kick the plug, etc., you can recover everything you've committed. The database has to write something to the disk every time you do a COMMIT.

A log file allows you to minimize the amount of data you write. In fact, if you're running in a multi-user environment —especially if you're getting into a high OLTP (Online Transaction Processing) situation—and there are a lot of users pounding at the database, it gets optimized even further by attempting to do a single write to COMMIT several transactions. I/O on COMMITs can be reducd to less than one I/O per COMMIT. The nature of your transactions will determine whether this optimization will affect your server.

Most PowerBuilder applications are either data entry or decision support. In either of those cases, the length of your transaction is due more to human interaction than to computer speed, and so the COMMIT time, whether it be 10 milliseconds or 500 milliseconds, is not significant to the operator. However, when you get into OLTP-type environments, it can be very important.

When using a log file, you should try to put the log file and the database file on separate physical disk drives. In most cases, separate devices will give you some performance improvements if your I/O system can handle the two devices at once.

Another reason to split the log file and the database file onto two different devices is that two devices give you some added security. If you lose one of your disks, you're in much better shape for recovery than if all your information was on one disk. If the database is destroyed due to a disk crash, your log file will still contain an up-to-the-moment backup.

If you lose the log file, the database will still be intact when you get the database up to the last checkpoint. (A log file backup is better.) Depending on how long you have set between checkpoints, you may lose only a couple of minutes' worth of work.

Q **Having a checkpoint often will slow Watcom SQL down a little, right?**

Frequent checkpoints can slow Watcom SQL down a little, although Watcom SQL tries to distribute the work for the checkpoint. As the checkpoint time nears, Watcom SQL starts to write out the checkpoint information during the time the server is not busy. As you get closer and closer to the checkpoint time, Watcom SQL gets a little bit more "excited" and starts "sneaking in" some writes between other people's operations. Ideally, when the checkpoint time hits, there will be very little work left to be done. This way, you don't get the big performance hit all at once.

Q **How does version 4.0 performance compare with versions 3.0/3.2 performance?**

Certainly, there has been some across-the-board performance improvement because the optimizer's been improved again. The biggest performance improvement has been on the network servers in environments like NT and NetWare, where there's a more sophisticated I/O system than in DOS. We've done a lot more work to take advantage of those. Version 3.2 took advantage of some of this, but in version 4.0, we made significant improvements.

We've run version 4.0 internally in our lab, and have gotten significant improvements on all the OLTP-type benchmarks that were reported in the *PC Magazine* benchmark that hit the streets in September, 1994.

> **Note**
>
> The *PC Magazine* article referred to is that for October 11, 1994. In that article, Watcom SQL *version 3.2* (not version 4.0) posted the fastest response time for any database with ad hoc queries. (Version 4.0 tends to run even faster than version 3.2.) Also, Watcom had the lowest price-per-user and the lowest transaction cost-per-user of any database.

Q **You were the fastest on response time for ad hoc queries in that review, right?**

Yes, and that's important to us. In one section on ad hoc queries, *PC Magazine* ran approximately 20 queries and added up the times. Watcom

SQL took about one hour and forty minutes to run the test. Approximately one hour and twenty minutes of that time was spent on two queries that were just big, monster queries. I suggested that they divide it up into two sections: one containing the real-time queries, which should have a response under ten seconds. The second would contain long queries—the hour-long sort of two million rows with no index. Because it's all left in the total, it doesn't matter if you took one or ten seconds on the short ones. All that matters is how long it takes you to do the two big queries.

Certainly the time we got on that with version 3.2 was significantly better than we had done before. Version 4.0 will be even better. Actually, it's a little disappointing that it didn't get more emphasis because ad hoc queries are the heart of decision support and data warehousing.

What's the best way to use caching to benefit performance?

Caching is important. The two biggest performance considerations when running any database operation are the number of I/O operations that have to be done and the amount of processing required. Caching plays an important role in reducing the number of real I/Os that happen.

Caching is a bit more complicated on a system like Windows. If you have an 8M machine, you can still ask for an 8M cache because it will use virtual memory. In Windows, in which there is a threshold that depends on what you are running and how Windows is set up, getting a large cache may actually slow things down because Windows does I/O operations to implement virtual memory.

Once you get beyond that, caching is really important for reducing the number of I/O operations. The optimizer is geared to try to reduce the number of I/O operations and then to reduce the amount of processing. Reducing processing becomes very important, depending on the type of query you're running and the size of the cache. There are a large class of queries and databases, in which all data for the query end up in the cache. Because cache has eliminated the need for external disk I/O, processing becomes really important.

There are several wrong ways to do a query, such as doing a JOIN and going through every table sequentially. This is inefficient, even if it's all in memory. You may have zero real I/Os, but the processing takes a real amount of time.

On the other hand, things change a lot once you get to queries whose data will not fit into cache. The optimizer tries to take that into consideration, and will choose different plans if you have different cache sizes.

The reduction in the number of I/Os is the biggest improvement we've made in version 4.0. Version 3.2 was designed for that first case, where a lot of the data was in cache and disk I/O was already optimized for us. Before version 4.0, we learned a lot about the impact of very large databases with relatively small caches and how to take that into consideration when creating the access plan.

Q One question is probably on every Watcom SQL user's mind. PowerSoft, which owns Watcom, was recently acquired by Sybase. Since Sybase has its own database, how will that affect future development?

Watcom will continue to operate and develop products under its own name, maintaining its business mandate, product mission and personnel at its current facilities. Sybase has recognized the rapidly growing need for an affordable database server that can be broadly deployed with little administrative support for single-user, workgroup and smaller departmental applications. With the Powersoft merger, Sybase can now offer the definitive product in this new database market segment to complement its enterprise server offerings. This new category of a "shrink-wrapped" database server extends and complements enterprise databases like the Sybase System 10 family.

Q Watcom SQL runs under QNX, right?

That's right. A lot of people are using it in embedded applications such as point-of-sales terminals. It's a real-time operating system, so people use it in settings such as shop floors and other areas that require a real-time response.

Even though QNX is a UNIX derivative, it works mostly in the PC environment, and it's for people who need the particular requirements of that operating system. QNX is particularly lightweight.

Q **What plans do you have to ease the migration from Watcom to Sybase?**

We plan to offer enhanced compatibility between Watcom SQL and Sybase SQL Server. In December 1994, Watcom demonstrated a version of Watcom SQL that executed Transact-SQL stored procedures. Further, we expect Watcom to leverage advanced Sybase enterprise capabilities, such as connectivity and replication technologies.

Note

You can use the data pipeline in PowerBuilder to convert from Watcom to another database. Included on this book's CD is a PowerBuilder program that converts from Watcom SQL to both Sybase and Oracle, including the security for the database!

Chapter 18

Distributing a Stand-Alone Version

Marvin Taylor is a supervisor at United Farm Bureau Insurance Companies in Indiana. He's been in the data processing industry for over 30 years. Currently, Taylor is in charge of PowerBuilder/Watcom development at Farm Bureau.

Michelle Lehman is a Senior Programmer Analyst at United Farm Bureau Insurance Companies in Indiana. Currently, she is team leader for PowerBuilder/Watcom development at Farm Bureau.

Q **Your department at United Farm Bureau Insurance Companies in Indiana distributed a stand-alone version of a Watcom SQL application. What was your business situation when you made this decision?**

Our company does most of its computer processing on a mainframe. Recently, however, our agency and marketing departments requested PC and laptop support. The reasons for this are obvious: with a laptop, an agent can process an application with a single visit to a client's home. Also, electronic processing of applications (as opposed to handwritten processing) will lead to fewer errors on applications, as well as less paperwork for the agent. All of these factors led our company to request a suite of applications that would run on a laptop.

The system would have to quote auto and homeowners' policies. We also needed to incorporate the current life insurance marketing system that was our only PC system at that time.

Techniques from the Pros

Interview with Marvin Taylor and Michelle Lehman by Chuck Wood

We faced numerous challenges:

- We had only one PC developer currently on staff. We determined that we would need at least five developers for this project.

- We had only four months to complete the first phase of this project—from requirements to implementation.

- Although there were auto system developers available, only one homeowners' system developer was available. We would have to train four out of five mainframe programmers on how to develop for the PC, and we would have to train two out of three developers on how to rate homeowners' policies. All of this had to occur within the four month time frame.

- We had limited resources available for consulting, and determined that we could only afford three weeks of consulting.

Q Why did you choose PowerBuilder with Watcom SQL?

We decided that the Windows environment would be ideal for the project. A Windows environment would mean our laptop application would require less training of our testers, customer service representatives, and, most of all, our agents. However, writing GUI-based applications is usually more difficult than writing standard text-based applications. Also, we had no experience in developing graphical systems or object-based development at Farm Bureau.

PowerBuilder and Watcom SQL solved a lot of our problems. We needed to choose a Windows development environment, as well as a PC database. We needed a development environment that met the following criteria:

- Our developers needed to learn the development environment rather quickly. We didn't allow much time for training.

- We needed a system that could be used by several developers at one time and supported some type of project management.

- We needed a robust development environment. Generating auto and dwelling quotes is a complex process, so the environment we chose had to be able to handle complex processes.

- We didn't have a two-year development cycle, so we needed a system that was *fast*. We needed an environment that could go from prototype to development quickly and easily.

- We needed the system to be fully integrated with a database that fit our needs.

PowerBuilder Enterprise Edition answered all these needs:

- Our developers were able to start developing after a one-week training class and were pretty accomplished after three months of PowerBuilder development. Sure, they still had things to learn about the environment, but, by-and-large, the development process was greatly enhanced.

- PowerBuilder supports multiple developers over a network with check-in/check-out capabilities. Also, several developers could each be working on different objects at the same time during development. This is necessary for a multi-developer project.

Choosing PowerBuilder was the hard decision. With several development environments out there—each claiming to be the easiest to develop with—choosing correctly can be difficult. Fortunately for us, the selection of PowerBuilder seems to have been a good choice.

By contrast, the database was the easiest to select, especially after choosing PowerBuilder as our development environment. Our database had to have the following features:

- It had to support multiple users. Because we are developing with multiple users, we wanted to all have access to the database at once. Therefore, a client/server database was a necessity.

- It had to be able to run on a laptop. Several client/server databases are not practical in a stand-alone environment. Our target user for our quoting system was an agent with a laptop. So not only did our database have to support client/server, it also had to function well as a stand-alone database.

- It should support SQL. Because all of our developers knew DB2 (an SQL database used on IBM mainframes), a database that supports SQL would have a flatter learning curve.

- We have a limited support staff, so the database had to be easy to install and support. The database should fit onto a laptop with little difficulty and then be (for the most part) self-optimizing and self-supporting. We needed a plug-and-play, out-of-the-box, shrink-wrapped database.

- Finally, the database had to be inexpensive, both at the development end and especially at the run-time end. We didn't have the resources to spend over $10,000 for a multi-user database, and each agent had to pay for his or her own laptop. We didn't want to charge the agent several hundred additional dollars for a run-time database.

Watcom SQL is the only database that meets of all these requirements:

- We started running the Watcom SQL database that comes with PowerBuilder, but this turned out to be annoying with all of us running and periodically merging our databases. Eventually, we purchased a client/server database, so we had little trouble running it over a network during development.

- Watcom SQL is one of the few client/server databases that will run on a stand-alone laptop.

- Watcom SQL supports SQL (of course). We also found some nice additions, such as bidirectional cursors and auto-increment fields, that are not present in other SQL databases like DB2.

- Watcom SQL is known for its ease of installation and self-support. It even optimizes itself.

- Even with all of its features, Watcom SQL is the least expensive per-user and per-transaction client/server database on the market today. This not only saved departmental budget money, but also helped keep the cost of the laptops down for our agents. There is a low one-time cost for unlimited use of the run-time version of Watcom SQL, so our agents had to pay nothing.

Because Watcom SQL answered all these needs, plus had a strong link to the PowerBuilder development environment, our choice of database was easy.

Q What were some challenges you had to resolve during development?

There were many challenges we had to resolve after choosing a PowerBuilder/Watcom SQL combination:

- Our requirement-developing techniques, system-analyzing techniques, and development techniques were all mainframe-centric, and not well suited for developing in an iterative environment such as PowerBuilder. Consequently, our programmers were forced to develop systems that conformed to our current methodology. This caused problems by using a design that wasn't centered around our development tool (PowerBuilder). Fortunately, we had a lot of input on the data model.

- Farm Bureau also wanted to support the mainframe users in our company who did not opt for the laptop program. Consequently, a mainframe quoting system was occurring at the same time as the laptop quoting system. Because management wanted similar functionality between the two systems, there was *a lot* of co-development and co-analysis. This not only reinforced much of the mainframe-centric techniques mentioned earlier, but developing (for the most part) exactly the same system on two different machines, operating systems, and languages was a monumental task, especially given the time frame with which the first phase of the product had to be completed.

- There was, and is, very limited documentation on PowerBuilder outside of the users' manuals. Your *Special Edition Using PowerBuilder 4* book wasn't out yet. Eventually, we found one third-party book on PowerBuilder, but that book didn't seem to meet our needs very well. We *really* needed a book on Watcom SQL. PowerBuilder 3 came with over 8,000 pages of documentation, but Watcom SQL documentation that comes with PowerBuilder is only around 200 pages. We looked all over to find a book on Watcom SQL, but didn't find *any*. I'm sure Watcom SQL developers all over are glad that this book is coming out.

    The lack of documentation, coupled with the limited consultation budget, really caused our developers some late nights trying to absorb the new technologies they were dealing with.

- There is a *huge* demand for PowerBuilder professionals in the Indianapolis market. Having personnel recruiters constantly calling your people and offering them employment elsewhere can put a lot of stress on a project (not to mention a supervisor or a team leader). The reasons PowerBuilder was such an easy fit with our development scheme make it a great match for other companies as well. Right now, there are not enough PowerBuilder developers to meet the demand in the Indianapolis area, and more companies are starting to use PowerBuilder to answer their PC development needs.

Q What third-party software did you use?

When developing a project, you should use resource-budgeting software, CASE software to help with data modeling, e-mail software to help communicate with each other, testers, users, management, and so on. Also, use version-control software, so that old versions of your PowerBuilder code are automatically saved.

We used Timeline and Guideline from Symantec to get a picture of the scope of the project. Guideline is good for reminding you of tasks that need to be completed; Timeline is good for tracking hours, resources, and completion dates. Also, Timeline can produce Gantt and Pert charts that graphically display your progress.

Because we're still a mainframe shop, all of our management, users, and testers had mainframe access, but few had LAN (Local Area Network) access. As a result, we had to use our mainframe mail package for scheduling and to communicate with each other. This was a little annoying to our developers, who had no need to access the mainframe except for scheduling and mail. Furthermore, there are PC mail packages available for LANs that are more robust, easier to use, and friendly. Consequently, communication suffered during the higher-stress coding areas.

We purchased ERwin to help with data modeling. In my experience, ERwin is the easiest CASE product to use. It also has a PowerBuilder version that interfaces well with PowerBuilder and Watcom SQL. Many would-be design flaws can be caught with a CASE product, so you don't have to go back and redesign or, even worse, try to implement design flaws by extra coding.

PowerBuilder comes with a check-in/check-out librarian feature that allows for some multi-user control. However, there is no archive control in PowerBuilder. Consequently, you probably need third-party software that hooks into PowerBuilder for version control. We purchased PVCS version control software, but with the hectic schedules of our developers and some turnover of trained individuals, we have yet to implement the PVCS software. I can't tell you much about it now, but we fully intend to implement it as soon as possible. Version-control software is a must for developers. It's too easy to overwrite some needed change by changing and updating a module.

Q What were some problems that occurred during implementation and distribution of a stand-alone Watcom SQL/ PowerBuilder system?

Implementing our system proved almost as difficult as developing it. First, we had to write an installation program to install our executable, the needed PowerBuilder DLLs, and our Watcom SQL database onto a laptop. This entailed adding files to the \WINDOWS\SYSTEM subdirectory, as well as setting up our own directory. Watcom SQL provided a run-time disk to help with the Windows setup. We had to include our own ODBC.INI and ODBCINST.INI files for the \WINDOWS\SYSTEM subdirectory. We encountered two particularly obscure problems when moving from our development environment to the laptop environment: the engine defined in the ODBC environment and the differences between the run-time version of Watcom SQL and the development version of Watcom SQL.

We currently have the challenge of bug fixes on the current version of our system while developing a new version of our system. Often, bug fixes have to be applied twice: once for the existing version and once for the new version. This can lead to inconsistancies between versions. It also forces testing twice for the same bug fix.

 What problems did you have with the engine definition?

The ODBC setup we used in our development environment was incorrect. PowerBuilder uses DB32W.EXE as its Watcom database engine. However, the run-time version did not come with DB32W.EXE. We ended up getting a cryptic message of `DB Error Code: -80 [WATCOM] [ODBC Driver] Unable to connect to database server: unable to start database engine`, as seen in figure 18.1.

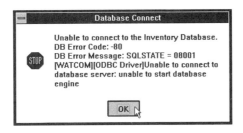

Fig. 18.1

You get this error dialog box when Watcom can't find your database engine program.

Eventually, we discovered that we had to change the laptop program to use RT32W.EXE. You can do this in one of two ways. One is to go into ODBC.INI in your \WINDOWS directory, find the database in question, and change the `Start=DB32W` to `Start=RT32W`. Although your ODBC.INI program could look different, depending on what databases and drivers you have loaded, the layout for the ODBC.INI file should look something like this:

▶ **See**
"Using DB32W.EXE, DBSTARTW.EXE, RT32W.EXE, and RTSTARTW.EXE," p. 612

```
[ODBC Data Sources]
Quote=WATCOM SQL 4.0

[Watcom SQL 4.0]
driver=C:\WSQL40\WIN\WOD40W.DLL

[Quote]
Driver=c:\WINDOWS\SYSTEM\WOD40W.DLL
UID=DBA
PWD=SQL
Start=C:\WSQL40\WIN\RT32W -d
DatabaseFile=C:\QUOTE
DatabaseName=QUOTE
AutoStop=yes
```

◀ **See**
"Using the Microsoft ODBC Admin-istrator," p. 24

Notice how the bold line uses the RT32W program to start the database. Editing your ODBC.INI file is the fastest way to change your database engine, but many are not comfortable using the editor to change an INI file. Furthermore, you run the risk of corrupting your database access if you handle the INI file incorrectly. Many prefer to go through the Windows ODBCADM program.

ODBCADM

To change your database engine through Windows, click the ODBCADM icon to open the ODBC administrator. The Microsoft ODBC Administrator dialog box opens, as seen in figure 18.2. Choose the database you are distributing using the Watcom SQL Runtime Edition and click **C**onfigure.

Fig. 18.2

You can use the ODBC Adminis-trator to configure database information, such as which engine to use.

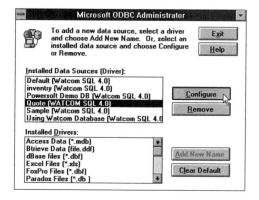

Information about your database will then be displayed. Be sure that **C**ustom is chosen in Database Startup, as seen in figure 18.3. Then choose **O**ptions.

Fig. 18.3

The Watcom SQL ODBC Configuration gives informa-tion about your current database defaults.

Now the Startup Options dialog box should appear. Notice that the Start Command listed is \WSQL40\WIN\db32w (see fig. 18.4). This tells the ODBC driver to look for DB32W.EXE to start your database.

Fig. 18.4

The Startup Options dialog box is where you enter information about your database engine.

As mentioned before, the run-time database is RT32W.EXE, so the Start Command must be changed from \WSQL40\WIN\db32w to \WSQL40\WIN\rt32w, as seen in figure 18.5.

Fig. 18.5

When distributing your program with the run-time version of Watcom SQL, you must change the Start Command to rt32w.

Now you should be able to connect to your database. Although using the ODBC Administrator to connect to your database is more cumbersome and time-consuming than editing the file yourself, using the ODBC Administrator is typically safer.

What were some problems that occurred when moving from development to run time?

▶ **See**
"Using DB32W.EXE, DBSTARTW.EXE, RT32W.EXE, and RTSTARTW.EXE," p. 612

Unknown to us at that time (and poorly documented in the PowerBuilder documentation), the run-time version of Watcom SQL does not allow certain SQL commands. So here we are, coding our SQL to make our quoting system work, when, after we move the command from the development environment to the run-time environment, it no longer functions.

▶ **See**
"COMMENT,"
p. 533

▶ **See**
"DROP,"
p. 548

▶ **See**
"GRANT,"
p. 555

▶ **See**
"REVOKE,"
p. 561

▶ **See**
"OUTPUT,"
p. 605

▶ **See**
"INPUT,"
p. 602

The run-time version of Watcom SQL (rt32w) does not support the ALTER, CREATE, COMMENT, or DROP commands. While the GRANT and REVOKE commands are allowed, they are severely restricted. This caused our installation program to fail when using the run-time versions of Watcom SQL, because we created tables during installation. We had to come up with a whole new method of distributing our application to our agent force. We've also discovered, much to our dismay, that the new version of Watcom SQL run time does not support stored procedures, and triggers or log files, so those new features have to be avoided when you're distributing your database.

To get around the limitations inherent when we were not allowed to create a table on a database, we had to perform the following steps:

1. Send a blank database to the agents.

2. Use OUTPUT to dump data from the existing database (if it is an update, as opposed to a new install).

3. Delete the existing database.

4. Copy the new database to their hard drive.

5. Use INPUT to import the data into the new database.

Of course, there are other methods we could have used, but this seemed to use the least amount of disk space of all the methods we thought of.

Q How do you maintain your quoting system?

Maintenance of our database consists of three major areas. First, we have to make changes to the existing system. Second, we have to maintain a test platform to test those changes. Finally, we have to distribute those changes to the agent force.

We keep a version on the LAN for major changes. Any minor changes made to the existing system must be copied here, and the major changes are applied to the system and released on a quarterly basis.

To make minor changes, we keep the last version of our application in a separate area on the LAN. Any problems or quick changes that need distributing get added here and then redistributed. Of course, we try not to use this version, and opt for a more scheduled release to avoid coding a change or problem fix twice.

To distribute, we take all of the read-write data the agent has and OUTPUT it to the hard drive. We then copy a blank database with the read-only information on it to the agent's hard drive, and then INPUT the read-write data back into the database. This allows the agent to keep their data from change to change.

Future enhancements to agent distribution will include an automatic backup and recovery options. These are important, in case something happens during installation that causes a database corruption.

Q What advice could you give to someone starting to develop a PowerBuilder/Watcom SQL application for the first time?

I would say that the major areas to watch out for are development and distribution. In development, understand that PowerBuilder is *event-driven,* not process-driven. Typical top-down, structured designs that worked well with COBOL and C don't work well with event-driven programming.

With PowerBuilder, the *user* controls the flow of the application. Because events are programmed for, PowerBuilder returns control back to the Windows environment when an event is finished. This is different than traditional programming, where the program has to stay in control the whole time until program termination.

Also remember that PowerBuilder is *iterative.* It seems that the typical design methodologies force an entire application (in its final form) to be developed at once. PowerBuilder is great at delivering sections of your application. When you want to add a section, it's a lot easier to do with PowerBuilder than it is with other languages (like COBOL and C). The event-driven nature of PowerBuilder makes your application naturally encapsulated, so that what is done in one window or command button rarely effects another.

If you're going to use several people to develop a system, be sure that you buy the multi-user platform of Watcom SQL. If you don't have a DBA to manage this database, assign one of the developers to be responsible for the database. Merging and overwriting data all the time is both dangerous and cumbersome.

Finally, be sure you review all of the new features in Watcom 4.0. The new features, such as temporary tables and auto-increment fields, can really help an application.

For distribution, be sure you test with *all* the components of your production environment. Our application would have failed if we didn't test it on a laptop prior to distibuting it to the agents.

Chapter 19

Using CASE to Develop and Design Your Watcom SQL Database

Dr. Ben Cohen is president and CEO of Logic Works, Inc.
Domenick Cilea is network manager of Set Marketing On, Inc.

Q Why is client/server technology becoming widely accepted?

Since the inception of PC technology over a decade ago, businesses and organizations have experienced tremendous growth in the raw power and utility of their information systems. Paralleling the current business philosophies toward decentralized management and resources, organizations of all sizes, shapes, and industries are trimming the layers between the decision makers and customers. In fact, more attention and resources are being placed on incorporating PC technology and networks into the workplace—creating distributed computing environments.

As aging mainframe and minicomputer technologies are being replaced by PCs, organizations are becoming increasingly interested in the emergence of cost-effective

Techniques from the Pros

by Dr. Ben Cohen and Domenick Cilea

client/server systems, products, services, and solutions. With the availability of sophisticated network operating software, database tools, and robust hardware server systems, client/server technology is the new paradigm for the next generation computing environment.

Q How is client/server development changing the role of CASE, and what place does component technology have in CASE tools?

Traditional CASE tools offer users a powerful system to design, review, tune, and change software applications. CASE provides a consistent way to build applications and manage them—as user needs and business requirements change.

Until recently, CASE technology was quite expensive because the tools were difficult to learn and use, and it often required dedicated staff to leverage the technology investment. Also, because many CASE systems were proprietary, they offered limited choices to expand and harness new technologies.

Today, PC-based client/server tools have emerged as low-cost, yet extremely powerful and easy-to-use alternatives. These new components include the client-side application development tools such as Powersoft's PowerBuilder, PC-based data and process modeling tools such as Logic Works' ERwin/ERX, and the server-based tools such as Powersoft's Watcom and Sybase's SQLServer.

Due to the availability of a wide range of databases and client/server technology, component-based tools are becoming an attractive option to developers because they provide an open, best-of-breed alternative that leverages existing technology investments. Component-based technology also enables developers to coordinate their application development efforts with the tools that specifically fit their environment.

Another benefit driving the market for component technology is that it provides developers with the ability to build cross-platform development environments—enabling these components to forward- and reverse-engineer existing X-based and SQL-based databases. This is ideal for upsizing business applications, and migrating to larger and more powerful database systems.

Today's CASE tools must support the customer's right to choose development technologies and standards. The open systems trend will continue to benefit products that can be used in conjunction with all leading client/server application development and database-management tools such as ERwin.

Q What's the difference between client- and server-side application development?

Client/server application development includes both client-side and server-side planning, design, and administration. *Client-side development* involves prototyping the screens and the front-end look and feel of an application. *Server-side development* involves the generation and synchronization of a database server.

By combining state-of-the-art data-modeling tools, such as ERwin, with PowerBuilder's popular client/server application development system, developers can have a unified framework for managing their organization's logical business model, physical database, and GUI-client design. For example, ERwin/ERX for PowerBuilder gives developers the ability to manage both client-oriented information such as PowerBuilder extended attributes, and server-oriented information such as triggers, stored procedures, and physical storage objects—all from within ERwin.

Providing a two-way link to the PowerBuilder dictionary (see fig. 19.1), ERwin lets you import, view, and modify an application's client-oriented attribute values in the same environment in which you model the server-oriented database schema.

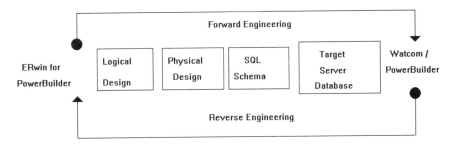

Fig. 19.1

The bi-directional link to Watcom SQL and/or to the PowerBuilder Data Dictionary provides read/write access to the database schema, as well as to PowerBuilder extended attributes.

Easy-to-use CASE tools, such as ERwin; and easy-to-use development tools, such as PowerBuilder, can form a complete database-design environment for client/server development. ERwin/ERX for PowerBuilder lets you use the best tool for each part of the development process:

- PowerBuilder for building sophisticated GUI client applications and for managing the connection between application objects and data sources.

- ERwin for developing the logical data model, including relationship descriptions, role names, foreign key migration, referential integrity rules, and other database design and maintenance functions, along with forward- and reverse-engineering (FRE), and a direct link to the database catalog.

On the other side of the application development spectrum is *server-side development*, which involves the generation and synchronization of a relational database server, such as Watcom SQL. Designing the back-end database server is essential for efficiently processing and servicing requests from front-end GUIs, and it is critical for overall system performance.

By utilizing a data-modeling tool like ERwin, developers can directly connect to a database's system tables, giving them the ability to quickly forward- and reverse-engineer desktop and SQL databases.

By directly connecting to the database system catalog, developers can eliminate the interim steps of creating, searching, maintaining, and manually loading SQL DDL script files through data administration tools. They can also convert a wide range of desktop and SQL databases by simply importing them into their data-modeling tool.

We designed ERwin to directly interface with widely used databases like Watcom SQL (as shown in figure 19.2). A direct interface into the database system tables eliminates the need for intermediate SQL processing. It also provides an excellent set of tools to reconcile the content of the data model with the system tables of an existing database.

Fig. 19.2

CASE tools like ERwin allow you to directly modify your database from your data model developed in your CASE design tool.

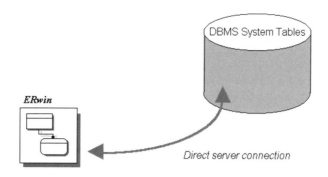

What benefits can data-modeling tools deliver to client/server development?

Model-driven application development allows users to visualize and design an application without spending a great deal of time and money. Using today's RAD (Rapid Application Development) tools, developers can quickly create a prototype — offering users a sample of what the finished product might look like. The prototype also gives developers an idea of how much application code is required before committing costly resources to fully build and deploy a client/server application development project.

By using a data-modeling tool to visually specify system requirements (see figure 19.3), users and developers can synchronize their needs and be involved in the overall design process. It's imperative that users be involved in the application design process because they are ultimately the people who will gauge its success or failure.

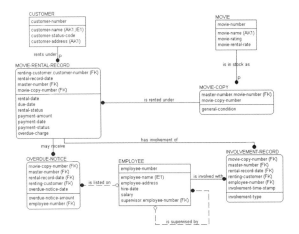

Fig. 19.3

ERwin data model.

A developer can use a model to explore what the system really looks like, and the user often gets to understand the real operation of the proposed system. A data-modeling tool can help generate a prototype that ultimately drives the design and implementation of the front-end interfaces and back-end database servers.

The other advantage of implementing data-modeling tools is that prototypes are easy to change and modify. From a data model, developers can constantly refine and hone the intricacies of their client/server application-development projects.

The beauty of data-modeling tools is that no matter where developers begin— either from scratch or from an existing database structure—they can forward- and reverse-engineer these data models, and continue to build and refine quality database applications.

Q How can data-modeling tools be used to assist organizations in the process of upsizing, downsizing, or rightsizing?

The current trend to upsize, downsize, rightsize, and re-engineer existing information systems to client/server computing environments is driving the need for powerful database design and modeling tools. Data-modeling tools such as ERwin give database administrators and application developers to create a detailed blueprint of their application development projects, tightly coupling client-side development activities with back-end servers. A comprehensive design will result in adherence to consistent, client/server development principles.

Today's developers are faced with tremendous challenges. As companies and organizations continue to evolve and re-engineer themselves (reducing personnel and redistributing resources), a greater emphasis is put on giving users the necessary tools to access information and communicate within the information technology infrastructure. Upsizers, downsizers, and rightsizers all share common issues— they must take a hard look at how their organizations are structured, and identify how data and processes are woven into this structure— taking both the human and technical issues into account. Then, they must deploy a system to equally fulfill the demands of the users and the organization.

Q How important is data modeling when migrating from one database to another (such as moving an X-based system to Watcom SQL)?

Utilizing data-modeling tools, developers can generate a multi-dimensional view of their database structure. After they get a clear picture of the structure, they can forward- and reverse-engineer data and process models.

For example, migrating from an X-based database to Watcom entails numerous tasks. With limited time and resources, developers need to understand what the objectives are for the development of a specific application, and identify what they need to do to meet these objectives.

Data-modeling software gives developers the essential toolset to drive the migration from one database to another. This software also provides a way for developers to upgrade or migrate from one version of an X-based or SQL-based database without writing trigger code, stored procedures, and schema—all while preserving the business rules and ensuring referential integrity.

Developers can easily reverse-engineer any existing database through the use of a data model, and then use a data model tool to re-engineer or migrate the database schema to a different target database—eliminating the need to write thousands of lines of trigger or procedure code.

Q How are the roles of developers changing as client/server application development increases?

Client/server application development is currently being implemented by a wide variety of developers, administrators, and users in many types of corporations and government agencies. Among the many users and application design approaches available today, all application-development projects must adhere to the following rules:

- Enforce business rules

- Improve productivity and performance

- Ensure data integrity

Today's client/server application designers fall into four categories. Interestingly enough, they all share similar needs and are dependent on component-based data and process modeling tools.

- *Application developers*. These are users who incorporate programs such as PowerBuilder to develop and manage client/server systems. Using a tool like ERwin for model-driven design, application developers can easily keep their applications "in sync" with the server database.

- *Data Administrators*. Also known as DAs, they model data and maintain data definitions and business rules. It's equally important for them to define, manage, and improve data integrity and consistency.

- *Database Administrators*. Also known as DBAs, their role is to model physical database design, manage design changes, generate database schemas, and synchronize the logical and physical schemas. The fact that ERwin can generate six month's worth of trigger code in minutes is a tremendous benefit to these DBAs.

- *Business/System Analysts*. These users define business rules, are heavily involved in re-engineering business processes, and develop a graphical blueprint of processes, functions, and activities.

What is reverse-engineering, and how important is it?

Reverse engineering is the process of creating a logical data model from an existing physical database. As technology changes, and new, more cost-effective methodologies such as client-server architecture are introduced, organizations require new vendor-independent migration tools such as ERwin to capture their legacy data so they can migrate it into the new environment.

Once the information structure is captured in a data model, it can be redesigned to take advantage of technical advances like triggers and stored procedures, and then quickly generated on a server platform that supports these new integrity and performance features. Because ERwin supports a direct connection to the target server and automatic datatype mapping between different vendors DBMS, migrating a database schema from one server to another is easily accomplished, as shown in figure. 19.4.

Fig. 19.4

Reverse engineering an Oracle database.

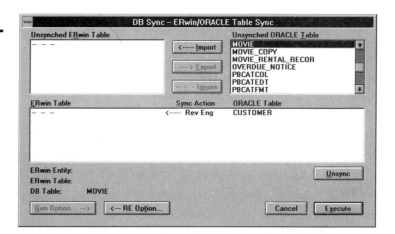

In the PC environment, there are major shifts occurring as business organizations establish new vendor relationships and standardize on different tool sets. By using ERwin's reverse-engineering capability to create a independent data model, an organization can develop a flexible migration strategy that supports simple version upgrades, moving from one DBMS vendor to another, or upsizing from an Xbase file-server environment to a robust client-server environment, based on an SQL database engine.

Q How important are open and independent client/server tools and databases?

Client-server architecture is based on a simple concept; use the right tool for the job. In a client-server environment, data-processing tasks are divided between the client application, which provides a well-designed interface so users can easily request, browse, and modify data; and the server DBMS, a high-performance engine designed to store and retrieve data in the most efficient manner. Both the front-end application and the back-end server are specialists that excel in one part of the data-management process.

The real benefit of client-server architecture is that it lets organizations build systems that exploit this type of specialization. For example, by separating the front-end application code from the database-engine code, you can use a variety of tools such as PowerBuilder, Visual Basic, or SQLWindows to build the user interface for a particular application. Because many development tools are available, you can choose the one that fits your needs best, based on your budget, the programming skills that are available in your organization, the features supported by a particular tool, the reputation of the vendor, etc.

For a data-modeling tool such as ERwin to be successful, it must be able to import and export information easily and communicate with a wide variety of front and back-end tools. ERwin currently supports schema generation and reverse engineering features for most popular SQL database engines, including Oracle, Sybase, Informix, Microsoft SQL Server, SQLBase, and Watcom SQL (as well as Access, Paradox, dBASE, FoxPro, and Clipper). Similarly, special ERwin versions support todays leading client application development tools.

Q What kind of reports can a data-modeling tool (such as ERwin) generate?

One of the main benefits of using a good data-modeling tool is the capability it gives you to quickly generate comprehensive system documentation. For example, ERwin/ERX is shipped with a set of standard report templates that generate detailed documentaion on all the entities, attributes, relationships, and constraints defined in your database schema. Using a built-in browser, you can filter these reports to include just the information you're currently interested in; and you can preview the information on-screen, save it as a text file, use DDE to send it to another Windows application, or send it directly to a printer.

In addition to displaying a graphical data model for easy analysis and design, a powerful tool like ERwin can help you quickly generate important documentation from the wealth of information that is captured in your data model (such as column datatypes, null status, primary and foreign keys, alternate keys, rolenames, business rules, and physical storage parameters). The ERwin report options also let you preview, save, or print our automatically-generated DDL (data definition statements) and SQL trigger code; as well as stored procedures, and pre- and post-schema generation scripts (see fig. 19.5.).

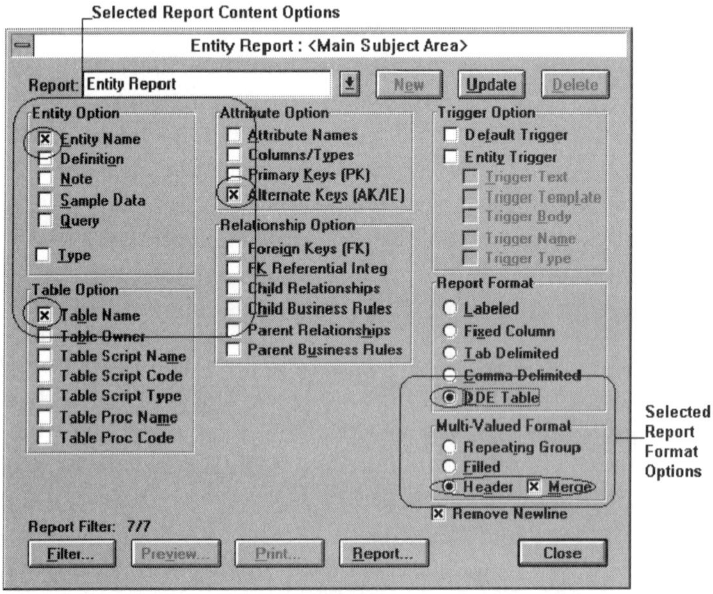

Fig. 19.5

ERwin report options.

To make this information easy to read, ERwin is currently bundling the new report writer, RPTwin, at no additional cost. RPTwin lets you define sophisticated reports with group, page, and report-level headers and footers; full support for Windows fonts; built-in drawing tools to create borders and break lines; a formula editor to manipulate text, number, time, and date information; and a variety of predefined layout styles. RPTwin turns a basic ERwin report into an informative, presentation-quality document.

Chapter 20

Using Watcom SQL with CA-Realizer

Elvira Peretsman is a senior software developer for Computer Associates International Inc., and is currently working on the next release of CA-Realizer for Windows and OS/2. Elvira joined Computer Associates in 1991, bringing with her over 10 years of experience and expertise in software development. Elvira holds a degree in Applied Mathematics and Computer Science from Riga University in Latvia.

Q What is CA-Realizer?

CA-Realizer is a development environment for Windows and OS/2 that lets the user create cross-platform applications. It's based on the BASIC language, but it has been expanded to include over 370 commands. Most of those commands are to support the built-in high level tools and to support all of the visual aspects of graphical operating systems.

> **Note**
>
> CA-Realizer is a BASIC-like language currently developed by Computer Associates (CA). The next version will include Watcom SQL, as well as an easy interface with the database.

Developing an application with CA-Realizer is pretty easy. You create the visual elements of your program— that's the windows, menus, forms, and the controls that are on them—by using the visual forms designer, FormDev. Then you add any supporting code to perform the actual processing. After that, you can create an executable application, complete with an installation disk set.

Techniques from the Pros

Interview with Elvira Peretsman by Charles A. Wood

Who uses CA-Realizer?

There are many types of users. They can range from individuals who want to create Windows or OS/2 applications for use at home, to developers creating applications for corporate-wide use—and just about everyone in between. There are also quite a few educational users as well.

 So it's for writing applications of any type, not just database applications?

That's right. It's pretty easy to develop just about any kind of application you can think of. Execution speed might be a factor. CA-Realizer is based on a p-code compiler that makes it faster than traditional BASIC interpreters, but somewhat slower than a native code compiler. In any situation, you have to weigh your goals to determine what tools you need to get there.

But when you compare CA-Realizer to other rapid development tools, it runs just as fast, if not faster. If you're doing a lot of calculations with numbers in arrays, CA-Realizer really flies! There is a special array shorthand that optimizes array manipulations and calculations. For most operations, it eliminates the need for looping through all the values in an array. This has made CA-Realizer popular with people doing financial and scientific work.

 How does CA-Realizer work with databases?

It depends on the version you're using. The 2.0 release relies on basic ODBC database access and add-ons such as DLLs. It has some built-in database functionality, but most people use an add-on such as Watcom SQL. Accessing DLLs, such as Watcom SQL, from within the CA-Realizer environment is easy using what we call *externals*. You just declare the functions in the DLL that you want to call from CA-Realizer before you make the call. Generally, you put all of these declarations in a single file that's called, for example, WATCOM.RLZ. At the beginning of your CA-Realizer applications, you make a call that says run watcom.rlz. This declares all the functions of the Watcom DLL in your application. After that, you can simply use the functions as if they where part of CA-Realizer's own language. But all of this gets much simpler and complete with the next release of the program.

How does data access work in your next version?

The next version, release 3.0 (which is due in the fall of 1995), has much more powerful database-access capabilities. We've built a complete set of database commands into the base language, and added custom tools and objects that make handling data almost automatic. If, you like, you can have full control over all the database functions or some mix of the two techniques. It really is several magnitudes better than release 2.0.

Release 3.0 builds on the strengths that already exist in the product and makes complex database applications very easy to write. The other major change is that you can handle all of your data access via ODBC. You can still access DLLs and add-ons using the external command syntax, but the integrated support relies on ODBC. So, even though all of your existing 2.0 programs will still work, you'll want to use the new API (application programming interface) to get the full benefits.

How does ODBC help in creating these applications? What made you choose this way?

ODBC offers a number of advantages to the developer of CA-Realizer applications, but the main benefit is database independence. By using the CA-Realizer database language, we provide a common API, so the developer can write fairly generic database code. You can develop a database application that works with any ODBC-compliant database. You connect, query, sort, add, and delete records the same way, no matter what database you choose. With ODBC, your CA-Realizer code becomes database-independent. You can develop by using a local database on your PC, but release it to people that will go against the corporate mainframe database. This also means that you can connect to multiple databases at the same time by using the same code. It really is powerful in that it can help you in database application design and development—and for creating a general front-end tool that can be used to access all of a company's data, it just can't be beat.

Can you say much about the next release of CA-Realizer?

Yes. It's been announced, and we've talked about the various new platforms we are supporting, in addition to Windows 3.x, Windows 95, Windows NT, Win32s, and OS/2. Not all at the same time, but fairly close together.

How do you write CA-Realizer 3.0 applications? Is it the same as for 2.0, and at what level are you coding?

It really is pretty much as I described earlier. You design your visual elements using FormDev, add any code that needs to be executed, and then run it. It can be that simple.

As to the level that you code, CA-Realizer is based on a greatly extended version of the BASIC language. One of the advantages of a language such as this is that it is fairly high-level. This helps cut down the development time needed to create applications. It also helps you by letting you invest a short period of time to get a pretty complete prototype up and running. You can make changes, add or delete features, or even scrap the entire idea before you've committed so much time and energy that you're trapped into using a particular design.

Of course, even though you program by using this high-level language, CA-Realizer still provides the features that allow you to have very fine control over how any individual feature works. For example, when you're making a query on a table, you can specify the minimum number of parameters, and get back a result that is based on a number of defaults. If, however, you want to specify all of the other parameters, you can. We try to keep the usability level of any feature high; if we find a way to ease the burden on the developer, we do it.

First, I'll talk about the development environment because there have been a lot of changes and additions made, and then I'll talk more about the data access specific features. The environment has been redesigned and enhanced to run and create true 32-bit programs. One of the advantages to this is that all the old DOS and 16-bit Windows memory limitations are gone. Array size restrictions, resource problems—these all go away with the flat memory model.

With version 3.0, we also introduce project-based development. It becomes much easier to control the process of managing various source codes, forms, and bit-map files. All of the files that go into a final executable program are gathered into the project and displayed in a graphical tree. The code editor is completely new, and it supports color coding of the various language elements such as comments, reserved words, and constants, as well as such things as what color to display an error line in the debugger (see fig. 20.1).

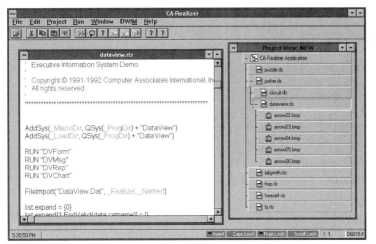

Fig. 20.1

The CA-Realizer 3.0 development environment.

CA-Realizer 3.0 also supports syntax checking, which can be a big help. The report generator is integrated into the environment now, and there's support for creating your own tool bar and status bar objects. The install manager is new. That lets you create complete install set disks, so you can distribute your program to other people—just as you would any commercial application. Again, it's not complex to do this, everything is pretty much point-and-click. The install manager does the hard work for you. There is a menu editor and an icon editor. Also, all of your controls can be shown in 3D, with either a raised or sunken appearance.

Along with the new database features, the biggest advance is with the addition of support for OLE (Object Linking and Embedding) 2.0 and OLE custom controls (OCXs). OLE can be a very complex thing to explain, but put very simply, it is a way for applications to talk and work with each other in a way that appears seamless to the user of the program.

Probably the most frequent example is a word processing document with a spreadsheet embedded in it. Even though the spreadsheet comes from another program, you can click it and make changes to it while you're still in your word processor. The two programs talk to each other and coordinate their individual functions. As soon as you select some text that you've written outside of the spreadsheet, the word processor takes over again.

But again, as a user, you don't see all of this communication between the applications take place. You just do what you want; the programs should handle all the details. Now, OCXs are OLE custom controls. They're built on this foundation of OLE 2.0, but think of them as plug-ins: individual little programs that you can add onto another application.

The best thing about these controls is that they can be attached to any program that can use an OCX, even though the two were written by different people in different companies. Word processors, spreadsheets, databases, or custom software packages (such as those you write with CA-Realizer) can all use the same OCX.

 You seem very excited about OLE and OCXs.

I am. They are technologies that open up CA-Realizer to all sorts of applications. There are already many developers who are creating OCXs, and that number will continue to grow. Also, many of these controls are targeted to do very specific things that would never be released on their own commercially. Companies and individuals can create an OCX, based on their very specific needs, and then quickly design a CA-Realizer application to contain it. The possibilities really are incredible.

 What about new database features?

That's the other major area where we added new capabilities. First, we added a number of commands to support database access and control. We added new CA-Realizer objects such as databases, tables, queries, records, and fields, and, of course, ways to use the two together. Quick Query is new (see fig. 20.2). It allows you to visually design your queries, based on a series of dialog boxes, and then it generates the proper SQL to execute. Not only is this simpler for the developer, it also allows end users to generate queries without having to know how to use SQL themselves.

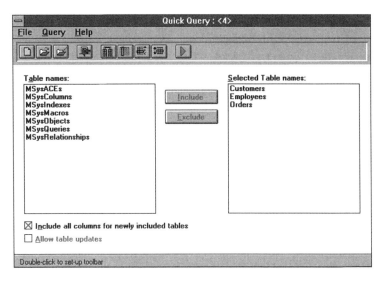

Fig. 20.2

You can generate SQL SELECT statements using the CA-Realizer Quick Query dialog box.

We implemented *bound data controls*, which allow you to attach a visual element such as an edit control to a specific field in a database. For example, you could have a person table where one of the fields is called name. You can create a control that would appear in a dialog box to the user to automatically display the contents of the field. Then, if the user changed that value (maybe changing the name from Bob to Sue), the control would update the field in the database for him. No code needs to be written, it's all done for you when you bind the control to the field.

We also have *db controls*: VCR-like controls that direct the movement of the database cursor through a set of records. Clicking the forward arrow advances the cursor to the next record in the set, and clicking the rewind arrow moves the cursor backwards a record in the set.

What makes all of this so powerful is that when you combine a db control with a number of bound controls, displaying or updating records can be done without any code. Using the person table example again, say that the form or dialog box has a bound edit control for each field (such as name, title, address, and phone number). Now, on that form, you add a db control (which looks similar to a VCR control panel, with arrows pointing forward and backward). When that form is displayed, it automatically puts the data from the current record—where the cursor is pointing—into each bound control. So the name control might get the value Philip. The title control gets and displays Manager. On and on, for as many bound controls as you have. Now, if the user selects the name and changes it to Debra, and then clicks the forward arrow, the bound control updates the field in the database and the change is committed. Then the form updates and displays the contents of the newly selected record. All of this is enabled with no coding required. Of course, if you want to have full control over each step, you can. It's your option.

One other thing with bound controls. Even though I used edit controls in the example, you can use other visual elements such as checkboxes, radio buttons, and lists. Many control types can be bound to a database field.

The other major database feature added to CA-Realizer is the *grid control*. This control looks very much like a spreadsheet, but it is a very powerful tool used to display data to the user. It also highly automates the process. Essentially, it can take an entire result set or group of records, and display them all. The user can then scroll through the list, add, delete, and modify fields, and then commit them to the database. With the database tools in CA-Realizer (such as the grid, db, and bound controls), creating a visual front end to a complex database really is an easy process.

 With all that in mind, how does the Watcom database integrate with CA-Realizer?

Absolutely great! The Watcom ODBC implementation is one of the most complete of any available. For example, it supports multiple cursors, random and backward cursor scrolling, transactions, and multi-concurrency. One of the many advantages to using Watcom SQL with our 3.0 release is that it enables everyone to focus on what they do best. We focus on the application design and development side, while the Watcom engine is focused on data access. Everybody wins, especially the user.

Q How do you create a CA-Realizer application using the Watcom engine?

At a really high level, you can break down the steps pretty easily. First, you need to connect to the database, which we actually refer to as a *datasource*.

Each datasource is the result of opening a specific database with a specific driver. After connecting, you might want to query the datasource to set up options for the application.

For example, you can query the datasource to get a list of tables in the database, or to check to see whether the database is read-only. You can query for isolation levels, the driver version, whether it is transaction-capable, and what the SQL conformance level of the database is. There are many other queries you can do, but that should give you a pretty good idea about the scope of the queries. Now, after you've set any specific options, you generate a solution set that is a set of records to operate on. There are a lot of options that include loading the entire table or performing a query that returns a subset of the records in the table.

Next, you can perform operations on the set (such as deleting records, adding them, and updating them). Depending on how your options are set, these changes can be committed to the database automatically, or you can collect all of these individual steps into a single transaction and manually commit them when you're ready to finish. Finally, you would disconnect from the datasource. That's all there is to it. When you look at an application, it can seem overwhelming—but when you break it down into steps, it becomes pretty clear.

Q Now let's get a more detailed view. How exactly do you connect to a database?

Again, first you need a datasource that is a driver and database combination. You get a datasource in CA-Realizer by calling DbControl with the DbConnect parameter. For example, you could call DbControl and pass in a driver name such as Watcom SQL, and a database name such as employee. This returns a database ID variable that is then used in your other calls. Say you've connected to the database, and you want to find out information about the employee database. You would call DbDatabaseQ and pass in the database ID and some CA-Realizer constant like DbTables. This would return a list of tables in that database.

Can you perform operations on those tables?

Right. If you wanted to load the entire table and browse through it, you would execute a DbTableLoad command, and pass in the database ID variable and a table name from the DbDatabaseQ result, say employee, which could be a table with individual employee records in it. This would return a set of records, which, in this case, would be all the records in that table. You could then change the last name field of the current record with a simple assignment statement, commit the changes to the database, and close the datasource connection by calling DbControl with the DbDisconnect parameter. The following CA-Realizer code gives you an idea of how the code is written:

```
db = DbControl(_DbConnect, "employee")
tables = DbDatabaseQ(db, _DbTables)
t = DbTableLoad(db, "employ")
t.lastname = "Williams"
DbControl(db, _DbCommit)
DbControl(_DbDisconnect, db)
```

How about building a form to show all of this to the user?

You build a form to show all of this to the user by using FormDev, the visual forms designer. It is very easy to use to create forms of any kind, but it has special features for creating database forms. Generally, you create a form by choosing **F**ile, **N**ew Form. This creates a form that looks just like a window in Windows or OS/2. You then add objects or controls by selecting them from the toolbar and dropping them onto the form. For example, you could add a button to the form by clicking the button tool and then clicking the upper right side of the form. FormDev puts a button control there. You could then, for example, change its text from the default to OK. You can also add CA-Realizer code that would get executed when someone clicked the button. You might choose to implement some sort of error-checking on the field values before they are committed to the database. A button is one place where you can add this code.

If you want to create a database form, FormDev will walk you through the process. First, FormDev asks you for a query to base the form on. Continue with the employee example. Using the Quick Query dialog boxes, you visually create a query that simply selects all of the records in the employee table. You then get a list of fields that make up each individual record in the table. From this list, you select the fields to place on the form (such as name, title, address, and phone). Then, choose a style that controls the way controls are visually presented: color, depth, and alignment. FormDev then creates the form and all of the controls needed to display the fields. It even creates control captions, and sets the form title and background colors.

You're not committed to the styles presented by FormDev; you can always change the forms after they have been created. With the form created, you can create the application and run it. You can browse through the records, make changes, and save them. You never had to write a line of code. It's the combination of FormDev and the high-level database tools that make building a complete application or creating a prototype so quick. They do the work and give you an attractive design that lets you concentrate on the specifics of your application—without losing time trying to get the form to look good.

Again, combining CA-Realizer with the Watcom database just makes it all the better; not only do you have a superior tool in CA-Realizer for building full applications and front-ends to databases, but you get a complete database back-end by using the Watcom database. Together, they are a great solution.

Chapter 21

David O'Hearn is a consultant for Computer Horizons Corporation. He has worked as a computer programmer and systems analyst for more than six years.

Mapping an Object-Oriented Design onto a Relational Database

Q What is Object-Oriented Technology and Object-Oriented Analysis?

Object-oriented technology (OOT) is the practice of developing and coding modules in a system that behave independently of other modules. In the early days of programming, functionality was stressed above data. Concentration on functionality gave us top-down or structured programming techniques. However, such concentration on programming techniques took away from the real importance of a system: namely, the data that the system contains and conveys. Data was *passive,* meaning that the data stayed in data stores waiting for functions to query or update. OOT allows the data to be *active* by tying functionality to the data. For example, a CAD (Computer Aided Drafting) object would contain data about the current draft or model as well as the code to display that model on the screen.

Techniques from the Pros

Interview with David O'Hearn by Charles A. Wood

OOT consists of three things: *object-oriented analysis* (OOA), where you define the objects and relationships that need to be designed based on requirements given to or developed by the analyst; *object-oriented design* (OOD), where you take the OOA and use it to define the functions that need to be coded as well as the appearance of any input or output; and, finally, *object-oriented programming* (OOP), which places the OOD in a program.

OOT can deliver a program that fits the needs defined by the requirements, just like any other development technique. However, there are other benefits when using OOT:

■ Unlike other techniques, OOT will eventually lead to a "warehouse" (or close to it) of stand-alone modules (also known as classes or objects) that you can use with other development *without changing a line of code*. Simply choose the pre-written objects you need for a system and plug them together. Therefore, new OOT development tends to speed up over time.

■ Maintenance of existing code is often more efficient. Because modules are independent, they tend to be isolated from each other. Because object-oriented systems are so modulated, it's often easy to track down any offending bug. Using OOT, maintenance consists of simply adding new independent modules or changing existing independent modules. Because modules tend to be isolated from each other, what occurs in one module will probably not effect other modules. This makes maintenance on existing programs faster to develop, easier to test, and more bug-free.

■ Iterative development is easier to accomplish. Any new modules that need to be written can be "inherited" from other similar modules to make the addition of needed modules more simplistic.

Q You've mentioned inheritance. Can you explain the main components of OOT?

The three main components of OOT are encapsulation, inheritance, and polymorphism:

■ *Encapsulation* is the act of designing a system in such a way that each module does not effect the performance of other modules. Encapsulation requires a conscious decision to not allow your module to effect any other module *and* to not allow any other module to affect your module.

Of course, there are levels of encapsulation. It's usually not feasible to have *every* module completely isolated from other modules. However, any time one module needs the existence of another module, then those modules need to "travel" together from system to system.

For instance, if you wrote an address module that needed a database access module, then every system that uses that address module would also have to access that database access module.

> **Note**
>
> What occurs in one module should not affect another module. Using the previous example, if you changed databases and therefore had to change the database access module, you should do so without having to change the address module *at all*. This is very important, and perhaps the heart of object-oriented technology. You should be able to completely replace an object without affecting the rest of the system.

- *Inheritance* is the act of reusing (not copying!) a section of code. Remember that with OOT, the data and the functionality are tied together. Inheritance allows subtyping of objects. Say you're designing an insurance company's policy system from the ground up. You would have several different types of policies to track (auto, home, life, and so on). These types of policies have definite similarities (customer information, effective date, and more) that could be "abstracted" into a parent policy class (see fig. 21.1).

> **Note**
>
> A *subtype* is a category of an object. For instance, an insurance policy object might have an auto insurance subtype, a dwelling insurance subtype, a life insurance subtype, and so on.

Now you could write functions and store data that relate to all policies in the Policy object. The Policy object can then be inherited into the Auto, Life, and Home objects. Auto, Life, and Home now contain all that is in the Policy object. You would then add data and functionality to Auto, Life, and Home to customize them to fit your needs. Any changes made to the Policy object are automatically reflected in the Auto, Life, and Home objects.

Fig. 21.1

You can use inheritance to share functionality between common objects.

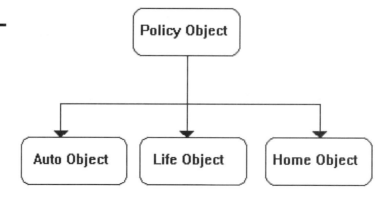

To use inheritance effectively, you must encapsulate the parent object. Remember that the Policy object *does not and should not* need to know how many or what type of descendants it has. If you wanted to sell the Policy object to a health insurance company, you should be able to do so without giving them the Auto, Life, and Home objects.

■ *Polymorphism* is probably the least understood of the three concepts. Polymorphism is the act of letting the data "decide" which function to execute. Say you have three display functions: date_display(value), dollar_display(value), and string_display(value). Depending on the value variable, you would execute one of these three programs just by coding a display(value) call.

You also use polymorphism to describe the act of executing a function based on its location in an ancestor-descendant relationship. For instance, if the Policy object mentioned previously were to call a rate function, *and* the rate function would execute depending on which descendant type were executed, then Policy would be using the object type as its basis for determining which function to execute.

My only caveat would be that these three features as well as the words "object," "object-oriented," and "OOA" have reached buzz-word status in the industry. These days, you rarely see "object-oriented" meaning truly object-oriented. Object-oriented *should* refer to a way of development as opposed to simply "containing objects."

For instance, although many Windows applications *claim* to be object-oriented, they are written in languages like BASIC or COBOL, which are *not* object-oriented languages. Furthermore, the tenets of encapsulation, inheritance, and polymorphism are often absent from development in these non-OOT languages.

Q What languages are object-oriented? Is PowerBuilder?

Your typical object-oriented languages include C++, Smalltalk, and Object Pascal. There's even talk of developing an object-oriented COBOL, which may be a little difficult to do (although it is my understanding that MicroFocus included links to a Smalltalk language inside their COBOL development).

PowerBuilder includes the three main components of object-oriented technology, so I would have to classify it as object-oriented, but only weakly so. You can encapsulate your code, but it's hard to encapsulate your objects from other users. They support inheritance, but have trouble deleting controls out of dependent objects if those controls are on the parent objects. Finally, they support a type of polymorphism, in that ancestor objects can trigger and execute descendent events and functions. However, they don't support true polymorphism—you can't define functions having the same name but different function parameters, and expect your data to "choose" which function to go to.

The data is active in object-oriented systems. PowerBuilder does have active data in that the data is combined with functionality (as with its DataWindow objects), so I would classify it as an object-oriented development system.

However, you don't need to have an object-oriented development environment to implement an OOA. It's just easier.

Q Why would OOT require different database considerations than traditional top-down systems?

Because objects are entities, development would be easier if you could map each object onto its own table. However, implementing an OOD with a relational database is difficult for several reasons:

- You have an inheritance structure where some data is in an ancestor and some is in a descendant. This is difficult to resolve using a single table to store an object.

- Objects may contain some iterative parts. For example, in the auto insurance object mentioned earlier, your car may have one or several drivers, and one or several loss payees. Iterations in a table layout are impossible using a single table to store an object.

- You have functionality that is combined with the data. The data may be meaningless without the functionality to interpret it, but it's difficult to store functionality on a database.

Q Why use object-oriented technology with a relational database like Watcom SQL when using an object-oriented programming language?

There are obvious benefits to object-oriented development. More and more, corporations are getting into it because of the obvious benefits (such as reusability and ease of maintenance). However, corporations are entrenched in their relational database and relational database models.

Even if corporations were not entrenched in their relational databases, object-oriented databases (OODBs) are still in their infancy. The benefits of OOT are often offset by the lack of features found in existing OODBs. One of the necessary features is data independence. Most OODBs require an object-oriented language with the proper class structure for access while most relational databases like Watcom SQL have many interfaces and can be accessed without the need for additional programming. Data integrity, database administration, and security are well-defined, easy to use, and stable with relational databases, especially in Watcom SQL (known for its ease of use). These features are not well-defined in most OODBs and are often poorly implemented when they exist.

▶ **See**
"Understanding Stored Procedures," p. 236

▶ **See**
"Understanding Triggers," p. 237

You are more likely to start finding object-oriented features in relational databases. Watcom SQL also allows complex objects (like graphics) to be stored in its BLOB data type. Also, in version 4.0, Watcom SQL allows stored procedures and triggers. Although these stored procedures are not object-oriented in nature, they allow the developer to tie some functionality to the data on a table. Watcom SQL delivers a lot of the features of an OODB while at the same time, Watcom SQL is a relational database and incorporates relational designs that are so important to corporations: data integrity, data independence, data administration and security, and concurrency. Watcom SQL incorporates all of the features you need to have in a small business or departmental database.

If you are going to have more than one application and/or use your data in more than one way, you'll get a lot more use out of a relational database like Watcom SQL. A relational database is a lot easier to use with non-object technologies. If you're just now starting to use object-oriented programming, you can still use your non-object-oriented code. Finally, relational databases like Watcom SQL use SQL as the database language. There is no standard language available for OODB databases yet. You can buy third-party software or use SQL consultants rather easily with Watcom SQL where you couldn't with an OODB database.

In conclusion, it's usually a lot better to go with a relational database like Watcom SQL even if you're starting to use OOT. There are just too many benefits right now when using a relational database.

Q Are there any situations in which you would forgo the benefits of a relational database and use an OODB?

Well, if you are doing a stand-alone project that doesn't relate to any other tables, then you don't have to worry about concurrency, data independence, or some of the other areas at which relational databases excel. If you need to use complex objects, as with a CAD/CAM system, and don't need to relate to any other application or database, then you *might* want to use an OODB. On the other hand, Watcom SQL, with its BLOB data type and stored procedures can perform much of the tasks of an OODB, and you get all the advantages of using a relational database.

Q When using OOT, how would you map standard objects onto a Watcom SQL database?

With more traditional development techniques, you would use a relational database to separate the data from the source code. The source code then performs functions on the data. With OOT, the code and the data reside together. This code/data combination needs to be resolved when using a relational database.

The way to resolve this conflict is to design your object-oriented system around your relational database and divide your objects into different areas depending on what they cover. For instance, you could first define your environment objects like your GUI-related (Graphical User Interface) objects, printing objects, and relational database objects. Then you define all business objects like payroll-objects, employee-objects, policy-objects, and so on. The business objects should then function regardless of the type of user interface, the type of device, and the type of database used. By dividing out your business objects, you allow their reuse even if the GUI, the printer, or the database changes.

Part of your database objects will include *storage objects*. Storage objects are contained in your other objects and are used to allow your business objects to communicate with a relational database. Using these objects, you query and update your database. Anything you normally do in an OODB you would define in your storage object. Soon, you'll have a layer of storage objects between your business objects, which hold the day-to-day processing of your business and your Watcom SQL database (see fig. 21.2).

Objects from your object model tend to have a one-to-one correspondence with your relational database tables. However, there are a lot of objects that are complex objects and don't map directly to tables. Complex objects will take up most of your time when you try to use an object-oriented system with your relational database.

Fig. 21.2

Business objects are separate from environment objects, with storage objects acting as a translator between business and database objects.

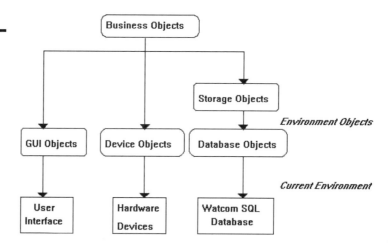

For example, you could have two objects that share a one-to-one correspondence. Say all of the software your organization purchased had some type of support policy. Also assume that it's your organization's policy to always purchase some type of support for every software package. You would want to keep track of the software (software vendor, package name, who used it, what version, and so on) and the support policy (software vendor, support company, what type, what cost, what time frame, and so on). On your object model, these two would be contained in two different objects, but each would have a one-to-one relationship—each software object would have one support object, and each support object would have one software object. On the database, however, you would probably place them in the same table because one-to-one tables tend to normalize into the same table.

When you store data in a one-to-many relationship, objects already have a relationship between them that is intrinsic in the object-oriented program. However, in a database, you must set up keys that match the intrinsic relationship between objects in your object-oriented program. For instance, assume you have a sales system where you have customers receiving items through invoices. Each customer could have several invoices, but each invoice could only be for one customer. In an object-oriented design, this one-to-many relationship would be defined through the internal processing of the objects, but in a database, you must establish a customer_number foreign key on your invoice table (which you did). In an object-oriented system, your storage objects must maintain this foreign key between one-to-many tables.

Many-to-many object relationships must also be handled somehow in your relational database. Referring back to the sales system, you had a many-to-many relationship with invoice and item: each invoice could contain several items, and each item could be ordered by several invoices. Because relational databases have a hard time with many-to-many relationships, you introduced an associative table called invoice_line that contained all the lines of the invoice. You therefore converted a many-to-many item-invoice relationship to two different relationships: a one-to-many invoice_line-item relationship and a one-to-many invoice_line-invoice relationship. Any associative tables that resolve many-to-many relationships must be maintained by your storage object.

In summary, your storage object must do the following:

- Maintain any one-to-one object relationships that you combine on the same table.

- Maintain any foreign keys on the "many" table in a one-to-many relationship.

- Maintain any associative tables that need to be introduced to your Watcom SQL database to resolve many-to-many relationships.

This covers that mapping of standard objects onto your relational database. Of course, the hard part of mapping an object-oriented is in mapping the complex objects that use inheritance or have iterative components.

Q So, how would you map complex objects that have iterative components onto a relational database?

A complex object can contain certain data that recurs in groups. Let's switch from the Inventory Tracking system to the insurance model discussed earlier. Say you had an auto insurance object. This object might contain several loss payees who loaned you money for the car, or several drivers. Drivers would be an iterative component of the object where internal arrays are maintained, but it is a problem for the relational database because relational databases can't handle dynamic arrays in a table.

To resolve iterative components of an object, you must create another table with the iterative component and a foreign key to the "main" object. Thus, you resolve internal iterative components by introducing a table with a many-to-one relationship with the object table. Like other database considerations, this must be maintained by the storage object.

Q How can you resolve inheritance in a relational database?

The problem with inheritance is that you have two (or more) objects: the ancestor object contains general information about the type of object you're using, and the descendent object contains detailed information specific to the object you're using.

To really bring out the effect of inheritance, let's expand the insurance object model talked about previously to include whole life insurance and term life insurance. Then break term life into increasing premium and level premium (see fig. 21.3).

This is a truly mammoth inheritance structure. Say you now want to store the level premium term insurance object onto a relational database. You now have to decide whether to "roll up" or "roll down" to store the object.

To roll up the database, you would store all policy information on a policy table, all life information on a life table, all term life information on a term table, all increasing premium term on a increasing premium table, and all level premium information on a level premium table. Each level of inheritance would have a one-to-one foreign key to the level above it, and each ancestor would have a zero-to-one relationship with its descendent (see fig. 21.4).

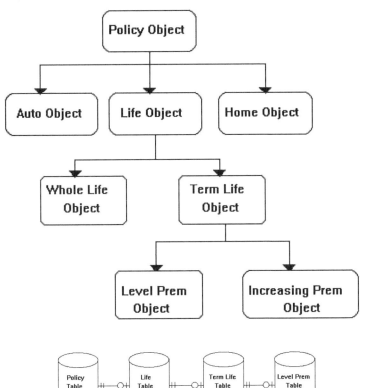

Fig. 21.3

Inheritance can often grow to be quite expansive.

Fig. 21.4

Rolling up allows common information between objects to be stored in their own table.

You would roll up the object design into the relational database if you intended to do a lot of processing at the ancestor level. For example, you may want to be able to easily list all of the policies of a system, all of the life policies of a system, all of the term life policies of a system, and all of the level premium term life policies of a system. The policy table would contain all life, auto, and home policies owned by a customer.

Another type of roll up would be where you actually combine the descendants with the ancestor. For instance, the difference between level premium term insurance and increasing term insurance is minimal from a system development standpoint. You could combine the two right into the term life table with a type indicator to indicate what type of insurance you have (see fig. 21.5).

Fig. 21.5

Combining objects during roll up can decrease the number of tables necessary.

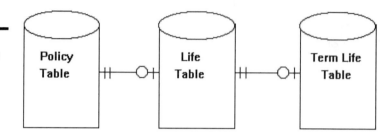

Conversely, you could roll down the database into it's descendent components. If this were the case, you would have many stand-alone tables with only descendent tables. Each descendent table would contain all the information about itself and its ancestors (see fig. 21.6).

Fig. 21.6

Rolling down duplicates common information on each table, but reduces the number of tables necessary.

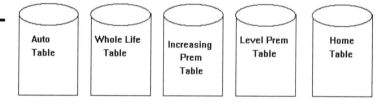

The roll down approach works especially well when you run every aspect of your business as a stand-alone unit. If you have an auto insurance division, a whole life division, and so on, then you would probably want the data to be centered around single divisions and processed as stand-alone tables. Rolling down also works well for distributed databases or for using data warehouses and PowerBuilder's data pipeline because data can then be centralized to location.

The most probable approach for most systems will be a hybrid roll up–roll down system. In this case, you would roll up part of the system and roll down the other part of the system. For instance, if you wanted to keep a policy base, but then wanted to isolate the rest of the information, you would roll up to the policy object, but roll down any intermediate objects between policy and the descendent objects. You also might want to combine certain objects into subtypes of the same table, as with level premium term and increasing premium term (see fig. 21.7).

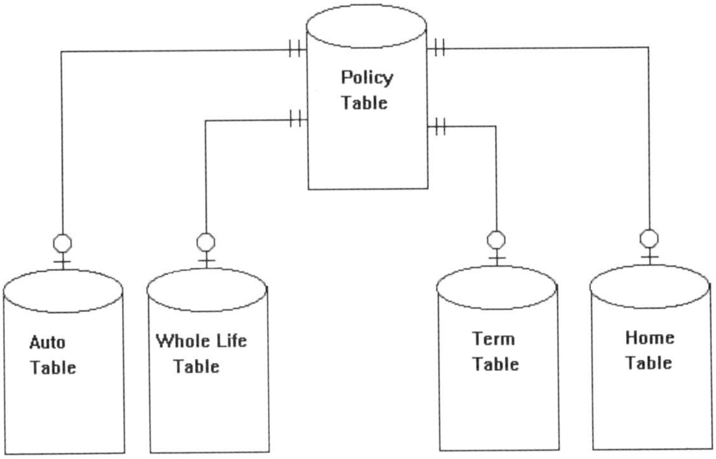

Fig. 21.7

Inheritance can be used to share functionality between common objects.

Sometimes the roll up or roll down decision is difficult, but it is important. Your decision will effect the capabilities of your database later on. It's something you really have to examine, and it's not that easy to decide.

At any rate, your roll up and roll down objects are defined.

Q How can you use stored procedures and triggers to ease the burden on your storage object?

Stored procedures and triggers are great. Although not truly object-oriented, they are greatly encapsulated. Using Watcom SQL's stored procedures and triggers allows you to reduce the complexity of your storage object while enhancing data integrity at the same time.

See "Understanding Stored Procedures," p. 236

See "Understanding Triggers," p. 237

Whereas storage objects are corporate-wide, stored procedures and triggers should be defined for the current data model. Triggers can enforce business rules at the application level with no work or even knowledge of the trigger that's being executed at that time. Triggers can even enforce a greater degree of verification than is feasible at the local developer level.

The enhancements made to Watcom SQL 4.0 really aid in several areas, and mapping an object-oriented design to a Watcom SQL database is one of them. The integrity and data independence available with Watcom SQL, along with the new features such as stored procedures and triggers, can really make a positive impact on object-oriented development.

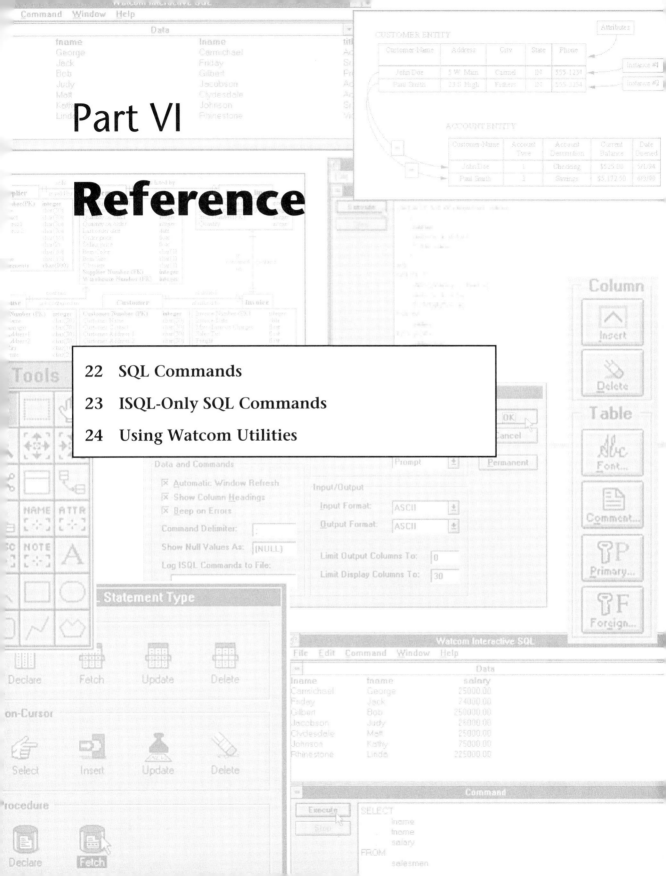

Part VI

Reference

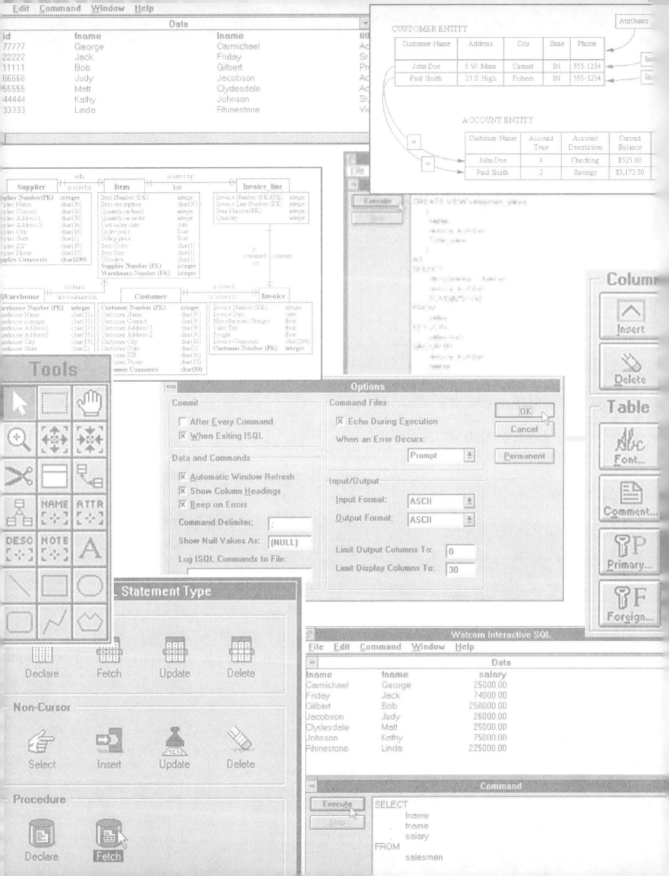

Chapter 22

SQL Commands

by John R. Zebrowski

The SQL language lets developers switch from database to database with less training time and costs for each database. Watcom SQL's implementation of the SQL language extends the standard language definition by adding SQL commands not available in other databases.

Watcom has divided SQL into two categories: *ESQL (Embedded SQL),* which is used inside programs, and *ISQL (Interactive SQL),* which is used inside the ISQLW environment.

SQL commands can be one of three types:

- *ESQL-only commands* are SQL commands that can only be used inside a program.

- *ISQL-only commands* are SQL commands that can only be used inside the ISQLW environment.

- *Standard SQL commands* are SQL commands that can be used both in-side a program and inside the ISQLW environment.

◀ See "Using ISQLW," p. 20

VI

This chapter lists all the standard SQL commands available in Watcom.

Expressions

Expressions are used in SQL statements. An *expression* can be a constant, a column name, a variable, a subquery, an if statement, or a function. Expressions also can consist of operations. Table 22.1 lists the types of expressions that exist. When the syntax of an SQL command calls for an expression, you can find it in Table 22.1.

Reference

Table 22.1   Types of Expressions

Expression Type	Description
constant	A constant can be an integer, number, string (enclosed in single quotes) or a host variable (preceded by a colon). You can also use special constants defined in Table 22.3 in the Special Constants section.
[table-name.]column-name	An expression can consist of a single column name.
variable-name	Using the CREATE VARIABLE command, you can create a variable to use with your Watcom SQL statements.
function-name (expression, ...)	Functions can also serve as expressions. Functions are reviewed in Chapter 5.
operations	Operations consist of string manipulation or mathematical expressions. Mathematical expressions include the unary minus (negative sign), addition, subtraction, multiplication, division, and expression. String manipulation consists of concatenation (||).
(subquery)	Subqueries are SELECT statements within other SELECT statements. These can be very useful, but can also cause inefficient processing.
if-expression	The if-expressions allow the user to test a condition and return the expression based on the truth value of that condition. (See the Conditions section for more information.) The format for an if-expression i s: `IF condition THEN expression [ ELSE expression ] ENDIF`

◄ See "Under-
standing
Watcom SQL
Functions,"
p. 122

Conditions

Conditions test for truth value (a condition will evaluate to either TRUE, FALSE, or UNKNOWN). Conditions contain relational operators, special constants, subquery operators, and conjunctions.

Relational Operators

Conditions are used to compare two values usually by using a relational operator. Relational operators are listed in Table 22.2.

Table 22.2	Relational Operators		
Operator	**Name**	**Example**	**Description**
=	Equal	a = b	Tests to see if two values are equal.
<	Less than	a < b	Tests to see if one value is less than another.
<=	Less than or equal to	a <= b	Tests to see if one value is less than or equal to another.
>	Greater than	a > b	Tests to see if one value is greater than another.
>=	Greater than or equal to	a >= b	Tests to see if one value is greater than or equal to another.
~=, !=, or <>	Not equal	a <> b a ~= b a != b	Tests to see if two values are not equal. ~=, !=, and <> all function identically.
BETWEEN	BETWEEN	a BETWEEN b AND c	Tests to see if one value is between two other values. The two following SQL conditions are equivalent: a BETWEEN b AND c a >=b AND a <= c
IS (boolean)	IS	a IS TRUE	Tests if a Boolean value or condition is TRUE, FALSE, or UNKNOWN. UNKNOWN is returned if the Boolean value tested is NULL.
LIKE	LIKE	a LIKE "d%g"	Tests to see if a string value matches a pattern. For any pattern string, an underscore indicates that the place holder can be equivalent to any one character. A percent sign indicates that the placeholder can be equivalent to zero, or more characters or spaces. In the example given, *a LIKE "d%g"* would test TRUE if *a* were "dog", "dig", "dug", ,"dg", "d1g", "d+g", and so on.

Special Constants

Conditions can also contain special *constants*, which are reserved words whose values are either defined as constant or dynamically determined at run time. The following is a list of the special constants defined for Watcom SQL:

Table 22.3 Special Constants

Special Constant	Description
CURRENT DATE	CURRENT DATE lets the user select or compare against the current date.
CURRENT TIME	CURRENT TIME lets the user select or compare against the current time.
CURRENT TIMESTAMP	CURRENT TIMESTAMP lets the user select or compare against the current date and time.
NULL	NULL tests if the value is a NULL.
SQLCODE	SQLCODE is only valid inside procedures. It lets the user test the return code of the previous SQL statement.
SQLSTATE	SQLSTATE is only valid inside procedures. It lets the user test the return state of the previous SQL statement.
USER	USER returns the current user connected to the database.
TRUE	TRUE is often used with Boolean variables. It allows the user to test a variable or expression for true or false values.
FALSE	FALSE is often used with Boolean variables. It allows the user to test a variable or expression for true or false values.
UNKNOWN	UNKNOWN is flagged if the field you want to select or compare against is a NULL value.

◀ See "Understanding NULLs," p. 51

Subquery Operators

Conditions can also contain *subqueries,* which are SELECT statements within other SQL statements. A subquery allows testing against a group of values already on the database. This type of condition utilizes a subquery and one of the subquery operators listed in Table 22.4.

Table 22.4 Subquery Operators

Special Constant	Example	Description
ANY (SELECT statement)	a > ANY (SELECT ...)	Tests a value against a group of values. In the example, TRUE would be set if *a* were greater than any value returned from the SELECT statement.
SOME (SELECT statement)	a > SOME (SELECT ...)	Same as ANY.

Special Constant	Example	Description
ALL (SELECT statement)	a > ALL (SELECT ...)	Tests a value against a group of values. In the example, TRUE would be set if *a* were greater than all values returned from the SELECT statement.

IN (SELECT statement)	a IN (SELECT ...)	Tests a value to see if it's equal to any value in a SELECT statement. The following two conditions function identically:
		
		`...a = ANY (SELECT`
		`customer_number FROM`
		`customer_table)...`
		`...a IN (SELECT`
		`customer_number FROM`
		`customer_table)...`

EXISTS (SELECT statement)	EXISTS (SELECT ...)	EXISTS tests to see if at least one row is returned from a SELECT statement.

Conjunctions

Conjunctions are used to join conditions together to form a new condition or, in the case of NOT, to change the value of a condition. Table 22.5 lists conjunctions.

Table 22.5   Conjunctions

Conjunction	Example	Description
AND	condition1 AND condition2	Returns TRUE if condition1 is TRUE and condition2 is TRUE. Returns FALSE if either one is FALSE. Returns UNKNOWN if either condition is NULL or if both conditions are NULL.
OR	condition1 OR condition2	Returns TRUE if either condition is TRUE. Returns FALSE only if both are FALSE. Returns UNKNOWN if either condition is NULL or if both conditions are NULL.
NOT	NOT condition	Reverses the value of a condition. If the condition is TRUE, FALSE is set. If the condition is FALSE, TRUE is set. If the condition is UN-KNOWN, nothing changes.

VI

Reference

You can view and compare conjunctions with the truth table shown in Table 22.6.

Table 22.6	Conjunctions				
Condi-tion_a	**Condi-tion_b**	**Con-junc-tion**	**Example**		**Return Value**
TRUE		NOT	NOT condition_a		FALSE
FALSE		NOT	NOT condition_a		TRUE
UNKNOWN		NOT	NOT condition_a		UNKNOWN
TRUE	TRUE	AND	condition_a AND condition_b		TRUE
TRUE	FALSE	AND	condition_a AND condition_b		FALSE
TRUE	UNKNOWN	AND	condition_a AND condition_b		UNKNOWN
FALSE	TRUE	AND	condition_a AND condition_b		FALSE
FALSE	FALSE	AND	condition_a AND condition_b		FALSE
FALSE	UNKNOWN	AND	condition_a AND condition_b		UNKNOWN
UNKNOWN	TRUE	AND	condition_a AND condition_b		UNKNOWN
UNKNOWN	FALSE	AND	condition_a AND condition_b		UNKNOWN
UNKNOWN	UNKNOWN	AND	condition_a AND condition_b		UNKNOWN
TRUE	TRUE	OR	condition_a OR condition_b		TRUE
TRUE	FALSE	OR	condition_a OR condition_b		TRUE
TRUE	UNKNOWN	OR	condition_a OR condition_b		UNKNOWN
FALSE	TRUE	OR	condition_a OR condition_b		TRUE
FALSE	FALSE	OR	condition_a OR condition_b		FALSE
FALSE	UNKNOWN	OR	condition_a OR condition_b		UNKNOWN
UNKNOWN	TRUE	OR	condition_a OR condition_b		UNKNOWN
UNKNOWN	FALSE	OR	condition_a OR condition_b		UNKNOWN
UNKNOWN	UNKNOWN	OR	condition_a OR condition_b		UNKNOWN

ALTER DBSPACE

You use the ALTER DBSPACE command to modify the main dbspace file or any additional database files that make up a database. You can use the command to increase the size of the dbspace files, in increments of pages, or change the name of the dbspace files, as stored in the SYSFILE table.

The syntax for ALTER DBSPACE is as follows:

```
ALTER  DBSPACE  [creator.]dbspace-name
    ... ¦ ADD  number      ¦
          ¦ RENAME  filename¦
```

- creator. Refers to the creator of the dbspace.

- dbspace-name. Refers to the dbspace that you want to modify. A database consists of one main dbspace and up to 11 additional dbspaces.

- ADD number. Increases the size of the specified dbspace in increments of pages. The ADD command allows you to pre-allocate space for the dbspace and thus to improve the performance of bulk loads.

- RENAME filename. Renames the dbspace in the SYSFILE table. The new file name should be fully qualified to indicate where the file is located, for example C:\PB4\EXAMPLES\PSDEMODB.DB.

Caution

The RENAME option of this command will not physically rename the dbspace file; the name change is internal to WATCOM. Be sure to check that the physical file name is the same as the file name listed in the SYSFILE table.

◀ See "CREATE DBSPACE," p. 242

ALTER TABLE

You use the ALTER TABLE command to modify an existing table in the database. The syntax for the ALTER TABLE command is as follows:

```
ALTER  TABLE  [table-creator.]table-name
          ¦ ADD  column-definition [column-constraint ...]   ¦
          ¦ ADD  table-constraint ¦
          ¦ MODIFY  column-definition ¦
          ¦ MODIFY  column-name  DEFAULT  default-value  ¦
          ¦ MODIFY  column-name  [ NOT ] NULL ¦
      ... ¦ DELETE  column-name   ¦ , ...
```

```
¦ DELETE   CHECK   ¦
¦ DELETE   UNIQUE   ( column-name, ... )     ¦
¦ DELETE   PRIMARY KEY   ¦
¦ DELETE   FOREIGN KEY role-name     ¦
¦ RENAME   new-table-name      ¦
¦ RENAME   column-name   TO   new-column-name      ¦
```

■ [table-creator.]table-name. The table-name is the name of the table. Table-creator can also be specified, but defaults to the user ID used to connect to the database.

■ ADD column-definition. Adds a new column to the table. The syntax for column-definition is as follows:

> column-name data-type [NOT NULL] [DEFAULT default-value]

column-name. This is the name of the column that you want to add to this table. No two columns in a table can have the same name.

data-type. Any data type supported by Watcom SQL.

[NOT NULL]. The table must be empty in order to specify NOT NULL and make the column-name a required column.

[DEFAULT default-value]. The value for a column will be set to the DEFAULT value on INSERT if no column value is supplied by the user. The other options for default-value besides a *string* or *number* are:

> AUTOINCREMENT. This option will automatically generate a unique numeric value for the column. It is typically used for surrogate primary keys.

> CURRENT DATE. This option will set the default column value to the current system date.

> CURRENT TIME. This option will set the default column value to the current system time.

> CURRENT TIMESTAMP. This option will set the default column value to the current system date and time.

> NULL. This option will set the default column value to null. Null is implied if no default value is specified for the DEFAULT keyword.

> USER. This option will set the default column value to the user ID performing the INSERT.

- [column-constraint]. A column-constraint can be any of the following:

    UNIQUE. The value of the column must be unique for all rows.

    PRIMARY KEY. The value of the column must be unique for all rows, and is usually the best identifier for a row.

    CHECK (condition). This constraint ensures that a row will fail on INSERT or UPDATE if the condition evaluates to false.

    REFERENCES primary-table-name[(primary-column-name)] [actions]. The column is a foreign key for primary_column_name in primary_table_name. The [actions] option can be one of the following:

    ON UPDATE CASCADE. This will update the foreign keys to match the updated value of the primary key.

    ON UPDATE SET NULL. This will set the foreign key values to NULL when the primary key is updated.

    ON UPDATE SET DEFAULT. This will set the foreign key values to the value specified by the primary key's DEFAULT clause.

    ON UPDATE RESTRICT. This will prevent a primary key value from being updated while foreign key values exist.

    ON DELETE CASCADE. This will delete the rows whose foreign key values match the deleted primary key.

    ON DELETE SET NULL. This will set the foreign key values to NULL when the primary key is deleted.

    ON DELETE SET DEFAULT. This will set the foreign key values to the value specified by the primary key's DEFAULT clause.

    ON DELETE RESTRICT. This will prevent a primary key value from being deleted while matching foreign key values exist.

- ADD table-constraint. Adds a constraint to the table. A table-constraint can be any of the following:

    UNIQUE (column-name,...). No two rows can have the same value in all of the named columns.

    PRIMARY KEY (column-name,...). This option can only be used if the table does not already have a primary key constraint.

VI

Reference

CHECK(condition). A row will fail on INSERT or UPDATE if the condition evaluates to false. The CHECK constraint is usually defined at the table level when it references more than one column.

- foreign_key_constraint. The syntax for a foreign_key_constraint is as follows:

```
[NOT NULL] FOREIGN KEY [role-name] [(column-name,...)]
REFERENCES primary-table-name [(primary-column-name,...)]
[actions] [CHECK ON COMMIT]
```

NOT NULL. The value of column-name cannot be NULL.

FOREIGN KEY [role-name][(column-name,...)]. The role-name is the name for the foreign key used to distinguish it from another foreign key to the same table. The column-name is the column that is a foreign key.

REFERENCES primary-table-name[(primary-column-name)] [actions]. The column is a foreign key for primary-column-name in primary-table-name. The [actions] options are the same as those previously listed for column constraints.

[CHECK ON COMMIT]. The integrity of the foreign keys will not be checked until a COMMIT is issued.

- MODIFY column-definition. Changes the length or data type of the column. An attempt to change the data type will cause Watcom to attempt a data conversion. If the data conversion fails, the column will not be modified.

- MODIFY column-name DEFAULT default_value. Changes the default value for column-name. To remove a default value, specify DEFAULT NULL.

- MODIFY column-name [NOT] NULL. Changes a required column into an optional column and an optional column into a required column.

- DELETE column-name. Deletes the column from the table.

- DELETE CHECK. Deletes all check constraints from the table.

- DELETE UNIQUE (column-name,...). Deletes a uniqueness constraint for the table and any foreign keys that reference the uniqueness constraint.

- DELETE PRIMARY KEY. Deletes the primary key constraint and all foreign keys that reference the primary key.

- DELETE FOREIGN KEY role-name. Deletes the foreign key with the specified role name.

- RENAME new-table-name. Renames the table.

- RENAME column-name TO new-column-name. Changes the name of an existing column to the new-column-name.

An example of the ALTER TABLE command is as follows:

```
ALTER TABLE employee
ADD        FOREIGN KEY (dept_id)
                REFERENCES department  (dept_id)
                ON DELETE RESTRICT
                ON UPDATE SET NULL;
```

This example will alter the employee table by adding a table constraint. The table constraint is a *foreign-key-constraint* that establishes the dept_id column on the employee table as a foreign key to the dept_id on the department table. Two [actions] are also specified. The first action prevents the deletion of a dept_id from the department table if any employee records exist with that dept_id value. For example, assume one row exists in the department table with a dept_id of 100 and *n* rows exist on the employee table with a dept_id of 100, (where *n* is any number greater than zero). The one row in the department table could not be deleted until all *n* rows were deleted from the employee table. The second constraint works as follows: if the value of the dept_id column in the one row of the department table was changed from 100 to any other value, then all *n* rows in the employee table would have their dept_id values changed from 100 to NULL.

◄ See "CREATE TABLE," p. 243

Troubleshooting

I am using an ALTER command, but I keep getting a message telling me that I have a syntax error. What's happening?

You may actually have a syntax error, or you may be using the run-time engine. If you are using RT32W and RTSTARTW as database engines, you are not allowed to alter tables.

CALL

The syntax for the CALL command is

```
CALL  procedure-name ( expression [ ,... ] )
CALL  procedure-name ( parameter-name = expression [ ,... ] )
```

You use the CALL command to invoke an existing procedure that has been created with the CREATE PROCEDURE command. You must have created the procedure, been granted EXECUTE privileges on the procedure, or have DBA authority to run the given procedure. You can execute the CALL command inside an application program or in another procedure. Arguments can be passed positionally or by keyword. The called procedure will return any INOUT or OUT parameter values.

Troubleshooting

I have a stored procedure that works fine when testing, but seems to be ignored after I distribute. What's happening now?

Unfortunately, Watcom SQL's run-time version does not support stored procedures. You'll have to implement your procedures inside your host language.

CHECKPOINT

Use CHECKPOINT to write out all updated pages of a database that are currently in memory to disk. If you are running the network version of the database, you must have DBA authority to issue a checkpoint.

The syntax for CHECKPOINT is:

```
CHECKPOINT
```

Note

Typically, there is no need for an application to issue a CHECKPOINT command because a CHECKPOINT will also occur for any of the following reasons:

- The database engine is stopped.

- The database is idle long enough to perform a checkpoint.

- A COMMIT is issued to a database that is running without a transaction log.

- The amount of time since the last checkpoint is about to exceed the CHECKPOINT_TIME option setting.

- The amount of time it would take to recover from a system failure exceeds the RECOVERY_TIME option setting.

> **Caution**
>
> If an application issues a CHECKPOINT while a backup is in progress, the CHECK-POINT will be suspended and the application will hang.

CLOSE

This closes a previously opened cursor in Embedded SQL, procedures, and triggers. The CLOSE command is typically issued after all rows have been fetched from the result set.

◀ See "DECLARE Command," p. 421

◀ See "OPEN Command," p. 423

◀ See "FETCH Command," p. 422

The syntax for CLOSE is as follows:

```
CLOSE cursor-name
```

- cursor-name. An identifier or host-variable that refers to the open cursor. The host-variable format can only be used in Embedded SQL.

The following is an example:

```
EXEC SQL CLOSE my_cursor;
```

> **Caution**
>
> Any cursors that are opened without the WITH HOLD option will be automatically closed at the end of a transaction.

COMMENT

The COMMENT command is primarily used for documenting database items by utilizing the "remarks" column found in the following database system tables: SYSTABLE, SYSINDEX, SYSCOLUMN, SYSFOREIGNKEY, SYSUSERPERM, SYSPROCEDURE, and SYSTRIGGER.

To assign a comment to a database item, you must be the creator of the item or have DBA authority.

The syntax for COMMENT is as follows:

```
COMMENT ON
            ¦ TABLE   [creator.]table-name ¦
            ¦ INDEX   [creator.]index-name ¦
```

VI

Reference

```
    ... ¦ COLUMN  [creator.]table-name.column-name    ¦ IS
          ➥comment
          ¦ FOREIGN KEY  [creator.]table-name.role-name   ¦
          ¦ USER  userid   ¦
          ¦ PROCEDURE  [creator.]procedure-name   ¦
          ¦ TRIGGER  [creator.]trigger-name   ¦
          ➥comment:
          ¦ string   ¦
          ¦ NULL   ¦
```

Tip

To remove comments, set the comment to NULL.

Example:

```
COMMENT ON  USER b6248 IS  "Chuck Boudreau"
COMMENT ON TRIGGER tr_employee_audit IS "This trigger puts a
➥timestamp on update"
```

> ### Caution
>
> The COMMENT command cannot be issued in a trigger or procedure, or inside the run-time version of Watcom SQL.
>
> Comments associated with tables and columns via the PowerBuilder database painter are stored in the PowerBuilder catalog tables, not in the "remarks" column of the WATCOM system tables.

COMMIT

Tip

COMMIT frequently to free up database resources; after a COMMIT, the rollback log is deleted and any locks held by the transaction are released.

Use the COMMIT command to end a transaction and make permanent changes to the database. A *transaction* can be defined as the work done on a single database connection between two successful COMMITs or between a ROLLBACK and a COMMIT.

In a two-phase COMMIT situation, the COMMIT is issued after a successful execution of the PREPARE TO COMMIT command.

The syntax for COMMIT is as follows:

```
COMMIT [WORK]
```

At the end of a transaction, the database should be in a consistent state. A database with invalid foreign keys is not in a consistent state and therefore cannot be committed; for example, the COMMIT command will fail.

> **Caution**
>
> The following commands will automatically perform a COMMIT: ALTER, COMMENT, CREATE, DROP, GRANT, REVOKE, and SET OPTION

◀ See "ROLL-BACK Statement," p. 173

CONNECT

Use the CONNECT command to establish a connection to a specific database running on a specific database engine or server. The command can be used in Embedded SQL and ISQL with no authorization required.

The syntax for CONNECT is as follows:

```
CONNECT  [ TO engine-name ]  [ DATABASE database-name ]
     ... [ AS connection-name ]
     ... [ USER ]  userid  IDENTIFIED BY password
engine-name:      identifier, string or host-variable
database-name:    identifier, string or host-variable
connection-name:  identifier, string or host-variable
userid:     identifier, string or host-variable
password:   identifier, string or host-variable
```

■ TO engine-name. Refers to the database engine that is running the database to which you want to connect. If no engine-name is specified and there are multiple local engines running, WATCOM will look for database-name to be on the default local engine, such as the first engine started. If there are no local engines running but DBCLIENT is running, then WATCOM will look for database-name to be on the default server.

■ DATABASE database-name. The name of the database to which you want to connect. If no database-name is specified, the default is the first database started on the given engine or server.

■ AS connection-name. By specifying this, you can simultaneously have multiple connections to a database, or multiple connections to multiple database servers. Each connection maintains its own transaction. Use the SET CONNECTION statement to change the active connection and the DISCONNECT statement to drop a connection.

■ USER userid IDENTIFIED BY password. Refers to the authorization level to be used for the connection. In Embedded SQL, the authorization level of the userid and password will be used for all dynamic SQL and all static SQL that was preprocessed via SQLPP without a specified userid and password.

Tip

If there are multiple engines running, and each engine is running multiple databases, utilize the optional TO and DATABASE keywords to avoid specified database not found errors.

VI

Reference

If no userid and password are specified, you will be prompted for the information. If you are connected via a userid that has DBA authority, you can connect via additional userids without specifying a password.

CREATE DBSPACE

Use CREATE DBSPACE to create additional database files for an existing database. The new database files can physically exist on a separate device from the root database file.

You cannot use this command in stored procedures or triggers; DBA authority is required and this command issues an automatic COMMIT.

The syntax for CREATE DBSPACE is as follows:

```
CREATE  DBSPACE  [creator.]dbspace-name  AS  filename
```

■ creator. Refers to the userid under which you want the dbspace created.

Tip

If you are using the Network Server for NetWare, you should use a volume name instead of a drive letter to qualify the filename parameter.

■ dbspace-name. Refers to the dbspace that you want to create. A database consists of one root dbspace, created via DBINIT, and up to 11 additional dbspaces. Each dbspace can be up to 2G in size for a maximum database size of 24G. However, any one table and its associated indexes must fit in the 2G limit of a dbspace.

■ filename. A string containing the physical file name of the dbspace. The database file does not have to exist on the same device as the root database file. If the filename is not fully qualified, the file will be created in the directory of the root database file. Any relative directory will be relative to the root directory. If you are running the network version of Watcom, filename refers to a file on the database server.

An example of the CREATE DBSPACE command is as follows:

Tip

To view a list of all the dbspaces for a particular database, connect to the database and then select * from SYS.SYSFILE.

```
CREATE DBSPACE finance as "c:\pb4\finance.db";

CREATE DBSPACE accounting AS accounting.db;
```

The first example creates a dbspace called finance, which will physically exist as finance.db in the c:\pb4 directory. The second example will create a dbspace called accounting, which will physically exist as accounting.db in the same directory as the main database file.

CREATE INDEX

Normal sequential access takes a long time with a large database. To *drastically* speed up queries (SELECTs), indexes should be defined for appropriate columns in the appropriate tables.

> **Note**
>
> Usually, you can assume that an index speeds up queries like the SELECT or cursor (OPEN...FETCH) statements. However, indexes typically slow down table updates done with INSERT, UPDATE, and DELETE. You should define your index to meet your needs; yet, for performance reasons, don't index every field (especially those not found in the WHERE clause in a query).

Tip

Primary keys are a type of index, but you *might* want to define an index for a primary key. See the interview with performance expert David Yach in Chapter 17 for an example.

The syntax for the CREATE INDEX command is as follows:

```
CREATE [UNIQUE] INDEX [index-creator.]index-name
    ON [table-creator.]table-name
    (column-name1 [ASC¦DESC], column-name2 [ASC¦DESC]...)
```

- `UNIQUE`. This is specified when the index will not allow duplicate values. The default is to allow duplicate indexes.

- `[index-creator.]index-name`. The `index-name` is the name of the index. `index-creator` can also be specified, but defaults to the userid used to connect to the database.

- `ON [table-creator.]table-name`. The `ON` clause is used to specify the `table-name` of the index. The `table-creator` should be specified if the creator of the table is different than the userid used to connect to the database.

- `column-name1 [ASC¦DESC]....` `Column-name` is the name of the column (or columns) that you want to use for this index. `ASC` for ascending or `DESC` for descending can be specified. (Ascending is assumed.)

An example of the CREATE INDEX command is as follows:

◄ See "Creating Procedures," p. 314

```
CREATE INDEX name_index
    ON customer
    (last_name ASC, first_name ASC)
```

The previous command creates an index called `name_index` on the customer table. The `name_index` uses the `last_name` and `first_name` as columns for the index. Duplicates are allowed because UNIQUE wasn't specified, and the userid is assumed to be the same userid that is connected to the database.

VI

Reference

CREATE TABLE

Tip
If you have
PowerBuilder, you
can "paint" a new
table in the data-
base painter and
then save the log
file out to disk.
The log file will
contain the actual
CREATE TABLE
syntax.

The syntax for the CREATE TABLE command is as follows:

```
CREATE  [ GLOBAL TEMPORARY ]  TABLE  [creator.]table-name
    ... (       ¦ column-definition [ column-constraint ... ]   ¦, ...
            ¦ ,table-constraint        ¦)
    ... [ IN [creator.]dbspace-name ]
    ... [    ¦ ON  COMMIT  DELETE  ROWS   ¦      ]
         ¦ ON  COMMIT  PRESERVE  ROWS  ¦
```

- [GLOBAL TEMPORARY]. If specified, the created table will be a temporary table and not a base table.

- [table-creator.]table-name. The table-name is the name of the table. Table-creator can also be specified, but defaults to the userid used to connect to the database.

- column-definition. The syntax for column-definition is as follows:

    column-name data-type [NOT NULL] [DEFAULT default-value]

    column-name. This is the name of the column that you want to define for this table. No two columns in a table can have the same name.

    data-type. Any data type supported by Watcom SQL.

    [NOT NULL]. Specify NOT NULL if you want to make column-name a required column.

    [DEFAULT default-value]. The value for a column will be set to the DEFAULT value on INSERT if no column value is supplied by the user. The other options for default-value besides a string or number are:

    AUTOINCREMENT. This option will automatically generate a unique numeric value for the column. It is typically used for surrogate primary keys.

    CURRENT DATE. This option will set the default column value to the current system date.

    CURRENT TIME. This will set the default column value to the current system time.

    CURRENT TIMESTAMP. This option will set the default column value to the current system date and time.

    NULL. Null is the default default value.

USER. This option will set the default column value to the userid performing the INSERT.

■ [column-constraint]. A column-constraint can be any of the following:

UNIQUE. The value of the column must be unique for all rows.

PRIMARY KEY. The value of the column must be unique for all rows and is usually the best identifier for a row

REFERENCES primary_table_name[(primary_column_name)] [actions]. The column is a foreign key for primary_column_name in primary_table_name.

◀ See "Understanding Referential Integrity," p. 236

The [actions] option can be one of the following:

ON UPDATE CASCADE. This updates the foreign keys to match the updated value of the primary key.

ON UPDATE SET NULL. This sets the foreign key values to NULL when the primary key is updated.

ON UPDATE SET DEFAULT. This sets the foreign key values to the value specified by the primary key's DEFAULT clause.

ON UPDATE RESTRICT. This prevents a primary key value from being updated while foreign key values exist.

ON DELETE CASCADE. This deletes the rows whose foreign key values match the deleted primary key.

ON DELETE SET NULL. This sets the foreign key values to NULL when the primary key is deleted.

ON DELETE SET DEFAULT. This sets the foreign key values to the value specified by the primary key's DEFAULT clause.

ON DELETE RESTRICT. This prevents a primary key value from being deleted while matching foreign key values exist.

CHECK (condition). This constraint ensures that a row fails on INSERT or UPDATE if the condition evaluates to false.

■ table-constraint. A table-constraint can be any of the following:

UNIQUE (column-name,...). No two rows can have the same value in all of the named columns.

VI

Reference

PRIMARY KEY (column-name,...). No two rows can have the same value in all of the named columns. A table can have only one primary key constraint.

CHECK(condition). A row will fail on INSERT or UPDATE if the condition evaluates to false. The CHECK constraint is usually defined at the table level when it references more than one column.

foreign-key-constraint. The syntax for a foreign-key-constraint is as follows:

```
[NOT NULL] FOREIGN KEY [role-name] [(column-name,...)]
REFERENCES primary-table-name [(primary-column-name,...)]
[actions] [CHECK ON COMMIT]
```

NOT NULL. The value of column-name cannot be NULL.

FOREIGN KEY [role-name] [(column-name,...)]. The role-name is the name for the foreign key used to distinguish it from another foreign key to the same table. The column-name is the column which is a foreign key.

REFERENCES primary_table_name[(primary-column-name)] [actions]. The column is a foreign key for primary-column-name in primary-table-name.

[actions]. These available actions are the same as those listed previously for column constraints.

[CHECK ON COMMIT]. The integrity of the foreign keys will not be checked until a COMMIT is issued.

■ [IN [creator.]dbspace-name]. The dbspace-name is the name of the dbspace in which you want the table created. creator can also be specified, but defaults to the userid used to connect to the database.

■ ON COMMIT DELETE ROWS. This option is for temporary tables only. The rows of the temporary table will be deleted on COMMIT.

■ ON COMMIT PRESERVE ROWS. This option prevents the rows of a table from being deleted on COMMIT. The rows will be deleted when the current connection ends.

An example of the CREATE TABLE command is:

```
CREATE TABLE Employee
     (employee_id          INTEGER NOT NULL,
      first_name           VARCHAR(30) NOT NULL,
      department_id        INTEGER NOT NULL,
      last_name            VARCHAR(30) NOT NULL,
      address              VARCHAR(60),
      city                 VARCHAR(30),
      state                CHAR(2),
      zip_code             CHAR(9),
      dept_id              INT,
      salary               DECIMAL(7,2)
                                CHECK (salary< 1000000),
      gender               CHAR(1)
                                CHECK (gender IN ('F', 'M')),
      ssn_no               CHAR(9) NOT NULL,
      birth_date           DATE NOT NULL,
      PRIMARY KEY (employee_id),
      FOREIGN KEY  (department_id)
             REFERENCES DEPARTMENT  (department_id)
             ON DELETE RESTRICT
             ON UPDATE RESTRICT
);
```

The previous example creates a table called Employee. The table has six required columns : `employee_id`, `first_name`, `last_name`, `ss_no`, `birth_date`, and `department_id`. The `PRIMARY KEY` is `employee_id`; `department_id` is a `FOREIGN KEY` to the Department table. Referential integrity will be maintained by restricting any attempts to change or delete a specific `department_id` on the Department table, while rows with that specific `department_id` still exist on the Employee table. The CHECK constraints will prevent employees from having salaries of one million dollars or more, and genders other than M for male, or F for female.

Tip

It's much easier to create tables via the PowerBuilder database painter or by forward engineering a logical table model in ERwin to a Watcom database.

Troubleshooting

When I distribute my Watcom SQL database, I try to create a table to hold my data. However, my distributed version fails. Why is that?

If you are using RT32W and RTSTARTW as database engines, then you are not allowed to use any CREATE command. The run-time version does not support this.

◀ See "Creating and Deleting Triggers," p. 346

VI

CREATE VARIABLE

Use the CREATE VARIABLE command to create an SQL variable of the specified data type that can be used anywhere that column names are allowed.

Tip

After using the
CREATE VARI-
ABLE for large
objects, use the
DROP VARIABLE
command to free
up disk space.

The following are true of created variables:

- Their default value is null until assigned a value using the SET VARI-ABLE command.

- Their scope is limited to the current connection, and they are accessible until the connection is disconnected or a DROP variable command is issued.

- They are unaffected by any COMMIT or ROLLBACK commands.

- They are useful for creating large text or binary objects for INSERT or UPDATE because embedded SQL host variables are limited to 32K.

The syntax for CREATE VARIABLE is as follows:

```
CREATE  VARIABLE  identifier  data-type
```

CREATE VIEW

The result set of a SELECT statement against one or more tables is another table. The result set table does not exist on its own, but is defined in terms of other tables. The CREATE VIEW command allows you to define such a table, known as a *view*, and store the definition (SELECT) in the database under a view name. When the view is used in an SQL command, the underlying SELECT is executed.

> **Note**
>
> A view can be specified as part of an UPDATE command, provided that its underlying SELECT statement does not contain a GROUP BY clause, a UNION, or any aggregate functions.
>
> A view can be specifed as part of an INSERT or DELETE command, provided that the previous criteria to update a view are met. Views are typically used for security purposes or to hide the complex joins that are necessary when generating reports from a fully normalized database.
>
> Because a view can be used in place of tables in a select statement, it is possible to create a view from one or more underlying views.

The syntax for the CREATE VIEW command is as follows:

```
CREATE VIEW [view-creator.]view-name [(column-name1,column-
name2,...)]
      AS select_without_order_by
```

- [view-creator.]view-name. The view-name is the name of the view to be created. view-creator can also be specified, but defaults to the userid used to connect to the database.

- [(column-name1,...)]. The column-names specified will be the column-names in the view definition. If column-names are not specified, the select list column names are used.

- AS select_without_order_by. The AS clause is used to specify the SELECT command from which the view will be derived. Note that the select is not allowed to have an ORDER BY clause.

An example of the CREATE VIEW command is:

```
CREATE VIEW  v_employee_public  (first_name, last_name,
department_name, gender )
  AS SELECT  emp_fname , emp_lname , dept_name, gender
      FROM  employee , department
      WHERE ( department.dept_id = employee.dept_id );
```

The previous command creates a view called v_employee_public with four columns: first_name, last_name, department_name, and gender. By creating a view, you can grant select privileges that allow everyone access to the previous column information, and prevent access to any confidential information that may be stored in the employee table.

The following example shows the previous view in use:

```
SELECT  first_name, last_name , department_name
      FROM  v_employee_public;
```

DECLARE CURSOR

The DECLARE CURSOR command defines a cursor to be used with a specified SELECT statement or CALL statement. The cursor, when OPEN, will act as a pointer into the result set of the specified SELECT or CALL statement.

> **Note**
>
> The DECLARE statement is a compiler directive; it does not get executed.

VI

Reference

The syntax for DECLARE CURSOR is as follows:

```
DECLARE  cursor-name  [ SCROLL ¦ NO SCROLL ¦ DYNAMIC SCROLL ]
        ...          ¦ CURSOR FOR  statement ¦
             ¦ CURSOR FOR  statement-name  ¦
        ... [ FOR UPDATE ¦ FOR READ ONLY ]
```

- `cursor_name`. The name of the cursor.

- `SCROLL`. The cursor is bi-directional, and will remember row ordering and whether or not a particular row has been updated.

- `NO SCROLL`. The cursor is not bi-directional; it is limited to FETCH NEXT and FETCH RELATIVE 0 operations.

- `DYNAMIC SCROLL`. This is the default setting. The cursor is bidirectional and more efficient than a SCROLL cursor.

- `CURSOR FOR statement`. The statement is either a SELECT or a CALL.

- `CURSOR FOR statement_name`. The `statement_name` is a statement that was prepared with the PREPARE command.

- `FOR UPDATE`. This option allows the cursor to be used in an UPDATE (positioned) or DELETE (positioned) operation.

- `FOR READ ONLY`. The cursor is not updateable.

DECLARE LOCAL TEMPORARY TABLE

Local temporary tables are tables that are created for a specific purpose and then dropped at the end of their use. Local temporary tables can be used to reduce the complexity of a join or to pass information from one application to another within the same database connection. This command establishes a temporary table.

> **Note**
>
> A local temporary table can be used to pass data from one part of the application to another.
>
> It is implicitly dropped at the end of an SQL connection.
>
> DROP TABLE and ALTER TABLE commands cannot be issued against a temporary table.

The syntax for the DECLARE LOCAL TEMPORARY TABLE command is:

```
DECLARE LOCAL TEMPORARY TABLE table-name
    ... (     ¦ column-definition [ column-constraint ... ]   ¦, ...
          ¦ ,table-constraint          ¦)
    ... [     ¦ ON COMMIT DELETE ROWS   ¦     ]
          ¦ ON COMMIT PRESERVE ROWS ¦
```

- `table-name`. The name of the temporary table.

- `column-definition`. The syntax for `column-definition` is as follows:

    `column-name data-type [NOT NULL] [DEFAULT default-value]`

    `column-name`. This is the name of the column that you want to define for this table. No two columns in a table can have the same name.

    `data-type`. Any data type supported by Watcom SQL.

    `[NOT NULL]`. Specify NOT NULL if you want to make `column_name` a required column.

    `[DEFAULT default-value]`. The value for a column will be set to the DEFAULT value on INSERT if no column value is supplied by the user. The other options for `default-value` besides a `string` or `number` are:

    > `AUTOINCREMENT`. This option automatically generates a unique numeric value for the column. This option is typically used for surrogate primary keys.

    > `CURRENT DATE`. This option sets the default column value to the current system date.

    > `CURRENT TIME`. This option sets the default column value to the current system time.

    > `CURRENT TIMESTAMP`. This option sets the default column value to the current system date and time.

    > `NULL`. This option is the default default value.

    > `USER`. This option sets the default column value to the userid performing the INSERT.

- `[column-constraint]`. A `column-constraint` can be any of the following:

    > `UNIQUE`. The value of the column must be unique for all rows.

VI

Reference

PRIMARY KEY. The value of the column must be unique for all rows and is usually the best identifier for a row.

REFERENCES primary-table-name[(primary-column-name)] [actions]. The column is a foreign key for primary-column-name in primary-table-name. The [actions] option can be one of the following:

ON UPDATE CASCADE. This option updates the foreign keys to match the updated value of the primary key.

ON UPDATE SET NULL. This option sets the foreign key values to NULL when the primary key is updated

ON UPDATE SET DEFAULT. This option sets the foreign key values to the value specified by the primary key's DEFAULT clause.

ON UPDATE RESTRICT. This option prevents a primary key value from being updated while foreign key values exist.

ON DELETE CASCADE. This option deletes the rows whose foreign key values match the deleted primary key.

ON DELETE SET NULL. This option sets the foreign key values to NULL when the primary key is deleted.

ON DELETE SET DEFAULT. This option sets the foreign key values to the value specified by the primary key's DEFAULT clause.

ON DELETE RESTRICT. This option prevents a primary key value from being deleted while matching foreign key values exist.

CHECK (condition). This constraint ensures that a row will fail on INSERT or UPDATE if the condition evaluates to false.

■ table-constraint. A table-constraint can be any of the following:

UNIQUE (column-name,...). No two rows can have the same value in all of the named columns.

PRIMARY KEY(column-name,...). No two rows can have the same value in all of the named columns. A table can have only one primary key constraint.

CHECK(condition). A row will fail on INSERT or UPDATE if the condition evaluates to false. The CHECK constraint is usually defined at the table level when it references more than one column.

foreign-key-constraint. The syntax for a foreign-key-constraint is as follows:

```
[NOT NULL] FOREIGN KEY [role-name] [(column-name,...)]
REFERENCES primary-table-name [(primary-column-name,...)]
[actions] [CHECK ON COMMIT]
```

NOT NULL. The value of column-name cannot be NULL.

FOREIGN KEY [role-name] [(column-name,...)]. The role-name is the name for the foreign key used to distinguish it from another foreign key to the same table. The column-name is the column that is a foreign key.

REFERENCES primary_table_name[(primary-column-name)] [actions]. The column is a foreign key for primary_column_name in primary_table_name. The [actions] option can be the same as those listed previously for column constraints.

[CHECK ON COMMIT]. The integrity of the foreign keys will not be checked until a COMMIT is issued.

- ON COMMIT DELETE ROWS. Any rows in the temporary table will be deleted on commit. This is the default.

- ON COMMIT PRESERVE ROWS. The rows in the temporary table will not be deleted on commit.

DELETE

DELETE is used to remove rows from a particular table

The syntax for DELETE is:

```
DELETE  FROM  [creator.]table-name  [WHERE  search-condition]
```

- [creator.]table-name. The table-name is the name of the table. creator can also be specified, but defaults to the userid used to connect to the database.

Tip
When designing applications that provide a graphical user interface, all delete requests from the user should be confirmed prior to issuing the actual DELETE command to the database.

VI

Reference

- [WHERE search-condition]. All rows for which the search-condition evaluates to TRUE will be deleted. If a search-condition is not specified, then all the rows from table-name will be deleted.

DELETE (POSITIONED)

DELETE (POSITIONED) is used to delete data when using an updateable cursor. The deleted row will be the row pointed at by the cursor.

The syntax for DELETE (POSITIONED) is

```
DELETE  [FROM  [creator.]table-name]
     ... WHERE  CURRENT  OF  cursor-name
```

◀ See "Using DESCRIBE with C++," p. 402

- [FROM [creator.]table-name]. This option is only specified if the cursor was declared for a joined query. The table-name is the name of the table from which you want to delete the current row. creator can also be specified, but defaults to the userid used to connect to the database.

- cursor-name. The name of the cursor.

DISCONNECT

Use the DISCONNECT command to drop a connection to the database.

The syntax for the DISCONNECT command is:

```
DISCONNECT  ¦ connection-name ¦
       ...¦ [ CURRENT ]  ¦
       ¦ ALL                        ¦
```

- connection-name. The name of the connection to be dropped.

- CURRENT. The current connection will be dropped. This is the default.

- ALL. This option is used in ISQL; it drops all of the connections held by the application.

DROP

The DROP command is used to remove any of the following database structures from the database: dbspaces, indexes, tables, views, procedures, and triggers.

All tables in a dbspace must be dropped before the dbspace can be dropped.

A table cannot be dropped if it is currently in use by another connection. When a table is dropped, all indexes and keys for that table are dropped, and the data is deleted.

The DROP command cannot be used in a trigger or procedure.

The syntax for the DROP command is as follows:

◀ See "DROP Command," p. 422

```
        ┆ DBSPACE   [creator.]dbspace-name   ┆
  DROP  ┆ INDEX   [creator.]index-name ┆
        ┆ TABLE   [creator.]table-name        ┆
        ┆ VIEW  [creator.]view-name           ┆
        ┆ PROCEDURE  [creator.]proc-name      ┆
        ┆ TRIGGER   [creator.]trigger-name    ┆
```

- ■ [creator.]. The creator of the database structure about to be dropped should be specified if the creator is different than the userid used to connect to the database.

- ■ DBSPACE [creator.]dbspace-name. The dbspace_name is the name of the dbspace about to be dropped.

- ■ INDEX [creator.]index-name. The index_name is the name of the index about to be dropped.

- ■ TABLE [creator.]table-name. The table_name is the name of the table about to be dropped.

- ■ VIEW [creator.]view-name. The view_name is the name of the view about to be dropped.

- ■ PROCEDURE [creator.]proc-name. The proc_name is the name of the procedure about to be dropped.

- ■ TRIGGER [creator.]trigger-name. The trigger_name is the name of the trigger about to be dropped.

The following are examples of the DROP command:

```
DROP DBSPACE  dba.employee

DROP INDEX    xak1employee

DROP TABLE  employee
```

VI

Reference

DROP OPTIMIZER STATISTICS

You use this command to reset the database optimizer statistics to default values.

The syntax for DROP OPTIMIZER STATISTICS is as follows:

```
DROP OPTIMIZER STATISTICS
```

Tip

It's a good idea to DROP OPTIMIZER STATISTICS after the testing phase in a project. The optimizer statistics may be set incorrectly because test data often doesn't have the same volume as production data. Also, if you notice your database running slowly, try the DROP OPTIMIZER STATISTICS to see if resetting your optimizer statistics improves performance.

◀ See "Execute Command," p. 422

> **Note**
>
> Watcom SQL is a self-tuning database. Each database starts off with a set of default statistics that are used by the query optimizer to generate data-access plans. As queries are run against the database, the statistics are updated to more accurately reflect the best access methods for that particular database. As the accuracy of the statistics improves, so does the performance of the database.

DROP VARIABLE

Use the DROP VARIABLE command to eliminate an SQL variable and release its resources.

The syntax for DROP VARIABLE is:

```
DROP  VARIABLE  identifier
```

EXPLAIN

The internal methods used to satisfy a query against a Watcom database are determined by the Watcom optimizer. The optimizer will determine in what order to search tables, and what indexes to use to construct a result set. The EXPLAIN statement allows you to gain access to the database's plan for data retrieval.

The syntax for the EXPLAIN statement is:

```
EXPLAIN PLAN FOR CURSOR cursor-name INTO host-variable
      ...¦ INTO host-variable ¦
      ¦ USING DESCRIPTOR sqlda-name ¦
```

- cursor-name. The name of an open cursor.

- [INTO host-variable]. The data from the cursor will be placed into the host-variable, which must be declared as string type.

■ ¦ USING DESCRIPTOR sqlda-name ¦. This option allows you to specify the
SQLDA.

FETCH

The FETCH command retrieves one row from a previously opened cursor.

> **Note**
>
> The DECLARE statement must appear before the FETCH, and the OPEN must be
> executed before the FETCH. If the cursor name is a host variable, then the DECLARE
> must be executed before the FETCH.

The syntax for the FETCH command is as follows:

```
FETCH      ¦ [ NEXT ]  ¦   cursor-name
           ¦ PRIOR     ¦
           ¦ FIRST     ¦
           ¦ LAST      ¦
           ¦ ABSOLUTE  row-count  ¦
           ¦ RELATIVE  row-count  ¦

     ... [      ¦ INTO  host-variable-list    ¦      ]
                ¦ USING DESCRIPTOR  sqlda-name     ¦
                ¦ INTO  variable-list  ¦
     ... [ PURGE ]  [ BLOCK n ]  [ FOR UPDATE ]
```

■ cursor-name. The name of the cursor.

■ [NEXT]. The cursor is advanced to the next row before the FETCH.

■ PRIOR. The cursor is positioned to the prior row.

■ FIRST. The cursor is positioned to the first row.

■ LAST. The cursor is positioned to the last row.

■ ABSOLUTE n. The cursor is positioned to row n. If n is 0, then the cursor
is positioned prior to the first row. If n is negative, then the cursor is
positioned n rows from the end.

■ RELATIVE n. The cursor is moved n positions from the current row. If n is
positive, then the cursor is moved forward; if n is negative, then the
cursor is moved backwards.

■ [INTO host-variable-list]. The data from the cursor is placed into the
host variables.

- USING DESCRIPTOR sqlda-name. The fetched data will be placed into the SQLDA descriptor array.

- INTO variable-list. The data from the cursor is placed in the variable list. This clause is for triggers and stored procedures only.

- [PURGE]. For multi-client environments, where block fetching is performed, the PURGE option clears any buffered rows on the client machine prior to the FETCH.

- [BLOCK n]. For block fetching, n indicates how many rows will be fetched by the application. If n is set to 0, then only one row will be retuned per fetch.

- [FOR UPDATE]. This option puts a write lock on the row in order for the data to be updated.

FROM

Use the FROM clause to specify the tables or views used in a SELECT or an UPDATE statement.

The syntax for the FROM clause is:

```
...FROM  table_expression1[, table_expression2, ...]
```

A table_expression can be any one of the following:

- ¦table_specification¦. A table_specification can be further defined as:

  ```
  [userid.] table-name [[AS] correlation-name]
  ```

- [userid.]table-name. The table-name is the name of the table from which you want to SELECT or UPDATE. The userid can be specified, but defaults to the userid of the connection.

- [[AS] correlation-name]. This option allows you to specify a temporary name for a table. Correlation names can also be used to distinguish between multiple instances of the same table in one select statement.

  ```
  ¦table_expression  join type  table_specification
  ➥[ON condition]¦
  ```

- join type. A join occurs between two tables and can be any one of the following types:

CROSS JOIN. This join type does not restrict any rows. If no WHERE condition is specified for a CROSS JOIN, a Cartesian product results. The following FROM clauses are equivalent:

```
FROM t1, t2

FROM t1 CROSS JOIN t2
```

[NATURAL ¦ KEY] JOIN. The NATURAL keyword implements the specified join by comparing columns with like names. The KEY keyword implements the specified join based on the foreign key, provided there is only one foreign key relationship.

[NATURAL ¦ KEY] INNER JOIN. All joins are either inner or outer joins. Inner joins are the default. In the example

```
FROM t1 INNER JOIN t2
```

each row in the result set will consist of data from t1 and t2, where the joining columns match. If a row from t1 does not have a match in t2, the unmatched row from t1 will not be in the result set.

```
[NATURAL ¦ KEY] LEFT OUTER JOIN
```

In the example

```
FROM t1 LEFT OUTER JOIN t2
```

all rows from t1 will be brought back, regardless of whether there is a matching row in t2. In the case of an unmatched row from t1, any columns in the select list from t2 will be NULL for that row.

```
[NATURAL ¦ KEY] RIGHT OUTER JOIN
```

In the example

```
FROM t1 LEFT OUTER JOIN t2
```

all rows from t2 will be brought back, regardless of whether there is a matching row in t1. In the case of an unmatched row from t2, any columns in the select list from t1 will be NULL for that row.

- [ON condition]. Use this option to specify a join condition. With INNER JOINs, the WHERE clause and the ON condition are equivalent means for specifying a join condition. With OUTER JOINs, the ON condition is part of the join operation.

- (table_expression,...). This just indicates that a table can be joined to multiple tables, as in t1 KEY JOIN (t2, t3).

VI

Reference

GET DATA

Use the GET DATA command to fetch long binary or long varchar fields from the current row of a cursor. It allows you to obtain pieces of the column to get around the 32K-limit of host variables.

The syntax for the GET DATA command is:

```
GET DATA cursor-name COLUMN column-number OFFSET start-offset
        ¦ USING DESCRIPTOR sqlda-name ¦
...     ¦ INTO host-variable ¦
```

- cursor-name. The name of the open cursor.

- column-number. The number of the column that you want to get from the cursor. The column's data type must be either string or binary.

- start-offset. The start-offset specifies the starting location, in bytes, for the next piece of data. Typically the start-offset starts at one and is incremented in a loop by the length of the host_variable into which the data is being fetched.

- ¦INTO host-variable ¦. The length of the host_variable determines the amount of data that will be fetched with each issuance of the GET DATA command.

- ¦ USING DESCRIPTOR sqlda-name ¦. This option allows you to specify the SQLDA for dynamic statements.

GET OPTION

The GET OPTION command returns the setting for a database option for a specified user ID. If no user ID is specified, then the user ID of the current connection is used.

The syntax for the GET OPTION command is:

```
GET OPTION[userid.]option-name
...     ¦ INTO host-variable ¦
        ¦ USING DESCRIPTOR sqlda-name ¦
```

- [userid.]. The user ID for whom you want to determine the option setting. You must have DBA authority in order to use this option with someone else's user ID.

- `option-name`. The name of the option whose setting you want to get.

- `¦ INTO host-variable ¦`. The value for the named option is returned to the `host-variable`.

- `¦ USING DESCRIPTOR sqlda-name ¦`. This option allows you to specify the SQLDA for dynamic statements.

GRANT

The GRANT command has four different formats, and is used to assign various privileges:

Format 1 of the GRANT command establishes new user IDs, or allows an existing user to change his or her password.

Format 2 of the GRANT command issues database privileges, creates groups, and maintains group membership.

Format 3 of the GRANT command grants privileges on individual tables or views. Multiple privileges can be granted at once. In order to grant privileges on a table or view, you must have DBA authority, be the owner, or have been granted the specific privilege WITH GRANT OPTION privileges.

Format 4 of the GRANT command allows the user to execute the named procedure. You must have DBA authority or be the creator of the procedure in order to grant this privilege.

The syntax for the GRANT command is:

Format 1:

```
GRANT CONNECT TO userid IDENTIFIED BY password
```

Format 2:

```
GRANT privileges TO userid,....
```

Format 3:

```
GRANT privileges  ... ON [creator.]table-name TO userid,.... [WITH
GRANT OPTION]
```

Format 4:

```
GRANT EXECUTE ON [creator.]procedure-name TO userid,...
```

VI

Reference

The following are the identifiers for Format 1:

- user ID. Refers to either a new user ID or an existing user ID whose password needs to be changed. To create a new user ID using Format 1, you must have DBA authority.

- password. The new password for the corresponding user ID. To change your own password, simply issue the GRANT command with your user ID and a new password. You will not be prompted for password verification. If no password is specified, connections to that user ID will not be possible.

The following are valid privileges for Format 2 of the GRANT command:

- DBA. Allows the userid to do anything in the database. Typically, this is the person responsible for the database. DBA authority is required to GRANT this privilege.

- RESOURCE. Allows the userid to create tables and views. DBA authority is required to GRANT this privilege.

- GROUP. Effectively creates a user group. The userid is given the privilege of having members added to it via the MEMBERSHIP IN GROUP keyword. DBA authority is required to GRANT this privilege.

- MEMBERSHIP IN GROUP userid. Allows the user to inherit the privileges that have been GRANTed to the group. DBA authority is required to GRANT this privilege unless you are adding members to your own userid.

The following are valid privileges for Format 3 of the GRANT command:

- ALTER. Allows the user to make changes to a table using the ALTER COMMAND.

- DELETE. Allows the user to delete rows from the table or view.

- INSERT. Allows the user to insert rows into the table or view.

- REFERENCES. Allows the user to create indexes on the named tables, and foreign keys that reference the named tables.

- SELECT. Allows the user to look at the data contained in the table or view.

- UPDATE [(column-name,...)]. If no column names are specified, this allows the user to update any columns from the table or view. If column names are specified, the user is only allowed to update those columns.

- ALL. Provides the user with all of the previously mentioned privileges.

- WITH GRANT OPTION. The user is allowed to GRANT the same privilege to other users.

Examples:

```
GRANT CONNECT TO Adam, Austin, JohnPaul IDENTIFIED BY Apple,
Banana, Cherry
```

```
The previous example establishes three new userids and their
respective passwords using Format 1 of the GRANT command.GRANT
CONNECT TO Purchasing IDENTIFIED BY
```

```
GRANT GROUP  TO Purchasing
```

```
GRANT MEMBERSHIP IN GROUP Purchasing TO Adam, Austin, JohnPaul
```

The previous three examples demonstrate how to set up a group user ID and add members to the group. The first GRANT command is Format 1, the second and third GRANT commands are Format 2.

```
GRANT SELECT, UPDATE, INSERT, DELETE ON order_master TO Purchasing
```

The previous example uses Format 3 of the GRANT command to grant privileges on the order_master table to all members of the Purchasing group.

INSERT

The INSERT command adds a single row (Format 1) or a set of rows (Format 2) into a table.

The syntax for INSERT is:

Format 1:

```
INSERT  INTO  [creator.]table-name  [( column-name, ... )]
     ... VALUES ( expression ¦ DEFAULT, ... )
```

Format 2:

```
INSERT  INTO  [creator.]table-name  [( column-name, ... )]
     ... select-statement
```

- [creator.]table-name. Table-name is the name of the table in which the insert is being made.

- [(`column-name,...`)]. Allows you to insert values in the order that the column names are specified. If column names are not specified, then the values will be inserted in the order that the table columns were created.

◄ See "Under-
standing
Nulls," p. 51

- `VALUES ( expression ¦DEFAULT,...)`. The `VALUES` keyword is followed by an expression or the keyword `DEFAULT` for every column value to be inserted. If `DEFAULT` is specified, then the default value for the column will be inserted.

- `select-statement`. For Format 2, you can specify a `select-statement` and the complete result set of the `select-statement` will be inserted into the table.

OPEN

◄ See "Using
PREPARE and
EXECUTE,"
p. 401

The OPEN command opens a previously declared cursor, and positions the cursor before the first row of the result set.

◄ See "Under-
standing the
SQLDA
Structure,"
p. 398

The syntax for the OPEN command is as follows:

```
OPEN   cursor-name
       ... [    ¦USING DESCRIPTOR  sqlda-name ¦     ]
                ¦ USING host-variable, ...     ¦
       ... [ WITH HOLD ]  [ ISOLATION LEVEL n ]  [ BLOCK n ]
```

- [USING DESCRIPTOR `sqlda-name`]. For dynamic cursors, you can specify an SQL descriptor.

- [USING `host-variable`, ...]. For dynamic cursors, you can specify a `host-variable`.

- [WITH HOLD]. This option will keep the cursor open until the connection to the database is terminated.

- [ISOLATION LEVEL *n*]. This option allows the cursor to be opened at a different isolation level than what was specified via the SET OPTION command.

- [BLOCK *n*]. This option allows you to specify the maximum number of rows that can be contained in a block.

PREPARE TO COMMIT

The PREPARE TO COMMIT command determines whether a COMMIT command can be performed without causing a database integrity problem. The command is typically used in situations in which the option `WAIT_FOR_COMMIT` is turned on. If any foreign key violations exist, they will be detected with this command, and a database error will be issued.

The syntax for PREPARE TO COMMIT is:

```
PREPARE TO COMMIT
```

The following example shows the use of the PREPARE TO COMMIT command:

```
SET wait_for_commit = on;
DELETE FROM customer WHERE customer_number = :custnumb;
PREPARE TO COMMIT;
```

In this code, we turn the `WAIT_FOR_COMMIT` option on. This forces Watcom SQL to wait until a COMMIT before checking the referential integrity of any command. We then issue a DELETE, which deletes a row off the customer table. `PREPARE TO COMMIT` then checks to see if a COMMIT is possible—and will return an error if it isn't.

PUT

PUT allows you to place a row on an open cursor. The format for the PUT command is:

```
PUT cursor_name
    [USING DESCRIPTOR sqlda_name]
    FROM :host_variable_list]
```

The `cursor_name` is the name of the open cursor. The `sqlda_name` is the name of the SQLDA descriptor area. The `host_variable_list` is a list of host variables used to add to the cursor.

The following command:

```
PUT customer_cursor FROM :customer_number, :customer_name
```

places the `customer_number` and the `customer_name` fields in the `customer_cursor`.

> **Note**
>
> The PUT command is not typically used. A good time to use the PUT command is when a function or procedure processes a cursor, and you want to place additional information on that cursor to be processed.
>
> If you find yourself using several PUT commands in an application, check for design errors. Chances are, you missed an easy way to do something and are now resorting to more difficult development techniques.

> **Caution**
>
> You *cannot* do a positional update or positional delete on a cursor row that has been PUT onto a cursor.

RELEASE SAVEPOINT

The RELEASE SAVEPOINT command releases a savepoint in the current transaction.

The syntax for RELEASE SAVEPOINT is:

```
RELEASE SAVEPOINT [savepoint_name]
```

- [savepoint_name]. The savepoint_name is the name that was specified when the SAVEPOINT command was issued in the current transaction. If no name is specified, then the last established savepoint is used.

RESUME

Use the RESUME command to continue the execution of a suspended procedure. The command is used in the context of a cursor that was declared and opened for a call to a procedure. After the RESUME command has been issued, the procedure can complete, and the cursor can be closed.

◀ See "Using Cursors," p. 323

The syntax for the RESUME command is as follows:

```
RESUME  cursor-name
```

- cursor-name. The name of the open cursor that was declared for a call to a procedure that returns a result set.

REVOKE

The REVOKE command is used to take away privileges that were established via the GRANT command. In order to REVOKE a privilege, you must have granted that particular privilege or have DBA authority. Like the GRANT command, the REVOKE command has several formats:

- Format 1 of the REVOKE command is used to remove user IDs, groups, and special permissions such as DBA and RESOURCE authority.

- Format 2 of the REVOKE command is used to take away table-related privileges.

- Format 3 of the REVOKE command takes away a user's ability to execute a procedure.

The various formats of the REVOKE command are as follows:

Format 1:

```
REVOKE privileges FROM userid,....
```

Format 2:

```
REVOKE privileges  ... ON [creator.]table_name FROM userid,....
```

Format 3:

```
REVOKE EXECUTE ON [creator.]procedure_name FROM userid,...
```

The following are the identifiers for Format 1:

- userid. Refers to the userid that is about to lose one of the privileges (the user Id from which privileges are about to be revoked).

The following are privileges that can be revoked via Format 1:

- CONNECT. The specified user loses all access to the database.

- DBA. The specified userid will lose DBA authority and all the privileges that it conveys.

- RESOURCE. The specified userid will lose the ability to create tables and views.

- GROUP. The specified userid will no longer be allowed to have members. All existing memberships will be removed.

- MEMBERSHIP IN GROUP group-userid. The specified userid will be removed from the group specified as group-userid.

VI

Reference

The following are table privileges that can be revoked via Format 2:

- ALTER. The specified userid will lose the authority to change the definition of the specified table or view.

- DELETE. The specified userid will lose the authority to delete rows from the specified table or view.

- INSERT. The specified userid will lose the authority to insert rows into the specified table or view.

- REFERENCES. The specified userid will lose the authority to create indexes on the named tables or create foreign keys that reference the named tables.

- SELECT. The specified userid will lose the authority to query against the table or view.

- UPDATE [(column-name,...)]. The specified userid will lose the authority to update any rows within the table. If column-names are listed, then the update restriction applies only to the named columns.

The following are examples of the REVOKE command:

```
REVOKE CONNECT FROM Templer

REVOKE    MEMBERSHIP IN GROUP Swoosh FROM Taylor, Oliver, Wolters

REVOKE ALL ON employee FROM Adam
```

ROLLBACK

Use the ROLLBACK command to undo any work since the last COMMIT or ROLLBACK.

The syntax for ROLLBACK is:

```
ROLLBACK [WORK]
```

ROLLBACK TO SAVEPOINT

The ROLLBACK TO SAVEPOINT command undoes any changes since the last savepoint.

The syntax for ROLLBACK TO SAVEPOINT is:

```
ROLLBACK TO SAVEPOINT [savepoint_name]
```

■ [savepoint_name]. The savepoint_name is the name that was specified when the SAVEPOINT command was issued in the current transaction. If no name is specified, then the last established savepoint is used. If any savepoints were established after the named savepoint, then the later savepoints are also undone.

SAVEPOINT

Use the SAVEPOINT command to establish a savepoint in the current transaction.

The syntax for SAVEPOINT is:

```
SAVEPOINT [savepoint_name]
```

■ [savepoint_name]. The name of the savepoint to be established.

SELECT

The SELECT command queries the database for information.

The SELECT command typically returns a set of information. If you need to process data one row at a time, you have to limit your result set to one row and specify the INTO clause, or utilize a cursor.

◀ See "Using Cursors," p. 323

> **Note**
>
> The GROUP BY clause must contain all columns that are specified in the SELECT list, the HAVING clause, and the ORDER BY clause.

> **Caution**
>
> If a join is not specified between tables in a FROM clause, your SELECT will result in a Cartesian product. For example, assume that tables A and B each have 100 rows. If you construct a SELECT statement and specify both tables on the FROM clause, and do not join them in the WHERE clause, you will get 10,000 rows returned (100 * 100).

The syntax for the SELECT command is:

VI

Reference

```
SELECT [ ALL ¦ DISTINCT ]  select-list
    ... [      ¦ INTO  host-variable-list      ¦      ]
           ¦ INTO  variable-list   ¦
    ... FROM  table-list
    ... [ WHERE   search-condition ]
    ... [ GROUP  BY  column-name, ... ]
    ... [ HAVING  search-condition ]
    ... ¦ [ ORDER  BY  expression  [ ASC ¦ DESC ], ... ]     ¦
           ¦ [ ORDER  BY  integer  [ ASC ¦ DESC ], ... ]  ¦
```

■ [ALL ¦ DISTINCT]. ALL is the default, and indicates that all the rows that meet the WHERE clause will be returned. If you want to eliminate duplicate rows, specify DISTINCT.

■ select_list. The select-list is a list of comma-separated expressions that can be any of the following:

table_name.* , expression [AS alias_name], -or table-name.column-
➥name

table_name.*. This option would bring back all the columns from the specified table.

expression [AS alias_name]. This option allows for aggregate functions or subselects to be specified as select items. The alias_name can be used to refer to the specific select item throughout the query. If as subquery is specified, it must be in parentheses.

table-name.column-name. The specified column-name would be brought back as part of the result set.

■ ¦ INTO host_variable_list¦. This applies to Embedded SQL SELECTs that return one row. The host_variable_list is a list of variables that will receive the values from the items in the select list. The number of host variables must match the number of items in the select list.

■ ¦ INTO variable_list¦. This applies to procedures and triggers only. The variable_list is a list of variables that will receive the result set values.

■ FROM table_list. The list of tables or views from which data is being selected.

■ [WHERE search-condition]. The search-condition limits what data will be selected from the tables in the FROM table list. It is also where joins are specified between tables in the table list.

■ [GROUP BY column_name,...]. The GROUP BY clause groups individual rows together that have matching values for the column or columns specified. The result set will then contain one row that represents each group.

- ■ [HAVING search-condition]. Whereas the WHERE clause filters out individual rows, the HAVING clause filters out grouped data that does not meet the search condition. The HAVING clause can only be used if there is a GROUP BY clause or if all the items in the select list are aggregate functions.

- ■ ¦ [ORDER BY expression[ASC ¦ DESC], ...]¦. This format of the ORDER BY clause determines the sort order for each item in the result set. Each item can be specified as either ASC for ascending or DESC for descending. The default is ascending.

- ■ ¦ [ORDER BY integer [ASC ¦ DESC], ...]¦. This format of the ORDER BY clause allows you to sort the result set by specifying the position of the select-list item. For example, to sort by the third item, specify 3 for the integer.

The following are examples of the SELECT command:

```
SELECT d.dept_name, e.last_name, e.first_name, e.salary_amt
    FROM department d ,
         employee  e
   WHERE ( department.dept_id = employee.dept_id ) and
         ( (e.salary_amt > (  SELECT avg(salary_amt)
                                        FROM employee )) )
ORDER BY e.salary_amt DESC


SELECT department.dept_name,  employee.*
       FROM employee, department
       WHERE ( employee.dept_id = department.dept_id )

SELECT count (*) INTO :count FROM department
```

SET OPTION

The SET OPTION command is used to set database options and ISQLW options. There are three formats for the SET OPTION command:

Format 1:

```
SET [TEMPORARY] OPTION
       [user_id. ¦ PUBLIC.]option_name = [option_value]
```

Format 2 (ISQLW Only):

```
SET PERMANENT
```

Format 3 (ISQLW Only)

> SET

SET PERMANENT (Format 2) is used in ISQLW only to set current ISQLW options permanently on the database for the userid connected to the database. SET by itself (Format 3) is used to display the current ISQLW options.

The clauses for Format 1 are as follows:

■ TEMPORARY. TEMPORARY is specified to change settings for this connection only.

> **Caution**
>
> TEMPORARY settings can only be used for the current user ID. If another user ID is specified or PUBLIC is specified, an error will result.

■ [user_id. ¦ PUBLIC.] option_name = [option_value]. This clause is used to specify an . option. Option_name specifies which option is set. Option_value is the setting for the option_name. If option_value is omitted, the option setting for the option_name is deleted, and the default (or PUBLIC) option setting is used. You can specify a userid or PUBLIC setting for the option. If omitted, the option setting is for the current userid only.

ISQLW options affect the ISQLW environment. Database options affect the database functionality. Valid options and settings can be seen in table 22.7.

Table 22.7   Valid Database and ISQLW Options

OPTION	Type	VALUES	DEFAULT
AUTO_COMMIT	ISQLW	ON,OFF	OFF
AUTO_REFETCH	ISQLW	ON,OFF	ON
BELL	ISQLW	ON,OFF	ON
BLOCKING	Database	ON,OFF	ON
CHECKPOINT_TIME	Database	number of minutes	60
COMMAND_DELIMITER	Database	string	';'
COMMIT_ON_EXIT	ISQLW	ON,OFF	ON

OPTION	Type	VALUES	DEFAULT
CONVERSION_ERROR	Database	ON,OFF	ON
DATE_FORMAT	Database	string	'YYYY-MM-DD' 'MM/DD/YYYY'*
DATE_ORDER	Database	'YMD','DMY','MDY'	'YMD''MDY'*
ECHO	ISQLW	ON,OFF	ON
HEADINGS	ISQLW	ON,OFF	ON
INPUT_FORMAT	ISQLW	ASCII, FIXED, DIF, DBASE, DBASEII, DBASEIII, FOXPRO, LOTUS, WATFILE	ASCII
ISOLATION_LEVEL	Database	0,1,2,3	0
ISQL_LOG	ISQLW	file-name	''
NULLS	ISQLW	string	'(NULL)'
ON_ERROR	ISQLW	STOP, CONTINUE, PROMPT, EXIT	PROMPT
OUTPUT_FORMAT	ISQLW	ASCII, FIXED, DIF, DBASEII, DBASEIII, FOXPRO, LOTUS, SQL, TEXT, WATFILE	ASCII
OUTPUT_LENGTH	ISQLW	integer	0
PRECISION	Database	number of digits	30
RECOVERY_TIME	Database	number of minutes	2
ROW_COUNTS	Database	ON,OFF	OFF
SCALE	Database	number of digits	6
STATISTICS	ISQLW	0,3,4,5,6	3
THREAD_COUNT	Database	number of threads	0
TIME_FORMAT	Database	string	'HH:MM:SS.SSS'
TIMESTAMP_FORMAT	Database	string	'YYYY-MM-DD HH:MM:SS.SSS'
TRUNCATION_LENGTH	ISQLW	integer	30
WAIT_FOR_COMMIT	Database	ON,OFF	OFF

The default if the database was created with a WATCOM SQL version earlier than 4.0.

VI

Reference

A description of each option can be viewed in Table 22.8.

Table 22.8	Database and ISQLW Option Descriptions
OPTION	**Description**
AUTO_COMMIT	AUTO_COMMIT gives you the choice of whether or not to COMMIT after every successful SQL command (ON or OFF) in your ISQLW environment. The default is OFF.
AUTO_REFETCH	AUTO_REFETCH allows you to choose whether (ON) or not (OFF) you want any query results in the ISQLW data window refetched and redisplayed after any INSERT, UPDATE, or DELETE SQL command. The default is ON.
BELL	BELL indicates whether or not (ON or OFF) a beep will sound if an error occurs in the ISQLW environment. The default is ON.
BLOCKING	
CHECKPOINT_TIME	
COMMAND_DELIMITER	The COMMAND_DELIMITER is the character (or characters) used to delimit multiple SQL commands in your ISQLW environment. The default is a semicolon (;).
COMMIT_ON_EXIT	COMMIT_ON_EXIT gives you the choice of whether or not (ON or OFF) to COMMIT when exiting your ISQLW environment. The default is ON.
CONVERSION_ERROR	
DATE_FORMAT	
DATE_ORDER	
ECHO	ECHO allows you to indicate whether or not (ON or OFF) your SQL commands will echo to the data window before execution in your ISQLW environment. The default is ON.
HEADINGS	HEADINGS allows you to indicate whether or not (ON or OFF) you want headings to be displayed with the results of a SELECT statement in the ISQLW environment. The default is ON.
INPUT_FORMAT	INPUT_FORMAT allows you to choose the input format of your file to be used with the INPUT ISQLW command. Valid values are ASCII, DBASE, DBASEII, DBASEIII, DIF, FIXED, FOXPRO, LOTUS, and WATFILE.
ISOLATION_LEVEL	
ISQL_LOG	ISQL_LOG allows you to log all SQL commands to a user-specified file in the ISQLW environment.

OPTION	Description
NULLS	NULLS lets you indicate how you want to display any NULLs that are SELECTed in your ISQLW environment. The default is '(NULL)'.
ON_ERROR	ON ERROR lets you choose how ISQLW will handle an error when reading from a command file. Valid values are STOP, PROMPT, CONTINUE, and EXIT.
OUTPUT_FORMAT	OUTPUT_FORMAT allows you to choose the output format of your file to be used with the OUTPUT ISQLW command. Valid values are ASCII, DBASEII, DBASEIII, DIF, FIXED, FOXPRO, LOTUS, SQL, TEXT, and WATFILE.
OUTPUT_LENGTH	OUTPUT_LENGTH allows you to control the length of the output file in an OUTPUT ISQLW command. Using this information, the OUTPUT command truncates the output to a desired length. A zero (0) used for OUTPUT_LENGTH indicates that no truncation will be done.
PRECISION	
RECOVERY_TIME	
ROW_COUNTS	
SCALE	
STATISTICS	STATISTICS lets you set the height of the statistics window in the ISQLW environment. The height is in lines. A value of 0 for STATISTICS turns the statistics window off. The default is 3.
THREAD_COUNT	
TIME_FORMAT	
TIMESTAMP_FORMAT	
TRUNCATION_LENGTH	TRUNCATION_LENGTH allows you to control the length of the columns displayed in the ISQLW environment. Using this information, any columns resulting from a SELECT SQL command are truncated to the specified column width in this text box. A zero value for TRUNCATION_LENGTH indicates that columns will be truncated to the length of the ISQLW data window.
WAIT_FOR_COMMIT	

The following SET OPTION command will turn the headings on in the ISQLW environment:

▶ See "INPUT," p. 602

```
SET OPTION HEADINGS = ON
```

VI

Reference

SET CONNECTION

Use the SET CONNECTION command to change the active database connection.

The syntax for the SET CONNECTION command is:

```
SET CONNECTION [connection_name]
```

- [connection_name]. The name of the connection that you want to become the active connection. If no connection name is specified and an unnamed connection exists, that connection will become active.

SET SQLCA

The SET SQLCA command tells the SQL preprocessor to use a SQLCA other than the default global SQLCA.

The syntax for the SET SQLCA command is

```
SET SQLCA[sqlca]
```

- [sqlca]. The C language reference to an SQLCA pointer.

SET (VARIABLE)

The SET (VARIABLE) command is used to assign a value to a variable that was created using the CREATE VARIABLE command.

The syntax for SET (VARIABLE) is:

```
SET  identifier  =   expression
```

- [identifier]. The previously created variable.
- [expression]. The variable will be set to the value of the expression.

UNION

Use the UNION clause to combine the result sets from multiple SELECT statements.

The syntax for the UNION clause is:

```
select UNION [ALL] select
[UNION [ALL] select],...
[ORDER BY integer [ASC¦DESC],...]
```

■ select. All select statements that are UNIONed together must have the same number of items in the select list, and none of the select can have an ORDER BY clause.

■ [ALL]. This combines all rows from all of the UNIONed select statements. If ALL is not specified, then duplicate rows will be eliminated.

■ [ORDER BY integer [ASC¦DESC],...]. This option allows the combined result set to be sorted, in either ascending or descending order, by specifying the select items by position number.

UPDATE

The UPDATE command modifies data from one or more tables in the database.

The syntax for UPDATE is:

```
UPDATE  table-list  SET
    ...  column-name = expression, ...
    ...  [ WHERE  search-condition ]
    ...  [ ORDER BY  expression  [ ASC ¦ DESC ] ,... ]
```

■ table-list. The list of tables to be updated.

■ SET column_name = expression. The column_name to be updated will be set to the value of the expression.

■ WHERE search_condition. Only the rows that satisfy the search condition will be updated.

■ ORDER BY expression [ASC ¦ DESC]. This option allows you to specify the order in which the update is performed.

UPDATE (POSITIONED)

Use the UPDATE (POSITIONED) command to modify data via an updateable cursor.

The syntax for UPDATE (POSITIONED) has two formats:

VI

Reference

Format 1:

```
UPDATE  WHERE  CURRENT  OF  cursor-name
      ... ¦ USING DESCRIPTOR sqlda-name ¦
            ¦ FROM host-variable-list        ¦
```

Format 2:

```
UPDATE  table-list  SET
      ...  column-name = expression, ...
      ...  WHERE  CURRENT  OF  cursor-name
```

- `cursor name`. The name of the cursor.

- `USING DESCRIPTOR sqlda_name`. `Sqlda-name` is a descriptor that has columns to match the columns in the cursor's select statement.

- `FROM host-variable-list`. The values in the `host-variable-list` will be used for the update.

- `table-list`. The list of tables to be updated.

- `SET column-name = expression`. The `column_name` to be updated will be set to the value of the expression

VALIDATE TABLE

Because Watcom operates under both DOS and Windows, which are unprotected operating environments, there is the possibility that your Watcom tables can inadvertently become corrupted. In order to verify that your tables have not been corrupted, you can issue the VALIDATE TABLE command.

The syntax for the VALIDATE TABLE command is

```
VALIDATE TABLE [creator.]table_name
```

- `[creator.]table_name`. The `table_name` is the name of the table that you want to have validated. `table_creator` can also be specified, but defaults to the `userid` used to connect to the database.

WHENEVER

The WHENEVER statement allows the programmer to specify how to handle errors. The WHENEVER statement is not an executable statement, but rather an SQL preprocessor directive to insert an IF (sqlcode) test after each Embedded

SQL statement. Each WHENEVER statement encountered throughout the C program listing overrides the previously encountered WHENEVER statement.

The syntax for the WHENEVER statement is:

```
¦ WHENEVER SQLERROR ¦
¦ WHENEVER SQLWARNING ¦
¦ WHENEVER NOTFOUND ¦
      ¦ GOTO label ¦
      ¦ STOP ¦
      ¦ CONTINUE ¦
      ¦ {c CODE;}  ¦
```

- SQLERROR. Allows you to specify how to handle conditions where the SQLCODE is less than zero.

- SQLWARNING. Allows you to specify how to handle conditions where the SQLCODE is greater than zero.

- NOTFOUND. Allows you to specify how to handle conditions where the SQLCODE is 100.

- ¦ GOTO label ¦. When one of the above conditions is encountered, go to the section of code labeled by the label.

- ¦ STOP¦. When one of the above conditions is encountered, stop execution.

- ¦ CONTINUE ¦. This is the default action to take when one of the above conditions is encountered. It specifies that program executions should continue.

- ¦ {c CODE;} ¦. When one of the above actions is encountered, execute the specified c code.

From Here...

This chapter discusses the most commonly used SQL commands. To find out about other SQL commands and Watcom SQL utilities, you can review the following chapters:

- Chapter 12, "Implementing Procedures and Triggers," discusses the use of stored procedures and triggers within the Watcom SQL environment. Included are SQL commands that affect procedures and triggers. Also included are several ESQL-only commands.

VI

Reference

- Chapter 14, "Implementing Watcom SQL with SQLPP (C and C++)," discusses using Watcom SQL in a C++ environment. Many ESQL-only commands are covered in this chapter.

- Chapter 23, "ISQL-Only SQL Commands," discusses commands available only within the ISQLW environment.

Chapter 23

ISQL-Only SQL Commands

by Charles A. Wood

The power of a database comes from its use inside a programming language. However, sometimes a developer will need to test an SQL command or view database information without the burden of writing a program to do so.

Most SQL databases have a utility program to run their SQL commands outside of a program. Watcom's utility that does this is called ISQLW. (*ISQLW* is an acronym for *Interactive Standard Query Language for Windows*.)

> **Note**
>
> The program discussed here is a Windows interactive SQL command processor called ISQLW. However, for DOS, QNX, and OS/2, the program is called ISQL, and commands that run in the ISQLW and ISQL environments are called ISQL commands.

While most SQL commands are available for inside applications, as well as in the ISQLW environment, there are several commands that are available only in the the ISQLW environment. This chapter discusses ISQL-only SQL commands.

◀ See "Using ISQLW," p. 20

CONFIGURE

You use the CONFIGURE command in the ISQLW program to set ISQL options that you normally set with the SET OPTION command. ISQL options effect the ISQLW environment, as well as any command files used in the RTSQLW utility program. When you issue the CONFIGURE command, the ISQL Options dialog box appears (see fig. 23.1). This dialog box allows you to use an on-line graphical window to set options in the ISQL environment.

▶ See "Using RTSQLW," p. 640

◀ See "SET OP- TION," p. 565

The syntax for CONFIGURE is

```
Configure;
```

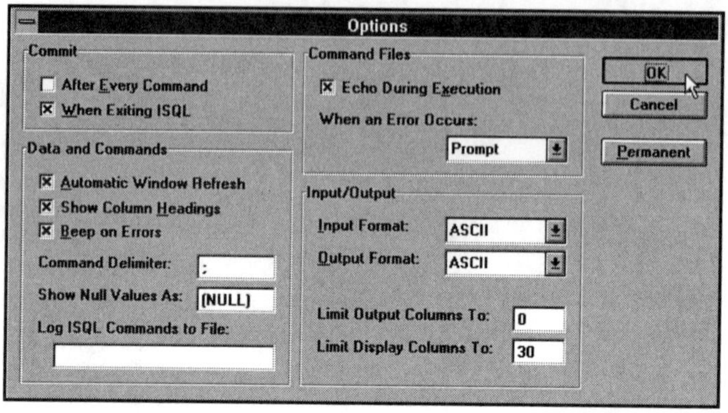

Fig. 23.1
The Options dialog box allows you to set ISQL options without having to code a SET OPTION SQL statement.

◄ See "SET OPTION," p. 565

Tip
A semicolon is the default *command delimiter*. The command delimiter separates multiple SQL calls in the ISQLW environment. If you execute only one SQL command, then a command delimiter is optional.

Tip
COMMITing after every SQL statement takes additional time. In a large SQL sequence, you may want to COMMIT only when you exit the ISQLW environment.

Note

The command delimiter (;) can be changed by using the CONFIGURE window shown in figure 23.1 and described later in this section.

Options set using the CONFIGURE command only effect the ISQLW environment; host languages such as PowerBuilder, Visual BASIC, or C++ are not affected by the CONFIGURE command. The Options dialog box offers the following options:

- **Commit**. You have the choice of either COMMITing after every SQL command or COMMITing only when you exit the ISQLW environment. By default, you COMMIT when you exit the ISQLW environment. This way, in the case of errors, you can use the ROLLBACK SQL command to automatically roll back your database changes to the point of the last COMMIT, or to the point where you entered the ISQLW environment.

- **Data and Commands.** These options control the way data and commands are displayed or captured. You can set the following options:

  Automatic Window Refresh. This allows you to indicate whether you want query results displayed again in the ISQLW Data window after any INSERT, UPDATE, or DELETE SQL command.

Show Column Headings. You can choose whether you want headings displayed with the results of a SELECT statement.

Beep on Errors. By checking this, you indicate that a beep will sound if an error occurs. If you do not check this option, a beep does not sound when an error occurs.

Command Delimiter. The command delimiter is the character (or characters) used to separate multiple SQL commands in the ISQL environment. The default is a semicolon.

Caution

If you permanently change the command delimiter, you could create some problems. First, other users must be told that the semicolon is no longer the command delimiter. Second, letters or numbers used as command delimiters require a space before them.

Show Null Values As. In this text box, you define how you want to display any NULLs that are SELECTed.

Log ISQL Commands to File. The ISQL environment allows you to log all SQL commands to a file you specify.

Caution

There are two situations you should be aware of when using an SQL log file:

1. The SQL log file erases any existing log file. *It deletes the previous log file without warning!*

2. The SQL log file saves at the end of the ISQL session. Therefore, the SQL log file *does not save all of your SQL.* It only saves the SQL in the ISQLW Command window when you exit the ISQLW environment.

Note

To review all the transactions done to your database over a period of time, you should use the transaction log file instead of the command log file.

◀ See "Transaction Log," p. 307

VI

References

■ **Command Files.** These options control the way commands are processed during the execution of SQL. You can set the following command-file options:

Echo During Execution. This indicates whether your SQL commands will echo to the Data window before executing in the ISQLW environment.

When an Error Occurs. This drop-down list lets you choose how ISQL will handle an error when reading from a command file. Valid values are:

Stop. ISQL stops reading commands from the file and returns to the Command window for additional commands (if any).

Prompt. ISQL asks the user whether he wants to continue.

Continue. The error is ignored and ISQL continues processing the next command. When using the INPUT ISQL command, the row in error is ignored and the INPUT command continues reading the rest of the rows.

Exit. The error causes ISQL to terminate.

■ **Input/Ouput.** The Input/Output group box allows you to select options that affect the way the results of queries made to the database (using the SELECT statement) are displayed. You can also control default formats of the INPUT and OUTPUT SQL statements in the Input/Output group box.

Input Format. This drop-down list allows you to choose what input format you want to use with the INPUT ISQL command. Valid formats are ASCII, DBASE, DBASEII, DBASEIII, DIF, FIXED, FOXPRO, LOTUS, and WATFILE. INPUT formats are explained in the OUTPUT SQL command section, later in this chapter.

Output Format. This drop-down list allows you to choose what output format to use with the OUTPUT ISQL command. Valid formats are ASCII, DBASEII, DBASEIII, DIF, FIXED, FOXPRO, LOTUS, SQL, TEXT, and WATFILE.

Limit Output Columns To. With this option, you can control the length of the output file in an OUTPUT ISQL command. The OUTPUT command truncates the output to the desired length. A zero (0) in this text box indicates that no truncation takes place.

Limit Display Columns To. This text box allows you to control the length of the columns displayed. Any columns resulting from a SELECT SQL command are truncated to the specified column width. A zero (0) indicates that columns truncate to the length of the Data window.

▶ See "SYSOPTION," p. 724

▶ See "SYSUSER-OPTIONS," p. 753

By clicking OK, you set the options only for that connection. By clicking **P**ermanent, you permanently set the options for your user ID.

DBTOOL

The DBTOOL command invokes one of the Watcom SQL utility programs described in Chapter 24, "Using Watcom Utilities." The syntax of each DBTOOL command depends on the function you want to access. After first discussing connection parameters, the following sections list each function of DBTOOL, the Watcom SQL utility program the DBTOOL command accesses, the DBTOOL command syntax, and an example of the DBTOOL command. At the end is a discussion of the Database Tools icon in your ISQLW environment.

Understanding Connection Parameters

You use *connection parameters* when you want to connect to a database. Even if you're connected to the database through ISQLW, you still need to provide connection parameters when required. This is because the DBTOOL commands invoke one of the Watcom SQL utility programs in a separate Windows session that runs outside of the ISQLW environment.

DBTOOL commands that use connection parameters are DBTOOL BACKUP TO, DBTOOL UNLOAD TABLES, and DBTOOL VALIDATE TABLES. (These commands are reviewed later in this section.) Table 23.1 lists the verbose keyword, the short form of the keyword, an example of how to use the connection parameter, and a description.

Table 23.1	Connection Parameters		
Verbose Keyword	**Short Form**	**Example**	**Description**
Userid	UID	UID=dba	The user ID defined in the Grant SQL statement.
Password	PWD	PWD=SQL	The password of the user ID.

(continues)

VI

References

Table 23.1 Continued

Verbose Keyword	Short Form	Example	Description
ConnectionName	CON	CON=conn	The name of the connection used to connect to the database (for multiple database connections).
EngineName	ENG	ENG=Sample	The name of the ODBC engine to start.
Database Name	DBN	DBN=Powersoft Demo DB	The name of the database assigned by the database configuration in the database painter.
Database File	DBF	DBF=\wsql\ sample.db	The file of the database.
DatabaseSwitches	DBS	DBS=-d	Switches used in the database.
AutoStop	AutoStop	AutoStop	(In PB.INI, use AUTOSTOP=TRUE.) Disconnects from the database after the command that's using the connection parameters is finished, if there are no other connections to the database.
Start	Start	Start=DB32W	The name of the Watcom program used to start the database engine.
Unconditional	UNC	UNC	(In PB.INI, use UNC=TRUE.) Starts the database, even if the log file cannot be used. If you are using a log file with your database and the log file gets corrupted, you can still open your database without accessing the log file by using UNC.

The following is an example of the use of connection parameters:

```
UID=dba;PWD=sql;ENG=sample
```

The above line is similar to the CONNECTSTRING parameter found in the PB.INI file. You can also connect by using positional parameters without qualifiers (as was necessary in Watcom version 3.2) as follows:

```
dba,sql,sample
```

Using the old positional connection parameters does connect to a database engine, but they disable the use of multiple databases running on one server. Running multiple databases on one server is a new feature of Watcom 4.0.

You can see an example of connection parameters with the following DBTOOL BACKUP TO command:

```
DBTOOL BACKUP TO f:\backup ALL FILES NOCONFIRM USING
UID=dba;PWD=sql;ENG=sample
```

DBTOOL ALTER DATABASE

DBTOOL ALTER DATABASE alters the status of the transaction log in a database. DBTOOL ALTER DATABASE executes the DBLOGW utility program. The following is the syntax for DBTOOL ALTER DATABASE:

```
DBTOOL ALTER DATABASE name NO [ TRANSACTION ] LOG
DBTOOL ALTER DATABASE name SET [ TRANSACTION ] LOG TO filename
```

◀ See "The Trans-
action Log,"
p. 292

▶ See "Using
DBLOGW.EXE,"
p. 630

- `name` refers to the name of the database.

- `NO LOG` or `NO TRANSACTION LOG` turns the transaction log off so you're no longer running with a transaction log.

> **Caution**
>
> Running a Watcom SQL database without a transaction log can slow down database performance. In addition, a transaction log allows the user the luxury of up-to-the-moment recovery of a corrupted database. Carefully consider this before you disable your transaction log.

- `SET LOG TO filename` or `SET TRANSACTION LOG TO filename` resets the database to use another log file.

DBTOOL ALTER WRITE FILE

DBTOOL ALTER WRITE FILE reports the status of a write file, and can assign a write file to a database. When a write file is used, all changes to a database are placed in the write file, leaving the original database untouched. DBTOOL ALTER WRITE FILE executes the DBWRITEW utility program.

Tip
Write files are good for testing. This way, the original contents of the database are untouched.

The following is the syntax for DBTOOL ALTER WRITE FILE:

```
DBTOOL ALTER WRITE FILE name
     [ REFER TO dbname ]
```

VI

References

▶ See "Using DBWRITEW. EXE," p. 639

- ■ name refers to the name of the write file.

- ■ REFER TO dbname. If the REFER TO clause is present, it alters the write file so that it becomes the write file of a new database. This erases the write file. If the REFER TO clause is not present, the DBTOOL ALTER WRITE FILE command only reports the status of the write file.

DBTOOL BACKUP TO

▶ See "Using DBBACKW.EXE," p. 621

DBTOOL BACKUP TO can backup the database and database log files, and it can write files, even if the database is being accessed by another user in a multi-user database setting. DBTOOL BACKUP TO executes the DBBACKW utility program.

> **Note**
>
> You cannot connect to a database using the single-user Watcom SQL version if another user is already attached.

The following is the syntax for the DBTOOL BACKUP TO command:

```
DBTOOL BACKUP TO directory
      [ DBFILE ] [ WRITE FILE ] [ [ TRANSACTION ] LOG ] [ ALL FILES
]
      [ RENAME [ TRANSACTION ] LOG ] ¦ [ TRUNCATE [ TRANSACTION ]
LOG ]
      [ NOCONFIRM ]
      USING connection_string
```

- ■ TO directory specifies what directory receives the backup file. The backed up database has the same name as the production database.

- ■ You can specify which part or parts of the database you want to back up. DBFILE backs up the database file with the .DB extension. WRITE FILE backs any write files. LOG or TRANSACTION LOG backs up the transaction log. Finally, ALL FILES backs up all files associated with the database.

- ■ RENAME LOG or RENAME TRANSACTION LOG backs up the log file and replaces the .LOG extension with a number starting with 001 (DBLOG.001). TRUNCATE LOG or TRUNCATE TRANSACTION LOG forces a backup of the transaction log and restarts the transaction log.

> **Caution**
>
> If you *never* truncate your transaction log, it will soon surpass the size of the
> entire database. It is a good idea to often truncate your transaction log when
> doing a full backup.

■ `NOCONFIRM` overwrites files without confirmation.

■ `USING connection_string` specifies the connection parameter.

DBTOOL COMPRESS DATABASE

The DBTOOL COMPRESS DATABASE command shrinks a database 40 to 60
percent of its original size. A compressed database can speed up your access
time, but you cannot update data on a compressed database. You must expand a compressed database before you can update it (unless you use a write
file). However, you can still execute a SELECT on a compressed database. (See
the "DBTOOL UNCOMPRESS DATABASE" section for information on how to
expand a compressed database.) DBTOOL COMPRESS DATABASE executes
the DBSHRINW utility program. The syntax for DBTOOL COMPRESS DATA-
BASE is as follows:

▶ See "Using
DBSHRINW.
EXE," p. 634

```
DBTOOL COMPRESS DATABASE database_file
     [ TO compressed_file ]
```

■ `database_file` is the name of the database to be compressed.

■ `TO compressed_file`. A compressed file clause allows you to name the
compressed file. The compressed file must not have the same name as
the database file. If you do not specify a compressed file name, it defaults to the database name with a .CDB extension.

DBTOOL CREATE DATABASE

DBTOOL CREATE DATABASE allows you to create a new database. It executes
the DBINITW utility program. The syntax for the DBTOOL CREATE DATA-
BASE command is as follows:

▶ See "Using
DBINITW.EXE,"
p. 628

```
DBTOOL CREATE DATABASE filename
     [ [ TRANSACTION ] LOG TO logname ] ¦ [ NO [ TRANSACTION ] LOG
]
     [ IGNORE CASE ] ¦ [ RESPECT CASE ]
     [ PAGE SIZE n ]
     [ COLLATION colname ]
     [ ENCRYPT ]
     [ TRAILING SPACES ]
```

VI

References

■ `LOG TO logname` or `TRANSACTION LOG TO logname` allows you to specify the transaction log used with the Watcom database. `NO LOG` or `NO TRANSAC-TION LOG` indicates that the database will run without a transaction log.

> ### Caution
>
> Running a Watcom SQL database without a transaction log can slow down database performance. In addition, a transaction log allows the user the luxury of up-to-the-moment recovery of a corrupted database. Consider carefully before you disable your transaction log.

■ `IGNORE CASE` does not take case into account when making comparisons. `RESPECT CASE` is new to version 4 of Watcom SQL, and was added to comply with ANSI standard SQL. `RESPECT CASE` takes case into account when making comparisons.

> ### ANSI Standard
>
> If you ever worked with DB2, Oracle, Sybase, or another SQL database, you probably noticed that the SQL is similar between them all. This is because the American National Standards Institute (ANSI) sets the standards for many popular languages like C++, BASIC, COBOL, and SQL.
>
> Watcom SQL is designed to be fully ANSI-compliant. That way, if you are familiar with other databases, you will have little trouble moving to Watcom SQL.
>
> ANSI standards allow some standardization across product lines, while at the same time giving software developers the freedom to enhance their product; thereby allowing themselves to be set apart from other databases.
>
> Most SQL databases add additional features to their SQL language, and Watcom SQL is no exception. ISQLW-only statements like CONFIGURE, DBTOOL, etc., are not part of the ANSI SQL standard, but are added in the Watcom SQL implementation to make the functionality of your database a little more robust.

■ `PAGE SIZE n`. Watcom SQL allocates disk space to all database tables and indexes based on page size. When you access information on your database, the information is swapped into memory, one page at a time. Valid page sizes, in bytes, are 512, 1024 (default), 2048, or 4096. A good rule is that the larger the page size is, the faster the database is. For large multi-user databases, use **4096**.

> **Caution**
>
> DBSTARTW and RTSTARTW are 16-bit database engines, and DB32W and
> RT32W are 32-bit database engines. 16-bit database engines cannot start a
> database with a page size larger than 1024. If you need to use 16-bit engines
> (for 286 machines), then keep the page size at 1024 and use DBSTARTW for
> developing. Otherwise, set the page size to 4096 and develop with DB32W.

■ `COLLATION colname`. The collation controls the sort order of the database.
Sort order controls which characters are placed before other characters in
an ORDER BY command. Changing the collation sequence is especially
useful when using Watcom SQL in non-English speaking countries.

◄ See "Making Different Collating Sequences," p. 238

■ `ENCRYPT`. Specifying `ENCRYPT` makes it harder to look at your database
with disk utilities and other programs outside Watcom SQL.

► See "SYSCOLLATION," p. 710

> **Caution**
>
> Some compression programs have a difficult time compressing encrypted files.
> This can affect the time and space needed to back up your database.

■ `TRAILING SPACES`. Specifying `TRAILING SPACES` causes Watcom SQL to
ignore trailing spaces for comparisons. For instance, "`Chuck Wood`" and
"`Chuck Wood  `" would compare the same.

DBTOOL CREATE WRITE FILE

You use the DBTOOL CREATE WRITE FILE command to assign a write file to
a database. When you use a write file, all changes to a database are placed in
the write file—leaving the original database untouched. This can be handy
for testing a database without corrupting the actual data contained in the
database. DBTOOL CREATE WRITE FILE executes the DBWRITEW utility
program. The syntax for DBTOOL CREATE WRITE FILE is as follows:

► See "Using DBWRITEW. EXE," p. 639

```
DBTOOL CREATE WRITE FILE writefilename
     FOR DATABASE databasename
     [ [ TRANSACTION ] LOG TO logname ]
     [ NOCONFIRM ]
```

■ `writefilename` is the name of the write file to be created. If
`writefilename` already exists, it is replaced and any information in the
old write file is lost. If no extension is given to `writefilename`, .WRT is
used.

VI

References

■ FOR DATABASE databasename. The FOR DATABASE clause assigns the write file to a database. The database name and the write file name must not be the same name.

■ LOG TO logname or TRANSACTION LOG TO logname allow you to specify the name of your log file. If you do not specify a log file name, the new log file for the database defaults to the database name with a .WLG extension.

■ NOCONFIRM forces DBTOOL CREATE WRITE FILE to overwrite any files without confirmation.

DBTOOL DBINFO DATABASE

The DBTOOL DBINFO DATABASE command displays information about the database, as seen in figure 23.2.

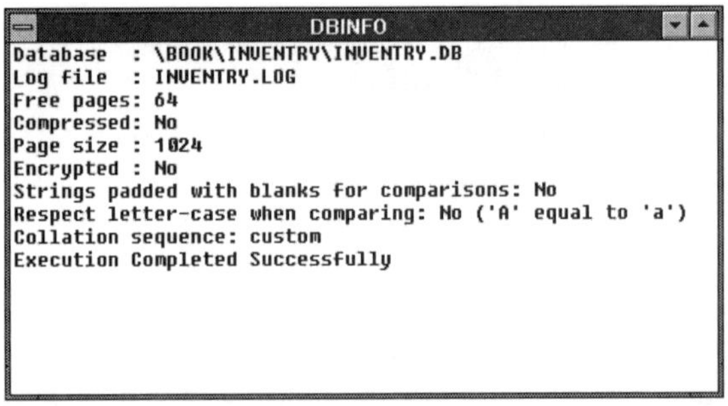

Fig. 23.2
You can find out the options set when your database was created by using DBTOOL DBINFO DATABASE.

```
┌─────────────────────── DBINFO ───────────────────────┐
│ Database  : \BOOK\INVENTRY\INVENTRY.DB                │
│ Log file  : INVENTRY.LOG                              │
│ Free pages: 64                                        │
│ Compressed: No                                        │
│ Page size : 1024                                      │
│ Encrypted : No                                        │
│ Strings padded with blanks for comparisons: No        │
│ Respect letter-case when comparing: No ('A' equal to 'a')│
│ Collation sequence: custom                            │
│ Execution Completed Successfully                      │
└───────────────────────────────────────────────────────┘
```

► See "Using DBINFOW.EXE," p. 628

DBTOOL DBINFO DATABASE executes the DBINFOW utility program. The syntax for DBTOOL DBINFO DATABASE is as follows:

```
DBTOOL DBINFO DATABASE database
     TO outputfile
     [ [ WITH ] PAGE USAGE ]
```

■ database is the name of the database file from which you want information.

■ TO outputfile. The TO outputfile clause redirects the output from the DBTOOL DBINFO DATABASE to an output file.

■ PAGE USAGE or WITH PAGE USAGE displays the page statistics on the database if Watcom SQL can establish a connection.

DBTOOL DROP DATABASE

The DBTOOL DROP DATABASE command erases a database. It executes the DBERASEW utility program. The following is the syntax for DBTOOL DROP DATABASE:

▶ See "Using DBERASEW. EXE," p. 627

```
DBTOOL DROP DATABASE name
     [ NOCONFIRM ]
```

- name is the name of the database you want to delete.

- Specifying NOCONFIRM turns off any verification of the database deletion.

DBTOOL TRANSLATE

The DBTOOL TRANSLATE command translates a transaction log into SQL. Using DBTOOL TRANSLATE is a good way to perform up-to-the-moment-of-failure recoveries if your database file is corrupt. DBTOOL TRANSLATE executes the DBTRANW utility program. The following is the syntax for DBTOOL TRANSLATE:

▶ See "Using DBTRANW. EXE," p. 635

```
DBTOOL TRANSLATE [ TRANSACTION ] LOG FROM logname
     [ TO sqlfile ]
     [ WITH ROLLBACKS ]
     [ USERS u1, u2, ... ] ¦ [ EXCLUDE USERS u1, u2, ... ]
     [ LAST CHECKPOINT ]
     [ ANSI ]
     [ NOCONFIRM ]
```

- LOG FROM logname or TRANSACTION LOG FROM logname indicates what log file will be translated to SQL.

- TO sqlfile lets you specify the name of the SQL file. If you omit this clause, the SQL file name defaults to the log file name with an .SQL extension.

- WITH ROLLBACKS includes transactions that were not COMMITed.

◀ See "COMMIT," p. 534

- USERS u1, u2, … allows you to specify what users' transactions will be included. EXCLUDE USERS u1, u2, allows you to include all users' transactions except the ones listed. The default is to include all users' transactions.

- LAST CHECKPOINT specifies that only transactions completed since the last checkpoint will be translated.

- ANSI generated ANSI standard SQL.

- NOCONFIRM indicates to replace SQL files (if applicable) without verification.

VI

References

To restore a database, complete the following steps:

1. Use DBTOOL DROP DATABASE to erase the current database (refer to the "DBTOOL DROP DATABASE" section, earlier in this chapter).

2. Using the Windows File Manager or the DOS COPY command, copy the backup of your database where Watcom SQL expects to find your current database.

3. Use DBTOOL TRANSLATE to translate your log file into an SQL file, as shown in the previous code.

4. Use the READ command to execute the newly created SQL file. Now your database should be recovered.

DBTOOL UNCOMPRESS DATABASE

▶ See "Using
DBEXPANW.
EXE," p. 627

The DBTOOL UNCOMPRESS DATABASE command expands a database that was compressed with the DBTOOL COMPRESS DATABASE command. It executes the DBEXPANW utility program. This is the syntax for DBTOOL UNCOMPRESS DATABASE:

```
DBTOOL UNCOMPRESS DATABASE compressed_database
        [ TO expanded_database ]
        [ NOCONFIRM ]
```

■ compressed_database lists the name of the compressed database. If you do not give an extension, a .CDB extension is used.

■ TO expanded_database lists the name of the target uncompressed database. If omitted, the expanded database name will be the compressed database name with a .DB extension. If no extension is listed with the expanded database name, a .DB extension is used.

■ NOCONFIRM replaces the expanded database, if it already exists and does not ask for verification.

DBTOOL UNLOAD COLLATION

◀ See "Making
Different Collat-
ing Sequences,"
p. 238

▶ See
"SYSCOLLATION,"
p. 710

DBTOOL UNLOAD COLLATION extracts a collating sequence or sequences from SYS.SYSCOLLATION. The following is the syntax for DBTOOL UNLOAD COLLATION:

```
DBTOOL UNLOAD COLLATION [ colname ] TO output_file
        [ EMPTY MAPPINGS ]
        [ HEX ¦ HEXADECIMAL ]
        [ NOCONFIRM ]
        USING connection-string
```

- `colname` is the name of the collation sequence you want to extract. The default is all collation sequences.

- `TO output_file` indicates where the collation sequences will be stored.

- `EMPTY MAPPINGS` allows for some older collations, where there were gaps between sort positions in the collating sequence. These gaps are represented by a colon if you specify `EMPTY MAPPINGS`. Otherwise, they are ignored.

- `HEX` or `HEXADECIMAL` allows for some collating sequences that use extended characters. Extended characters with an ASCII value greater than hex 7F may not appear correctly on your screen. When you specify HEX, it translates those characters to \x*nn*, where *nn* is the hexadecimal number of the character.

- `NOCONFIRM` overwrites the `output_file` if it exists, and does not ask for verification.

DBTOOL UNLOAD COLLATION executes the DBCOLLW utility program.

DBTOOL UNLOAD TABLES

The DBTOOL UNLOAD TABLES command unloads all the tables in a database to an SQL file. You can then execute this SQL file to reload all of the tables. It executes the DBUNLOAW utility program. This is the syntax for DBTOOL UNLOAD TABLES:

```
DBTOOL UNLOAD TABLES    TO directory
       [ RELOAD FILE TO sqlfile ]
       [ DATA ¦ SCHEMA ]
       [ UNORDERED ]
       [ VERBOSE ]
       USING connection-string
```

- `TO directory` specifies where the unloaded data files with the database data will be located.

- `RELOAD FILE TO sqlfile` specifies the name of the SQL file. If you omit this clause, the SQL file defaults to RELOAD.SQL.

- Specifying `DATA` only unloads statements pertaining to data. No CREATE statements will be included. Specifying `SCHEMA` unloads the CREATE statements only. No INSERT data statements will be loaded. The default is for both `DATA` and `SCHEMA` to be unloaded.

▶ See "Using DBCOLLW.EXE," p. 625

▶ See "Using DBUNLOAW.EXE," p. 636

VI

References

- UNORDERED unloads data without accessing the primary key. Normally, you could use this option to unload a database with a corrupt index. This option is also faster than unloading data in primary key order, which is the default.

- If you specify VERBOSE, the table name and how many rows are being unloaded is specified.

- USING connection-string connects you to a database. Valid values for a connection-string are discussed in "Understanding Connection Parameters," earlier in this section.

DBTOOL VALIDATE TABLES

▶ See "Using DBVALIDW. EXE," p. 638

DBTOOL VALIDATE TABLES validates all indexes of a table (or tables) in a database. The command executes the DBVALIDW utility program. The syntax for DBTOOL VALIDATE TABLES is as follows:

```
DBTOOL VALIDATE TABLES [ t1, t2, ... ]
        USING connection-string
```

- t1, t2, specifies what tables will have their indexes validated. The default is all tables.

- USING connection-string connects you to a database. Valid values for a connection-string are discussed in "Understanding Connection Parameters," earlier in this section.

Database Tools

The DBTOOL commands can be implemented inside a SQL command file, as well as within the ISQLW environment. However, most users will prefer using the Database Tools that come with ISQLW. The Database Tools duplicate the functionality of the DBTOOL command, and tend to be much easier to use. To enter the Database Tools, click on the Database Tools icon. This will display the Database Tools dialog box (see fig. 23.3).

The Database Tools dialog box includes a Tools list box, which allows you to select the tool you want to use. The button right next to the Tools list box (where the pointer is in figure 23.3) changes, depending on which tool you currently have highlighted. In addition to the tools, the Database Tools dialog box allows you to specify connection parameters required by some tools or to connect and disconnect from a database.

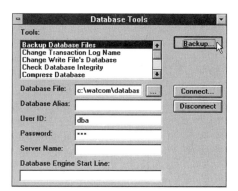

Fig. 23.3
The Database Tools
dialog box allows
you to graphically
implement the
Watcom SQL
DBTOOL com-
mands.

Troubleshooting

I'm in ISQLW. Why can't I find the Database Tools icon?

It's there. You probably have one of your windows on top of the icon. Try temporarily minimizing your Data Window, your Statistics Window, and your Command
Window. The icon will then show up.

Database Tools will graphically prompt you for the information needed for
the equivalent DBTOOL command. This section covers the new Watcom SQL
Database Tools.

Backup Database Files
By clicking Backup Database Files in the Database Tools dialog box, typing in
the database file you want to back up with a user ID and password, and clicking **B**ackup, you open the Backup Database Files dialog box (see fig. 23.4).

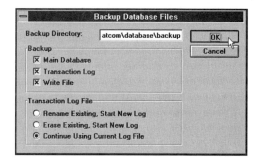

Fig. 23.4
The Backup
Database Files
dialog box allows
you to back up a
database and
manipulate its
transaction log.

In the Backup Database Files dialog box, do the following:

■ You must enter the directory in which you will place the backup files in the Backup Directory text box.

■ You must choose what to back up in the Backup group box. You can choose to back up your main database, your transaction log, your write file, or any combination of the three.

■ You may choose to manipulate your transaction log. You can rename the transaction log file (thereby starting a new transaction log with a new name), erase the existing transaction log file (thereby starting a new transaction log with the same name), or continue using the current log file with no changes.

> **Note**
>
> Even if you did not choose to back up the transaction log in the Backup group box, if you rename or erase the existing transaction log, Watcom SQL will force a backup of the existing transaction log.

Change Transaction Log Name

By clicking on Change Transaction Log Name in the Database Tools dialog box, typing in the database file you want to change, and clicking Change, you open the Change Transaction Log File dialog box, shown in figure 23.5.

Fig. 23.5
The Change Transaction Log File dialog box allows you to manipulate your transaction log.

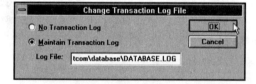

The Change Transaction Log File dialog box allows you to discontinue the use of the transaction log by clicking on **N**o Transaction Log. By clicking **M**aintain Transaction Log, you can use a new transaction log by clicking the name of the new transaction log in the Log File text box.

Change Write File's Database

By clicking on Change Write File's Database in the Database Tools dialog box, typing in the database write file you want to change, and clicking Change, you open the Change Write File's Database dialog box (see fig. 23.6).

Fig. 23.6
The Change Write
File's Database
dialog box allows
you to use your
write file for a
different database.

In the Refers to Database text box, enter the name of the database that you
want the write file attached to. The write file will then start to function only
for that database.

Check Database Integrity

By clicking on Check Database Integrity in the Database Tools dialog box,
typing in the database file you want to check, along with a user ID and password, and clicking Check, you open the Check Database Integrity dialog box
(see fig. 23.7).

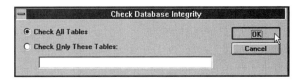

Fig. 23.7
The Check
Database Integrity
dialog box allows
you to validate the
indexes of a
database or certain
database tables.

In the Check Database Integrity dialog box, you click Check **A**ll Tables to
validate the indexes of an entire database, or you can click on Check **O**nly
These Tables and enter the table names you want to validate (separated by
commas). When you click OK, the Database Validation Progress window
opens, displaying the progress of your validation (see fig. 23.8).

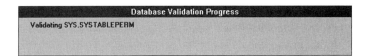

Fig. 23.8
The Database
Validation Progress
window displays
each table as it is
being validated.

VI

Troubleshooting

*I'm trying to validate my table, and I enter my fully qualified table name with my user ID. I
receive an error saying my table does not exist, but I know it does. What am I doing wrong?*

The Check Database Integrity database tool does not allow you to enter user IDs. If
you specify a table, the Check Database Integrity database tool will search first for the
table under your user ID and then check other user IDs for the same table.

(continues)

(continued)

If you need to validate a table under another user ID but can't get to it because you have a table with the same name under your own user ID, try validating the whole table instead.

Compress Database

By clicking Backup Database Files in the Database Tools dialog box, typing in the database file you want to compress, and clicking Compress, you open the Compress Database As dialog box (see fig. 23.9).

Fig. 23.9

The Compress Database As dialog box allows you to specify the file name and path of the compressed database file.

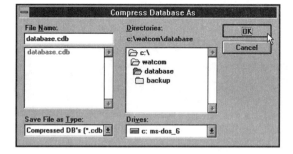

After choosing the name and path of your compressed database file, click OK. The Compress Database tool will create a compressed version of your database. When Watcom SQL has finished compressing your database, the Compression Information window will appear with compression information, as shown in figure 23.10.

Fig. 23.10

The Compression Information window displays a before and after snapshot of the effects of compression on your database.

Type	Pages	Bytes	Compressed	Comp
Tables	85	87040	37038	
Indices	42	43008	10914	
Other	7	7168	2376	
Free	34	34816	0	
Total	168	172032	50328	

Database: c:\watcom\database\database.db
Compressed Into: C:\WATCOM\DATABASE\DATABASE.CDB

Create Database

By clicking on Create Database in the Database Tools dialog box, typing in
the database file you want to create, and clicking Create, you open the Create
Database dialog box (see fig. 23.11).

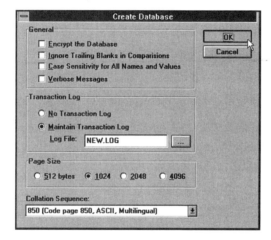

Fig. 23.11
The Create
Database dialog
box allows you to
specify the
creation options of
your database.

The following creation options can be specified by using the Create Database
tool:

- Clicking **E**ncrypt the Database allows you to password-protect your
  database so that only those users authorized to view the data can do so.
  This disables some utilities that can access database files outside of the
  Watcom SQL environment.

◀ See "Making Different Collating Sequences," p. 238

▶ See "Using DBCOLLW.EXE," p. 625

▶ See "SYSCOLLATION," p. 710

■ Clicking on **I**gnore Trailing Blanks in Comparisons will cause database comparisons to compare equal if one has trailing blanks. With this, "Chuck Wood" and "Chuck Wood   " will be considered equal.

■ Clicking on **C**ase Sensitivity for All Names and Values will cause database comparisons to compare equally. If this is clicked off, "Dr. Smith," "dr. smith," and "DR. SMITH" will be considered equal.

■ Clicking on **V**erbose Messages will cause verbose messages to be returned during a database error inside the ISQLW environment.

■ You can click on **N**o Transaction Log to turn off the transaction log, or you can click on **M**aintain Transaction Log and specify a log file to turn a log file on.

■ You can specify 512, 1024, 2048, or 4096 as the page size.

■ You can specify the collation sequence.

Create Write File

By clicking on Create Write File in the Database Tools dialog box, typing in the name of the database file for which you want to create a write file, and clicking Create, you open the Create Write File for Database dialog box (see fig. 23.12).

Fig. 23.12
The Create Write File for Database dialog box allows you to create a write file and specify a write file log for a database.

After entering the write file name and a write file transaction log file name, click on OK to create the write file and return to the Database Tools dialog box.

Database Information

By clicking on Database Information in the Database Tools dialog box, typing in a database file along with a user ID and password, and clicking Display, you open the Database Information dialog box (see fig. 23.13).

By clicking on Page Usage, you open the Page Usage window (see fig. 23.14). The Page Usage window shows how many pages were allocated to each table and index, how much of that page allocation is being used, and the percentage of the database that each table/index combination occupies.

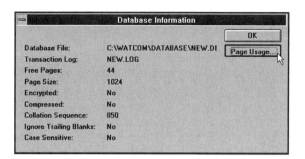

Fig. 23.13
The Database Information dialog box displays useful information about your database.

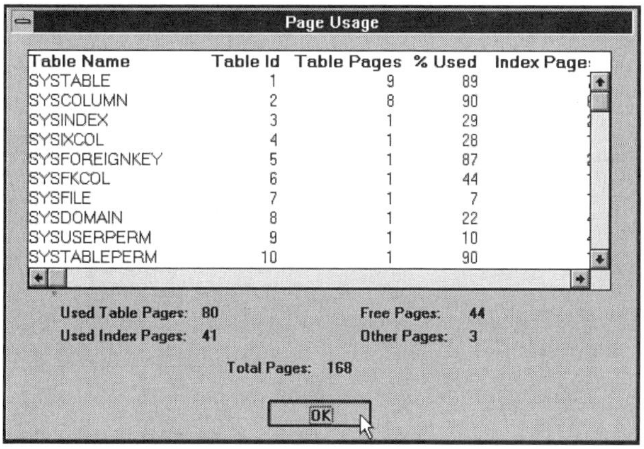

Fig. 23.14
The Page Usage window shows useful disk-allocation information, broken down by table and index.

Erase Database or Write File

By clicking on Erase Database or Write File in the Database Tools dialog box, typing in a database file name, and clicking Erase, you open the Erase Database or Write File dialog box (see fig. 23.15).

Fig. 23.15
The Erase Database or Write File dialog box lets you specify which database file you want to erase.

VI

References

In the Erase Database or Write File dialog box, you can specify whether you want to delete the database or write file, and/or delete the database transaction log file.

► See "Using
DB32W.EXE,
DBSTARTW.EXE,
RT32W.EXE,
and
RTSTARTW.EXE,"
p. 612

> **Caution**
>
> If you only erase the log file of a database, you must open the database engine (DB32W, DBSTARTW, RT32W, or RTSTARTW) with an -f parameter to force open the database without a log file, or click on Change Transaction Log Name, described earlier in this section, to allow the database to have no log file.

Extract Collation from Database

By clicking on Extract Collation from Database in the Database Tools dialog box, typing in a database file name along with a user ID and password, and clicking Extract, you open the Extract Collation from Database dialog box (see fig. 23.16).

Fig. 23.16
The Extract
Collation from
Database dialog
box allows you to
pull off the
collation sequence
used in the
database into a
text file for
viewing and
editing.

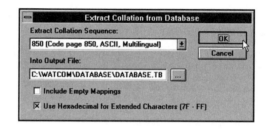

The following information is asked for in the Extract Collation from Database dialog box:

- The Extract Collation Sequence drop-down list box allows you to choose which collation sequence to extract. The default is the collation sequence currently used for your database.

- The Into Output File text box allows you to enter the file in which you want to store the collation sequence.

◄ See "Making
Different Collat-
ing Sequences,"
p. 238

► See "Using
DBCOLLW.EXE,"
p. 625

► See
"SYSCOLLATION,"
p. 710

- The Include Empty Mappings checkbox allows for some older collations where there were gaps between sort positions in the collating sequence. These gaps are represented by a colon if you click Include Empty Mappings. Otherwise, they are ignored.

- Clicking on the Use Hexadecimal for Extended Characters (7F - FF) allows for some collating sequences that use extended characters. Extended characters with an ASCII value greater than hex 7F may not appear correctly on your screen. When you click on this checkbox, it translates those characters to \xnn, where nn is the hexadecimal number of the character.

Rebuild Database

By clicking on Rebuild Database in the Database Tools dialog box, typing in a database file name along with a user ID and password, and clicking Rebuild, you open the Rebuild Database dialog box (see fig. 23.17).

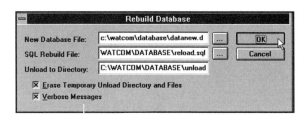

Fig. 23.17
The Rebuild Database dialog box allows you to create a database based on information in another database.

In the Rebuild Database dialog box, you specify the following information:

- The New Database File text box is where you specify the name of the database to be rebuilt from the old database.

- The SQL Rebuild File text box is where you specify the name of the SQL command file that is created during the rebuild and used to rebuild the new database.

- The Unload to Directory text box is where you specify the directory to store the SQL command file and the .DAT files resulting when the unloading of the old database occurs.

- The Erase Temporary Unload Directory and Files checkbox indicates whether or not you want to delete the .DAT, .SQL, and the unload directory when Watcom SQL finishes rebuilding your database.

- The Verbose Messages checkbox indicates that all messages that appear will be descriptive rather than short.

Translate Transaction Log to SQL

By clicking on Translate Transaction Log to SQL in the Database Tools dialog box, typing in a transaction log file name, and clicking Translate, you open the Translate Transaction Log to SQL dialog box (see fig. 23.18).

The following information is specified in the Translate Transaction Log to SQL dialog box:

- The Translate Log to an SQL File Named text box lets you enter the name of the SQL command file that the log file will be translated into.

Fig. 23.18
The Translate
Transaction Log to
SQL dialog box is
used to translate a
log file to
executable SQL.

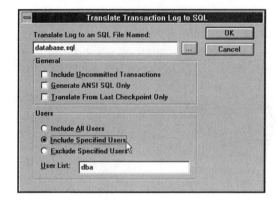

- The Include **U**ncommitted Transactions checkbox lets you include even those transactions that have not yet been COMMITed. Otherwise, only the COMMITed transactions will be translated.

- The **G**enerate ANSI SQL Only check box generates SQL that complies with the ANSI SQL standard.

- Clicking on Include **A**ll Users allows you to translate transactions from all users. You can also click on **I**nclude Specified Users or **E**xclude Specified Users, based on a user list containing users separated by commas.

Uncompress Database
By typing in a compressed database file name, clicking on Uncompress Database in the Database Tools dialog box, and clicking Uncompress, you open the Uncompress Database dialog box (see fig. 23.19).

Fig. 23.19
The Uncompress
Database dialog
box lets you
specify the name
of the target
database name.

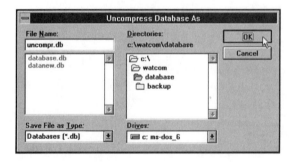

In the Uncompress Database dialog box, you click on the path and type in the name of the database that will be created when the compressed database is translated into an expanded database.

Unload Database

By typing in a database file along with a user ID and password, clicking on
Unload Database in the Database Tools dialog box, and clicking Unload, you
open the Unload Database to Text Files dialog box (see fig. 23.20).

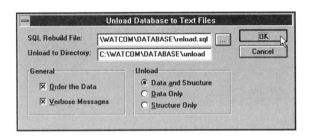

Fig. 23.20
The Unload
Database to Text
Files dialog box
allows you to
unload your data
from your database
to .DAT files with
SQL used to reload
the data.

Using the Unload Database to Text Files dialog box, you specify the following
information:

- The SQL Rebuild file text box contains the name of the file that will
  contain the SQL needed to reload the unloaded data into a new database.

- The Unload to Directory text box is where you specify the directory to
  store the .DAT files resulting when the unloading of the old database
  occurs.

- The **O**rder the Data checkbox unloads the data in primary-key order
  from each table. Ordering the data is not as efficient as unordered data,
  and requires that an intact index be present.

- The **V**erbose Messages checkbox indicates that descriptive messages will
  be displayed during the unload process.

- In the Unload group box, you can choose to unload **D**ata Only, which
  unloads the data without the CREATE statements needed to re-create
  the database; **S**tructure Only, which unloads the CREATE statements
  needed to re-create the database but does not unload any of the data
  itself; and Data **a**nd Structure, which unloads both the data and the
  CREATE statements needed to re-create the database.

EXIT, QUIT, BYE

EXIT, QUIT, or BYE all leave the ISQLW environment; there isn't a difference
between the three commands, and no additional parameters are used. These

VI

References

◀ See "Under-
standing Trans-
actions," p. 168

commands execute a COMMIT on your database if you selected the
COMMIT_ON_EXIT option. (See the CONFIGURE section, earlier in this chapter.)
Otherwise, a ROLLBACK is executed.

◀ See "COM-
MIT," p. 534

The formats for EXIT, QUIT, and BYE (respectively) are as follows:

◀ See "ROLL-
BACK," p. 562

```
Exit

Quit
```

◀ See "SET OP-
TION," p. 565

```
Bye
```

HELP

HELP accesses the ISQLW help file. This is the syntax for HELP:

```
HELP [topic]
```

The topic is not required. If you use topic, HELP displays information on
that topic. Otherwise, an index of HELP topics is displayed for you to choose
from. The following is an example of the HELP command:

```
HELP DBTOOL
```

INPUT

INPUT allows you to import data from an input data file into your database.
The syntax for the INPUT command is as follows:

```
INPUT INTO tablename
      [FROM filename ¦ PROMPT]
      [FORMAT inputformat]
      [BY ORDER ¦ BY NAME]
      [DELIMITED BY delimiter]
      [COLUMN WIDTHS (colwidth1, colwidth2, ...)]
      [NOSTRIP]
      [(columnname1, columnname2, ...)]
```

The following list explains the components of the INPUT command:

- INTO tablename. This specifies the table that will receive the input.

- FROM filename. This specifies the file name where the data to be input
  resides. If a FROM clause is not present, PROMPT is assumed. The user will
  be prompted for the name of the input data file.

- FORMAT inputformat. The input format is the format of the input file. If
  you do not specify the input format, the default input format (usually
  ASCII) is used. Valid values for the input format are:

■ **ASCII.** ASCII format is regular text format. Rows are separated into lines, and columns are separated by commas or by the delimiter specified by the DELIMITED BY clause on the INPUT SQL statement. Any string may be enclosed in either single or double quotes.

If you want to INPUT a string column containing a comma (or other specified delimiter), you *must* enclose that string in single or double quotes. To include a quote symbol, enclose the field in that quote symbol and place two quote symbols where you want to include the single or double quote.

Watcom also recognizes some C++ special characters denoted by a backslash. "\n" represents a carriage return–line feed combination. This is often called the *newline character*. "\xDD" represents a character using a hexadecimal character where DD is located. Finally, to import a backslash, "\\" must be used.

■ **DBASE.** The INPUT file is in either dBASE II or dBASE III format. Watcom tries to determine what format the file is in before processing. If the table doesn't exist that is on the dBASE file, it will be created.

■ **DBASEII.** The INPUT file is in dBASE II format. If the dBASE II table doesn't exist on the Watcom SQL database, it will be created.

■ **DBASEIII.** The INPUT file is in dBASE III format. If the dBASE III table doesn't exist on the Watcom SQL database, it will be created.

■ **DIF**. The INPUT file is in Data Interchange Format. If the DIF table doesn't exist on the Watcom SQL database, it will be created.

■ **FIXED.** INPUT rows are in fixed format, with each row starting on a new line. If you did not specify COLUMN WIDTHs in the INPUT command, then the widths have to be the maximum widths allowed by the data type in use.

■ **FOXPRO.** The INPUT file is in FoxPro format. If the FoxPro table doesn't exist on the Watcom SQL database, it will be created.

> **Note**
>
> The only difference between dBASE and FoxPro formats is the memo fields.

Tip
Although ASCII is usually the default input format, it can be changed by using CONFIGURE or the SET OPTION SQL commands.

VI

References

■ **LOTUS**. The file is in Lotus 1-2-3 format. INPUT assumes that the first row of the spreadsheet is the column name. If a table does not exist with the specified column names, it will be created.

> ### Caution
>
> Creating tables from Lotus 1-2-3 files may create data types and column widths that are not what you expect. This is because the data types are based on the spreadsheet cell, not a database field definition.

■ **WATFILE.** The input will be a WATFILE file. If the WATFILE table doesn't exist, it will be created. WATFILE is a tabular file format available from Watcom.

■ BY ORDER ¦ BY NAME. The BY clause allows the user to either import the data from the input file BY ORDER (default), in which the columns from the input file are matched up to the columns in the target table based on their sequential order; or BY NAME, in which the names of the columns are matched up with the names of the columns of the input file.

> ### Note
>
> Not all input formats have column names. The BY NAME clause is only allowed for DBASE, DBASEII, DBASEIII, DIF, FOXPRO, LOTUS, and WATFILE input formats.

■ DELIMITED BY delimiter. This clause lets you specify the delimiter for an ASCII input file. The default is a comma. Non-ASCII file formats ignore the DELIMITED BY clause.

■ COLUMN WIDTHS (colwidth1, colwidth2,). The COLUMN WIDTHS clause lists the column widths for a FIXED input format. If you do not specify the COLUMN WIDTHS, the widths used are the maximum widths for each data type in the target table.

■ NOSTRIP. The INPUT command automatically strips trailing spaces when using an ASCII input format. You can specify NOSTRIP to allow trailing spaces in the target table if they exist on the ASCII input file.

■ (columnname1, columnname2,). If the input format allows it, you can list the column names of the columns you want to import. This creates a table (if one doesn't already exist) with the same column name and column types used in the input file.

> **Note**
>
> As mentioned earlier, not all input formats have column names. Column name listings are only allowed for DBASE, DBASEII, DBASEIII, DIF, FOXPRO, LOTUS, and WATFILE input formats.

Some typical INPUT commands are as follows:

```
INPUT INTO customer FROM customer.dat FORMAT ASCII;

INPUT INTO orders FROM order.dbf  FORMAT DBASEIII BY NAME
(customer_id, item_number, order_quantity, order_date)
```

OUTPUT

The OUTPUT command allows you to export the contents of a SELECT or INPUT command to a file. If no SELECT or INPUT command precedes the OUTPUT command, an error message will be reported. The following is the syntax for the OUTPUT command:

```
OUTPUT     TO filename
     [ FORMAT outputformat ]
     [ DELIMITED BY delimiter ]
     [ QUOTE quote_character [ ALL ] ]
     [ COLUMN WIDTHS (colwidth1, colwidth2,...) ]
```

The following list explains the components of the OUTPUT command:

■ TO filename. This specifies the output data file name where that data will be written.

■ FORMAT outputformat. The output format is the format of the output file. If you do not specify an output format, the default output format (usually ASCII) is used. Valid values for the output format are:

  ■ **ASCII.** The output will be in ASCII format, with one row per line. ASCII is the default OUTPUT format.

  Columns will be separated by commas (or the user-defined column delimiter using the DELIMITED BY clause in the OUTPUT SQL statement).

All strings will be enclosed in single quotes (or the string defined in the QUOTE clause in the OUTPUT SQL statement). If you specify ALL in the OUTPUT SQL statement, then all columns (not just strings) will be in quotes.

Watcom also recognizes some C++ special characters denoted by a backslash. "\n" represents a carriage return–line feed combination. (This is often called the newline character.) "\xDD" represents a character using a hexadecimal character where DD is located. "\\" indicates a single slash.

■ **DBASEII.** The output from the OUTPUT SQL statement will be in dBASE II format.

■ **DBASEIII.** The output from the OUTPUT SQL statement will be in dBASE III format.

> **Caution**
>
> dBASE II output can have a maximum of only 32 columns, and dBASE III and FoxPro can have a maximum of only 128 columns. Also, any strings longer than 255 characters will be truncated in dBASE II and dBASE III.

■ **DIF.** The output from the OUTPUT SQL statement will be in standard Data Interchange Format.

■ **FIXED.** The output from the OUTPUT SQL statement will be in fixed columns, determined by the COLUMN WIDTHS clause in the OUTPUT statement. If you omit the COLUMN WIDTHS clause, the column width will be the maximum width allowed for each column's data type.

> **Note**
>
> No headings will be displayed with FIXED output.

■ **FOXPRO.** The output from the OUTPUT SQL statement will be in FoxPro format.

> **Caution**
>
> dBASE II output can have a maximum of only 32 columns, and dBASE III and FoxPro can have a maximum of only 128 columns. Also, any strings longer than 255 characters will be truncated in dBASE II and dBASE III.

■ **LOTUS.** Output will be in Lotus 1-2-3 format with headings along the top of the spreadsheet.

> **Caution**
>
> There is no limit to the size of spreadsheet Watcom SQL can produce. However, many spreadsheets have limitations on the size of the spreadsheet they can work on or produce. If you are using OUTPUT to take the data from the database to a spreadsheet, make sure the spreadsheet is large enough to handle the file's size.

■ **SQL.** Output is formatted into an ISQL INPUT command, required to replace the information on the file.

■ **TEXT.** This format is similar to the FIXED format; however, headings are stored in the output file in column format along with tab-delimited columns.

■ **WATFILE.** The output will be a WATFILE file. WATFILE is a tabular file format available from Watcom.

■ DELIMITED BY delimiter. This clause lets you specify the delimiter for an ASCII output file. The default is a comma. Non-ASCII file formats ignore the DELIMITED BY clause.

■ QUOTE quote_character. The QUOTE clause lets you specify the quote character. If omitted, the quote character default is a single quote. If ALL is added to the QUOTE clause, all output will be in quotes.

■ COLUMN WIDTHS (colwidth1, colwidth2,). The COLUMN WIDTHS clause lists the column widths for a FIXED output format. If COLUMN WIDTHS are omitted, the widths used are the maximum widths for each data type in the source table of the SELECT or INPUT command preceding the OUTPUT command.

VI

References

An example of the OUTPUT command is as follows:

```
SELECT * FROM customer;
OUTPUT TO customer.dat FORMAT TEXT;
```

The above statement will SELECT all records from the customer table and output them to the CUSTOMER.DAT file in TEXT format.

> **Note**
>
> As an alternative to the OUTPUT command, Watcom SQL also supports output *redirection*. Redirection is achieved by using a greater than sign followed immediately by a pound sign and the filename with no spaces (such as ">#filename"). The following command SELECTs all records from the customer table and puts the output in the file CUSTOMER.DAT:
>
> ```
> SELECT * FROM customer >#customer.dat
> ```

PARAMETERS

Using the READ SQL command, you can pass parameters to an SQL command file. PARAMETERS are used to identify the parameters to the SQL command file. The following READ SQL statement starts processing the SQL in the sqlfile.sql SQL command file:

```
READ sqlfile.sql 50
```

In this command, the number 50 is passsed to the SQL command file for processing. Inside the SQL command file, a PARAMETERS clause must be present to process the parameter. The following SQL is a typical example of an SQL command file that expects a parameter:

```
PARAMETERS number_of_orders;
       . . .
SELECT orders.customer_id, customer.customer_name, count(*)
      FROM customer, orders
      WHERE orders.customer_id = customer.customer_id
      GROUP BY orders.customer_id
      HAVING count(*) >= {number_of_orders}
      >#bestcust.dat;
```

The previous SQL SELECTs every customer_id that has a number of orders greater than the passed number_of_orders. The output is redirected into BESTCUST.DAT. If no parameters are passed to the SQL command file, PARAMETERS will prompt the user for the value of the parameters.

READ

The READ command reads SQL commands from an SQL file. The SQL file contains any valid ISQL commands, including other READ statements. Thus, you could have several SQL files read at once. The syntax for the READ command is as follows:

```
READ sqlfile [parameters]
```

READ searches for the `sqlfile` in the current director, then searches the path specified by the environment variable SQLPATH, and then searches the path specified by the PATH environment variable.

If a PARAMETERS clause is specified in the SQL command file, READ can pass parameter values to the SQL command file, or the user is prompted for the parameter values. The following is an example of the READ command:

```
READ bestcust.sql 10
```

The above READ command will execute the SQL command file BESTCUST.SQL. In addition, a parameter value of 10 will be passed to the BESTCUST.SQL command file where a PARAMETERS clause (hopefully) will be present to process the parameter. (If no PARAMETERS clause is present, any parameters passed will be ignored.)

> **Note**
>
> RTSQLW automatically issues a READ command to execute SQL command files. The following command will READ the CLEANDB.SQL command file:
>
> ```
> RTSQLW cleandb.sql
> ```

▶ See "Using RTSQLW.EXE," p. 640

SYSTEM

SYSTEM is not available with Windows programs. However, if you're running the DOS or QNX version of Watcom SQL, use the SYSTEM command to run DOS commands or QNX commands. The format for the SYSTEM command is as follows:

```
SYSTEM [operating-system-command]
```

If you do not specify an operating system, SYSTEM opens an operating system shell. To exit the shell and return to your ISQL environment, type **EXIT** in DOS or press Ctrl+D in QNX.

An example of the SYSTEM command is as follows:

```
SYSTEM FORMAT A:
```

This above command will format a floppy in drive A: in the MS-DOS environment using the DOS version of Watcom SQL.

> **Note**
>
> Although there is no way to run another program from the Watcom SQL Windows environment, you can use Watcom SQL in conjunction with PowerBuilder, and use the PowerBuilder RUN function as follows:
>
> ```
> RUN ("FORMAT A:")
> ```

From Here...

The ISQLW environment and ISQL commands make administering a database much easier. For related topics, check out the following chapters:

- Chapter 12, "Implementing Procedures and Triggers," discusses the use of stored procedures and triggers within the Watcom SQL environment. Included are SQL commands that affect procedures and triggers. Also included are several ESQL-only commands.

- Chapter 14, "Implmenting Watcom SQL with SQLPP (C and C++)," discusses using Watcom SQL in a C++ environment. Many ESQL-only commands are covered in this chapter.

- Chapter 22, "SQL Commands," discusses standard SQL commands that can be used within computer programs, as well as within the ISQLW environment.

- Chapter 24, "Using Watcom Utilities," describes the utility programs that come with Watcom SQL. These programs can be used interchangably with the DBTOOL SQL commands discussed in this chapter.

Chapter 24

Using Watcom SQL Utilities

by Charles A. Wood

Watcom SQL includes several utilities that help you administer a database. These utilities allow you to perform functions outside your database in a Windows environment without needing to write a program. Also, if you want to distribute your Watcom database, a Windows run-time version is available with many utility programs.

The following topics are covered in this reference chapter:

■ The utilities included with Watcom SQL, their syntax, and descriptions of their use

■ Accessing your Watcom SQL database engine via the ODBC interface

■ Accessing your Watcom SQL database engine via the PowerBuilder database painter

■ Using utilities to help you run your Watcom SQL database as a network server

> **Note**
>
> As with the rest of this book, the Windows programs are used as a default. However, there are also DOS, QNX, and OS/2 versions of Watcom SQL that do not have the W extension in the program name. For instance, the DOS version of DBINITW.EXE is DBINIT.EXE.

◀ See "Understanding Connection Parameters," p. 579

VI

Reference

> **Note**
>
> Several of these programs require you to specify a connection string, also known as connection parameters. Connection parameters are discussed in Chapter 23.

> **Note**
>
> DBTOOLSW.EXE is no longer included with Watcom SQL. The functionality was added to ISQLW.EXE.

Using DB32W.EXE, DBSTARTW.EXE, RT32W.EXE, and RTSTARTW.EXE

A *database engine* is a program that controls access to a database. Watcom SQL comes with four database engines. Each engine uses the same parameters and performs basically the same function. The Watcom SQL database engines are:

- **DB32W.EXE.** DB32W.EXE is the default database, which is used to read and write a Watcom SQL database with 32-bit access. DB32W requires an 80386 chip or higher; 32-bit access requires that Windows be run in Enhanced mode.

◀ See "DBTOOL CREATE DATA-BASE," p. 583

> **Note**
>
> *32-bit access* takes advantage of the advanced architecture of the Intel 80386 chip (and later versions of Intel processors) to increase the amount of data that can be transferred at once. 32-bit access can dramatically speed up your disk access.
>
> *Enhanced mode.* You can run Windows 3.1 in two modes: Standard or Enhanced. Standard mode allows access to extended memory and task switching. Enhanced mode allows 32-bit disk access and sets up virtual memory by using free space on your hard drive. Enhanced mode is usually faster for disk-intensive applications due to its 32-bit disk access. In addition, Enhanced mode leaves more memory for the current task—thereby reducing the out of memory application errors.

- **DBSTARTW.EXE.** DBSTARTW.EXE is the database to use for 16-bit access to your Watcom SQL database. Functionally, DBSTARTW.EXE is equivalent to DB32W.EXE, except that the page size defined in the DBINITW program cannot exceed 1024 bytes, and DBSTARTW tends to run slower than DB32W.

- **RT32W.EXE.** RT32W.EXE is a 32-bit run-time version of Watcom SQL. RT32W.EXE has disabled some commands, like the CREATE and ALTER SQL commands.

- **RTSTARTW.EXE.** RTSTARTW.EXE is a 16-bit run-time version of Watcom SQL. RTSTARTW.EXE has all the capabilities and limitations of RT32W.EXE, except that RTSTARTW.EXE runs a little slower and can't access any database with a page size larger than 1024 bytes.

The syntax for the Watcom SQL engines is as follows:

```
engine_name  [engine_switches] [database_file [database_switches]]
```

engine_name can be DB32W, RT32W, DBSTARTW, or RTSTARTW. If you have a 386 or 486 machine, you should use RT32W or DB32W.

database_file is the name of your database file on your hard drive. If you omit the extension of the database file, it searches for a WRT extension followed by a DB extension. The *database_file* can be a Watcom 4.0 database or a Watcom 3.2 database.

Tip

If you can use DB32W and RT32W instead of DBSTARTW and RTSTARTW, then do so. DB32W runs faster and can access databases with a higher page size than DBSTARTW.

Troubleshooting

I have no trouble attaching to my 3.2 database using my 3.2 Watcom SQL engine. However, I cannot attach to my database using my 4.0 engine. What's wrong?

Watcom SQL version 3.2 has been "patched" to level E. If you have an earlier version of Watcom SQL 3.2, such as 3.2A or 3.2B, you may have trouble attaching to your 3.2 database or upgrading it. Some earlier versions of Watcom SQL let errors (especially index errors) exist in the database. These errors were not allowed to exist in the later patches. Try unloading your 3.2 database with your current 3.2 engine with the data only option, then reloading your database with either your "patched" 3.2 engine or your 4.0 engine. Your 4.0 engine can then be used to access your 3.2 database.

Be cautious. If you reload your database using your 4.0 engine, your 3.2 engine can no longer access your database. See "Using DBUNLOAW.EXE" and "Using DBUPGRDW.EXE," later in this chapter.

VI

Reference

> **Note**
>
> *Patches* are minor upgrades and bug fixes to a program. When Watcom (the company) encounters a bug in the Watcom SQL program, they often fix it as a patch and then release the patch (via CompuServe or their own bulletin board) to be downloaded and applied. Instructions on how to apply each patch are in a READ.ME file contained in the download.

engine_switches	**The engine switches in use are as follows:**
-a translog	Apply the transaction log named by translog. This option applies the log and then terminates.
-b	Use bulk mode. Although this is handy for large quantities of data at a time, I do not recommend it for everyday use because it's not as safe as normal operations and only allows one user.

> **Note**
>
> *Bulk mode* is used for moving large volumes of data. Using bulk mode saves time because ROLLBACK logs and transaction logs are not kept. In bulk mode, no records are locked and no automatic COMMITs are performed after data definition commands.
>
> Running a database in bulk mode is a little risky. Since there is no automatic COMMIT, ROLLBACK statements roll back the database to the last explicit COMMIT. Because there is no rollback log, you can't use savepoints; aborting a command will always cause the database transaction to roll back to the last explicit COMMIT. Finally, with no transaction log, there is no log of the changes.
>
> If you must use bulk mode, be sure to back up first.

Tip

The -a and -f database switches are often used for database recovery.

-c cache-size	Set cache-size. This number sets the size of the cache. Any cache size less than 10,000 is assumed to be kilobytes. If an M is at the end of the number, megabytes is assumed. By default, the database uses 2M cache.
-f	Force-start the database. This starts the database without a log, and immediately terminates. This is handy for clearing the database after the log has been lost.
-ga	Forces the database to shut down after the last database disconnects in a multi-user environment.
-gc num	Sets the maximum length in minutes that the database engine can run without performing a CHECKPOINT.

engine_switches	**The engine switches in use are as follows:**
-gd level	Sets the database permission. Valid levels of permission include the following:
dba	Only users with DBA authority can start new databases.
all	All users can start new databases.
none	No new databases can be started. The default is dba.
-gf	Starts the database but disables all triggers.
-gi num	Sets the maximum number of concurrent I/O requests that the database engine can process. The default is one.
-gn num	Sets the number of concurrent execution threads that the database engine can process at once. For DB32W, the default is 20.

Tip
Increasing the number of concurrent I/O requests can significantly improve performance.

> **Note**
>
> An *execution thread* is a request that the database engine will process. Using the -gn switch with the Watcom SQL engine determines the number of concurrent requests that the database can process at one time.

-gp size	Sets the maximum page size allowed. Valid values of size are 512, 1024, 2048, or 4096.

> **Caution**
>
> The database engine can fail if the engine opens databases of different sizes. Try to open the databases with the largest page size first to avoid this problem, or specify `-gp 4096` in your DB32W or RT32W engine command line.
>
> DBSTARTW and RTSTARTW only allow a size of 1024 bytes.

◀ See "SET OP-
TION," p. 565

◀ See "Backing
Up and Recov-
ery," p. 289

◀ See "Recovery
from System
Failure," p. 302

-gr num	Sets the estimated recovery time to restore all pages to the most recent checkpoint using the checkpoint log, and to apply any changes made from the checkpoint log to the time of failure from the transaction log in the event of a disk failure. This option sets your checkpoint frequency of your database.
-gs size	Sets the stack size of every thread in the engine. Size signifies the number of bytes in the stack.

(continues)

VI

Reference

engine_switches	**The engine switches in use are as follows:**
-n name	Sets the name of the database engine. By default, the engine name is the name of the database file. (For the Inventory Tracking system, the default is INVENTRY.)
-noems	Doesn't use expanded memory.
-noext	Doesn't use extended memory.
-nofar	Doesn't use DOS 640k for extra cache.

> **Caution**
>
> You need to use the -nofar option when using certain compilers and applications, such as Borland C++, that require contiguous additional memory to allocate.

-noxms	Doesn't use XMS memory.
-q	Quiet mode. Doesn't print any messages.
-u size	Uses only size bytes of lower (640K) memory. Use this option if your application takes up too much lower memory space, but it can really slow down your database. Never set the size lower than 200K. Any size less than 10,000 is assumed to be kilobytes.

database_switches	**The database switches in use are as follows:**
-d	Uses normal DOS input and output instead of direct BIOS input and output. DOS calls can be faster than BIOS calls when you have a small database (less than 3M), and you have disk-caching software running. If your database is over 10M, don't use this flag.
-n name	Sets the name of the database. By default, the name of the database is the name of the database_file with the path and the extension removed. (For example, the name of C:\WSQL40\WIN\SAMPLE.DB is sample.)
-v	Logs old values of columns on SQL updates, as opposed to only enough information to uniquely identify the key. Use this if you're working on a copy of the database.

Accessing Your Database Engine through the ODBC Interface

When using the ODBC interface, as in PowerBuilder, you can choose what database engine you want to use for each database. First, click the OCBCADM in your Windows environment. The Microsoft ODBC Administrator dialog box appears, as shown in figure 24.1.

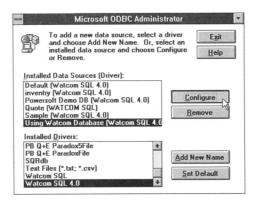

Fig. 24.1
Use the Microsoft ODBC Administrator dialog box to configure your Watcom SQL database to the Microsoft ODBC standard.

From here, choose Watcom SQL 4.0 and then your database. Click **C**onfigure to open the Watcom SQL ODBC Configuration dialog box (see fig. 24.2).

Fig. 24.2
The Watcom SQL ODBC Configuration dialog box is used to specify information about your Watcom SQL database.

VI

Reference

From here, select **Cu**stom in the Database Startup group, and then click **O**ptions. The Startup Options dialog box appears, as shown in figure 24.3.

Fig. 24.3
You can specify
the database
engine and
switches using the
Startup Options
dialog box.

In the Startup Options dialog box, specify the database engine name and any engine switches in the Start Command text box, and any database switches in the Database Switches text box. Now, when you use ODBC to open your Watcom SQL database, your database starts with the proper engine, as well as the proper switches.

Accessing Your Database Engine through the PowerBuilder Interface

The database engines are the only Watcom SQL program you can run in PowerBuilder. To define your database engine, access the database painter by clicking the Database icon. Then open the File menu, and choose Configure ODBC (see fig. 24.4).

Fig. 24.4
You can do any
database configu-
ration when you
access the
Configure ODBC
menu option.

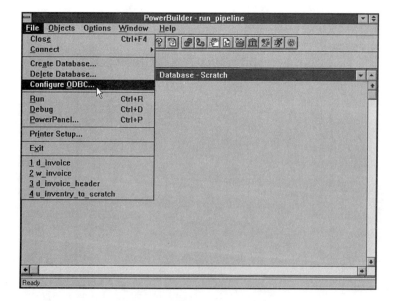

The Configure ODBC dialog box appears (see fig. 24.5). Select the database driver for your database and choose your data source (database).

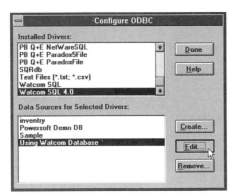

Fig. 24.5
The Configure ODBC dialog box allows you to choose what database and database driver to use.

Click on **E**dit. This pulls up the WATCOM SQL ODBC Configuration dialog box (refer to fig. 24.2). From here, you configure your database the same way you did in figures 24.2 and 24.3.

Troubleshooting

My Watcom SQL program works fine on my computer and on all computers with PowerBuilder or Watcom SQL installed, but when I try to make a stand-alone version to distribute my PowerBuilder application, the distributed version can't access the database. What should I do?

When you install PowerBuilder, your Watcom databases are configured to use DB32W as the starting program. The run-time version does not have DB32W or DBSTARTW. Therefore, you must run RT32W or RTSTARTW when using the Watcom run-time version. Be sure you change it if you are distributing Watcom's run-time SQL version with your program.

Now you have to set up a profile to connect to your new database inside PowerBuilder. Choose **F**ile, **C**onnect, and then **S**etup (see fig. 24.6).

You should now see the Database Profiles dialog box shown in figure 24.7. To define a new database, click **N**ew.

The Database Profile Setup dialog box appears (see fig. 24.8). Enter the profile name you want to use in PowerBuilder, the database driver you'll be using (ODBC), your user ID and password, and the database name. Then click OK.

Fig. 24.6
Click on **F**ile,
Connect, and then
Setup to create or
define an existing
ODBC setup to
your PowerBuilder
environment.

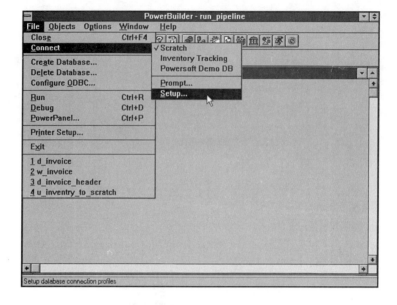

Fig. 24.7
The Database
Profiles dialog box
lets you edit an
existing database
profile or create a
new one.

Fig. 24.8
The Database
Profile Setup
dialog box allows
you to enter
profile informa-
tion about your
database for use in
PowerBuilder.

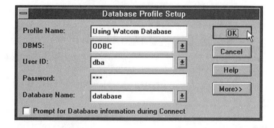

When you click OK, the SQL Data Sources dialog box appears (see fig. 24.9).
PowerBuilder needs to know what data source to use. Pick the database you're
defining and click OK.

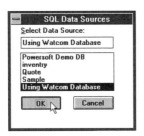

Fig. 24.9
You choose what database to connect to in the SQL Data Sources dialog box.

Troubleshooting

I can't find the database I want to connect to in the SQL Data Sources dialog box. What's wrong?

If you can't find your data source in the SQL Data Sources dialog box, then you haven't defined your database to ODBC. Make sure you created your database using **F**ile, **C**reate Database, the DBTOOL CREATE DATABASE command, or the DBINITW.EXE utility, and then define your database to ODBC using the examples in figures 24.1, 24.2, and 24.3. Your database will then appear in the SQL Data Sources dialog box. See "Using DBINITW.EXE" later in this chapter.

◀ See "DBTOOL," p. 579

The Database Profiles dialog box now lists the PowerBuilder database profile you developed (see fig. 24.10). When you select that database and click OK, PowerBuilder connects to the database for you.

Fig. 24.10
The Database Profiles dialog box lists all profiles created so far, including any new ones just created.

VI

Reference

Using DBBACKW.EXE

DBBACKW makes a backup copy of all the files that make up a single database, which includes all tablespaces and log files. The only difference between using DBBACKW.EXE and the DOS COPY command, or the Windows File Manager is that DBBACKW allows you to back up your database when another database is running, and DBBACKW lets you erase and restart your transaction file. The syntax for the DBBACKW.EXE utility is as follows:

```
DBBACKW [switches] directory
```

The directory is the directory on disk where DBBACK copies your database and database files.

Valid switches for the DBBACKW command are:

Flag	Description
-c connection_parameters	Supplies database connection parameters (see Chapter 23 for more details).
-d	Does not back up the transaction log. Specifying -d backs up all database, dbspace, and write files.
-q	Quiet mode. Suppresses all output.
-r	Renames and restarts the transaction log. The old transaction log has the same name as the current transaction log, but with the first available number for an extension starting with 000. The first transaction log file name is tranlog.000 (where tranlog is the name of the transaction log), then tranlog.001 on the next backup, then tranlog.002, tranlog.003, and so on. This option forces a transaction log backup, even if you specify -d or -w.

Troubleshooting

You said I could back up my entire database using DBBACKW when the database is in use. However, when I try, the backup doesn't finish until I kick everyone off the database. Why is that?

If you specify the -r flag to rename and restart the transaction log, DBBACKW waits until all transactions are committed before allowing the backup. With certain database designs or with extremely heavy usage, the database is rarely committed until everyone disconnects from the database.

-s "cmd"	-s specifies the command line to start the database engine or network requester (DBCLIENW). If you don't use this flag, it checks the environment variable SQLCONNECT. If SQLCONNECT is not defined, the default is DBSTARTW -q %d (where %d is the database name).

Flag	Description
-t	Only backs up the transaction log.

> **Note**
>
> You will often use transaction log backups to incrementally back up a database since the last full backup. If you manage the transaction log properly, it's easy and quick to do a transaction log backup.

Flag	Description
-w	Only backs up the write file without backing up the database, dbspace, or transaction log files. See "Using DBWRITEW.EXE" later in this chapter.
-x	Deletes and restarts the transaction log. This forces a transaction log backup, even if you specify -d or -w.
-y	Replaces any existing files without confirmation.

◀ See "DBTOOL CREATE WRITE FILE," p. 585

Troubleshooting

I need to back up my database, but I receive an error message that says I do not have permission. What can I do?

You need DBA authority to back up a database. There are two ways to get around this restriction. First (and best), have your Database Administrator grant you DBA authority, or (even better) pawn off the backup responsibility to the Database Administrator. If you can't receive DBA authority but still need to back up the database, you can copy the database, transaction log, and write files (if applicable) using the DOS COPY command or the Windows File Manager. However, this method does not let you restart your transaction log.

Tip
All database files will be backed up unless you specify the -d, -t, or -w switch.

An example of the function call is as follows:

```
\wsql40\win\DBBACKW.exe -y -c UID=dba;PWD=sql;DBF=mydb.db c:\backup
```

Using DBCLIENW.EXE

DBCLIENW starts up the network requestor. DBSERVEW must already be running before DBCLIENW will function. DBCLIENW then accesses the server database identified by DBSERVEW using the server name.

VI

Reference

The syntax for DBCLIENW is as follows, in which `server name` is the name given to your server database defined using DBSERVEW:

```
DBCLIENW  [switches]  server_name
```

The DBCLIENW switches are as follows:

-c	Purges previous connections from this client computer. If a client machine is turned off or rebooted while connections still exist to the server, these connections may be left open unless closed by the server. The -c switch can close these connections.
-e	Encrypts all packets passed over the network. Unencrypted packets can pose a security risk. If you are concerned about network security, use this switch.

> **Caution**
>
> Encrypting network packets by using the -e switch can slow down database performance.

-p packet-size	Sets the maximum size of communication packets. The default is 512 bytes, and the minimum is 200 bytes. Typically, the larger the packet size, the faster the database access, *but* the larger the impact on the rest of the server.
-q	Operates in quiet mode. Do not print messages.
-r	Disables blocking by fetching only one row per network request. This can slow down your database access and increase your network traffic.

> **Note**
>
> *Blocking* allows the user to retrieve more than one index or more than one row at a time. Typically, most users process information sequentially based on an index. Watcom SQL tries to block these requests to speed up the database access and network traffic.

-s buffer_space	Specifies the amount of space to use for network buffers (in kilobytes). The default is 64K.
-t timeout	Specifies the amount of time in hundredths of a second before the client will reissue a request if there has been no response from the server. The default is 25 and is usually adequate.

> **Caution**
>
> Setting a timeout too low can affect the entire network because requests will be coming in from the client at a faster rate.

-x network_list Uses only the listed network drivers (NamedPipes, NetBIOS, TCP/IP, or IPX). The default is to try all network drivers.

Using DBCOLLW.EXE

DBCOLLW extracts a *collation* (sorting sequence) from your database, suitable for use with DBINITW, to create a database using a custom collation. This is for the really advanced database power user. A *custom collation* is a sort order that is not ascending or descending. For instance, if you want the city name to appear in ZIP code order when indexing your file, you can use a custom collation. DBCOLLW extracts that collation, if one exists.

The syntax for DBCOLLW is as follows:

```
DBCOLLW [flags] output_file
```

output_file is the file where the collating sequence is stored. The flags in use are as follows:

Flag	Description
-c connection_parameters	Supplies database connection parameters (refer to Chapter 23 for more information).
-e	Includes empty mappings. Normally, collations don't specify the actual value that a character is to sort to. Instead, each line of the collation sequence sorts to one higher than the last one. However, older collations have gaps between some sort positions. DBCOLLW skips these gaps unless you specify the -e flag.
-q	Quiet mode. Suppresses all output.
-s "cmd"	-s specifies the command line to start the database engine or network requester (DBCLIENW). If you don't use this flag, it checks the environment variable SQLCONNECT. If it doesn't define SQLCONNECT, the default is DBSTARTW -q %d (where %d is the database name).

(continues)

VI

Reference

Flag	Description
-x	Use hex for extended characters. Some sites support extended characters, especially for foreign languages. If an extended character goes above hex 7F, this flag converts the character to a two-digit hexadecimal number in the form of \xdd.
-y	Replaces any existing files without confirmation.
-z col-seq	Specifies the collating sequence label. Use this if the label is different than the one being used by the database.

Available collating sequences that come with Watcom SQL are as follows:

Collating Sequence	Description
437EBCDIC	Code Page 437, EBCDIC
437LATIN1	Code Page 437, Latin 1
437ESP	Code Page 437, Spanish
437SVE	Code Page 437, Swedish/Finnish
850CYR	Code Page 850, Cyrillic
850DAN	Code Page 850, Danish
850ELL	Code Page 850, Greek
850ESP	Code Page 850, Spanish
850ISL	Code Page 850, Icelandic
850LATIN1	Code Page 850, Latin 1
850LATIN2	Code Page 850, Latin 2
850NOR	Code Page 850, Norwegian
850RUS	Code Page 850, Russian
850SVE	Code Page 850, Swedish/Finnish
850TRK	Code Page 850, Turkish
852LATIN2	Code Page 852, Latin 2
852CYR	Code Page 852, Cyrillic
855CYR	Code Page 855, Cyrillic

Collating Sequence	Description
856HEB	Code Page 856, Hebrew
857TRK	Code Page 857, Turkish
860LATIN1	Code Page 860, Latin 1
861ISL	Code Page 861, Icelandic
862HEB	Code Page 862, Hebrew
863LATIN1	Code Page 863, Latin 1
865NOR	Code Page 865, Norwegian
866RUS	Code Page 866, Russian
869ELL	Code Page 869, Greek

Using DBERASEW.EXE

DBERASEW erases a database, log file, or write file. It's useful because
Watcom SQL databases and log files are marked read-only. The format for
DBERASEW is as follows:

```
DBERASEW [flags] filename
```

filename is the name of the log file, database file, or write file you want to
delete. The flags in use are as follows:

Flag	Description
-q	Quiet mode. Suppresses all output.
-y	Erases files without confirmation.

Using DBEXPANW.EXE

DBEXPANW expands a compressed database created by DBSHRINW, which is
a good method for distribution. The format for DBEXPANW is:

```
DBEXPANW [flags] compressed_file database
```

compressed_file is the name of the compressed file created by DBSHRINW. If
you don't list an extension, it uses the CDB extension. database is the name

VI

Reference

of the database you want to create. If you don't list an extension, it uses the DB extension. The flags in use are as follows:

Flag	Description
-q	Quiet mode. Suppresses all output.
-y	Replaces any existing files without confirmation.

Using DBINFOW.EXE

DBINFOW displays information about a database file or write file, including the options used to create the database, the name of the transaction log file, and other information. The database engine shouldn't be running when you run DBINFOW. The format for DBINFOW is:

```
DBINFOW [flags] filename
```

filename is the name of the database or write file you want information about. The flags in use are as follows:

Flag	Description
-c connection_parameters	Supplies database connection parameters (see Chapter 23 for more detail).
-q	Quiet mode. Suppresses all output.
-s "cmd"	-s specifies the command line to start the database engine or network requester (DBCLIENW). If you don't use this flag, it checks the environment variable SQLCONNECT. If it doesn't define SQLCONNECT, the default is DBSTARTW -q %d (where %d is the database name).
-u	Outputs page-usage statistics along with the rest of the output.

Using DBINITW.EXE

DBINITW.EXE creates a new database. The syntax for DBINITW is as follows:

```
DBINITW [flags] new-database-file
```

new-database-file is the name of the database file being created. The flags for DBINITW are as follows:

Flag	Description
-b	Specifying -b causes Watcom to ignore trailing spaces when doing comparisons. For instance, "Chuck Wood" and "Chuck Wood " would compare the same. The default is to take trailing spaces into account when doing comparisons.
-c	-c takes case into account when making comparisons. The default is to not take case into account when comparing. For instance, "Chuck Wood" and "CHUCK WOOD" would compare the same.
-e	Specifying -e encrypts your database. This makes your database harder to look at with disk utilities and other programs outside Watcom SQL.

> **Caution**
>
> Some compression programs have a difficult time compressing encrypted files. Since encryption adds a random element to your database, you'll find that encrypted files don't compress nearly as small as non-encrypted files. Also, compression on encrypted files takes longer.

-l	Lists available collating sequences.
-n	Causes your database to run with no transaction log.

> **Caution**
>
> Running a Watcom SQL database without a transaction log can slow down database performance. In addition, a transaction log allows the user the luxury of up-to-the-moment recovery of a corrupted database. Consider carefully before you disable your transaction log.

-p page-size	-p sets the page size. A page is a buffer set aside by Watcom SQL in lower memory for swapping data in and out. Valid page sizes (in bytes) are 512, 1024 (default), 2048, or 4096. A good rule of thumb is the larger the page size, the faster the database. For large multi-user databases, use 4096.

VI

Reference

(continues)

Flag	Description

Tip
You especially
need to change
the collation
sequence when
using Watcom
SQL in non-
English speaking
countries. See
"Using
DBCOLLW.EXE"
later in this
chapter.

> **Caution**
>
> DBSTARTW and RTSTARTW are 16-bit database engines, while DB32W and RT32W are 32-bit database engines. 16-bit database engines (DBSTARTW and RTSTARTW) cannot start a database with a page size larger than 1024. If you need to use 16-bit engines (for 286 machines), then keep the page size at 1024 and develop with DBSTARTW. Otherwise, set the page size to 4096 and develop with DB32W.

Flag	Description
-q	Quiet mode. Suppresses all output.
-s "cmd"	-s specifies the command line to start the database engine or network requester (DBCLIENW). If you don't use this flag, it checks the environment variable SQLCONNECT. If SQLCONNECT is not defined, the default is DBSTARTW -q %d (where %d is the database name).
-t log-name	Use -t to specify your transaction log file name. The default transaction log file name is the database name with a LOG extension.
-z col-seq	-z specifies a collating sequence. You use a collating sequence for comparisons and ordering.

◀ See "Making
Different Collat-
ing Sequences,"
p. 238

▶ See
"SYSCOLLATION,"
p. 710

An example of DBINITW that creates a database called MYDBASE.DB is as follows:

```
DBINITW -p 4096 mydbase
```

Using DBLOGW.EXE

Use DBLOGW to display, change the name of, or disable the transaction log. Its format is as follows:

```
DBLOGW [flags] database
```

database is the name of the database you want to access. The flags in use are as follows:

Flag	Description
-n	Does not use a transaction log.

Flag	Description

> **Caution**
>
> As mentioned earlier, running a Watcom SQL database without a transaction log can slow down database performance. In addition, a transaction log allows the user the luxury of up-to-the-moment recovery of a corrupted database. Consider carefully before you disable your transaction log.

-q	Quiet mode. Suppresses all output.
-t log_name.	Changes the name of the transaction log file to log_name.

Using DBSERVEW.EXE

DBSERVEW starts the database on the network server. Users then attach to the server database using DBCLIENW command discussed earlier. DBSERVEW can manage many clients simultaneously. DBSERVEW and DBCLIENW take the place of DB32W and DBSTARTW in a network environment.

The syntax for DBSERVEW is as follows, in which *database_file* is the name of your database file on your hard drive. If you omit the extension of the database file, it searches for a WRT extension followed by a DB extension. The *database_file* can be a Watcom 4.0 database or a Watcom 3.2 database.

```
DBSERVEW  [server_switches] database_file [database_switches]
```

The DBSERVEW server switches are as follows:

-a translog	Apply the transaction log named by translog. This option applies the log and then terminates.
-b	Use bulk mode. Although this is handy for large quantities of data at a time, I do not recommend it for everyday use because it's not as safe as normal operations and only allows one user.
-c cache-size	Set cache-size. This number sets the size of the cache. The database server will use extra memory for caching database pages. Any cache size less than 10,000 is assumed to be kilobytes. If an M is at the end of the number, megabytes is assumed. By default, the database server uses 2M of cache.

(continues)

VI

Reference

-d	Use normal DOS input and output rather than direct I/O. By default, the network uses low-level direct I/O calls, which can be much faster than normal DOS I/O. However, when your database is small (under 3M) and caching is enabled, DOS calls can be faster. Because of potential slow-downs, it is never recommended to use this switch with extremely large databases (over 10M).
-e	Encrypt all packets passed over the network. Unencrypted packets can pose a security risk. If you are concerned about network security, use this switch.

Tip

The -a and -f database switches are often used for database recovery.

> **Caution**
>
> Encrypting network packets by using the -e switch can slow down database performance.

-f	Force-start the database. This starts the database without a log, and immediately terminates. This is handy for clearing the database after the log has been lost.
-ga	In a multi-user environment, forces the database to shut down after the last database disconnects.
-gc num	Sets the maximum length, in minutes, that the database engine can run without performing a CHECKPOINT.
-gd level	Sets the database permission. Valid levels of permission are:

Tip

Increasing the number of concurrent I/O requests can significantly improve performance.

	dba	Only users with DBA authority can start new databases.
	all	All users can start new databases.
	none	No new databases can be started.

The default is dba.

-gf	Starts the database, but disables all triggers.
-gi num	Sets the maximum number of concurrent I/O requests that the database engine can process. The default is one. This option is only available on the NT and OS/2 versions of the server.
-gn num	Sets the number of concurrent execution threads that the database engine can process at once. For DB32W, the default is 20.
-gp size	Sets the maximum page size allowed. Valid values of size are 512, 1024, 2048, or 4096.

> **Caution**
>
> The database engine can fail if the engine opens databases of different sizes. Try to open the databases with the largest page size first to avoid this problem, or specify -gp 4096 in your DB32W or RT32W engine command line.
>
> DBSTARTW and RTSTARTW only allow a size of 1024 bytes.

◀ See "Backing Up and Recovery," p. 289

◀ See "Recovery from System Failure," p. 302

◀ See "SET OPTION," p. 565

-gr num	Sets the estimated recovery time to restore all pages to the most recent checkpoint using the checkpoint log, and to apply any changes made from the checkpoint log to the time of failure from the transaction log in the event of a disk failure. This option sets your checkpoint frequency of your database.
-gs size	Sets the stack size of every thread in the engine. size signifies the number of bytes in the stack.
-i minutes	Disconnects clients that have not submitted a request for a given number of minutes.

> **Note**
>
> A client machine in the middle of a database transaction will hold locks until the transaction is ended or the connection is terminated. Therefore, if a user accessing the database leaves in the middle of a transaction, no other user can access any locked records and the number of users on a database is limited.
>
> Using the -i flag will prevent a user from monopolizing the resources unless that user is actually working.

-l password	Locks the server keyboard with the specified password.
-n name	Sets the name of the database server. By default, the server name is the name of the database file. The server name specifies the name that is used by DBCLIENW when a client starts up a database. It is also used on the connect statement issued by client applications.
-o filename	Print all server message windows to an output file, in addition to displaying it on the screen.
-p packet-size	Set the maximum of communication packets (the default is 512 bytes; the minimum is 200 bytes). Typically, the larger the packet size, the faster the database access, *but* the larger the impact on the rest of the server.

(continues)

VI

Reference

-r	Disable blocking by fetching only one row per network request. This can slow down your database access and increase your network traffic.
-t time	Shuts down the server at a specified time. This is useful for automated off-line backups. The format for time is HH:MM with HH being 1-23, and MM being 1-60. A date can also be specified in the format "YYYY/MM/DD HH:MM."
-x network_list	Use only the listed network drivers. (NamedPipes, NetBIOS, TCP/IP, or IPX.) The default is to try all network drivers.

The database switches are as follows:

-n name	Sets the name of the database. By default, the name of the database is the name of the database_file with the path and the extension removed. (For example, the name of C:\WSQL40\WIN\SAMPLE.DB is sample.)
-v	Logs old values of columns on SQL updates, as opposed to only enough information to uniquely identify the key. Use this if you're working on a copy of the database.

Using DBSHRINW.EXE

DBSHRINW compresses a database that you can later expand using DBEXPANW. This is a good method for distribution. The format for DBSHRINW is:

```
DBSHRINW [flags] database [compressed_file]
```

database is the name of the database you want to compress. If you don't list an extension, it uses the DB extension. compressed_file is the name of the compressed file to be created. This defaults to the database name with a CDB extension. If you don't list an extension, it uses the CDB extension. The flags in use are as follows:

Flag	Description
-q	Quiet mode. Suppresses all output.
-y	Replaces any existing files without confirmation.

Using **DBSTOPW.EXE**

DBSTOPW.EXE stops the database engine or the multi-user client (DBCLIENW). All resources return to Windows. The format for DBSTOPW.EXE is as follows:

```
DBSTOPW [flags] database_name
```

> **Note**
>
> Don't use *database_name* when you use the DBSTOP.EXE program in the DOS version of Watcom SQL.

database_name refers to the name of the database engine or the multi-user client (DBCLIENW) currently running. The flags used are as follows:

Flag	Description
-c	Causes the DBSTOPW utility to fail if there are any active connections.
-q	Quiet mode. Suppresses all output.

> **Caution**
>
> -q also suppresses error messages in DBSTOPW.EXE. If this happens, you may not know whether DBSTOPW.EXE was successful.

> **Note**
>
> The QNX version of Watcom SQL also supports a *-p pswd* switch in the QNX-related program, DBSTOP. The *-p pswd* switch allows you to specify the password to unlock the server.

Using **DBTRANW.EXE**

DBTRANW.EXE translates the transaction log file into an SQL command file. You often use DBTRANW.EXE for recovery of a database. The format for DBTRANW is as follows:

```
DBTRANW [flags] transaction_log [SQL_log]
```

VI

Reference

transaction_log refers to the transaction log of the database. *SQL_log* specifies the SQL command file created by DBTRANW.EXE. The flags used with DBTRANW.EXE are as follows:

Flag	Description
-a	Includes transactions in the SQL_file that have not yet been committed.
-f	Only includes transactions in the SQL_file that have been completed since the last checkpoint.
-r	Removes uncommitted transactions. (This is the default.)
-s	Produces ANSI standard SQL transactions, which is handy for converting to another database. The default is to use Watcom SQL transactions.
-t	Includes trigger-generated transactions in the SQL_file. This normally isn't done through SQL, although if your database has the same triggers defined, you don't need this flag.
-u user1, user2,...	Selects transactions for listed users. The default is all users.
-x user1, user2,...	Excludes transactions for listed users. The default is no exclusions.
-y	Replaces any existing files without confirmation.
-z	Includes trigger-generated transactions in the SQL_file as comments.

The following is an example of a DBTRANW command that converts all transactions, as well as uncommitted transactions, from MYDBASE.DB to MYDB.SQL:

```
DBTRANW -a MYDBASE MYDB.SQL
```

Using DBUNLOAW.EXE

You use DBUNLOAW to unload a database into an ASCII file containing SQL statements called RELOAD.SQL (unless you use the flags described here to change the name of your output file). The following is the syntax of DBUNLOAW:

```
DBUNLOAW  [flags] directory
```

directory refers to the output directory where the database unloads. The flags used with DBUNLOAW.EXE are as follows:

Flag	Description
-d	Unloads data only. Doesn't unload the schema commands (CREATE TABLE, CREATE INDEX, and so on). RELOAD.SQL (or your user-defined SQL command file) contains INSERT statements only, and only reloads data into an existing database.
-n	Unloads schema definition only (CREATE TABLE, CREATE INDEX, and so on). RELOAD.SQL (or your user-defined SQL command file) contains the commands to rebuild the database structure only, and doesn't include INSERT statements.
-q	Quiet mode. Suppresses all output.
-r reload-file	-r allows you to specify the name of the generated SQL command file to reload the database. If you don't specify -r, RELOAD.SQL is the default.
-s "cmd"	-s specifies the command line to start the database engine or network requester (DBCLIENW). If you don't use this flag, it checks the environment variable SQLCONNECT. If SQLCONNECT is not defined, the default is DBSTARTW -q %d (where %d is the database name).
-u	Normally, the data to be INSERTed unloads in primary key format. Specifying -u speeds up the unload, as well as ignores any indexing problems.
-v	Verbose output. Displays any additional status messages.
-y	Replaces any existing files without confirmation.

An example of DBUNLOAW is as follows:

```
DBUNLOAW -c UID=admin;PWD=school;ENG=sample \unload
```

This command creates RELOAD.SQL in the \unload directory, which contains SQL calls to duplicate the sample database from the last backup.

Using DBUPGRDW.EXE

DBUPGRDW.EXE upgrades a 3.2 database to a 4.0 database. Running DBUPGRDW.EXE on a database allows the user to add 4.0 features to his database, such as stored procedures. The format for DBUPGRDW.EXE is as follows:

```
DBUPGRDW [flags] database
```

database refers to the database being upgraded. The flags for DBUPGRDW are as follows:

Flag	Description
-c connection_parameters	Supplies database connection parameters (see Chapter 23 for more detail).
-q	Quiet mode. Suppresses all output.

> **Caution**
>
> While Watcom SQL 4.0 can access Watcom SQL 3.2 databases, the reverse is not true. After you convert a database to version 4.0, any user running version 3.2 cannot access your database.

An example that upgrades the sample database from 3.2 to 4.0 using DBUPGRDW.EXE is as follows:

```
DBUPGRDW -c UID=admin;PWD=school;ENG=sample sample.db
```

Using DBVALIDW.EXE

Tip
Use DBVALIDW in conjunction with DBBACKW before backing up, so any index problems are caught before the backup.

DBVALIDW validates all indexes on a table in the database, and reports any problems.

The syntax for DBVALIDW.EXE is as follows:

```
DBVALIDW [flags] [table_name]
```

table_name is the name of the table you want to validate. If you omit *table_name*, DBVALIDW.EXE validates all tables in the database. The flags for DBVALIDW.EXE are as follows:

Flag	Description
-c connection_parameters	Supplies database connection parameters (see Chapter 23 for more information).
-q	Quiet mode. Suppresses all output.
-s "cmd"	-s specifies the command line to start the database engine or network requester (DBCLIENW). If you don't use this flag, it checks the environment variable SQLCONNECT. If SQLCONNECT is not defined, the default is DBSTARTW -q %d (where %d is the database name).

An example of DBVALIDW, which validates the student table in the sample database, follows:

```
DBVALIDW -c UID=admin;PWD=school;ENG=sample student
```

Using **DBWATCHW.EXE**

DBWATCHW starts the server-monitoring facility. The network requestor (DBCLIENW) must be running prior to issuing the DBWATCHW command. DBWATCHW displays the database server screen on the client machine. It is useful to check who is logged on the database server. You can also use it to display both the server and client statistics on your client machine.

The syntax for DBWATCHW is as follows:

```
DBWATCHW [switches]
```

The valid switches for DBWATCH are as follows:	
-c connection_parameters	Supplies database connection parameters.
-s "command"	Specifies the command string that will be used to start the network requestor (DBCLIENW). The command should contain a %d. The %d will be replaced with the database name. If this option is not specified, the environment variable SQLSTARTW is checked. If there is no SQLSTARTW environment variable defined, the default is "DBCLIENW -q %d."

Using **DBWRITEW.EXE**

You use DBWRITEW.EXE to manage database *write files*, which are files that contain all the changes to a particular database, leaving the original database unchanged. The syntax for DBWRITEW.EXE is as follows:

```
DBWRITEW [flags] database_name [write_name [log_name]]
```

The *database_name* is the name of the database that needs a write file established. *write_name* is the name of the write file. If you don't specify a *write_name*, the write file defaults to the database file name with the WRT extension. You can only specify *log_name* if you specify *write_name*. *log_name* refers to the name of the log file. If you don't specify a *log_name*, then the log file defaults to the *write_name* with the WLG extension. The flags used with the DBWRITEW.EXE utility are as follows:

Flag	Description
-c	Specifying -c creates a new write file. If a write file exists with the same name, it loses all data from the old write file.
-d	-d indicates that the write file is currently in use. -d points an existing write file to a different database.
-q	Quiet mode. Suppresses all output.
-s	Reports write file status only.
-y	Replaces any existing files without confirmation.

Tip

Write files are good to use for testing because they don't allow corruption or data manipulation of the database.

An example of starting up a write file using DBWRITEW, which creates a write file for the sample database, is as follows:

```
DBWRITEW -c \wsql40\win\sample.db \wsql40\win\sample.wrt
```

Using RTSQLW.EXE

RTSQLW allows you to run ASCII files containing interactive run-time SQL statements. The format for RTSQLW is as follows:

```
RTSQLW [flags] SQLfile
```

Tip

RTSQLW is really useful for installation programs. With RTSQLW, you can issue ISQL commands that aren't available to you in Power-Script, such as INPUT and OUTPUT.

The SQLfile is a text file containing the SQL commands to be executed. Flags that can be used with RTSQLW are as follows:

Flag	Description
-b	Does not print the banner. Currently, Watcom ignores this flag.
-c connection_parameters	Supplies database connection parameters (see Chapter 23 for more information).
-q	Quiet mode. Suppresses all output.
-s "cmd"	-s specifies the command line to start the database engine or network requester (DBCLIENW). If you don't use this flag, it checks the environment variable SQLCONNECT. If SQLCONNECT is not defined, the default is DBSTARTW -q %d (where %d is the database name).
-v	Verbose output. Displays additional status messages.
-x	Specifying -x causes RTSQLW to perform a syntax check only without executing any commands.

Troubleshooting

I have an SQL command file that works fine when I run RTSQLW on my computer. However, when I try to distribute the command file to my clients, I get a syntax error. Why?

The RTSQLW program can process every command the ISQLW program can process. However, if you try to use the RTSQLW when distributing your database with the RT32W or RTSTARTW engine, your ALTER and CREATE commands won't work. Try to accomplish your distribution without using the ALTER and CREATE commands.

For instance, if you're trying to create a new table and populate it with data from an old table, instead of using a CREATE statement and filling in the data, ship a blank table and use the INPUT and OUTPUT commands to populate the new table with the old table's data.

Using ISQLW.EXE

Using ISQLW, you can enter SQL commands interactively. You can also execute any single SQL command or an SQL command file (such as the one generated by DBUNLOAW.EXE). The syntax for ISQLW is as follows:

◀ See "Using ISQL with Windows and Windows NT," p. 205

```
ISQLW [flags] [isql_command ¦ SQL_command_file]
```

The `isql_command` is a single SQL command. The `SQL_command_file` is a text file containing SQL statements. If you omit both the `isql_command` and the `SQL_command_file`, it displays the ISQLW environment. The flags for ISQLW are as follows:

Flag	Description
-b	Does not print the banner. Currently, Watcom ignores this flag.
-c connection_ parameters	Supplies database connection parameters (see Chapter 23 for more detail).
-q	Quiet mode. Suppresses all output.
-s "cmd"	-s specifies the command line to start the database engine or network requester (DBCLIENW). If you don't use this flag, it checks the environment variable SQLCONNECT. If SQLCONNECT is not defined, the default is DBSTARTW -q %d (where %d is the database name).
-v	Verbose output. Displays additional status messages.
-x	Specifying -x causes RTSQLW to perform a syntax check only without executing any commands.

VI

Reference

Using REBUILD.EXE

Note

REBUILD.EXE is *not* available in the Windows version of Watcom SQL. It is included here in case you're using another operating system to run your Windows database.

REBUILD.EXE is available on DOS, Windows NT, QNX, or OS/2. REBUILD.EXE rebuilds an old database into a new database. The format is as follows:

```
REBUILD old_database new_database [dba_password]
```

old_database is the source database. *new_database* is the destination database. If you specify *dba_password*, the new database uses the new password for access. You must specify the *dba_password* if the password to the DBA userid in the old-database is not SQL.

REBUILD runs the UNLOAD, DBINIT, and ISQL commands with the default command line options.

Using SQLPP.EXE

SQLPP is an acronym for the SQL preprocessor. When you add Watcom SQL commands to C or C++, the code must go through a preprocessor to convert the SQL commands to C or C++ function calls. The SQLPP preprocessor utility does this.

PowerBuilder does not include SQLPP. However, SQLPP can come in handy when developing C++ user objects inside PowerBuilder. The format for the SQLPP.EXE utility is:

```
SQLPP [flags] C++_program [output_program]
```

The C++_program is the C or C++ program containing the SQL commands. Normally, this has an extension of SQC. The *output_program* is where the new C or C++ program with the SQL calls translated into C function calls is located.

If you omit *output_program*, the *output_program* defaults to the *C++_program* with a C extension (if the *C++_program* doesn't already have a .C extension). If the *C++_program* already uses a C extension, SQLPP places the output in a file with the same name as the *C++_program* with a CC extension.

The format for the flags are as follows:

-c	Tells SQLPP to favor code size. This limits code size and increases execution speed. This is the default.
-d	Tells SQLPP to favor data size. This limits the data size by reusing data structures and initializing variables at run-time. This option might slow down your program and increase code size.
-f	Places the *far* C and C++ keyword before SQLPP generated code.

Note

Use the -f flag for programs written in Borland or Turbo C or C++ using the large and huge memory models, or your SQL might not work and your program might not compile.

-l userid,pswd	Specifies the user ID and passwords for authorization of static SQL statements.
-n	Generates line number information in the C file. If your C++ compiler supports the *#line* meta-variable in C/C++, then this option generates the exact lines in error in your output_program, as opposed to the SQL call in your C++ program.
-o operating_system	The -o flag specifies the Watcom SQL engine type. Valid values for operating_system are: DOS: MS-DOS or DR-DOS DOS32: 32-bit DOS extended program DOS286: 286 DOS extended program WINDOWS: Microsoft Windows WIN32: 32-bit Windows OS232: 32-bit OS/2 WINNT: Microsoft Windows NT NETWARE: Novell NetWare QNX: 16-bit QNX QNX32: 32-bit QNX
-r	Generates reentrant code. It's necessary when you manage multiple SQLCAs.
-q	Quiet mode. Suppresses all output.

VI

Reference

(continues)

The format for the flags are as follows:

-s string_len	Sets the maximum string size that SQLPP places in the C or C++ output_program. This option exists because many C and C++ compilers have an upper limit on the size of strings.

Appendix A

Watcom SQL Reserved Words

Table A.1 lists Watcom SQL reserved words. If these reserved words are used as identifiers in an SQL statement, they should be enclosed in quotation marks.

Table A.1	Watcom SQL Reserved words
Reserved Word	**Function**
ABSOLUTE	ABSOLUTE is used in the FETCH SQL command to retrieve an exact row from a CURSOR, regardless of the CURSOR's current position.
ADD	ADD is used in the ALTER TABLE command to add columns to a table definition.
AFTER	AFTER is used when defining triggers to signify whether the trigger is to take place BEFORE or AFTER a database event.
ALL	ALL PRIVILEGES, or just ALL, is used in the GRANT command to give all table authority to a user. ALL is also used in a SELECT statement as a default that is the opposite of DISTINCT. ALL indicates that all rows that meet the WHERE criteria are to be SELECTed. ALL also is used in a WHERE conditional expression, such as the compare ALL subquery in the following expression. The two uses for ALL can be seen in the following SQL statement:

```
SELECT ALL Customer
    FROM custtable
    WHERE order_cost > ALL (SELECT
    order_cost
        FROM custtable
    WHERE district = 'A');
```

(continues)

Table A.1 Continued	
Reserved Word	**Function**
ALTER	ALTER is an SQL command used in ALTER TABLE and ALTER DBSPACE.
AND	AND is used as a conjuction in a WHERE clause.

ANY	ANY is similar to ALL when used in a subquery as follows:
	
	`SELECT Customer`
	`        FROM custtable`
	`        WHERE order_cost = `**`ANY`**` (SELECT`
	`        order_cost`
	`                FROM custtable`
	`                WHERE district = 'A');`

AS	AS is used to give an expression an alias in the SELECT statement. It also is used in the CAST expression (CAST varname AS datatype).
ASC	ASC is used in the CREATE INDEX command to indicate an ascending index.
ATOMIC	ATOMIC is used inside a compound statement (in a BEGIN and END block). Specifying ATOMIC after BEGIN forces Watcom SQL to view your compound statement as one atomic statement. If any statement fails, all statements fail when ATOMIC has been specified.
AUTOINCREMENT	AUTOINCREMENT is used in the CREATE TABLE clause to declare a column to be AUTOINCREMENT. This is useful for keys that must be unique.
BEFORE	BEFORE is used when defining triggers to signify if the trigger is to take place BEFORE or AFTER a database event.
BEGIN	BEGIN marks the beginning of a compound statement inside a procedure or trigger.

BETWEEN	BETWEEN is used in a WHERE clause indicating that a value is between two other values:
	
	`        . . .`
	`        WHERE order_cost `**`BETWEEN`**` 10000 and 20000`

BINARY	BINARY is a data type identical to CHAR except BINARY is case sensitive, while CHAR is not.
BLOCK	BLOCK is a clause in a FETCH statement that gives the client and server a hint as to how many rows may be fetched by the application.
BY	BY is used in the GROUP BY and ORDER BY clauses in a SELECT statement.
CACHE	CACHE is reserved for Watcom SQL future use.

Reserved Word	Function
CALL	CALL is used to execute a procedure subroutine from within another procedure.
CASCADE	CASCADE is an option used with the CREATE TABLE command to indicate that rows on the table will be deleted if the row on the foreign key table is also deleted.
CASE	CASE is a decision structure used in procedures.
CAST	CAST is used to force data type conversions.
CHAR	CHAR or CHAR(size) defines a character string data type. Size defaults to 1 but can be any value from 1 to 32,767.
CHARACTER	This is the same as CHAR.
CHECK	CHECK is used in the CREATE TABLE and ALTER TABLE commands to add a validity check to a column.
CHECKPOINT	Performs a checkpoint on the database.
CLOSE	CLOSE is used to close a cursor.
COLUMN	COLUMN is used in the GET DATA SQL command.
COMMENT	The COMMENT command stores a comment about a table, index, column, foreign key, user, procedure, or trigger on the database.
COMMIT	COMMIT is used to finalize transactions after an SQL command.
CONNECT	CONNECT is the SQL command used to connect an application to a database.
CREATE	CREATE is used in the CREATE DBSPACE, CREATE INDEX, CREATE PROCEDURE, CREATE TABLE, CREATE TRIGGER, and CREATE VARIABLE commands.
CROSS	CROSS JOIN is used in the FROM clause in a SELECT statement.
CURRENT	CURRENT is used in a positioned UPDATE or positioned DELETE in the WHERE CURRENT OF clause.
CURSOR	DECLARE CURSOR is used to process a multi-row SELECT statement inside a host language or a procedure.
DATE	DATE is a data type used to store dates.
DBA	DBA is an authority granted using the GRANT SQL command.

(continues)

VII

Appendixes

Table A.1 Continued

Reserved Word	Function
DBSPACE	CREATE DBSPACE is used to create a separate file that contains database tables, columns, and indexes.
DEC	This is the same as DECIMAL.
DECIMAL	DECIMAL declares a floating point data type.
DECLARE	DECLARE is used in the DECLARE CURSOR and DECLARE TEMPORARY TABLE commands.
DEFAULT	DEFAULT is used to set default values for NOT NULL columns if a program is attempting to update the column with a NULL. DEFAULT is declared in the CREATE TABLE command.
DELETE	DELETE is an SQL command used to delete rows from a table.
DESC	DESC is used in the CREATE INDEX command to indicate a descending index.
DISTINCT	DISTINCT is used in a SELECT statement to eliminate duplicate rows.
DO	DO is used as a compound statement BEGIN marker of a FOR loop inside a procedure.
DOUBLE	This is the same as FLOAT.
DROP	DROP is used in the DROP DBSPACE, DROP INDEX, DROP PROCEDURE, DROP TABLE, DROP TRIGGER, DROP OPTIMIZER STATISTICS, DROP STATEMENT, DROP VARIABLE, and DROP VIEW statements.
DYNAMIC	DYNAMIC SCROLL is a clause used in the FETCH statement to indicate what FETCH commands are allowed.
EACH	EACH is reserved for Watcom SQL future use.
ELSE	ELSE is used in the IF...ELSE..ENDIF decision structure in a stored procedure.
ELSEIF	ELSEIF is used in the IF...ELSEIF..ENDIF decision structure in a stored procedure.
END	END is used to terminate a compound statement in a procedure. It is always coupled with BEGIN.
ENDIF	ENDIF is used in the IF...ELSEIF..ENDIF decision structure in a procedure.

Reserved Word	Function
ESCAPE	ESCAPE can be used with a LIKE clause in a WHERE condition to specify escape expressions in a string.
EXCEPTION	EXCEPTION is used as an error handling clause inside a compound statement in a procedure.
EXCLUSIVE	EXCLUSIVE is reserved for Watcom SQL future use.
EXECUTE	EXECUTE runs a procedure.
EXISTS	EXISTS is an expression that returns TRUE if a subquery returns at least one row, or FALSE if the subquery returns no rows.
FALSE	FALSE can be placed on a WHERE clause in the following format:
	`... WHERE condition IS [NOT] FALSE ...`
FETCH	FETCH is an SQL command that retrieves rows from a CURSOR.
FIRST	FIRST is used in a FETCH statement to retrieve (or retrieve again) the first row in a cursor.
FLOAT	FLOAT is a double precision floating-point number ranging from 2.22507385850720160e-308 to 1.79769313486231560e+308.
FOR	FOR is in a procedure as a combination CURSOR and loop processing command.
FOREIGN	FOREIGN is used in the FOREIGN KEY declarations inside CREATE and ALTER TABLE SQL commands.
FROM	FROM is used to signify a table name in a SELECT command.
FULL	FULL is reserved for Watcom SQL future use.
GLOBAL	The GLOBAL TEMPORARY clause is used in the CREATE TABLE command to create a temporary table.
GRANT	GRANT is an SQL command used to grant authority to users.
GROUP	GROUP is used in the GROUP BY clause in a SELECT statement.
HAVING	HAVING is a group-selection clause used in a SELECT statement.
HOLD	HOLD is an option while opening a CURSOR that locks selected records on a table.

VII

Appendixes

(continues)

Table A.1 Continued

Reserved Word	Function
IDENTIFIED	IDENTIFIED is used to specify a password in a CONNECT statement.
IF	IF is used in the IF...ELSEIF..ENDIF decision structure in a stored procedure.
IN	IN is used in a SELECT statement in conjunction with a subquery to test if a column value is contained in a result set of another SELECT statement. IN is also used to declare input parameters in a procedure.
INDEX	INDEX is used in a CREATE INDEX command.
INNER	INNER is used in a SELECT statement to signify an inner join.
INOUT	INOUT is used to declare input-output parameters in a procedure.
INSERT	INSERT is an SQL command that adds rows to a table.
INSTEAD	INSTEAD is reserved for Watcom SQL future use.
INT	INT declares a data type to store an integer of values -2,147,483,648 to 2,147,483,647.
INTEGER	This is the same as INT.
INTO	INTO is used to place the results of a SELECT statement in a host variable or procedure variable. INTO is also used in the INSERT command to describe the table being updated.
IS	IS is used on a WHERE statement to test for IS TRUE, IS FALSE, and IS UNKNOWN, as shown below: ... WHERE condition IS [NOT] FALSE ...
ISOLATION	The ISOLATION LEVEL allows a CURSOR to be opened at a different isolation level than is set by the SET OPTION command.
JOIN	JOIN is used on a SELECT statement to automatically join two tables through their primary key and foreign key relationships.
KEY	KEY is used in PRIMARY KEY and FOREIGN KEY clauses in the CREATE TABLE and ALTER TABLE commands. KEY JOIN is also used in the FROM clause in a SELECT statement.
LAST	LAST is used in a FETCH statement to retrieve (or retrieve again) the last row in a CURSOR.

Reserved Word	Function
LEAVE	LEAVE is used in a procedure to leave a loop or compound statement.
LEFT	LEFT OUTER JOIN describes the join in a FROM clause in the SELECT STATEMENT.
LEVEL	The ISOLATION LEVEL allows a CURSOR to be opened at a different isolation level than is set by the SET OPTION command.
LIKE	LIKE is used in a WHERE clause to select records that match a pattern.
LOCAL	LOCAL is reserved for Watcom SQL future use.
LOCK	LOCK is reserved for Watcom SQL future use.
LONG	LONG is used in VARCHAR and BINARY declarations to give string lengths of up to 2G.
LOOP	LOOP is used in conjunction with WHILE to create a loop inside a stored procedure.
MATCH	MATCH is reserved for Watcom SQL future use.
MEMBERSHIP	MEMBERSHIP is used in a GRANT statement to grant a user membership in a user group.
MODE	MODE is reserved for Watcom SQL future use.
MODIFY	MODIFY is used in the ALTER TABLE command to modify a column definition in a table.
NAMED	NAMED is reserved for Watcom SQL future use.
NATURAL	NATURAL JOIN is used in the FROM clause in a SELECT statement.
NEW	NEW is reserved for Watcom SQL future use.
NEXT	NEXT is used in a FETCH statement to retrieve (or retrieve again) the next row in a CURSOR.
NO	NO SCROLL is a clause used with the FETCH command to limit the direction of the FETCH.
NOT	NOT is used in conditions to switch the true and false values. NOT NULL is also used in the CREATE TABLE command to not allow INSERTs or UPDATEs to a column using a NULL value.
NULL	NOT NULL is also in the CREATE TABLE command to not allow INSERTs or UPDATEs to a column using a NULL value.

VII

Appendixes

(continues)

Table A.1 Continued

Reserved Word	Function
NUMERIC	This is the same as DECIMAL.
OF	OF is used in a positioned UPDATE or positioned DELETE in the WHERE CURRENT OF clause.
OFFSET	OFFSET is used in the GET DATA command.
OLD	OLD is reserved for Watcom SQL future use.
ON	ON table-name is a clause used in the GRANT command.
ONLY	FOR READ ONLY is used in the FOR statement in a stored procedure.
OPEN	OPEN is used to open a cursor.
OPTION	OPTION is used in the WITH GRANT OPTION clause. It is also used in the SET OPTION SQL command.
OPTIONS	See OPTION.
OR	OR is used as a conjunction in a WHERE conditional clause.
ORDER	ORDER BY returns rows from a SELECT statement in a specific order.
OTHERS	OTHERS is reserved for Watcom SQL future use.
OUT	OUT is used to declare output parameters in a procedure.
OUTER	OUTER is used to define outer joins in a SELECT statement.
PRECISION	PRECISION is used in the SET OPTION command to set the default precision for the Watcom SQL database.
PREPARE	The PREPARE clause is used to set up a dynamic SQL statement in a host language (such as C++).
PRESERVE	PRESERVE is reserved for Watcom SQL future use.
PRIMARY	PRIMARY KEY clauses are used in the CREATE TABLE and ALTER TABLE commands.
PRIOR	PRIOR is used in a FETCH statement to retrieve (or retrieve again) the previous row in a CURSOR.
PRIVILEGES	ALL PRIVILEGES, or just ALL, is used in the GRANT command to give all table authority to a user.
PROCEDURE	DECLARE PROCEDURE sets up a procedure in a database.

Reserved Word	Function
PURGE	PURGE is a clause in the FETCH statement that causes the client to flush its buffers of all rows and then send the fetch request to the server.
READ	FOR READ ONLY is used in the FOR statement in a stored procedure.
REAL	REAL is a single precision floating-point number ranging from 1.175494351e-38 to 3.402823466e+38.
REFERENCE	See REFERENCES.
REFERENCES	REFERENCES refers to the table a foreign key references using the CREATE TABLE and ALTER TABLE commands.
REFERENCING	See REFERENCES.
RELATIVE	RELATIVE is used in the FETCH SQL command to retrieve a row from a CURSOR relative to the current CURSOR position.
RELEASE	RELEASE SAVEPOINT resets a SAVEPOINT.
RENAME	RENAME is used in the ALTER TABLE command to rename a table or column.
RESIGNAL	RESIGNAL allows you to leave a compound statement containing an EXCEPTION clause with the error still active to be captured by a higher-nested EXCEPTION, or by the database.
RESOURCE	The GRANT RESOURCE gives a user the authority to create and drop tables.
RESTRICT	RESTRICT is used in the foreign key definition of a CREATE TABLE command to create RESTRICT referential integrity.
RESULT	RESULT is used in the CREATE PROCEDURE command to create result sets to be returned to the user.
RESUME	RESUME resets a CURSOR or procedure.
REVOKE	The REVOKE command takes authority away from a user.
RIGHT	RIGHT OUTER JOIN describes the join in a FROM clause in the SELECT STATEMENT.
ROLLBACK	ROLLBACK erases all INSERTs, UPDATEs, and DELETEs since the last COMMIT statement.
ROW	ROW is reserved for Watcom SQL future use.
ROWS	ROWS is reserved for Watcom SQL future use.

(continues)

Table A.1   Continued

Reserved Word	Function
SAVEPOINT	The SAVEPOINT command establishes a savepoint in the current transaction.
SCHEDULE	SCHEDULE is reserved for Watcom SQL future use.
SCROLL	SCROLL, NO SCROLL, and DYNAMIC SCROLL are clauses used in the FETCH statement to indicate what FETCH commands are allowed.
SELECT	The SELECT SQL statement queries the database for information.
SET	SET is used in the SET CONNECTION, SET OPTION, SET SQLCA, and SET variable commands.
SHARE	SHARE is reserved for Watcom SQL future use.
SIGNAL	The SIGNAL command forces an error exception in a procedure.
SMALLINT	SMALLINT is a data type whose variables can be between -32,768 and 32,767.
SOME	SOME is reserved for Watcom SQL future use.
SQLCODE	SQLCODE is a system constant that returns the current SQLCode.
SQLSTATE	SQLSTATE is a system constant that returns the current SQLSTATE code.
STATEMENT	STATEMENT is reserved for Watcom SQL future use.
STATISTICS	The DROP OPTIMIZER STATISTICS command resets optimizer statistics.
SUBTRANS	SUBTRANS is reserved for Watcom SQL future use.
SUBTRANSACTION	SUBTRANSACTION is reserved for Watcom SQL future use.
TABLE	TABLE is used in the CREATE TABLE and ALTER TABLE commands.
TEMPORARY	The GLOBAL TEMPORARY clause is used in the CREATE TABLE command to create a temporary table.
THEN	THEN is used in the IF...ELSEIF...ELSE...ENDIF decision structure in a procedure.
TIME	TIME is a data type used to store times.

Reserved Word	Function
TIMESTAMP	TIMESTAMP is a data type used to store date/time combinations.
TO	TO userid is a clause used in the GRANT command.
TRIGGER	TRIGGER is used in the CREATE TRIGGER and ALTER TRIGGER commands.
TRUE	TRUE can be placed on a WHERE clause in the following format: `... WHERE condition IS [NOT] TRUE ...`
UNION	UNION is used in a SELECT statement to combine two tables before selecting information.
UNIQUE	UNIQUE is used when creating an index or foreign key to force a unique value.
UNKNOWN	UNKNOWN is used to test if a NULL value is present. UNKNOWN can be placed on a WHERE clause in the following format: `... WHERE condition IS [NOT] UNKNOWN ...`
UPDATE	The UPDATE command changes the column values in a row.
USER	USER is used in the CREATE USER and GRANT commands.
USING	The USING DESCRIPTOR clause is used when a descriptor is called for inside a host language (such as USING SQLCA).
VALIDATE	VALIDATE TABLE is an SQL command used to validate rows and indexes in a table.
VALUE	See VALUES.
VALUES	VALUES is used in the INSERT command to tell what values are to be inserted.
VARCHAR	This is the same as CHAR.
VARIABLE	VARIABLE is used in the CREATE VARIABLE and DROP VARIABLE commands.
VARYING	VARYING is included in Watcom SQL as a data type to provide ANSI compatiblity with CHAR data type declarations. It has no effect.
VIEW	VIEW is used in the CREATE VIEW and DROP VIEW commands.

(continues)

VII

Appendixes

Table A.1 Continued

Reserved Word	Function
WHEN	WHEN is used in conjunction with a CASE evaluation in a procedure.
WHERE	WHERE is a clause used in several SQL statements that allows selection of specific rows that meet a certain criteria.
WHILE	WHILE is a looping structure used in procedures.
WITH	WITH HOLD is an option while opening a CURSOR that locks selected records on a table.
WORK	WORK is reserved for Watcom SQL future use.

Appendix B

Watcom SQL Limitations

Watcom SQL is designed to handle any database—from a small single-user database to a large multi-user corporate database. Although some limitations exist (listed in table B.1), these limits are usually not reached before the memory and disk space run out of capacity.

Table B.1 Watcom SQL Limitations	
Category	**Limit**
Database Size	2G per tablespace, 12 tablespaces per file
Number of Tables Per Database	32,767 (32K)
Table Size	2G (must be in one tablespace)
Number of Columns Per Table	999
Field Size	2G
Number of Indexes	32,767 per table

There is no limit to the number of tables referenced by transaction or index-entry size. The number of rows per table and the row size are both limited by the size of the table. The number of rows per database is limited by tablespace size.

Appendix C
Database Error Messages

Watcom SQL comes with database error messages. When an application program executes an SQL statement, it returns a numeric code. This code is referred to as an SQLCODE. From the SQLCODE, you can determine whether the application has an error or warning. The SQLCODE has three values that it can use: if the SQLCODE returns a zero, the SQL was successful; if the SQL statement was in error, the value of the SQLCODE is a negative one; if the value is +100, a warning about a row not being found is given.

For a more specific error message the SQLDBCODE is used. The SQLDBCODE works along the same respects as the SQLCODE. The major difference is that the SQLDBCODE defines the errors more specifically. The error messages are negative numbers, and the warning messages are positive numbers. A value of zero refers to having no errors or warnings—a successful completion.

This appendix is divided into four sections. The first section is an alphabetically sorted list of all of the error messages and their corresponding SQLCODE. The second section is a list of SQLSTATE codes with their corresponding SQLCODE. This section is sorted by SQLSTATE. The third section describes the errors and messages. It isn't sorted in numeric order, but it's close. If you don't know the category, you should still be able to find it. The fourth section deals with SQLPP error and warning messages. The SQLPP (SQL preprocessor) error and warning messages are sorted by the SQLPP codes. The messages and probable cause are listed with the SQLPP code.

The percent symbol (%) accompanies some of the messages. This represents a string that Watcom passes back to the application.

Alphabetical List of Error Messages and SQLDBCODE

This first section is listed alphabetically by the error message. This will help you primarily if you are sending the SQLSTATE codes back from the transaction. Because the SQLSTATE codes have a broader meaning, you can use the description to correspond to an SQLCODE. The SQLCODE could give you a better understanding of the error.

SQLDBCODE	Description of Message
–210	'%s' has the row in %s locked
–134	'%s' not implemented
–110	'%s' already exists
–120	'%s' already has grant permission
–140	'%s' is an unknown userid
–123	'%s' is not a user group
0	no error and no message
–150	aggregate functions not allowed on this statement
–307	all threads are blocked
–125	ALTER clause conflict
–407	an argument passed to a WSQL HLI function was invalid
–298	attempted two active database requests
–98	authentication violation
–160	can only describe a SELECT statement
–127	cannot alter a column in an index
–105	cannot be started—'%s'
–157	cannot convert '%s' to a '%s'
–269	cannot delete a column referenced in a trigger definition
–270	cannot drop a user that owns procedures in runtime engine

VII

Appendixes

–128	cannot drop a user that owns tables in runtime engine
–183	cannot find index named '%s'
–191	cannot modify column '%s' in table '%s'
–106	cannot open log file '%s'
–190	cannot update an expression
–212	CHECKPOINT command requires a rollback log
–88	client/server communications protocol mismatch
–113	column '%s' in foreign key has a different definition than primary key
–149	column '%s' cannot be used unless it is in a GROUP BY
–144	column '%s' found in more than one table—need a correlation name
–195	column '%s' in table '%s' cannot be NULL
–143	column '%s' not found
–267	COMMIT/ROLLBACK not allowed in ATOMIC compound statement
–273	COMMIT/ROLLBACK not allowed in trigger actions
–85	communication error
–108	connection not found
–99	connections to database have been disabled
–142	correlation name '%s' not found
–172	cursor already open
–170	cursor has not been declared
–180	cursor not open
–241	database backup not started
–96	database engine already running
–100	database engine not running
–89	database engine not running in multi-user mode
–77	database name not unique

(continues)

SQLDBCODE	Description of Message
–87	database name required to start engine
–266	database was initialized with an older version of the software
–97	database's page size too big
–231	dblib/database engine version mismatch
–138	dbspace '%s' not found
–306	deadlock detected
–304	disk full transaction rolled back
–121	do not have permission to '%s'
–78	Dynamic memory exhausted
–184	error inserting into cursor
–107	error writing to log file
–251	foreign key '%s' for table '%s' duplicates an existing foreign key
–145	foreign key name '%s' not found
–305	I/O error '%s' transaction rolled back
–250	identifier '%s' too long
–242	incomplete transactions prevent transaction log renaming
–196	index '%s' for table '%s' would not be unique
–111	index name '%s' not unique
–199	INSERT/DELETE on cursor can modify only one table
–301	internal database error '%s' transaction rolled back
–263	invalid absolute or relative offset in FETCH
–159	invalid column number
103	invalid data conversion
–81	invalid database engine command line
–156	invalid expression near '%s'

–155	invalid host variable
–79	invalid local database switch
–187	invalid operation for this cursor
–192	invalid operation on joined tables
–200	invalid option '%s'—no PUBLIC setting exists
–95	invalid parameter
–133	invalid prepared statement type
–272	invalid REFERENCES clause in trigger definition
–201	invalid setting for option '%s'
–130	invalid statement
–161	invalid type on DESCRIBE statement
–104	invalid userid and password on preprocessed module
–103	invalid userid or password
–209	invalid value for column '%s' in table '%s'
–405	invalid WSQL HLI callback function
–400	invalid WSQL HLI command syntax
–401	invalid WSQL HLI cursor name
–403	invalid WSQL HLI host variable name
–404	invalid WSQL HLI host variable value
–402	invalid WSQL HLI statement name
–262	label '%s' not found
–135	language extension
–139	more than one table is identified as '%s'
–197	no current row of cursor
–181	no indicator variable provided for NULL result
–194	no primary key value for foreign key '%s' in table '%s'
–211	not allowed while '%s' is using the database

(continues)

SQLDBCODE	Description of Message
–101	not connected to SQL database
–182	not enough fields allocated in SQLDA
–86	not enough memory to start
–188	not enough values for host variables
–152	number in ORDER BY is too large
–114	number of columns does not match SELECT
–122	operation would cause a group cycle
–119	primary key column '%s' already defined
–198	primary key for row in table '%s' is referenced in another table
–193	primary key for table '%s' is not unique
–265	procedure '%s' not found
105	procedure has completed
–215	procedure in use
–274	procedure or trigger calls have nested too deep
–76	request denied—no active databases
–75	request to start/stop database denied
–222	result set not allowed from within an atomic compound statement
–221	ROLLBACK TO SAVEPOINT not allowed
104	row has been updated since last time read
–208	row has changed since last read—operation canceled
100	row not found
–300	runtime SQL error—'%s'
–220	savepoint '%s' not found
–213	savepoints require a rollback log
–153	SELECT lists in UNION do not match in length
–185	SELECT returns more than one row

−232	server/database engine version mismatch
−84	specified database is invalid
−83	specified database not found
−132	SQL statement error
−230	sqlpp/dblib version mismatch
−299	statement interrupted by user
−151	subquery allowed only one select list item
−186	subquery cannot return more than one result
−131	syntax error near '%s'
−118	table '%s' has no primary key
−141	table '%s' not found
−112	table already has a primary key
−126	table cannot have two primary keys
−214	table in use
−116	table must be empty
−302	terminated by user transaction rolled back
−74	the selected database is currently inactive
400	the supplied buffer was too small to hold all requested query results
−109	there are still active database connections
−261	there is already a variable named '%s'
−147	there is more than one way to join '%s' to '%s'
−146	there is no way to join '%s' to '%s'
−102	too many connections to database
−268	trigger '%s' not found
−271	trigger definition conflicts with existing triggers
−243	unable to delete database file
−189	unable to find in index '%s' for table '%s'

(continues)

SQLDBCODE	Description of Message
–80	unable to start database engine
–82	unable to start specified database
–240	unknown backup operation
–148	unknown function '%s'
–297	user-defined exception signaled
102	using temporary table
–158	value '%s' too large for destination
101	value truncated
–260	variable '%s' not found
200	warning
–154	wrong number of parameters to function '%s'
–207	wrong number of values for INSERT
–264	wrong number of variables in FETCH
–406	WSQL HLI internal error

SQLSTATE Codes

A second type of error code that Watcom SQL supports is SQLSTATE code. The SQLSTATE codes are defined by ANSI SQL-92. Each SQLSTATE code is a five character string that relates back to a corresponding SQLCA number. The characters are made up of letters A through Z and numbers 0 through 9. A value of 00000 indicates a successful completion.

In Watcom, there are two ways to get the SQLSTATE values. You can retrieve them through SQLCA or ODBC. The SQLCA returns an SQLSTATE value that is specific to the type of error received. The ODBC defines a more broad SQLSTATE value. For this reason, there can be more than one SQLSTATE value returned in ODBC. The SQLCA method might be more suited to your needs than the ODBC because the SQLCA method gives a more specific error message.

The SQLSTATE and ODBC SQLSTATE codes are mostly used when swapping between databases. If this isn't the case in your development, it might be easier to use the SQLCODE. Personal preference and experience will help you decide which is best for you.

SQLSTATE	Number
00000	0
01000	200
01004	101
01W02	102
01W03	103
01W04	104
01W05	400
01W06	105
02000	100
07001	–188
07002	–182
07005	–160
07W01	–161
07W02	–130
07W03	–133
08001	–105
08003	–101
08004	–140
08W01	–100
08W02	–108
08W03	–102
08W04	–99
08W05	–106

(continues)

SQLSTATE	Number
08W06	−109
08W07	−80
08W08	−81
08W09	−82
08W10	−83
08W11	−84
08W12	−85
08W13	−86
08W14	−87
08W15	−88
08W16	−89
08W17	−107
08W18	−230
08W19	−231
08W20	−232
08W21	−98
08W22	−97
08W23	−96
08W24	−95
08W25	−79
08W26	−78
08W27	−77
08W28	−76
08W29	−75
08W30	−74
09W01	−184

09W02	–187
09W03	–197
09W04	–199
0A000	–134
0AW01	–135
21000	–185
21W01	–186
22002	–181
22003	–158
22W01	–407
22W02	–208
23502	–195
23503	–194
23505	–196
23506	–209
23W01	–193
23W05	–198
24501	–180
24502	–172
24W01	–170
26501	–132
26W01	–402
28000	–103
28W01	–104
2D501	–273
34W01	–401
37505	–154

(continues)

SQLSTATE	Number
3B001	−220
3B002	−221
3BW01	−213
3BW02	−222
40000	−300
40001	−306
40W01	−301
40W02	−302
40W03	−304
40W04	−305
40W06	−307
42501	−121
42W01	−120
42W02	−122
42W03	−123
42W04	−131
42W05	−148
42W06	−150
42W07	−155
42W08	−156
42W09	−403
42W10	−404
42W11	−400
42W12	−405
42W13	−159
42W14	−260

42W15	−261
42W16	−200
42W17	−201
42W18	−210
42W19	−211
42W20	−212
42W21	−214
42W22	−298
42W23	−215
42W24	−262
42W25	−263
42W26	−264
42W27	−266
42W28	−267
42W29	−274
52002	−144
52003	−143
52009	−119
52010	−110
52012	−139
52W01	−141
52W02	−142
52W03	−183
52W04	−111
52W05	−126
52W06	−251
52W07	−145
52W08	−147

(continues)

SQLSTATE	Number
52W09	−265
52W10	−268
52W11	−271
52W12	−272
52W13	−138
53002	−207
53003	−149
53005	−152
53008	−191
53011	−114
53018	−157
53023	−151
53026	−153
53030	−113
53W01	−125
53W02	−190
53W03	−192
53W04	−146
53W05	−127
53W06	−269
54003	−250
55008	−118
55013	−112
55W02	−116
55W03	−128
55W04	−270
57014	−299

99999	−297
WB001	−240
WB002	−241
WB003	−242
WB004	−243
WI005	−189
WI007	−406

Error Message Descriptions

This section gives you the probable cause to the SQLDBCODE you receive. Along with the SQLDBCODE, the SQLSTATE code and the ODBC state code are given. You only need the ODBC state code if you are using the ODBC interface.

◄ See "Using ODBC," p. 436

The constant applies when you are using Visual Basic or C++. The constants are in a copybook and can be referenced while using these languages.

Warnings

The warnings notify you of certain conditions taking place. They don't terminate processing.

The ODBC driver handles all ODBC state codes.

Code	Constant	State	ODBC State	Probable Cause
0	SQLE_NOERROR	00000		No error and no warning messages were indicated.
100	SQLE_NOTFOUND	02000		Did not find the row to be retrieved.
101	SQLE_TRUNCATED	01004		Attempted to insert, update, select, or fetch a value in the database that was too large to fit in the destination.

(continues)

Code	Constant	State	ODBC State	Probable Cause
102	SQLE_TEMPORARY_ TABLE	01W02		Created a temporary table to satisfy the query. This can only occur on an OPEN statement.
103	SQLE_CANNOT_CONVERT	01W03		The database was not able to convert a value to the required type.
104	SQLE_ROW_UPDATED_ WARNING	01W04		This indicates that the row from the table was previously updated. A FETCH retrieved a row from a cursor declared as a SCROLL cursor, the row was previously fetched from the same cursor, and one or more columns in the row were updated since the last fetch.
105	SQLE_PROCEDURE_ COMPLETE	01W06		An OPEN or a RESUME has caused a procedure to execute to comple tion or a cursor has attempted to RESUME on a SELECT statement.
200	SQLE_WARNING	01000		This warning message indicates the condition that caused the warning.
400	SQLE_HLI_MORE_DATA_ AVAILABLE	01W05		The buffer supplied by the calling application was too small to contain the entire query. The attempt to get the query result was set using the WSQL HLI function wsqlquerytomem.

Environment Errors

The environment errors are primarily database errors; these can be severe database problems. Your database could be corrupted.

Code	Constant	State	ODBC State	Probable Cause
–80	SQLE_UNABLE_TO_ START_ENGINE	08W07	08001	The database engine multi-user client was not able to start. Either there was not enough memory to run the database engine or the executable command could not be found.
–81	SQLE_INVALID_ COMMAND_LINE	08W08	08001	The database engine or multi-user client was not able to start due to an invalid command line.
–74	SQLE_DATABASE_NOT_ ACTIVE	08W30	08001	The selected database was in an inactive state. This state occurs during database initialization or shutdown.
–75	SQLE_START_STOP _DATABASE_DENIED	08W29	08001	The engine denied permission to start or stop a database.
–76	SQLE_REQUEST_DENIED_ NO_DATABASE	08W28	08001	The engine denied the request because there are currently no databases loaded.
–77	SQLE_ALIAS_CLASH	08W27	08001	There is a conflict with the name of the current database against the name of a previously loaded database.
–79	SQLE_INVALID_ LOCAL_OPTION	08W25	08001	An invalid local database switch was found in the DBS option.
–82	SQLE_UNABLE_TO_ START_DATABASE	08W09	08001	The database engine or multi-user client was started but was unable to find the specific database or server name. No specific reason is known.

(continues)

Code	Constant	State	ODBC State	Probable Cause
–83	SQLE_DATABASE_NOT_ FOUND	08W10	08001	The database engine or multi-user client was started but was unable to find the specific database or server name. The database file cannot be opened or the specified server could not be found on the network.
–84	SQLE_INVALID_ DATABASE	08W11	08001	The database engine was started but the specified database file was invalid.
–85	SQLE_COMMUNICATION_ ERROR	08W12	08S01	A communication problem between the multi-user client and server has occurred. This commonly occurs when the multi-user client is unable to start because a communication error occurred while trying to locate the server.
–78	SQLE_DYNAMIC_ MEMORY_EXHAUSTED	08W26	S1001	The allocation of dynamic memory failed.
–86	SQLE_NO_MEMORY	08W13	S1001	The database engine or multi-user client executable was loaded but was unable to start due to not having enough memory to run properly.
–87	SQLE_DATABASE_ NAME_REQUIRED	08W14	08001	The name for the database engine or multi-user client was not specified.
–88	SQLE_PROTOCOL_ MISMATCH	08W15	08S01	The multi-user client was unable to start because the protocol versions of the client and the running server do not match. The client and server software need to be the same version.

| -96 | SQLE_ENGINE_
ALREADY_RUNNING | 08W23 | S1000 | The database engine with the same name as the database engine you're trying to start is already running. Only one can be running on a server at a time. |
| -89 | SQLE_ENGINE_
NOT_MULTIUSER | 08W16 | 08001 | The database was started for bulk loading (the –b switch) and cannot be used as a multi-user engine. Stop the database, and start again without –b. In the DOS version of Watcom SQL Version 3.0, the database engine was not started in multi-user mode. |

Connection Errors

Because ISQL is not initially connected to the database, you must make a connection. Connection errors occur when a connection is not successful.

Code	Constant	State	ODBC State	Probable Cause
-95	SQLE_INVALID_ PARAMETER	08W24	08004	An error occurred while translating an SQL command into separate parameters while attempting to start your database engine. This usually occurs in a C++ program. The string parameter associated with this is one of the entry points: db_start_engine(), db_start_database(), db_stop_engine(), db_stop_database(), or db_string_connect().
-97	SQLE_PAGE_SIZE_ TOO_BIG	08W22	08004	There was an attempt to start a database with a page size that exceeded the maximum page size of the running engine.

(continues)

Code	Constant	State	ODBC State	Probable Cause
–98	SQLE_AUTHENTICATION_ VIOLATION	08W21	08001	There was an attempt to connect to an engine or server that has been authenticated for exclusive use with a specific application.
–99	SQLE_CONNECTIONS_ DISABLED	08W04	08005	The multi-user server connections were disabled on the server console. You receive this error until you enable the server console again.
–100	SQLE_ENGINE_NOT_ RUNNING	08W01	08001	The database engine or the network requester have not been run or the interface library is unable to find it.
–101	SQLE_NOT_CONNECTED	08003	08003	The database has not been connected, or a DISCONNECT command has been executed and the database has not been reconnected.
–102	SQLE_TOO_MANY_ CONNECTIONS	08W03	08004	One of three possibilities: the number of computers allowed to connect to the server by the license agreement for the multi-user client has been exceeded; the connection limit of two for the DOS engine was exceeded; or the Windows engine connections exceeded the limit of 10.
–103	SQLE_INVALID_LOGON	28000	28000	The userid or password were invalid or incorrect. ISQL handles this error by presenting a connection dialog.
–104	SQLE_INVALID_MODULE_ LOGON	28W01	28000	The userid or password was invalid when the module was preprocessed.

VII

Appendixes

−105	SQLE_UNABLE_TO_CONNECT	08001		The specified database environment could not be found. If the environment is a database name, the database could be corrupt, does not exist, is not a database, or could be an invalid format.
−106	SQLE_CANNOT_OPEN_LOG	08W05	08003	The database engine was unable to open the transaction log file. This could be because the log file name specifies an invalid device or directory. If this is the case, use the DBLOG utility to find where the transaction log should be and change it if necessary.
−107	SQLE_ERROR_WRITING_LOG	08W17	S1000	The database engine received an I/O error writing the log file. Possibly because the log file is full or the log file name is invalid.
−108	SQLE_CONNECTION_NOT_FOUND	08W02	08003	The specified connection name on a DISCONNECT or SET CONNECTION statement was invalid.
−109	SQLE_STILL_ACTIVE_CONNECTIONS	08W06	S1000	An application requested shutdown the database using the db_stop() function when there are still active connections to the database.

Creation Errors

The creation errors occur when you attempt an unsuccessful modification on an existing table or create a new table unsuccessfully. The reason for these errors is not syntax.

Code	Constant	State	ODBC State	Probable Cause
–110	SQLE_NAME_NOT_UNIQUE	52010	S0001	Attempted to create a table, view, column, or foreign key with a name that already exists.
–111	SQLE_INDEX_NAME_ NOT_UNIQUE	52W04	S0011	Attempted to create an index with a name that already exists.
–112	SQLE_EXISTING_ PRIMARY_KEY	55013	23000	Attempted to add a primary key on a table that already has a primary key defined. To add a new primary key, the current primary key must first be deleted.
–113	SQLE_INVALID_ FOREIGN_KEY_DEF	53030	23000	The data type of the column in the foreign key is not the same as the data type of the column in the primary key. One of the columns needs to have its definition changed using the ALTER TABLE command.
–114	SQLE_VIEW_ DEFINITION_ERROR	53011	21S01	An INSERT command contains a SELECT with a different number of columns than the INSERT.
–116	SQLE_TABLE_MUST_BE_ EMPTY	55W02	S1000	Attempted to modify a table, and Watcom SQL can only perform the change if there are no rows in the table.
–118	SQLE_NO_PRIMARY_KEY	55008	23000	Attempted to add a foreign key that refers to a table without a primary key. A primary key needs to be added to the table before a foreign key can refer to the table.
–119	SQLE_PRIMARY_KEY_ COLUMN_DEFINED	52009	23000	A column name was listed twice in the definition of a primary key.

−125	SQLE_ALTER_ CLAUSE_CONFLICT	53W01	S1000	The ALTER TABLE command can have only one of the following clauses: primary key clause, foreign key clause, or uniqueness clause.
−126	SQLE_PRIMARY_KEY_ TWICE	52W05	23000	The primary key was specified twice in the CREATE TABLE command.
−127	SQLE_COLUMN_IN_INDEX	53W05	S1000	Attempted to delete or modify the definition of a column that is part of a primary or foreign key. This error can also come from an attempt to delete a column that has an index on it. If this is the case, DROP the index or key, perform the ALTER command, and add the index or key again.
−128	SQLE_USER_OWNS_ TABLES	55W03	37000	The runtime engine reported an attempt to drop a user that owns tables. Because the runtime engine cannot drop tables, the operation is not allowed. The development engine is better suited for this operation.
−250	SQLE_IDENTIFIER_TOO_ LONG	54003	37000	An identifier is longer than 128 characters.
−251	SQLE_DUPLICATE_ FOREIGN_KEY	52W06	23000	Attempted to define a foreign key that already existed.
−183	SQLE_INDEX_NOT_FOUND	52W03	S0012	A DROP INDEX command named an index that does not exist. Check for spelling errors or whether the index name must be qualified by a userid.

VII

Appendixes

Permission Errors

The permission errors are due to a lack of authority to perform the command. Check with the DBA to get authority to complete your task.

Code	Constant	State	ODBC State	Probable Cause
–120	SQLE_ALREADY_ HAS_GRANT_PERMS	42W01	37000	The SQL GRANT command attempted to give a user the GRANT OPTION that already the OPTION.
–121	SQLE_PERMISSION_ DENIED	42501	42001	Permission was not granted to use a table that belongs to another userid.
–122	SQLE_GROUP_CYCLE	42W02	37000	Attempted to add a member to a group that results in a member belonging to itself (perhaps indirectly).
–123	SQLE_NOT_A_GROUP	42W03	37000	Attempted to add a member to a group that has not been granted the GROUP special privilege.

Prepare Errors

You receive these errors primarily when executing the PREPARE command. The PREPARE command is an embedded SQL command.

Code	Constant	State	ODBC State	Probable Cause
–130	SQLE_INVALID_ STATEMENT	07W02	S1000	The statement identifier (generated by PREPARE) passed to the database is invalid.
–131	SQLE_SYNTAX_ERROR	42W04	37000	The database engine does not understand the command being executed. If the command is a keyword (such as DATE) for a column name, try enclosing the keyword in quotation marks ("DATE").

VII

Appendixes

−132	SQLE_STATEMENT_ ERROR	26501	S1000	The statement identifier (generated by PREPARE) passed to the database is invalid.
−133	SQLE_INVALID_ STATEMENT_TYPE	07W03	S1000	This is an internal C language interface error. If this error occurs, report it to Watcom.
−134	SQLE_NOT_IMPLEMENTED	0A000	S1000	The requested operation or feature is not implemented in Watcom SQL.
−135	SQLE_LANGUAGE_ EXTENSION	0AW01	S1000	The requested operation is not valid in Watcom SQL.

Semantic Errors

The semantic errors occur when the command cannot be understood by the system. This happens most often when a name is misspelled.

Code	Constant	State	ODBC State	Probable Cause
−138	SQLE_DBSPACE_NOT_ FOUND	52W13	S0002	The dbspace name was not found.
−139	SQLE_CORRELATION_ NAME_AMBIGUOUS	52012	SG001	The same correlation name was used to identify two tables in the same FROM clause.
−140	SQLE_UNKNOWN_USERID	08004	28000	The name of the userid does not exist.
−141	SQLE_TABLE_NOT_ FOUND	52W01	S0002	The name of the table does not exist. The name of the table might be misspelled or connected with a different userid and the table name was not qualified with a user name.

(continues)

Code	Constant	State	ODBC State	Probable Cause
–142	SQLE_CORRELATION_NAME_NOT_FOUND	52W02	S0002	Could not find the correlation name. In this case, the correlation name may be misspelled, or a table name was used instead of the correlation name.
–143	SQLE_COLUMN_NOT_FOUND	52003	S0022	Could not find the column name. The column name may be misspelled, or Watcom may have looked in the wrong table for the column.
–144	SQLE_COLUMN_AMBIGUOUS	52002	SJS01	A column found in more than one table was not assigned a correlation name. A correlation name allows the system to assign the correct column to the correct table.
–145	SQLE_FOREIGN_KEY_NAME_NOT_FOUND	52W07	37000	Could not find the foreign key. The name may be misspelled or the foreign key may not exist.
–146	SQLE_CANNOT_JOIN	53W04	37000	Attempted to join two tables that cannot be joined. If the attempt was a KEY JOIN, there must be a foreign key on one of the tables that references the primary key of the other table. If the attempt was a NATURAL JOIN, check to see if there is a common column name between the tables.

VII

Appendixes

−147	SQLE_AMBIGUOUS_JOIN	52W08	37000	The system found more than one way to attempt a KEY JOIN. Either there are two foreign keys from one table to the second table or each table has a foreign key to the other table. In both cases, you can resolve this error by using a correlation name for the primary table that is the same as the role name of the desired foreign key relationship.
−148	SQLE_UNKNOWN_FUNC	42W05	37000	The function name is not a database function. The database function may be misspelled or used in an incorrect manner. An example of this is using MINIMUM instead of MIN.
−149	SQLE_INVALID_GROUP_SELECT	53003	37000	You left a column name out of GROUP BY. To correct this error, either place the column name in the GROUP BY or use an aggregate function on the SELECT statement.
−150	SQLE_AGGREGATES	42W06	37000	An aggregate function was used in an UPDATE statement. An aggregate function is any of the following: MIN, MAX, SUM AVG, or COUNT.
−151	SQLE_SUBQUERY_SELECT_LIST	53023	37000	The subquery has more than one column in the select list. Modify the select list to have only one column.
−152	SQLE_INVALID_ORDER	53005	37000	An integer used in an ORDER BY list is larger than the number of columns in the SELECT list.

(continues)

Code	Constant	State	ODBC State	Probable Cause
−153	SQLE_INVALID_UNION	53026	37000	A UNION was specified, but the SELECT statements involved in the union do not have the same number of columns in the select list.

Expression and Function Errors

These errors occur when the system cannot understand the expression or function. Check the parameters used and the set up of the function.

Code	Constant	State	ODBC State	Probable Cause
−154	SQLE_WRONG_ PARAMETER_COUNT	37505	37000	The number of parameters to a database function is incorrect. Check the syntax and try again.
−155	SQLE_VARIABLE_ INVALID	42W07	37000	The host variable is invalid. The host variable was supplied to the database using the C language interface as either a host variable or through an SQLDA.
−156	SQLE_EXPRESSION_ ERROR	42W08	37000	There is an expression that the database engine cannot interpret. An example of this might be adding two dates together.
−157	SQLE_CONVERSION_ ERROR	53018	07006	The value that was supplied to or fetched from the database was invalid. This could occur if the value was an alpha character (W) and a numeric character was required.

−158	`SQLE_OVERFLOW_ERROR`	22003	22003	The value that was supplied to or fetched from the database was too large for the destination column or host variable. An example of this is if the value was 100 and the field that you're sending it to is defined DEC(3,2).

−159	`SQLE_INVALID_`
	`COLUMN_NUMBER`
	`GET_DATA`
		42W13	S1000	The column number in a command is invalid.

Describe Errors

You receive these errors primarily when executing the DESCRIBE command. The DESCRIBE command is an embedded SQL command.

Code	Constant	State	ODBC State	Probable Cause
−160	`SQLE_DESCRIBE_` `NONSELECT`	07005		In the C language interface, an attempt was made to describe the select list of a statement other than in a SELECT statement.
−161	`SQLE_INVALID_` `DESCRIBE_TYPE`	07W01		This is an internal C language interface error. Report the problem to Watcom.

Open Errors

These errors occur when you use the OPEN statement of a cursor incorrectly.

Code	Constant	State	ODBC State	Probable Cause
−170	`SQLE_CURSOR_NOT_` `DECLARED`	24W01	24000	Attempted to OPEN a cursor that has not been declared.

(continues)

Code	Constant	State	ODBC State	Probable Cause
–172	SQLE_CURSOR_ ALREADY_OPEN	24502	24000	Attempted to OPEN a cursor that has already been opened.

Fetch Errors

These errors occur when data is being retrieved from a cursor using a FETCH command.

Code	Constant	State	ODBC State	Probable Cause
–180	SQLE_CURSOR_NOT_ OPEN	24501	34000	Attempted to OPEN a cursor that has not been declared.
–181	SQLE_NO_INDICATOR	22002	S1000	A NULL value was retrieved from a database that did not have an indicator variable. The indicator variable holds the value of the NULL.
–182	SQLE_SQLDA_TOO_ SMALL	07002		There are not enough fields in the SQLDA to retrieve all of the values.
–184	SQLE_PUT_CURSOR_ ERROR	09W01	S1000	An error occurred while inserting into a cursor.
–185	SQLE_TOO_MANY_ RECORDS	21000	S1000	An Embedded SELECT statement returned more than one result. A cursor may need to be used in this case.
–186	SQLE_SUBQUERY_ RESULT_NOT_UNIQUE	21W01	37000	More than one row was retrieved from a subquery. This could be the case if you were using a WHERE clause with your subquery. You might want to change to an IN, ANY, or ALL.
–187	SQLE_CURSOROP_ NOT_ALLOWED	09W02	24000	An operation was not allowed on a cursor.

−188	SQLE_NOT_ENOUGH_ HOST_VARS	07001		There were not enough host variables for either the number of bind variables, the command, or the number of select list items. Look at the list of host variables again.
−189	SQLE_NOT_FOUND_ IN_INDEX	WI005	S1000	This is a Watcom SQL internal error and should be reported to Watcom. It should be possible to get around this by dropping and recreating the index.

Update and Insert Errors

These errors occur during an invalid modification of a table using the UPDATE or INSERT commands.

Code	Constant	State	ODBC State	Probable Cause
−190	SQLE_NON_ UPDATEABLE_COLUMN	53W02	37000	Attempted to update a column in a query that was a database expression.
−191	SQLE_CANNOT_MODIFY	53008	37000	The column cannot be modified. Either you do not have authority to modify the column, or the table is a view and the column in the view is defined as an expression.
−192	SQLE_NON_ UPDATEABLE_VIEW	53W03	37000	Attempted to delete from a query involving more than one table.
−193	SQLE_PRIMARY_KEY_ NOT_UNIQUE	23W01	23000	Attempted to duplicate a primary key. This error can occur if you try to add a new row with a primary key that already exists. The incorrect row is not added to the database.

(continues)

Code	Constant	State	ODBC State	Probable Cause
–194	SQLE_INVALID_ FOREIGN_KEY	23503	23000	Attempted to insert or update a row that has a foreign key for another table. The value of the foreign key is not NULL and there is not a corresponding value in the primary key.
–195	SQLE_COLUMN_CANNOT_ BE_NULL	23502	23000	The setup of the column requires a value to be present in the column. The value of the column that was retrieved was NULL.
–196	SQLE_INDEX_NOT_ UNIQUE	23505	23000	The name of the index was not unique. This could happen during an INSERT or UPDATE when a row has the same value as another row in some column, and there is a constraint that does not allow duplicate indexes.
–197	SQLE_NO_CURRENT_ROW	09W03	24000	Attempted to perform an operation on the current row of a cursor, but the current row is not there. This error could take place if the current row is before the first row of the cursor, after the last row of the cursor, or on a row that has already been deleted.
–198	SQLE_PRIMARY_KEY_ VALUE_REF	23W05	23000	Attempted to modify or delete a primary key that is referenced else-where in the database.
–199	SQLE_ONLY_ONE_TABLE	09W04	37000	Attempted to modify more than one table at a time. This could involve trying to INSERT into a cursor and have specified values for more than one table. Another example could be trying to DELETE from a cursor involved in a join.

−209	SQLE_INVALID_ COLUMN_VALUE	23506	23000	Attempted to modify a table in which the value for a column violated a CHECK constraint.
−208	SQLE_ROW_UPDATED_ SINCE_READ	22W02		Attempted a modification on a cursor declared as a SCROLL cursor after the row had already been previously updated since the last time the row had been read. This should eliminate the "lost update" problem.
−207	SQLE_WRONG_NUM_OF_ INSERT_COLS	53002	37000	The number of values used in an INSERT command do not match the number of columns specified in the INSERT command or the number of columns in the table if no columns are specified.

Variable Errors

These errors occur when you use a variable incorrectly. This usually happens when you misspell a variable name or try to create a variable name that already exists.

Code	Constant	State	ODBC State	Probable Cause
−260	SQLE_VARIABLE_NOT_ FOUND	42W14	37000	Attempted to DROP or SET the value of an SQL variable that was not created or was previously dropped.
−261	SQLE_VARIABLE_EXISTS	42W15	37000	Attempted to CREATE a variable with a name that was not unique. Change the name to a variable that does not already exist.

Appendixes

VII

Procedure Errors

Procedures and triggers are features that store procedural SQL statements in the database for use by all applications. The following errors occur when the procedural SQL statements do not perform successfully.

Code	Constant	State	ODBC State	Probable Cause
−262	SQLE_LABEL_NOT_FOUND	53W02	37000	Did not find the statement label referenced in a LEAVE statement.
−263	SQLE_INVALID_ FETCH_POSITION	53008	37000	The offset specified in a FETCH was invalid or NULL. This can occur if the absolute or relative offset positioned the cursor before the first row, after the last row, on a row that has already been deleted.
−264	SQLE_WRONG_NUM_OF_ FETCH_VARIABLES	53W03	37000	The number of variables specified in the FETCH statement was not equal to the number of variables in the SELECT list of items of the DECLARE statement.
−265	SQLE_PROCEDURE_NOT_ FOUND	23W01	S0002	The name of the procedure could not be found. Either you have misspelled the name of the procedure or you have forgotten to qualify the procedure name with a user name after connecting with a different userid.
−266	SQLE_OLD_DBINIT	23503	37000	The database is missing some system table definitions due to an invalid or older version of Watcom SQL. The database should be unloaded and reloaded into a database that has been initialized with a newer version of Watcom SQL.

-267	SQLE_ATOMIC_OPERATION	23502	37000	Encountered a COMMIT or ROLLBACK statement while executing in an atomic operation. Atomic operation statements do not permit the COMMIT, ROLLBACK, and ROLLBACK TO SAVEPOINT.
-268	SQLE_TRIGGER_NOT_FOUND	23505	S0002	Could not find the name of the trigger. Either you misspelled the name of the trigger or you forgot to qualify the trigger name with a user name after connecting with a different userid.
-269	SQLE_COLUMN_IN_TRIGGER	09W03	S1000	Attempted to delete a column that is referenced in a trigger definition. To correct this error, DROP the trigger before performing the ALTER command.
-270	SQLE_USER_OWNS_PROCEDURE	23W05	37000	Attempted to drop a user that owns procedures was reported by the runtime engine. This operation results in dropping procedures. The runtime engine cannot drop procedures. The develop engine should be used.
-271	SQLE_TRIGGER_DEFN_CONFLICT	09W04	S0001	Could not create a trigger definition because there was a conflict with an existing trigger definition. That trigger name might already exist.
-272	SQLE_INVALID_TRIGGER_COL_REFS	23506	37000	The REFERENCE clause in a trigger definition is invalid. This can occur if you specify an OLD correlation name in a BEFORE INSERT trigger, or a NEW correlation name was specified in an AFTER DELETE trigger.

(continues)

VII

Appendixes

Code	Constant	State	ODBC State	Probable Cause
−273	SQLE_INVALID_ TRIGGER_STATEMENT	22W02	37000	Attempted to execute a statement that is not allowed while performing a trigger action. Triggers are only fired due to an INSERT, UPDATE, or DELETE statement.
−274	SQLE_NESTING_TOO_ DEEP	53002	37000	You may have defined a procedure or trigger that caused an unlimited recursion (possibly an infinite loop).

Option Errors

Option errors occur when the SET OPTION command is invalid.

Code	Constant	State	ODBC State	Probable Cause
−200	SQLE_INVALID_OPTION	42W16	37000	There is an invalid option name in the SET OPTION command. This can be either a misspelled option name or failure to have the DBA define the option as a PUBLIC value.
−201	SQLE_INVALID_ OPTION_SETTING	42W17	37000	There is an invalid value for an option in the SET OPTION command. You need to check the values to see if the values match the options.

Concurrency Errors

These errors occur when transactions that are running at the same time lock out other transactions.

Code	Constant	State	ODBC State	Probable Cause
−210	SQLE_LOCKED	42W18	40001	Attempted to read or write a row that was locked by another user. You receive this error only if you set the database option BLOCKING to OFF. The resource becomes available when the row lock is released.
−211	SQLE_MUST_BE_ ONLY_CONNECTION	42W19	40001	Attempted to CREATE or DROP a dbspace that had other active users of the database. There cannot be any other users of the database when you issue these commands.
−212	SQLE_CHECKPOINT_ REQUIRES_UNDO	42W20	40001	You cannot use a CHECKPOINT command when the database engine is running in bulk mode without a rollback log.
−214	SQLE_TABLE_IN_USE	42W21	40001	Attempted to ALTER or DROP a table that had other active users of the database. There cannot be any other users of the database when you issue these commands.
−215	SQLE_PROCEDURE_IN_ USE	42W23	40001	Attempted to DROP a procedure that had other active users of the database. There cannot be any other users of the database when you issue these commands.

VII

Appendixes

Savepoint Errors

These errors occur when SAVEPOINTs are used incorrectly.

Code	Constant	State	ODBC State	Probable Cause
–220	SQLE_SAVEPOINT_ NOTFOUND	3B001	S1000	Attempted to rollback to a savepoint that does not exist or could not be found.
–221	SOLE_ROLLBACK_ NOT_ALLOWED	3B002	S1000	A ROLLBACK TO SAVEPOINT in an atomic operation is not allowed to rollback to a savepoint established before the atomic operation.
–222	SQLE_RESULT _NOT_ALLOWED	3BW02	S1000	A SELECT statement with no INTO clause or a RESULT CURSOR statement are not allowed with an atomic compound statement.
–213	SQLE_SAVEPOINTS_ REQUIRE_UNDO	3BW01	S1000	You cannot use Savepoints when the database engine is running in bulk mode without a rollback log.

Version Checking Errors

These errors are due to an incompatible version in the software being used. Check the versions of the software for compatibility.

Code	Constant	State	ODBC State	Probable Cause
–230	SQLE_PP_DBLIB_ MISMATCH	08W18	08001	The SQL preprocessor does not match the database interface library.
–231	SQLE_DBLIB_ENGINE_ MISMATCH	08W19	08001	The database interface library does not match the version number of the database engine.
–232	SQLE_SERVER_ENGINE_ MISMATCH	08W20	08001	The version of the database server software is not compatible with the version of the database engine.

Backup Errors

These errors occur when there is an unsuccessful backup of the database.

Code	Constant	State	ODBC State	Probable Cause
−240	SQLE_UNKNOWN_ BACKUP_OPERATION	WB001	S1000	An invalid backup command operation was specified in a call to db_backup.
−241	SQLE_BACKUP_ NOT_STARTED	WB002	S1000	Could not start a database backup. Either you do not have DBA authority or another backup is still running.
−242	SQLE_BACKUP_CANNOT_ RENAME_LOG_YET	WB003	S1000	The database engine was unable to rename the transaction log after the last page was returned. This error could have occurred do to an active connection still present. To correct the error, reissue the request until you receive an SQL_NOERROR.
−243	SQLE_BACKUP_UNABLE_ TO_DELETE_FILE	WB004	S1000	Could not delete the database file. The filename should not be the same as any database file currently in use.

Miscellaneous Errors

These errors are user-defined errors. The system allows for the user to use these error codes. They are not specific to a certain category.

Code	Constant	State	ODBC State	Probable Cause
−297	SQLE_USER_DEFINED_ EXCEPTION	99999	S1000	A stored procedure or trigger signaled a user-defined exception. This error state is reserved for use within stored procedures or triggers to signal an exception that can be guaranteed not to have been caused by the database engine.

(continues)

Code	Constant	State	ODBC State	Probable Cause
–298	SQLE_DOUBLE_REQUEST	42W22	S1000	In embedded SQL, there was an attempt to start a database request while there was still another request processing.

User Interruption Message

This error occurs when the user initiates a termination command.

Code	Constant	State	ODBC State	Probable Cause
–299	SQLE_INTERRUPTED	57014	S1000	The user issued an abort operation to stop the current processing and prompt for the next command. The database stopped the operation without doing a rollback. If the aborted statement was one that modified the table and the engine was not running in bulk operations mode, all changes made to the table during the current command are undone. If the abort is detected during a data definition command, the current command is canceled, but the COMMIT that is automatically performed before the command starts is not canceled.

◀ See "ROLL-BACK," p. 173

Errors that Cause Rollbacks

These errors are internal database problems that are severe enough to cause a rollback.

Code	Constant	State	ODBC State	Probable Cause
–300	SQLE_ERROR	40000	S1000	This error indicates an internal database error,

VII

Appendixes

				and should be reported to Watcom.
–301	SQLE_DATABASE_ERROR	40W01	S1000	This error indicates an internal database error, and should be reported to Watcom. A ROLL BACK WORK command automatically executes.
–302	SQLE_TERMINATED_ BY_USER	40W02	S1000	A command was issued to abort while the database was executing. A ROLLBACK WORK command automatically executes. This can happen when the engine is running in bulk mode and you abort an INSERT, UPDATE, or DELETE operation.
–304	SQLE_DEVICE_FULL	40W03	S1000	The hard disk is out of free space. A ROLLBACK WORK command automatically executes.
–305	SQLE_DEVICE_ERROR	40W04	S1000	Watcom SQL detected a problem with the hard disk. If you cannot find a hardware error using the operating system disk check utility, report the problem to Watcom. A ROLLBACK WORK command auto-matically executes.
–306	SQLE_DEADLOCK	40001		Attempted to read or write a row that was locked by another user. This is a deadlock situation. Watcom SQL automatically cancels the last transaction that became blocked.
–307	SQLE_THREAD_DEADLOCK	40W06	40001	Attempted to read or write a row that was locked by another user. When all threads are blocked, it is a deadlock situation. Watcom SQL automatically cancels the last transaction that became blocked.

Errors Specific to WSQL HLI

◀ See "Implementing Watcom SQL HLI," p. 417

These errors deal directly with the WSQL HLI. These errors do not have ODBC state codes.

Code	Constant	State	ODBC State	Probable Cause
−400	SQLE_HLI_BAD_SYNTAX	42W11		The command string sent to wsqlexec is invalid. Check the command string for misspelled keywords. If that is not the case, check to see if the variable names are too long.
−401	SQLE_HLI_BAD_CURSOR	34W01		The cursor name in the command is not valid. The cursor name might be misspelled or was never declared.
−402	SQLE_HLI_BAD_ STATEMENT	26W01		The statement name in the command is not valid.
−403	SQLE_HLI_BAD_HOST_ VAR_NAME	42W09		The host variable callback function does not recognize the host variable being used.
−404	SQLE_HLI_BAD_HOST_ VAR_VALUE	42W10		The value of the host variable is too long.
−405	SQLE_HLI_BAD_ CALLBACK	42W12		WSQL HLI needed to use a callback function, but the function has not been registered using the wsqlregister- funcs entry point.
−406	SQLE_HLI_INTERNAL	WI007		This is a Watcom SQL internal error and should be reported to Watcom.
−407	SQLE_HLI_BAD_ ARGUMENT	22W01		One of the arguments passed to a WSQL HLI function was invalid. This may indicate that a pointer to a command string or result buffer is the null pointer.

Internal Errors (Assertion Failed)

The Watcom SQL engine comes with many internal checks. They detect any database errors. If the system comes back with an `Assertion Failed` message, the database may be corrupt. Do not use the database engine until the message is resolved. You should report the error displayed on the screen to Watcom. If the database file is corrupt, you can reconstruct it from your backups and transaction logs.

Errors and Warnings Specific to SQLPP

These errors and warnings deal primarily with the SQL preprocessor.

◀ See "Running the SQL Preprocessor (SQLPP)," p. 386

Warnings Specific to SQLPP (C and C++)

The embedded SQL statements intermixed with C and C++ source code are translated by the embedded SQL preprocessor (SQLPP). The following are warnings that are produced by SQLPP. These warnings might cause an error when sent to the database engine.

◀ See "Using SQLPP.EXE," p. 642

Code	Message	Probable Cause
2660	into clause not allowed on declare cursor — ignored	An into clause on a SELECT statement was specified in a DECLARE cursor. The into clause is ignored.
2661	unrecognized SQL syntax	An SQL statement will probably cause a syntax error when the statement is sent to the database engine.
2662	unknown sql function '%s'	An SQL function unknown to the preprocessor will probably cause an error when the statement is sent to the database engine.
2663	wrong number of parms to sql function '%s'	An SQL function with the wrong number of parameters will probably cause an error when the statement is sent to the database engine.

(continues)

Code	Message	Probable Cause
2664	`"static"`	You have used the SQLPP utility program with the –r flag to pre-process a static SQL statement. Watcom names all C++ static SQL calls and gets confused about which program is performing the SQL call. Try reformatting your static SQL call into a dynamic SQL call by placing the SQL call in a host variable.

Errors Specific to SQLPP (C and C++)

The embedded SQL statements intermixed with C and C++ source code are translated by the embedded SQL preprocessor (SQLPP). The following errors are produced by SQLPP. With the errors being caught in the preprocessor, you can correct them before they reach the database engine.

Code	Message	Probable Cause
2601	`subscript value %ld too large`	Attempted to index a host variable that is an array with a value too large for the array.
2602	`combined pointer and arrays not supported for hosttypes`	There was an array of pointers as a host variable.
2603	`only one dimensional arrays supported for char type`	There was an array of characters as a host variable. This is not a legal host variable type.
2604	`VARCHAR type must have a length`	Attempted to declare a VARCHAR or BINARY host variable without specifying a size for the array.
2605	`arrays of VARCHAR not supported`	Attempted to declare a host variable as an array of VARCHAR or BINARY. This is not a legal host variable type.
2606	`VARCHAR host variables cannot be pointers`	Attempted to declare a host variable as a pointer to a VARCHAR or BINARY. This is not a legal host variable type.

2606	`initializer not allowed on VARCHAR host variable`	You cannot specify the C variable initializer for a host variable of type VARCHAR or BINARY. It must be initialized in regular C executable code.
2608	`FIXCHAR type must have a length`	The DECL_FIXCHAR macro was used to declare a host variable of type FIXCHAR without specifying a length.
2609	`arrays of FIXCHAR not supported`	Attempted to declare a host variable as an array of FIXCHAR. This is not a legal host variable type.
2610	`arrays of int not supported`	Attempted to declare a host variable as an array of ints. This is not a legal host variable type.
2611	`precision must be specified for decimal type`	You must specify the precision when declaring a packed decimal host variable using the DECL_DECIMAL macro.
2612	`arrays of decimal not allowed`	Attempted to declare a host variable as an array of DECIMAL. This is not a legal host variable type.
2613	`unknown hostvar type`	A host variable type was declared that the SQL pre-processor could not understand.
2614	`invalid integer`	An integer was expected in an embedded SQL statement, but the preprocessor could not convert the value into an integer.
2615	`'%s' host variable must be a C string type`	A C string was expected in an embedded SQL statement, but the value supplied was not a C string.
2617	`'%s' symbol already defined`	Attempted to create a host variable that already exists.
2618	`invalid type for sql statement variable`	A host variable that was used as a statement identifier is an invalid type. The host variable needs to be of the type a_sql_statement_number.

(continues)

VII

Appendixes

Code	Message	Probable Cause
2619	`cannot find include file '%s'`	The specified include file cannot be found. Note that the pre-processor uses the INCLUDE environment variable to search for include files.
2620	`host variable '%s' is unknown`	Cannot find the host variable. Check to see if the host variable was declared in a declare section.
2621	`indicator variable '%s' is unknown`	There is an indicator variable in a statement that was not declared in the declare section.
2622	`invalid type for indicator variable '%s'`	There is an indicator variable that has an invalid type. The indicator variables must be of the type *short int*.
2623	`invalid host variable type on '%s'`	The host variable type was invalid. The preprocessor was expecting a host variable of a string type, but received something other than a string type.
2625	`host variable '%s' has two different definitions`	The same host variable name was defined with two different types in the same module.
2626	`statement '%s' not previously prepared`	An embedded SQL statement name was used without first being prepared.
2627	`cursor '%s' not previously declared`	An embedded SQL cursor name was used without first being declared.
2628	`unknown statement '%s'`	Attempted to drop an embedded SQL statement that cannot be found.

2629	host variables not allowed for this cursor	Host variables are not allowed on the declare statement for the cursor. If the cursor name is provided through a host variable, use full dynamic SQL and prepare the statement.
2630	host variables specified twice - on declare and open	The host variables for a cursor were specified on the declare and the open statements. The host variable should be specified on the declare statement for static SQL. For dynamic SQL, the host variable should be specified on the open statement.
2631	must specify a host list or using clause on '%s'	The statement requires host variables to be specified either in a host variable list or from a SQLDA.
2633	no into clause on select statement	An embedded static SELECT statement was specified without an INTO clause.
2636	incorrect embedded sql syntax	There is a syntax error in an embedded SQL specific statement.
2637	missing ending quote of string	There is a string constraint in an embedded SQL statement without an ending quote before the end of the line or end of the file.
2639	token too long	The maximum token length of 2K for the SQL preprocessor was exceeded. For excessive length constant strings in embedded SQL, use string concatenations.
2640	'%s' host variable must be an integer type	There was a host variable that was not an integer type in a statement where only an integer type host variable was allowed.

Appendix D

SQL System Tables

Both Watcom SQL and PowerBuilder have system tables. In addition, Watcom SQL has system views. *System tables* are database tables you use to keep track of the database and to enhance the execution speed and development speed of a database application. *System tables* help Watcom SQL determine access rights and function more efficiently. Watcom SQL system tables are used to store the following:

- User names and passwords

- Table names and table information, such as creator and remarks

- Column names and information such as data type, width, and whether NULLs are allowed

- Information about primary keys, foreign keys, and indexes such as column name and whether duplicates are allowed

- Access rights to the database, each table, and each column in a table

- User-defined stored procedures

- Database options such as page size, encryption, and case sensitivity

- Collation sequences that tell Watcom SQL in what order to store and retrieve keys and indexes

- Triggers

Because these tables are owned by SYS, they can only be read. Rows in the table cannot be updated with SQL INSERT, UPDATE, or DELETE commands. Similarly, the table definitions cannot be changed with an SQL ALTER or DROP command.

> **Note**
>
> The Watcom SQL system tables are listed in alphabetical order. However, you may want to review two tables, SYSTABLE and SYSUSERPERM, before the other tables. SYSTABLE and SYSUSERPERM play an intricate role in the system tables, and are referenced quite frequently by other system tables.

There are 20 system tables, as seen in figure D.1. The tables listed in figure D.1 show the system table with its primary key. If that primary key contains a foreign key to another table, the column name is followed by an (FK) notation. Also, if a table depends on another table (i.e. a table contains a foreign key to another table), then a line connects the two tables with a dot on the dependent table. This section describes each system table in detail.

Fig. D.1
Watcom SQL's 20 system tables (primary keys only) and how they relate to each other.

Tip
A dependent table is a table with a foreign key to another table. This is denoted with a dot on the dependent table in figure D.1.

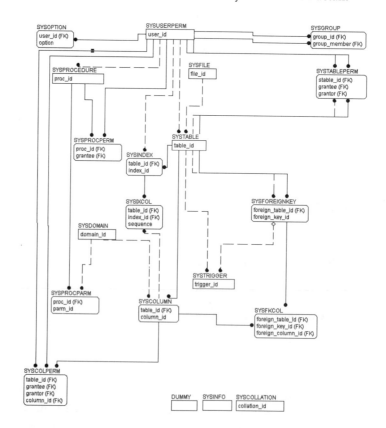

VII

Appendixes

- **PERM** in the table name indicates that it is a permission table. Access rights are defined in these tables.

- **FK** in the table name indicates that the table has something to do with the foreign keys in a database.

- **PROC** in the table name indicates that the table has something to do with stored procedures.

- **COL** in the table name means that the table has something to do with the column definition (except the SYSCOLLATION table, which has to do with collation sequences).

- **TABLE** in the table name indicates that the table has something to do with the table definition.

DUMMY

SYS.DUMMY is not used to store information. SYS.DUMMY was included so that the developer could query the database without having to access a table. For instance, if the user wanted to store the current user ID in a user_id local variable, he or she would use the following SELECT statement:

```
SELECT USER
    INTO :user_id
    FROM SYS.DUMMY;
```

In the SELECT USER statement, the program retrieves the user_id. SELECT USER requires no specific table, yet every SELECT requires a table name in the FROM clause. Therefore, Watcom included SYS.DUMMY to indicate that the information retrieved was not from a table. Table D.1 shows the layout for the SYS.DUMMY table. The SYS.DUMMY table has no primary key and no valuable columns. This table was created with dummy_col as a column because you cannot create a table without at least one column.

Table D.1   The Layout of SYS.DUMMY

Column Name	Column Datatype	Options	Description
dummy_col	INTEGER	NOT NULL	Dummy_col is never used and contains inconsequential data. It was added because Watcom SQL makes every table have at least one column.

SYSCOLLATION

Several times in an SQL Select, you must specify an order by using the ORDER BY clause. Although most SQL programmers take it for granted, Watcom SQL defaults to an ASCII format to determine the proper order for building and retrieving from a database.

Sometimes, especially in languages other than English, you may want a different sort order. To accomplish this, you use a different *collating sequence*. A collating sequence tells the database in what order to retrieve information, how to build indexes for the quickest access possible, and how to compare two columns.

Table D.2 shows the layout of the SYS.SYSCOLLATION table.

Table D.2   Layout of SYS.SYSCOLLATION

Column Name	Column Datatype	Options	Description
collation_id	SMALLINT	PK, NOT NULL	Collation_id is a unique number identifying the collating sequence.
collation_label	CHAR(10)	NOT NULL	Collation_label is a string that identifies each collating sequence. It is used with the -z option in the DBINITW command to define the collating sequence for a database.
collation_name	CHAR(128)	NOT NULL	Collation_name is the name of the collating sequence.
collation_order	BINARY(1024)	NOT NULL	Collation_order is a 256 element array defining the order of rows in the database.

You can't determine the collating sequence inside PowerBuilder. You must instead establish the collating sequence when you create the database using the DBINITW command (outside PowerBuilder) with the -z option and the collation_label. For instance, if you want to use the Canada-French collation sequence in a newly created database called Yourdb, you create your database outside PowerBuilder by running DBINITW with the following parameters:

```
DBINITW -z 863 yourdb.db
```

Table D.3 lists the available collating sequences in Watcom SQL.

Table D.3   Collation Sequences in Watcom SQL

collation_id	collation_label	collation_name
1	437	Code page 437, ASCII, United States
2	850	Code page 850, ASCII, Multilingual
3	852	Code page 852, ASCII, Slavic/Latin II
4	860	Code page 860, ASCII, Portugal
5	863	Code page 863, ASCII, Canada-French
6	865	Code page 865, ASCII, Norway
7	EBCDIC	EBCDIC
8	437EBCDIC	Code Page 437, EBCDIC
9	437LATIN1	Code Page 437, Latin 1
10	437ESP	Code Page 437, Spanish
11	437SVE	Code Page 437, Swedish/Finnish
12	850CYR	Code Page 850, Cyrillic
13	850DAN	Code Page 850, Danish
14	850ELL	Code Page 850, Greek
15	850ESP	Code Page 850, Spanish
16	850ISL	Code Page 850, Icelandic
17	850LATIN1	Code Page 850, Latin 1
18	850LATIN2	Code Page 850, Latin 2

(continues)

Appendixes

VII

Table D.3	**Continued**	
collation_id	**collation_label**	**collation_name**
19	850NOR	Code Page 850, Norwegian
20	850RUS	Code Page 850, Russian
21	850SVE	Code Page 850, Swedish/Finnish
22	850TRK	Code Page 850, Turkish
23	852LATIN2	Code Page 852, Latin 2
24	852CYR	Code Page 852, Cyrillic
25	855CYR	Code Page 855, Cyrillic
26	856HEB	Code Page 856, Hebrew
27	857TRK	Code Page 857, Turkish
28	860LATIN1	Code Page 860, Latin 1
29	861ISL	Code Page 861, Icelandic
30	862HEB	Code Page 862, Hebrew
31	863LATIN1	Code Page 863, Latin 1
32	865NOR	Code Page 865, Norwegian
33	866RUS	Code Page 866, Russian
34	869ELL	Code Page 869, Greek

SYSCOLPERM

Unlike other SQL permissions, Watcom SQL allows you to GRANT update access at the column level. This is done with the following SQL command:

```
GRANT UPDATE ( mycolumn ) ON mytable TO myuser
```

Every time access is granted at the column level, a record is inserted in the SYS.SYSCOLPERM table. The layout for the SYS.SYSCOLPERM table is shown in Table D.4.

VII

Table D.4	Layout for SYS.SYSCOLPERM		
Column Name	Column Datatype	Options	Description
table_id	SMALLINT	PK, FK1, NOT NULL	Table_id references the table of the column update access. The table_id, along with the column_id, is a foreign key of the SYSCOLUMN table.
grantee	SMALLINT	PK, FK2, NOT NULL	Grantee is the user ID of the user who granted the update permission. It is a foreign key of the SYSUSERPERM table.
grantor	SMALLINT	PK, FK2, NOT NULL	Grantor is the user ID of the user who is granted update permission. It is a foreign key of the SYSUSERPERM table.
column_id	SMALLINT	PK, FK1, NOT NULL	Column_id references the column where the access is granted. The column_id, along with the table_id, is a foreign key to the SYSCOLUMN table.

Caution

Granting permission can be tricky. At many companies, there are security positions or even departments whose only task is to administer security to the database.

There are several points you must consider when granting security:

- You can grant database, table, or column access to a user.

- You can grant SELECT, UPDATE, DELETE, or INSERT (as well as ALTER or DROP) access to a user for any database or table.

- Table access overrides column access. If you grant table access to an individual, that access supersedes specific column access. Also, if you grant Alter, Drop, Delete, or Insert access to a table, the user can access those SQL functions, no matter what column access he is given. For instance, if a table has three columns (columns 1, 2, and 3), and if I have Drop and Column Update access, I can still Drop a row off a table, no matter what my column access is.

SYSCOLUMN

Every table must have at least one column. These column definitions are stored in the SYS.SYSCOLUMN table. By accessing this table, the end user can determine a column's datatype, width, and other options that are set when a column is defined. Table D.5 describes the SYS.SYSCOLUMN layout.

Table D.5	**Layout for SYS.SYSCOLUMN**		
Column Name	**Column Datatype**	**Options**	**Description**
table_id	SMALLINT	PK, FK1, NOT NULL	Table_id is a foreign key describing the table where the column resides. Table_id, along with column_id, forms the primary key for SYS.SYSCOLUMN.
column_id	SMALLINT	PK, NOT NULL	Column_id is a sequence number that uniquely identifies the column.
pkey	CHAR(1)	NOT NULL	Pkey contains a Y or N, determining whether this column is a primary key or is part of a primary key.
domain_id	SMALLINT	FK2, NOT NULL	Domain_id is a number determining the datatype of the column. Domain_id is a foreign key to SYSDOMAIN.
nulls	CHAR(1)	NOT NULL	Nulls contains a Y or N, indicating whether this column allows NULLs.
width	SMALLINT	NOT NULL	Width can contain the number of characters in a string column, the precision in a numeric column, or the number of bytes allocated for this column.
scale	SMALLINT	NOT NULL	Scale contains the number of digits after the decimal place for numeric columns or a zero for all other column data types.
estimate	INTEGER	NOT NULL	This column is used for self-tuning by Watcom. The more you access your database, the better the performance should be.

VII

Appendixes

Column Name	Column Datatype	Options	Description
column_name	CHAR(128)	NOT NULL	The name of the column.
remarks	LONG VARCHAR		The remarks of the column.
default	LONG VARCHAR		The default value of this column that is only set during an insert.

SYSDOMAIN

A datatype is also known as a *domain*. The SYS.SYSDOMAIN table lists Watcom SQL's available datatypes and allows the user to choose the domain (or datatype) for each column based on those available. Table D.6 shows the layout for SYS.SYSDOMAIN.

Table D.6   Layout for SYS.SYSDOMAIN

Column Name	Column Datatype	Options	Description
domain_id	SMALLINT	PK, NOT NULL	Domain_id is a unique key describing the domain.
domain_name	CHAR(128)	NOT NULL	Domain_name is the name of the domain data type.

The SYSCOLUMN and SYSPROCPARM tables have foreign keys to the SYSDOMAIN table for their data access. Table D.7 lists the available domain data types.

Table D.7   Available Domains (Datatypes) in Watcom SQL

Domain ID	Name	Domain Bytes	Range
1	smallint	2	-32768 - 32767
2	integer	4	-2,147,483,648 - 2,147,483,647

(continues)

Table D.7   Continued

Domain ID	Name	Domain Bytes	Range
6	date	4	1/1/0001 - 12/12/9999
7	char(string_size)	string_size	0 to 32767 bytes (string_size)
9	varchar(string_size)	string_size	0 to 32767 bytes (string_size)
8	char(string_size)	string_size	0 to 32767 bytes (string_size)
10	long varchar	8	Database size**
11	binary(string_size)	string_size	0 to 32767 bytes (string_size)
12	long binary	8	Database size**
13	timestamp	8	YYYY:MM:DD HH:MM:SS:PPPP
14	time	8	HH:MM:SS:PPPP

*"a" is the number of digits after the decimal while "b" is the number of digits before the decimal.

**The current maximum database size is two gigabytes.

SYSFILE

Most databases only use one file. However, Watcom SQL lets you split your files into several different physical files. These files are called *tablespaces* or *dbspaces*. Dbspaces allow you to expand a database larger than one physical disk drive. To create a dbspace, use the CREATE DBSPACE SQL command as follows:

```
CREATE DBSPACE my_new_file AS 'newfile.db'
```

When you create a table, you can place that table in a dbspace other than SYSTEM if you specify the existing dbspace, as follows:

```
Create Table my_new_table (
    my_number      integer
) IN my_new_dbspace
```

The layout for SYS.SYSFILE is shown in Table D.8.

Table D.8 Layout for SYS.SYSFILE

Column Name	Column Datatype	Options	Description
file_id	SMALLINT	PK, NOT NULL	A number that uniquely identifies the database file. All databases have at least one file, identified by 0, where the system tables are stored.
file_name	LONG VARCHAR	NOT NULL	This is the complete name of the database file, including the path.
dbspace_name	CHAR(128)	NOT NULL	This is the name of the dbspace. For the first file (with file_id of 0), the dbspace_name is SYSTEM. For other dbspaces, the dbspace_name is determined by the CREATE DBSPACE SQL command.

SYSFKCOL

A *foreign key* is a relationship between two tables—a *foreign table* and a *primary table*. Every foreign key relationship is described by a row in SYS.SYSFOREIGNKEY and one or more rows in SYS.SYSFKCOL.

SYS.SYSFKCOL lists all the foreign key to primary key relationships. SYS.SYSFKCOL lists all the columns in the database that are used for or part of a foreign key. This table makes use of a *logical* foreign key (as opposed to a *physical* foreign key). A physical foreign key is a foreign key that is expressly declared during the creation of a table. A logical foreign key is a relationship between two tables that is not reflected by an actual foreign key declaration.

SYS.SYSFKCOL makes use of two physical foreign keys. A logical foreign key is a foreign key that is implied but not expressly declared. Primary_column_id, along with the related primary_table_id in SYS.SYSFOREIGNKEY (described after this), forms a foreign key to SYS.SYSCOLUMN. Because the two columns that form the foreign key come from two different tables, there is no way to expressly declare a physical foreign key. However, a logical foreign key relationship is definitely present.

Because logical foreign keys are implied but not expressed, referential integrity is not tightly enforced except through programming. The logical foreign key relationship is shown as a foreign key in parenthesis.

◀ See "Understanding Keys," p. 48

Table D.9 shows the layout for SYS.SYSFKCOL.

Table D.9 Layout for SYS.SYSFKCOL			
Column Name	**Column Datatype**	**Options**	**Description**
foreign_table_id	SMALLINT	PK, FK1, FK2 NOT NULL	Foreign_table_id describes the table where the foreign key resides. It is part of three keys: foreign_table_id, foreign_key_id, and foreign_column_id. These form the primary key for SYSFKCOL. Foreign_table_id and foreign_key_id form a foreign key to SYSFOREIGNKEY. Finally, foreign_table_id and foreign_column_id form a foreign key to SYSCOLUMN.
foreign_key_id	SMALLINT	PK, FK1, NOT NULL	Foreign_key_id describes the sequence number of the foreign key found in SYSFOREIGNKEY. Foreign_key_id is part of the primary key, and is also part of a foreign key to SYSFOREIGNKEY.
foreign_column_id	SMALLINT	PK, FK2, NOT NULL	Foreign_column_id describes the column where the foreign key exists. Foreign_column_id is part of the primary key and is part of a foreign key to SYSCOLUMN.
primary_column_id	SMALLINT	NOT NULL, (FK3)	Primary_column_id describes the column in the primary table where the relationship to the foreign table exists. Primary_column_id, along with the primary_table_id in SYSFOREIGNKEY, is part of a logical foreign key to SYSCOLUMN.

SYSFOREIGNKEY

As mentioned in the SYSFKCOL description, every foreign key is described by a row on the SYS.SYSFOREIGNKEY table. You can see the layout for SYSFOREIGNKEY in Table D.10.

Table D.10   Layout for SYS.SYSFOREIGNKEY

Column Name	Column Datatype	Options	Description
foreign_table_id	SMALLINT	PK, FK1, Index1, NOT NULL	Foreign_table_id describes the table where the foreign key resides. Foreign_table_id is part of three keys. Foreign_table_id and foreign_key_id form the primary key for SYSFOREIGNKEY. Foreign_table_id also is a foreign key to SYSTABLE. Finally, a unique index is defined on role and foreign_table_id.
foreign_key_id	SMALLINT	PK, NOT NULL	Foreign_key_id is part of the primary key, and is the sequence number of the foreign key.
primary_table_id	SMALLINT	FK2, (FK3), NOT NULL	Primary_table_id describes the table where the primary key relating to this column's foreign key resides. It also serves as a logical foreign key with primary_column_id in SYSFKCOL to the SYSCOLUMN table.
root	INTEGER	NOT NULL	Foreign keys are stored in a binary-tree format. A *binary-tree format* is a fast indexing method used by Watcom SQL for quick retrieval. Root describes the root to the binary tree where any search should begin.
check_on_commit	CHAR(1)	NOT NULL	Check_on_commit is a Y or N, determining whether this table should wait until a commit before checking for referential integrity.
nulls	CHAR(1)	NOT NULL	Nulls describe whether this foreign key can be NULL. If you allow your foreign key to be NULL, then you imply a zero-to-many relationship with the primary table. If you don't allow NULLs in your foreign key, you imply a one-to-many relationship with the primary table.

(continues)

Table D.10	Continued		
Column Name	**Column Datatype**	**Options**	**Description**
role	CHAR(128)	Index1, UNIQUE, NOT NULL	Role is the name of the relationship between a foreign table and a primary table. A unique index is defined using role and foreign_table_id.
remarks	LONG VARCHAR		Remarks is a string of comments.

SYSGROUP

A *user group* is a collection of users. When using the GRANT SQL command, a user group is considered a single user. However, a group has several members in itself. Every user group–member combination is defined in the SYS.SYSGROUP table shown in Table D.11.

◀ See "GRANT," p. 555

User groups and members have a many-to-many relationship. A user group contains several members and a member may be in several groups.

Table D.11	Layout for SYS.SYSGROUP		
Column Name	**Column Datatype**	**Options**	**Description**
group_id	SMALLINT	PK, FK, NOT NULL	Group_id is the identification of a group. Groups are considered users and therefore Group_id is a foreign key to SYSUSERPERM.
group_member	SMALLINT	PK, FK, NOT NULL	Group_member is the user id of the member of a group. Group_member is also a foreign key to SYSUSERPERM.

To define a group, you first define a user group as a single user with the following SQL Grant statement:

◀ See "Using the GRANT and REVOKE SQL Commands," p. 229

```
GRANT CONNECT TO user_group IDENTIFIED BY asdfasdf
```

You have now created a user named user_group with a password of asdfasdf. Next, you define user_group as a group with the following SQL command:

```
GRANT GROUP TO user_group
```

Now you can add members to your user group with the following SQL command:

```
GRANT MEMBERSHIP IN GROUP user_group TO cwood
GRANT MEMBERSHIP IN GROUP user_group TO dohearn
GRANT MEMBERSHIP IN GROUP user_group TO jrang
GRANT MEMBERSHIP IN GROUP user_group TO phoran
```

You have now added cwood, dohearn, jrang, and phoran to user_group. Any access granted to user_group will also be granted to all of its members.

SYSINDEX

Indexes are created either with the UNIQUE clause in the Create Table statement, or with the CREATE INDEX statement. An index can be one of three types:

- *Unique constraint.* A unique constraint is an index that must not have any duplicate values. NULLs are not allowed in unique constraints.

- *Unique index.* A unique index is an index that cannot have any duplicate values unless that value is NULL. A NULL in an unique index implies that no index exists for the row being queried.

- *Non-unique index.* Columns that are non-unique indexes can duplicate each other and/or contain NULL.

When you create an index, a row is created in SYS.SYSINDEX describing the index. You can see the layout for SYS.SYSINDEX in Table D.12.

Table D.12	Layout for SYS.SYSINDEX		
Column Name	**Column Datatype**	**Options**	**Description**
table_id	SMALLINT	PK, FK1, NOT NULL	Table_id describes the table that the index belongs to. It is part of the primary key and is a foreign key to SYSTABLE.
index_id	SMALLINT	PK, NOT NULL	Index_id is a sequential number of the index.

(continues)

Table D.12   Continued

Column Name	Column Datatype	Options	Description
root	INTEGER	NOT NULL	Indexes are stored in a binary-tree format. A binary-tree format is a fast indexing method used by Watcom SQL for quick retrieval. Root describes the root to the binary tree where any search should begin.
file_id	SMALLINT	NOT NULL	File_id is the file or dbspace containing the index. (Currently, this field is not used, and the index is always contained in the same file as the table.)
unique	CHAR(1)	NOT NULL	Unique indicates whether the index is a unique index (Y), a non-unique index (N), or a unique constraint (U).
creator	SMALLINT	FK2, Index, NOT NULL	Creator describes the user that created the index. It is a foreign key to SYSUSERPERM.
index_name	CHAR(128)	Index, NOT NULL	Index_name is the name given to the index. No two indexes can have the same name. It forms an index with creator.
remarks	LONG VARCHAR		Remarks are comments about the index.

SYSINFO

SYS.SYSINFO (see Table D.13) contains the system information for the database that is set when you create the database. Because of its nature, SYSINFO does not have a primary key and only has one record per database.

Table D.13   Layout for SYS.SYSINFO

Column Name	Column Datatype	Options	Description
page_size	SMALLINT	NOT NULL	Page_size is the number of bytes in lower memory reserved for each transaction. Typically, the larger the page_size, the

Column Name	Column Datatype	Options	Description
			faster the processing. However, the 16-bit engines (DBSTARTW and RTSTARTW) may not be able to access page sizes over 1024.
encryption	CHAR(1)	NOT NULL	Encryption is Y or N, indicating whether your database is encrypted. It protects your sensitive data, but can be corrupted by some compression packages. Certain disk-search programs cannot access your database.
blank_padding	CHAR(1)	NOT NULL	Y or N, indicating whether trailing spaces are to be considered when performing string comparisons with your database.
case_sensitivity	CHAR(1)	NOT NULL	Y or N, indicating whether case is to be considered when performing string comparisons with your database.
default_collation	CHAR(10)		String specifying one of the provided collating sequences in SYSCOLLATE (default "850").
database_version	SMALLINT	NOT NULL	Database_version is a small integer describing the Watcom SQL database version where this database was created.

SYSIXCOL

SYS.SYSIXCOL lists all columns that are part of an index, as seen in Table D.14.

Table D.14	Layout for SYS.SYSIXCOL		
Column Name	**Column Datatype**	**Options**	**Description**
table_id	SMALLINT	PK, FK1, FK2, NOT NULL	Table_id references the table that the index is for. Table_id, index_id, and sequence are the primary key for SYSIXCOL. Table_id also serves as foreign keys to (with index_id) SYSINDEX and to (with column_id) SYSCOLUMN.
index_id	SMALLINT	PK, FK1, NOT NULL	Index_id is a sequential number of the index. It acts as a foreign key, along with table_id, to SYSINDEX.
sequence	SMALLINT	PK, NOT NULL	Sequence is the relative importance of the primary key in the index.
column_id	SMALLINT	FK2, NOT NULL	Together with table_id, column_id identifies the column that is the index. Table_id and column_id form a foreign key to SYSCOLUMN.
order	CHAR(1)	NOT NULL	Order is A or D to indicate that the index is kept in either ascending or descending order.

SYSOPTION

◀ See "SET OP-TION," p. 565

◀ See "Using DBINITW.EXE," p. 628

Each user is allowed to set her own options by using the SET command. For example, if you want to ignore conversion errors, you should use the following SQL statement:

```
SET OPTION CONVERSION_ERROR = "OFF"
```

When you set your own options, the options get stored in the SYS.SYSOPTION table under your user id. Table D.15; Table D.16 shows the layout for the SYS.SYSOPTION table.

VII

Appendixes

Table D.15 Layout for SYS.SYSOPTION

Column Name	Column Datatype	Options	Description
user_id	SMALLINT	PK, FK, NOT NULL	User_id identifies the user whose settings are set. It is part of the primary key and is a foreign key to the SYSUSERPERM table.
option	CHAR(128)	PK, NOT NULL	Option is a character string describing the option set by the user. It is part of the primary key.
setting	LONG VARCHAR	NOT NULL	Setting is a character string describing how the option is set.

Table D.16 User Options in SYS.SYSOPTION

Option	Initial Setting	Description
Auto_commit	Off	Auto_commit is set to ON or OFF, indicating whether a COMMIT and a ROLLBACK are performed after each successful command.
Auto_refetch	On	Auto_refetch is set to ON or OFF, indicating whether queries in the ISQLW window will be refetched after an Insert, Delete, or Update.
Bell	On	Bell is set to ON or OFF, indicating whether a beep will sound when an error occurs.
Blocking	On	Blocking is set to ON or OFF, indicating whether a user cannot use a locked table and must wait until that table becomes available, or a locked table will return an error code.
Checkpoint_time	60	Checkpoint_time is the number of minutes before an automatic checkpoint is issued.
Commit_on_exit	On	Commit_on_exit is set to ON or OFF, indicating whether a commit is done when leaving the ISQLW environment.

◄ See "Maintaining Consistency and Integrity through Isolation Levels," p. 276

(continues)

Option	Initial Setting	Description
Conversion_error	On	Conversion_error is set to ON or OFF, indicating whether to report conversion errors or to process conversion problems by placing a NULL in the field that is generating the error.
Date_format	YYYY-MM-DD	This mask sets the date format. You could also use *f* for French days and months. For instance, a format of *YYYY ffffffffffffffff DD* will list the year, the name of the month in French, and the day.
Date_order	YMD	Indicates the sort order of dates: YMD, DMY, or MDY.
Echo	On	Echo is set to ON or OFF, indicating whether comments are echoed to the ISQLW environment before they are executed.
Headings	On	Headings is set to ON or OFF indicating whether headings will be displayed after execution of a Select statement in ISQLW.
Input_format	ASCII	Controls the format for the Input SQL command. Valid values are ASCII, DBASE, DBASEII, DBASEIII, DIF, FIXED, FOXPRO, LOTUS, and WATFILE.
Isolation_level	0	Sets the isolation level. Valid values are 0, 1, 2, and 3. ISQL_log is a string containing the name of the file where all SQL commands in the ISQLW environment are to be logged.
NULLS	(NULL)	NULLS is a string describing how NULLs are to be displayed in the ISQLW environment.
On_error	Prompt	On_error controls what happens when an error occurs during a Read, RTSQL execution, or DBSQL execution. Valid values are STOP, PROMPT, CONTINUE, and EXIT.
Output_format	ASCII	Controls the format for the Output SQL command. Valid values are ASCII, DBASEII, DBASEIII, DIF, FIXED, FOXPRO, LOTUS, SQL, TEXT, and WATFILE.
Output_length	0	Controls the length (through truncation) of the output file from the Output SQL command. The default is 0 (no truncation).

Table D.16   Continued

Option	Initial Setting	Description
Precision	30	Precision specifies how many significant digits are allowed after a mathematical operation.
Recovery_time	2	Sets the maximum length of time in minutes that a system takes to recover from system failure before aborting the recovery.
Row_counts	Off	Row_counts is set to ON for actual or OFF for estimate, indicating how the number of rows retrieved from a query will be stored in a transaction object or variable.
Scale	6	Scale specifies the minimum number of digits a value is allowed before truncating (if necessary) because of exceeding precision.
Screen_format	Text	Screen_format allows you to set the format of the screen.
Statistics	3	Represents the height of the statistics window in lines in the ISQLW environment. A 0 in the Statistics field turns the statistics window off.
Thread_count	0	Sets the maximum number of concurrent requests being processed by the database in a multi-user database format. 0 defaults the engine used: if you are using 16-bit DOS, the thread count will default to 3. If you are using 16-bit QNX or 16-bit Windows, the thread county will default to eight. Finally, if you are using a 32-bit engine, the number of threads increases to 20.
Time_format	HH:NN:SS.SSS	Time_format is an edit mask that sets the default for all time datatype displays.
Timestamp_format	YYYY-MM-DD HH:NN:SS.SSS	Timestamp_format is an edit mask that sets the default for all timestamp datatype displays.
Truncation_length	30	Controls the truncation of the results of a Select SQL statement in the ISQLW environment.
Wait_for_commit	Off	Wait_for_commit is set to ON if you want to check foreign key referential integrity immediately after all Delete, Insert, or Update statements. It is set to OFF if you want to check referential integrity only when a Commit is issued.

◄ See "Imple-
menting Proce-
dures and
Triggers,"
p. 313

SYSPROCEDURE

Watcom now allows stored procedures. You can set up these procedures to be accessed from within Watcom SQL or from programming languages that use Watcom SQL. All procedures have a row declared in SYS.SYSPROCEDURE. Table D.17 shows the layout for SYS.SYSPROCEDURE.

Table D.17 Layout for SYS.SYSPROCEDURE			
Column Name	**Column Datatype**	**Options**	**Description**
proc_id	SMALLINT	PK, NOT NULL	Proc_id is a unique sequence number that identifies the stored procedure for the current database. It is the primary key of SYSPROCEDURE.
creator	SMALLINT	FK, Index, NOT NULL	Creator is the user id of the owner of the procedure. It is a foreign key to SYSUSERPERM.
proc_name	CHAR(128)	Index, NOT NULL	Proc_name is the name of the stored procedure. Each creator can have only one proc_name. Proc_name and creator form a unique index.
proc_defn	LONG VARCHAR		Proc_defn contains the command used to create the procedure.
remarks	LONG VARCHAR		Remarks are comments made about the stored procedure by the creator.

SYSPROCPARM

Stored procedures hold all of the parameters that are passed to the stored procedure in SYS.SYSPROCPARM. See Table D.18 for the layout of SYS.SYSPROCPARM.

Table D.18 Layout for SYS.SYSPROCPARM

Column Name	Column Datatype	Options	Description
proc_id	SMALLINT	PK, FK1, NOT NULL	Proc_id is a number that uniquely defines the procedure in SYSPROCEDURE. It is part of the primary key of SYSPROCPARM and is a foreign key to SYSPROCEDURE.
parm_id	SMALLINT	PK, NOT NULL	Parm_id is a sequence number of the parameter number of a stored procedure. Proc_id and parm_id make up the primary key of SYSPROCPARM.
parm_type	SMALLINT	NOT NULL	The parameter type can be 0 (normal parameter), 1 (result), 2 (SQLSTATE error value), and 3 (SQLCODE error value).
parm_mode_in	CHAR(1)	NOT NULL	Y or N indicates whether this parameter supplies a value to the stored procedure.
parm_mode_out	CHAR(1)	NOT NULL	Y or N indicates whether this parameter is returned to the calling procedure.
domain_id	SMALLINT	FK2, NOT NULL	Identifies the data type. Domain_id is a foreign key to SYSDOMAIN.
width	SMALLINT	NOT NULL	Width is the number of characters in a string, the precision of numeric values, and the number of bytes of storage for all other passed variables.
scale	SMALLINT	NOT NULL	Scale is the number of digits after the decimal place in numeric parameters. Scale is set to zero if it isn't applicable.
parm_name	CHAR(128)	NOT NULL	The name of the parameter.
remarks	LONG VARCHAR		A string containing comments of this parameter.

SYSPROCPERM

Like tables, procedures can be restricted. Authority for stored procedures is stored in the SYS.SYSPROCPERM table. Table D.19 shows the layout for the SYS.SYSPROCPERM table.

Table D.19 Layout for SYS.SYSPROCPERM			
Column Name	**Column Datatype**	**Options**	**Description**
proc_id	SMALLINT	PK, FK1, NOT NULL	Proc_id identifies the procedure whose authority is granted. It is part of the primary key and is a foreign key to SYSPROCEDURE.
grantee	SMALLINT	PK, FK2, NOT NULL	Grantee is the user number of the person receiving access to the stored procedure. Proc_id and grantee make up the primary key. Grantee is a foreign key to SYSUSERPERM.

SYSTABLE

Tip
Dependent tables have foreign keys to other tables.

Most other system tables are dependent on SYS.SYSTABLE, SYS.SYSUSERPERM and/or SYS.SYSCOLUMN. For every table or view defined in your database, there is a corresponding row in the SYS.SYSTABLE table. Table D.20 shows the layout for SYS.SYSTABLE.

Table D.20 Layout for SYS.SYSTABLE			
Column Name	**Column Datatype**	**Options**	**Description**
table_id	SMALLINT	PK, NOT NULL	A sequence number identifying the table. It is the primary key of SYSTABLE.
file_id	SMALLINT	FK1, NOT NULL	File_id is the file identifier of the file or dbspace where the table resides. It is a foreign key to SYSFILE.
count	INTEGER	NOT NULL	Count is the number of rows in the table updated during each successful CHECKPOINT. This number is used by Watcom SQL for optimizing performance.

Column Name	Column Datatype	Options	Description
first_page	INTEGER	NOT NULL	A Watcom SQL database is always divided into pages. This describes where to locate the first page of the table.
last_page	INTEGER	NOT NULL	The last page containing information about the table.
primary_root	INTEGER	NOT NULL	Primary keys are stored in a binary-tree format. A binary-tree format is a fast indexing method used by Watcom SQL for quick retrieval. Primary_root describes the root to the binary tree where any search should begin. (Please note that first_page, last_page, and primary_root will all be zero for views.)
creator	SMALLINT	FK2, Index, NOT NULL	Creator is the user id of the creator of the table or view. It is a foreign key to SYSUSERPERM.
table_name	CHAR(128)	Index, NOT NULL	Table_name is the name of the table. Table_name, along with creator, form a unique key. No user can create two tables with the same name.
table_type	CHAR(10)	NOT NULL	Table_type has four possible values: BASE for base tables, VIEW for views, GBL TEMP for global temporary tables, and LCL TEMP for local temporary tables.
view_def	LONG VARCHAR		For views, view_def contains the CREATE statement used to create the view. For tables, this column will contain any CHECK constraints for the table.
remarks	LONG VARCHAR		Remarks are a string of comments about the table. Remarks are set by the COMMENT ON SQL command.

SYSTABLEPERM

SYS.SYSTABLEPERM, as broken down in figure D.21, lists the permissions available for each user on each table.

Table D.21 Layout for SYS.SYSTABLEPERM

Column Name	Column Datatype	Options	Description
stable_id	SMALLINT	PK, FK1, NOT NULL	Stable_id is the table number of the table or view that permission is granted for. It is part of the primary key, and is a foreign key to SYSTABLE.
grantee	SMALLINT	PK, FK2, NOT NULL	Grantee is the user id who has been granted access to the table or view. It is a foreign key to SYSUSERPERM.
grantor	SMALLINT	PK, FK3, NOT NULL	Grantor is the user id who granted access to the grantee for the table or view. It is a foreign key to SYSUSERPERM.
ttable_id	SMALLINT	FK4, NOT NULL	Currently, ttable_id is not used. It has the same value as stable_id, and is a foreign key to SYSTABLE.
selectauth	CHAR(1)	NOT NULL	Selectauth can be Y to indicate that the grantee has select authority, N to indicate that the grantee does not have this authority, and G to indicate that the grantee can grant this authority to others.
insertauth	CHAR(1)	NOT NULL	Insertauth can be Y to indicate that the grantee has insert authority, N to indicate that the grantee does not have this authority, and G to indicate that the grantee can grant this authority to others.
deleteauth	CHAR(1)	NOT NULL	Deleteauth can be Y to indicate that the grantee has delete authority, N to indicate that the grantee does not have this authority, and G to indicate that the grantee can grant this authority to others.
updateauth	CHAR(1)	NOT NULL	Updateauth can be Y to indicate that the grantee has update authority, N to indicate that the grantee does not have this authority, and G to indicate that the grantee can grant this authority to others.

Column Name	Column Datatype	Options	Description
updatecols	CHAR(1)	NOT NULL	Updatecols can be Y to indicate that the grantee has been granted or denied specific column update capability in SYSCOLPERM. N indicates that no such authority has been specified.
alterauth	CHAR(1)	NOT NULL	Alterauth can be Y to indicate that the grantee has alterauth authority, N to indicate that the grantee does not have this authority, and G to indicate that the grantee can grant this authority to others.
referenceauth	CHAR(1)	NOT NULL	Referenceauth can be Y to indicate that the grantee has reference authority, N to indicate that the grantee does not have this authority, and G to indicate that the grantee can grant this authority to others. Reference authority indicates that the grantee is allowed to reference this table with a foreign key from another table.

SYSTRIGGER

One row on the SYS.SYSTRIGGER table (see Table D.22) describes declared triggers. SYS.SYSTRIGGER also contains triggers that are automatically generated when foreign key/referential integrity actions are required by the database.

◀ See "Using Triggers," p. 344

Table D.22   Layout for SYS.SYSTRIGGER

Column Name	Column Datatype	Options	Description
trigger_id	SMALLINT	PK, NOT NULL	This is a sequence number that identifies the trigger. It is the primary key for SYSTRIGGER.
table_id	SMALLINT	FK1, Index1, Index2, NOT NULL	Table_id identifies the table where the trigger is applied to. Table_id is a foreign key to SYSTABLE.

(continues)

Table D.22 Layout for SYS.SYSTRIGGER

Column Name	Column Datatype	Options	Description
event	CHAR(1)	Index1, Index2 NOT NULL	Event describes the action that causes the trigger to fire. Valid values are D (Delete), I (Insert), U (Update), C (Update of column).
trigger_time	CHAR(1)	Index1, NOT NULL	Trigger_time describes when the trigger will fire in relation to the event. Valid values are B (Before the event) and A (After the event).
trigger_order	SMALLINT	Index1	Trigger_order is a sequence number that determines the order of the trigger in relation to other triggers that fire at the same event and trigger_time.
foreign_table_id	SMALLINT	FK2, Index2	Foreign_table_id identifies the table where the foreign key definition has caused a referential integrity action.
foreign_key_id	SMALLINT	FK2, Index2	Foreign_key_id identifies the foreign key where the foreign key definition has caused a referential integrity action. Foreign_table_id and foreign_key_id form a foreign key to SYSFOREIGNKEY.
referential_action	CHAR(1)		This is the referential integrity action defined by a foreign key. Valid values are C (CASCADE), D (DELETE), N (SET NULL), and R (RESTRICT).
trigger_name	CHAR(128)	Index3	Trigger_name is the name of the trigger. Two triggers can't have the same name.
trigger_defn	LONG VARCHAR	NOT NULL	Trigger_defn is the command used to create the trigger.
remarks	LONG VARCHAR		Remarks is a comment string describing the trigger.

SYSUSERPERM

SYS.SYSUSERPERM, as seen in Table D.23, identifies the user. It is referenced by all creator and authority type fields in the system tables.

Column Name	Column Datatype	Options	Description
Table D.23 Layout for SYS.SYSUSERPERM			
user_id	SMALLINT	PK, NOT NULL	User_id is a sequence number that uniquely defines the user. It is the primary key for SYSUSERPERM.
user_name	CHAR(128)	Index, NOT NULL	User_name is the name of the user. It is how a user logs on to the database.
password	CHAR(128)		Password is the password required by the user.
resourceauth	CHAR(1)	NOT NULL	Resourceauth is set to Y or N, indicating whether the individual has the right to create tables.
dbaauth	CHAR(1)	NOT NULL	Dbaauth is set to Y or N, indicating whether the individual has the right to grant access to other users. This is a very powerful access to grant.
scheduleauth	CHAR(1)	NOT NULL	Scheduleauth is set to Y or N to see if the user has scheduling authority. This is not currently used by Watcom SQL.
user_group	CHAR(1)	NOT NULL	User_group is a Y or N, indicating if this is an individual user or a user group.
remarks	LONG VARCHAR		Remarks is a comment string describing the user.

Appendix E

Watcom SQL System Views

Views are a way to present read-only information to a user in a format that may be easier to understand than direct table access. Additionally, views can be used to restrict viewing access on a table to only specific columns. Hence, views can allow accessibility to data as well as enhance sensitive data security.

Due to the nature and design of database management systems, many system tables use sequence numbers, codes, and other ambiguous entries to describe the database. Watcom SQL provides system views to help ease the burden and ambiguity of using system tables.

If you need to access the system tables to determine user or column information, Watcom SQL system views present system information more clearly. It is often easier than directly accessing the system tables.

◄ See "Using Views," p. 52

◄ See "CREATE VIEW," p. 542

This appendix describes each view, lists the columns of each view with its origin and a description, and lists the SQL that Watcom used to create each view.

> **Note**
>
> Even for SQL gurus, the SQL used to create some of these Watcom SQL system views can get pretty advanced. Still, it's a good way to learn some very complicated SQL SELECT statements. Coupled with a list and description of the view columns, you should have no trouble using the system views.
>
> Remember, Watcom SQL creates these views for you. You don't have to create the views yourself. The list of SQL statements used to create the views is only to show you the SQL commands needed to create system views. Also, as with all views, the Watcom SQL system views are read-only and, like the system tables, cannot be directly modified by the database user.

SYSCATALOG

The SYS.SYSCATALOG view lists all the tables and views in SYS.SYSTABLE in a more readable format. You can see the columns of SYS.SYSCATALOG in Table E.1.

Table E.1   Columns in the SYS.SYSCATALOG View

Column Name	Column Table	Original Column	Description
creator	SYSUSERPERM	user_name	Creator is the user_name of the user who created the table. User_name is the name of the user. It is how a user logs on to the database.
tname	SYSTABLE	table_name	Tname is the name of the table. You cannot create two tables with the same name.
dbspacename	SYSFILE	dbspace_name	Dbspacename is the name of the dbspace. For the first file (with file_id of 0), the dbspacename is SYSTEM. For other dbspaces, the dbspace_name is determined by the CREATE DBSPACE SQL command.
tabletype	See Description	See Description	Tabletype is the table_type of the table found in SYSTABLE. However, all BASE entries have been converted to TABLE.

Column Name	Column Table	Original Column	Description
ncols	See Description	See Description	Ncols is a count of the number of columns in the table. It is derived from the number of entries in SYSCOLUMN.
primary_key	See Description	See Description	Primary_key is set to Y or N depending on whether there is a primary key for this table.
check	See Description	See Description	Check will contain any CHECK constraints for the table. If there are no check constraints or this is a view, check is set to null.
remarks	SYSTABLE	remarks	Remarks are a string of comments about the table.

The SQL used to create SYS.SYSCATALOG is as follows:

◀ See "SELECT," p. 563

```
CREATE VIEW SYS.SYSCATALOG (creator, tname, dbspacename, tabletype,
ncols, primary_key, "check", remarks)
AS SELECT
        (select user_name from SYS.SYSUSERPERM where
user_id=SYSTABLE.creator),
        table_name,
        (select dbspace_name from SYS.SYSFILE where
file_id=SYSTABLE.file_id),
        if table_type='BASE' then 'TABLE' else table_type endif,
        (select count(*)from SYS.SYSCOLUMN where
table_id=SYSTABLE.table_id),
        if primary_root=0 then 'N' else 'Y' endif,
        if table_type<>'VIEW' then view_def endif,
        remarks
FROM SYS.SYSTABLE
```

SYSCOLAUTH

The SYS.SYSCOLAUTH view presents column-update information found in SYS.SYSCOLPERM in a more readable format. Notice in Table E.2 that, although SYS.SYSCOLAUTH is driven by the SYS.SYSCOLPERM, no columns from SYS.SYSCOLPERM are present in SYS.SYSCOLAUTH. More readable columns found in related tables replaced all columns from SYS.SYSCOLPERM.

Table E.2   Columns in the SYS.SYSCOLAUTH View

Column Name	Column Table	Original Column	Description
grantor	SYSUSERPERM	user_name	Grantor is the user_name of the user who granted permission for column update to the grantee.
grantee	SYSUSERPERM	user_name	Grantee is the user_name of the user who was granted column update permission.
creator	SYSUSERPERM	user_name	Creator is the person who created the table.
tname	SYSTABLE	table_name	Tname is the name of the table containing the column to which the grantee has access rights.
colname	SYSCOLUMN	column_name	Colname is the name of the column to which the grantee has access rights.

The following is the SQL used to create SYS.SYSCOLAUTH:

```
CREATE VIEW SYS.SYSCATALOG (grantor, grantee, creator, tname,
colname)
AS SELECT (select user_name from SYS.SYSUSERPERM where
user_id=SYSCOLPERM.grantor),
     (select user_name from SYS.SYSUSERPERM where
user_id=SYSCOLPERM.grantee),
     (select user_name from SYS.SYSUSERPERM join SYS.SYSTABLE
where table_id=SYSCOLPERM.table_id),
     (select table_name from SYS.SYSTABLE where
table_id=SYSCOLPERM.table_id),
     (select column_name from SYS.SYSCOLUMN where
table_id=SYSCOLPERM.table_id and column_id=SYSCOLPERM.column_id)
FROM SYS.SYSCOLPERM
```

SYSCOLUMNS

The SYS.SYSCOLUMNS view presents the column information found in SYS.SYSCOLUMN in a more readable format. Table E.3 shows the columns in SYS.SYSCOLUMNS.

Table E.3 Columns in the SYS.SYSCOLUMNS View

Column Name	Column Table	Original Column	Description
creator	SYSUSERPERM	user_name	Creator is the user_name of the table in which the column being described resides.
cname	SYSCOLUMN	column_name	Cname is the name of the column being described.
tname	SYSTABLE	table_name	Tname is the name of the table in which the column being described resides.
coltype	SYSDOMAIN	domain_name	Coltype is the datatype of the column.
nulls	SYSCOLUMN	nulls	Nulls describe whether a column can be NULL.
length	SYSCOLUMN	width	Length can contain the number of characters in a string column, the precision in a numeric column, or the number of bytes allocated for this column.
syslength	SYSCOLUMN	scale	Syslength contains the number of digits after the decimal place for numeric columns or a zero for all other column datatypes.
in_primary_key	SYSCOLUMN	pkey	In_primary_key contains a Y or N, determining whether this column is a primary key or is part of a primary key.
colno	SYSCOLUMN	column_id	Colno is the sequence number of the column being described.
default_value	SYSCOLUMN	"default"	Default_value is the default of the column being described if a user tries to insert a NULL into the column.
remarks	SYSCOLUMN	remarks	Remarks is a string of comments about the column.

The SQL used to create SYS.SYSCOLUMNS is as follows:

```
CREATE VIEW SYS.SYSCOLUMNS (creator, cname, tname, coltype, nulls,
length, syslength, in_primary_key, "colno", default_value, remarks)
AS SELECT (select user_name from SYS.SYSUSERPERM where
user_id=SYSTABLE.creator),
       column_name,
       table_name,
       (select domain_name from SYS.SYSDOMAIN where
domain_id=SYSCOLUMN.domain_id),
       nulls,
       width,
       scale,
       pkey,
       column_id,
       "default",
       SYSCOLUMN.remarks
from SYS.SYSCOLUMN join SYS.SYSTABLE
```

SYSFOREIGNKEYS

The SYS.SYSFOREIGNKEYS view presents the information found in the SYS.SYSFOREIGNKEY and SYS.SYSFKCOL tables in a more readable format. The columns in SYS.SYSFOREIGNKEYS are listed in Table E.4.

Note

The columns in SYS.SYSFOREIGNKEYS that begin with "foreign_" refer to the *foreign table*, or the table where the foreign key exists. The columns that begin with "primary_" refer to the *primary table* or the table where the primary key exists that the foreign key in the foreign table references.

Table E.4   Columns in the SYS.SYSFOREIGNKEYS View

Column Name	Column Table	Original Column	Description
foreign_creator	SYSUSERPERM	user_name	Foreign_creator is the user_name of the user who created the foreign table.
foreign_tname	SYSTABLE	table_name	Foreign_tname is the name of the foreign table.
primary_creator	SYSUSERPERM	user_name	Primary_creator is the user_name of the user who created the primary table.

Column Name	Column Table	Original Column	Description
primary_tname	SYSTABLE	table_name	Primary_tname is the name of the primary table.
role	SYSFOREIGNKEY	role	Role is the name of the relationship between a foreign table and a primary table.
columns	See Description	See Description	Columns lists all the primary key to foreign key relationships, separated by commas with the word IS between them. For instance, the columns entry between SYSFKCOL and SYSCOLUMNS would be listed as `foreign_table_id IS table_id, foreign_column_id IS column_id.`

The SQL used to create SYS.SYSFOREIGNKEYS is as follows:

```
CREATE VIEW SYS.SYSCOLUMNS (foreign_creator, foreign_tname,
primary_creator, primary_tname, role, columns)
AS SELECT (select user_name from SYS.SYSUSERPERM join SYS.SYSTABLE
where table_id=foreign_table_id),
      (select table_name from SYS.SYSTABLE where
table_id=foreign_table_id),
      (select user_name from SYS.SYSUSERPERM join SYS.SYSTABLE
where table_id=primary_table_id),
      (select table_name from SYS.SYSTABLE where
table_id=primary_table_id),
      role,
      (select list(string(FK.column_name,' IS
',PK.column_name))from SYS.SYSFKCOL join SYS.SYSCOLUMN as
FK,SYS.SYSCOLUMN as PK where
foreign_table_id=SYSFOREIGNKEY.foreign_table_id and
foreign_key_id=SYSFOREIGNKEY.foreign_key_id and
PK.table_id=SYSFOREIGNKEY.primary_table_id and
PK.column_id=SYSFKCOL.primary_column_id)
FROM SYS.SYSFOREIGNKEY
```

SYSGROUPS

Groups are pools of authors that have similar (or identical) access rights. SYS.SYSGROUPS lists the member names by group name for easier access. A column listing of the SYS.SYSGROUPS view can be seen in Table E.5.

Table E.5 Columns in the SYS.SYSGROUPS View			
Column Name	Column Table	Original Column	Description
group_name	SYSUSERPERM	user_name	Group_name is the user_name of the group.
member_name	SYSUSERPERM	user_name	Member_name is the user_name of the group member.

The SQL used to create SYS.SYSGROUPS is as follows:

```
CREATE VIEW SYS.SYSGROUPS (group_name, member_name)
AS SELECT g.user_name,u.user_name
FROM SYS.SYSGROUP,SYS.SYSUSERPERM as g,SYS.SYSUSERPERM as u
WHERE group_id=g.user_id and group_member=u.user_id
```

SYSINDEXES

The SYS.SYSINDEXES view presents index information in a more readable format than that found in SYS.SYSINDEX. A column listing of the SYS.SYSINDEXES view can be seen in Table E.6.

Table E.6 Columns in the SYS.SYSINDEXES View			
Column Name	Column Table	Original Column	Description
icreator	SYSUSERPERM	user_name	Icreator is the user name of the creator of the index.
iname		index_name	Iname is the name of the index.
fname	SYSFILE	file_name	Fname is the dbspace where the index is located.
creator	SYSUSERPERM	user_name	Creator is the creator of the table where the index resides.
tname		table_name	Tname is the name of the table where the index resides.
indextype	SYSINDEX	See Description	In SYSINDEX, if the value of the unique column is N, the indextype is non-unique. If the value of the unique column is U, the index type is unique constraint. Otherwise, it's just unique.

Column Name	Column Table	Original Column	Description
colnames	See Description	See Description	This is the column name(s) of the index followed by ASC or DESC, for ascending or descending. For example, the SYSFOREIGNKEY entry colnames read role ASC, foreign_table_id ASC.
interval	See Description	See Description	Currently always 0. Reserved for future use.
level_num	See Description	See Description	Currently always 0. Reserved for future use.

VII

Appendixes

The SQL used to create SYS.SYSINDEXES is as follows:

```
CREATE VIEW SYS.SYSINDEXES (icreator, iname, fname, creator, tname,
indextype, colnames, interval, level_num)
AS SELECT (select user_name from SYS.SYSUSERPERM where
user_id=SYSINDEX.creator),
       index_name,
       (select file_name from SYS.SYSFILE where
file_id=SYSINDEX.file_id),
       (select user_name from SYS.SYSUSERPERM where
user_id=SYSINDEX.creator),
       table_name,
       if "unique"='N' then 'Non-unique' else if "unique"='U' then
'UNIQUE constraint' else 'Unique' endif endif,
       (select list(string(column_name,if "order"='A' then ' ASC'
else ' DESC' endif))from SYS.SYSIXCOL join SYS.SYSCOLUMN where
index_id=SYSINDEX.index_id and
SYSIXCOL.table_id=SYSINDEX.table_id),
       0,
       0
FROM SYS.SYSTABLE join SYS.SYSINDEX
```

SYSOPTIONS

The SYS.SYSOPTIONS view is identical to the SYS.SYSOPTION table, except for one thing. Instead of finding a user_id on the SYS.SYSOPTION table, the SYS.SYSOPTIONS view gives you a user_name. A column listing of the SYS.SYSOPTIONS view can be seen in Table E.7.

Table E.7	Columns in the SYS.SYSOPTIONS View		
Column Name	**Column Table**	**Original Column**	**Description**
user_name	SYSUSERPERM	user_name	User_name is the name of the user who set the option and who the option is for.
option	SYSOPTION	option	Option is a character string describing the option set by the user.
setting	SYSOPTION	setting	Setting is a character string describing how the option is set.

The SQL used to create SYS.SYSOPTIONS is as follows:

```
CREATE VIEW SYS.SYSOPTIONS (user_name, "option", "setting")
AS SELECT (select user_name from SYS.SYSUSERPERM where
user_id=SYSOPTION.user_id),
        "option",
        "setting"
FROM SYS.SYSOPTION
```

SYSPROCAUTH

The SYS.SYSPROCAUTH table is a table that lists the creator and the grantee access rights of a procedure. A column listing of the SYS.SYSPROCAUTH view can be seen in Table E.8.

Table E.8	Columns in the SYS.SYSPROCAUTH View		
Column Name	**Column Table**	**Original Column**	**Description**
grantee	SYSUSERPERM	user_name	Grantee is the user name of the user who was granted authority to execute this procedure.
creator	SYSUSERPERM	user_name	Creator is the user name of the user who created the procedure.
procname	SYSPROCEDURE	proc_name	Procname is the name of the procedure.

The SQL used to create SYS.SYSPROCAUTH is as follows:

```
CREATE VIEW SYS.SYSPROCAUTH (grantee, creator, procname)
AS SELECT (select user_name from SYS.SYSUSERPERM where
SYSPROCPERM.grantee=SYSUSERPERM.user_id),
      (select user_name from SYS.SYSUSERPERM where
SYSPROCEDURE.creator=SYSUSERPERM.user_id),
      proc_name
FROM SYS.SYSPROCEDURE join SYS.SYSPROCPERM
```

SYSPROCPARMS

The SYS.SYSPROCPARMS view shows the same information found in the SYS.SYSPROCPARM table, except the SYS.SYSPROCPARMS view is more readable. A column listing of the SYS.SYSPROCPARMS view can be seen in Table E.9.

Table E.9	Columns in the SYS.SYSPROCPARMS View		
Column Name	**Column Table**	**Original Column**	**Description**
creator	SYSUSERPERM	user_name	Creator is the user name of the user who created the procedure.
parmname	SYSPROCPARM	parm_name	Parmname is the name of the parameter.
procname	SYSPROCEDURE	proc_name,	Procname is the name of the procedure.
parmtype	SYSPROCPARM	parm_type,	The parameter type can be 0 (normal parameter), 1 (result), 2 (SQLSTATE error value), and 3 (SQLCODE error value).
parmmode	SYSPROCPARM	See Description	In SYSPROCPARM, if parm_mode_in =Y and parm_mode_out=N, then parmmode is IN. If parm_mode_in=N and parm_mode_out=Y then parmmode is OUT. If both parm_mode_in and parm_mode_out equal Y, then parmmode is INOUT.
parmdomain	SYSDOMAIN	domain_name	Parmdomain is the datatype of the procedure parameter.

(continues)

VII

Appendixes

Table E.9	Continued		
Column Name	Column Table	Original Column	Description
length	SYSPROCPARM	width	Length is the number of characters in a string, the precision of numeric values, and the number of bytes of storage for all other passed variables.
remarks	SYSPROCPARM	remarks	Remarks is a string containing comments about the procedure.

The SQL used to create SYS.SYSPROCPARMS is as follows:

```
CREATE VIEW SYS.SYSPROCPARMS (creator, parmname, procname,
parmtype, parmmode, parmdomain, length, remarks)
AS SELECT (select user_name from SYS.SYSUSERPERM where
user_id=SYSPROCEDURE.creator),
        parm_name,
        proc_name,
        parm_type,
        if parm_mode_in='Y' and parm_mode_out='N' then 'IN' else if
parm_mode_in='N' and parm_mode_out='Y' then 'OUT' else 'INOUT'
endif endif,
        (select domain_name from SYS.SYSDOMAIN where
domain_id=SYSPROCPARM.domain_id),
        width,
        SYSPROCPARM.remarks
FROM SYS.SYSPROCPARM join SYS.SYSPROCEDURE
```

SYSTABAUTH

The SYS.SYSTABAUTH view lists the user authority by table. You can see the columns for SYS.SYSTABAUTH in Table E.10.

Table E.10	Columns in the SYS.SYSTABAUTH View		
Column Name	Column Table	Original Column	Description
grantor	SYSUSERPERM	user_name	Grantor is the user name of the person who granted authority to the table.
grantee	SYSUSERPERM	user_name	Grantee is the user name of the person who received authority of the table.

VII

Appendixes

Column Name	Column Table	Original Column	Description
screator	SYSUSERPERM	user_name	Screator is the person who created the table where authority was granted.
stname	SYSTABLE	table_name	Stname is the name of the table whose access rights are being GRANTed.
tcreator	SYSUSERPERM	user_name	Tcreator is not yet used, and is the same person as screator.
ttname	SYSTABLE	table_name	Ttname is not yet used, and is the same table as stname.
selectauth	SYSTABLEPERM	selectauth	Selectauth can be Y to indicate that the grantee has select authority, N to indicate that the grantee does not have this authority, and G to indicate that the grantee can grant this authority to others.
insertauth	SYSTABLEPERM	insertauth	Insertauth can be Y to indicate that the grantee has insert authority, N to indicate that the grantee does not have this authority, and G to indicate that the grantee can grant this authority to others.
deleteauth	SYSTABLEPERM	deleteauth	Deleteauth can be Y to indicate that the grantee has delete authority, N to indicate that the grantee does not have this authority, and G to indicate that the grantee can grant this authority to others.
updateauth	SYSTABLEPERM	updateauth	Updateauth can be Y to indicate that the grantee has update authority, N to indicate that the grantee does not have this authority, and G to indicate that the grantee can grant this authority to others.
updatecols	SYSTABLEPERM	updatecols	Updatecols can be Y to indicate that the grantee has been granted or denied specific column update capability in SYSCOLPERM. N indicates that no such authority has been specified.

(continues)

Table E.10	Continued		
Column Name	**Column Table**	**Original Column**	**Description**
alterauth	SYSTABLEPERM	alterauth	Alterauth can be Y to indicate that the grantee has the authority to alter the table, N to indicate that the grantee does not have this authority, and G to indicate that the grantee can grant this authority to others.
referenceauth	SYSTABLEPERM	referenceauth	Referenceauth can be Y to indicate that the grantee has reference authority and, therefore, can query the table, N to indicate that the grantee does not have this authority, and G to indicate that the grantee can grant this authority to others.

The following is the SQL used to create SYS.SYSTABAUTH:

```
CREATE VIEW SYS.SYSTABAUTH (grantor, grantee, screator, stname,
tcreator, ttname, selectauth, insertauth, deleteauth, updateauth,
updatecols, alterauth, referenceauth)
AS SELECT(select user_name from SYS.SYSUSERPERM where
user_id=SYSTABLEPERM.grantor),
     (select user_name from SYS.SYSUSERPERM where
user_id=SYSTABLEPERM.grantee),
     (select user_name from SYS.SYSUSERPERM join SYS.SYSTABLE
where table_id=SYSTABLEPERM.stable_id),
     (select table_name from SYS.SYSTABLE where
table_id=SYSTABLEPERM.stable_id),
     (select user_name from SYS.SYSUSERPERM join SYS.SYSTABLE
where table_id=SYSTABLEPERM.ttable_id),
     (select table_name from SYS.SYSTABLE where
table_id=SYSTABLEPERM.ttable_id),
     selectauth,
     insertauth,
     deleteauth,
     updateauth,
     updatecols,
     alterauth,
     referenceauth
FROM SYS.SYSTABLEPERM
```

SYSTRIGGERS

The SYS.SYSTRIGGERS view lists all expressly declared (non-foreign-key) triggers in a more readable format than that found in the SYS.SYSTRIGGER table. A column listing of the SYS.SYSTRIGGERS view can be seen in Table E.11.

Table E.11 Columns in the SYS.SYSTRIGGERS View

Column Name	Column Table	Original Column	Description
owner	SYSUSERPERM	user_name	Owner is the creator of the trigger.
trigname	SYSTRIGGER	trigger_name	Trigname is the name of the trigger.
tname	SYSTABLE	table_name	Tname is the name of the table where the trigger resides.
event	SYSTRIGGER	See Description	If the event on SYSTRIGGER is I, U, C, or other, then the event on the SYSTRIGGERS view is INSERT, UPDATE, UPDATE, or DELETE, respectively.
trigtime	SYSTRIGGER	See Description	If the event on SYSTRIGGER is A, B, or other, then the trigtime on the SYSTRIGGERS view is AFTER, BEFORE, or INSTEAD OF, respectively.
trigdefn	SYSTRIGGER	trigger_defn	Trigdefn is the command used to create the trigger.

The SQL used to create SYS.SYSTRIGGERS is as follows:

```
CREATE VIEW SYS.SYSTRIGGERS (owner, trigname, tname, event,
trigtime, trigdefn)
AS SELECT (select user_name from SYS.SYSUSERPERM where
user_id=SYSTABLE.creator),
     trigger_name,
     table_name,
     if event='I' then 'INSERT' else if event='U' then 'UPDATE'
else if event='C' then 'UPDATE' else 'DELETE' endif endif endif,
     if trigger_time='B' then 'BEFORE' else if trigger_time='A'
then 'AFTER' else 'INSTEAD OF' endif endif,
     trigger_defn
FROM SYS.SYSTRIGGER join SYS.SYSTABLE
WHERE foreign_table_id is NULL
```

SYSUSERAUTH

The SYS.SYSUSERAUTH view lists all the columns of the SYS.SYSUSERPERM table, except for the user id and remarks. Because this view contains the password, only those with DBA authority can access information on the SYS.SYSUSERAUTH. A column listing of the SYS.SYSUSERAUTH view can be seen in Table E.12.

Table E.12   Columns in the SYS.SYSUSERAUTH View

Column Name	Column Table	Original Column	Description
user_name	SYSUSERPERM	user_name	User_name is the name of the user. It is the way a user logs on to the database.
password	SYSUSERPERM	password	Password is the password defined for the user.
resourceauth	SYSUSERPERM	resourceauth	Resourceauth is set to Y or N, indicating whether the individual has the right to create tables.
dbaauth	SYSUSERPERM	dbaauth	DBAauth is set to Y or N, indicating whether the individual has the right to grant access to other users. This is a very powerful access to grant.
scheduleauth	SYSUSERPERM	scheduleauth	Scheduleauth is set to Y or N to see whether the user has scheduling authority. This is not currently used by Watcom SQL.
user_group	SYSUSERPERM	user_group	User_group is a Y or N, indicating whether this is an individual user or a user group.

The SQL used to create SYS.SYSUSERAUTH is as follows:

```
CREATE VIEW SYS.SYSUSERAUTH (name, password, resouceauth, dbaauth,
scheduleauth, user_group)
AS SELECT user_name,
      password,
      resourceauth,
      dbaauth,
      scheduleauth,
      user_group
FROM SYS.SYSUSERPERM
```

SYSUSERLIST

The SYS.SYSUSERLIST view contains all the fields of the SYS.SYSUSERAUTH view except the password. All users have access to the SYS.SYSUSERLIST view, while only those with DBA authority have access to the SYS.SYSUSERAUTH view. A column listing of the SYS.SYSUSERLIST view can be seen in Table E.13.

Table E.13   Columns in the SYS.SYSUSERLIST View

Column Name	Column Table	Original Column	Description
user_name	SYSUSERPERM	user_name	User_name is the name of the user. It is the way a user logs on to the database.
resourceauth	SYSUSERPERM	resourceauth	Resourceauth is set to Y or N, indicating whether the individual has the right to create tables.
dbaauth	SYSUSERPERM	dbaauth	DBAauth is set to Y or N, indicating whether the individual has the right to grant access to other users. This is a very powerful access to grant.
scheduleauth	SYSUSERPERM	scheduleauth	Scheduleauth is set to Y or N to see whether the user has scheduling authority. This is not currently used by Watcom SQL.
user_group	SYSUSERPERM	user_group	User_group is a Y or N, indicating whether this is an individual user or a user group.

The SQL used to create SYS.SYSUSERLIST is as follows:

```
CREATE VIEW SYS.SYSUSERLIST (name, resourceauth, dbaauth,
scheduleauth, user_group)
AS SELECT user_name,
        resourceauth,
        dbaauth,
        scheduleauth,
        user_group
FROM SYS.SYSUSERPERM
```

SYSUSEROPTIONS

The SYS.SYSUSEROPTIONS view contains all user-option settings. If a user has not specifically set a user option, the SYS.SYSUSEROPTIONS view lists the public option. A column listing of the SYS.SYSUSEROPTIONS view can be seen in Table E.14.

Table E.14	Columns in the SYS.SYSUSEROPTIONS View		
Column Name	**Column Table**	**Original Column**	**Description**
user_name	SYSUSERPERM	user_name	User_name is the name of the user whose options are being listed.
option	SYSOPTIONS	option	Option is a string containing the name of the user option.
setting	SYSOPTIONS	option	Setting is the individual user setting. If the user has not set this option, setting is the public default for this option.

The SQL used to create SYS.SYSUSEROPTIONS is as follows:

```
CREATE VIEW SYS.SYSUSEROPTIONS (user_name, "option", "setting")
AS SELECT u.name,
        "option",
        isnull((select "setting" from SYS.SYSOPTIONS as s where
s.user_name=u.name and s."option"=o."option"),"setting")
FROM SYS.SYSOPTIONS as o,SYS.SYSUSERAUTH as u
WHERE o.user_name='PUBLIC'
```

SYSUSERPERMS

The SYS.SYSUSERPERMS view contains all the fields of the SYS.SYSUSERPERM table except that password. All users have access to this view, while only those with DBA authority have access to the SYS.SYSUSERPERM table. A column listing of the SYS.SYSUSERPERMS view can be seen in Table E.15.

Table E.15	Columns in the SYS.SYSUSERPERMS View		
Column Name	**Column Table**	**Original Column**	**Description**
user_id	SYSUSERPERM	user_id	User_id is a sequence number that uniquely defines the user.
user_name	SYSUSERPERM	user_name	User_name is the name of the user. It is how a user logs on to the database.
resourceauth	SYSUSERPERM	resourceauth	Resourceauth is set to Y or N, indicating whether the individual has the right to create tables.

Column Name	Column Table	Original Column	Description
dbaauth	SYSUSERPERM	dbaauth	DBAauth is set to Y or N indicating whether the individual has the right to grant access to other users. This is a very powerful access to grant.
scheduleauth	SYSUSERPERM	scheduleauth	Scheduleauth is set to Y or N to see if the user has scheduling authority. This is not currently used by Watcom SQL.
user_group	SYSUSERPERM	user_group	User_group is a Y or N, indicating if this is an individual user or a user group.
remarks	SYSUSERPERM	remarks	Remarks is a comment string describing the user.

The SQL used to create SYS.SYSUSERPERMS is as follows:

```
CREATE VIEW SYS.SYSUSERPERMS
AS SELECT user_id,
       user_name,
       resourceauth,
       dbaauth,
       scheduleauth,
       user_group,
       remarks
FROM SYS.SYSUSERPERM
```

SYSVIEWS

The SYS.SYSVIEWS view lists only views. When dealing with views, SYS.SYSVIEWS may be easier to use than the SYS.SYSTABLE table because the view listing is restricted to only views. A column listing of the SYS.SYSVIEWS view can be seen in Table E.16.

Table E.16   Columns in the SYS.SYSVIEWS View

Column Name	Column Table	Original Column	Description
vcreator	SYSUSERPERM	user_name	Vcreator is the creator of the view.

(continues)

Table E.16	Continued		
Column Name	**Column Table**	**Original Column**	**Description**
viewname	SYSTABLE	table_name	Viewname is the name of the view.
viewtext	SYSTABLE	view_def	View text is the CREATE VIEW statement used to create the view.

The SQL used to create SYS.SYSVIEWS is as follows:

```
CREATE VIEW SYS.SYSVIEWS (vcreator, viewname, viewtext)
AS SELECT user_name,
       table_name,
       view_def
FROM SYS.SYSTABLE join SYS.SYSUSERPERM
WHERE     table_type= 'VIEW'
```

Appendix F

PowerBuilder System Tables

Like Watcom SQL, PowerBuilder uses five system tables called *Powersoft Repository Tables* to keep track of extended attributes for the tables and columns when developing an application. These tables do not have a primary key, and do not physically relate to each other or to the Watcom system tables. Many logical relationships do exist, however. This appendix describes these five tables.

> **Note**
>
> When a table has no primary keys, that table becomes read-only to PowerBuilder. PowerBuilder replaces their primary keys with indexes so that the Watcom SQL database can only be modified internally.

PBCATCOL

The PBCATCOL table describes the extended attribute defaults defined for each column in the database painter. Table F.1 defines the layout for the PBCATCOL table.

Table F.1 Columns in the PBCATCOL Table			
Column Name	**Column Datatype**	**Options**	**Description**
pbc_tnam	CHAR(129)	Index, NOT NULL	Pbc_tnam is the name of the table where the column being described resides. Pbc_tnam, pbc_ownr, and pbc_cnam all form an index to PBCATCOL.
pbc_tid	INTEGER		Pbc_tid is the SQL Server object id of the table. It is not used or defined in Watcom SQL.
pbc_ownr	CHAR(129)	Index, NOT NULL	Pbc_ownr is the user name of the creator of the table. Pbc_tnam, pbc_ownr, and pbc_cnam all form an index to PBCATCOL.
pbc_cnam	CHAR(129)	Index, NOT NULL	Pbc_cnam is the column name of the column being defined. Pbc_tnam, pbc_ownr, and pbc_cnam all form an index to PBCATCOL.
pbc_cid	SMALLINT		Pbc_cid is the SQL Server column id. It is not used in Watcom SQL.
pbc_labl	VARCHAR(254)		Pbc_labl is the label defined in the database painter for the column.
pbc_lpos	SMALLINT		Pbc_lpos is the label position. Valid values are 23 (column is left-justified), 24 (column is right-justified). If there is no label, 0 can also occur.
pbc_hdr	VARCHAR(254)		Pbc_hdr is the heading of the column being defined.
pbc_hpos	SMALLINT		Pbc_hpos is the justification of the heading. Valid values are 23 (heading is left-justified), 24 (heading is right-justified), and 25

VII

Appendixes

Column Name	Column Datatype	Options	Description
			(heading is center-justified). If there is no heading, 0 can also occur.
pbc_jtfy	SMALLINT		Pbc_jtfy is the justification of the column. Valid values are 23 (column is left-justified), 24 (column is right-justified), and 25 (column is center-justified). 0 indicates that justification has not been chosen for this column.
pbc_mask	VARCHAR(31)		Pbc_mask is the display format name.
pbc_case	SMALLINT		Pbc_case controls the case of the column. Valid values are 26 (actual), 27 (upper), and 28 (lower).
pbc_hght	SMALLINT		Pbc_hght is the column height in PowerBuilder units.
pbc_wdth	SMALLINT		Pbc_hght is the column width in PowerBuilder units.
pbc_ptrn	VARCHAR(31)		Pbc_ptrn is the validation rule name.
pbc_bmap	CHAR(1)		Pbc_bmap is Y or N, indicating whether the column is a bitmap.
pbc_init	VARCHAR(254)		Pbc_init is the initial value of the column.
pbc_cmnt	VARCHAR(254)		Pbc_cmnt is the comments of the column being defined.
pbc_edit	VARCHAR(31)		Pbc_edit is a character string defining the edit style of the column.
pbc_tag	VARCHAR(254)		Pbc_tag is reserved, but not used yet by PowerBuilder.

PBCATEDT

The PBCATEDT table describes all edit styles, both user-defined and those provided by PowerBuilder. Table F.2 describes the PBCATEDT table.

> **Note**
>
> *Edit styles* are formatted variables used for easier viewing and data entry. Examples of edit styles include drop-down data lists (DDDLs), radio buttons, edit masks, and check boxes.

Table F.2   Columns in the PBCATEDT Table

Column Name	Column Datatype	Options	Description
pbe_name	VARCHAR(30)	Index, NOT NULL	Pbe_name is the name of the user-defined edit style. Pbe_name and pbe_seqn form a unique index to PBECATEDT.
pbe_edit	VARCHAR(254)		Pbe_edit is the format string of the edit style. Depending on the edit style type, pbe_edit can contain an edit mask, a code table entry, a field constraint, or a prompt.
pbe_type	SMALLINT		Pbe_type is a small integer describing the type of edit style. Some valid values include 85 (check box), 86 (radio button), 87 (drop-down list box), 88 (drop-down data window), 89 (edit format), and 90 (edit mask).
pbe_cntr	INTEGER		Pbe_cntr is the revision counter for the edit style. Pbe_cntr gets incremented every time the edit style is modified.
pbe_seqn	SMALLINT	Index, NOT NULL	Pbe_seqn is the row number of the edit style. Most edit styles require several entries in the PBECATEDT table.

Column Name	Column Datatype	Options	Description
			Pbe_name and pbe_seqn form a unique index to PBECATEDT.
pbe_flag	INTEGER		Pbe_flag is a flag used by PowerBuilder products for internal use.
pbe_work	CHAR(32)		Pbe_work is an extra field used by PowerBuilder for internal use.

PBCATFMT

The PBCATFMT table describes all format definitions used in PowerBuilder. Table F.3 describes the PBCATFMT table.

Table F.3	Columns in the PBCATFMT Table		
Column Name	Column Datatype	Options	Description
pbf_name	VARCHAR(30)	Index, NOT NULL	Pbf_name is the name of the display format.
pbf_frmt	VARCHAR(254)		Pbf_frmt is the mask used to format the output.
pbf_type	SMALLINT		Pbf_type is the data type of the format. Valid values are 82 (Date), 81 (Number), 80 (String), 83 (Time), and 84 (Timestamp).
pbf_cntr	INTEGER		Pbf_cntr is the concurrent-usage flag.

PBCATTBL

The PBCATTBL table describes all table-display options, including font pitch, type, and height that are used in all data, heading, and label displays. Table F.4 defines the PBCATTBL table.

Table F.4   Columns in the PBCATTBL Table

Column Name	Column Datatype	Options	Description
pbt_tnam	CHAR(129)	Index, NOT NULL	Pbt_tnam is the name of the table being described. Pbt_tnam and pbt_ownr form an index to PBCATTBL.
pbt_tid	INTEGER		Pbc_tid is the SQL Server object id of the table. It is not used or defined in Watcom SQL.
pbt_ownr	CHAR(129)	Index, NOT NULL	Pbt_ownr is the creator of the table being described. Pbt_tnam and pbt_ownr form an index to PBCATTBL.
pbd_fhgt	SMALLINT		Pbd_fhgt is the data font height in PowerBuilder units when the table is being displayed.
pbd_fwgt	SMALLINT		Pbd_fwgt is the weight of the data font. Valid values are 400 (normal) and 700 (bold).
pbd_fitl	CHAR(1)		Pbd_fitl is Y or N, indicating whether the data font is in italics.
pbd_funl	CHAR(1)		Pbd_funl is Y or N, indicating whether the data font is underlined.
pbd_fchr	SMALLINT		Pbd_fchr is the character set for the data font. Valid values are 0 (ANSI), 2 (Symbol), 255 (OEM).
pbd_fptc	SMALLINT		Pbd_fptc is the data font pitch and family*.
pbd_ffce	CHAR(18)		Pbd_ffce is the data font typeface.
pbh_fhgt	SMALLINT		Pbh_fhgt is the heading font height in PowerBuilder units when the table is being displayed.
pbh_fwgt	SMALLINT		Pbh_fwgt is the weight of the heading font. Valid values are 400 (normal) and 700 (bold).
pbh_fitl	CHAR(1)		Pbh_fitl is Y or N, indicating whether the heading font is in italics.

VII

Appendixes

Column Name	Column Datatype	Options	Description
pbh_funl	CHAR(1)		Pbh_funl is Y or N, indicating whether the heading font is underlined.
pbh_fchr	SMALLINT		Pbh_fchr is the character set for the heading font. Valid values are 0 (ANSI), 2 (Symbol), 255 (OEM).
pbh_fptc	SMALLINT		Pbh_fptc is the heading font pitch and family.
pbh_ffce	CHAR(18)		Pbh_ffce is the heading font typeface.
pbl_fhgt	SMALLINT		Pbl_fhgt is the label font height in PowerBuilder units when the table is being displayed.
pbl_fwgt	SMALLINT		Pbl_fwgt is the weight of the label font. Valid values are 400 (normal) and 700 (bold).
pbl_fitl	CHAR(1)		Pbl_fitl is Y or N, indicating whether the label font is in italics.
pbl_funl	CHAR(1)		Pbl_funl is Y or N, indicating whether the label font is underlined.
pbl_fchr	SMALLINT		Pbl_fchr is the character set for the label font. Valid values are 0 (ANSI), 2 (Symbol), 255 (OEM).
pbl_fptc	SMALLINT		Pbl_fptc is the label font pitch and family.
pbl_ffce	CHAR(18)		Pbl_ffce is the label font typeface.
pbt_cmnt	VARCHAR(254)		Pbt_cmnt is the string containing comments about the table.

*Font pitch is derived by adding the pitch constant with the family constant. The pitch constant is 0 (Default), 1 (Fixed), and 2 (Variable). The family constant is 0 (Don't care), 16 (Roman), 32 (Swiss), 48 (Modern), 64 (Script), and 80 (Decorative).

PBCATVLD

The PBCATVLD table contains all validation rule information. Table F.5 describes the PBCATVLD table.

Note

In PowerBuilder, validation rules keep your column from losing focus if that value entered does not meet the criteria you defined for that column. For example, if you have an order price field, you can make a validation rule that order price cannot be negative.

Table F.5   Columns in the PBCATVLD Table

Column Name	Column Datatype	Options	Description
pbv_name	VARCHAR(30)	Index, NOT NULL	Pbv_name is the name of the validation rule.
pbv_vald	VARCHAR(254)		Pbv_vald is the validation rule.
pbv_type	SMALLINT		Pbv_type is the data type of the validation rule. Valid values are 82 (Date), 81 (Number), 80 (String), 83 (Time), 84 (Timestamp).
pbv_cntr	INTEGER		Pbv_cntr is the concurrent-usage flag.
pbv_msg	VARCHAR(254)		Pbv_msg is the validation error message.

Appendix G

What's on the CD?

The CD-ROM included with *Special Edition Using Watcom SQL* contains a number of useful utilities and demos. It also includes a run-time version of Watcom SQL, and the databases and Watcom SQL applications used throughout this book. The material on the CD-ROM is arranged in three directories:

- *DATA*. The source files for the large databases and Watcom SQL application examples described in this book.

- *WATCOM*. The run-time version of Watcom SQL.

- *APPS*. The demos and applications.

You can run all of the demos and applications right from the CD-ROM. However, some require that you create a working file directory so you can write your changes to it. If this is the case, simply copy the directory of the demo or application you want to your hard drive and run the executable file from there.

The Source Files

The DATA directory contains the source files for examples described throughout the book. The CD-ROM icon you see in the margin here indicates that the example being discussed appears on the CD-ROM.

Product Name: Watcom SQL Run-Time Version

Price: $199 (Single User Version)

Provided by:

Watcom International Corp
415 Philip Street
Waterloo, Ontario, N2L 3X2
Phone Number: 519-886-3700
Fax Number: 519-747-4971

Product Description

◀ See "RTSQLW," p. 640

Throughout this book, the Watcom SQL database was discussed. Included on the CD-ROM, in the \WATCOM directory, is the run-time version of Watcom SQL. With the Watcom SQL run-time version, you can use the RTSQLW package to run SQL commands against your Watcom SQL database. This is especially useful if you don't currently own a copy of Watcom SQL and would like to try it out.

A certain functionality of the Watcom SQL developer's version and multi-user versions (described in this book) is not present in the run-time version of Watcom SQL included on the CD-ROM. The run-time version does not allow CREATE, ALTER, COMMENT, or DROP commands. Also, procedures and log files are disabled. This should not stop you from trying out SQL commands with the databases provided on the CD.

Also included in the run-time version of Watcom SQL are several Watcom SQL utilities described in Chapter 24. These utilities can help you manage your run-time databases.

Product Name: Andyne GQL

Provided by:

Andyne Computing Unlimited
552 Princess Street
Kingston, Ontario, K7L1C7
Phone Number: 613-548-4355
Fax Number: 613-548-7801

Product Description

Andyne GQL is an ad hoc query tool for organizations managing SQL database access in a client/server environment. Powerful and easy to use, Andyne GQL makes current data accessible and meaningful to end users while maintaining corporate security and control.

Andyne GQL is also a good decision support tool. It sends up-to-the-minute information directly to the desktop, where users can make informed decisions quickly. With Andyne GQL's graphical point-and-click interface, users understand what to do and how to do it. And, with the capability to build their own queries, produce professional reports, and integrate data with other applications, users work with exactly the information they want—in the form they want it. It's what decision-makers have always needed: easy access to usable information.

Andyne GQL is fully customizable. It can be tailored to meet the needs of every user in an organization—whatever her computer skills or business needs. Database administrators determine what information and facilities should be available to users, and they present the information in a sensible manner. Users can then focus on obtaining and using the information that is relevant only to them, without struggling with the complexity typically associated with SQL database access.

Andyne GQL is a graphical front end for ODBC database access (see fig. G.1). This package can ease the task of graphically reviewing your data. To launch the application, type **gqluser.exe** from the \apps\gql_demo directory on your CD.

Fig. G.1
Andyne GQL
provides a very
slick front end to
your ODBC
database.

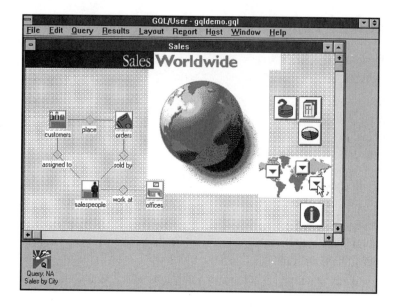

Product Name: BrioQuery

Provided by:

Brio Technology
650 Castro Street, Suite 500
Mountain View, CA 94041
Phone Number: 415-961-4110
Fax Number: 415-961-4572

Product Description

BrioQuery is a complete, ad hoc, multi-dimensional query tool, with built-in crosstabs and power reporting for Windows and Macintosh computers. You can use this tool to locate, analyze, and present information from any data warehouse. BrioQuery includes three distinct modules for querying, reporting, and analysis. Each shares a common user interface and common data, promoting easy movement between these different tasks. Users can combine several analyses and reports into a single document to present complete drill-down analysis.

BrioQuery's graphical interface enables users at all levels to perform ad hoc queries, construct reports, and complete an instant analysis. Its graphical query system enables users to easily access information from virtually any SQL relational database. Prompted constraints and a context-sensitive advisor in a familiar layout make ad hoc queries both quick and easy.

To access your Watcom SQL database from BrioQuery, you must first state that you are using ODBC as your database. (Watcom SQL is an ODBC database.) After starting BrioQuery, choose **D**ataModel, **C**onnection Preferences, as seen in figure G.2.

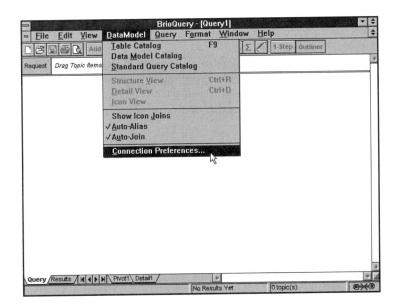

Fig. G.2
You must change your connection preferences to attach to a Watcom SQL database from BrioQuery.

This opens the Connection Preferences dialog box shown in figure G.3.

Click the Connection button to open the Configure Connection Software dialog box, as seen in figure G.4. Click the Exclude All button to turn off all other connections. Then double-click ODBC. Repeat this procedure using the Database command button. Click OK to return to the BrioQuery Query window.

Fig. G.3
Use the Connec-
tion Preferences
dialog box to tell
BrioQuery which
database to attach
to.

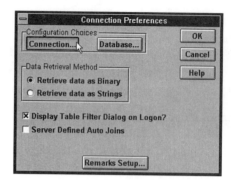

Fig. G.4
Use this dialog
box to define
connections and
database types for
BrioQuery.

Next, choose **D**ataModel, **T**able Catalog. This pulls up the ODBC Logon dialog box shown in figure G.5. Leave the User and Password text boxes blank
and click Change.

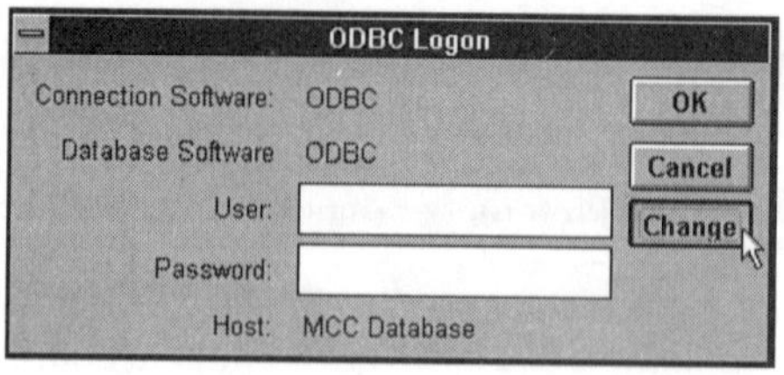

Fig. G.5
This dialog box
lets you choose the
connection type
and the database
for each server.

Now the Server Chooser dialog box appears (see fig. G.6). Make sure the connection type and the database are both ODBC and click OK.

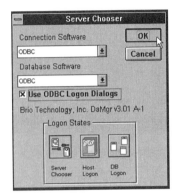

Fig. G.6
The Server Chooser dialog box lets you pick your connection type and your database type from any types previously declared in the Configure Connection Software dialog box.

Now the SQL Data Sources dialog box appears (see fig. G.7). Here, you can choose any Watcom SQL database you have previously created as your data source.

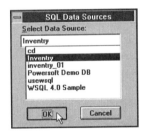

Fig. G.7
The SQL Data Sources dialog box lists all defined databases.

After asking for your user ID and password, BrioQuery returns you to the Host Logon window. Click OK to return to the Query painter. The Query window now has a Table Catalog child window, where you can drag tables to your Query window to manipulate and define tables and columns, as shown in figure G.8.

Fig. G.8

The Query window allows you to define queries with existing tables and columns.

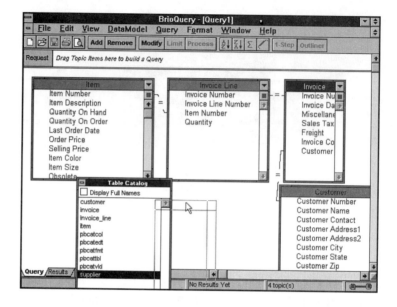

You don't have to know programming or be an SQL database expert to retrieve database information with BrioQuery. BrioQuery's multi-dimensional analysis tool helps users understand data, spot trends, compare results, and even define new categories on-the-fly. With this cross tab analysis module, users can summarize, compute percentages, add subtotals at any level, or gain new perspective by simply pivoting an axis or changing the hierarchy of any nested layer.

BrioQuery also provides a sensible way for IS professionals to manage and control the ad hoc query environment. With BrioQuery's repository-based data models and master queries, IS can distribute predefined views of the database. Information managers can also use BrioQuery to grant power users direct access to data in data warehouses. For less experienced users, they can set up and mandate predefined business data models.

BrioQuery also makes deployment and maintenance easy with Automatic Distributed Refresh (ADR). This feature, combined with a central repository, ensures that information managers can build and deploy data models and master queries only once, regardless of the number of users supported. ADR automatically delivers the most current version to every single user, whether they are running Windows or Macintosh.

The BrioQuery Test Drive included on the CD-ROM provides the following functionality:

- Immediate access to database tables

- A structured view and control of the database

- Push-button, pre-built reports (see fig. G.9)

The BrioQuery Test Drive has some functionality disabled and limits you to 50 rows returned from your query.

Type **brioqry.exe** to get started. The BrioQuery Test Drive will ask you for your serial number. Click Cancel, and the BrioQuery Test Drive informs you that you're a non-registered user (see fig. G.10). Click Continue to start the program.

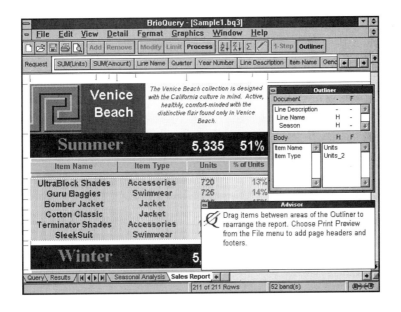

Fig. G.9
The BrioQuery Test Drive can produce professional and colorful reports.

Fig. G.10
BrioQuery tries to determine if you have a registered serial number. If not, this message appears telling you where to obtain a registered copy.

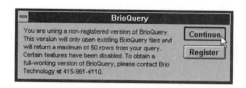

Product Name: Chen DB Designer

Provided by:

Chen & Associates
4884 Constitution Ave., Suite 1-E
Baton Rouge, LA 70808
Phone Number: 800-448-2436
Fax Number: 504-928-9371

Product Description

The enclosed demo is a self-guided tour. Type **SGT** to run the program.

The Chen PowerBuilder Companion is a CASE tool for optimal database design. The user can launch a PowerBuilder script to implement the design on the host DBMS. Schema changes are supported, as are links to the CHEN ER-Modeler Workbench, which includes data and process modeling, and reverse engineering for more than 30 DBMSs. Migration/conversion is supported. Dictionary reports are produced. The sophisticated Chen Normalizer can decompose records and relations into more desirable formats, including 3NF. Links to major data dictionaries and CASE tools are provided. Stand-alone and network operations are supported.

Type **sgt.bat** in the \apps\chendb directory on your CD to start the demo.

Caution

To run this demo, you must be running at 640×480 resolution. Otherwise, the demo will not run properly and your screen will flicker. If this happens, press Alt+F then X, and again Alt+F then X, and press Enter to exit out to Windows. Restarting Windows clears this problem.

Product Name: Crystal Reports Pro Price: $395

Provided by:

Crystal Services
1050 West Pender Street
Vancouver, BC, Canada V6E 3S7
Phone Number: 604-893-6329
Fax Number: 604-681-2934

> **Note**
>
> The shareware version of Crystal Reports does not support Watcom SQL, although the Crystal Reports Pro does. Crystal Reports is included to show what kind of reports you can generate with a report generating package.

Product Description

Included on the CD-ROM is a complete and working version of Crystal Reports, version 3.0. The latest version of Crystal Reports, version 4.0, is described below.

Crystal Reports is a Windows-based application that provides for report design and analysis. Using drag-and-drop, you can easily build band-based reports that join as many tables as you need. You can sort and subtotal in one step, sort on groups, export reports to many file formats, and distribute reports via integrated e-mail. In addition to the complete report writer, developers can access Crystal's powerful report engine using enhanced Visual Basic custom controls, OLE controls, the Report Engine DLLs, and open APIs.

Crystal Reports version 4.0 has the following enhancement over the included version 3.0:

- *Much greater speed.* Crystal Report's redesigned report engine with "smart engine" technology generates reports that are two to 10 times faster. SQL reports can be processed even faster with version 4.0's new support for stored procedures and the product's capability to sort data on the SQL Server.

- *Easier report design.* Version 4.0 includes Experts, which prompt the user for choices and then automatically perform reporting tasks. The user interface has been improved with a new tab interface, ruler, Best Fit button, Automatic Styles, and all new Grid.

- *Increased report analysis capabilities.* These include fully integrated, flexible graphing that provide visual presentation of data. Twelve styles are seamlessly integrated in the package, eliminating the need to go into another program to graph. Querying is also much simpler with the new Select Records Interface. Option tabs enable you to refine a query until the user has the information they want. Also, drill-down capabilities give the user detailed data analysis by allowing him to simply double-click a summary field and see a window of the detailed data.

- *More report engine control.* Version 4.0 adds more control over the report engine. More than 20 new direct calls have been added, for a total of over 80. Visual Basic users can take full advantage of the report engine via an enhanced, full-featured VBX with more than 80 properties—plus an all-new OCX with an easy-to-use property page interface for even faster integration of reports.

Crystal Reports works with ODBC databases to generate reports. By allowing you to place fields on different bands (heading, detail, or footer) and including functions (SUM, AVG, and so on) that are useful in reports, Crystal Reports is a quick way to generate a report (see fig. G.11). The Crystal Reports applications include a tutor and an easy way to generate quick reports from your Watcom SQL database.

To run the tutorial, run **ptutor.exe** in the \apps\crystal directory on your CD. To start the application itself, type **crw.exe** in the \apps\crystal directory on your CD.

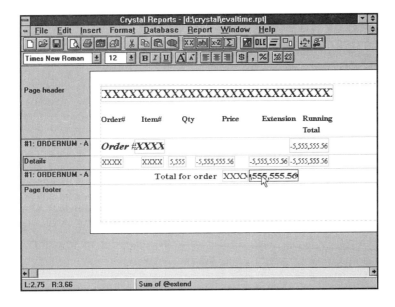

Fig. G.11

Crystal Reports can build reports from any ODBC database, such as Watcom SQL.

VII

Appendixes

Note

Crystal Reports will ask you to fill in a registration and user survey when you start (see fig. G.12). If you are not ready to register, choose Cancel.

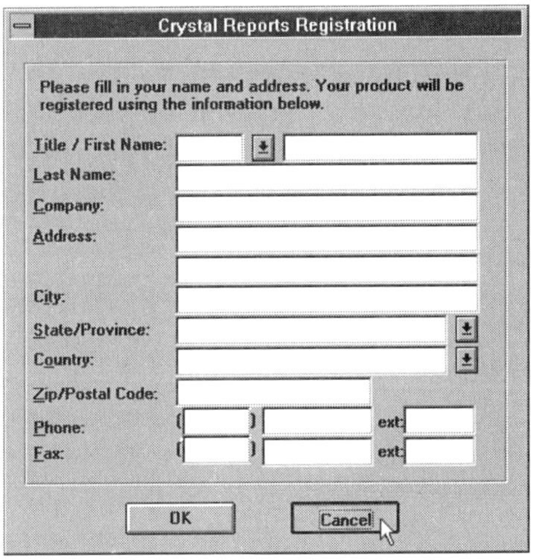

Fig. G.12

The Crystal Reports Registration dialog box lets you fill in information to become a registered user of Crystal Reports.

Product Name: DataEdit

Provided by:

Brio Technology
650 Castro Street, Suite 500
Mountain View, CA 94041
Phone Number: 415-961-4110
Fax Number: 415-961-4572

Product Description

DataEdit provides the power to update relational databases through a graphical forms building environment with a point-and-click interface. DataEdit uses a centralized data model to ensure database integrity and maintain complex relationships—even across tables.

DataEdit is ideal for those users who have an SQL database and lots of data, but little time for building data entry forms. From database design to full-featured applications, DataEdit supports the entire process, without programming or re-creating database structures locally. DataEdit includes the following features:

- *Quick building of database systems.* DataEdit's direct access approach removes the need for redefining databases on client machines. System designers need only to access the database, set cardinalities between tables, and define desired field domain values. You can drag fields directly from a visual representation of the database onto the form under construction. This eliminates confusing intermediary layers. The drag-and-drop interface automatically reads the centralized data dictionary to integrate field names, sizes, and domain values without any additional typing.

- *SQL database management.* DataEdit users retrieve, update, and insert data records using proven graphical interface concepts incorporated in electronic data entry forms. DataEdit forms respect and enhance server-level security through features such as read-only fields, pop-up menus for limited valid-value sets, and built-in browse lists generated directly from the database. A free-floating palette of standard buttons enables users to take advantage of DataEdit's built-in insert and update logic. Multi-windows and form-to-form data-transfer capabilities streamline tasks and eliminate redundant data entry procedures.

■ *Flexibility and power.* Expert users add real value to this already powerful tool by taking advantage of DataEdit's scripting language. Button and form scripts include field value manipulations, as well as SQL statements with embedded field value references. Such powerful buttons make specialized data entry functions easy.

Run **demo.bat** from the `\apps\dataedit` directory on the CD to start the demo.

Caution

To run this demo, you must be running at 640×480 resolution. Otherwise, the demo will not run properly and your screen will flicker. If this happens, press Alt+F then X, and again Alt+F then X. Press Enter to exit to Windows. Restarting Windows clears this problem.

Product Name: EasyCASE Price: $1,295

Provided by:

Evergreen CASE Tools, Inc.
8522 154th Ave. NE
Redmond, WA 98052
Phone Number: 206-881-5149
Fax Number: 206-883-7676

Product Description

EasyCASE is an easy-to-use, low cost, highly functional Computer Aided Software Engineering (CASE) tool that supports a wide range of methods for process event and data modeling. It is used primarily during the analysis and design phases of system development. It can be used for logical and physical data modeling, which results in the generation of SQL database creation scripts, and supports forward and reverse engineering of xBase databases.

EasyCASE allows you to data model using several different design methods, such as IDE1FX, Bachman, Martin, and so on. Although EasyCASE is not for the beginner, you can use this tool for some great documentation of your database (see fig. G.13).

Fig. G.13
EasyCASE supports some popular design methods and structures, such as the data flow diagram started here.

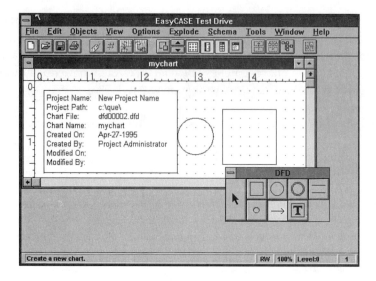

To start the application, run **ecwin.exe** from the \apps\easycase directory on your CD.

> **Note**
>
> Be sure you run your projects from your C drive. EasyCASE needs to be able to write to your project, and you can't write to a CD.

Product Name: InfoModeler
Price: $24.95

Provided by:

Asymetrix Corp.
110 110th Ave. NE, Suite 700
Bellevue, WA 98004
Phone Number: 800-448-6543
Fax Number: 206-454-7696

Product Description
InfoModeler is a set of visual design tools for database professionals. Info-Modeler uses conceptual modeling tools based in ORM (Object Role Modeling), which help to communicate and automate the process of building sound relational database management systems. Designers and end users use English business rules and sample data to build the information model. InfoModeler then automatically generates a correct, normalized database.

The InfoModeler Demo takes you through some of the features of InfoModeler. For database modelers, InfoModeler is one of the most cost effective packages.

To launch the InfoModeler Demo, run **cplshow.exe** from the `\apps\infmodlr` directory on the CD.

Product Name: ProReports

Provided by:

Software Interfaces, Inc.
1400 Broadfield, Suite 600
Houston, TX 77084
Phone Number: 713-492-0707
Fax Number: 713-492-0725

Product Description
ProReports for Windows and X/Motif is a powerful and easy-to-use information access and delivery system for enterprise-wide use. As a GUI tool, ProReports is easy to use for the novice or the expert, and it incorporates all of the features of both ad hoc and production report writers. It also allows powerful access and reporting on heterogeneous database data, plus other data, all in the same report.

ProReports allows reports to be created on a client and run on any client or server, and retain the identical formatting attributes, including fonts, images, and layout. This gives organizations the ability to match their computing resources to their business needs. For example, a customized telephone billing report can be created quickly and easily on a PC using ProReports for Windows, and then sent to any server attached to a heavy duty printer that can print the thousands of pieces of correspondence required overnight.

ProReports is designed so that everybody in an organization, from a simple end user to a corporate developer, can use the same tool to develop all types of ad hoc and production reports. ProReports' method for building reports means that the beginning user does not have to know SQL or database design. It intuitively walks the user through the querying and report-generating processes. From the beginner to the expert, ProReports' powerful and sophisticated ad hoc querying and reporting capabilities allow users to quickly and easily manipulate data to produce valuable information and create presentation-quality reports.

ProReports also allows users to perform multiple queries on heterogeneous data sources in the same report. Plus, it allows users to perform operations on the results of those queries, and these results can then be incorporated in the same report. This allows previously impossible ways to access, view, analyze, and present information with an easy-to-use GUI tool. For example, with a few clicks of a mouse, a user can combine manufacturing data from ORACLE, purchasing information from DB2, and forecasting information from Microsoft Access—all in the same report. ProReports allows all levels of users to do these many operations without heavy 4GL programming and with the ease of a GUI-based tool.

Data sources accessible natively include: DB2 (all members), INFORMIX, INGRES, MS SQL Server, ORACLE, Rdb/VMS, and SYBASE. Middleware access is offered through EDA/SQL, SequeLink, and any ODBC source to databases such as Watcom, Paradox, Microsoft Access, dBASE, and more. Client platforms include: Microsoft Windows 3.1 and NT, X/Motif on SunOS, Solaris, HP, and RS/6000. Server support includes: SunOS, Solaris, HP, RS/6000, and VAX/VMS. In 1995, support will be added for an expansive variety of desktop servers to large IBM mainframes.

Before you run the demo, you must first run **pptview.exe** in the \apps\proreprt directory on your CD to start a viewer from which you can see the demo. Then you can start the demo by opening the file PROREP10.PPT.

Product Name: R&R Report Writer Price: $249

Provided by:

Concentric Data Systems
110 Turnpike Rd.
Westborough, MA 01581
Phone Number: 508-366-1122
Fax Number: 508-366-2954

Product Description

R&R Report Writer puts information at your fingertips. With this product, you'll have the power to select, analyze, summarize, and present information easily and quickly. R&R Report Writer comes in two versions: one for connecting to xBase ($249), and one for SQL ($395). To create a report, you click the picture of the report you want, and R&R Wizards walks you through the design steps. R&R Report Writer can quickly turn raw data into views you use. You can:

- Create professional-quality business reports and forms, financial statements, directories, form letters, and labels.

- Make better decisions for using data analysis tools that let you rank customers, profile sales, summarize operations, and build crosstabs and charts in Excel 5 via OLE automation.

- Print finished reports, view them on-line, send via e-mail, and export to other desktop applications.

Programmers can customize report templates, wizards, dictionaries, predefined calculations, user-defined functions, and run-time report parameters for maximum control.

Link production reports into Visual Basic, C++, xBase, and other Windows applications. Or launch reports from Program Manager icons. R&R Runtime makes it easy with EXE, DLL, and VBX interfaces. The Runtime is royalty-free.

Note that you must have at least 450K of conventional memory to run this program. To launch the program, run **demo.exe** in the \apps\r&r.rept directory on the CD.

Product Name: S-Designor

Provided by:

SDP Technologies
One Westbrook Corp Center, Suite 805
Westchester, IL 60154
Phone Number: 708-947-4250
Fax Number: 708-947-4251

Product Description

S-Designor database modeling tools empower users to draw entity-relationship diagrams, and customizable physical data models. Users can also create scripts, reverse engineer, and produce quality documentation for over 40 databases. The two-level design process starts with the user's conceptual model. Then S-Designor generates the physical model, in which users can enhance tables, references, integrity rules, indexes, and extended attributes. The bi-directional bridge to the target database transfers column formats, validation rules, and edit styles. Other features include seamless reverse engineering through ODBC, alter table commands, integrity triggers, and sub-models. The network version, S-Designor Corporate, couples work-group management with an SQL-based central dictionary, allowing team members to share complete design information.

This demo version is fully functional, except that it cannot save models.

S-Designor Pro is a graphical interface to ODBC databases like Watcom SQL. S-Designor Pro allows you to model and then apply it to your ODBC-compliant database. The professional version of S-Designor Pro can perform the following tasks:

- Direct database generation via ODBC

- Direct trigger and stored procedure generation via ODBC

- Direct database modification via ODBC

- Direct SQL execution via ODBC

- 4GL reverse engineering for PowerBuilder and TeamWindows extended attributes via ODBC

- 4GL generation for PowerBuilder and TeamWindows extended attributes via ODBC

You'll find the design capabilities of the S-Designor Pro demo easy to use and fully featured (see fig. G.14). To start the demo, run **sdpro.exe** from the \apps\sdesignr directory on your CD.

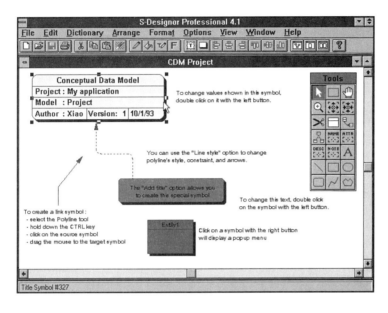

Fig. G.14
S-Designor Pro allows you to model your ODBC database with colorful symbols and descriptive help.

Product Name: SQLASSIST

Provided by:

Software Interfaces, Inc.
1400 Broadfield, Suite 600
Houston, TX 77084
Phone Number: 713-492-0707
Fax Number: 713-492-0725

Product Description

SQLASSIST is a powerful and sophisticated decision-support system with ad hoc querying, analysis, and data-conversion facilities. SQLASSIST offers an integrated solution for the novice end user who needs quick and easy data access and analysis tools, and for the expert database administrator who needs state-of-the-art performance and functionality.

With SQLASSIST, users can easily locate, access, and analyze data from hundreds of relational database tables. For non-technical users, SQLASSIST's drop-down menus and dialog boxes shield them from having to know complex database design and the SQL query language. SQLASSIST optimizes queries, joins, and paths in the background. Querying is intuitive and simple, from querying on-the-fly to querying with predefined templates using run-time variables or with data in pop-up lists. A Query Advisor guards against users sending inefficient or potential runaway queries.

For database experts, SQLASSIST creates correct, efficient, and complex SQL statements, and can read previously written SQL statements so that valuable investment is not lost. Because SQLASSIST runs directly against the database engine, there is no need to set up or maintain a separate data dictionary. An interactive SQL mode is also available for writing, editing, and viewing SQL statements in the traditional manner. SQLASSIST supports the major database vendors' SQL extensions, plus primary and foreign keys. Executives and managers can convert the query data to Excel, Lotus 1-2-3, dBASE, WordPerfect mail merge, delimited, and many other formats. In a single step, researchers can convert query data into advanced statistical applications such as RS/1 and the SAS System. These fast and easy conversions can save an organization thousands of hours in reformatting and rekeying.

SQLASSIST protects and maximizes the performance of information system resources. SQLASSIST is a read-only data access tool, so users cannot corrupt valuable data. SQLASSIST enforces the database and system restrictions on tables, columns, and rows, and provides table and column restrictions from within SQLASSIST. It also runs directly against the database engine, so there is no performance loss.

SQLASSIST's design philosophy allows an organization to leverage its existing information systems' investment, as well as to take advantage of emerging technologies. Databases currently supported via their native APIs include DB2, INFORMIX, INGRES, MS SQL Server, ORACLE, Rdb/VMS, and SYBASE. EDA/SQL and ODBC support provides access to databases such as Watcom, Paradox, dBASE, Excel, and more. Platforms and operating systems supported include VAX/VMS, DEC/ULTRIX, DEC/Alpha, HP, RS 6000, Sun/OS, and Sun/Solaris. SQLASSIST is available for character-based, Microsoft Windows, and OSF/Motif environments, and supports multiple network protocols.

To start the demo, you must run **pptview.exe** in the \apps\sqlasst directory on your CD. Then you can start the demo by opening the file SQLAPRM4.PPT.

Index

Symbols